PUBLICATIONS ON RUSSIA AND EASTERN EUROPE
OF THE SCHOOL OF INTERNATIONAL STUDIES
UNIVERSITY OF WASHINGTON
VOLUME 12

THE BALKAN CITY, 1400–1900

NIKOLAI TODOROV

UNIVERSITY OF WASHINGTON PRESS

SEATTLE AND LONDON

*Sponsored by the Russian and East European Program
of the School of International Studies
University of Washington*

This book has been published with the assistance of a grant from
the Andrew W. Mellon Foundation.

Frontispiece(Plate 1): 17th-century Belgrade.
Courtesy of Gennadion Library, Athens.

LIBRARY OF CONGRESS CATALOGING IN PUBLICATION DATA

Todorov, Nikolaĭ.
   The Balkan City, 1400-1900.

   (Publications on Russia and Eastern Europe of the
School of International Studies ; v. 12)
      Translation of: Balkanskiiat grad.
      Bibliography: p.
      Includes index.
      1. Cities and towns--Balkan Peninsula. 2. Balkan
Peninsula--Economic conditions. I. Title.
II. Series: Publications on Russia and Eastern Europe
of the School of International Studies, University
of Washington ; v. 12.
HT145.B3T6313   1983   307.7'64'09496   82-21836

ISBN 0-295-95897-9

CONTENTS

ILLUSTRATIONS

Plates

Figures

TABLES

FOREWORD

In 1972 *Balkanskiiat Grad, XIV-XIX Vek* was first published in
Sofia. This volume has rapidly attracted the world-wide attention of historians, economists, sociologists, urbanists,
and area specialists interested in the Balkan Peninsula and
the Ottoman Empire. Soon after its publication, references
to this work appeared in the studies of these scholars, and
it became obvious that this work should be made accessible to
the widest possible academic audience. Following the publication of a Russian translation in 1976 and two French translations in 1977 and 1980, the need for an English version
became apparent.

   The Balkan City, 1400-1900 is the twelfth volume to appear in the Publications on Russia and Eastern Europe Series
of the School of International Studies of the University of
Washington. However, it is the first translated work to
appear in this series. This fact alone testifies to the

importance which those responsible for the series attached to
this study. Based primarily on original Ottoman sources,
The Balkan City presents to the reader the administrative and
economic organization of the city during this period and the
numerous changes which took place in the various localities of
the Balkans during these centuries. The volume provides economic information concerning production, commerce, prices,
profits, local specialization, and public works, as well as
demographic information about the religious, ethnic, professional, and everyday lives of the people. The author has
brought together in these pages a wealth of data and information which gives the most complete and detailed picture offered
thus far on life in the Balkan cities during these five
centuries.

      The author, Nikolai Todorov, holds doctoral degrees
both in the historical sciences and in medicine. He is
a member of the Bulgarian and Soviet Academies of Sciences
and serves as the vice-president of the Bulgarian Academy.
He is an historian and Ottomanist by training, as well as
a linguist versed in all the languages of the region, including Greek and Romanian. A scholar of international
repute, Academician Todorov has earned his colleagues'
respect not only as an author of numerous books and articles,
but also as one of the founders and ex-presidents of the
Association internationale des études du sud-est européen,
as senior research associate of the Bulgarian Institute of
History, as director of the Bulgarian Institute for Balkan
Studies, and as founder and secretary general of the Centre
internationale d'information sur les sources de l'histoire
balkanique et méditerranéenne. His accomplishments have
been recognized by his election to membership in the Association d'histoire moderne et contemporaine (Strasbourg), the
Commission internationale d'histoire des villes (Toulouse),
the Union internationale des études orientales et asiatiques
(Paris), and the Société d'histoire démographique (Paris).

      Dr. Todorov's contributions to international coopera-
tion have gone beyond the academic. He also has served as
Bulgarian Ambassador first to UNESCO and then to Greece. We
feel honored to have been asked by this distinguished scholar
to publish the English version of his outstanding work.

                              Professor Peter F. Sugar
                              University of Washington

PREFACE

The study of the development of cities on the Balkan
Peninsula from the fifteenth through the nineteenth century is
important to both Balkan and general historical scholarship.
However, despite a certain number of studies on individual
cities or on some aspects of urban material and cultural life,
the fundamental problems of the socioeconomic and demographic
development of the Balkan city have not yet been elaborated in
monograph form. Neither the urban economy nor the social
structure of the urban population in the Balkans has been ade-
quately studied or defined. Also lacking are presentations of
sufficient material for a comparative analysis of the cities
on the peninsula that could serve as the basis for theoretical
generalization.

The relatively uniform socioeconomic and political conditions of the lands that fell within the framework of the

Ottoman state permit the investigation of trends and regularities (*zakonomernost*, *Gesetzmässigkeiten*) inherent in the urban
system of the Balkans as a whole. The presence of a common
feudal system and political superstructure provides the chronological and territorial backdrop to such issues as the number
and size of cities, state regulation and the urban economy,
the role of the city in the emergence and development of capitalist relations, property and social differentiation, and the
relationships among and between the various categories of the
urban population. Differences in the evolution of cities and
differences in the disintegration of feudalism and the genesis
of capitalist relations may find a successful explanation when
considered against the background of concrete economic and
geographical conditions as they affected individual cities in
different parts of the Balkans.

     The investigation and clarification of these issues,
however, is doubly complex. Not only do both feudal and capitalist trends of development clash in a single city, but two
civilizations clash as well. The Muslim civilization enjoyed
both the support of the state and the entire political and
economic machinery of central and local authorities. But the
culture that the Turks found on the Balkans was also distinguished by profound traditions and by a development strong
enough to place its imprint on newly emergent social and
economic forms.

     This work, then, is a study of the development of the
city in the former Balkan provinces of the Ottoman Empire, excluding Wallachia, Moldavia, and the western parts of the pen-
insula--territories where different and special conditions existed. The one deviation from these parameters--a comparison
of the cities of the Danubian *vilâyet* (an administrative unit;
after 1850 the largest in the Ottoman Empire) with Serbian and
Greek cities in the nineteenth century (i.e., after the formation of independent states)--will, through an extension of the
data base, contribute even more towards revealing certain general regularities.

     To describe the different institutions of the city and
to investigate events and processes inherent in the entire urban population requires the use of a multitude of criteria,
and this has determined both the plan of attack and the methods adopted. The primary goal has been to clarify basic processes and regularities, which requires the use of a massive
body of material--if possible material of the same type. It
is for this reason that we have used source material that was
suitable for statistical processing. It would be superfluous
to emphasize the importance of such data and its advantages
over fragmentary and individual pieces of information. Material extracted from census records, tax registers, and similar
documents is particularly significant for research in the

socioeconomic history of the Balkan peoples, where to date it
has remained to all intents and purposes unused. Its inherent
shortcomings--the oversimplification of phenomena and the
emphasis of only the most characteristic features--may be compensated by confronting it with information of a different
origin and also by the parallel study of individual phenomena
and facts.

Unfortunately, the extensive use of statistical methods
for the period under study has encountered additional difficulties: the insufficiency of the data and the absence of
serial documents for the entire period or for a given period
of time, for the better part of the Balkan Peninsula. These
difficulties have compelled us to make the fullest possible
use of the collections of sources that are available for particular areas and cities: tax registers, information about
sales and estates, census returns, guild registers, and the
ledgers of entrepreneurs. We have grouped the material from
these sources into series. Insofar as possible, we have also
used information both of other types and from different areas
for the sake of comparison and as something of a check on the
accuracy of the conclusions drawn from the quantitative
analysis.

To reveal the composition of those urban strata that
might otherwise become lost in the common mass of the urban
population, we have placed great attention on the analysis of
a number of individual cases. Without the study of particular
cases of certain kinds of crafts and guild organizations, of
the representatives of different milieus, and of the transformation of individual artisans and merchants into entrepreneurs, one cannot arrive at a full characterization of this or
that social group. We have not deemed it expedient, however,
to cite fragmentary documentary material for all cities, but
have focused our attention on the clarification of essential
features in the development of the Balkan city. Nor have we
examined certain questions connected with the urban economy
that constitute a theme of their own (for example, foreign
trade and its role). In this way, by mutual supplementation
and comparison, the quantitative and qualitative aspects of
the documentation acquire their true value.

* * *

Previous studies of the agrarian relations and the demographic composition of the Balkan Peninsula that have been
based on data from the Turkish archives have shown that the
various Ottoman registers, despite all their shortcomings, are
a most important source for the study of the socioeconomic
life of the Ottoman Empire. It is not an exaggeration to
state that the solution to a number of questions connected

with the study of the Balkan city may be expected only after
the publication and processing of data from the registers preserved in the rich Turkish archives and in those of the Balkan
countries. This, however, is such a remote prospect that by
necessity researchers must proceed with the gradual elucidation of separate aspects of the problems noted above, doing so
by extracting and processing the maximum possible amount of
data from the archives that are accessible to them.

     The richest and fullest collections of Turkish documents
are contained in the Central Turkish State Archives (the *Başvekâlet Arşivi*) and in the other eighteen archival centers of
Istanbul and Ankara. Sizable collections exist, however,
outside Turkey's borders--in the state archives, museums, li-
braries, and other cultural institutions of a number of countries that were once part of the Ottoman Empire or maintained
lively ties with it.

     The bulk of the Ottoman documents in Bulgaria are gath-
ered in the Oriental Department of the Cyril and Methodius
National Library in Sofia. These records are documents from
the archives of the Turkish central government in Istanbul
(chiefly from the archives of the grand vizier and the *Defterhane* or state treasury), from the archives of the government
of the Danubian vilâyet in Ruse, and from the archives of the
*mutasarrif*s (the administrative and military heads of the
imperial subdivisions known as *sancak*s) of Vidin, Tŭrnovo,
Tulcea, Silistra, Sofia, Plovdiv, and so on. They cover
nearly the entire period of Ottoman rule in the Balkans--from
the fifteenth through the nineteenth century.[1]

     We have tried to make the fullest possible use of this
rich documentary base. Primary attention has been paid to
massive amounts of kindred archival material that offered
data on relatively large areas--one or several sancaks--or for
the entire Balkan Peninsula, and material that also covers a
prolonged period, thus being relatively stable in form and
suitable for statistical processing. The basic sources containing information in bulk are the various registers or *defter*s. The varied character and content of these records reflect the different purposes and occasions for which they were
compiled (political, financial, economic, military, etc.).
Here we will briefly touch on those kinds of registers that
contain data on the socioeconomic development and appearance
of the Balkan city.

     All the registers drawn up for fiscal purposes are simi-
lar in character, irrespective of the designation of the revenue. These are inventories of fief holdings, registers of
certain categories of the population, and registers of fiscal
units.

     Listed in the inventories of fief holdings (*timar ve
zeamet defteri; hasha-i padisah defteri; icmal defteri*) are

all the localities included in a given holding, the number of
households, the sum of the revenue in *akçe*s (a small silver
coin), and the general recapitulation. A unique subgroup of
this type are the "detailed registers" (*mufasal defteri*).
These provide the fullest listing of the original distribution
of the lands in the Ottoman Empire into fief holdings, and
they record the changes that regularly occurred over the
course of time. They state not only the total number of
households but also a name-by-name listing of the population
as well as the size and type of the tax paid.

The *timar* (feudal fief holding) registers kept in Sofia
possess all these characteristics. Most of them refer to the
European provinces of the Ottoman Empire and they are an extremely valuable source of data of land relations, the form
and size of the feudal rent, the ethnic character of population, and the history of individual settlements. However,
although they offer the researcher abundant data, they are
primarily concerned with villages. It is for this reason that
we have made but limited use of them (only if they contain
information about certain cities incorporated in one type of
fief holding or another or if they throw light on the relationship between the city and the village).

The "summary registers" of the population (*nüfus defteri*) offer information on civil status: age structure,
family and property status, and taxes paid in kind and cash.
Here, however, it is not a case of registers covering the entire population of the empire, but only of lists of separate
categories of the population subject to a different tax obligation (e.g., the non-Muslim male population obligated to pay
the poll tax, the *cizye*) or laden with special duties--for
example, the peasants conscripted for regular auxiliary troops
(*voynugan*, Turkish, *voynuk*; *sokolar*, Turkish, *dŏganci*), and
the *celepkeşan*s, the livestock contractors.

In the Oriental Department there are several registers
drawn up for the collection of the cizye in various regions of
the Ottoman Empire. One of them, which refers to the year
1490-91 (or 896 in the Muslim calendar based on the Hegira),
contains data on the entire Balkan Peninsula. By comparing
the data from this register with data published by the Turkish
researchers O.L. Barkan, T. Gökbilgin, and H. İnalcık, and by
the Yugoslav historians H. Šabanović, A. Handžić, M. Sokoloski
and O. Zirojević, it has become possible to map certain basic
moments in the demographic situation of the Balkans, the movement of the population, and its ethnic composition in the earliest period of Ottoman rule. Finally, on the basis of data extracted from these fiscal registers and from the publications
of the authors cited, we have classified Balkan cities by size
and studied their growth.

The sicils (*kadı* registers) differ somewhat from the documents noted so far. They constitute a unique register of all central notices (*fermans*, *berats*, *buyrultus*, etc.)[2] sent to the kadı and to other local authorities so that they might be brought to the attention of the population. They include a record of all petitions, complaints, and inquiries addressed by private individuals to the central authorities, and, in addition, offer valuable material on the everyday life of the population. They record all cases of an economic, social, and even personal character that required some sort of arbitration. Specifically, these are the minutes or protocols of civil cases: sales, exchanges, leases, settlements of family and marital relations, estate inventories, and so on. The broad scope of the sicils suggests that a thorough familiarity with the information they offer could be of help in clearing up individual aspects of social relations and of urban economic life, and in ascertaining certain trends within them.

In this book a thorough use has been made of the protocols of the kadı registers preserved in the Oriental Department for the cities of Vidin, Sofia, and Ruse.[3] These quite complete collections cover an almost uninterrupted period from the middle of the seventeenth to the third quarter of the nineteenth century. In the 163 registers (66 for Vidin, 55 for Sofia, and 42 for Ruse), we have discovered a considerable number of documents concerning such things as state regulation of commerce, the role and place of guilds, and the relations among the individual branches of the craft industry. Records of sales and of estate inventories have thrown light on the property and social differentiation of the urban population and on certain trends in the socioeconomic development of the cities. The multitude, the uniformity, and the constant annual repetition of such documents have permitted a comparative analysis as well as the study of processes over an extended period of time. Material concerning 6,000 cases of sales and estates has been taken and processed from the sicils of the three cities of Sofia, Vidin, and Ruse.

With the aid of data from official censuses in Greece, Serbia, and in the Ottoman state, all carried out after the 1830s, we have examined the movement of the whole population in the nineteenth century, its ethnic composition, and its age structure. The returns of the census conducted by Midhat Paşa in the 1860s (and discovered by us), contain comprehensive data on the cities of the Danubian vilâyet, the size of their population, and the type and total value of urban property.

To analyze the occupational composition and the property status of the urban population, we have processed the receipts for taxes paid, the *esnaf tezkeresi* (permits to exercise a trade) and other documents preserved in the Oriental Depart-

ment of the National Library in Sofia. They concern some
15,000 persons.

On the basis of the same data, several more avenues of
research have opened up. First, it has become possible to examine the professional employment of the urban population and
to determine the proportion of craftsmen, merchants, persons
engaged in farming, servants, and other wage earners. Furthermore, we have been able to differentiate the population on
the basis of income and occupation and to examine the status
and differentiation of property. For this purpose, we have
employed both the assessments of houses and the markedly more
varied assessments (through sales and inheritances) of shops,
workshops, and warehouses.

To set up categories of the urban population by size of
income and by property status so that they would correspond to
definite social groups changing in time, we have drawn upon
numerous local sources--guild registers, the registers of the
millet-related municipal community organizations (obshtinas),
and personal archives. Those relevant documents are kept in
the Bulgarian Historical Archive of the National Library or
have appeared in various scholarly publications.

Another basic source on which this work has been based
is the Gümüşgerdan archival fund in the Central State Historical Archive in Sofia.[4] This collection of more than 33,000
documents, practically all in Greek, describe the economic
activity of the Gümüşgerdan family from the beginning to the
end of the nineteenth century. Of the greatest interest have
been the defters providing an account of the manufacture of
woolen cloth in the mountainous areas of the Rhodope region
and in a mill near Plovdiv, as well as ledgers on the sale and
purchase of wool, the finished local cloth (*aba*, a coarse
woolen cloth used for cloaks and other clothing) and the
hooded cloaks that were made on orders placed by the Turkish
government. This archive has permitted the clarification of
a number of problems of the greatest importance in the socioeconomic history of nineteenth-century Bulgaria. It has also
shed light on the relationship between Turkish authorities and
wool and aba producers in practically the whole central part
of the Balkans, as this relationship was affected and mediated
through entrepreneurs such as the Gümüşgerdans.

The guild registers kept in the Bulgarian Historical
Archive of the National Library form a special part of the
sources used. The analysis of the data they contain has made
it possible to establish the character of the guild organization and its place in the socioeconomic life of the city in
the late eighteenth and in the first half of the nineteenth
century.

There is no need to mention here the extremely valuable

published documents to which we have also referred or the different kinds of individual documents located in various other
archives.

Naturally, the use of source material so diverse in origin and nature presupposes that this documentation be subjected to an extensive critical analysis to establish its au-
thenticity, and that it also be subjected to whatever correc-
tives prove necessary. This careful approach holds particularly true for Ottoman Turkish fiscal documents. Accordingly,
a concrete analysis of the documentation has been made in
appropriate sections of the book.

In covering such a large number of historical issues and
problems, it has proved impossible to summarize the characteristic views of every author who has touched on this or that
aspect of the questions examined. Besides, many authors simultaneously publish sources, offer important conclusions, and
in certain cases put forth concepts that have to be refined or
corrected. It is for these reasons that no comprehensive cri-
tique has been made of the historiography, although, where
appropriate, a historiographical review of the fundamental
questions accompanied by references and a critical stance towards certain individual publications has been included.
Here, we shall limit ourselves to a few general remarks.

In Balkan historiography, most of the information on the
socioeconomic position of the city is found in literature on
individual cities and villages. Some monographs on individual
cities possess great scholarly value, and most of them contain
interesting (though fragmentary) data, chiefly for cities in
the nineteenth century. Also of considerable scholarly interest are the materials contained in various museum yearbooks
and in other regional publications. For some of the large
cities of the Balkan Peninsula--for example, Istanbul, Edirne
(Adrianople), Sofia, Salonika (Thessalonike), Belgrade (Beograd), and Sarajevo (Serajevo)--separate works have appeared.
Collections by teams of authors have also been published that
contain vast quantities of factual material covering various
periods of time. For this kind of work special credit goes to
T. Gökbilgin, Ö. L. Barkan, G. Gülübov, N. Svoronos, H. Kreševljaković, N. Mikhov, and J. Tadić.

Here, we should also stress the importance of a small
number of books on the economic history of the Balkan peoples
(for Bulgaria by Zh. Natan, for the Socialist Federal Republic
of Yugoslavia by N. Vučo). The appearance of these books represented a significant historiographical advance, for they
have contributed to and have continued to assist the ability
to develop a correct grasp of a whole complex of questions,
and they have facilitated the elaboration of these questions
in monographic form. It is fitting also to emphasize the
great importance of the multivolumed general and summary works

on the history of Balkan countries. These works are the result of years of effort by large teams of authors, and they
reflect the latest scholarly findings concerning questions of
socioeconomic development. Such works on the history of Bulgaria, Yugoslavia, and Albania have been published almost
simultaneously in those countries and in the Soviet Union.
The histories of Greece published at different times by such
prominent authors as Ya. Kordatos, A. Vakalopoulos, D.
Zakitinos, and N. Svoronos are also of great importance.

       The works of a number of researchers could be introduced
for each of the questions examined in this book, and indeed, a
large number of books, studies, and articles devoted to different aspects of the socioeconomic and demographic development of the Balkan city are examined in the course of the
narrative. The criticism offered in certain cases is not
meant to reject or to disparage a particular study. There are
views, however, that have been rejected as obsolete owing to
the accumulation of new material, to the enrichment of historical exploration, and sometimes because they represent a
one-sided examination of the subject in question.

PART ONE

The Balkan City under Ottoman Feudalism, 1400-1800

Plate 2. A view of Istanbul. Reprinted from H. Inalcik, *The Ottoman Empire; the Classical Age, 1300-1600* (London, 1973).

Plate 3. 17th-century Gallipoli. Courtesy of Gennadion Library, Athens.

Pre- and Early Ottoman Rule

1. THE PRE-OTTOMAN URBAN TRADITION

The character and the unique aspects of Ottoman feudalism have not yet been sufficiently elaborated in Ottoman and Balkan historiography, nor have the common features and differences that existed in the structure of the individual parts of the huge Ottoman Empire, which spread over three continents. Despite the progress that has been made in the research on this issue, we do not yet know the extent to which the structure of Ottoman feudalism was influenced by medieval Muslim societies and by Byzantium. Still less is known about the direct impact on cities of the heritage and practices of the medieval Balkan states whose population and territory made up practically the entire European part of the Ottoman realm.

In the last few years, widespread discussion has been taking place on precapitalist societies and in particular on the so-called Asian way of production and Asian feudalism.

This discussion has been joined by scholars from the Soviet
Union and other Socialist countries, from Turkey, and from
many other European countries. As a result scores of studies
have appeared in periodicals, and several collections have
been published in different languages.[1] The basic issues
have involved not only agrarian relations in their entirety
(the forms of ownership, the character of land utilization,
and irrigation systems), but also relations of dependence and
the role of the state in economic life as a whole. The discussion has included as well a number of theoretical issues:
the periodization of social development, the regularities
that characterize feudalism as a whole and its variants, and
types of society in the same formation.

It is not our task here to continue this discussion, but
simply to note that some scholars include the economic system
of the Ottoman Empire in the "Asian" category noted above.
The Turkish scholar S. Divitçioğlu has taken up the task of
establishing an economic model of Ottoman society in the
fourteenth and fifteenth centuries. He has based himself on
the works of Marx and Engels, and on the achievements of
contemporary historiography, in order to construct an ab-
stract model of the "Asian way of production" and to compare it
with the specific model of the socioeconomic structure of
Ottoman society. His results show that both models coincide
with respect to the form of ownership, the form of exploitation, and class structure, but differ in such other areas as
the form of the division of labor between the city and the
village and the form of public works construction (particularly in the irrigation network). Divitçioğlu's work is a
contribution to the Marxist clarification of the economic
history of the Ottoman Empire.[2]

On the other hand, E. Antoniadis-Bibicou, in a well-
argued article whose conclusions may be extended to the
other states in the Byzantine sphere of influence,[3] has
rejected the view that Byzantium could have belonged to the
countries in which the "Asian way of production" and "Asian
feudalism" existed. As long as we lack scholarly clarification of the heritage assimilated by the Ottoman feudal
system, and of the impact of closer or more distant social
structures of the formation of Ottoman society, the origin
and evolution of a number of Ottoman institutions cannot be
definitively explained, and such questions cannot be put to
rest.

Let us then turn our attention to some of the principles
of the structure of the pre-Ottoman city insofar as they are
related to the tradition adopted by the Ottoman state.

The socioeconomic history of Byzantium and the states
in the territory that later formed the Ottoman Empire raises

some thorny problems. Although part of the ancient slave-
owning world, Byzantium escaped the fate of the Roman Empire.
For ages its existence and cultural values stimulated the development of Europe. It knew periods of upsurge and decline,
but retained unchanged its general role as a primary factor
in the development of areas of Southeastern Europe and Asia
Minor along the road of feudalism. Soviet Byzantology, which
at present is leading in the study of the Byzantine city, has
noted that "the study of feudalism in Byzantium cannot suc-
ceed without a determination of (the city's) role in this
process."[4] It is not a question solely of Constantinople,
the fabled city that drew the dreams of monarchs and merchants, of knights and men of culture of both East and West,
but of cities in general and the city as such.

Soviet historians have continued to discuss the place of
the cities of Byzantium in the transition from slave-owning
antiquity to feudalism. There exists, among some Soviet
historians, the view that there was a complete continuity of
the institution of the cities. The cities were preserved,
and they continued to strengthen themselves as centers of
commodity relations, of strongly developed handicrafts and
commerce, and with established forms of exploitation of the
producing population.[5] Other authors believe that, with the
exception of a few larger cities, in the period from the
fourth to the ninth century a crisis occurred in the slave-
owning polis; this form of city subsequently died, and the
feudal city gradually emerged in its place. The ruralization
that took place in the life of the empire had by the ninth
and tenth centuries turned practically all its cities into
large villages.[6]

The state of the late Byzantine city, which has been
inadequately studied, is also under discussion. The question
that has divided historians is whether the prerequisites
and elements of capitalist development had been established
in the Byzantine city by the eve of the Turkish conquest.
Although they will admit that the thirteenth and fourteenth
centuries saw a slow development of productive forces, some
authors have paid greater attention to what they see as the
paralyzing impact of feudal relationships of production on
Byzantium--an impact that caused the Byzantine city to wane.
The flourishing of individual export-related crafts did not
imply a general economic advance, and in no case can one
speak of the emergence of capitalist relations (or even of
the prerequisites for the appearance of capitalist production) in the Byzantine cities. Still less would this be true
for the cities of the neighboring Balkan states that were
following the same path of development.[7]

Other authors have argued that capitalist relations did

emerge in the economic life of Byzantium, but with respect to
the city, either these writers have claimed the appearance of
only a few elements of a capitalist means of production or
they have denied their existence on the grounds that in the
thirteenth and fourteenth centuries feudal lords, together
with the representatives of commercial and interest (chiefly
foreign) capital, had taken the upper hand in the cities.[8]

In its taxation system and method of obtaining feudal
rent, Byzantium stood closer to the Eastern states than to
those of Western Europe. It was only in the period of late
Byzantine feudalism, when large-scale private landownership
increased, that the character of the feudal rent also
changed. By that time, however, Byzantium had lost so much
territory that the "country of cities" was left with only a
few.

The Byzantine city was distinguished by highly developed
handicrafts and commerce. Small-scale artisan production of
a commodity character was prevalent. Large artisan shops belonged to the state. A guild organization existed with
elaborate rules pertaining to the variegated activities of
its affiliated producers. Along with cities that had such an
appearance (one that was common to many cities large or
small, situated deep in the interior of the peninsula or on
the coast) there were also purely commercial cities. These
centers promoted intensive transit and import-export trade,
to which certain types of production were subjected. This is
the most universally accepted portrait of the Byzantine
city.[9]

But as one probes more deeply into the features of the
city, differing appraisals begin to appear. Assuming that
from the ninth and tenth centuries the city was as we have
depicted it, historians have been divided in their appraisal of the nature of artisan production and guild organization. Some Soviet scholars have asserted that, together with the free artisan petty producer, slave labor was
still used in the larger workshops. At that time the guilds
were relatively too weak to overcome the competitive
struggle among individual artisans and to curb their entrepreneurial spirit. These scholars have used a broad background to examine the city, its socioeconomic structure, and
its internal social struggles. They have felt that the
process of feudalization accepted the heritage of the
Hellenistic world, but modified it as dictated by the new
conditions. An opposing point of view has been taken by
other Soviet scholars who have considered the Byzantine city
after the ninth century to be fully feudal. They have regarded the guild organization that had emerged as an expression of feudal domination, as in the city of Western Europe.

What distinguished the Byzantine city from the city of Western Europe was the presence of a developed system of state
regulation that limited the initiative of the corporative
institutions and influenced the course of urban social struggles. The complicated contradictions within the Byzantine
city set different strata and segments of the urban popu-
lation--the organized and unorganized, the privileged, hired
labor, and the owners--against each other and, separately or
jointly, against the state institutions.

The development of artisan production and trade in
Constantinople--set apart by a number of specific circumstances connected with its predominance as the capital city
of an empire and its position as a central commercial artery
connecting the East with the West--has been studied in detail.
Here, the commanding role of the state over the existing
corporations was most pronounced.

What has been said to this point refers only to the
position of the Byzantine city up to the thirteenth century,
in that we lack comprehensive studies concerning the period
immediately before the Turkish invasion.

The drift toward urban self-government was intensified
after the Latin conquest of Byzantium. This did not, however,
produce an upsurge of the late Byzantine city, since power in
the city proved to be almost entirely in the hands of the
feudal aristocracy,[10] a group that denied to the representatives of the merchants and other groups of the producing
population access to leadership in the urban organs of power.
In this also the late Byzantine city and the city of Western
Europe were different. There has been unanimity in the
historiography on the question of the decline of the city,
where feudal elements and the representatives of commercial
and interest capital now took the upper hand. Nevertheless,
from the analysis of material relating to artisan production
in a number of cities of the Balkan Peninsula, it is evident
that this industry reached great perfection in many branches,
particularly those that manufactured goods for export. This
upsurge of production was also reflected in the way of life
of the urban stratum that was differentiating itself from
the rest of the population. The houses of the urban well to
do were painted and decorated on the outside with gold and
multicolored stones and an exceptionally large amount of
sculpture was used in their adornment. However, these houses
had no more than two stories and only in some large cities
were buildings of three or more stories erected. With the
concentration in the city of a substantial layer of poor
hired labor and persons employed in all kinds of unskilled
work (the urban plebs), there began widespread construction of
rental housing in which the poor population was increasingly

accomodated and thus further exploited by the entrepreneurial
stratum.

Words that expressed divisions of the urban population
into rich, middle, and poor entered into the contemporary
vocabulary. In the fourteenth century the middle class
emerged as a differentiated category. In this respect,
Constantinople and Salonika, the two leading cities in the
Byzantine state, have been studied in the greatest detail.
In conjunction with the consideration of concrete material
that reveals the state of handicrafts, commerce, and the
economic progress or decline of a given period, the study
of these cities has also shown the weakened role of the
guilds and the retreat of a number of Byzantine institutions
in the face of the ever increasing competition of powerful
Italian merchant guilds that consolidated themselves into
a position of strength.

The regularities we are talking about here hold generally true both for the purely Byzantine city and for the Slav
city in the Balkans.[11] In a most general sense, the studies
on the medieval Bulgarian, Serbian, Dalmatian, Croatian, and
other cities have not facilitated a solution of the problem.
Only the literature on the Dalmatian cities and on urban
centers of the western Balkans has provided a comparatively
exhaustive picture of the internal structure and economic
life of the city. For the other parts of the Balkan Peninsula, existing studies have concentrated more on the administrative structure of the cities and on the life of the
feudal aristocracy--that is, on precisely those aspects of
urban life that underwent the greatest changes after the
establishment of Ottoman rule. Nor can one really use the
literature just mentioned on the Dalmatian and Croatian
cities, since these cities developed under the strong influence of Italy and other places, and their evolution was
different from that of the cities in the central and eastern
parts of the Balkans. The different territorial distribution
of the cities located in the interior, or along big rivers,
or on the coasts of the three seas, lends them a number of
special features. As a whole, however, they represent a
differentiated group of Balkan cities--differing typo-
logically both from the West European and from the Muslim
city.

Practically all students of Muslim society share the
conclusion that "the medieval Muslim culture was above all
an urban culture." The authors of a two-volume work on
Islamic society, H. A. R. Gibb and H. Bowen, have written
that the contrast between the city and village--as the representatives of two entirely different worlds--was nowhere
more sharply expressed than in Islamic society.[12] Even the

relationship of the Muslim conquerors to the city and the
village was different. Although they did not introduce
changes in the life and the external appearance of the villages, they considerably altered the outward appearance of
the cities and placed on them their lasting imprint.

Scholars who have studied the Muslim city in the Arab
world are unanimous in the definition of its most general
and characteristic features (without neglecting, it should be
noted, to establish its typology according to the place and
role of its inherited material and spiritual culture).[13]
The medieval Muslim city was distinguished by the absence
of an organic structural unity. It lacked the unified municipal structure so characteristic of the European city, but
consisted of self-governing groups. The theocratic principle
on which the Muslim state was based contributed even more to
this theme of self-government since it required the organization of the population by religious profession. The
population, joined by a common religion or a common occupation, usually lived in self-sufficient quarters with their
own places of worship, public baths, and stores and shops.
This principle also applied to the occupational division of
the population into separate quarters or *mahalle*s. The
differentiated mahalle was one of the typical features of the
Muslim city. The city had a central street with merchant
stalls (the *çarşı*) where different types of production and
trade were concentrated and where there were several bazaars
with large commercial houses (*bezistan*s), inns, storehouses,
and so forth.[14] Dominating the entire urban complex were
religious and cultural institutions and the administrative
center--the palace, administrative offices, and buildings of
the army and police. As a rule, these institutions were
situated in the fortified part of the city, the fortress.

The Arab traveler Ibn Batuta, who visited Asia Minor in
the 1330s, left quite an interesting description of Konya
(Konia) and other Seljuk cities.[15] (At that time the Seljuk
Turks had already acquired a settled urban life and culture.)
The account reveals a unified urban structure, with the
castle of the feudal prince on the highest place, with a
mosque, *medrese*,[16] *zaviye*,[17] and other public buildings.
The population lived in quarters separated from each other
by walls. The quarters of the local non-Turkish population
were also walled. The merchants, who along with the landed
feudal aristocracy formed a powerful social group, enjoyed
the greatest kind of respect. Foreign merchants also formed
a separate quarter, set off by walls whose gates were closed
at night and on Turkish holidays. The artisans were also
concentrated in one place according to their occupation and
their membership in an appropriate guild.[18] Fortress walls

encircled the entire city. The gates were closed at night
for fear of the nomadic population whose tents sometimes
spread to the very wall of the fortress. This was the general picture of such large cities as Konya, Sivas, Kayseri
(Kaisaria), and tens of smaller ones in Asia Minor.

A second essential feature of the Muslim city was the
direct interference in economic life, through legislation and
control, of the central power. From the viewpoint of Muslim
legislation, the population was made up of two categories:
first, representatives of power and those who maintained its
authority--the administration, the tax-exempt military and
religious officials; and second, the ordinary subjects, the
reaya (*râya*), who created material goods. Part of the reaya
cultivated the land, another engaged in handicrafts, and a
third part in trade. What united these three kinds of reaya
was the payment of taxes and the right to acquire wealth.
But an essential difference did exist among them: Muslim
legislation controlled the activities of both the farmer and
the artisan, restricting the sale price, the rate of profit,
the supply of raw materials, and the volume of production;
the activity of the merchant, on the other hand, saw all
sorts of encouragement. This attitude towards trade also
found expression in an Ottoman *nasihatname* (or instruction)
written in the second half of the fifteenth century. "Look
with favour on the merchants in the land; always care for
them; let no one harass them; let no one order them about;
for through their trading the land becomes prosperous,
and by their wares cheapness abounds in the world; through
them, the excellent fame of the *Padişah* is carried to surrounding lands, and by them the wealth within the land is
increased."[19]

The state took an interest in the activities of merchants not only because they supplied necessary consumer
goods and raw materials required for production. They also
concentrated in their hands enormous funds, accessible in
times of need both to state institutions and to the population when it needed money to pay its taxes on time. It
was for this reason that Muslim legislation contained
numerous provisions concerning the acquisition of wealth,
its utilization, and moneylending.

As is evident, what was involved here was chiefly wholesale, interregional and foreign trade. Special names
designated wholesale dealers in seasonal goods, merchants
involved in overland and sea trade with distant markets, and
so forth. Legislation also elaborated the forms of partnership between merchants, their mutual rights and obligations
when they were located in different places, and methods of
payment.[20]

The legislation concerning the activities of producers among the population was not worked out in such detail. The aspiration of the artisans for enrichment was condemned, the maximum profit was fixed at 10 percent (with exceptions for certain branches of production up to 25 percent); and competition was forbidden. Care was taken to create equal conditions in the supply of raw materials, and toward this end, in many cases, common deliveries and equal distribution of raw materials were carried out. Special persons supervised trade in the market places and kept an eye on the supply of staple commodities to the population.

Guilds became an important feature of Ottoman urban life, but there are certain episodes in the history of the pre-Ottoman guild that have to be noted before one can explain a number of features and aspects of their later organization. After the defeat of the Middle and Near Eastern Muslim Empire by the Mongol invasion in the middle of the thirteenth century and with the wane of central state power, the guilds acquired new functions thanks to their affiliation with certain political and religious societies. They thus fell under the strong influence of the *Futuwwa* (Fütüvvet)--an organization of a religious and social character that appeared in the Muslim countries of the Near East. This association strengthened the guilds' moral rules and their almost religious ritual. Finally it even gave the guilds a name, so that, at least for a certain period of time, Futuwwa and guild became synonymous. V. A. Gordlevskii, in his major work on the history of the Seljuk state, has explained the merger of the Futuwwa and the guild organization by the emergence of a new political factor in Anatolia, the organization of the so-called *ahis*.[21] According to Gordlevskii and other researchers, the ahis represented the knightly estate in Seljuk society that assumed the task of maintaining social order during the political disorganization that followed the establishment of Mongol rule in the Near East. The ahis introduced a strict military order into their organization, brought up a number of principles of social equality and fraternity, and in order to ensure public support, linked themselves with the guilds. It was precisely at that point that rules based on ideals of social justice and fraternity, as proclaimed by the Futuwwa, were codified. Each guild was headed by an ahi or *şeyh* who presided over ceremonial assemblies, particularly those festive assemblies lasting several days, when new members were admitted to the guilds.[22]

Such were some of the general principles of state theory and practice of pre-Ottoman Muslim society, particularly as they relate to trade and the guild organization in the Near

East.   As noted above, there were considerable differences in
the urban tradition of pre-Ottoman Muslim societies and of
Byzantium, and in the practice of the Slavic Balkan states.
In one respect, however, these societies showed great similarity.   Despite the development of the process of feudalization in the Balkans, the role of the state in Byzantium
and the Balkan lands was considerable.   It was precisely
that role, which permeated the entire life of the country
and imparted a special character to the feudal structure of
society (with a centrally apportioned feudal rent and with
the awarding of privileges in obtaining and collecting
taxes), that was inherent in both Byzantine and Muslim tradition and practice.

The question of the continuity of urban life and institutions of the Balkan and Near Eastern peoples into the
Ottoman era would have been resolved long ago had sufficient
material been available.   Unfortunately, concrete information
about urban social relations and institutions is lacking
precisely for the critical first century and a half of
Ottoman rule when the reorganization of social relations was
taking place and new institutions were emerging.

2. BALKAN CITIES, 1400-1600

The generally accepted view in the historiography on the Ottoman conquest is that the destructive force of invasion turned numerous areas of the Balkans into a desert for a prolonged period, and that the local population, routed by the invader, exterminated, or taken away into slavery, declined to the extent that all the more fertile plains became populated by Turks. During the frequent waves of conversions to Islam in the fifteenth and the sixteenth centuries, those urban Greeks, Bulgarians, Serbs, and others who survived chose to withdraw to inaccessible mountains where they founded new settlements. In this way, most of the existing cities also became Turkish.

One of the first (and for a long time the sole) Balkanists of the late nineteenth and the early twentieth centuries to expound this thesis was K. Jireček. In his *Istoriia Bolgar* Jireček characterized the period up to the beginning

of the Bulgarian National Revival (*Vŭzrazhdane*) as the "sad-
dest and darkest period in Bulgarian history."[1] According to
Jireček many of the cities were destroyed and "the inhabitants of the plain fled to the mountains and there founded
new cities."[2] V. Zlatarski, a Bulgarian historian, has also
written about the flight of the population "to out-of-the way
and impregnable places under the impact of the first shock
after the catastrophe and during the incessant wars for conquest of the peninsula."[3] Parallel with this flight was
Ottoman colonization of the eastern and southern Bulgarian
lands, those Zlatarski considered "as the most depopulated."[4]
It was only later, in his opinion, that the Bulgarian population began gradually to descend from the mountains to the
plains and to resettle in the cities.

   Even the most recent surveys do not go beyond these
conclusions. For instance, in *Istoriia na Bŭlgariia* (in
both of the editions put out by the Historical Institute of
the Bulgarian Academy of Sciences), the question of the city
in the Bulgarian lands between the fifteenth and the seventeenth century is not treated in very much detail. The
author of this section limits himself to noting that "some
of the cities fully changed their national appearance," and
that in others the population "was mixed, in most cases with
the Turkish element prevailing."[5] This conception of the
cities in the Bulgarian lands seems to be responsible for the
description of the rebellions of the fifteenth to the seventeenth centuries, despite their obviously urban character, as
spontaneous rural uprisings.[6] The Soviet *Istoriia Bolgarii*,
meanwhile, refers to the consistent displacement of the
Bulgarian population from the cities in the fifteenth and
sixteenth centuries, while the percentage of the Turkish
inhabitants rose to two-thirds of the urban population.[7] Only
recently, in several publications, has an attempt been made
to reassess this question in the light of new data.[8]

   In Yugoslavia, there were differentiated regions of urban
development, due to the various ways in which these regions developed. The literature on urban development along the
Dalmatian coast forms a special part of the historiography
on the cities. The complex fate of these cities--with their
life under Ottoman, then Venetian, and then Austrian dom-
ination--offers a picture of urban development that differs
significantly from that which occurred in the other regions
of modern Yugoslavia.[9] In the region of Bosnia, urban life
developed mostly under the impact of factors that emerged
later in the conditions of the Ottoman feudal system. Because
it was one of the principal Muslim cities in the western
parts of the Balkan Peninsula, Sarajevo continues to attract
the attention of many scholars.[10] The development of the

Serbian cities, however, was rather different. In connection
with the shifting frontier between the Ottoman Empire and
Central Europe, these cities underwent continuous changes.[11]
Thus, Yugoslav literature, together with its findings concerning the destruction of most of the Serbian, Bosnian,
and other cities, and the carrying off or conversion to Islam
of the urban population, also contains conclusions that posit
a considerable urban development during the sixteenth century.

The demographic consequences of the Ottoman invasion
and conquest of Greece are examined in the recently published detailed history of Greece of A. Vakalopoulos. The
author has summed up the results of the research of Greek
historians, has made wide use of the accomplishments of the
scholars of other Balkan lands, and has himself looked into
these questions.[12] Although unable to provide concrete
data on the size of Greek relocation, Vakalopoulos has
established several streams of migration that accompanied the
advance of the Turks in Asia Minor and the Balkans. The
greatest number of Greeks went to Venetian-controlled lands
and islands in the eastern Mediterranean. There was a considerable Greek migration to Italy and also to the Caucasus.
In addition, Vakalopoulos has written about the withdrawal
en masse of the population to mountains and other inaccessible areas as well as to the few "secure" cities such
as Salonika and Ioannina (Yannina), which enjoyed special
privileges. In the Peloponnesus, where the Venetians
continued to rule for a longer period in a few of their fortified ports, people gathered from different places--"Greeks,
Albanians, Albano-Vlachs and even Gypsies, who mixed with
the Franks." The result was a considerable reduction in the
Greek population in the undefended lands.[13]

The demographic and social changes that occurred in
Cyprus after its occupation by the Turks are described
in a generalizing monograph by the Cypriot historian
T. Papadopoulos.[14]

Albanian historiography has also taken up the study of
the socioeconomic development of the Albanian people from
the fifteenth to the seventeenth century.[15] In connection
with attempts to write a new history of Albania, a number
of studies have been undertaken to determine the character
of the Albanian lands both before and after the establishment of Turkish rule. In an article devoted to the position
of cities in the first two centuries of Turkish domination
in Albania, Z. Shkodra has noted "the complete destruction"
of many "flourishing cities and fortresses." Furthermore,
"the big cities of Shköder (Shkodra), Lesh (Alessio), Krujë
(Croia), Durrës (Durazzo), Berati (Berat), Vlona (Vlorë,

Avalone), Gjinokastër (Argyrokastron), and others were either
destroyed and rendered uninhabitable, or reduced to villages
and strong-points where military garrisons were established."[16] However, Shkodra has provided copious information that an economic revival and even a general upsurge
of the cities in which the Albanian element predominated had
already begun in the sixteenth century.[17]

We will not dwell in detail on the negative consequences
of the Turkish conquest or on a general appraisal of the
negative role of Ottoman domination on the development of the
Balkan peoples. These questions have been elaborated in
numerous studies in all Balkan languages and in the major
European languages, and they have been reflected in many
documentary collections. However, the lack of sufficient
data, as explained above, has led people to generalize for
the whole period of Ottoman rule from the well-known facts
concerning the destructive character of the Ottoman invasion,
the original colonization of the Balkans, and the flight of
the local population.

Similar extreme conclusions can be found in Turkish
historiography on the results of Turkish colonization,
the decline of the cities, and the general depopulation of
the Balkans. In the works of the Turkish scholar Ö. L.
Barkan, for example, which are otherwise distinguished by
conscientious research and treatment of sources, there are
some theses that are not fully substantiated. Barkan has
described what he calls the total collapse of the cities
of the Balkan Peninsula. When they subsequently reappeared
in the fifteenth and sixteenth centuries, these cities arose,
in his opinion, as almost a new phenomenon and as a systematic settlement of the Turkish population carried out by the
central authorities. "In this way and contrary to a very
great number of cities in Western Europe," Barkan has argued,
"there is no question at all of a *spontaneous emergence* of
the cities (in the Ottoman Empire); rather, their creation
was a matter of the sultan's will. The sultans, who had at
disposal all the resources of the Empire, ordered that, with
the aid of the means they had amassed, all buildings and installations that a city needed should be constructed."[18] On
this basis Barkan has written that Balkan cities "were, so
to speak, *created anew*," since they "*were populated and
colonized in a systematic manner by the state*"; and he has
characterized "*the most important cities of the Ottoman
Empire* (as) *Turkish and Moslem in their population*" (emphasis
in the original).[19]

Arguing that there was a total break in the urban life
of previous centuries, Barkan has attributed the turkification of cities and the rise of new cities to the increase

in the Muslim population of the Balkan Peninsula, particularly in the cities. In other words, the Turkish invasion
is paradoxically described as an event that brought to an
end that civilization that had given birth to the city in the
first place.[20] It should be pointed out that, thanks to
increased scholarly contacts with Balkan scholars, current
Turkish historiography has toned down some of the above
conclusions.[21]

Extreme interpretations in the opposite sense are encountered in the historiography of other Balkan peoples.
After emphasizing the relative "backwardness of the Turkish
population," which was "at a lower stage of its socioeconomic
development," several scholars have put forward the thesis
that the Ottoman conquest caused a reversal or stagnation,
an expression of which was the almost total ruralization of
the Balkan Peninsula. The presence of several major centers
of consumption, and of Istanbul in particular, has been emphasized to mitigate even more the role of the other cities.
These cities have usually been regarded as strategic fortresses or administrative centers containing only an insignificant non-Muslim population kept there only to provide
for the needs of the auxiliary personnel required by the
Turkish garrison and the parasitic Muslim stratum. The
Turks in the city have generally been regarded as a nonproducing part of the population.

The scholarly treatment of this problem also requires
a reassessment of the widespread thesis concerning the
primitive character of Ottoman feudalism in the Balkans.
Such a view reduces socioeconomic relationships and the
political life of the Ottoman Empire to the level of individual Turkic seminomadic tribes that formed only part of the
Ottoman strike force, and that in the Balkans did not play
the same colonizing role as they did in Anatolia. Moreover,
such a view impoverishes the historical process in that it
does not take into consideration the material base and
culture of the countries and peoples incorporated into the
Ottoman state system; nor does it take into account the
corresponding level of development attained by the upper
levels of the Ottoman ruling class, which in the first centuries of Ottoman rule was to a great extent made up of persons who had assimilated the high culture of Byzantium, the
Middle East, and the Balkans.

* * *

Marxist historical science does not take a static view
of the city, but examines its development in connection with
the social division of labor. Furthermore, in accord with
the predominance of this or that urban feature, it introduces

a different manner of establishing the typology of the cities
in a given social system. Marxists consider the productive
functions to be the determinant factor. Speaking in a very
general way, we would accept the following definition of a
city: an agglomeration of people, to a greater or lesser
extent detached from farming and engaged in industrial and
commercial activity, and possessing a definite administrative
status. In the feudal city under consideration, the concentration of craftsmen did not, of course, imply the absence
of craftsmen in the surrounding villages, and similarly, the
predominance of artisan, manufacturing, and commercial
activity in the city did not exclude the semiagrarian character of a number of urban settlements.

The absence of sufficient source material is not the
sole stumbling block facing the student of the Balkan city
in the classical period of Ottoman feudalism. The one-
sidedness of the material makes it nearly impossible to
formulate accurate criteria for determining the true urban
character of each of the inhabited localities that are called
cities in various documents and accounts. What we are
referring to here is the lack of sufficient data on the
economic side of urban life and on the productive activity
of the population. The study of the Balkan city is still
in the stage where even the most general questions are yet
to be resolved: the number of cities, the size and structure
of the urban population, the place of the city in the
feudal economy, and so on.

Furthermore, the state of historiography on the medieval
Balkan city fails to provide the researcher with a firm
point of departure for investigating, in the period preceding
the Turkish invasion, the processes that were to continue
after the Turkish settlement in the Balkans, which are precisely the object of this present discussion. Nevertheless,
various bits of evidence in the medieval sources, when
combined with archaeological data, do permit certain conclusions about the toponymy of the urban localities, their
general appearance, and certain aspects of their internal
life. On the whole, these sources indicate a considerable
spread of urban life as an inherent feature of feudalism
in the Balkan lands, and such a conclusion is supported by
later travel accounts. Before starting their journeys
through the Balkan lands under Turkish rule, many travelers
had first familiarized themselves with information about
the settlements through which they were to pass, and in their
accounts they attached great importance to the remnants of
the ancient and medieval past.

But circumstances demand that, in attempting to answer

(to the extent possible) the question of the distribution, composition, and nature of cities, one must inevitably refer most of all to Turkish sources. To employ, however, a comparative analysis of the documentary material on cities from the Turkish sources requires one to resort to the classification of settlements adopted by the Ottoman administration.

However incomplete the juridical grounds used by the state for proclaiming a given settlement to be a city and not a village, the legislative documents of most countries often mention the numerous administrative, political, and other considerations involved in making such decisions. The legislation of the reign of Mehmed II "The Conqueror" (1451-81) and of Süleyman "The Magnificent" (1520-66), however, which is rather detailed on all other basic questions, contains practically no direct information on the status of the city. This legislation regulates trade in the majority of commodities, covers the rendering of various artisan and other services, and defines the difference in the status of the urban and rural population. But it says nothing about the criteria applied by Ottoman authorities to delineate the city as a definite entity.[22]

Here of course one might refer to general Muslim practice, which had already been adopted and codified at the time of the first Muslim conquests. The pre-existing division and status of the population of cities and villages was preserved by means of definite obligations (the *haraç*, a land tax on non-Muslims; and the cizye) meant to emphasize the basic distinction between the faithful (the *müslim*, a person "surrendered to God") and the infidel (the *kâfir*). The Muslim tradition accordingly contained no religious and dogmatic obstacle preventing the Ottoman state from adopting the existing material base--and hence the existing differentiation between cities and villages--of Byzantine times and of the period of the independent Balkan states. Such a continuity of Balkan urban life was eased by the general similarity of feudalism in the Balkan lands in the pre- and postinvasion periods; indeed, one of the characteristic features of both periods in the development of the Balkans was the spread of the cities. Unfortunately, having noted this connection, we have to add that it fails to bring us any closer to a solution, since the question of the status of the medieval Balkan and late Byzantine city has not been particularly well researched. Furthermore, the mechanical use of categories from another epoch, one distant not only chronologically but also in terms of the major changes that took place in all of Balkan life in the intervening period of the

fourteenth and fifteenth centuries, can even more quickly
lead one astray.[23]

Such, then, are the considerations that have compelled
us to adopt, with all of its conventionality, the Ottoman
conception of the cities. In doing so we at least possess
unified initial material. Difficulties do arise, however, in
how to interpret the designation encountered most frequently
in the documents, *nefs*.[24] In literal translation nefs means
"the very," "the very place," and it indicates the center of
a *nahiye* (i.e., an administrative entity that was a component
part of the larger territorial unit known as the *kaza*). Additional clarification, therefore, must be sought in the
Turkish documents to ascertain the true character of the settlements so designated.

In the Ottoman state, the administration not only
clearly distinguished the status of the city from that of the
village, but it also introduced a certain classification of
the urban settlements themselves.

In the Muslim world the generally accepted term for
designating a city was *şehir*.[25] In Ottoman documents this
term denoted a fully developed city. There was a separate
term for a fortress, *kale*, which denoted both the city fortress (the citadel) and a fortified city itself.[26] The city
(şehir) usually had a fortified part housing the Turkish administration, the guard, Christian families entrusted with
special duties, and (if there was one) the garrison.

The term *kasaba*[27] was used in the documents to denote a
settlement of an urban type that had exceeded a village in
size and importance, but which had not yet reached the
dimensions and appearance of a city (şehir). The kasaba was
an unfortified settlement whose population engaged in trade
and handicrafts. Like every city, its territory had fixed
boundaries, but it possessed only a minimum number of public
buildings.[28] It took a royal order to proclaim a settlement
to be a kasaba, since this matter involved changes in the
status and tax obligations of the urban population (which was
chiefly Muslim).

In and of itself, the *palanka* could not have the status
of a city, since it simply represented a place fortified with
embankments and stakes, of the kind seen both in kasabas and
villages. Palankas emerged in the second half of the
sixteenth century and particularly in the seventeenth century
in connection with an increase in the frequency of *haydut*
raids.[29] In the early seventeenth century (1621) an anony-
mous French author wrote that most villages in Serbia and
Bulgaria had fortified stockades--that is, palankas.[30] Their
outward appearance and the manner of their construction are
well known from the accounts of foreign and Turkish travelers.

The *varoš* represented a suburb of the medieval Balkan
city, and in Ottoman times it was the Christian part of the
city.

More frequently in the western parts of the Balkan Peninsula than in the east, one encounters as well the names
tărg and *pazar*--the Slavic and Ottoman (of Persian origin)
names for small towns of the kasaba type--for settlements
differing considerably from the village thanks to the presence of a regular market, but still without the status of
a kasaba.[31]

When documents (most often fiscal) used different de-
signations for the same city, what was usually at issue were
references to a definite group of the population living
either in the kale, in the varoš, or in the remaining part
of the city. In some cases these terms were used in one and
the same context.[32]

For the late fifteeenth and the early sixteenth century,
over two-hundred settlements on the Balkan Peninsula under
Ottoman rule are listed as cities in Turkish registers. This
figure does not include all of the cities of that time, since
the information on which the figure is based has been drawn
from sources that are not exhaustive concerning all settlements. Furthermore, cases are still coming to light of villages that were proclaimed kasabas at the beginning of or in
the course of the sixteenth century. As noted, the greatest
difficulty consists in determining to what extent settlements that the registers designated as nefs were really
cities or represented small mining settlements, market
places, and fortresses (some even in a state of decline).
Thus, a mid-fifteenth century register of the sancak of
Nikopol indicates as distinct from the villages (and apart
from such sixteenth century and later cities of Nikopol,
Tŭrnovo, Svishtov, Ruse, Vratsa, etc.), such settlements as
Pleven, Riakhovo, Cherven, Gigen, Reselets and Kurshuna.[33]
Some of these settlements failed to develop into cities, and
others, such as the Bulgarian medieval stronghold of Cherven,
faded completely. Only Pleven and Riakhovo consolidated
themselves and subsequently developed as urban centers.
Other sancaks provide similar examples. In any event, the
absolute number of cities is not particularly important here.
Any such number would differ insignificantly from the already
established number, and since our analysis is based only on
the available data on the settlements (which cover about
half of them), the absence of an absolute number of cities
will hardly affect the conclusions that we are drawing about
the character of the city and the relative spread of urban
settlements on the Balkan Peninsula.

* * *

The Turkish conquest of the Balkans was carried out in
several consecutive stages. Fifty years passed from the
first lodgment of the Turks on the Gallipoli Peninsula (the
mid-fourteenth century) to the occupation of the eastern and
central parts of the Balkans. The second stage of Turkish
consolidation in the Balkans had begun by the middle of the
fifteenth century. It took about three decades to seize the
remaining Greek lands on the peninsula, and Bosnia, Hercegovina, and the hitherto unoccupied Serbian lands. In the
early decades of the sixteenth century the Turks directed
their attack at Croatia and at Hungary, which possessed
territory south of the Danube. Belgrade fell in 1521 and
Buda (now Budapest) in 1541. The remaining western parts
of the peninsula were annexed a little later. Thus, before
the end of the sixteenth century, the Ottoman state incorporated within its boundaries the entire Balkan Peninsula
and parts of Central Europe.

Simultaneously with the seizure of territories, the
Turks set up their administrative organization. The basic
administrative unit of the Ottoman Empire was the sancak
(although in the frontier areas a slightly different territorial status was introduced). The term "sancak" in Turkish
(or *liva* in Arabic), which translates as "standard" or
"flag," is evidence of how the administrative division in
the Ottoman state followed military lines. The administrative governor simultaneously commanded the *sipahi* feudal
cavalry force and other troops recruited in the territory
of the sancak. The size of a sancak depended on many factors
--on the course of the conquest itself, on the existing
political and administrative structure, on geographic conditions, and on considerations of military strategy. Accordingly, changes occurring in the frontier areas also led to
changes in the sancaks of the interior.

A certain number of sancaks, joined together by both a
common administrative and military subordination, formed the
largest administrative unit--the *beylerbeylik* (or *eyalet*)
headed by a *beylerbeyi* ("bey of beys"). Despite possible
differences in territorial extent, in the number of troops
recruited, and in the amount of taxes collected, the
various sancaks that together formed a beylerbeylik were all
equal to one another in a legal and administrative sense and
were equally subordinate to the beylerbeyi. The sancak,
however, that served as the seat of a beylerbeyi was called
a "paşa sancak" after the title of the beylerbeyi (who was
usually called a *paşa* and later a *vezir*).[34]

In its turn, the sancak was divided into smaller units
called nahiyes--districts. The nahiye stood closest to the
existing administrative organization and was composed of a
few villages and a fortress or town, usually a small one.

The administrative governor resided in the central settlement, which might also be a large village.

The kaza or *kadılık* was originally a territory covered
by the judicial authority of a kadı. Insofar as the kadı
was also entrusted with extensive administrative power, however, the kadılıks or kazas soon became administrative units
of their own, ranking between the nahiye and the sancak.
Unlike the nahiyes and sancaks, which were present everywhere, kadılıks were found only where a Muslim population
was present.[35]

The Balkan Peninsula was divided into some thirty
sancaks whose number and territorial size were subject to
change with the expansion of Ottoman terriory. Until the
fall of Buda (1541), all sancaks in the European part of the
Ottoman Empire formed the beylerbeylik of Rumelia, which was
the first beylerbeylik of the Ottoman Empire. (The term
"Rumeli"--"Roman country" in the Byzantine sense--was used to
denote the territories north of the Dardanelles and the
Bosporus.) As a differentiated administrative unit, the
beylerbeylik of Rumelia was founded after the conquest
of Edirne (1362 or 1371), which was proclaimed the capital.
Gelibolu (Gallipoli) and Plovdiv were also the seats of a
beylerbeyi until the occupation of Constantinople (1453)
and its adoption as capital of the Ottoman Empire; later,
Edirne and Sofia (from the sixteenth century) were also seats
of a beylerbeyi.

Cities also played a definite role in the establishment
of the administrative system. As a rule, administrative
units were named after the larger cities that fell within
their boundaries, cities that were also the seat of the
territory's administrative-judicial and military authorities.
This coincidence of the administrative hierarchy with the
hierarchy of cities was also linked to unique features of the
Ottoman military-fief system.[36]

The first sancak in the Balkans, Gelibolu, originally
encompassed only the Gallipoli Peninsula; it later also included the islands of Imroz (Imbros), Lemnos, Samothrace,
Thasos, and Bozcaada (Tenedos). As a *has* of a *kapudan paşa*
or admiral,[37] this sancak also embodied the districts situated on the Aegean coast, at first as far as Komotinē
(Gümüljina). At the time of Kaireddin Barbarossa (1483-
1546), who took over the command of the Ottoman navy as
kapudan paşa with the title of beylerbeyi, a new eyalet,
Cezair, was set up. In addition to the Gallipoli Peninsula,
it included the entire Thracian coast, parts of the coasts
of central and western Greece, the islands of Euboea
(Evvoia), Lesbos (Mytilene, Mytilini), Rhodes (Rodos), Chios
(Khios), Andros, and the area of Izmir (Smyrna).

Also located in eastern Thrace was the sancak of Vize--

the European hinterland of Constantinople--with about ten
cities (Babaeski, Vize, Derkos, Ereğli, Inces, Kırklareli
[Kirk-Kilissa, Lozengrad], Lüleburgaz, Silivri, Hayrobolu,
Çorlu); and the sancak of Chirmen, which comprised the lands
between the Sredna Gora Mountains and the Stara Planina (Balkan Mountains), the territory east of the Strema River (Stri-
ama River), and along the left bank of the lower reaches of
the Arda River (with the cities of Kazanlŭk, Yenice [Chirpan],
Nova Zagora, Khaskovo, and Chirmen [Chernomen]). The sancak
of Edirne was the largest in the beylerbeylik of Rumelia, and
for a certain period of time it was even identified with it.
As a sancak of a beylerbeyi it is better known in the literature as *Paşa Sancak* because it was under the direct rule of
the beylerbeyi. It spread over the remaining part of eastern
Thrace and took in the entire massif of the Rhodope Mountains,
the Aegean coastal region, the valley of the Maritsa River
(in Greece the Evros; in Turkey the Meriç), and the valley of
the Vardar River (in Greece the Vardares) up to the western
Macedonian mountain range. Here is how an account of 1530
described the settlements of this sancak: "Account of the left
and right sides of *Liva Paşa* which has: 32 kadılıks, 9 fortresses, 35 cities proper and kasabas, 3,859 villages."[38]
Nine of the cities were located in Thrace (from Ipsala to
Tatar Pazardzhik); eleven were situated on the Aegean coast
(from Enez [Aenos] to Salonika and in the north up through
Nevrokop); and fifteen were found in Macedonia. Originally
forming a frontier area (an uc), the city of Skopje (Skoplje,
Üsküb) joined the Paşa Sancak about 1463. A separate sancak
of Skopje was formed in 1553.[39]

In the late fourteenth century an administrative organ-
ization was carried out of the lands north of the Balkan
Mountains (northeastern Bulgaria), Epirus, and Thessaly.
The sancak of Sofia was formed for the area that included the
following cities: Berkovitsa, Breznik, Ikhtiman, Samokov,
Sofia, Chiprovtsi and Pirot (Şehir-köy). The sancak of
Kiustendil extended over the Vranja area and Pomoravia and
took in part of Macedonia. It included the cities of Vranja,
Dupnitsa (now Stanke Dimitrov), Kratovo, Melnik, Nugeric,
Petrich, Radomir, Strumica, Štip, and Kiustendil.

Northern Bulgaria was divided into three sancaks: the
sancak of Vidin, which comprised the valley of the Timok
River (with three cities); the sancak of Nikopol, from the
Belogradchik and Vratsa Mountains to a line to the east
between Silistra and Shumen (with a dozen cities); and the
sancak of Silistra. The sancak of Silistra, established
probably in the fifteenth century, occupied a territory that,
after the Ottoman conquest of part of Bessarabia, extended
from south of the Balkan Mountains north beyond the Danube;

it included the Black Sea coast from the mouth of the Danube
to the Veleka River and the Sakar Mountains to the south, the
whole of the Dobruja, the eastern part of the Balkan Mountains, and northeastern Thrace. It therefore encompassed, in
addition to the Black Sea cities of Pomorie (Ankhialo), Varna,
and Nessebŭr (Messembria), and the Danubian cities of
Silistra, Turtucaia (Tutrakan) and Hirşova, the cities of
Provadiia, Karnobat, and Iambol.

The sancak of Ohrid extended to cover northern Albania
(with the city of Krujë). In the 1430s central and southern
Albania were merged into the sancak of Arvanid with the city
of Gjinokastër as its center.[40] The liberation movement led
by Georgi Castrioti Scanderbeg that broke out some ten years
later restored the country's independence for about half a
century. In the second half of the fifteenth century (1466),
the Turks founded the city of Elbasani (Elbasan) and occupied
the northern areas of Albania including the city of Shkodër
(1479). In the early sixteenth century , the Albanian lands
were divided into the sancaks of Elbasani, Vlona, Shkodër,
Prizren, and Ohrid. These sancaks contained eleven cities
and twenty-three fortresses.

The region between southern Albania and Thessaly formed
a separate sancak of Ioannina with the cities of Arta,
Kónitsa, Përmet, Rinasa, Ioannina, and Rogos. Also located
in Thessaly was the sancak of Trikkala with a number of previously existing cities such as Agrafa, Domokos, Elasona,
Navpaktos (Inebahti), Trikkala, Phanarion (Fanarion), the
newly founded Yenişehir (Larissa), and Catalça (Pahrsalus).
Together with the island of Leukas (Leucadia), the regions
of Arcadia and Aetolia in the western coastal parts of Greece
formed the sancak of Karliili (Preveza). The sancak of
Florina (Phlórina), with the city of the same name (also
called Lerin), was the smallest sancak.

The final conquest of the Greek lands on the Balkan
Peninsula was completed after the fall of Constantinople.
It was then that the sancak of Agribos was formed. It was
composed of the island of Euboea and the part of central
Greece opposite it, with the cities of Athens, Karystos
(Karistos, Kizilhisar), Lamia (Izdin, Zituni), Lebadeia
(Levádeia), Salona (Amphissa), and Thebes (Thevai). The
Peloponnesus formed the separate sancak of Peloponnesus and
included about ten cities and fortresses.

The greatest changes took place in the administrative
organization of the western parts of the Balkan Peninsula.[41]
By the middle of the fifteenth century, the Serbian lands
and the greater part of Bosnia and Hercegovina were finally
conquered. The sancak of Smederevo, which comprised the
former region of Belgrade and Braničevo plus Šumadija, was

the largest sancak in the Serbian lands. It included the
most important fortresses on the Danube and several mining
settlements. Although the seat of the *sancakbeyi* was transferred to Belgrade after that city's occupation in the early
sixteenth century, the sancak retained the name of Smederevo
until the eighteenth century. The sancak of Vuk, known later
as the sancak of Vučitrn, was formed from the lands of the
last Serbian king; it ran along the left banks of the rivers
Sitnica and Ibar and took in four cities: Vučitrn, Novo Brdo,
Priština, and Trepča. The right banks of the same rivers
formed the territory of the sancak of Prizren, which also
included Metohija. The basins of the lower reaches of the
two Morava rivers and part of the basin of the Nišava River
were incorporated into the sancak of Alaça Hisar (Kruševac),
which included the cities of Kruševac, Bolvan, Zaplanina,
Leskovac, Kuršumlija, Medvedza, Plana, and Prokuplje (Urkup).

The first seat of the Bosnia sancakbeyi was the city of
Jajce, but after the establishment of Sarajevo as a kasaba
(1461-62) the sancakbeyi moved there. The sancak of Hercegovina was set up in 1470 with the town of Foča as its center,
and in 1480 the sancak of Zvornik was established (after the
city of the same name).

In the early sixteenth century and finally in the 1520s
and 1530s, many Hungarian possessions in the Balkans were
seized and joined to the sancaks of Zvornik and Bosnia. The
conquered cities and strongholds met different fates. Some
of them were destroyed and abandoned, others were fortified
and enlarged. In the early sixteenth century, there were
more than ten cities in Bosnia: Banja Luka, Visoko, Višegrad,
Novi Pazar, Konjič, Livno, Olovo, Sarajevo, Travnik, Jajce,
and so on. The sancak of Hercegovina was smaller and
contained fewer cities: Foča, Cajniče, Prijepolje, Plevlja,
Mostar, Goražde, and Blagaj. The sancak of Zvornik incorporated a few cities: Zvornik, Srebrenica, Sremska Mitrovica,
Gračanica, Gorna Tuzla, and Dolna Tuzla.

After the fall of Belgrade and the conquest of Srem
(Syrmia), the sancak of Osijek or Srem was founded with its
seat in Osijek and later in Ilok. In 1537 the sancak of
Požega was set up, but in 1580 its territory was attached to
the sancak of Bosnia. With the expansion of the Ottoman
possessions beyond the Danube, a new eyalet of Budim was
founded (1541). The new eyalet included some of the sancaks
of the Rumelian beylerbeylik, specifically those of Smederevo,
Zvornik, and the newly established sancaks of Srem and Požega.

The successful advance of the Turks on Slavonia in the
middle of the century resulted in the formation of the sancak
of Začasna, known also as Čazma or Pakrac after the name of
the settlements where the sancakbeyi resided. Some Bosnian

lands were attached to these sancaks. After new acquisitions,
another sancak, Krk (1580), was separated from the sancak of
Klis, which had been founded in the late 1530s in the Croatian lands.

The expansion of captured territory and the particular
attention that was attached to the western sancaks in defending the Ottoman provinces on the Balkan Peninsula produced
a new eyalet known as the Bosnian *paşalık*. It was established in 1589 with its seat in Banja Luka. It incorporated
the sancaks of Bosnia (Paşa Sancak); those of Hercegovina,
Klis, Pakrac, and Krk, which were taken from the beylerbeylik
of Rumelia; and the sancaks of Zvornik and Požega, now
transferred from the eyalet of Budim. In the sixteenth
century along with the changing fortunes of Ottoman arms
against Austria, other changes occurred in the territorial
breakdown of the lands in the western parts of the Balkan
peninsula.

Information on the population of cities is even scantier
than our knowledge of the number of cities (or at least that
can be established by using the names of urban settlements).
The Ottoman authorities started the registration of the
population as early as the first half of the fifteenth
century, but such registrations became regular only in the
second half of the century, taking place at intervals of
from ten to twenty years. The registration of a given
sancak took from one to two years.[42] The data from registers
used for taxation of the population or for the allocation
of feudal revenue provide a basis for calculating the size
of cities throughout the fifteenth and the sixteenth
centuries. However, due both to the insufficiency of these
data and to their character, determining the absolute number
of the urban population at that stage is impossible. In
those same centuries accidental factors played a significant
role in the uneven development of cities: some of them
remained depopulated, others expanded as a result of their
temporary role as frontier towns with the accompanying influx
of troops and auxiliary groups (and then, with the shifting
of frontiers, they declined). It must be regretted that
contemporary registrations were not conducted simultaneously
all over the territory, and that the surviving registers
are not exhaustive enough to permit a determination of
the absolute size of the population for a given period.

The data on taxable households are also insufficient
to establish the absolute number of the population. It is
necessary both to discover new sources and to analyze very
carefully the position of the individual household, which
varied greatly during that period in the Balkans.[43] Even
for individual areas, we still lack studies on the average

size of a household. There are no reliable data for the tax-
exempt part of the population either. Along with permanent
residents and the representatives of the ruling stratum who
were exempt on various grounds, this nontaxable population
included segments of the military and semi-military sectors
(an extremely variable factor due to frequent military operations). Accordingly, we have refrained from making calculations and drawing conclusions about the absolute size of the
urban population; rather, we have focused our efforts on
establishing the kinds of cities, their classification, and
the ratio of the urban to the nonurban taxable population.
The categories of contemporary demography rank cities as
small (10,000 to 50,000 inhabitants), medium (50,000 to
100,000), and large (over 100,000).   For the Middle Ages
most observers divide cities into small (up to 2,000 inhabitants), medium (from 2,000 to 10,000), and large (over
10,000). Some authors add more groupings, for example, a
category of pocket cities (*gradove dzhudzheta*), which
contained from several tens of inhabitants to several hundreds; others rank cities in terms of the geometric progres-
sion of their population (starting with cities with 200 to
400 inhabitants); and a third group prefers to take into
account the socioeconomic and political role of the city.[44]
      No attempt has yet been made to classify Balkan cities
by size of population. Taking into account the available
data and the accepted division of European cities, we have
attempted this kind of classification on the basis of the
number of taxable households or houses rather than in terms
of the total size of the populations (see table 1). In the
Ottoman Empire the household or the house was the taxable
entity. When referring to the fifteenth and sixteenth
centuries, this taxable entity (called the *hane* from the
word for house) may be identified with a household represented by the head of the family. As well as with the help
of certain other kinds of evidence, this identification has
been made on the basis of numerous comparisons of enumera-
tions and changes in the number of hanes ("newly found,"
"deceased," "converted to Islam").[45] In certain cases the
records provide the occupation of the person taxed, thus
permitting an even more accurate determination of the
correspondence between hane and household. Contemporary
historians of the Balkans have adopted this method.[46]
      The use of three different periods permits greater
accuracy by making it possible to employ kindred eras to
group cities for which information is available only at
certain times; or, one can compare the three periods. (A
number of cities are repeated over the three periods, but
in the absence of complete data, one cannot draw conclusions

DISTRIBUTION OF BALKAN CITIES IN THE 15TH AND 16TH CENTURIES
ACCORDING TO THE NUMBER OF HOUSEHOLDS

Period	Total number of cities		Size						
			Up to 400 Households		401-800 Households		801-1,600 Households		Over 1,600 Households
	Number/Percentage		Number/Percentage		Number/Percentage		Number/Percentage		Number/Percentage
15th century	48	100.0	38	79.2	7	14.6	2	4.2	1	2.0
16th century (first half)	86	100.0	47	54.7	26	30.2	10	11.6	3	3.5
16th century (second half)	36	100.0	12	33.3	5	13.9	11	30.6	8	22.2

SOURCE: T. Gökbilgin, "Kanunî Sultan Süleymen Devri başlarinda Rumeli eyaleti livalari, şehir ve kasabalari," *Belleten* 20 (1956): 261-85; idem, *XV-XVI inci asirlarda Edirne*, pp. 37-68; İnalcik, *Hicrî 835 Tarihi*, pp. i, xvii, xxxv, 1, 4, 5, 28, 30; Ö. L. Barkan, "Essai sur les données statistiques des registres de recensement dans l'Europe Ottoman aux XVe et XVIe siècles," *Journal of Economic and Social History of the Orient* 1, no.1 (1957): 34-36; idem, "Tarihi demografi araştirmalari ve osmali tarihi," *Tarihi Mecmuasi* 10 (1953): 22; M. Sokoloski, "Le développement de quelques villes dans le sud des Balkans aux XVe et XVIe siècles," *Balkanica* 1 (1970): 83, 89, 93, 95, 96, 98-105; Handžić, "Zvornik," pp. 176-91; idem, "Grad Šabac i nijegova nahija u prvoj polovini XVI vijeka," *Članci i grada za kulturnu istoriju istočne Bosne* (Sarajevo, 1961) pp. 97-108; Šabanović, *Bosanski pašaluk*, pp. 115-228; Shkodra, "Qytetet shqiptare," p. 71; *Turski izvori* 2: 161, 165, 187, 193, 199, 233, 243, 245, 253, 271, 333, 389.

about the general increase in the number of cities. This
matter of growth in the number of cities is examined in a
separate section below, where information from more dates is
compared.) Here we are simply establishing the categories of
the city by size, and for each of the different eras, determining how, in terms of size, these cities are distributed
in percentage terms. The figures cited below for the number
of inhabitants is tentative, but we can affirm that if a
five-member household is taken as the basis the numbers
indicated are not only conservative but would form the lowest
possible limit of the urban population.

The first group comprises settlements with up to 400
taxable households (or with a population ranging from several
hundred to 2,000 people); the next--cities with between 401
and 800 taxable households (and a population of up to 4,000-
5,000 people); the third--cities with between 801 and 1,600
taxable households (and a population of up to 8,000-10,000
inhabitants); and the last--cities with more than 10,000
inhabitants.

For the fifteenth century, more than three-fourths of
the cities for which we have information belong to the first
group, which might be defined as the group of small cities.
For the sixteenth century, however, the relative number of
cities in this group decreases nearly twofold; it now comprises
only about one-third of the total number of cities surveyed.

As the range of this first group includes cities of
very small size, it is necessary to examine the internal
distribution of the settlements included, and proceeding
from the number of households, to determine which cities
accurately convey the typical image of the small city.

For the fifteenth century the group of small cities
includes 7 settlements with up to 100 taxable households (or
18.4% of the total of this group), 14 cities with between 101
and 200 households (36,8%), 11 cities with between 201 and 300
households (28.9%), and 6 settlements with between 301 and
400 households (15.8%). This data thus reveals that cities
with between 100 to 300 households are the decisive element
in defining the group of small cities. For the fifteenth
century such cities comprise 65.7% of the total number
of settlements in the group of small cities; for the second
half of the sixteenth century this share rises to 85%. For
the sixteenth century, furthermore, cities with up to 100
households considerably decrease in number.

The figures show that even the group of small cities
was dominated by settlements in which the taxable population
numbered about 1,000 people or more. In their size--and
without taking into account the tax-exempt population and
the representatives of the feudal class, the administration,

and the various categories of military personnel--these settlements fully corresponded to the small cities of medieval
Western Europe.

The next two groups, containing cities with from 401 to
1,600 taxable households, comprise cities of medium size.
Taken together, for the fifteenth century these groups account
for 18.8% of the total number of cities surveyed--a figure
that increases to 41% for the first half of the sixteenth
century and to 44.5% for the second half. As indicated by
the percentage increase, settlements of this size were becoming significantly more widespread. The sixteenth-century
increase in the number of such cities is due not only to the
availability of more information about the cities of that
period; it also reflects the movement of a number of small
cities into the higher category during this era. Ruse, for
example, which in the middle of the fifteenth century had
243 households, by 1520-30 had grown to 668 households. The
two Albanian cities of Berati and Ioannina, which in the 1430s
had some 200 households each, came in the early sixteenth
century to exceed 500 households. By the 1570s the number
of households in Kiustendil had increased from 375 to 833.
Sarajevo also showed a rapid development; twenty years after
its founding it had 181 households, a number that, in the
first half of the sixteenth century, increased to 1,024, and
in the second half of the same century reached 4,270. In
one century Nikopol grew from 754 households to 1,243 (in the
1530s). There was also an increase in the number of households of many settlements that remained within the category
of the medium-sized city.

Cities with more than 1,600 taxable households form
the group of large cities. (We are excluding Istanbul from
this group because of its unique development as the capital
of the empire). Certain characteristic features in the
classification of Balkan cities are thrown into better
relief when one also takes into consideration the number of
households these cities contained. What stands out from
table 1 is that the number of households in the medium-sized
cities, although fluctuating, shows no constant increase or
decrease over the three periods included. At the same time,
however, the number of households in the large cities
increased many times over. This well-represented category
illustrates one of the unique features of the urban network
in the Balkans: the widespread distribution of settlements
with several thousand inhabitants. This feature can be
explained by the level of Balkan economic development, and
in particular its potential for supplying the urban
populace with agricultural produce.[47]

Although the categories used here do reflect the size

of the city, they still fail to provide an accurate idea of
the true importance of this or that individual city in that
epoch. As noted by R. Mols, a prominent expert in the demographic history of the West European city: "In point of fact,
there is no parallelism between the importance of a town in
the past and the absolute number of the population." In the
period of their great splendor from the thirteenth to the
fifteenth century, when they were the uncontested metropo-
lises of northern Germany and Belgium, Lübeck, Cologne,
Brussels, and Antwerp had modest populations of 10,000,
15,000, 40,000, and 80,000 inhabitants.[48]

The Balkan cities of relatively comparable importance in
the fifteenth and the early sixteenth century were Edirne
and Salonika (each with more than 5,000 households), Sarajevo
(which in the second half of the sixteenth century exceeded
4,000 households), Athens (with more than 2,000 households in
the early sixteenth century), and Vidin and Nikopol (which in
the second half of the sixteenth century also had over 2,000
households each). Only Istanbul surpassed these cities; as
early as the 1470s it had 16,024 households.[49] In their number and the size of their populations, this group of large
cities on the Balkans did not generally differ from the category of large cities in Western Europe. In the European
states of that time cities numbering 20,000 inhabitants or
more were exceptions; only capitals had populations several
time more numerous than those of the other cities. By 1500
six cities in Europe had over 100,000 inhabitants: Paris,
Naples, Venice, Milan, Istanbul, and Moscow.[50]

In comparison with Western Europe, however, the small
city was less strongly represented on the Balkans. In
early sixteenth-century Germany, for example, there were
some 150 cities with a population of from 1,000 to 2,000
people and about 2,500 (often cities in name only) with
populations below 1,000 people.[51] With the exception of
about 10 settlements, all of the 160 cities of mid-sixteenth-
century Russia had from 1,000 to 2,000 inhabitants.[52] In
Brabant, one of the most developed regions of today's
Belgium, where at the end of the fifteenth century (1496)
about 45% of the entire population was concentrated in the
cities, 37.7% of the urban population lived in small cities.[53]

* * *

The Balkan city possesses its own unique architectural
and planning features, and it had these attributes not in the
nineteenth and twentieth centuries, but in earlier centuries
as well.

Accounts that have been preserved from the fifteenth and
sixteenth centuries reveal a number of features that distinguish both the Balkan Muslim city from other Muslim cities,

and the Balkan Christian city from the city of Western Europe.
Contemporary travelers were usually representatives of court
and business circles of Western Europe and had for the most
part been entrusted with a diplomatic or other mission.[54]
Their descriptions, however much they differ in their authors'
interest in the present and past of the lands through which
they passed, and in the wealth and depth of the impressions
they gleaned, do coincide in several respects.

The travelers were generally disappointed by the destruction or absence of the fortress walls of Balkan cities. For
the Western traveler, it was the fortress wall that essentially symbolized and distinguished the city. He rarely
failed to note the absence of fortress walls in Balkan settlements as the basic difference setting these cities apart
from those of Western Europe. "There is," noted one traveler, "no fortified wall to shelter the frightened one."[55]
This circumstance made travelers skeptical about the status
of the settlements they entered. For them, the remains of
ancient or more recent ramparts were practically the only
grounds on which they would accept the "open" settlement
as a city.

The absence of multistoried stone buildings puzzled them
no less. Practically all travelers noted that they had
failed to see "any house resembling tall castles" and that
the buildings were low, single-storied, and, moreover, "made
of planks." They were disappointed with the squat wooden
houses they encountered, and it was with "grief" that they
viewed the "deplorable appearance" of houses constructed of
wattle and daub.

Such appraisals of Ottoman cities held true regardless
of their size; even Istanbul was no exception. Hans Dernschwam, one of the most well-educated travelers (his description of life in the sixteenth-century Ottoman Empire ranks as
one of the more interesting, genuine, and faithful accounts),
summarized what he had seen in 1553 to 1555 in the capital
and in the Balkan provinces thus: "The buildings are of wood,
single-storied, built directly on the ground and on a level
with it, without underground or vaulted cellars which are
lacking in all these countries." Continuing with a description of Plovdiv, he added: "One does not see noteworthy buildings, or, except mosques and public baths, beautiful urban
residences. The other buildings are all artisan's sheds
or shops, as in Istanbul and Edirne." About Sofia, Dernschwam wrote: "The city is large and long, is not walled
and the houses are clayed, as in Istanbul."[56] Another well-
known traveler, Reinold Lubenau, who in the 1580s traveled
over the entire Balkan Peninsula and Asia Minor, was also
taken aback by the squat houses in Belgrade and in most
other Balkan cities.

According to these and other observers, however, most of
the cities mentioned were well populated, even densely so, and
noteworthy for their intensive commercial and artisan life.
Lubenau remarked about Belgrade that "in its shops a person
can obtain everything that he desires, as in the most advanced
cities of Italy and Germany." He extended this characteristic
to include Sofia and other well-known Ottoman cities.[57] Those
who passed through or stopped over in Sofia remarked that it
was "in our time a famous market place" and characterized it
as "large and with numerous merchants." And an early seventeenth century traveler named Wehner found Sofia to be a
"well-populated commercial city, as large as the German city
of Worms."[58]

The appearance of the Balkan city, which the travelers
found so unusual, helps greatly to explain the view that
came to prevail concerning the turkification of cities as a
result of the Ottoman conquest. Both the squat houses that
were so very different from those in the Western medieval
city and the small number of large stone buildings (which
in turn were converted into mosques and public baths) lent
an eastern flavor to the city. It was always hard for these
travelers to see the workshop of the non-Muslim--externally
it did not particularly differ from the Muslim workshop. In
a brief stay, and given such factors as the general suspi-
ciousness toward foreigners, the oppression of the Christian
population, and finally that administrative power and the
chief urban posts were firmly in the hands of the dominant
Muslims, it was not easy for the traveler to grasp the non-
Muslim base of the city and the true numerical relationships
among the individual components of the population.

* * *

If we are to resolve the major question of the direct
consequences of the establishment of the Turkish rule on
Balkan lands and cities, we need concrete studies on the
real changes that occurred, rather than vague conclusions on
general consequences. This can only be done through studies
on particular areas, the compilation of which will lead to
more comprehensive generalizations. Of considerable interest
in this respect is the information on settlements located
along the Constantinople road. The discovery of demographic
changes and of the emergence of new settlements and their
transition from one category into another--that is, the
study of the changes that took place along one of the best
maintained and protected highways in the Balkans--is of
primary importance for clarifying the question of the ways
the Turkish invasion influenced Balkan settlements.

The fate of the Constantinople road, which was used

during Roman times and throughout the Middle Ages, and then
in the period of Ottoman domination of the Balkans, was a
matter of great interest to members of various diplomatic
missions and travelers who happened to pass along it. Military and economic considerations compelled neighboring countries, Austria in particular, to send well-trained experts to
study the conditions of the road and the settlements situated
along its route.

The material that was gathered was used in numerous
travel accounts, and also in several published scholarly
works. The Yugoslav turcologist O. Zirojević has written
a book on the Constantinople road from Belgrade to Sofia from
the middle of the fifteenth to the end of the seventeenth
century.[59] Comparing the information provided by travelers
with data from the Ottoman Turkish registers, Zirojević has
recaptured the picture of contemporary life on one of the
most important arteries in Southeastern Europe.

The frequent Turkish military campaigns in Central
Europe and the support of strong garrisons in the western
frontier zones of the Balkans demanded that the Constantinople road be maintained in good condition. In speaking
of "maintenance," however, one should bear in mind the
rather loose meaning of this concept. The efficient Roman
system of keeping the road in good condition did not exist
in Turkish times. The Ottoman authorities were primarily
concerned with the safety of the road's traffic, and they
sought this goal by granting a special status to the population (given the title *derbentçi*) who lived along the most
vulnerable sections of the road. In exchange for reduced
taxes, this part of the population had to assure the protection of gorges, passes, and river fords or bridges; they
were also obligated to pursue *haydut*s and brigands. A
concern for security was also indicated by detours away from
the bed of the Roman road. These detours (which, if possible,
took the road away from the forests) were used according to
the season and the state of the road. Prior to any significant Turkish advance, road crews numbering from a few hundred
to several thousand men cleared and leveled the road for the
transport of equipment and food, and for passage of Turkish
troops.

The use of this road linking Istanbul with the Balkans
and Central Europe more than other routes explains the additional measures undertaken to provide for the support and
maintenance of bridges and places for sleeping and resting.
All travelers, however critical they might otherwise be of
the condition of the road, noted that there were fords and
usually bridges spanning the numerous rivers. The Turkish
authorities maintained caravansaries for merchants and

travelers, as well as a regular mail service with the necessary modest way stations and horses it required.

For the section of the Constantinople road between
Belgrade and Sofia, Zirojević has established the existence
of 108 villages and 7 cities. (Two of the cities had been
former villages that in the mid-sixteenth century became
kasabas). This group of settlements also included those
along branches of the road running along both banks of the
Morava River between Smederevo and Paraćin, as well as on
other minor branches located along further stretches of the
road.

On the basis of archaeological data, references in medieval sources, and other information, one can fix the existence
prior to the Turkish invasion of some 70 of the villages
mentioned by Zirojević. Nothing definite can be said about
the origins of the remaining 30 or so villages. For about
64 of the roughly 70 settlements whose medieval origins can
be established, information exists that indicates their
immediate fate in the first decades following their fall under
Turkish rule. Seventeen villages were destroyed, deserted,
and left lifeless, and the population of about half of those
villages moved to neighboring areas where they founded new
villages.

The conquered villages (or to be more precise, populated
villages existing at the time of the first Turkish registrations) numbered 47, and thus represent about three-fourths
of the 64 settlements for which information is available.
These villages make up nearly half of all the villages counted
by Zirojević. Most had a few dozen households, many had over
50 and some had even over 100 households. There was a continuity in the development of these villages; it is important
to stress that an influx of new settlers and conversions to
Islam were neither characteristic nor decisive for their
survival.

Having exhausted itself in the eastern and central parts
of the Balkan Peninsula, the wave of Turkish colonization
could not pull Turkish settlers to the west and northwest.
Accordingly, colonization here involved the settlement of
groups of people from the Balkan lands who were granted a
special status corresponding to their semimilitary functions.
In the Serbian lands this role was played chiefly by means
of Vlachs who, as stock raisers, were a very mobile group.
Islamization proceeded apace with the settlement of Vlachs
and included a certain part of both the Vlach population and
of the existing Serbian element. The extent of this process
in the Serbian lands, however, hardly compares with the scale
of conversions that occurred farther west, in Bosnia and
other parts of the Balkans.

All this indicates the concern of the Turkish authorities to prevent the depopulation of the Constantinople road.
Evidence that Ottoman rule attempted to retain the local
population is numerous and diverse: the readiness to grant
exemptions from some taxes, the introduction of a derbentçi
status for half of the villages even when not required by
local conditions, the preservation of many patrimonies in
different villages, and the presence of numerous Christian
sipahis.

Unique terrain and other conditions allow one to differentiate four sections of the Constantinople road between Belgrade and Sofia: between Belgrade and Smederevo,
from Smederevo to Ćuprija and Paraćin, from Paraćin to Niš,
and from Niš to Sofia. The development of the villages from
the last quarter of the fifteenth century to the end of the
sixteenth century reveals certain differences along these
four sections. We shall dwell on these differences in detail.

From Belgrade to Smederevo was a level and a peaceful
road, relatively protected by the Danube. The villages
situated there, despite fluctuations in the number of households, generally retained their size. Only two villages show
a drop in the number of households (in both cases a drop of
as many as 10 households). For the late sixteenth century,
5 of the villages fall into the category of settlements
having up to 50 households, 1 had 65 households, and for 1
village there is no information. (The documents make no
additional mention of the Vlachs quartered in the villages
of Leštani and Bolec who in the late 1520s numbered 37 and
144 households respectively.)

The second section (Smederevo to Ćuprija and Paraćin)
contained 48 villages situated along the branches of the
road on both banks of the Morava River. These villages
were economically linked with Belgrade and Smederevo. Of the
30 villages for which there is information that allows comparison over time, 8 remained practically unchanged, 6 more
than doubled in size, and the remaining 16 decreased in size.
The latter group involved decreases ranging from a few dozen
households to reductions so large that they left the villages
with only one-third or even one-fourth of its former population.

Vlachs were registered in almost all the villages on
this section of the road. Their increase in numbers in the
1520s was connected with intensified concentration of auxiliary military settlers in the immediate proximity of the
frontier areas. Used both for colonizing deserted villages
and for increasing the population of existing ones, the
Vlachs enjoyed a special status that differed markedly from
the status of the reaya. They were exempt from many taxes,

paid the tithe only at half rate, were not subject to contributions under the *devşirme*,[60] and enjoyed far greater self-
government than the reaya. Their duties, furthermore, did
not outweigh their privileges. The later shift of the frontier areas westward reduced both households linked with servicing the army and the auxiliary military population, Vlachs
in particular. The only Vlach households that remained were
those that had already assumed a sedentary life and had become a permanent farming and stock-raising population of the
sancaks of Smederevo and Vidin.

    In connection with these changes in population movement,
and perhaps for other reasons as well, most of the villages
in this section underwent great fluctuations and decreases
in size, and some went into a total decline. The village
of Lugavčina, near Smederevo, had only 10 households at the
first registration in 1476-78 and it was entered as 2 villages, Gorna and Dolna Lugavčina. In 1516 these villages were
settled with Vlachs, with the number of reaya households
remaining about the same (12). In the late 1520s both villages together contained 52 Vlach and 72 Christian households.
But beginning in the 1530s the number of households dropped
to a total of 47, and in the second half of that century it
decreased to 30. In the later registers the Vlachs were not
indicated separately, but a certain number of Muslim households did appear.[61] Also indicative was the development of
the village of Radovanije, south of Smederevo. Having been
left with 2 households at the time of the registration of the
population in 1476-78 (the other inhabitants had fled across
the river), by the 1520s the village had grown to 71 Christian
and 2 Muslim households. It also contained inhabitants with
Vlach status (47 Christian households and 1 Muslim household).
But by the 1530s a sharp decline set in, the number of households dropping 3 times. Toward the end of the century, however, the village again contained more that 50 households.
The village of Batočina, which in 1516 had been populated
solely by Vlachs, in the late 1520s numbered 114 Vlach, 81
Christian, and 6 Muslim households, but in 1536 there remained only 25 Christian and 3 Muslim households and the village continued to decline throughout the century. The development of a number of neighboring villages followed a similar
course.[62]

    But not all the villages met the same fate. For example,
the village of Miloševac, very near the village of Lugavčina,
in 1476-78 numbered 244 Christian households, making it the
largest village in Serbia at that time. In the late 1520s
the number of households rose to 318, and 24 Vlach households
were also registered. The village kept growing throughout
the sixteenth century. Without changing its status as a
village, it came to number 357 households.[63]

In the second half of the fifteenth century, Jagodina, which occupied a central position between Smederevo and Niš, remained a large village. It was also the location of a weekly market and fair that attracted outside craftsmen and merchants. In 1476-78 it had 155 households, 105 Christian and 50 Vlach. It attracted sipahi fief holders who settled in it, and the great Turkish feudal lord Derviş Aǧa, on his withdrawal from Szeged (Szegedin) in Hungary, chose Jagodina as his residence. In the middle of the sixteenth century he erected a mosque, a clock tower, and a *saray* (court). He also settled 50 Hungarian families in Jagodina's environs. In the 1560s the village expanded to 172 households, of which 110 were Muslim and 62 Christian, and it then obtained the status of a kasaba. In the 1580s the number of Muslim households dropped several times (there remained 27), while the number of Christian households rose to 77.

The third section of the road (from Paraćin to Niš) also ran through a prosperous area, with 27 villages. Unlike the section of the road examined above, however, in the 1520s the villages in this section decreased in size, followed by a stabilization in subsequent decades.

The last section (from Niš to Sofia) incorporated 23 villages, of which 8 showed an increase in number of households, 7 retained approximately the same size, and 8 decreased in size. The larger villages increased by several tens of households, and the smaller settlements grew by 2 or 3 times over. In certain cases the decline in the number of households almost eliminated the village. Generally speaking, in the 1570s the number of households had risen in comparison with the beginning of the century, a phenomenon not observed in the other sections of the Constantinople road.

A comparison of the data over different years reveals that the villages of the first section retained a fairly constant average number of households (from 39 to 34) over a prolonged period. In the next section, the development of villages was uneven: in the late 1520s they rapidly increased in size (to an average of 84 households), but in the following decades they sharply declined (down to an average of 34 households). This decrease was felt even more markedly in the third section (from 76 to 33 households). In spite of fluctuations, in some instances very abrupt ones, the villages of the last section showed a tendency to grow (to an average of 66 households).

In its entirety, the development of the settlements examined along the Constantinople road over a prolonged period involved considerable ups and downs, but in the long run these fluctuations did not lead to a permanent and massive decline of the settlements along the road. Cases of the complete extinction of villages are rare.

It is difficult to isolate the specific causes of the
fluctuations in village size. Although the factors involved
cannot be determined for each individual case, the general
course of events shows that a number were at work: the settlement and subsequent ebb of semimilitary parts of the population; the inclination of the reaya to resettle farther away
from the road (a phenomenon revealed by the state's willing-
ness to grant derbentçi status without requiring the corresponding obligations in the area of local security); still
later, at the end of the sixteenth century, the decline of
the derbentçi status itself; and finally, the grave consequences for the population of the incessant movement of
troops, natural disasters, and to a certain extent, the
resettlement deliberately undertaken by the central authorities to strengthen specific sections of the road and other
areas.

By the 1570s and 1580s, the decades for which the data
is fullest, the development of the villages along this
stretch of the Constantinople road had the dimensions shown
in table 2.

The bulk of villages were small settlements of up to
50 households. In the last section of the road, where such
villages were fewer in number than in the second or third
sections, they formed half of all villages listed for that
part of the road. Large villages usually did not contain
more than about 100 households. True, there were larger
villages between Pirot and Sofia, but it should be pointed
out that the other sections had also included larger villages.
For example, the village of Jagodina, located in the section
between Smederevo and Paraćin had reached 172 households
before it became a kasaba.

Comparison with other areas in the Balkans show that
they too were dominated by small villages. Of a total of
about 200 villages in the area of Sofia, Samokov, and
Salonika, small villages made up from 66.3% (Sofia) to 72.1%
(Salonika). In these areas villages with up to 100 households
represented between 20% and 30% of the total number of
villages, and those with over 100 households numbered from
2.5% of the villages in the area of Sofia to 5.4% of the
villages in the region of Salonika (and up to 10% of the
villages in particular parts of the Sofia and Samokov
regions). As these examples show, the villages along the
Constantinople road did not differ markedly in size from
those in other areas of the Balkans.

In the 1470s there were 1,160 households in the cities
situated along the Constantinople road between Belgrade and
Sofia and these urban households accounted for some 20% of
the total number of households located along the roads.[64]

TABLE 2

DISTRIBUTION OF VILLAGES ALONG THE CONSTANTINOPLE ROAD
CIRCA THE 1570s AND 1580s

Number of Households in a Village	CONSTANTINOPLE ROAD							
	1st Section Villages		2nd Section Villages		3rd Section Villages		4th Section Villages	
	Number	Percentage	Number	Percentage	Number	Percentage	Number	Percentage
Up to 20	2	33.33	8	26.7	10	37.0	5	21.7
21 to 50	2	33.33	17	56.7	10	37.0	6	26.1
51 to 100	2	33.33	4	13.3	6	22.2	7	30.4
101 to 150	-	-	-	-	1	3.8	2	8.7
151 to 200	-	-	-	-	-	-	1	4.4
Over 200	-	-	1	3.3	-	-	2	8.7
Total	6	100.0	30	100.0	27	100.0	23	100.0

SOURCE: Information contained in Zirojević, *Carigradski drum*, pp. 112-93.

Of the cities situated on the Constantinople road only Smederevo, the center of the sancak, enjoyed the status of a şehir.
Until the mid-sixteenth century this city, which had been
one of the strong medieval fortresses in the Balkans (built
on the model of the fortress of Constantinople), remained the
most important frontier base for the Turkish advance in the
west. From 1488 to the 1540s the size of its permanent
military garrison--composed of *müstahfiz*es,[65] *azaps*[66] and
*topçu*s[67] (all of them Muslims), and the *armatoles*[68] (Christians)--fluctuated between 1,690 and 757 persons. The Turks
strengthened the fortress, constructing a number of workshops
and storehouses for military needs. With the fall of Belgrade
(1521) and the Banat (1551-52), Smederevo lost its military
importance. By the end of the century the garrison had
dropped to about 200 men and the fortress was fully neglected.
The city, however, retained its significance as an important
trading center throughout almost the whole of the sixteenth
century.

    The population of Smederevo developed in the following
manner. According to the registration lists, in the early
sixteenth century the city had 7 mahalles containing 181
houses, 76 shops (of which 21 had been destroyed), and 48
*oda*s (rooms) used as artisan workshops. By 1616 the Christian
mahalles numbered 7, with 162 households, and there were 3
Muslim quarters containing 65 households--a total of 227
households. There were also 23 merchants from Dubrovnik.

In the 1670s the registers listed 15 mahalles containing a
total of 302 households. In this period Smederevo, thanks
to its trade and port, was undergoing intensive development
and was not inferior to Belgrade. At that time it possessed
367 shops and workshops, and the number of merchants from
Dubrovnik had increased. At the close of the century,
however, the number of mahalles in Smederevo dropped to 11,
and the total number of households to 201.[69]

Up to the end of the sixteenth century, four settlements
along the Constantinople road had the status of kasaba: the
preinvasion fortified cities of Niš and Pirot and two
villages that had been raised to *kasaba* status, Jagodina and
Paraćin. Niš, which had fallen to Turkish forces once before
(in 1386), was finally seized in 1428. As a fortress that
fell within the boundaries of the Ottoman Empire as early as
the first century of Turkish rule, it lost all its strategic
importance, although it did retain a position as a small
commercial and artisan town and as a center of transit trade.
In 1498 Niš had 313 households, and this number remained
practically constant until the end of the sixteenth century,
when it dropped to 223. The size of sixteenth-century Pirot
also stayed fairly constant; from a mid-century size of about
200 households, it increased to 240 households at the century's close. A great predominance of Muslim households
characterized both cities. Toward the middle of the century,
Paraćin, formerly a non-Muslim village and then a mixed settlement, became a fully Muslim kasaba with some 70 households.
In Jagodina, which kept a relatively stable total number of
households (from 130 to 170 in the course of the sixteenth
century), the Christian population suffered a twofold decrease
as a result of conversions to Islam. The stronghold of
Gročka, or Hisarlik, failed to retain its importance, and
throughout the sixteenth century its population amounted to
but a few dozen households.

The information thus presented on the settlements along
the Constantinople road reveals a distinct continuity in
their development. Their names, the composition of the
population, and the number of households attest to their
pre-Ottoman origins and the preservation of the local population. Given that the Ottoman conquest was rapid and followed
the main roads, and given contemporary means of transportation,
the flight of the population that can be observed at that
time did not lead to resettlement at great distances away.
In certain places the invasion did produce a population ebb
of some shorter or longer duration, but these shifts did
not qualitatively alter the general demographic situation.
The villages both along the Constantinople road and in the
interior of the peninsula retained an approximately equal

average number of households, testifying to the presence of
common conditions and the effect of constant factors on
socioeconomic development. Fluctuations in the population
growth of individual villages, even where there was considerable interference by the central authorities, did not markedly alter the essentially general course of population movement. The development of cities testifies to the same fact.

In the course of two centuries only two villages acquired the status of kasaba, one of which actually remained
a medium-sized village and obviously owed its kasaba status
to the entirely Muslim character of its population. That
development failed to lead to the emergence of at least one
more or less important city, a city that the Ottoman administration would honor with the title of "şehir"--or in general
failed to produce a qualitatively new urban structure for
such a long period of time--is eloquent testimony to the
point we are making. Accidental factors could not lead to
the emergence of cities. Both the size of urban settlements
and their location at fixed intervals along the Constantinople road show that these cities developed in connection with
local market conditions, both with regard to foodstuff supply
and to the opportunities for marketing artisan products. The
location of caravansaries and smaller markets indicates the
same thing. Each city had several caravansaries, some of
which were located at appropriate distances between cities.
Markets and bazaars appeared in those villages that were
located far away from cities and accordingly required their
own market.

The specific features of the development of settlements
on the Balkan Peninsula, as engendered by the Ottoman
social system and as they were influenced by the new conditions that arose after the establishment of Ottoman rule,
do not contradict the basic regularities of the socioeconomic
processes inherent in every feudal society.

Pre- and Early Ottoman Rule

3. DISTRIBUTION OF THE URBAN POPULATION BY RELIGION

Considerable migrations of the local population, both forced and voluntary, to various parts of the Balkan Penin-sula and beyond accompanied the establishment of Turkish domination in subsequent decades. Furthermore, there was a relocation of Turkic peoples from Asia Minor to the Balkans. Although one can determine the over-all scope of the Turkish colonization of the Balkans and the eastern Mediterranean, published information does not permit studying the course of this relocation at the level of individual settlements.[1] The publication of information listed on a name-by-name basis from the extensive Ottoman tax regis-ters makes it possible to determine the basic ethnic com-position, the incoming and original population, and the course of conversions to Islam for certain nahiyes and san-caks. But such a piecemeal approach can hardly produce a satisfactory demographic portrait of the settlements.

44

The difficulty here arises not only because there is
little real likelihood of the publication of even part of
the registers preserved for the fifteenth to the seventeenth
century, but it springs from the Ottoman documentation differentiating the population exclusively on the basis of religion. Even the use of names in these documents, therefore,
fails to provide a very reliable criterion for determining
the ethnic affiliation of either Muslims or non-Muslims. To
begin with, common Christian names prevailed over specifically Bulgarian, Serbian, Croatian, Greek, and Albanian
names; furthermore, it is impossible to distinguish Muslim
Turks from those Balkan people who converted. Only in those
isolated cases where a clerk entered the ethnic identity
along with a person's name can one discover the person newly
converted to Islam or can one draw conclusions about mixed
ethnic composition. For example, a register of the population in the Sofia and Samokov areas for the third quarter of
the fifteenth century lists the names of the heads of the
households in thirty-eight villages. Among the hundreds of
names of Bulgarians that are given without indicating their
nationality, "Vlach" occurs twice after a name, "Greek" once,
"Kuman" once, and "Serb" twenty-four times. Obviously, here
were persons who, in a given area, had an origin that set
them apart from the basic ethnic inhabitants. This example
shows that the infrequent ethnic designation (when it was not
an incidental sobriquet) should be used more to determine
certain Balkan migration patterns than to serve as a basis
for general conclusions about the ethnic composition of the
population.[2] These, then, are some of the reasons why we
have chosen to entitle this chapter "Distribution of the
Urban Population by Religion." We are aware that, given the
present state of historiography and the sources, the examination of the ratio between Muslims and non-Muslims in the city
is the best means of determining at least in part the ethnic
distribution of the urban population in the Balkans.

In a certain sense the presence of a mixed urban population held true for all Balkan peoples despite the varying
extent of Turkish colonization and Islamization they experienced, and, as we have seen in the review of the literature,
this question is still producing lively debate. According
to the latest information, the scope and dimension of
Turkish colonization was far less than what might be suggested by the size of the Muslim population in the nineteenth
century, and Turkish historians have set about refuting
standard views on the origin of the Ottoman Empire and on
the role of different nationalities in its creation.

Starting with J. Hammer and ending with H. A. Gibbons
and N. Jorga, a number of historians who authored major works

on the history of the Ottoman Empire expounded the thesis
(which received almost universal acceptance) that not only
was the Ottoman Empire created chiefly after a Byzantine
model, but that its very creation was the work of non-Turks,
mainly Greeks and Slavs. These assertions went so far as
to attribute even the Ottoman military successes to the
work of conquered peoples, who were said to have formed the
major component of the Ottoman armed forces. On this basis,
Gibbons, identifying the Ottomans as different from the
Turks, wrote that it was not the Turks who were the conquerors of European soil, but rather a new nationality, one
formed of both Turks and numerous representatives of Christian peoples.[3] One might also recall Hammer's well-known
comments that the Turkish successes were actually the result
of the ingenuity and skill of the Greeks and Slavs, the
valor of the Albanians, and the endurance of the Bosnians
and Croats--in other words, Turkish successes were due to
the qualities and talents of the conquered peoples themselves.[4] In a well-known work, N. Jorga presented his view
that the fall of Constantinople brought about a change only
in the form of the state (and, in part, a change of religion)
--in essence, Byzantine institutions remained and continued
their evolution.[5] Even R. Grousset, one of the prominent
contemporary students of the Seljuk Empire and of the early
development of the Ottoman state, similarly explained the
conquest of the Balkan Peninsula. Having noted the accumulation of considerable Turkic masses in Anatolia, he wrote:
"By attracting to their side various renegades, by abducting
and recruiting numerous Christian children for military
service, and by abducting as well numerous Greek and Slav
girls designed to mother new Ottoman generations, the Turkish
troops conquered the Balkans thanks to Balkan elements."[6]

It is against these views that Turkish historians have
taken up the challenge. To demonstrate the Turkish character
of various institutions of the Ottoman Empire, a number of
studies have been written examining both the origin and
movement of the Turkic tribes and the establishment of Turkic
states in Central Asia and the Near East. Other works have
appeared attempting to prove a continuity in culture and the
material bases of society from the Turkish tribes to the
Ottomans and various hypotheses have also been elaborated on
the material preconditions that caused the establishment of
Turkish domination in Asia Minor and on the Balkan Peninsula.[7] The point of greatest importance in this argument,
however--especially as presented in the works of the well-
known Turkish historian Ö. L. Barkan--cites the numerical
strength of the Turkish population as a determining factor
in the victory of Muslim society over Byzantium and the
Balkan peoples.

It would be worthwhile to dwell in greater detail on
the views of Barkan, who has written a special work on
Turkish colonization of the Balkan Peninsula. After pointing
out that it would have required a miracle for a seminomadic
tribe of a few hundred tents to impose itself in a linguistic
and ethnic respect on such an impressive empire as Byzantium,
Barkan finds that the fundamental shortcoming of previous
researchers was their failure to take into account the
manpower resources of the Turks and of the Muslim world
in general. The change from the Byzantine to the Ottoman
Empire was not a matter of replacing some dynasties and
ruling strata with others, or of the mass conversion of
Christians to Islam, but rather of major changes in the
ethnic distribution of the population in Asia Minor and the
Balkans, as a result of the permanent colonization of these
lands by the newcomers. The Turks established themselves
in new territories, founded lasting colonies, and thanks to
their numerous offspring, transformed conquered lands into
their own fatherland. In Barkan's opinion, therefore, the
Turkish conquest was not simply a sequence of military
successes, but rather the result of a struggle between two
civilizations that had come into contact with each other, and
if one of these civilizations imposed its language and
religion on the other, that victory was due to the "numerical
and potential preponderance of one of the populations over
the other." Barkan's basic conclusion, therefore, comes to
this: the history of the Ottoman Empire must be defined as
the history of the migration of large masses of people, a
migration in which the chief place was taken by a Turkish
colonization that was well planned and deliberately conducted
by the central power.[8]
    This study is not concerned with the general question of
Turkish colonization or with the settlement of various Turkic
tribes in Asia Minor. Turkish colonization of the Balkans is
an incontrovertible fact, and together with conversions to
Islam, explains the presence, as early as the fifteenth and
sixteenth centuries, of considerable numbers of Muslims in
the Balkans. One cannot, however, accept certain conclusions
about the fate of the non-Muslim population and of the
non-Muslim city.

                          * * *

    A significant part of the Turkish settlers in Rumelia
was composed of Yuruks (nomadic Turkic tribes). In terms of
their place of origin or settlement, these Yuruk settlers in
Rumelia can be grouped as shown in table 3.
    The overwhelming majority of the Naldöken Yuruks settled
in the areas of Stara Zagora and Plovdiv. There were 91
"hearths" (Bulgarian *odzhak*) in the region that included

TABLE 3

DISTRIBUTION OF YURUKS IN RUMELIA
(In numbers of hearths)

Place of origin or settlement	1543	1556	1585
Naldöken	196	216	242
Tanridağ	328	-	424
Salonika	500	-	-
Ovče Pole	-	97	-
Vize	39	41 (1557)	-
Kocacik	126	-	154

SOURCE: The information provided here and in the text about the settlement of Yuruks is taken from Gökbilgin, *Rumeli'de Yürükler*, pp. 50, 70, 71, 74, 80-84, 91-99. One hearth numbered from 10 to 40 persons; consequently, the general number of Yuruks in the Balkans--about 40,000--corresponds to Barkan's figure of 37,435. The Naldöken group, for example, in 1585 showed 1,210 *eşkincis* (a group of the population freed from other obligations in return for ancillary service to the army); 4,950 assistant eşkincis; 1,410 assistant *zaims* (a zaim was a feudal lord given a land grant in return for service); 884 assistant *seraskers* (a serasker was a military commander)--all headed by 10 seraskers and 1 zaim (ibid.,p. 64).

Stara Zagora, Iambol, and Kazanlŭk; and 65 hearths in the area around Plovdiv and Tatar Pazardzhik. Some of these Yuruks (19 hearths) also settled in the territory from Shumen to the mouth of the Danube, and several hearths of Naldöken Yuruks were encountered in the region of Tŭrnovo (4) Ikhtiman (6), Khaskovo (3), Edirne (4), and Elkhovo (4).

The settlement of the Tanridağ Yuruks took two chief directions: one (158 hearths) along the Aegean littoral from Drama to Keşan, and the other (103 hearths) toward north-eastern Bulgaria and the Dobruja (from Tŭrnovo to Hirşova and Tekirg'ol). A smaller part of the Tanridağ hearths gathered around Elkhovo.

As their name implies, the third group of Yuruks, the
Salonika Yuruks, settled both in Macedonia, primarily in its
southern parts, and in Greece. A total of 329 hearths
gathered in the area of Yenişehir, Çatalca, Serfiçe, Florina,
and as far north as Bitolj; another 28 hearths near Salonika
in the districts of Yenice Vardar, Kilkis, and up to
Strumica. [9] Part of the Yuruks of this group also settled on
the Thracian plain (29 hearths) and in northeastern Bulgaria
(26 hearths).

The Yuruks of Ovče Pole settled mostly in Macedonia
(89 hearths), but a small group of them did stop in Thrace.
All of the Vize Yuruks were settled in eastern Thrace.

The final group of Yuruks, those from Kocacik, also
settled in the eastern parts of the Balkan Peninsula, in an
area from Edirne to Hirşova.

Besides the above, there were 88 hearths of Tatar settlers. These Tatar settlers were distributed territorially
in much the same way as the Yuruks, predominantly in the
Bulgarian lands.

We have provided these details to show that many of the
Muslims who came from the outside and settled in Rumelia
were Yuruks and Tatars. These were the groups who formed
the compact mass of the Muslims in the valleys of the
Maritsa and Vardar rivers and in the lands along the Black
Sea coast. One should also note a very characteristic
trend involving changes in the number of these settlers.
As Gökbilgin pointed out, if for the sixteenth century the
Yuruks were tending to increase, the reverse was true in
the following century, when their numbers were generally on
the decline. Thus, in 1609 the Naldöken group numbered 112
hearths, less than half those existing in 1585. In the
Stara Zagora area, to be more specific, the number of
hearths dropped from 66 to 16, in the region of Plovdiv from
46 to 21, and in the region of Tatar Pazardzhik from 19 to
9. The Tanridağ Yuruks, who were twice as numerous as those
from Naldöken, retained their numbers over a longer period.
Until the end of the sixteenth century their numbers increased, and in the mid-seventeenth century they numbered
220 hearths in the sancaks of Nikopol and Silistra together
with the Dobruja. At the very beginning of the seventeenth
century, the Ovče Pole and Vize groups of Yuruks underwent
a certain decrease in their numbers (respectively, from 97
to 88 hearths and from 39 to 30 hearths). By the mid-seventeenth century, the Kocacik group had declined to a mere
18 hearths. This decrease, it seems, was an expression of
general changes in the direction of the expansion of the
Ottoman Empire and of a decline in the military-fief system
in the sixteenth and seventeenth centuries, factors that
caused the withdrawal of the Yuruks to other parts of the

empire. This withdrawal marked most clearly the end of mass
Turkish colonization in the Balkans. The original influx--
mass migrations from Asia Minor--had ceased as early as the
sixteenth century. [10]

* * *

From this survey of information about the Yuruks and
Tatars (the main reserve of colonization) who settled in the
Balkans, it is evident that their settlement cannot in itself
explain either the large numbers of Muslims in the sixteenth
century or the ever-increasing growth of the Muslim population in the following centuries.

There is no need here to cite material about the conversions to Islam that constantly occurred in the upper class
of the Ottoman Empire up through the nineteenth century. [11]
A considerable number of Balkan peoples adopted the new
religion. Through forced Islamization of both large groups
and individuals, and by means of the devşirme system, Ottoman
authorities not only terrorized the Balkan peoples, they also
created a nucleus of loyal followers and supporters. Furthermore, heavy ethnic oppression and discrimination could not
help but foster in certain strata of the enslaved peoples
a desire to free themselves of incessant acts of violence and
humiliation and to try to become socially and politically at
one with the Muslim population. This was possible only
through a change of faith, for more than any other medieval
European state, the Ottoman was a theocratic entity. From
the sultan down to the ordinary subject, all were soldiers
of the Prophet. Relationships among groups of the population
were regulated by the Koran and by other sacred books that
were the sources of religious norms and of legislation. The
sole right of organization granted to the non-Muslim peoples
in the Ottoman Empire was the right to set up ecclesiastical
community organizations or obshtinas, the most important of
which--the Eastern Orthodox--were headed by the patriarchs of
Constantinople. [12]

Let us examine those conversions to Islam that produced
a much quicker and more irreversible assimilation of the non-
Muslim population--that is, the voluntary, individual conversions.

Not infrequently a change of faith resulted from a
desire to change one's social position. It has been established that, to preserve not only their lives but also their
privileges and social position, a considerable part of the
feudal strata of the conquered people took up Ottoman
service. [13] These elements gradually merged with the Ottoman
ruling class, with most of them accepting Islam. In other
layers of the population the change of religion was sometimes
the result of a desire to escape ethnic discrimination.

There is a great deal of information about this phenomenon in one of the earliest registers for the cizye collection
in the Balkan Peninsula. This document concerns the years
1491-92, and it reveals the numbers of households converted
(by vilâyet over the course of one year): Iambol and Aitos--
5; Plovdiv--3; Ohrid--4; Debar--3; Prespa--5; Mokra--4;
Prizren--1; Tetovo (Kalkandilen)--4; Strumica--5; Višegrad
and several other vilâyets in Bosnia--26; Visoko and Sarajevo
(again in Bosnia)--31; Zeta (in Montenegro)--30; Olovo (in
Bosnia)--2; Gjinokastër and Zagora (in Albania)--14; Euboea--
3; the Gypsies in Komotinē and Serres--12 households.[14] An
analogous process formed the basis of the conversion to
Islam of a considerable part of the population of the Rhodope
Mountains.[15]

In Bosnia and Hercegovina Islamization took place without massive Turkish colonization. The first individual conversions accompanied the Turkish invasion and affected mostly
the ruling class. The Christian sipahis were the first to
accept Islam. In the next few decades the process came to
encompass broad social layers--about 30% of the entire population by 1533, and 40% by the middle of the sixteenth
century. Islamization involved both the original population
and many of the Vlach cattle breeders settled by the Turkish
authorities. In some places more than half of these Vlachs
accepted the new faith.[16] Both the Islamization of the
Vlachs and a gradual increase in the number of Muslim households in the Christian villages following upon the conversion
of one or two of their inhabitants can be observed in all the
registers published by Yugoslav authors.

Instances of the secret profession of Christianity
after the acceptance of Islam testify to the wide scope of
conversions under the pressure of difficult conditions, a
circumstance that has recently attracted the attention of
a number of scholars.[17] When to these kinds of conversions
one adds forced abductions of girls and women (a practice
that became widespread),[18] it becomes clear that factors
that at first glance seem insignificant slowly but steadily
fostered the expansion of the Muslim population on the Balkan
Peninsula. All of this, furthermore, indicates not only the
intricacy of the ethnic relations in the fifteenth and
sixteenth centuries and later, but also the complexity of the
origin of the Islamic population of the peninsula.

* * *

The numerical relationship between the non-Muslim and
Muslim taxable households of the Balkan Peninsula can be
seen from the data that Barkan has compiled for the beginning
of the sixteenth century (see table 4).

The households comprising the non-Muslim population in-

TABLE 4

DISTRIBUTION OF THE TAXABLE HOUSEHOLDS ON THE BALKAN PENINSULA
BY RELIGIOUS AFFILIATION, 1520-1535

SANCAKS	H O U S E H O L D S (by numbers and percentage)						
	Christian		Muslim		Jewish		Total number
Paşa	183,512	72.5	66,648	26.3	2,998	1.2	253,194
Smederevo*	106,861	97.8	2,367	2.2	-	-	109,228
Trikkala	57,671	82.0	12,347	17.5	387	0.5	70,405
Kiustendil	56,988	89.4	6,640	10.5	49	0.1	63,677
Morea	49,412	97.0	1,065	2.1	464	0.9	50,941
Nikopol	31,891	77.4	9,122	22.1	206	0.5	41,219
Bosnia	19,619	54.0	16,935	46.0	-	-	36,554
Euboea & coastal area	33,056	98.0	663	2.0	-	-	33,728
Ohrid	32,748	98.0	641	2.0	-	-	33,389
Ioannina	32,097	98.0	613	2.0	-	-	32,710
Kruševac	25,759	96.7	881	3.3	-	-	26,640
Sofia	24,341	94.0	1,569	6.0	-	-	25,910
Shkodër	23,859	95.5	1,116	4.5	-	-	24,975
Silistra	6,615	28.0	17,295	72.0	-	-	23,910
Vize	9,467	44.0	12,193	56.0	-	-	21,660
Vidin	19,517	95.5	914	4.5	⁊	-	20,438
Vučitrn	18,914	96.5	700	3.5	-	-	19,614
Prizren	18,382	98.0	359	2.0	-	-	18,741
Hercegovina**	9,588	58.0	7,077	42.0	-	-	16,665
Zvornik	13,112	83.5	2,654	16.5	-	-	15,766
Chirmen	1,578	11.0	12,686	89.0	-	-	14,264
Karliili	11,395	100.0	7	-	-	-	11,402
Elbasani	8,916	94.5	526	5.5	-	-	9,442
Gelibolu	3,901	43.7	5,001	56.0	23	0.3	8,925
Montenegro	3,446	100.0	-	-	-	-	3,446
Dukakin	1,829	100.0	-	-	-	-	1,829
Gypsies	10,294	59.9	6,897	40.1	-	-	17,191
Total:	814,777	81.0	186,952	18.6	4,134	0.4	1,005,863

SOURCE: Ö.L. Barkan, "Osmanlı Imparatorluğunda bir iskân," 15 (1953-54): 237.
  ^This figure includes, as Barkan indicates, 80,000 armatoles, voynuks and Vlachs, concentrated as auxiliary army groups in the sancak of Smederevo (ibid., p. 236).
  **There is no information about three kazas in the sancak of Hercegovina.

cluded 7,851 voynuks.[19] In addition, there were 82,692 armatoles and Vlachs stationed in the area of Smederevo. The
Muslim population incorporated 12,105 *müsellems*[20] (and another
1,252 müsellems with a rather special status), and 37,435
Yuruks (of whom 23,000 were linked to the military organization).[21] To these numbers should be added an additional
40,000-50,000 persons who made up the sipahi force that consisted of *timariots* (holders of timars), *cebelis*,[22] and garrison troops. This data, which clarifies somewhat the special
groups of the population at the time when such groups were
most numerous, indicates that in the first decades of the sixteenth century the total of the various types of Muslim and
non-Muslim military and paramilitary categories was about 20%
as large as the entire taxable population of the Balkans.

The principal conclusion that can be drawn from the above data is that at the time of the greatest concentration of Turkish settlers in the Balkans, and at the time when the invasion was still producing a significant displacement of the local population and causing it to withdraw to more secluded and inaccessible areas, the ratio of the Muslim to the non-Muslim households was approximately one to four. Furthermore, a considerable portion of the Muslim population was formed of recent converts from the conquered peoples.

Without looking for a special system in the distribution of the Muslim population, one cannot but note its concentration in strategically important places. In the eastern part of the Balkan Peninsula this population formed an uninterrupted belt that was in contact with the Tatars who hovered just beyond the Danube. Large numbers of Muslims also settled along the valley of Maritsa River (the principal thoroughfare of the Balkan Peninsula, one leading to the approaches of Istanbul), and along the Vardar River (the second major water thoroughfare leading to the south). The concentration of Muslims was, for the same reasons, extremely high in the northeastern parts of Bosnia and Hercegovina, the point of further Turkish expansion toward Central Europe, and in Albania and the other frontier regions where the authorities feared both incursions from the outside and uprisings. One could hardly doubt, therefore, the strategic significance of the settlement of tribes such as the Yuruks and the Islamization of the population in northeast Bulgaria, Thrace, and the western parts of the Balkan Peninsula.

* * *

Let us now take up an analysis of the concrete information we have on the cities. We have at our disposal information about 113 cities in various sancaks drawn from the works of Gökbilgin, Barkan, Inalcık, Sokoloski, Zirojević, Handžić, from some other Yugoslav publications, and also from the Turkish sources kept in Sofia. For the majority of the cities, the data provided by various authors coincide. There are certain discrepancies, however, owing to the failure to include in the registers widows or Jewish households and, as Sokoloski has shown, to occasional errors in the documents themselves.

All of the information available to us about the ratio of Muslims to non-Muslims in the population is represented in summary form in table 5.

The data represented in table 5 characterizes the trend of development of the two components of the urban population in the fifteenth and sixteenth centuries. As early as the first half of the sixteenth century, there was a marked increase in the Muslim population. Although one

TABLE 5

DISTRIBUTION OF THE URBAN POPULATION BY
RELIGION, 15TH-16TH CENTURIES

Number of cities	Periods	Households (by number and percentage)			
		Christian	Muslim	Other	Totals
44	15th c.	9,680 72.29	3,577 26.71	133 1.00	13,390 100
84	16th c. (1st half)	24,067 51.11	18,881 40.09	4,145 8.80	47,093 100
29	16th c. (2nd half)	9,426 36.07	15,922 60.93	785 3.00	26,133 100

cannot determine the exact amount of the increase, its connection with conversion to Islam, or the extent to which it
was an expression of colonization or of changes in the numerical relationships on the peninsula as a whole as a result
of independent growth in the Muslim population, the trend
itself is beyond dispute.

Of 44 cities in the fifteenth century, 28 had a Muslim
population (that is, more than half), but the percentage of
Muslims in the general population was not high. Muslims
prevailed over the non-Muslim element in only 6 cities,
whereas the non-Muslim population dominated in 38. Furthermore, of these 6 cities only Kiustendil had a particularly
noteworthy Muslim domination--over 70%. In the remaining 5
cities it did not exceed 70%. The Christian population, on
the other hand, featured higher concentrations. Thus, 16
cities were completely non-Muslim: Berati, Gjinokastër,
Goražde, Kalavrita, Kanina, Klisura, Corinth, Krujë, Livno,
Mostar, Përmet, Prepolje, Turtucaia, Holumiče, Cherven, and
Jagodina. Another 9 cities were almost exclusively Christian,
with this group constituting from 90 to 100% of the total
population; only in 4 cities did the Christians fail to
exceed more than 70% of the population. The size of
the cities under consideration made no difference in the
ratio between the two indicated groups of the population.
Both non-Muslims and Muslims were concentrated in small and,
in part, in medium-sized cities.

The data for the first half of the sixteenth century
cover 84 cities, revealing that in 60 (or 71% of the
total) the non-Muslim population prevailed, with the Muslims
dominant in 21 (25%), and that 3 cities had considerable
populations representing other religious groups, chiefly
Jews and Gypsies. Although the non-Muslim population prevailed both in absolute numbers of households and in the number of cities in which it was a predominant element, there was

a considerable increase in the number of Muslims. Muslims now
lived in 72 cities, or almost everywhere. The number of completely non-Muslim cities dropped to 9--Agrafa, Gjinokastĕr,
Delvinĕ, Kanina, Klisura, Pĕrmet, Prilep, Tŭrgovishte (Eski
Dzhumaia), Jagodina; and there were now 11 cities where Christians comprised from 90 to 100% of the population--Athens,
Berati, Biglista, Varna, Dolna Tuzla, Domokos, Kostur, Livno,
Melnik, Petrich, and Serfiçe. There was a considerable
increase in the number of cities in which the non-Muslims comprised up to 70% of the population (19) and from 70 to 80% of
the population (21). The number of cities with a predominant
Muslim population rose to 21 and entirely Muslim cities
appeared--Yenice Karasu and Sarajevo. The city of Yenice
Vardar also took on an almost fully Muslim character. There
was a particularly strong increase (to 11) in the number of
cities with a marked preponderance of Muslims (over 70%). In
the other 7 cities Muslims formed up to 70% of the population.

The increase in the number of Muslim households came
about through Muslim concentration in medium-sized cities
and particularly in cities containing from 800 to 1,600
households (see also table 6). Of the 21 cities with a predominant Muslim population, 9 (43%) were cities with up to
400 households and 11 (52%) were with 801 to 1,600 households. Of the contemporary cities with a Christian majority,
36 (60%) belonged to the small city category and 23 (38%)
to that of the medium city (that is, cities with up to
1,600 households).

The concentration of Muslims in comparatively larger
cities was even more clearly expressed in the second half
of the sixteenth century. At that time 7 of the 16 cities
with a predominant Muslim population fell into the category
covering from 801 to 1,600 households and 3 of the 16 were
in the group with over 1,600 households (Sarajevo, Sofia,
and Vidin). At the same time only 23% of the cities with
a Christian majority (3 of a total of 13) were in the group
of cities containing 800 to 1,600 households and 2 cities
(Varna and Ruse) fell into the group of cities with more than
1,600 households.

* * *

The evolution of the ratio of Muslims and non-Muslims in
the capital of the Ottoman Empire is a matter of great interest. Istanbul was not only the political center of the
Ottoman state. The conquest of Constantinople, which had the
prestige of a world capital, realized the most treasured
Muslim expectations. In its significance as the new seat of
the caliph, Istanbul now became the premier Muslim city, a
city as marvelous as the ancient capital of the Arab caliphs
at Baghdad. To it flowed the enormous wealth provided by

TABLE 6

DISTRIBUTION OF CITIES BY SIZE AND BY RELIGIOUS
AFFILIATION OF POPULATION, 16TH CENTURY

Size of city (by number of households)	No. of cities	(By number and percentage)					
		Non-Muslim		Muslim		Total	
Up to 400	55	7,758	70.8	3,201	29.2	10,959	100
401-800	17	7,412	75.0	2,475	25.0	9,887	100
801-1,600	12	5,756	44.3	7,229	55.7	12,985	100
More than 1,600	4	13,452	48.8	14,095	51.2	27,547	100
TOTAL	88	34,378	56.0	27,000	44.0	61,378	100

victorious wars, by contributions, by the continuous inflow
of taxes and other imposts, by gifts, and by the income
that resulted from a widespread commerce. Thanks to its
key geographic position--at the crossroads of several major
land and sea commercial thoroughfares--and to the privileges and facilities that it had enjoyed for several centuries, Istanbul was transformed into the largest city in
Europe. Here stood the sultan's court in all its splendor;
here lived the most exalted officials, the richest representatives of the Ottoman ruling stratum, and the greatest
merchants. Istanbul saw the construction of the largest
mosques, palaces, and business buildings, and it housed the
greatest number of Muslim religious, charitable, and educational establishments.
    With its institutions controlled directly by the
supreme power, Istanbul became the model that influenced
the formation of other cities. True, part of the Balkan
Peninsula had been incorporated into the boundaries of the
Ottoman state prior to the fall of Constantinople, and
adapting these regions to the Ottoman regime had been
effected or begun several decades earlier. But it was only
the capture of Constantinople and its transformation into a
capital that ushered in the era of the construction of the
Ottoman pyramid of power. It was now that the state codified
and distributed throughout the whole empire the legislation
that consolidated and amplified the established practice
regulating the relationships among the different strata of
the population, between the original population and the
state, between individual parts of the huge state, and between the provincial cities and the capital.

On the fall of Constantinople in 1453, most of the surviving Greeks were expelled to Edirne, Bursa, Gelibolu, and
Plovdiv. In their place Mehmed II brought in Turks and
other Muslims from Asia Minor and the Balkans, Greeks from
the Peloponnesus, the Aegean islands, and several cities in
Asia Minor and the Balkans, and Armenians from different
parts of Anatolia. Inhabitants representing other Balkan
nationalities were also settled in Istanbul and the surrounding villages. The Sultans Bayezid II, Selim I, and Suleyman
"the Lawgiver" also settled Istanbul with considerable groups,
chiefly craftsmen from the newly conquered lands outside
the Balkans.

A 1540 register of the Istanbul population reveals the
near and distant origins of the peoples who either came or
were brought to the capital. Thus, the Greeks (1,457 households) originated from Karaca to Yenice Foça, from the island
of Lesbos, from Feodosiya (Kaffa), and Trabzon (Trebizond);
the Armenians (807 households) came from Trabzon and other
cities of eastern, central, and western Anatolia; the Jews
(1,522 households) resettled here from nearly thirty Balkan
cities, from Spain, and from the German states.[23]

According to a census in Stambul and Galata,[24] in 1478
there were 9,486 Muslim and 6,538 non-Muslim households (of
which 1,647 were Jewish), comprising respectively 58.11%
and 41.89% of the total number of households. The population
amounted to from 65,000 to 80,000 persons. In 1489 the
number of non-Muslim households had grown to 10,865 (including
2,491 Jewish households). For the period from 1520 to 1530,
the data provided by Barkan indicates 46,635 Muslim, 25,292
Christian, and 8,070 Jewish households (or a total of 80,000
households and about 400,000 inhabitants; 58.3% of this
population was Muslim and 41.7% was non-Muslim). About 1550,
Cristobal Villanon, physician of Sinan Paşa, estimated the
number of households at about 104,000. Census data for the
seventeenth century is lacking. The information from
travelers as cited by R. Mantran provides population figures
that fluctuate from 800,000 to 1,000,000 inhabitants, with
the same breakdown between Muslims and non-Muslims that
existed in the sixteenth century. For the end of the century
(1690-91), Mantran, using data from two registers giving the
cizye levied on 62,000 households, has calculated the population as ranging from 600,000 to 700,000. Taking into account
the suburbs, including Üsküdar, the population was about
800,000, which made Istanbul the largest city in Europe and
the Near East in the seventeenth century.[25]

From the fifteenth to the end of the seventeenth century,
the population of the capital increased several times over,
but the ratio of Muslims to non-Muslims remained unchanged.
The non-Muslims were not transferred to special parts of the

city, to closed districts. It is true that as a rule Muslims
and non-Muslims lived in separate quarters, but these quarters alternated with one another and were immediate neighbors,
and the artisan and commercial part of the city was basically
common. This was the essential difference between the medieval Muslim city in general and the city in the Ottoman
Empire, especially in those Ottoman territories where, as in
the Balkans, the local population continued to constitute a
majority.

Greeks made up the basic component of the capital's
non-Muslims. They settled in numerous districts in Istanbul,
in Galata, and in the suburbs outside the city walls. The
location of the more compact groups of the Greek population
can be seen in the distribution of Greek churches, which in
the seventeenth century numbered about thirty. With the
transfer of the patriarchate in 1601 to the Phanar, this
district became the center of the emerging Greek aristocracy
and bourgeoisie. Greeks began to build stone houses, in
sharp contrast to the surrounding single-story wooden homes,
and these in a sense served to emphasize the importance of
the nascent Greek stratum. Thanks to the extensive network
of middlemen scattered in the ports all over the eastern
Mediterranean and the Black Sea, the Greeks gradually
succeeded in establishing almost complete maritime and commercial supremacy. The Greeks in Istanbul were sailors,
fishermen, and boatmen, and they engaged in various specialized crafts. They also made up a big part of the taverners
and innkeepers.

Jews represented the next most numerous group of non-
Muslims in Istanbul. Here more than anywhere else different
Jewish communities struggled with one another for dominance.
The Jews expelled from Spain found in Istanbul a considerable
group of Jews who had settled there in Byzantine times; later
they were joined by Jews coming from the German countries.
In Istanbul the Jews lived along the Golden Horn in about ten
neighborhoods, and with the influx of new Jewish settlers they
formed compact groups in other parts of the old city and on
the opposite shore of the Golden Horn. The Jews had a
reputation for their participation in international commerce,
their role as middlemen in various transactions, as
appraisers and informants, and particularly for their
financial activity.

Armenians also formed a sizable part of the population
of Istanbul. They had been transferred there at the time of
Mehmed II, who ordered the Armenian patriarch to move from
Bursa to the new capital. Their number increased with the
renewed involvement of Persia and the Middle East in eastern
Mediterranean trade and the use of Istanbul as a transship-
ment place of oriental goods bound for Europe. In Istanbul,

the Armenians were concentrated principally in the eastern
parts of the city. (The Armenian mule drivers who carried
merchandise to Edirne formed a whole district.) Although
they started out as middlemen in international trade, the
Armenians did not limit themselves to this role but became the
financial mainstay and guarantors of Armenians coming from
other places, expanding the scope of their operations so that
in subsequent centuries they formed a powerful stratum of
bankers. They also engaged in a number of crafts.

In the capital there lived representatives of many other
peoples mentioned in the documents: relatively numerous
Albanians, Gypsies, and "Egyptians" (a general name denoting
the Arab population), Persians, Vlachs, Serbians, Bulgarians,
and others--all engaged in construction or in occupations connected with feeding the population of the capital.

Turks made up the majority in Istanbul and its suburbs
and produced the mass of state employees at all levels. They
also provided most of the troops stationed in the palace and
the city, but most of the Turkish population was made up of
small shopkeepers and artisans. The Turks engaged in all
types of handicrafts, save those prohibited by their religion
(e.g., running an establishment for the sale of spirits).

What has been said so far reveals a number of significant features of the capital of the empire that have a more
general importance. Despite the real opportunity for
Istanbul to become a purely Turkish and Muslim city through
the extermination and expulsion of its Greek population, the
Turkish sultans resettled it with Christians in such numbers
that they almost equaled the Muslims. Istanbul differed
markedly from those cities where the non-Muslims formed a restricted minority and were compelled to move and live within
strictly defined conditions, showing that the Turkish rulers
did not strive to create a closed Muslim society even in their
own capital. The existence in Istanbul of considerable numbers of conquered peoples was something dictated from above;
it was reaffirmed by law, and the coexistence of the ruling
and the subjugated nationalities was regulated and controlled
by the sultans themselves and by the central authorities. The
center of the state reflected the empire as a whole, a society
of many ethnic groups thoroughly intermixed.

* * *

To summarize, the establishment of Turkish domination in
the Balkans led to many changes in the ethnic and religious
composition of the urban population in various areas of the
Balkan Peninsula. The existing Christian population, however,
was not ousted from the cities nor did it lose its position
as the basic urban productive population. Though deprived of
its own political and administrative power and subjected to

the strong and centralized military-theocratic organization
of the Ottoman Empire, it nevertheless preserved itself in
the majority of the cities in numbers exceeding not only the
resettled Turkish population, but the Muslim population in
general.   In the sixteenth century, despite heavy losses
during the Turkish invasion, despite the forced transfer of
the urban non-Muslim population from the Balkans to Asia
Minor, and despite the continuous process of Islamization,
the overwhelming majority of the Balkan cities retained the
non-Muslim character of their population.

However, if we want to depict the full picture of the
socioeconomic life of the Balkan city, we must also analyze
the professional composition and the economic activity of its
two components (non-Muslims and Muslims) and the character
and role of the social, cultural, and religious institutions
of the entire urban population, irrespective of the ethnic
origin of the city and the time at which either component
might have been dominant.

Pre- and Early Ottoman Rule

4. TRENDS IN URBAN GROWTH

The total absence of information about birth and mortality rates makes it impossible to calculate the natural increase of the population in the Balkans under Ottoman rule. Given that the study of the process of migration has only just begun, it is also not possible to study the growth of the urban population that resulted from it. Therefore, to determine trends in urban growth, we have compared information over several consecutive periods for some forty cities, grouping these cities (to the extent possible) according to their geographical proximity.

Some of the earliest data on taxable non-Muslim and Muslim households concerns Albanian cities in the sancak of Vlona (see table 7). Vlona, Kanina, Berati, and Gjinokastër fell to the Turks as early as 1417-19; Krujë, Lesh, Shkodër, and Drish in 1478-79; and Durrës in 1501. Some of the urban settlements and fortresses in the Albanian lands were almost

TABLE 7

POPULATION MOVEMENT OF SEVERAL CITIES IN THE SANCAK OF
VLONA, 15TH AND 16TH CENTURIES

Cities	NUMBER OF HOUSEHOLDS			
	1431-32		1506-7	
	Non-Muslim	Muslim	Non-Muslim	Muslim
Gjinokastër	163	--	143	--
Kanina	237	--	514	--
Berati	227	--	395	11
Klisura	113	--	244	--
Përmet	42	--	260	--

SOURCE: The table is composed on the basis of data drawn
from İnalcık, *Hicrî 835 Tarihi, Sûret-i Defter-i Sancak-i Ar-*
vanid, pp. i, xxvii, xxxv; as supplemented with data from
Shkodra, "Qytetet schqiptare gjatë dy shekujevë të parë të
sundimit turk," *Ekonomia popullore*, no. 5 (1965), p. 71.

fully destroyed and were unable to recover. Others declined
because of the great migration of the local (chiefly urban)
population to Italy (about 200,000 persons) and the resulting disruption of the economic ties--which in the preceding
century had been quite lively--with cities in Italy and
Europe.

Over a period of 75 years, the number of taxable households in all of the cities (save Gjinokastër) increased. In
Kanina, Berati, and Klisura, the increase was nearly twofold,
or an average annual rate of growth of 10.5, 7.9, and 10.4
per 1,000, respectively. Përmet's increase was more striking
--a sixfold growth, or an average of 36.2 per 1,000 per
year. In the period under consideration, there was a decrease
in number of households only in Gjinokastër, which had an
average annual drop of 1.8 per 1,000. Additional information
for this city for 1583, however, indicates that the number
of households had increased. There were now 434 households
(implying an average annual growth rate of 14.7 per 1,000).

The quickening of economic life in Albanian lands
that can be noted for the early sixteenth century suggests
that urban growth rates were not uniform over the whole period
under review, but rather intensified in its closing decades.
This trend was also reflected in the rapid development of
the newly founded (in 1466) town of Elbasani. In the 1470s

Elbasani's walls contained more than 1,000 Muslim households,
and its varos̆ housed a mixed population of considerable size.
Elbasani became one of the most important economic and
administrative centers of Albania. At the same time the other
cities were also developing, and the growth of two of them--
Kanina and Berati--resulted in their metamorphosis into
medium-sized cities. (About 1570 Berati already numbered
1,050 households.) Vlona also grew rapidly. At the end of
the fifteenth century about 500 Jewish families settled
there, and by the mid-sixteenth century it had become a
vigorous commercial center.

Information can be compiled by periods for the urban
settlements of the sancak of Paṣa also, and table 8 shows
the number of taxable households in several cities of this
sancak.

There was also an increase in number of households in
the cities of this group (except Kostur). Their average
annual rate of growth was: Skopje--2.9 per 1,000; Bitolj--
8.9 per 1,000; Veles (Köprili)--3.3 per 1,000; Serres--8.7
per 1,000; and Kic̆evo--8.7 per 1,000. Only in Kostur was
there a decrease in the number of households (at an average
of 4.6 per 1,000 annually). From the mid-sixteenth century,
however, there is information that the number of households
in Kostur rose to 1,077 (1,003 Christian households, 57
Muslim, and 17 Jewish). But toward the end of the sixteenth
century, the number again declined (to 909), largely at the
expense of the Christian part of the population.

Later information on the number of households is also
available for Bitolj, Skopje, and Veles. In the quarter of
a century following 1519, the annual average rate of growth
for Veles and Skopje increased to equal 4.7 and 8.3 per 1,000,
respectively. Skopje continued to grow in the second half
of the sixteenth century as well. From 1528 to 1571-80, the
number of taxable households rose from 1,027 to 1,794, that
is, by an average of 11.6 per 1,000 per year. In the same
period Bitolj showed a considerably lower rate of growth
(1.5 per 1,000) with a decline in the numbers of both
Muslim and Christian households. That it enjoyed a slight
absolute increase was due mainly to an increased number
of Jewish and (to a lesser extent) of Gypsy households.

In the cities examined, the total number of households
increased at relatively similar rates, with differences among
the individual components of the population. Thus, the rates
of growth in the number of Muslim households were very high--
86.7 per 1,000 in Kic̆evo, 28.3 per 1,000 in Kostur, and 26.8
per 1,000 in Veles. In Tetovo, which grew from 248 in 1458
to 275 households in 1477, or by 7.6 per 1,000, however,
the number of non-Muslim households rose by 12.5 per 1,000,

TABLE 8

POPULATION CHANGE IN SEVERAL CITIES IN THE SANCAK OF PAŞA,
15TH AND 16TH CENTURIES

Cities	Years	N U M B E R	O F	H O U S E H O L D S			
	Years	Non-Muslim	Muslim	Total	Years	Non-Muslim	Muslim	Total
Skopje	1455-60	339	551	850	1519	302	717	1,019
Bitolj	1469	185	295	480	1521-30	205	640	845
Veles	1460	229	9	238	1519	247	42	289
Kostur	1477	940	22	962	1518	732	67	799
Serres	1465	--	--	817	1518	--	--	1,283
Kičevo	1475	145	31	176	1519	145	111	256

SOURCE: The table has been compiled on the basis of information contained in
Ö. L. Barkan, "Tarihi demografi araştırmaları ve osmanlı tarihi," *Tarihi Mecmuası*
10 (1953):22; T. Gökbilgin, "Kanunî Sultan Süleyman," p. 262; and M. Sokoloski,
"Le développement de quelques villes dans le sud des Balkans aux XVe e XVIe
siècles," *Balkanica* 1 (1970): 83, 89, and "Devri başlarında Rumeli eyaleti livaları şehir ve kasabaları," *Belleten* 20 (1956): 262.

while the number of Muslim households went down at an average
of 21.4 per 1,000 per year. The explanation for this deviation in the growth of the two groups of the population--a
phenomenon observable in a number of other cities as well--
should be sought in the effects both of conversions to Islam
and of those factors that led to a more intensive migration.
        Concrete examples can serve to illustrate how these
deviations occurred in strategically important areas.
Zvornik, also called "The Key to the Drina," had already
developed as a city of medieval Bosnia but its location made
it particularly important after its capture by the Turks in
1460. As an important junction of roads to Dubrovnik, Serbia,
and the Hungarian lands, and for a time situated in the
frontier zone, Zvornik had great strategic significance for
the Turks. They made new fortifications, enlarged the fortress several times over, and garrisoned it with permanent
troops, including about one hundred Christian armatoles and
several hundred Muslim müstafhizes, azaps, topçus, and
horsemen. A 1512 census of Zvornik's population counted 150
Christian and 70 Muslim households, and including the military, the city totaled 580 households. Two decades later
the number of Muslim households had risen to 113, and the
number of Christian households had dropped from 150 to 29.
In 1548 there were still 30 households, but by this time the
number of Muslim households had grown to 432 (that is, nearly
a fourfold increase) at the expense of the Muslim population
of the surrounding villages. At the end of the sixteenth
century the Turkish conquest of Hungarian lands reduced
Zvornik's military and strategic significance. The garrison

withdrew from the city, reducing the number of households by half: out of 432 Muslim households, only 212 remained; and of the 30 Christian households, there remained but 6. Meanwhile, other urban settlements in Bosnia had been growing in importance, and part of the urban population of Zvornik resettled in those cities.

Having lost its importance as a frontier base, sixteenth-century Smederovo survived as an ordinary city, with Belgrade rising at its expense. The number of households in Belgrade rose from 239 in 1536 to 420 in 1560, and to 953 in 1577. Toward 1577, its average annual rate of growth was 30.3 per 1,000, and especially striking was the sevenfold increase in the number of its Muslim households (an average annual rate of growth of 57.9 per 1,000).

The Muslim city of Sarajevo also developed rapidly, and by the second half of the sixteenth century it had become one of the most populated cities of the western part of the Balkan Peninsula. Over roughly a fifty-year period the number of households there increased fourfold, or on an average of 30.1 per 1,000 per year.

Some other Serbian, Bosnian, and Croatian cities declined in numbers of households and others grew. For over half a century Novi Pazar recorded an average annual rate of growth of 18.2 per 1,000, and Užice's rate of growth was 11.4 per 1,000. In some 40 years the population of Vučitrn shot up abruptly--at an average yearly rate of 30.2 per 1,000-- chiefly because of the increase of non-Muslim households. On the other hand, the data on the cities of Olovo, Goražde, and Novo Brdo indicate decreases in the growth rates (respectively, by 0.2, 5.6, and 23.6 per 1,000).

Greater fluctuations in the growth of cities (and particularly where these pertained to the different components of the urban population) were characteristic chiefly of frontier areas and areas with intensive Islamization.

Let us also examine the growth of four Bulgarian cities in the sancak of Nikopol that in the period under study underwent fewer fundamental changes (see table 9). Over nearly a century these four cities showed the following increases in number of households: Nikopol--489; Tŭrnovo-- 81; Lovech--61; and Vratsa--37. That gives an average annual rate of increase of 1.0, 1.5, 2.4, and 0.9 per 1,000. Data for non-Muslim and Muslim households indicate little difference in the rate of growth: the rate ranged for the Muslim households from 1.9 per 1,000 (Vratsa) to 9.7 per 1,000 (Lovech), and the non-Muslim households ranged from 0.2 per 1,000 (Tŭrnovo) to 5.6 per 1,000 (Nikopol). The number of Christian households averaged an annual decrease of 0.4 per 1,000 in Vratsa and a decrease of 1.3 per 1,000 in Lovech.

TABLE 9

POPULATION CHANGE IN SEVERAL CITIES IN THE
SANCAK OF NIKOPOL, 15TH AND 16TH CENTURIES

| | H O U S E H O L D S | | | | | |
| | 1425-30 | | | 1520-35 | | |
Cities	Non-Muslim	Muslim	Total	Non-Muslim	Muslim	Total
Nikopol	446	308	754	775	468	1,243
Tŭrnovo	372	132	504	379	206	585
Vratsa	368	23	391	354	74	428
Lovech	177	51	228	156	133	289

SOURCE: The table is based on data contained in *Turski izvori za bŭlgarskata
istoriia* 2 (1966): 161, 165, 253, 271; Gökbilgin, "Kanunî Sultan Süleyman,"
pp. 268-69; and Ö. L. Barkan,"Essai sur les données statistiques des registres
de recensement dans l'Empire Ottoman aux XVe et XVIe siècles," *Journal of
Economic and Social History of the Orient* 1, no. 1 (1957):36.

The frequent coincidence of the growth rates of these
Bulgarian cities--both in terms of the numbers of Muslims and
non-Muslims and their over-all growth--leads us to believe
that this was related to the presence of generally uniform
conditions. What differences there were did not result
from such temporary factors as, for example, momentary acts
of massive Islamization, of colonization, or of an ebb of the
population.

For comparison, let us introduce data available for
several large cities for the subsequent fifty years (table
10). Very high rates of growth (respectively, 19, 22.7,
and 24.2 per 1,000) occurred in the three port cities of
Ruse, Varna, and Vidin. (By comparison, in Sofia and
Plovdiv at that time the growth rate equaled, respectively,
4.7 and 4.3 per 1,000.) There were considerable differences
in the development of the two basic groups of these cities.
Ruse's rapid growth in the period under study appears to have
been primarily the result of a tenfold increase in the number
of Muslim households (an average of 47.4 per 1,000 annually).
The Muslim population of Varna grew at an even higher rate--
53.1 per 1,000, and that of Vidin, too, experienced a high
growth rate--24.2 per 1,000. It should immediately be
added that, relative to the experience of other cities, the
Christian population of these three cities also increased
greatly: in Ruse Christian households grew at a rate of
8.4 per 1,000, in Varna at 17.8 per 1,000, and in Vidin at
23.0 per 1,000. The Christians increased at a much slower
rate than the Muslim population, however. The increase in
the number of Muslims and non-Muslims in Plovdiv proceeded
at practically the same rate, 5 and 5.8 per 1,000, respectively.

TABLE 10

POPULATION CHANGE IN SEVERAL CITIES
IN THE BULGARIAN LANDS, 16TH CENTURY

Cities	NUMBER OF HOUSEHOLDS					
	1520-30			1571-80		
	Non-Muslim	Muslim	Total	Non-Muslim	Muslim	Total
Ruse	574	81	668	875	824	1,699
Varna	534	34	568	1,295	453	1,748
Vidin	287	356	650	897	1,207	2,152
Sofia	280	971	1,291	204	1,376	1,638
Plovdiv	119	761	987	153	1,019	1,226

SOURCE: This information from registers preserved in Istanbul has
been personally given to the author by Ö. L. Barkan, and we extend
our thanks to him. The table specifies information only on Muslims
and Christians. The totals, however, include other components of
the population that do not fall into these categories or whose
nationality is not shown. In the individual cities these groups
break down as follows:
    1520-30: Ruse, 13 widows; Vidin, 7 Jews; Sofia, 40 widows;
Plovdiv, 94 Jews, 13 widows.
    1571-80: Vidin, 48 Jews; Sofia, 6 widows, 52 Jews; Plovdiv,
54 Jews.

    In Sofia the development of Muslim and non-Muslim house-
holds differed again. In the period under review the number
of Christians was declining on an average of 6.3 per 1,000
per year, while the number of Muslims rose 7.9 per 1,000.
There is no doubt that this reflects conversions to Islam,
something that was also expressed in the local folklore.
(By way of comparison with Sofia, over the same period Athens
showed an annual average rate of growth of 8.1 per 1,000:
from 2,297 households in 1520-30 to 3,203 households in
1571-80.)
    Let us dwell in somewhat greater detail on Salonika,
whose growth was linked to a considerable influx of Jews,
and on Edirne, the former capital of the empire. A migration
of the Jewish population from the cities of Asia Minor to
Turkey's European possessions occurred even before the final
Turkish conquest of the Balkan Peninsula. In the second
half of the fourteenth century, the Ashkenazim (a Hebrew
term meaning German Jews) were among the Jews expelled
from Hungary and the German lands. They found for themselves a refuge in the Danubian cities of Bulgaria and
Romania. But it was a major wave of Jewish immigration
from Spain and Sicily in the last decade of the fifteenth

century--the Sephardim (from the Hebrew word *Sĕphārad*, which
referred to a region usually identified as Spain)--that truly
produced a compact Jewish population in the more vigorous
centers of the empire. In the sixteenth century there arrived new reinforcements of Jews who had been driven out or
who were fleeing persecution. The strongest wave came in
1568 when the marranos (Jews who had accepted Christianity),
driven from Portugal, Italy, and southern France by the
cruel persecution of the Inquisition, augmented the Jewish
colonies in Salonika, Skopje, Sofia, Belgrade, and Sarajevo.
The marranos succeeded in bringing most of their possessions,
and their arrival invigorated trade in the cities where they
settled.[1]

Actually, in the sixteenth and the seventeenth centuries
Jews turned Salonika into the chief commercial city of the
eastern Mediterranean. In the first half of the sixteenth
century, the number of Jewish households fluctuated from
2,500 to 3,500. In 1518 there were 3,143 Jewish households
(at a time when there were 1,374 Muslim and 1,087 non-Muslim
households).[2] In the following decades the number of
Salonika's Jewish households dropped, which in all probability was the result of the withdrawal of the already
established Jewish population and other groups to the capital
and to other cities in the interior of the country. In the
late sixteenth century in Salonika, the non-Muslim population
(not counting the Jews) living in ten mahalles amounted to
1,234 households. They were contained as special groups of
the population (for example, there were 62 households in the
fortress). To this sum should be added 93 bachelor households and 470 households of widows, which, taken together,
increased the number of households of this part of the
population by about 150.[3]

In 1529 Edirne had 3,269 Muslim households. The non-
Muslims (472 households) were concentrated in 19 Christian
mahalles and included 7 bachelor households, 6 households
of widows, and 4 of voynuks. In the Muslim mahalles there
were an additional 46 Christian households.[4] Edirne's
8 Jewish mahalles contained 201 households (and 6 bachelor
households).[5] Over the next half century (from 1521-30 to
1571-80), according to Barkan's data, Edirne showed an
increase of 619 households, representing an average annual
rate of growth of 6.1 per 1,000.

* * *

These data on some forty cities show that over nearly a
century practically every city had a population increase, and
one must question the source of this growth.

There are certain processes that are characteristic
of any historical epoch. Although there are differences in

the extent to which they reveal themselves, these processes
have been present throughout all of Europe. For the sixteenth and seventeenth centuries, it has been established
that European city dwellers had a lower life expectancy
than villagers and, for all age groups, a much higher
mortality rate.[6] It had been found that most European cities,
particularly the larger ones, sometimes existed for centuries
on end in an endemic state of constant deficit in the
natural increase of their population.[7] Left to themselves,
such cities would inevitably have declined and disappeared--
and not necessarily as the result of cataclysms or epidemics
that might quickly take the lives of tens of thousands of
people. These cities survived, grew, and even flourished
because of an uninterrupted influx of population from the
outside. Seeing what was happening, contemporaries compared
the cities both to graveyards and to mythical monsters constantly devouring the blood tax offered by the surrounding
population as a sacrifice to the urban minotaur.[8]

That migration had a strong effect on the Balkan city
is shown by marked differences in the growth rates of
these cities generally and of separate groups of the urban
population. It is also revealed by the uneven development
of the same city in different periods.

The question comes down to this: was this increase due
largely to an individual wave of colonization or to movements of the population linked to socioeconomic processes
that drew the surrounding rural population to the city? The
population increase of cities situated all over the Balkan
Peninsula--including regions where there were few Turkish
settlers--attests to the operation of permanent forces
that ensured a continuous human influx into the city.

We know, for example, the place of origin of 1,973
persons (more than half of the total involved) who worked on
the construction of the Süleymaniye mosque and imaret in
Istanbul. Of these workers, 51.6% (607 Christians and 411
Muslims) were from Istanbul and its vicinity, 23.5% (311
Muslims and 153 non-Muslims) came from Asia Minor, and the
remaining 24.9% (300 non-Muslim and 191 Muslims) were from
Rumelia and islands of the Aegean Sea.[9]

In the mid-sixteenth century several hundred master
craftsmen and unskilled hands gathered in Istanbul where
for years they worked far away from their birthplaces. They
came from all parts of the Balkan Peninsula and from the
islands. It is recorded that 47 persons came from Edirne,
33 from Salonika, 25 from the Peloponnesus, 24 from Bosnia,
24 from Gelibolu, 18 from Skopje, 18 from Serres, 16 from
Silivri, 15 from Ereğli, and so on. And, of course, this
was not the only building project under way at that time.
In every smaller or larger city construction was taking

place on bezistans, inns, caravansaries, and mosques--proj-
ects engaging the labor of tens and hundreds of builders.
These workers too had assembled from different regions, for
it was by continuous movement from place to place that they
could find work. Considering the trades of such individuals,
furthermore, we have reason to believe that they did not have
urban origins, but rather sprang from the district surrounding the city in question. The movement of these workers
was dictated primarily by economic factors and the possibility of finding work. When corvée work was ordered by the
state, the contractual fulfillment of a given order was
based on a preliminary study of available manpower, skilled
and unskilled. The recruitment of workers, artisans, and
master builders was carried out in an established manner and
for a fee. In a centralized state such as the Ottoman Empire,
it was natural for major construction projects to involve the
regulation of both the manner of recruiting workers and
artisans and their pay--and to regulate these matters without
changing the nature of labor itself.

The use of such fairly large groups of skilled and
unskilled workers on centrally sponsored projects, and in
urban work in general, raises the question of the circumstances in which manpower might leave the village to work
and even to stay in the city. Could the existing restrictions
on leaving the land--restrictions that some authors regard as
a manifestation of serfdom--seriously restrict the movement
of the rural population and its resettlement in the city?
Insofar as they can be studied, surviving legal documents
and what we know about actual practice permit an answer to
this question.

It seems that at the end of the fifteenth century and
in the sixteenth century, the social division of labor was
fairly advanced in the countryside. Numerous provisions of
Ottoman legislation concerned the duties of precisely
those peasants who had gradually become artisans (tailors,
shoemakers, carpenters, ironsmiths), or who, as peasants,
simultaneously worked as carters, charcoal burners, fishermen,
or even as farm hands.

The laws provided that a village craftsman could, with
or without simultaneously being engaged in farming, work in
his village and totally support himself on the income from
his craft. Thus in accordance with a 1488 *kanunname* (or
collection of laws) of Mehmed II, if a village carter
(*kiraçi*) had been registered as "with the occupation of
carting," he was fully entitled to abandon the cultivation
of his land and was exempted from the duty to sow the established amount of seed. In return, he was obligated to carry
salt and other items for his sipahi and to pay 50 akçe a
year.[10] In a 1526 law for the sancak of Sofia, these 50 akçe

were termed the *çift bozan* ("tax for leaving the land"), and
were levied "from reayas who leave their land and go to work
in another place."[11] Persons who did not work the land paid
the çift bozan at the rate of 50 akçe for Muslims and 62
akçes for non-Muslims, who also had to pay an *ispence* of 25
akçe.[12] The village craftsman could also choose not to give
up the cultivation of his land; he could work it as before,
sowing the required *mut* of seed and paying the appropriate
taxes (the tithe on production, and so forth).[13] The law
freed him from "paying anything as an artisan working with
a cart in the town," so nothing additional could be levied
from him. How strictly the law differentiated this individual's work as a village artisan from his farming is seen
when, due to poverty or old age, he left his land uncultivated, the sipahi had no right to oppress him or to seek
compensation from his earnings as an artisan. The sipahi
only had the right to give the neglected land to another
reaya.[14]

Numerous cases of this kind show that even in the period
of so-called classical Ottoman feudalism the village was
forming an artisan stratum. This development necessitated
both the enumeration of the types of artisan activity and
the regulation of their legal position. "The artisans,
weavers, tailors, slipper makers, ironsmiths, charcoal
burners, their likes and others living in the village will
annually pay 3 *hizmets* [services] and 3 akçe," reads a 1488
kanunname of Sultan Mehmed II "the Conqueror." It was
forbidden to compel artisans to produce above the norms.
Their manufactured goods could not be seized by force, but
could be taken only if the artisans themselves consented
to provide them voluntarily and for payment in accordance
with "local prices."[15] Village artisans were also allowed
to practice their trade in other vilâyets.[16]

In other words, with the regular payment of the çift
bozan, artisans could establish even permanent residence
in a new place until sufficient time had passed for them to
be included in another category of the taxable population--
as artisans, but now as the residents of a city. Naturally,
such a transformation could come about only if their profession had provided the expected economic guarantees and
material advantages over farming. The new trade had to
produce sufficient earnings for the artisan to meet expenses
for support of his family and for the simultaneous payment of
both the tax for leaving the land and the additional levies
on the new profession.

But the growth of the urban population cannot be
explained solely by the settlement of rural artisans in the
cities. The substantial growth of the cities that we have
already established also supposes a continuous influx of a

certain number of peasants. The documents tell us that
through the intervention of a kadı peasants who had fled or
abandoned their land could be compelled to return. The
law, however, put restraints on the forced return of
peasants when fifteen or twenty years had elapsed since they
had settled in a new location.[17]

The question, therefore, stands as follows: what pre-
dominated--the desire to keep rural inhabitants bound to the
soil or the wish simply to ensure the regular receipt of the
feudal rent? The measure mentioned above, in our opinion,
has to be seen more as a guarantee against arbitrary
abandonment of the land rather than as a measure designed to
prevent each and every departure from the village.

In essence, the existing agrarian relations rendered
a system of serfdom superfluous. The feudal rent was
centrally established and centrally allotted.[18] Only its
actual appropriation was divided: fiscal agents collected
one part, while the collection of the other part was ceded
by the state to holders of land grants (e.g., a timar, a
zeamet, or an has). The ratio between the portions of
rent collected by the state and by private individuals
changed in the course of time, as did the distribution of
the feudal rent among the representatives of the ruling class
itself. But such changes had no effect on the status of
the peasants, whose basic obligation it was to pay the feudal
rent and taxes. For the state, in its capacity as supreme
arbiter of the feudal rent, it sufficed to assure continuous
revenue from peasant obligations and to avoid major
quantitative changes in that revenue. This explains why the
Ottoman ruling class and the state failed to impose any
particular restrictions on the widespread practice of the
purchase and sale of land, together with its encumbrances,
among peasant farmers.

The law itself, therefore, made it possible to practice
a nonagricultural occupation openly and, given certain
conditions, also to change a place of residence. It
sufficed for the agricultural producer regularly to pay the
sum required in such cases (the çift bozan), or to find a
buyer to whom to transfer the land with all its encumbrances.
The land law of 1609 envisaged the annual payment of 300
akçe in the case of a whole *çiftlik* (in the sense of the
arable land allotted for cultivation by one household), 150
akçe where the land equaled half a çiftlik, and 75 akçe for
smaller plots of land.[19]

The craftsman who made up his mind to leave his village
or the peasant who wanted to set up his farm near the city
or to work as a hired hand took into consideration this whole
complex set of conditions to avoid the effect of the law that

might return him to his village. This careful approach
is shown in kadı registers, which contain only rare examples
of the forced return of peasants who had previously abandoned
their land. In the sixteenth- and seventeenth-century registers for Sofia, there are only isolated complaints from
sipahis about peasants who had left their land and fled.
Requests for the return of peasants usually went unheeded
owing to the passage of ten, fifteen, or twenty years since
the peasants had left their original village.[20] At the same
time, these registers mention a greater number of cases of
the liquidation of village property or of the acquisition of
houses in the city. The sale of a village house cannot be
regarded as the final step in the breaking off of ties
with the village.[21] In an article about late seventeenth
century Vidin, a Bulgarian historian has noted the same kind
of influx of rural population into the city. He has brought
to light information that illustrates that Bulgarians bought
more plots and houses from Turks than from their compatriots.
Furthermore, he has noted that "the rural origin of several
Vidin Bulgarians is indicated textually."[22]

The register of the Ruse kadı includes instructions that
reveal the reluctance and perhaps even the inability of the
authorities to force the rural population to remain in
place. An instruction of March 28, 1587, addressed to the
kadıs of Tŭrnovo, Lovech, Nikopol, and Pleven, noted that
the population of the hasses of the grand vizier had begun to
resettle in the adjacent kadılıks, a dispersal of the reayas
that was harming production on has properties. Nevertheless,
the reayas who had abandoned their land were required only to
pay the cizye and the extraordinary tax. The instruction
explicitly decreed that those peasants who had left their
land "not be driven from their new location of residence
and not be resettled."[23] A zaim named Salih reported that
many reayas and sons of reayas in numerous Ruse villages had
left their native places to settle in cities. In reply to
this complaint, in 1698 an order was sent to the kadı in
Nikopol to have these persons sent back, but only if less
than ten years had passed since they had left their native
villages.[24] There were many examples of peasants gradually
settling in Ruse--a phenomenon demonstrated by their purchase
of houses, shops, workshops, plots, and so forth, and by
the liquidation of village property.[25] Here again the sipahis
complained to the kadıs, but with no results.

Both the legislation mentioned and, even more so, everyday practice indicate that the measures that provided for
the return of the peasants who had abandoned their land
failed to be effectively applied. The complete liquidation
of a farm by means of a sale and legalized by a deed could

not be challenged. (Quite another question, of course, was
the economic feasibility of such a step. Even in the face
of the strongest possible desire to avoid oppression, a
peasant decided to take such an extreme step--selling out his
farm--only after assuring himself of adequate and reliable
sources of income from some other occupation.) All of this
supports the conclusion that, provided the economic prerequisites were favorable, there were no insurmountable obstacles
to the movement and settlement of the rural population in
the cities.

     Study of Ottoman laws also permits certain conclusions
about the differences in the registration of urban and rural
inhabitants. Laws neither provided the grounds for the
classification of settlements as "cities" or "villages,"
nor did they state the conditions through which a village
became a palanka or a city. Nevertheless, the distinction
between an urban and a rural inhabitant was drawn very
strictly.

     On the whole, and regardless of its creed, the rural
population was called reaya.[26] The inhabitants of palankas
and kasabas continued to be entered in the reaya registers
despite the essential difference in their position from
villagers. Even the reaya who had lived in a city for ten
years or more and who could not be compelled to return to his
sipahi, and who was thus freed from his peasant obligations,
went on being entered in the lists of the reayas.[27] Such
a person was registered as a townsman (şehirli) only when
a general description and census of the whole vilâyet was
made, and a new register of city dwellers compiled.
Süleyman's legislation contained a provision that also
envisaged cases of direct registration in urban fiscal
registers. If a person had stayed in a given city for fifty
years, he was registered as an "added citizen" without having
to wait for a general description of the population and
without being included in the reaya lists.[28]

                              * * *

     The data considered here on the growth of 40 cities
indicate that, when examined over a period of years and for
different parts of the Balkans, there was an increase in the
number of households in most of the cities. The rates of
this increase differed considerably--from 1 to 30 per 1,000
per year. From a comparison of the average number of households of about 100 cities in the fifteenth and sixteenth
centuries, it is evident that this number nearly doubled in
the first half of the sixteenth century and about trebled
in the second half. The growth of the cities was primarily
the result of an influx of the population from the surround-

ing countryside. The sharp fluctuations also noted in the urban population were caused by special circumstances: such things as strategic considerations, which produced a temporary influx or withdrawal of considerable groups of the urban population, the establishment of new administrative centers for whole regions, and the intensive development of certain cities and ports as primary crossroads of inter-Balkan trade and of the expanding trade between the Ottoman Empire and Europe.

Plate 4. A sketch by F. D. Witt of 17th-century Zarnata in
the Peloponnesus. Courtesy of Gennadion Library, Athens.

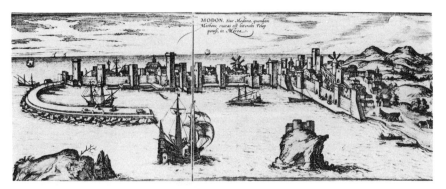

Plate 5. The harbor of 17th-century Modoni from Jacobus
Peters, *Description des principales villes . . . de la
Grèce. . . .* Courtesy of Gennadion Library, Athens.

Plate 6. The ancient agora of Corinth. Courtesy of Gennadion
Library, Athens.

Plate 7. 17th-century Saloniki. Courtesy of Gennadion
Library, Athens.

Plate 8.   Ainslie, Turkey.   Courtesy of Gennadion Library, Athens.

Plate 9.   Berati, Albania.

5. THE CITY IN THE FEUDAL SYSTEM

The Balkan city entered the Ottoman feudal system in a completed form--as a feudal category that had already taken shape. The onset of Ottoman rule does not involve questions of any kind of transition from one socioeconomic structure to another, nor does it raise questions about that stage of socioeconomic development when the division of labor has severed handicrafts from agriculture and has given rise to the feudal city as a new economic and social phenomenon. The medieval city in the Balkans already had its own centuries-old history as an economic center of a rural area, as a fortress and focal point of military and administrative authority, and as a commercial junction and crossroads for thoroughfares leading to other parts of Europe and Asia Minor.

The indisputable continuity of Balkan urban life through the pre-Ottoman and Ottoman periods does not, however, mean that the development of the city was totally uniform. Balkan

cities continued developing as feudal cities in accordance
with the basic regularities of that process--but under the
influence of new conditions that produced different tempos of
development and manifested certain unique aspects. With the
formation of the Ottoman state, conditions in the Balkans
changed considerably. This followed upon the creation of a
uniform political community for the entire Balkan Peninsula,
ethnic and religious changes, shifts in the principal economic and military thoroughfares, and the imposition of a
system of feudal relations wherein the state played a dominant role even in land. Although Ottoman rule did not affect
the feudal essence of the relationships already existing in
the Balkans, it did alter the social structure of Balkan
societies by promoting a new feudal class and by imposing on
the area its own religious, cultural, and educational institutions. We have already indicated some of the changes that
took place in the appearance and role of the Balkan city; let
us now examine the place of the city in the Ottoman feudal
structure and the most characteristic aspects of the state's
influence on urban economic life.

Feudal rent in the Ottoman state was apportioned in a
centralized manner into timars (with receipts of up to 20,000
akçe), zeamets (with receipts of from 21,000 to 100,000
akçe), and hasses (with receipts of over 100,000 akçe). The
distribution was carried out in accordance with the division
of the ruling class into a military-fief stratum for which
the timars were designated, a commanding military and administrative layer that received the zeamets, and an elite comprising both senior military and administrative ranks and the
courtiers who received has holdings.

All populated settlements in the Balkans regarded as
cities formed, either separately or sometimes with the
neighboring rural area, has holdings and zeamets, and some of
these settlements were also divided into timars. Thus at the
beginning of the sixteenth century, 177 Balkan cities for
which data are available were apportioned in the following
manner:

hasses of the sultan--------------------------------45
hasses of *vezirs*,[1] beylerbeyis,
    and sancakbeyis----------------------------------88
zeamets of *subaşis* and several others--------------26
timars--9
vakifs---9
                                         TOTAL 177

Urban receipts were appropriated by the elite of the
Ottoman ruling class. About one-fourth of these receipts
went to the support of the sultan himself, about half went
to the vezirs, beylerbeyis, and sancakbeyis, and the remain-

der went to the support of high military and administrative
officials in the provinces.

The sultan's has holdings included large cities (Edirne,
Salonika, Sofia, Plovdiv, Skopje, and Bitolj); ports (Vlona,
Messene [Koronē], Patras, and Durrës); all mining cities
(e.g., Srebrenica, Planina, Zaplanina, Olovo, Rudnik, Jejne,
Kratovo, Breznik, and Chiprovtsi); and about twenty other
cities of various sizes scattered about the Balkan Peninsula.
These included a few whose receipts also made up part of
the has holdings of beylerbeyis or sancakbeyis.[2]

There were only a few cities whose revenues formed
vakıfs. These cities included settlements in eastern Thrace
(Tekirdağ [Rodosto], Inces, Derkos, Silivri, Ereğli, and
Enec), as well as some cities in other parts of the Balkans
(e.g., Varna and Ikhtiman).

It is necessary to note that has holdings that were once
the direct possession of the sultan could pass into the hands
of senior officials--beylerbeyis, sancakbeyis, and subaşis--
and that has holdings and zeamets of individual persons could
once again become a has of a padişah. For instance, in 1526
the city of Karitena was a subaşi's zeamet and, fifty years
later, became the has of a beylerbeyi. At the beginning of
the sixteenth century Athens was the timar of a kadı, in
1526 the has of Ibrahim Paşa, and in the 1540s a sultan's
has. Toward the 1520s, Sofia, formerly a sultan's has,
became the has of the Rumelian beylerbeyi. At the time of
Mehmed II, Malgara was a has of the *mir-i alem*[3] of Gelibolu,
later the residence of a sancakbeyi, and in 1526 the possession of a beylerbeyi.[4]

As possessions of individual persons, urban has holdings
varied in size. Changes in the size of the has and in the
corresponding amount of urban revenue designated for the
feudal lord could follow a promotion in the hierarchy or
the loss of trust that had been invested in him by an official.
The size of urban has holdings and zeamets was increased or
decreased as a result of the allocation of urban receipts
among several holders or by subtracting or adding parts. In
this way the size of a sancakbeyi's has could be altered in
keeping with the position of the sancakbeyi himself. Thus,
in 1572 the has of the sancakbeyi of Požega amounted to
353,610 akçe; two years later, when Sinan Paşa became
sancakbeyi, it was raised to 468,475 akçe, and later, although still under Sinan Paşa, it was reduced to 387,564
akçe.[5] To obtain the sum earmarked for a particular beylerbeyi or other dignitary, the receipts from a number of cities
were often combined. Kasim Paşa, a beylerbeyi of Rumelia,
a vezir, and later a beylerbeyi of Morea, thus commanded
receipts from the cities of Serfiçe, Veroia (Karaferieh),

Voden, Yenice Karasu, Korçë (Korytsa), Vize, and other has
holdings. According to one register, Kasim's share of the
receipts from Veroia amounted to 55,000 akçe. Two other
parts of this city's receipts--of 22,000 and 40,000 akçe--
were allotted to Mustafa Paşa and to Ayas Paşa; and the
largest share, 445,000 akçe, made up a has of the padişah.[6]

Because the feudal lords lacked inheritance rights to
has holdings, zeamets, and timars (and also lacked close ties
with the land) they could not consolidate in a legal and
estate sense either as large feudal lords or as a small an-
cestral nobility in the manner that was typical for the medieval European state.

It is difficult to contain within a strict system the
state finances of the Ottoman government together with the
feudal revenues of Istanbul's ruling elite, of the provincial
feudal aristocracy, and of the military fief holders. It is
similarly difficult to relate the system of receipts to all
of the taxes paid by the subordinate population in general
and by urban and rural producers. Historians have not yet
clarified questions related to the structure and the size of
taxation or to the manner of the collection and allocation
of the great number of regular and extraordinary taxes levied
by the state for the benefit both of the treasury and the
class of feudal lords. We do have an over-all idea of the
allocation of the revenues designated for the treasury and
for the sultan and his court as we do for Ottoman holders of
fiefs of various size. The complexity, however, of both the
technique of allocation and of the manner in which various
items in the state budget are expressed in the documents
makes it impossible to establish the exact dimensions of
individual types of revenue and their total for a given area
or for a particular settlement.

The Defterhane, one of the departments of the Grand
Vizierate, dealt with the financial affairs of the Ottoman
Empire. It was headed by a chief *defterdar* with the rank
of a beylerbeyi who was responsible for Rumelia (the European
domains of the Ottoman state). Later he was joined by two
assistants, one of whom was responsible for Anatolia and the
other for the coastal regions of Anatolia and Rumelia, and
for Istanbul. The Defterhane included a system of offices
that handled the revenue items of the budget. From the few
published samples of the budget, one can conclude that this
complicated scheme of office organization changed constantly,
both in the number of offices (which fluctuated from four to
thirty-two) and in their internal distribution.[7]

Budgetary tables that have been preserved contain information only on receipts from the has possessions of the
sultan, revenues that were collected in the name of, and on

behalf of, the state treasury. According to Barkan's calculation, in the early sixteenth century these receipts
amounted to 51% of the total revenue of the country. Broken
down by areas, this represented 48% of the receipts from
Rumelia, 26% of those from Anatolia, 31% of Diarbekir's,
48% of those of Aleppo and Damascus, and 86% of the receipts
from Egypt.[8] The remaining portion of the revenue items
of the budget were allotted for distribution among the representatives of the class of Ottoman feudal lords in the form
of both fiefs and various rewards and privileges. The expenditures of the central state administration were covered
only by the receipts from the has holdings of the sultan,
which explains such a structure in the budgetary tables.

Of the budgets uncovered until now, only the budget for
1527-28 shows, as well as the has possessions of the sultan,
the receipts of the has holdings of other persons and of the
timars of sipahis and müstafhızes.[9] The total revenue from
all parts of the empire amounted to 537,929,006 akçe, of
which 198,206,192 came from Rumelia (yet another--and perhaps
the most convincing--proof of the leading role of the Balkan
lands in the economic life of the empire). Half of the
receipts from Rumelia were designated for the sultan and the
central authorities. The revenue items of the budget of
Rumelia were entered in the following manner: has holdings
of the padişah provided 94,784,238 akçe; has possessions of
vezirs and of other high dignitaries and military figures,
82,452,427 akçe; and the timars of the sipahis and müstafhızes in the fortresses, 10,086,683 akçe. The remaining sum
(about 11,000,000 akçe) was revenue from vakıfs. Thus, the
elite of the state and the commanding cadre of the Ottoman
military-feudal class appropriated roughly 46% of the revenues from Rumelia. The sum allocated to the forces stationed
in fortresses was relatively small and was distributed among
6,620 fiefs. Each fief holder was obligated to assure the
upkeep of one or two auxiliary soldiers.[10]

First among the sources of these revenues were the
mukataas, special state levies of considerable size that were
farmed out for collection.[11] The mukataas from the sultan's
has holdings amounted to 45,920,383 akçe, and represented
almost half (48.44%) of the total amount covered by these has
possessions. Here are some particulars: in 1445, the
mukataas from Plovdiv, Tatar Pazardzhik, and their surrounding area--a rice-growing region--yielded 1,679,920 akçe; in
1480, 2,650,000; in 1487, 3,400,000; and in 1688, 3,666,466
akçe. From the mines in Skopje and Kratovo in 1688 the
mukataas produced 5,990,940 akçe; from Vidin and its surroundings in 1688--4,186,000; from the salterns in Pomorie--
2,200,000; from Wallachia and Smederevo--2,563,392; from

Salonika--7,050,000; from the Siderokapsa mine near Salonika--
1,600,000; and from the mukataas on the fisheries in Istanbul,
from coffee, and from the roasting of coffee--7,734,720 akçe.

Collections from customhouses and ports were among the
most important revenues obtained through the mukataa system.
In 1688-89, the Istanbul customhouse yielded 39,838,800 akçe
(with the duty on the tobacco imported into Istanbul itself
producing 11,400,000). The customhouse of the port of Durrës
yielded 2,200,333 akçe; the port in Holumiče produced
2,310,000; the port in Messene--826,666; the port of Motoni--
594,444; and in 1583 the ports in Tulcea, Isaccea, and Macin
yielded 3,000,000 akçe.[12]

The next item of budgetary revenue was made up of the
cizye poll tax (from non-Muslims) and a land tax paid in
money, the ispence.[13] The general budgetary total also included a tax on vineyards and a tax paid by auxiliary military units, for example the Vlachs and others (although the
auxiliary paramilitary units enjoyed a number of privileges,
they did pay certain taxes).

Yet another item of revenue in the sultan's has possessions was the tax on tezkeres (trade permits) and berats
(1,797,625 akçe or 1.89%). These has holdings also included
other receipts to a general total of about 5,000,000 akçe
(from feudal possessions freed by the death of their holders,
and from the property of proprietors who died without heirs).

The sultan's has possessions included revenue sources
of the greatest potential and sources that by and large were
not related to agriculture. The greater part of these
revenues formed mukataas, which through a system of tax
farming were assigned for a definite period of time to private
individuals in return for a sum paid in advance to the
state treasury. State authorities, however, continued to
carry out the collection of these revenues.

The category of has possessions of other persons included
fiefs of different sizes that were distinguished from the
sultan's has holdings in that the revenues they represented
were collected by their proprietors on their own behalf and
for their own benefit. Has holdings formed from the revenues
from sancaks were granted to sancakbeyis, to some high officials of the court, and to the grand vizier. Although these
has possessions were not identical in terms of comprising
all the revenues from a given sancak, in general their size
did express the material possibilities of the sancak, something that makes it possible to compare them on a sancak-by-
sancak basis (see table 11).

In size, the has possessions of the sancaks of Rumelia
(excluding the has holdings of the Paşa Sancak) in 1521-22
were distributed as follows: up to 200,000 akçe--3; from

TABLE 11

HAS HOLDINGS BY SANCAK IN RUMELIA, 1521-1522

Sancak	Holder of Has	Size of Has (in akçe)
Bosnia	Mustafa Paşa	739,000
Smederevo	Bali Bey, son of Yahiya Paşa	622,000
Morea	Sinan Paşa	606,000
Vidin	Mesih Bey, keeper of standards	580,000
Hercegovina	Mustafa Bey, son of Davud Paşa	560,000
Silistra	Mustafa Bey, keeper of standards	560,000
Ohrid	Kasim Bey	535,000
Vlona	Transferred to Şadi Bey by inheritance	535,000
Ioannina	Husrev Bey, officer of palace gates	515,000
Shkodër	Iskender Bey, son of Evrenos	512,000
Gelibolu	Çafer Bey, chief of white eunuchs	500,000
Kiustendil	Transferred to Hayri Bey by inheritance	500,000
Nikopol	Mehmed Bey, son of Mihal	457,000
Sofia	Ali Bey, son of Mustansir	430,000
Trikkala	Ahmed Bey, son of Yahşi Bey	372,000
Kruševac	Ahmed Bey, son of Sinan Paşa	360,000
Vučitrn	Mehmed Bey, officer of palace gates	350,000
Zvornik	*Hacı* Mustafa Bey	264,000
Prizren	Ali Bey, son of Aranid	263,000
Karliili	Mehmed Bey, son of Ahmed Aǧa	250,000
Euboea	Lutfi Bey, officer of palace gates	250,000
Chirmen	Mahmud Bey, son of Mihal	250,000
Vize	Mehmed Bey	250,000
Florina	Hasan Bey, son of Isa Bey	200,000
Elbasani	Huseyn Bey, relative of Sinan Paşa	200,000
Karadaǧ	Iskender Bey, son of Çerne	100,000

SOURCE: Ö. L. Barkan, "H. 933-934," p. 304.

201,000 to 400,000--9; from 401,000 to 600,000--11; more than 600,000--3.

     Almost half of the possessions--rather large in size--
yielded about 500,000 or more akçe each. The largest has
holdings included the coastal and Danubian sancaks containing
ports (e.g., Morea [Peloponnesus], Gelibolu, Nikopol,
Silistra, and Smederevo), and several sancaks located in the

interior of the peninsula (Shkodër, Ioannina, Bosnia). The
majority of small has possessions represented the sancaks of
the interior (Montenegro, Prizren, Chirmen, Elbasani, and
Karliili).

The sancak of Paşa, which spread over a large territory
and contained some of the most important cities and ports,
comprised a great number of possessions, some of which
yielded as much as two or more million akçe.

* * *

A substantial part of all the revenue examined here,
revenue that constituted both the income of feudal lords
and the budget of the state, came from cities. For the reasons cited above, it is impossible to draw conclusions about
the total volume of receipts from a given administrative
territory; it is also not possible to compare for each sancak
the receipts from a city against those from its surrounding
rural area. Thus, additional study of this material must
inevitably follow the line of an analysis of individual
indicators.

Appendix 1 provides lists, on a sancak-by-sancak and a
city-by-city basis, that show the urban receipts commanded
by representatives of the Ottoman ruling class for the years
1526 to 1528. In terms of amounts of revenues from these has
holdings and zeamets, the distribution of the 177 cities
listed in Appendix 1 is: receipts of up to 20,000 akçe--50
cities (28.3%); between 20,000 and 100,000--94 cities (53%);
over 100,000--33 cities (18.7%).

Of the total receipts, the share of timars, zeamets, and
the smaller has holdings amount to about one-third. Very few
of the cities, however, yielded receipts that were small
enough to be on a par with those of several of the larger
villages, which shows that in the general dimension of revenues, the city differed from the village (the nature of the
urban revenue will be discussed later in this chapter). More
than half of all the cities fall into the group that produced
a revenue of from 20,000 to 100,000 akçe. But the distribution of such cities--again in terms of revenue yielded--is
not even. Most of them are concentrated in a subgroup of
cities yielding receipts up to 60,000 akçe. After that
point one can observe a gradually decreasing incidence in the
number of cities yielding higher revenues.

In the next group (cities yielding more than 100,000
akçe in revenue), we can see a concentration providing
revenues of from 100,000 to 300,000 akçe. Included here are
mining cities (e.g., Kratovo, Siderokapsa, Zaplanina,
Rudnik), coastal and Danubian ports spread about the whole
Balkan Peninsula (eleven cities in all), and a considerable

number of cities in the interior regions of the peninsula
including such important administrative, commercial, and
artisan centers as Sofia, Athens, Ioannina, Trikkala, Bitolj,
Mistra, and others (twelve in all). This group also includes
cities that formed has holdings yielding revenues higher than
1,000,000 akçe--Plovdiv, Vlona, Edirne, and Salonika.

The great difference in receipts between some cities and
most urban settlements lies in several unique sources of
revenue. These special factors include busy ports with an
intensive commercial turnover and large customs receipts
(such as Salonika, Vlona, and several other, though smaller,
port cities on the coast and on the Danube); the presence of
certain highly remunerative branches of production (rice
cultivation in the Plovdiv and Serres region; mines in such
cities as Srebrenica, Siderokapsa, Zaplanina, and others,
which had important has holdings despite their relatively
small populations); and also the presence of a number of
lively commercial and artisan centers with significant concentrations of urban population and prosperous surrounding
districts (e.g., Edirne, Bitolj, Plovdiv, Skopje).

The remaining cities listed in Appendix 1 are distributed on a gradually rising scale, that is, their receipts
relied on constant sources of urban revenue depending on size
and on several economic and geographic conditions that
affected the city's productive life.

In general, we get the same distribution of cities if we
compare the size of their receipts by households. Thus, in
comparing the receipts included in the above-mentioned has
possessions with the number of households of some 40 of the
cities, we find that in 11 of these cities (or 27%) the
average amount of the revenue yielded per household is less
than 100 akçe (and only in 2 cities--Trepca and Novo Brdo--is
it less than 50), while in 23 cities (57%) the average
receipts per household range from 100 to 200 akçe. A comparatively higher revenue yield per household of from 300 to 400
akçe holds true for Salonika and Edirne, as well as for such
mining settlements as Olovo and Siderokapsa. In some of
these cities where receipts from mining activity are distributed over a small number of households (as in Zaplanina), the
average receipts surpass 1,000 akçe.

Data from the mid-fifteenth century for about 10 cities
in northern Bulgaria produces similar results. The average
receipts per household of nearly two-thirds of these cities
are around 100 akçe; and in the remainder they fluctuate
between 150 and 200.

* * *

A comparison of the data provided above with the average

receipts from villages permits one to establish what these
values represented and at the same time raises the question
of the nature of these urban receipts. An essential difference existed between the urban and the rural economy, and in
the extent of taxation imposed on the population in the two
types of settlement. On the basis of information for fifty-
two villages in the regions of Sofia, Samokov, Vidin,
Salonika, Ksanti, and Drama, we have attempted to establish,
for these regions, the average rate of taxation of a rural
household, the correlation of separate types of budgetary
revenues, and also the nature of the village economy.[14]

Average receipts per household of from 50 to 100 akçe
are typical for 26 of these villages; for 7 of them the
average receipts go up to 110 akçe; and for yet another 2
villages, this figure reaches 120 akçe. Very few villages
have average receipts per household exceeding 120 akçes (10
villages in all, or 20% of the total) and only 2 villages in
the Salonika region have average receipts per household
exceeding 200 akçe.

Agricultural production represented the basic source of
receipts in all of these villages. The tithe on various
kinds of agrarian production usually amounted to more than
75% of the total receipts from the village, and in several
cases comprised more than 90% of the revenue. The remainder
of the receipts usually came from the ispence paid by the
non-Muslim households, the bad-i hava tax (of from 2 to 2.5
akçe per household), the *resmihuk* tax, the tax on marriages,
the *niyabet* and others.[15]

The structure of agricultural production clearly expresses an extensive mode of farming. Cereals, primarily
wheat and barley, dominated, with a smaller amount of cultivation of oats, rye, vetch, millet, and so forth. The grain
yield determined the size of the household income. As a rule,
the households of those villages with an average output of
from 2 to 4 *kile*[16] of wheat and of from 1.5 to 2.5 kile of
barley had an income of about 100 akçe. A higher income was
chiefly the result of more cereal production.

Instances where a very low income from cereals was
compensated for by the production of some other crop were
relatively rare. In the village of Rusile, for example,
where the average income per household was 50 akçe, an extremely low level of wheat and barley production (0.1 kile
per household) was compensated for by income from vineyards.
In the village of Bistritsa, the income from sheep was considerably higher, and so on. Information on the remaining
villages shows that there were certain differences in the
cultivation of individual crops. What was common to all
these villages, however, and what is particularly striking,

was how rarely they practiced intensive cultivation. Only in certain regions did other types of production--vineyards, vegetables, fruits, flax, and cotton--represent the more important sources of income. Beekeeping was developed in some villages, and in the environs of Sofia as well as in individual villages around Salonika, so was animal husbandry.[17]

For a number of villages there are indications that feudal receipts were produced by additional activities. These were chiefly *Shop* villages--that is, in the district of Sofia. Thus, in the village of Radichkov Samokov, 15% of the village's total receipts came from five water-driven forges (producing a taxable income of 750 akçe). In Srŭbski Samokov, the receipts from five such forges and two furnaces amounted to 580 akçe, or 13% of the village's total receipts.[18] The income from such auxiliary activities failed to have any decisive effect on the average receipts per household, which in these cases too were determined by the amount of cereal production.

There was only one village whose basic economic activity and source of revenue was something other than farming. This was the iron- and hardware-producing village of Saslar (of 79 households and located in the Vidin region). Saslar's receipts amounted to 5,720 akçe, 2,020 of which went to the timariot (the holder of the timar), and 3,700 of which went to the Vidin fortress. As metalworkers, the inhabitants of Saslar did not pay either the tithe or ispence. Their annual tax obligation consisted of 200 bars of iron for the fortress and 190 spearheads for the timariot. In 1466, by agreement with the peasants, the village was taxed through the mukataa arrangement. It paid 400 bars of iron and 210 spearheads for the fortress, and for the timariot, 30 houseshoes and 190 spearheads.[19]

The comparison between urban and rural receipts, therefore, reveals that per household, the average receipts from the city were approximately twice as large as those from the village. It should not be forgotten, however, that the average village receipts (established at about 100 akçe) included only the basic rural payments. The villages probably yielded more--through forced requisitions, extraordinary state levies (the *avarizes*), and also through the cizye. (But these taxes rested equally on the backs of both the villager and the city dweller). It is also true that the data provided above on urban revenues similarly fail to include the totality of payments, since in addition to revenues that made up state collections for the central budget, there was a whole category of collections spent on the maintenance of officials--the kadı, the *muhtesib* (or assistant kadı), and other representatives of specific urban posts

connected with the supervision of the market. These collections have not been reflected in the receipts identified
above; accordingly, the actual size of urban receipts was
considerably higher than what we have shown. One must also
keep in mind the essential difference in the character of
the receipts--in the village, farming was the source of the
basic part of feudal revenue; in the city it had a limited
significance.

The feudal receipts of several cities are recorded in
the documents. The records for the city of Vize, for example, show that in 1526 its receipts included the tax on
cereals; the ispence; the tax on flour mills; the tithe on
wine, beehives, gardens, and meadows; half of the niyabet of
the nahiye; fines; market dues; and the yield from neighboring fields.[20] In about the same year the receipts from
Novo Brdo consisted of the ispence and of revenues from the
mines and from the mukataas.[21] In 1527 the revenue from
Trepča included the tithe on cereals and the receipts from
the mine and from the city, but in 1544 it was composed only
of the latter receipts.[22] Several other examples reveal that
the receipts designated as proceeds for the central budget,
although not shown in detail, usually included the following:
market dues; the niyabet; the tithe on farm produce; various
duties on fishing, salt, marriage, and so forth; and, in a
number of cases, the ispence as well.

Information about certain cities in Macedonia, as published by a Yugoslav historian, permits one to examine the
ratio among individual items of budgetary revenue there.[23]
This information covers several years, making it also possible to study the dynamics of these revenues. Of decided
significance among them were market dues, the niyabet, and
the tithe on vineyards. Combined, they made up half and even
as much as three-fourths of the total receipts of these
cities.

The breakdown of the basic elements of revenue differed
in various cities. In 1477 in Veles, for example, the market
dues and the niyabet formed about 10% of the receipts; in
Prilep these items represented 16.6%; and in Tetovo and
Kostur, 28.2%. In about the same year in Veles the tithe
on vineyards constituted more than half the revenue, while
in Tetovo, Prilep, and Kostur, vineyards yielded, respectively, 45.6%, 48.6%, and 24.2% of the total receipts, indicating how that tithe represented one of the principal items
of budgetary revenue in these cities. In comparison, the
revenue from cereals was two times less, and sometimes even
smaller: for Veles, 18.6% of the total receipts, for Prilep
20%, for Tetovo 15.2%, and for Kostur 3.4%. In Bitolj, it
accounted for no more than 15% of the revenue. But this city

also had few vineyards, and at this time over 80% of its receipts consisted of market dues and other imposts. Only in
Skopje do we have a situation where (in 1477) the sum of
revenue from cereals exceeded half the total receipts (but
this sum was entered together with other taxes from the city
and from adjacent villages).

Farming continued to occupy an important place in the
cities just mentioned. But even in these regions, located as
they were deep in the interior and relatively distant from
the sea, taxes on domestic trade alone yielded from 10 to 40%
of the feudal dues and taxes in the second half of the fifteenth century. From one-third to one-half of the remaining
part of the receipts came from taxes on vineyards (which
should be regarded as supplementary sources of income and
livelihood for urban artisans and merchants). But these were
not the only monetary payments. If we add to them the revenue
collected by the treasury[24] (primarily the cizye and various
taxes on income from artisan production and from trade), we
are left with the picture of a comparatively well-developed
monetary turnover that had become part of the everyday life
of the urban population.

* * *

An analysis of the socioeconomic aspects of the Balkan
city requires additional material on the professional distribution of its population. Since the impressions of travelers,
however vivid, cannot really be used to reveal patterns of
urban production, we shall use data from Turkish sources to
describe the professional employment of the population of
several cities.

In 1546 the Muslim inhabitants of Skopje included:[25] 15
fortress guards, 166 akincis (mounted Turkish irregulars), 26
berat holders, 14 invalids and aged persons, 18 celepkeşans,
58 muezzins, 66 muhassıls (tax collectors in service to a
sipahi), 71 imams, 2 clerks, 1 kadı, 2 müdürs (administrators), 3 şeyhs, 9 dervişes (members of a Muslim religious order), and 6 servants in the mosque. Besides this group,
which included representatives of the Turkish garrison, the
administration, and the staff of the various Muslim institutions, the remainder of the Muslim population were artisans
and merchants. The group of shoemakers (89 individuals) was
composed of the following masters of different types of footwear: 36 başmakçıs, 25 papukçis (cobblers), 19 çizmecis
(bootmakers), 5 haffafs, and 4 kunduraçıs. There were 42
tailors, 5 abacıs (sewers of clothes made from coarse wool),
2 çukacıs (broadcloth makers), and 27 capmakers producing a
special skullcap (the takye). There were 8 artisans making
kebe (thick woolen cloth), 10 spinners, 4 thread makers, 4

*keçeci*s (horsecloth makers), 10 *mutafçı*s (makers of cloth
from goats' wool), 3 *hallaç*es, 19 harness makers, and 8 saddlers. There were 7 dyers and 3 wool combers. The group of
tanners was quite large, numbering 81 individuals. There
were 4 goldsmiths, 7 master metalworkers, 5 cutlers, 4 coppersmiths, 1 axmaker, 10 farriers, 11 carpenters, 4 potters,
and 10 potters specializing in cups. The Muslim artisans
also included 16 grocers, 21 butchers, 8 soap boilers, 2
chandlers, 4 bakers, 5 *halvacı*s (makers of sweets), 1 pie-
maker, 1 innkeeper, 1 *ambarcı* (barnkeeper), 20 shopkeepers,
16 druggists, 1 surgeon, 3 barbers, 1 bathkeeper, and 15 bath
attendants. There were 25 wholesale merchants, 5 slave traders, 4 hardware merchants, 1 salter, 1 carter, 1 bricklayer,
3 stonecutters, 5 old-clothes men, and 3 persons whose occupation is not clear. City dwellers involved in agricultural
work consisted of: 46 farmers (including 7 sowers and 4 rice
cultivators), 2 shepherds, and 3 millers. Several persons
worked at the mint: 4 master minters, 1 servant, 1 treasurer,
1 bookkeeper, and 1 guard. There was 1 Muslim who was proprietor of weights and measures. In addition, there was 1
overseer of the imaret and 1 tax collector.
    The city also had 216 Christian households. Barkan has
provided the occupations of the heads of only 16 of these
households: 9 tailors, 1 mutafçi, 4 fishmongers, 1 cobbler,
and 1 ironsmith. He notes that the heads of the remaining
households were chiefly engaged in agricultural work.
    Among the Muslims there was a decisive preponderance
(554 persons) of gainfully employed people representing a
great variety of handicrafts and of small mercantile operations. If to this group we add the celepkeşans (18), those
associated with agriculture (48), and the staff of the mint
(8), we have a situation where the population directly connected with production was one-and-a-half times greater than
the remainder of the populace. By adding to this group the
200 heads of non-Muslim households, most of whom were farmers, it becomes obvious that in the first half of the sixteenth century Skopje possessed the full appearance of a
medieval city. Ideally such a city would have part of the
population engaged in agriculture and an economy that also
represented all of the crafts typical of that time, which in
most cases would employ several dozen people.
    In 1548 there were 462 households in Zvornik. Further-
more, as an important frontier center, the city also housed
a considerable garrison. Islamization made speedy progress
there: in the course of 10 years, 90 households became
Muslim, leaving a mere 30 of them Christian--and in a short
time they too disappeared among the mass of Muslims. Evi-
dently the crafts practiced by the Muslim productive
population (432 households) were entirely connected with ful-

filling military contracts. This city had 104 tailors, 91
tanners, 33 carpenters, 24 saddlers, 19 mutafcıs, 18 horsecloth makers, and 53 butchers, grocers, bakers, and farriers.
Together with the representatives of the administration and
the müstafhizes, the artisan and merchant estate possessed
225.5 *dönüms* of vineyards.[26]

According to one register, in the second half of the sixteenth century, the heads of 1,702 Muslim households in
Salonika included 265 artisans, 80 merchants, 39 clerics and
educators, 26 individuals with various official posts, and 3
farmers. The occupation of the remainder of the population
is not shown. As noted in the same register, at that time in
Salonika there were 141 freed slaves and 32 converts to
Islam.[27]

In many respects the lists provided above are quite revealing. Above all, they provide evidence for what was a
typical phenomenon of the Ottoman Empire--the complete monop-
olization of the administrative apparatus by the ruling
nationality. Two other influential groups also stood out in
the Muslim upper stratum: the military, consisting of the
feudal forces and the fortress guard, and the representatives
of culture who also controlled education. Together with the
administration, these groups formed about 20% of the Muslim
urban population.

Artisans and small traders formed the bulk of the active
productive population in the city, both among Muslims and the
non-Muslims. As early as the period of classic Ottoman feudalism (the fifteenth and sixteenth centuries), when agriculture still occupied an important place in the urban economy,
much of urban feudal receipts came from marker dues, several
other urban imposts, and the tax on vineyards. The ruling
feudal class in the city was made up of military fief holders
and the representatives of Ottoman administration and culture.
They were gradually joined by Muslim and non-Muslim merchants
and artisans, as these individuals also accumulated sufficient
wealth and participated in municipal self-government and craft
guilds.

* * *

Urban receipts, as the most concentrated form of rent,
were given to the elite of the Ottoman feudal class. The
Balkan city, therefore, was part and parcel of the Ottoman
feudal system. It was not, however, the feudal possession
of any single individual, not even of the sultan. The city
was a feudal dependency of the state. As an aggregate feudal
lord, the state established the size and method of collecting
the revenues from the city. It determined the type and size
of the urban has holdings, zeamets, and timars, and granted
them to senior military figures and administrators for fixed
periods of time according to their ranks and responsibilities.

6. THE URBAN MARKET AND STATE REGULATION

The presence of numerous cities, some of which had heavily concentrated populations, required special measures to assure a normal supply of foodstuffs and to regulate their
relations with agricultural districts and with other supply
centers. The constant need to look after the supplies to
large cities (and particularly Istanbul) dictated, much more
than any particular Muslim tradition, the rigid centralization
of the state apparatus and its interference in economic life.
It was a matter involving the introduction of strict organization into the entire process of supply: the purchase of raw
goods from the immediate producer, the delivery of these goods
to large cities and to Istanbul, their storage, their distribution and additional processing, and finally, their sale to
the consumer. To avoid any interruption in the flow of
foodstuffs, this system had to function with the utmost effi-

94

ciency, and if for some reason or another there was a breakdown in delivery, the mechanism had to assure that the cities
had a sufficient reserve to last for a certain period of time.
To be able to forestall popular uprisings provoked by famine
or by a shortage of critical staples, it was also necessary
to prevent (or at the very least limit) speculation in food
products in different seasons, in years of drought, and in the
event of accidental shortages.

The Medieval rulers strove (as any rulers must) to avoid
social disturbances, particularly in the capital where they
would constitute a direct threat to power. But other major
centers could also become dangerous hotbeds of rebellion, and
the Ottoman government, in addition to its main concern of
assuring food for the capital, was also concerned with the
situation in other parts of the Balkans and in Asia Minor.
Given the then existing situation of insufficiently developed
market relations and slow shipment of goods, any interruption
in the supply of foodstuffs to the many thousands of people
in the capital or other large cities could produce serious
discontent.

The activity of the administrative and economic system
created to assure the provisioning of the cities depended
equally on the purposefulness of the decisions made by the
central authorities, and on how effectively these decrees
were executed in the provinces, for the sultan's orders and
the procedures established for the collection and delivery of
foodstuffs also required supervision and equally active measures by local authorities. Accordingly, a single system
linked Istanbul with the provinces and their cities.

Mehmed II (1451-81) carried out the first codification
of Ottoman laws that affected the social structure of the
empire within the population's various feudal obligations.
The two copies of these laws that have survived to the present
are not identical; one of them represents what seems to be a
provincial copy. The next codification, much more complete
than the first, was compiled in the reign of Süleyman I (1520-
66), who also issued a number of kanunnames for individual
cities and sancaks. The official texts of the laws of
Süleyman I have also not survived, and they are known only
in the form of copies. Published a number of times, the
kanunnames of Mehmed II and Süleyman I have been translated
into Bulgarian and issued in the series entitled Sources for
the History of Bulgarian Law.[1]

The oldest of the kanunnames regulating prices were
issued in 1501 by Bayezid II (1481-1512) and concerned the
three capital cities--Istanbul, Bursa, and Edirne.[2] Ö. L.
Barkan, who has discovered and published these documents, has
noted that the Ottoman archives also contain individual

documents for a later time. The earliest date for which he
has discovered similar legislation in the kadı registers of
Istanbul is 1776. There are, however, several registers that
record decisions about the establishment of price norms made
in the second half of the seventeenth century.[3]

Before publishing his kanunnames, Bayezid II issued--
with the help of a special inquiry--a ferman on the compilation of a list of the prices existing in Bursa. This list
was subsequently sent to Istanbul where it had to be examined
and discussed by those involved, and then it was incorporated
in the kanunname. Barkan believes that all three kanunnames
were drawn up by such decrees. This shows that Ottoman legislative practice took local conditions into account and
that, insofar as possible, the appropriate kadıs defended the
interests of producers before the central authorities.

A Soviet historian has recently discovered in Leningrad
a new copy of the laws of the time of Selim I (1512-20).[4] A
number of the provisions of this book of laws coincide with
the decrees on bazaars and market places issued at the time
of Bayezid II. Accordingly, it is possible to study more
fully the question of continuity in the drafting of legislative norms in the Ottoman state.

A comparison of the laws of Mehmed II and Bayezid II
(the second half of the fifteenth century), with the laws of
Selim I (the early sixteenth century), Süleyman II (the mid-
sixteenth century), and Mehmed IV (the second half of the
seventeenth century), provides insights into a number of important issues: the manner in which the state's regulatory instructions were put into practice, the actions of various
organs in establishing and regulating prices, the nature of
the rights and duties of producers and merchants, the kind of
market taxes paid on the import and sale of various commodities, and the manner in which the whole administrative
apparatus was maintained.

In view of the intervention of central authorities,
whose prerogatives included a direct say in the city's management, the administration of Istanbul differed fundamentally from that of other cities.[5] The grand vizier was the
supreme administrator of the capital. Kept busy, however,
with the affairs of the whole realm, he limited this function
to a traditional weekly tour of Istanbul's market places at
the conclusion of this or that *divan* meeting--that is, a public sitting of a judge. The frequent changes of viziers made
even more passing their participation in city government.
Actually, the prerogatives of the grand vizier fell to his
kaymakam, or deputy. Since the grand vizier accompanied the
sultan on his campaigns up to the sixteenth century, and
subsequently he himself commanded troops in the numerous wars

of the empire, he was often absent from the capital, and the
kaymakam became Istanbul's permanent acting administrator for
the city. Once a week the kaymakam met with those responsible for such things as the administrative and police
affairs of the capital. After the session they jointly
visited the market places and bazaars, supervising production
and trade and dispensing justice to those found guilty of
infringements.

A "religious-judicial institution," if one might call it
that, occupied a central place in Ottoman administration.
Its major task consisted of the exercise of controls and the
dispensation of justice on the basis of the religious norms
of the *şeriat* (the system of religious-civil law). This role
was entrusted to the kadıs.

The profoundly theocratic character of the Muslim institutions that formed the foundations of the Ottoman state did
not prevent the Turkish sultans from introducing necessary
amendments into Muslim legislation so that it might respond
to those constantly arising practical needs unforeseen by the
şeriat. By issuing special kanunnames formally sanctioned by
the head of the religion, the sultans could give the official
force of law to a number of local customs and existing norms
in the practice of the vanquished peoples. Accordingly, the
sultans could more easily assure the adaptation of the heritage of these peoples to the principles of Muslim state structure.

The kadıs put these kanunnames into practice, thus becoming not only the interpreters of religious rules and
judges of matters relating to the şeriat, but also administrative representatives of the central power. The kadıs exercised a many-sided administrative control. Their jurisdiction included the adjudication of disputes between individuals, marriage and divorce, and the probating of wills and
they were responsible for implementing the decisions that had
been made on all complaints that merchants and artisans addressed to the grand vizier. The kadıs exercised control
over corporations. They also supervised the market and producers and merchants supplying goods to the capital. This
varied and complex post was reserved only for competent
persons who had had the relevant training. The office of
kadı could not be purchased; rather, kadıs were appointed
from among a number of persons who had studied in a medrese.
The length of this training depended on the scholarly degree
that a given individual wanted to obtain, with fifteen to
twenty years of study required to receive the highest degree.

In the official hierarchy, the highest such posts were
those of the *kadıaskers*[6] of Rumelia and Anatolia and of the
kadı of Istanbul. Next in line were the kadıs of the holy

cities of Mecca and Medina, of the former capitals of Bursa
and Edirne, and of Cairo, Jerusalem, Damascus, and Aleppo.
The next ranking kadıs were those of Salonika, Plovdiv, Sofia,
Belgrade, Smyrna, Baghdad, and the remaining three kadıs of
Istanbul--those of Galata, Eyup (a purely Muslim district
located beyond the fortress walls of Istanbul), and Üsküdar.

The kadı's first assistant and deputy in the area of his
jurisdiction was the *naib*. In smaller administrative
entities such as the nahiyes, the naib performed an independent function that fully corresponded to that of a kadı.
Another assistant of the kadı was the *muhtesib*, who, while
retaining certain supervisory functions over the Muslim
observance of religious obligations, had the chief duty of
supervising the guilds, other organizations, and the market.
In return for the payment of a sum called the *bedel-i mukataa*,
the muhtesib purchased from the state both the right to collect the municipal dues known as the *ihtisab* for a year and
a berat for his appointment as a muhtesib. He himself had to
support the agents who collected the various duties from the
shopkeepers. In Istanbul the kadı was also able to use other
officials (e.g., the *şahbender*, who was responsible for wholesale trade and supervised the big merchants). Administrative-
related policing duties were carried out by military units
quartered in the cities. These units enforced the kadı's
sanctions. The religious-judicial nature of the Ottoman-
administration is thus seen in the wide range of the kadıs'
duties and in the pervasiveness of the şeriat in the life of
the empire.

* * *

Trade in wheat illustrates one of the unique features of
the economic life of the Ottoman Empire. Although the state
did not monopolize this trade, it put it into a definite
framework in the interests of the population and of small
producers, and yet also provided big capital with sufficient
opportunities for profit. With the size of the transactions
involved, and given the need of long-distance transportation,
the wheat trade permitted the acquisition of high profits
by those who held monetary capital--big merchants, representatives of the ruling strata, state functionaries who lent
money for the purchase of wheat, and shipowners who invested
money in this lucrative business. The state did not restrict
the activity of smaller grain suppliers, provided they observed the established requirements.

The export of grain from the Ottoman Empire was prohibited; it was permitted solely as an exception and even then
only with the permission of the grand vizier. The state did
not intervene in the transportation of wheat from the pro-

ducing areas to the capital, to other centers of consumption, or to those regions and islands where grain was not produced, but to avoid the diversion of large amounts of grain to places from where it could be smuggled abroad, and to prevent grain speculation in general, it designated the regions where it had to be supplied. In making such arrangements the geographical proximity of regions and the possibilities of transportation were taken into account. First to be met were the requirements of the center of the given grain-producing region and of the territory and islands located in its immediate proximity, and only then were the needs of more distant regions considered. Istanbul received the grain it needed from Rumelia (chiefly from southern Bulgaria), from the Danubian principalities, from regions located along the Asia Minor coast of the Sea of Marmara, and from the Smyrna area. The grain was assembled in several ports--Ruse and Silistra on the Danube, Varna and Burgas on the Black Sea, and Tekirdağ on the Sea of Marmara--from where it was shipped by sea. In the event of a shortage of grain in these areas, it was brought from other parts of the Balkan Peninsula and from Egypt.[7]

Having thus established the regions and allotted the basic volume of the grain supply, the state assigned to merchants the right to handle its subsequent purchase and transit. Beyond this point state interference subsided to controlling prices and delivery. For this purpose, the kadı of Istanbul provided a merchant with a patent (or permission) for the supply of wheat, a permit that was to be countersigned by the kadı of the locality where the purchase was made. The local kadı noted the amount of wheat purchased, its price, the name of the ship, the surname of its captain, the day the grain was loaded, and the day of sailing. Since the selling price of this grain (as both wheat and bread) depended on the purchase price, the latter figure was fixed by the grand vizier after consultation with the local kadı, other local interested persons, and with the kadı and the bakers and merchants of Istanbul. In the case of significant quantities of wheat, the consignment was accompanied by a guard, for the authorities wanted to be sure that the grain ship actually reached its intended destination.

According to calculations of a Turkish scholar who has authored a specialized study on the supply of Istanbul with cereals in the eighteenth century, about 90% of the wheat necessary for feeding the capital was supplied in the manner just described.[8] The remaining 10% represented that part of the grain directly provided by the state to meet the needs of the court and the garrison, and to serve as a reserve. According to another researcher, much the same breakdown held true for the seventeenth century as well, but this scholar has noted that in preceding centuries the state took a greater role in wheat purchases. For financial considerations, however, it had reduced its direct share in these wheat purchases.[9]

The text of the law on the provisioning of flour and bread was particularly categorical: "Watch that the Muslims suffer no hardship on account of a failure of flour to reach the market . . . and that there be sufficient bread, promptly delivered." For this purpose it was envisaged that each baker would have enough flour for two months (at the very least for one month). The bakers themselves were obligated "to work in cleanliness in accordance with the regulations, and [to bake] bread that is tasty and that is not below measure or insufficiently baked. If caught with burnt or soggy bread, [the baker] is to be caned on the heels."[10] Travelers were strongly impressed with the delivery of fresh bread every day by the bakers. Dernschwam, who spent more than a year (1553-55) in Istanbul, wrote: "The Turks want only freshly baked bread every day. The simple bakers, therefore, have to keep this circumstance in mind in baking, so that they are left with little or with no old bread. Otherwise they would have to sell three loaves for one asper, whereas two loaves of [fresh] bread cost one asper."[11]

* * *

The supply of meat followed similar lines. The Bulgarian lands and the Danubian principalities were again the main suppliers, but considerable numbers of sheep were also brought from Anatolia. The sheep were purchased by celepkeşans who had to register formally with the local kadı as sheep merchants. Some of the sheep purchasers were themselves flockowners and breeders, while others simply found that deals on the sheep market were a profitable investment for their money.[12] Here, too, prices were determined through the intervention of state authorities. The ranks of the sheep purchasers or celepkeşans included big suppliers whose area of activity included whole sancaks and who were themselves the owners of large flocks, attesting to the large profits produced by trade in sheep.

In 1674 Istanbul received for slaughter 199,900 buffalo, 3,965,760 sheep, and 2,877,400 lambs. In the same year, 325,228 sheep and lambs were supplied to the sultan's court and to the Janissaries. Although the number of livestock might have fluctuated from year to year, these differences were hardly significant. Istanbul was truly one of the most important meat-consuming centers.[13] The number of sheep required to supply the capital was established by decree and

entered in the appropriate defters. Accordingly, the kadı's
first task, in which he was assisted by the muhtesib, was to
make a count of the sheep imported by the celepkeşans, and
then to dispatch them for slaughter at the slaughterhouse and
at the meat shops. Only after the slaughter of the stock did
the kadı and the muhtesib give the celepkeşans a document
(called a *hüccet*) affirming the delivery. Such a double in-
ventory--counting the sheep before and after slaughter--was
designed to avoid any possibility of concealing the actual
number of sheep supplied. The hüccet recorded only the number
of sheep actually supplied; if more sheep were required, then
the kadıs were required to cooperate in an additional purchase
to meet the number stipulated in the decree. The celepkeşans
were strictly forbidden from replenishing their own flocks
with sheep brought by private individuals for sale in the
city.

The laws are silent on the kind of tax paid on sheep
brought to Istanbul by the celepkeşans. The legislation of
Mehmed II, however, does contain a provision concerning sheep
destined for sale: a tax of one akçe was paid for each pair
of sheep brought in from the outside. But if the sheep were
supplied by local butchers and slaughtered, then one akçe was
paid for each four sheep.[14] In the fifteenth and sixteenth
centuries this law became effective over the whole Balkan Peninsula. The legislation of Süleyman I and a number of other
kannunames for individual cities from Thrace to Sarajevo
repeated this regulation: one akçe for a pair of sheep, but
from local butchers, one akçe for every four sheep.[15] In a
law pertaining to Morea there was yet another provision concerning butchers who were outsiders. If such butchers slaughtered sheep or lambs, they paid two akçe for a tax called the
kantar akçesi.[16]

The meat obtained in this fashion was sold at meat shops
to the population at strictly fixed prices, although the law
did take into account the season and the type and quality of
the product. Thus, in the winter and spring, one akçe could
buy 250 *dirhem*[17] of mutton, and 300 dirhem in the summer. At
the end of summer and the beginning of fall, when meat was
plentiful, this price could buy 360 dirhem, but in the two
final months of fall the amount of mutton purchased by one
akçe again fell to 300 dirhem. During the same seasons, one
akçe bought 50 dirhem more of goat's meat than of mutton, and
50 dirhem less of lamb.[18] The muhtesib was required to assure
that mutton was not mixed with cheaper goat meat, and that the
meat sold at these established prices was not short-weighted
or substandard. The fines were quite severe: one akçe for
each dirhem under weight.

* * *

The instructions concerning cooks, vendors of brains, soupmakers, piemakers (*aşçılar*, *başçılar*, *büryancılar*, *börek-çiler*), and others had the same strict character. They had to sell food that was sufficiently cooked and hygienically prepared. Once used, plates and bowls had to be washed with water and wiped with a clean cloth. The food itself was not to be cooked in suet. Similar instructions concerned other kinds of dishes, roasted meat, and tripe soup. Also required was the regular tinning of vessels. Violators of the law were liable not to a fine, but to physical punishment.[19]

* * *

A strict system was also established for the delivery, storage, distribution, and sale of other foodstuffs. It was primarily the muhtesib who, acting in the name of the kadı, had to examine products to prevent suppliers from exaggerating their quality and from demanding an inflated price.[20] Expenses were taken into account in the determination of prices. A weight check preceded the removal of goods from storage, and these goods were taken out in the same order in which they had arrived. If carts arrived bearing large quantities of butter or honey, their loads were handed over to the storehouse of the market, where they had to remain for three days. Apparently, this was done so that the arrival of these goods could become known to all those interested. Anyone who tried to buy butter or honey directly from the cart was punished.[21]

One might also note the great availability of vegetables, milk, and cheese. Both Muslims and non-Muslims used these products much more than meat. Istanbul and other cities secured these in part from urban inhabitants directly engaged in their production, but mainly from the surrounding agricultural area. For larger centers and for Istanbul, such provisions, especially those that had been processed and could endure long transportation (dried fruit, cheese, etc.), were also brought from further away. Rumelia supplied good *kashkaval* (yellow cheese) and white cheese, and Wallachia and other regions supplied cheese wrapped in skins. The state did not directly control this trade; rather, private persons were required to observe the system laid down for urban trade --to deliver vegetables and other foodstuffs to predetermined places and to pay the appropriate taxes.

The law did not establish a strict price list for seasonal fruit and vegetables, and the kadı and the muhtesib were empowered to determine such prices in accordance with costs of transportation. But profits from the sale of these products were strictly regulated on the basis of the established norm, which allowed a profit of up to 10%. The

greater movement of fruit and vegetable prices was inevitable
in view of the variety and seasonal character of the majority
of these products: "Cucumbers, watermelons, sugarmelons,
apples, pears, broad beans, grapes, chickpeas, lentils, and
whatever else there is of this kind shall be sold according
to the season, and the price must be set with the assistance
of the kadı."[22]

* * *

Similar price controls covered all other consumer goods
and artisan services. The prices of leather products, and
particularly of footwear, were elaborated in the greatest
detail. Bootmakers (haffaf and çizmecis) sold several types
of high boots (çizme). These boots differed in style and in
color, and for each category boots were sold according to one
of three levels of quality: low, medium, and high. Boots of
given quality were to be sold at prices ranging from 26 to 28
akçe. There were also boots priced at 12 to 13 akçe, 13 to
14 akçe, and 15 to 17 akçe. The price of special boots in
"Bulgarian" color ranged from 22 to 26 akçe. There were two
types of shoes made from saffian leather that sold at prices
ranging from 15 to 20 akçe and from 23 to 27 akçe. Simple
slippers made without a counter (papuç) were also sold at
three levels of quality--from 5 to 6 akçe, 7 to 8 akçe, and
9 to 10 akçe a pair. A type of soft slipper (çehli) was
twice as expensive and depending on the quality, sold at
prices ranging from 14 to 15 akçe, 16 to 17 akçe, and 18 to
20 akçe.[23]

Such an elaborate price list for footwear presupposed a
no less detailed elaboration of prices for shoemaking materials. Sole leather made from buffalo skin was supplied to
bootmakers and to shoemakers at three levels of quality at
prices ranging from 160 to 200 akçe. Oxhide was priced at
from 20 to 80 akçe and cowhide at from 22 to 30 akçe. Heavy-
duty sole leather cost 10 akçe more for every quality and
sort. If dyed red, saffian leather from goatskin sold for 18
to 20 akçe; for other colors the price ranged up to 15 akçe.
Most expensive was mauve-colored saffian leather, the price
of which reached 25 akçe. Moroccan leather cost from 3 to 6
akçe. Processed horsehide was divided into several levels
of quality and had various prices--from 10 to 70 akçe.[24]

The masters who produced footwear received finished
material that had been furnished by livestock merchants and
by traders in skins and then processed by the city's curriers
or tanners. The curriers dressed the hides of livestock
slaughtered in the city as well as all imported skins (which
could be sold only to these curriers). After tanning the
skins, the curriers bypassed merchants and sold the finished

leather, including sole leather, directly to the producers--
the shoemakers and bootmakers. Only after the needs of shoemakers had been satisfied were merchants entitled to trade in
leather provided by the tanners or to buy the currier's merchandise. Furthermore, merchants were even limited to a 5%
profit margin on the sale of several types of leather (e.g.,
sole, saffian, and morocco leather). This restriction indicates the power of the curriers in the public life of the
city. Most of the undressed hides brought to Istanbul--and
the most highly valued ones--were imported from Wallachia
and Moldavia. Sheepskins from these regions, for example,
cost 2.5 akçe apiece, at a time when the same skins brought
from Zagorie (a region in the southern Balkan Mountains and
the *Sredna Gora*) cost 2 akçe apiece, and those from the
Dobruja cost 1.5 akçe apiece. Depending on its quality, raw
oxhide sold at prices ranging from 50 to 120 akçe.[25]

Even more detailed were the prices of the goods produced
by the harness makers and saddle makers: bridles, reins, and
various saddles, especially horse saddles. The brilliantly
polished bright red "Ottoman" saddles sold at prices ranging
from 350 to 600 akçe, and the greater the ornamentation, the
higher the price. Depending on their style and design, other
saddles cost from 80 to 250 akçe. Good reins of various
types and variously ornamented cost from 40 to 80 akçe, with
the cheapest costing from 8 to 10 akçe. There were two types
of blinkers, "Mongolian" (42 to 50 akçe) and "Bulgarian" (40
to 45 akçe). Chained double halters went for between 10 and
14 akçe; horseshoes sold for 5 akçe and shoes for donkeys for
3 akçe.[26]

Prices and norms were established for other commodities.
Merchants selling fabrics, headwear, and other goods had the
right to a 10% profit. For combers, the obligatory price of
150 dirhem of cotton was from 1 to 2 akçe. Woolen yarns had
to have a regular thread and to be mixed with cotton. Goods
produced from goatskin bore prices established on the basis
of their size: while a simple goatskin bag sold at 3 to 5
akçe, horsecloths 2 spans long and 6 spans wide cost 30 akçe;
and so forth. The price of caftans ranged from 15 to 20
akçe. A fur-lined caftan cost from 40 to 45 akçe. Armor-
ers had the right to sell long thin swords and "Damascus"
swords at various prices depending on the finish and deco-
ration. Good scabbards cost from 40 to 70 akçe. The finished work of coppersmiths and tinsmiths was also subject to
price norms overseen by the muhtesib.[27]

Lumber could not be purchased directly from the villages, and those who infringed this regulation were punished.
Lumber suppliers sold their merchandise at prices set according to the width and length of the planks and logs.

Cartage rates were also fixed. Cartage by horseback cost
up to 2 akçe over long distances, 1.5 akçe for medium distances, 1 akçe for short distances, and .5 akçe for very short
distances. The law required that special care and attention
be paid to horses, mules, and donkeys used for the transportation of goods. Their limbs had to be checked and the saddles examined, and they were not to be laden with more than
the established weight "because a beast has no language and
cannot speak."[28]
    Also regulated was the service of bath attendants and
barbers. They were particularly required to observe hygiene,
with an apparent religious (or really ethnic) discrimination:
the same towel or apron could not be used for both Christians
and Muslims. A similar discrimination can be seen in the
regulations governing the work of cooks and eating houses.[29]
Even the work of the doctor failed to escape the system of
controls. Physicians, pharmacists, and surgeons also found
themselves under the supervision of the muhtesib.

                            * * *

    As can be seen, the prices of nearly all staple goods and
of the widely needed consumer goods that were produced for
sale were regulated by the central power and by the kadıs, and
were supervised by the muhtesibs. The prices included a
profit margin, usually envisaged as 10%. Only in a "craft
that is very difficult is it permitted that 10 [akçe] can become 12"--that is, a 20% increase in the profit margin.[30]
    This state control had to be exercised in a regular
manner. For some goods, this control was a weekly affair; for
others the supervision was more occasional. But at least once
a month the kadı had to check to see whether prices were being
observed. The muhtesib also supervised the sales carried out
by guild elders, including instances where these transactions
were effected in the name of, and in the interests of, the
whole guild. As well, the muhtesib supervised the lending of
money at interest, the rate of which could not surpass 20%.
    Regulation and control extended even to the pay of labor.
The work of goldsmiths was remunerated at the rate of one akçe
for each dirhem of weight of the item in question. In the
summer, carpenters and masons were to be paid ten akçe for
their work and two akçe for food; in the winter, the rates
were eight akçe for the work and two for the food.[31] The
sewing of clothes was also regulated according to established
prices and norms. Thus, from a span of broadcloth, tailors
had to produce two shirts. A collar, however, had to be sewn
from a piece of cloth measuring half an *arshin*.[32] The cuts
were also established.
    There were special requirements with regard to footwear.

Shoes had to be made in such a way that their endurance corresponded to the sum paid at the ratio of two days' wear for
each akçe of cost. If shoes wore too quickly, a fine was
paid equal to their full value. If the shoe came apart at
the stitching, the fine was paid by the shoemaker who had
sewn them; if the sole leather or saffian leather became torn,
then the tanner or currier paid the fine.[33]

These price norms were the ones established for Istanbul,
Bursa, and Edirne, but when communicated by the sultan's decree to the kadıs of other cities, they had the force of law,
and they guided the local authorities of these cities. That
this was so is shown by the enactments of subsequent sultans
who referred to the kannunames mentioned above in those cases
where, at the request of the population or for some other
reason, it was necessary to resolve disputes.

One of the kadı's most important tasks was to participate
in the determination of price norms (nahr) and the fixing of
market prices for the city concerned. For this purpose the
kadı summoned the muhtesib, other experts, and the leaders of
the relevant guilds for a joint discussion of prices. Where
price norms had already been established, the market prices
were determined by the amount of raw material available and by
what kind of crop--good or bad--had been gathered. The profit
margin of merchants and craftsmen was also taken into consideration. Kadı registers contain records of the decisions
taken. Accordingly the data preserved in these registers
can be used for throwing light on the question of the extent
to which it was possible to adjust prices in the localities.

Price norms themselves were established in a centralized
manner. The norms established a price ceiling, that is, they
defined the maximum permissible price but did not prohibit the
sale of merchandise at lower prices. Furthermore, these norms
were worked out to be effective for a long period, which is
shown by a consistent adherence to roughly the same norms
over the course of decades and even centuries. Each new
sultan reaffirmed the norms, and they were also reaffirmed in
certain circumstances where there was a disruption in the
normal supply of goods--such as difficulties in finding and
delivering foodstuffs or sharp changes in the value of currency.

* * *

As this survey makes clear, the maintenance alone of the
several hundred thousand residents of the capital and of the
sultan's court with its guard--and also of the population of
other large cities--required a control and coordination that
encompassed all spheres of activity: production, exchange,
and supply. All of this significantly expanded the functions
of the organs of the state in economic life, and this devel-

opment, in its turn, inevitably limited the freedom of other
economic institutions. This all-embracing state regulation
was one of the most characteristic features of Ottoman feudalism.

7. Guild Organization and State Regulation

The guild (*esnaf*)[1] was the most all-embracing economic
and social organization in the Ottoman feudal system. The
state backed the guild for fiscal reasons and from a desire
to regulate economic life. The population relied on it for
its own professional and social support. The guilds brought
together people who shared the same occupation and who had a
kindred material position and interests. Some of the guilds
were established without regard to religious differences; in
other cases there existed parallel (i.e., Christian and
Muslim) guilds (and occasionally artisans who were not members of guilds).

Contemporary scholarship cannot confidently answer questions on guild organization in the fifteenth and sixteenth
centuries, how extensively they were spread throughout the
Balkan provinces of the empire, and how much of the urban

population the guilds at that time included. For that period (and, indeed, for later periods as well), not a single guild statute has as yet been discovered.[2] The earliest code of rules we have for the Balkan provinces of the Ottoman Empire (which still cannot be considered a full statute, but does speak of an already existing guild organization) is a 1657 collection of rules of the tanners of Elbasani. With its invocations to Ahi Evran Veli, the protector of tanners, this code reflects the religious elements that were characteristic of the Muslim guild. Its articles on economic activity concern the obligatory delivery of all goods necessary for tannery production (hides, dyes, etc.) to one place, from which the *yiğitbaşi* (the second-ranking person in the guild after the elders), with the help of the elders, had to distribute them among all members.[3]

The oldest preserved guild register (or *kondika*) is that of the aba-makers' guild of Plovdiv. Kept in Greek, it contains information from 1675 to the middle of the nineteenth century, chiefly on the acceptance of apprentices and journeymen and on the proclamation of masters. It also contains entries on individual duties (which have a statutory character), indications of applications for assistance, accounts for various payments, loans, and so on.[4]

Despite inadequate documentation, the guilds represent an important topic in the study of the urban economy and the social system of the Balkans, and they have attracted the greatest interest on the part of researchers. Accordingly, we should take a more detailed look at how historians have dealt with them.

Marx and Engels clearly and fully characterized the essence of the guild organization and how it was engendered in Western Europe: "The necessity for association against the organized robber-nobility, the need for communal covered markets in an age when the industrialist was at the same time a merchant, the growing competition of the escaped serfs swarming into the rising towns, the feudal structure of the whole country: these combined to bring about the guilds."[5] Brought to life by the needs of feudal society, the guilds in their own structure also represented a feudal institution.[6] Naturally, different conditions left their individual imprints on the structure of the guild and on its role in the economic and social life of each country.

The guilds in the Ottoman Empire emerged and developed in conditions different from those existing in the West. Accordingly, although they resembled western medieval corporative organizations, they had markedly distinct origins and experienced a number of unique features in their development. J. Sauvaget, one of the leading experts of the literature on

the history of the Muslim world, has with full justification
cited the state of the art as it relates to the history of
guilds as an example of how incomplete studies of Muslim institutions are: "Serious gaps exist in our knowledge of
Muslim institutions," he has noted. "Let us limit ourselves
to one example: the history of corporative organizations
escapes us almost completely."[7] In the extensive literature
that exists on the Islamic guilds generally, or that covers
various aspects of their organization in the Ottoman Empire
(in particular in Anatolia and Turkey's European possessions),
there are still various theories about their origin and
character, and these questions remain unresolved.[8] Some researchers have studied the Islamic guild as a natural continuation of Byzantine corporative organizations that were
adopted by the Arabs after the conquest of Syria and Egypt,
or by the Seljuk and Ottoman Turks in conquering Asia Minor
and Constantinople. Others have found the sources of the
emergence of the guilds in Islamic society itself, Arabic and
Seljuk. In their opinion the fundamental founding principle
of the guild was a powerful social movement for equality that
in the tenth and eleventh centuries shook the Muslim city
in the Near East. Despite its religious form, this movement
had a relatively liberal content.

Considerable credit goes to V. A. Gordlevskii for having
revealed the character of the guild organization in the
period of the Seljuk state and in the initial period of the
Ottoman Empire.[9] A. Gölpinarlı has published a great deal of
new material on the movement of the Muslim religious organization called the Futuwwa and on the unique knightly organization of the ahis. This material has been useful for the
ultimate clarification of the early period of the emergent
guild organization in Asia Minor.[10] B. Lewis, who in the
late 1930s summed up the different theories of the origin of
the Muslim guild, also attempted to provide a characterization of the guild organization in the Muslim world and in
particular in the Ottoman Empire. In trying to discover the
unique features of this organization and to compare it with
European guilds, he found that while the latter fulfilled
public functions and were recognized and administered by a
political authority (be it seignorial, municipal, or royal),
the guilds in Muslim countries were not created in response
to the needs of the state; rather, they constituted social
institutions in their own right and were brought to life by
and for the producers themselves. Thus, throughout the whole
of their history they retained a profound antiauthoritarian
sentiment and a hostile attitude, overt or covert, toward the
state. In connection with this feature of their development,
and more generally with the stagnant character of the economy

of the Muslim countries, the guild's masters, apprentices, and
journeymen formed a homogeneous social group that retained an
element of close personal contact that did not lead to that
sharp differentiation of masters and assistants into two
hostile social groups that occurred in European guilds. Another specific feature of the guilds in the Muslim world was
that they were open to Jews, Christians, and Muslims.[11]

Apart from those conclusions that have already become
outdated in the inexorable development of scholarship, we
must note that several theses have developed that require
serious corrections or totally fail to correspond to the
actual development of the guild organization in the Balkans.

In its general evaluation and characterization of the
guild, Balkan historical scholarship has repeated the conclusions of its European counterpart, citing new arguments
to support some of the positions that have been advanced.
Turkish researchers have occupied a special place in this,
and it is from precisely them that one should expect the
greatest results in the clarification of the role of the guild
organization in the socioeconomic life of the Ottoman Empire.
These scholars have directed their efforts chiefly to the
study of the historical roots of the guilds in Asia Minor--in
both pre-Ottoman times and in the early period of the Ottoman
state.[12]

Greek authors, meanwhile, have for the most part been
studying the cultural and political activity of the Greek
population in cities scattered about the Balkan Peninsula.
While occupied with the search for documents on the Greek
municipal organizations, they have also discovered numerous
registers containing information on the development of handicrafts and trade. Several studies have also been written on
Greek guilds and on the history of individual Greek municipal
community organizations.[13] In general, Greek historiography
has presented the guild organizations in the Greek lands (and
also in Constantinople, Edirne, Plovdiv, and in the coastal
cities of the Balkan Peninsula) as a natural continuation of
corporations that had begun to play an independent role during
the declining period of the Byzantine Empire. Subsequently
these corporations experienced the influence of Muslim institutions. A. Vakalopoulos has suggested that the strong influence of Muslim guilds was due to the diffusion of the Christian population and to Muslim colonization.[14]

Yugoslav historians have likewise paid serious attention
to guilds. They have published several monographs and a
number of other studies on the spread of the guild and on its
role, chiefly in the nineteenth century, in various cities
and regions of Yugoslavia (especially in Serbia, Bosnia, and
Hercegovina).[15]

Recently, the Albanian historian Z. Shkodra has in several studies examined the guild's legal position. He has shown that the complicated question of the character and development of the Balkan guilds will find its solution only through simultaneous comparison of information drawn from such varied sources as kannunames, kadı registers, _fütüvet-names_ (or medieval guild statutes), and guild codes. Having analyzed material for the Albanian lands, Shkodra has concluded that guilds appeared in the Balkans in the sixteenth century and that as early as the seventeenth century they possessed their own statutes and rules, which had been composed, consolidated, and put down in writing.[16]

Bulgarian bourgeois historians also searched for a model of the craft guilds. Some found it in the Byzantine guild, and others, the majority, in the Arab-Turkish guild.[17] Unlike the historians of other Balkan countries, Bulgarian researchers traced the structure of the guild in the Bulgarian lands to a 1772 ferman of Sultan Mustafa III (translated into Bulgarian by D. Ikhchiev and used for the first time by B. Tsonev).[18]

Bulgarian Marxist historical scholarship has contributed fresh clarification of the historical development of the guilds. Both Tsonev and N. Todorov have looked into the changes in craft guilds in the period of the Bulgarian National Revival (in comparison with the position of the guilds in previous centuries).[19]

As this brief survey indicates, a scholarly answer is pending not only for the question of the origin of the guild organizations in Ottoman society, but also, and even more so, for the questions of their character and role in the early centuries of Turkish rule on the Balkan Peninsula. Only the concerted efforts of the historians of all the Balkan countries will be able to resolve this problem. Here we shall present only several general considerations that, in our view, should be kept in mind in examining the role of the guild in the Balkan part of the Ottoman Empire.

To begin with, an inexact formulation of the question of the character and role of the guilds in the early centuries of Turkish rule would seriously impede the study of later changes in their structure. Researchers who do not take into account the historical development of the guilds sometimes plunge into unconvincing analogies with the guilds in the West, and draw unwarranted conclusions.

The problem of the origin of the guild is of considerable interest in its own right. It would be wrong, however, to stress the formal dispute (i.e., formal in the sense of the present state of the sources) that continues over what elements of the guild the Turks found, what they inherited, or what they introduced, and thus to ignore the study of

the development of the socioeconomic life of the Balkan
lands from the fifteenth to the seventeenth century, a period
of development that filled the guild with content and determined its form. It is natural for a new state system to introduce and impose its innate institutions and also to make
use of forms that it has just found. The aftermath of the
establishment of the Ottoman Empire, however, saw not only
changes but, to a considerable extent, the appearance of a
new totality of socioeconomic conditions that imparted a
different character both to the institutions just introduced
and to those already in existence. Such was the case, for
example, with the role of the state in the economic life of
the conquered Balkan lands, and with the relationships between the guilds and the organs of the state. In no case did
Ottoman state institutions and other public organizations
emerge as true copies of either Byzantine or other Muslim
institutions. The Turkish state and Ottoman feudalism must
both be examined as a complex synthesis of various influences
that had already taken place in Asia Minor but took their
final form only after the conquest of the Balkan Peninsula.

Finally, we can associate ourselves with the general
conclusion already made by Inalcık that, together with the
Byzantine impact on the pre-Ottoman Muslim state, there also
existed a direct Byzantine-Balkan influence on the Ottoman
state, an influence that found its expression "in the reaf-
firmation and preservation of a certain number of taxes and
privileges of some cities and layers of the population, of
former military and administrative structures--in a word,
of institutions to which the population had in the course of
centuries become accustomed."[20]

* * *

The documents of the seventeenth and eighteenth centuries testify to a great uniformity in the structure of guilds
throughout the whole Balkan Peninsula. Since guild structure
is one of the most frequently studied questions in the
historical literature of all the Balkan peoples, we will
limit ourselves here to a brief outline of the relationships
among its individual elements.

Throughout the entire period of its existence, the guild
possessed a structure containing three principal units: the
usta or master, the *kalfa* or journeyman and assistant master,
and the *çirak* or apprentice. In the period under consideration, their mutual rights and obligations did not change.
The apprentice took up work with a master to learn the trade,
and his work either went unpaid or was rewarded only mini-
mally. But without this apprenticeship with a master to
become, in the course of time, a member of the guild, the

ordinary producer could not be accepted into the urban society of that time. The advancement of an apprentice to journeyman fully depended on the master, who at a meeting of masters personally proclaimed his apprentice to be a journeyman.
The length of training in the different crafts varied, but
usually required several years. This amount of time was required not so much to master the craft (which in itself might
not be particularly complicated), but to pass through the
obligatory period of work as a servant in the workshop and
home of the master, becoming familiar with the existing rules
and developing the work habits and principles that lent so
much strength and vitality to the estate of craftsmen. In
commercial establishments the length of service was shorter.

     The journeyman, whose social status was that of a hired
worker, was in essence the master's assistant and a future
continuer of his business. In a period when a restricted
number of journeymen were admitted, promotion to the rank of
master was strictly regulated. For a journeyman to receive
the right to become a master required several years of work
with a particular master. His promotion, however, depended
not only on his own master but required the consent of the
general assembly of masters and the fulfillment of definite
conditions, the most important of which were the giving of
presents to the elders and--in a number of cases--the
production of a special product (a masterpiece) or the fulfillment of an order under the supervision of the masters.
The final proclamation of the journeyman to master took place
in solemn circumstances at a special general meeting called
a *testir*, which took place periodically at intervals of from
one to several years. Very often several guilds shared the
expenses of such ceremonies.

     Special permission was required to open a store or work-
shop, since for many handicrafts the number of shops was
fixed and could be increased only through a great deal of
effort. Most often the newly promoted master had to acquire
the so-called *gedik*, a document for the right of shop ownership. Mention is made of the gedik in the sources for the
seventeenth century and especially for those of the eighteenth century. It was a once-and-for-all document and thus
could be transferred by inheritance from father to son
(provided that the son had acquired the right to practice
his father's craft). In the absence of direct continuity
it is not possible to know what happened to the gedik. Could
it be ceded or sold to other persons? Under what conditions?
Did the family choose the new proprietor or was this done
through the intercession of the guild? It is impossible to
answer these questions.

     The existence of ownership rights to shops and workshops

that could pass to different people opened up the way for the
concentration of the ownership of stores and workshops in the
hands of one person. This procedure likewise permitted the
penetration of the artisans and merchant milieu by representatives of other layers of the population--the military
(particularly the Janissaries), officialdom, people close to
the sultan's court, and others. The gedik, furthermore,
provided the state with yet another opportunity to regulate
the opening of new workshops and stores in accordance with
rising needs.

The leading organs of the esnaf bore names from the pre-
Ottoman guild. By now, however, the religious and knightly
principle that dated to the period of the establishment of
the guilds in Asia Minor had been fully displaced, and in the
seventeenth century this principle had become only a conven-
tion. For example, from the end of the seventeenth century
to the beginning of the nineteenth century, the şeyhs, the
official leaders of the guilds, were mentioned more by tradition than by anything else. From time to time they took
part in ceremonial ritual.

The real head of the guild was the *kethüda* or *kâhya*,
who was elected from among the elders of the esnaf at a guild
assembly and was confirmed by the kadı. The next ranking
person was the yiğitbaşi, also elected at a general assembly
and confirmed by the kadı. The kethüda could be either a
Muslim or a non-Muslim, but in mixed guilds the general rule
was for the kethüda to be a Muslim. In such cases, however,
the non-Muslims always had their own yiğitbaşi. The *çavuş*
was one who carried out the authority of the guild by helping
to implement the decisions of the general assembly. The
supreme organ of the guild, however, was the council of elders. The most authoritative and experienced masters participated in the council and took part in resolving all questions concerning the life of the guild.

It should be pointed out that this structure made it
possible for the guild to adapt itself to the complex social
relations in the Ottoman Empire and to the changes that took
place in the empire's social life over the course of several
centuries. The independence of the guild in choosing its
leading organs, and in defending the interest of its members
and of the guild as a whole before the administrative
authorities and the central power, lent it a more or less
democratic character, and that attribute in turn attracted to
the guild all layers of the population regardless of their
ethnic affiliation. The official recognition of the guild as
part of the social structure of Ottoman society lent the
guild additional public influence. Accordingly, in a number
of disputes between representatives of the administration and

the guilds, the arbitration of the central power was relatively impartial and very often found the guilds to be in the
right. It was precisely this feature--which increased the
public functions of the craft guild--that to a large extent
assured the guild's existence up to the very end of the
Ottoman Empire. It was simultaneously a source of the
guild's strength and of its stagnation.

* * *

Let us now examine, on the basis of concrete examples,
the legal and economic relationships between the esnafs and
organs of the state. An analysis of these relationships is
essential to an understanding of the role that the guilds
began to play in the eighteenth and nineteenth centuries.

In Ottoman feudalism, control and regulation of the
production and sale of finished goods--that is, the activities that were the most characteristic economic features of
guild life--were closely interwined with the regulatory
activity of the Ottoman state and of local authorities. Most
of the available documents from the early period are fragmentary and concern different branches of artisan production.
Only a few are directly interrelated and deal with the same
kind of question over the course of a whole century (specifically, from the early sixteenth century to the beginning of
the seventeenth). These are documents drawn from kadı registers that concern the position of the tanners and furriers
of Sofia. If analogous documents about the guilds in Ruse
are added to this material, broader and more general conclusions can be developed, for both cities were situated on
important trade routes, both engaged in brisk commerce, and
both had a mixed population of Muslims and non-Muslims.

The production and processing of hides was a trade that
had undergone a widespread development both before and after
the Ottoman conquest of Bulgaria.[21] Undressed hides were
already an important item of export during the period of the
independent Bulgarian state. After the Turkish conquest, the
export of undressed hides increased and, it seems, passed
almost entirely into the hands of merchants from Dubrovnik.[22]
Hides from the Balkan countries, and in particular from
Bulgaria, assured the supply of raw material for the established handicraft industry of Dubrovnik and Italian cities.[23]
Not only undressed hides, but also the Bulgarian-supplied
processed leather called cordovan won great popularity on the
foreign market.[24] K. Tsen (1550) and P. Contarini (1580),
both of whom left relatively detailed descriptions of Sofia,
wrote that the various types of leather goods and arms produced in Sofia were sufficient to equip a large army.[25]

In late 1521 the tanners of Sofia sent their representa-

tive to Istanbul to complain before the sultan's court of a
violation in Sofia of the custom by which all of the dressed
hides of the city were at their disposal and that only after
their needs were met could any be sold to outsiders. In
January 1522, the Sofia tanners received a ferman that prohibited the free sale of skins until their own needs had been
fully satisfied. This ferman was entered in the register of
the Sofia kadı under the year 1550.[26] Immediately following
this ferman the register contains an entry on the minutes of
the decision of the Sofia kadı to warn butchers not to sell
hides suitable for tanning to outsiders until the Sofia
tanners had assured themselves of the number of hides they
needed.[27] Both the reference to custom in the suit and
favorable outcome for the tanners indicate that this kind of
practice had existed for a long time, but since the register
mentioned starts only in 1550, it is impossible to determine
whether this practice had been introduced earlier through
royal decree or whether it was based on regulations pertaining to the capital and applied by the kadı in this
specific case.

     In 1605 the Sofia tanners again complained that persons
from other regions of the empire were coming to buy hides and
thus infringing the interests of the local tanners. A ferman
issued on this occasion again restricted the right of outside merchants to buy hides needed by local artisans.[28]
In the same year the Sofia tanners secured another new ferman
that decreed that hides brought into Sofia had to be distributed among the tanners of Sofia as before, and that they were
not to be sold to other tanners at higher prices.[29]

     In 1611 a large number of tanners (on this occasion
about ten non-Muslim names are listed) met with the kadı of
Sofia, the leaders of the butchers' guild (i.e., the
kethüda and the yiğitbaşi), and many butchers. They stated
that for many years the price of the skins of the sheep that
had been slaughtered had been subject only to seasonal
fluctuation, changing three times a year, but had otherwise
remained the same over different years irrespective of the
amount of livestock killed. Recently, however, the tanners
charged, the butchers had begun to raise the prices of the
skins. The butchers admitted that they had violated the
custom and stated that in the future they would abide by past
practice.[30]

     The available sources also tell of a 1619 decision of
the Sofia tanners to send a representative to Istanbul. Once
again their complaint was based on "alien"--that is, non-
Sofian--tanners paying inflated prices for skins suitable
for processing. In connection with this complaint the kadı
was instructed to look into the matter and to assure the

Sofia tanners the opportunity to buy skins at established prices.[31]

Such documents shed light on the relationships among the furriers, tanners, and butchers in the use of the local market. The amount of skins provided by the slaughter of livestock in the city proved insufficient to meet the growing demand, and furthermore, the interference of outsiders also prompted increases in prices. This compelled the Sofia furriers and tanners to resort to the kadı's assistance to assure themselves the necessary amount of raw material. In conditions where exchange and internal trade links were limited, the artisans of Sofia sought a solution for their problem in a monopolistic use of the local market and in regulation.

On the basis of these documents, one cannot determine whether the outsiders in question were artisans who had come from the surrounding villages and cities or merchants in search of raw materials for export. But the documents do contain information both about individual merchants and about individual artisans. In 1619, for example, a certain merchant named Konstantin, the son of Manol of Melnik, bequeathed two buildings in Sofia.[32] Sources of the sixteenth and seventeenth centuries contain information on certain artisans who resettled in Sofia. Thus, a prominent and skillful goldsmith named Georgi Novi Sofiiski came from Kratovo to Sofia, where toward the year 1515 he died a martyr's death for refusing to accept Islam.[33] Also characteristic is the information provided by another document that describes how in 1611 Hüseyin Bey declared in court that a non-Muslim tanner, the son of Stanislav and an inhabitant of Sofia, had been born in one of his villages in his zeamet, but had left the village some twenty years previously to settle in Sofia. As provided for by the law, Hüseyin Bey demanded that the tanner pay the obligatory tax for the right to abandon the land. The accused admitted the justice of Hüseyin's demand and paid the tax.[34] The kadı registers of Sofia contain several similar petitions, but demands that residents be returned to villages remained without consequence in view of the long period of time that had usually elapsed. (We might also add that in the period under consideration the number of non-Muslim households in Sofia rose from about 238 in the sixteenth century to 327 by 1645.)[35]

The reaction of the craft guilds to the activity of incoming artisans might also be judged from the following incident that occurred in Sofia in 1612. In that year the kethüda of the *takyecis* (the oldest guild of the capmakers), accompanied by ten Turks and eleven Bulgarian craftsmen, complained to the kadı that newcomers had opened shops and

were practicing the trade although they "had not mastered it
and had not received the right to be independent masters."
The newcomers were thus infringing the interests of the guild.
The kadı's decision ordered the restoration of the old order
under the threat of punishment.[36] At the same time craftsmen
of Ruse were also complaining about the competition from
newcomers and persons outside the guild. In 1698 the guild in
Ruse whose members soled shoes sent the central authorities a
complaint against "several persons alien to the estate" who,
without being members of the guild, were making boots and
shoes.[37]

It is clear that in the late sixteenth century and in the
early seventeenth century artisans arriving from outside
settlements had already formed a considerable stratum, for
their activity was producing complaints, for example, on the
part of the entire guild of capmakers. It can be assumed that
one of the chief reasons for the complaint of the tanners and
furriers as well was the manufacturing activity of incoming
artisans. But because the production of these craftsmen was
not limited to the local market, the measures taken in response to the complaints concerned more the supply of raw
materials than the conditions of production or its limitation.

As suggested by the cases mentioned above, an increase
in the number of artisans produced complaints only when the
guild saw this growth as threatening the root interests of its
members. Take the incident concerning the group of new shoemakers in Ruse. For a whole group of new artisans to decide
to take up work in their own shops and to dare to compete
with existing artisans hints that the gradual opening of
artisan shops did not encounter serious opposition. The
presence of twenty-one capmakers in a single small city, to
cite another example, similarly leads one to believe that the
number of artisans was not rigidly controlled. And it is in
this sense too that one should understand a kadı's decision
to restore the "old order." This order cannot be taken to
mean a total closure of the new shops and the expulsion of
their owners; rather, it should be seen as a compulsory
measure of subordinating these new enterprises to the regime
of the guild organization. A number of documents offer evidence that a kadı's decision thus had the effect of assuring
the observance of established principles for exercising a
craft.

The 1612 complaint of the Sofia capmakers clearly reveals
the need of all artisans to observe the established order in
both the supply of raw materials and in the production of
goods. When this entire guild, headed by their elders, pro-
tested the activity of the incoming artisans, the craftsmen
themselves explained the nature and functioning of the ex-

isting order. They also dwelt on the question of the supply
of raw materials, by which the guild's elders distributed the
broadcloth supply in a way that assured each craftsman his
share and with it the obligation to work conscientiously and
to avoid the production of shoddy goods.[38] In 1550 the Sofia
masters who processed horsehides turned to the city authorities for assistance. On this occasion help was sought against
their own colleagues who were not following the established
order concerning the equal supply of horsehides, but who were
buying more hides than the other masters.[39]

The documents cited, it is true, do not provide sufficient evidence to warrant conclusions on the regulation of
production as a whole. But there can be no doubt that the
technical aspects of production were also regulated in some
detail. It is also evident that regulation covered all goods
and not just those that served the needs of the state.

In 1550, for example, the shoemakers in Sofia appeared
en masse before the kadı and stated that some masters had
begun to make shoes for the "infidels" that featured innovations and broke with existing style. The kadı thereupon
prohibited the innovations in question, with violators of this
decree held liable both to a fine of one hundred akçe and to
fifty blows with a cane.[40] A similar order was issued by the
central government on the basis of a 1571 report of the nazır
(supervisor) of Plovdiv. The decree forbade the guild of
abacıs from producing pieces of cloth eight to nine arshin in
size; rather, they had to keep to the established size of
twelve arshin.[41] In 1698 in Ruse, to cite another example,
several silk producers of Armenian descent (Manas, Aidin,
Evanos, and Perseh) complained about colleagues who had become
masters but who did not process the primary material in a
satisfactory manner and who produced silk of an inferior quality. This complaint prompted the intercession of the central
authorities and the issuance of a ferman--a step that was
necessary since previous measures had proven ineffective in
resolving the dispute in favor of the old norms.[42]

* * *

A careful examination of the material that characterizes
the state of the guild operations in the period under review
creates the impression that the artisans of Sofia turned to
the state for assistance in resolving questions that in
European countries usually fell within the competence of the
guilds themselves. Furthermore, the involvement of the state
in such cases did not result simply in the registration or
affirmation of decisions that the guild had already made for
itself. The documents are quite clear in this and always
indicate distinctly the causes of the dispute as well as the

grounds on which a given decision was taken. Even the right
to elect a kethüda, an *ustabaşı* (eldest master), and other
leaders of a particular guild--a right that was established by
ferman and represented one of the most important prerogatives
of the general assembly of the artisans--was subjected to the
approval of the kadı. For this purpose the kadı would draw up
a special protocol; therefore, it was necessary for the whole
guild or for a representative group to appear before him and
to declare, before the court of the şeriat, the election of
the guild leadership. This requirement held true for all
guilds regardless of their ethnic composition. In Sofia, for
example, all non-Muslim mutafçis appeared before the kadı for
the registration of their kethüda; in 1657 the Muslim coopers
of Ruse, representing their guild, registered their ustabaşı.[43]
And again in 1682 in Ruse, Bulgarian members of the guild of
fur-capmakers reelected as their kethüda Dimitŭr, the son of
Kiro, and then registered him. (Actually these artisans were
residents of the village of Arnaut located near Razgrad, but
members of the guild of Ruse.)[44]

These examples from various cities and for various guilds
demonstrate that the Ottoman state acted both as arbiter and
as active participant in the composition of esnaf rules and in
the conditions of artisan production. This participation
followed the spirit of the general organization of the economic system in the Ottoman Empire, where the state controlled
many facets of economic life.

In this vein, furthermore, the authorities very often
resorted to compulsory state contracts and work, particularly
in connection with military needs. Artisans, for example,
were required to work on the construction of fortresses,
bridges, and roads.[45] It reached the point where persons who
failed to carry out their specific obligations to the army
were forbidden to exercise their trade. Thus, a group of six
Jewish sellers of herbal medicines were forbidden to practice
their profession because they had refused to help the army
(probably by not agreeing to accompany it). To restore their
rights, they not only had to shoulder their obligation to the
army, but were also required to come before the kadı together
with a kethüda named Suleyman Çelebi and two Turks so that an
appropriate decision might be made. These military obligations fell on the craftsmen of smaller settlements as well as
on the artisans from the larger cities, something that led to
the disruption of the economic life of the small settlements.
Thus, in April of 1684 the craftsmen of Kiustendil asked the
Sublime Porte to rescind an order of Ehrem Mustafa Paşa
demanding for the army two bakers, a farrier, a saddler, a
cook, and a harness maker.[46] The implementation of such an
order would have placed Kiustendil's population in difficult

straits; for the city required three or four bakers, four or
five harness makers, five or six blacksmiths, and one saddler.
For this reason the Kiustendil guild, which also stated that
artisans had not been taken from the city for the army in the
past, and which agreed to pay a sum of 4,000 to 5,000 kuruş,
asked for royal intervention in rescinding the order.[47] Individual artisans sometimes used the military connection in
pursuit of their own interests. In 1617 three farriers,
citing a ferman for the production of horseshoes for the army,
purchased more iron than they needed and began to resell it.
This led to a protest from the blacksmith guild, which brought
the matter to the kadı. The court decided in favor of pre-
serving the existing order.[48]

* * *

Some authors consider the character of the craft guild
and its relations with the central power as a manifestation of
customary law. In his richly detailed *History of the Bulgarian Feudal State and Law*, M. Andreev has enumerated those
cases where Bulgarian customary law was incorporated as an
element in the Ottoman legal superstructure.[49] He stated the
belief that the administration of justice by the Bulgarian
guilds was also entirely influenced by the norms of Bulgarian customary law.[50] Although such a general conclusion
concerning the incorporation of Bulgarian customary law
into the system of Ottoman feudal law is acceptable (particularly in the sphere of family and property relations),
we cannot agree that the independent activity of the guild
can be regarded as primarily a manifestation of Bulgarian
customary law. One of the most important foundations for
such an assertion is the frequent reference to custom in
the Turkish documents themselves. In point of fact, what
the ordinary artisans and guild representatives had in
mind by custom were rules established and sanctioned by the
local and central authorities. They thus turned to the
legislation and to the practice of a huge state that had managed to consolidate itself and make its presence known. An
example of what we are talking about concerns a 1617 incident
with the Sofia bakers. In that year the bakers referred to
custom in what they alleged was an unjust fine imposed by the
muhtesibs. The bakers won their case when they produced a
ferman that envisaged all possible cases where fines would be
appropriate and specified their rates.[51] In this case, the
custom to which the Sofia bakers referred was actually a
regulation introduced by the state. Tens of similar cases
can be given for various cities. The repeated approaches to
the central government by the artisans of Sofia to obtain a
document that would detail the conditions of production speaks

for itself in identifying the initiators of this kind of regulation. All the more was this true when we consider that the
information cited by the bakers about the existing practices
in Sofia fully coincided with the rules established by Suléy-
man's legislation.

In this manner, then, an entire system was created to
regulate and control the urban economy. Naturally, this
system was the result of the complex development of the Ottoman state, which in its practice borrowed a great deal from
the existing institutions of the conquered peoples. However,
it was Ottoman authority that legally consolidated the ultimate formation of the guild and the rights and limitations of
its activity. In the period under consideration, therefore,
the guilds can hardly be examined as an expression of Bulgarian law or of customary law in general.

The question of the scope of customary law in this period
has yet to be resolved. It is known that the new law, which
was connected with the development of commodity-monetary
relations and of trade, emerged in the cities primarily as the
natural result of urban autonomy. This law originally took
shape, however, not as a general urban law, but as the differentiated law of separate corporations, one that combined
special provisions on the means of production and on trade
with, at least in part, provisions of a purely civil character.
The development of the majority of cities--for example, the
cities of Bulgaria up to the Turkish conquest--had apparently
not yet led to the differentiation of a commercial-industrial
urban population with a corresponding Bulgarian regulation of
production and exchange.[52]

* * *

The conclusion that can be drawn from an analysis of
concrete material is that it was primarily the Ottoman state
that created the public norms within whose framework handicrafts developed. The status of the guilds of the several
cities examined above did not in principle differ from their
position in other parts of the Balkan Peninsula. Speaking in
the most general way, the nature of the guild was determined,
on the one hand, by the mutual relations between the guild
and the productive activity of the Muslim population and on
the other, by the practice and productive activity of the non-
Muslim urban population. Consequently in this study we have
tried to answer the question of the relationships of the guild
organizations in Sofia with the Ottoman state irrespective of
the ethnic character of these guilds. Our assumption has been
that in this period ethnic composition made no difference in
principle in the position of the craft guilds.

It remains impossible, however, fully to resolve such

problems as the emergence of the guild, its spread and original structure, the extent to which it embodied the productive urban population in the fifteenth and sixteenth centuries, and the ethnic distribution of the artisans of common
guilds. The century and a half that it took for the final
Turkish conquest of the Balkan lands, and the different conditions in which this conquest took place, could not but leave
an imprint on the appearance of those institutions introduced
immediately after the establishment of Turkish rule. Time was
required to achieve unity in the administrative structure of
the various provinces and to bring about unity in the institutions located therein.

    We are equally unable to answer satisfactorily the ques-
tion of how much restrictive provisions impeded the process of
differentiation within the guilds. It can be assumed that the
predominance of the state's equalizing regulations meant that
the social differentiation of the artisans did not achieve the
necessary development. This question, however, has another
facet that can be examined apart from the issue of the role
of regulation in the process of production and in the opportunities for enrichment for certain members of the guild. Of
no less importance was the public significance of these
functions. The interference of the state in the independent
activity of the craft guild in Ottoman society--that is, the
element that distinguished it so fundamentally from the European guild--in this case became one of the major attributes of
the craft organization. In conditions of foreign rule, the
sanction of the state created real preconditions for the
development of artisan production among the subjugated peoples.
It lent public significance to the labor of non-Turkish
artisans, something that permitted them henceforth to increase
their role in the economic and social life of the cities of
the Ottoman Empire. At the same time, of course, both
stringent state regulation and state support of the guilds
(and of other obsolete feudal institutions) held back the
development of productive forces and of capitalist relations
in the Ottoman Empire. (Such issues as changes in the guilds
at the end of the eighteenth century and in the first half
of the nineteenth century, the relationships between guilds
and entrepreneurs, and the extent to which guilds impeded
the development of capitalist relations will be discussed in
Part 2.)

Plates 10 and 11. *Above*, the fortress of Silistra; *below*, the
town and fortress of Nikopol. Reprinted from *Donau Ansichten
nach dem Laufe des Donaustromes* (Vienna, 1862).

Plates 12 and 13. *Above*, the town and ruins of Svishtov; *below*, the town and fortress of Hirşova. Reprinted from *Donau Ansichten nach dem Laufe des Donaustromes* (Vienna, 1862).

8. Prices and the Assessment of Real Estate

Contemporary historical scholarship pays a great deal of
attention to notarial deeds, to inventories of personal estates, to deeds on purchases and sales, and to other property
records as sources of primary importance for determining the
material position and differentiation of the population in
given countries and periods. In the practice of the Ottoman
state, the sicils, which were kept by kadıs, were used to
register both estates and deeds for the purchase and sale of
property. Special registers were used in recording the estate
inventories of only certain groups, mainly the military.[1] The
Oriental Department of the National Library in Sofia houses
none of these inheritance registers per se. Instead, we have
drawn information on inheritances and sales from 101 eighteenth-century kadı registers, of which 52 pertain to Vidin,
38 to Sofia, and 11 to Ruse.

Table 12 provides a breakdown of these registers by number of recorded cases, place, and year. The data on Vidin are
the most complete. They cover sixty-six years of the eighteenth century, with an average of fifty-nine sheets per annum,
the number of sheets or pages being one sign of the volume of
registrations. The number of sheets fluctuates from an average of forty-six per year (from 1711 to 1720) to eighty-one
per year (from 1761 to 1770). The decade from 1731 to 1740 is
somewhat exceptional; for it, there is an average of only
thirty-one sheets per year. In any event, even more indicative than the number of sheets is the number of registered inheritances and deeds. Over the century, entries average
thirty-three per year. The distribution of these cases by
period is comparatively uniform, with the incidence ranging
from thirty to fifty per year. However, the average number of
registered cases is lower for the period from 1711 to 1720 and
for the decade from 1731 to 1740.

The kadı registers of Sofia and Ruse contain considerably
less information. As can be seen from table 12, the Sofia
registers possess but half of the data provided by the Vidin
registers both in number of years covered and in number of
recorded cases of estates and sales. The data for Ruse cover
only twelve years in all. Nevertheless, since the eighteenth
century has been the least studied period not only of Bulgarian history but in Balkan history generally, there is an obvious need to analyze all the available information about this
epoch, no matter how scanty. The unique character of the kadı
registers requires an attentive treatment of the data they
contain, and the analysis of these data demonstrates a similarity for all three cities in the distribution, both by assessment and by period, of different kinds of property. It is
precisely this similarity that substantiates a combined analysis for all three cities of the information that is available on a given type of property. In doing so, of course, we
will note deviations from the patterns in the individual
cities.

Of course, one has to be mindful that the registers do
not contain information on the property of all those who had
died. The kadı registered the movable and real property of
the deceased testator only when asked to do so by its heirs,
Muslims or non-Muslims, or by just one of them (i.e., when a
judicial division of the estate was required). The şeriat
also required the kadı's registration and distribution of all
estates left to infants and to minors, as well as those for
which surviving heirs simultaneously included both minors and
individuals who had reached the age of majority. Moreover,
Christians, Jews, and Armenians usually resolved their inheritance questions in accordance with the inheritance laws of
their own communities.

TABLE 12

THE REGISTRATION OF PROPERTY TRANSFERS IN KADI REGISTERS
OF VIDIN, RUSE, AND SOFIA DURING THE 18TH CENTURY

Periods	Vidin			Ruse			Sofia		
	Number of years covered	Volume, in sheets	Number of entries	Number of years covered	Volume, in sheets	Number of entries	Number of years covered	Volume, in sheets	Number of entries
1701-10	--	--	--	--	--	--	1	26	21
1711-20	8	364	93	4	124	68	--	--	--
1721-30	5	232	143	--	--	--	6	239	145
1731-40	6	188	148	4	378	71	2	72	52
1741-50	7	390	211	1	95	44	4	81	2
1751-60	6	371	303	1	59	13	3	103	37
1761-70	7	565	239	--	--	--	4	172	63
1771-80	9	663	353	1	101	18	3	192	33
1781-90	8	526	333	1	19	7	1	32	35
1791-1800	10	569	360	--	--	--	6	230	89
TOTAL	66	3,868	2,183	12	776	221	30	1,147	477

A considerable difference existed between the inheritance
law under the şeriat and the Byzantine law that was accepted
by the Eastern Orthodox church. The şeriat strictly fixed the
shares of inheritable property according to descending and
ascending lines. For example, a son who was the sole survivor
inherited all the property, but if he had a sister, he inherited only two-thirds of it. A surviving husband inherited
one-fourth of an estate, a surviving wife one-eighth, and so
on. In other words, inheritable shares varied, with male
legatees having a decided advantage. On the other hand, in
accordance with the rules adopted by the Eastern Orthodox
church and by the Christian ecclesiastical communities
(obshtinas) in the Ottoman state, all children had an equal
right to an inheritance regardless of sex.[2]

The data in question, unfortunately, contain certain
inaccuracies and lacunae that prevent conclusions of a demographic character, or conclusions about the absolute dimensions of the property of the urban population. Examples
include lacunae that make it impossible to establish the
number of testators, gaps that leave only limited data on
Christian estates, and difficulties arising from the subjec-
tive character of the assessments of a major part of the
property. Nevertheless, information on inheritances remains
particularly suitable both for a comparative analysis of the
varied categories of the urban population and for examining
the changes that took place in the position of these urban
groups over a relatively long period of time.

* * *

In using kadı registers to carry out research on questions related to the property differentiation of the urban
population, we encountered a great many individual assessments
of real estate, livestock, home furnishings, foodstuffs, and
so on. Since this information covers the entire eighteenth
century, it has been necessary to subject these various
assessments to the proper kind of analysis and control to
establish the extent to which the material position of urban
residents might have been affected by price fluctuations or
by changes in the value of money. Accordingly, a comparison
of the prices of real estate with the prices of foodstuffs,
livestock, and other items has been carried out to see how
these prices might have been changed by various factors, both
general and specific. The outward effect of changes in the
currency rate have been studied through the use of recent
work comparing the kuruş with the Venetian ducat.

The eighteenth-century practice of setting prices, as
revealed in the registers of Sofia, Vidin, and Ruse, continued the practice of previous centuries. The prices of food-

stuffs and of other staples were fixed at assemblies by the
guilds and the leading citizens of the city. Once approved
by the kadı and entered in the sicils, these prices became
obligatory. (In the kadı registers of Sofia, Vidin, and Ruse,
we have not discovered any instructions from the central
authorities in Istanbul that governed the method for setting
prices in the localities.) There are numerous examples of
this practice employed in the establishment of prices in these
three cities. The kadı, having noted the date of the general
assembly, would then list the names of those guildsmen having
full rights and the price that was established. (There
would also be an indication of how long the price would be
valid for seasonal goods--e.g., six months for meat.) One of
the more detailed registrarial protocols was compiled in Ruse
in December 1736.[3] Since this protocol enumerates eight
guilds (with their members), it is cited here in full:

Guild of the bakers

Esseid Mehmed; Hüsiyn çelebi (he has been elected as head
of the guild of bakers); Yono, the son of Georgi; Simeon,
the son of Stan; Kurgan, the son of Tomo; Agop, the son
of Baçik. The bakers subsequently registered: Yusuf beşe;
Arab Mehmed beşe; Molla Mustafa; the non-Muslims Dimitür
[and] Simeon.

180 dirhem of bread = 1 akçe

Guild of bunmakers

Hasan beşe; Anastas; the non-Muslim Ferdo

115 dirhem of buns = 1 akçe.

Guild of the butchers

Rifat, the son of Hasan beşe; Mustafa aga; Menlya Ahmed;
Osman beşe.

1 *okka*[4] of beef = 5 akçe.

[Note:] This fixed price of 5 akçe is established 44 days
after St. Dimitür's day--on 16 *şaban* 1149 [December 20,
1736].

[Note:] This fixed price is established for the time
from 16 *şaban* 1149 to St. Iuri's day [from December 20,
1736, to May 6, 1737].

Guild of the grocers

Elhac Mehmed, head of the market; Haci Mehmed; Elhac
Ibrahim; Mehmed çelebi; Mustafa beşe; Menlya Ibrahim; Ali
beşe; Ahmed çelebi; Topal Yusuf; Halil çelebi; Menlya
Salih; Molla Ismail.

1 okka of pure butter at from 40-54 akçe
1 okka of pure honey at from 17-20 akçe; at the very
   least for 15 akçe
1 okka of cheese at 12 akçe
1 okka of fat dried meat at 9 akçe
1 okka of Egyptian rice at 15 akçe
1 okka of cheap dried meat at 8 akçe
1 okka of Plovdiv rice at 13 akçe
1 okka of "kotu" grapes at 16 akçe
1 okka of "turia" grapes at 15 akçe
1 okka of red grapes ["?"] at 15 akçe
1 okka of black grapes at 15 akçe
1 okka of chick-peas at 9 akçe
1 okka of almonds at 40 akçe
1 okka of olive oil from 45-36 akçe

On the 4th of *zilhicce* 1149 [April 5, 1737].

Guild of the chandlers and soap boilers

Mustafa beşe, the son of Ahmed [and] kethüda of the
chandlers; Elhac Mehmed; Ali beşe; Mustafa; Ali.

[Note in the text] Second price-fixing--5 *şaban elmuazam*
1150 [December 8, 1737].

[Note in the text] It is written here that on 25 *receb*
1149 [November 29, 1736] the grocer Mehmed çelebi, the
son of Ali beşe, was appointed market head of the grocers
by general consent.

1 okka of sesame oil at 30 akçe
1 okka of linseed oil at 30 akçe
1 okka of lemon water at 20 akçe
1 okka of Izmir soap at 36 akçe
1 okka of white flax at 45 akçe
1 okka of ash-colored flax at 38 akçe
1 okka of figs at 10 akçe
1 okka of figs in boxes at 14 akçe
1 okka of yellow figs at from 8-12 akçe
1 okka of chick-peas at 15 akçe

1 okka of hazelnuts at 10 akçe
1 okka of pepper at 180 akçe
1 okka of raisins [price not indicated]

Guild of the carders

Esseid Mustafa beşe--carder; Elhac Omer--carder; Elhac
Yusuf--carder; Menlya Hasan--carder; Elhac Mehmed--
carder.

1 okka of thick cotton yarn at 110 akçe
1 okka of undampened cotton at 42 akçe
1 okka of raw cotton at 50 akçe
1 okka of ginned cotton for clothiers and yarn at 60
   akçe
1 okka of good black yarn at 100 akçe

Guild of the metalworkers

Elhac Yusuf--metalworker; Abdel Halilzade Elhac Halil--
metalworker; Kalaycioglu Mustafa beşe, son of Abdel
Halilzade--metalworker.

1 okka of iron at 15 akçe
1 okka of European steel at 50 akçe

Guild of mutafçıs

Mehmed beşe--kethüda of the mutafçıs; Ahmed beşe; Hüseyn
beşe; Hasan beşe; Cafer beşe; Mustafa bey; Huseyn çelebi; Master Mustafa; Osman Halife; another Hasan beşe;
Halil beşe; Mehmed beşe.

Goat wool sacks; horse blankets, bags; belts; cruppers.

This, then, was how the guilds and the kadıs set prices over
the course of the whole century.
    The registers, however, did not always list the names
of the guildsmen. There were many occasions when the decision of the general assembly was stated and recorded through
mention of only the date and an enumeration of the various
goods and their prices. This procedure was most often
followed for bread, meat, and several other products in
great demand. The existing regulatory system could not
prevent the fluctuation of prices caused by shortages of
goods or by the speculation in these goods that shortages
produced, but the constant recourse to the assistance of the
kadı and to measures of public influence reveal a determined

effort to retain a practice that was favored by the people
and supported by the state. Occasionally, prices were an-
nounced when a new kethüda took office. Thus, for example,
at the election of Ismail Paşa as kethüda of the Vidin bakers
for 1715 to 1718, the price of bread was fixed at 1 akçe for
130 dirhem.[5]

This practice had become so much a part of the way of
life of the urban population that it demanded the establishment of price norms for goods that were not customarily
included in the inventory of available goods and prices. The
documents frequently note such individual price decisions,
although they do not indicate the length of time for which
they were to be effective. In 1762, for example, the people
of Vidin petitioned the kadı to stop speculation in charcoal,
and a public crier was soon informing the population of the
established price of three okkas for one *para*.[6] What happened was that the charcoal had been imported into the city
and bought up by a few citizens who, using their resulting
monopoly, had thereupon raised its selling price. There are
many similar examples that show the force of tradition and
the results of the kadı's intercession, an assistance that
was frequently sought by the population.

Both the mechanism and continuing practice of price
setting that existed throughout the whole eighteenth century
can thus be established with sufficient clarity. There was
an obvious effort to set prices in accordance with both the
purchasing power of the population and the interests of the
producers and merchants. However, how well this practice
succeeded in balancing both sides of the exchange process is
yet to be studied and would require prolonged research.

The establishment of price norms, it should be noted,
did not exclude competition between the guild as a whole and
other producers and suppliers of goods. Nor did it prevent
a market struggle in general. But such a struggle had to
take place in the aftermath of the relevant sanctions of a
kadı. Since the entire system of equalizing regulation
stood in opposition to changes in the conditions of production and sale, instances involving competitive practice
would seem to have been more often the exception than the
rule. An example from Vidin illustrates some of the conditions that might permit a change in selling prices. The
head of the Vidin butchers, Halil beşe, with the consent of
the other twenty-seven owners of butcher shops, appeared
before the kadı to inform him that although the price of one
okka of mutton had been set at ten akçe, the butchers' guild
would be ready to lower the price to eight akçe provided that
its members were guaranteed a right of monopoly in the
slaughter of livestock.[7] In proposing to lower prices, the

guildsmen were thus seeking compensation in the form of a
monopolistic right. At the same time, the guild would be
retaining equal conditions for its members.

Regulation could not of course maintain a stable price
level when there were fluctuations in the currency rate or
when currency was undergoing devaluation. Nevertheless, this
regulation did seek to preserve existing ratios in commodity
prices and to restrict the use of currency fluctuations for
speculative purposes.

* * *

To examine the movement of prices for certain essential
commodities, we have assembled cases where price norms were
established and were registered in sicils. By years and by
city, these cases break down as follows:[8]

> Ruse--1715, 1736-1737, 1742, 1753, 1778-1779, 1790-1791
> Vidin--1705-1713, 1730, 1741-1742, 1742-1744, 1762-1773,
>   1766-1767
> Sofia--1744-1745, 1752, 1761-1762

On the basis of these data, diagrams have been compiled on the
movement of prices of several of the most widely used foodstuffs and groceries. In figure 1 the line describing the
movement of meat prices shows the greatest fluctuation for
the city of Vidin. From a price of 3 akçe in 1705, the
price of beef rose to 18 akçe in 1730--a sixfold increase.
From 1741 to 1744 beef had a fluctuating price of between
10 and 18 akçe. In 1766 it dropped to 6 akçe, but by 1772 it
had increased once again. The price of mutton fluctuated
from 6 to 24 akçe, the movement following the curve of beef
prices. The price of lamb also fluctuated.

For Sofia and Ruse, the price curve was relatively
gradual: for beef, from 4 to 6 akçe in Sofia, and from 5 to
9 akçe in Ruse; for both cities the price of mutton fluctuated from 10 to 12 akçe. Lamb prices also had an even rate
of growth, going from 6 akçe to an end-of-the-century price
of 12 akçe (i.e., a 100% increase). There were no sharp
fluctuations here, but information is lacking for precisely
those years that were so critical for Vidin. Thus, we are
unable to say whether we are dealing with a phenomenon common
to all three cities, or with differences caused by some
purely local factors.

In all three cities the prices of bread had a greater
stability, with prices ranging between 1.56 and 3.90 akçe
(fig. 2). The only sharp increase occurred in 1736 in Ruse.
Generally speaking, the price of a sweet white bread called
simid followed the same curve as did ordinary bread.

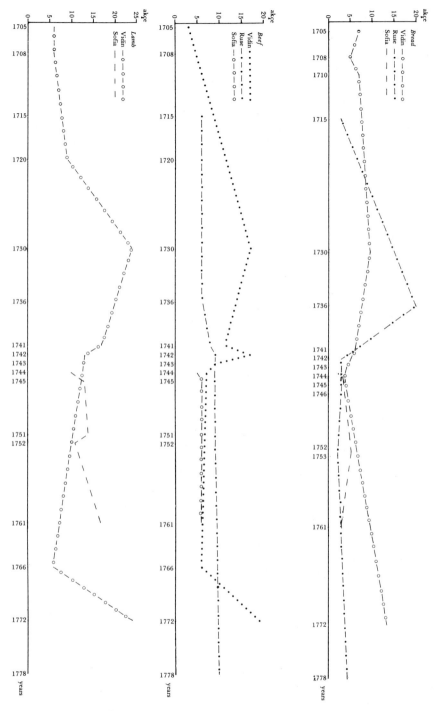

Fig. 1. Movement of meat prices
in the eighteenth century in Vidin, Ruse, and Sofia

Fig. 2. Movement of bread prices in the
eighteenth century in Vidin, Ruse, and Sofia

The price of white cheese in all three cities fluctuated
between 6 and 12 akçe (see fig. 3). Only in Vidin did the
price of cheese show an abrupt increase, going up to 18 akçe
in 1742. The price of butter was also fairly stable, and
ranged between 20 and 40 akçe in Vidin and Sofia. But, as
with the cheese, there was a threefold price increase in
Vidin in 1742. The price of olive oil ranged from 30 to 60
akçe. The greatest increases occurred in 1743 in Vidin when,
in comparison with the initial price (1705), the price of
olive oil doubled, and in 1790 in Sofia, when the price rose
to 72 akçe.
    In addition to these items, the sicils also record the
prices of a number of other foodstuffs such as fish, olives,
vegetables, and fruit. In most cases these were individual
prices set for one year or for only one city. We will give
only a few examples of these prices, using products that are
encountered in the price lists for all three cities. These
examples reveal certain price similarities.
    Fruit was sold at different prices according to the sea-
son, the size of the crop, and the effect of other local
factors. Thus, in Ruse in 1736, one okka of grapes had a
fixed price of 15 to 16 akçe, and in Sofia in 1744 the price
was 20 akçe. The price of figs in all three cities ranged
between 10 and 14 akçe. It should be noted that two kinds of
prices were established in Sofia specifically for figs,
grapes, and hazelnuts: producers sold at 4 akçe less than
the market price charged by grocers (respectively, the market
prices of these items were 16, 24, and 24 akçe).
    As well as foodstuffs, tallow (made both from calf and
sheep fat), candles, soap, and cotton were also in wide
demand. Information on the price of tallow is available for
all three cities. Early in the century one okka of tallow
cost 21 akçe in Vidin and 20 akçe in Ruse. By 1741 the price
had risen to 30-32 akçe, but in 1744 in both cities it again
dropped to 24 akçe. In the 1750s in Sofia one okka of
tallow cost 26 akçe. In comparison with the price at the
beginning of the century, the cost of candles had doubled by
the 1740s, and in 1772 it increased fourfold. The price of
soap increased from 10 akçe in 1705 to 20 akçe in 1741.
Over the following three years (to 1744) the price of soap
varied from 15 to 18 akçe (along with this "black" soap,
there was also a better quality soap that cost nearly twice
as much). In 1736 in Ruse, cotton cost from 38 to 45 akçe;
in 1738 in Vidin the price was 36 akçe. In Sofia in 1745
one cubit of cotton cloth cost from 10 to 34 akçe, depending
on its type.
    These examples of the prices of some of the most needed
and widely used commodities present a picture of prices that

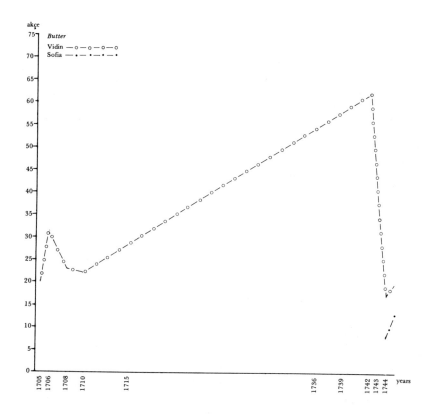

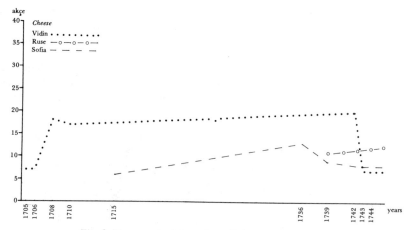

Fig. 3. Movement of the prices of cheese and butter
in the eighteenth century in Vidin, Ruse, and Sofia, 1705-1744

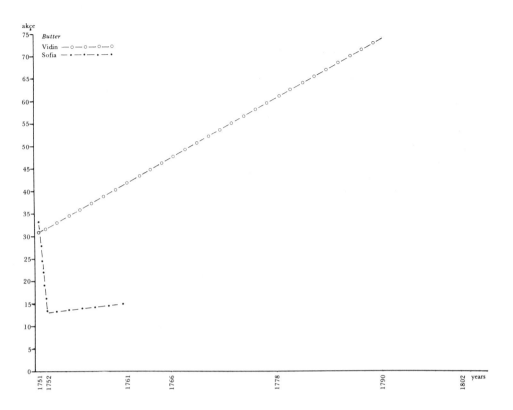

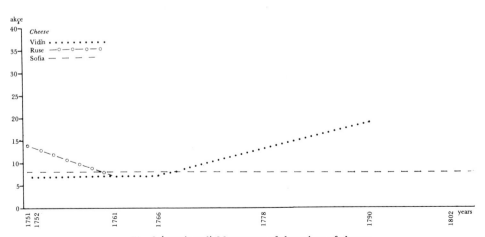

Fig. 3 *(continued).* Movement of the prices of cheese
and butter in the eighteenth century in Vidin, Ruse, and Sofia, 1751-1802

were more or less in a state of flux. In some years there
were sharp fluctuations, and the amount of the price change
differed in both cities and products. Thus, the price of
meat in Vidin increased three to six times over and the
price of cheese and butter rose threefold. The prices of
other foodstuffs, however, increased no more than one or two
times over. The available data indicate that in all three
cities the greatest fluctuations took place in 1741 to 1743
and again in 1772. It is clear that prices mirrored serious
disturbances in the country's economic and political life,
but the insufficiency of data prevents us from painting a
full portrait of price fluctuations or from determining the
reasons for these changes. One can only note that the greatest price increases for foodstuffs in all three cities
coincided with wars being waged by the Ottoman state in their
proximity.

Despite all these fluctuations, however, during most of
the eighteenth century one can see a constant effort to
restore prices to their original level. It cannot be determined whether this trend was the result of factors with
constant effect (including the mechanism for regulating
prices described above) or whether it was the result of the
direct and ad hoc interference of the state. Such state
intercession might have been motivated by both the personal
interests of the ruling classes or the need to avoid up-
heavals of the urban masses who might become dissatisfied
because of fluctuating prices resulting from speculative
practices. Whatever the cause, these factors tended to
bring prices into line (if not fully at least approximately)
with the norms established previously. Thus, in the last
quarter of the century the prices of half of the nearly
twenty types of goods we have examined were approximately
the same as they were at the beginning of the same century.
For those goods whose prices remained higher toward the end
of this period, seven items had a price increase of less
than 200%, and only five increased in price by as much as
200-500%.

* * *

To broaden this presentation of prices as reflected in
kadı registers, and to determine to what extent we are talking about general trends in price formation, let us also
examine the assessed value of several components of inheritances: quilts (one of the most frequently cited of household goods included in inventories of estates), livestock,
and vineyards. To study the price movement of these items
over the whole century, about ten cases have been drawn from
the sicils for each of the three cities for the following

years: 1698-99 (in view of the lack of data for the first
years of the eighteenth century); 1720; 1729; 1730-31; 1736;
1737-39; the first and last years of the 1740s; the beginning of the 1750s; 1776-78; and the end of the century.[9]

Until the 1770s the assessed worth of a quilt varied
from 1 to 5 kuruş in all these cities. At the end of the
1770s, higher prices appeared (from 10 to 20 kuruş), prices
that became typical by the end of the century when the average assessed value in the cases examined stood at about 10
kuruş (i.e., an increase in price of between 200 to 300%).

There was also stability in livestock prices, with the
inevitable upward trend again appearing about the 1770s.
Until this point the assessed value of a cow ranged from 2
to 10 kuruş, and only toward the end of the 1770s did this
price rise to between 10 and 20 kuruş. Only rarely--chiefly
toward the end of the century--were there cases where the
stated value of a cow stood higher than 20 kuruş. An ox
usually cost from 10 to 20 kuruş, and the assessed value of
a team of oxen ranged from 16 to between 30 and 40 kuruş. No
particular deviations are noticeable for the different
periods or for the individual cities. Throughout the whole
century in all three cities the assessed worth of a sheep
ranged from 0.5 to 2-3 kuruş.

The greater differences in the assessed prices of
horses--anywhere from 4 to 450 kuruş--were related to the
type of horse and to the kind of work for which it was
intended: for riding (*at*), as a draft animal (*beygir*), or for
herding (*hergele*). Where very high prices were paid (120,
137, 150, 200, 215, and 450 kuruş), the sicils indicate that
they were for saddle horses (specifically, stallions). The
stated price of most draft horses ranged from 10 to 20 kuruş
or an average of about 15-17 kuruş. Only in the 1770s was
there an increase in the number of horses priced higher than
20 kuruş, with the average price then standing at about 30-
35 kuruş, a figure that was to become higher by the end of
the century.

The assessed price of a dönüm of vineyard ranged from
3-4 kuruş up to 50, but this wide price range was to last
throughout the whole period. Actually, only rarely was a
dönüm of vineyard valued at a price higher than 20 kuruş.
In all three cities the average price was usually 10-15
kuruş, with somewhat higher prices appearing only toward
the end of the century.

The data just analyzed thus demonstrate that the eighteenth century was characterized by relative stability in the
prices of household goods, of livestock, and of certain types
of real estate. Up to almost the 1770s there were no visible
changes and only toward the end of the 1770s was there an

increase in prices, an increase that was to become larger
during the last quarter of the century.

Prices are of interest here primarily in relation to the
study, in the following chapter, of inheritances and of real
estate as signs of social differentiation. For now, however,
it might be worthwhile to note that inheritances and property
transfers were areas that tended even more to reflect the
restraining impact of established tradition and practice.

* * *

In the meantime, it is first necessary to consider the
question of changes in the value of the currency--one of the
most sensitive indicators of the economy. This study is
required both because the value of money had a bearing on
prices and because inheritances themselves included large
sums of money (and tended to include relatively larger
amounts of it as time went on). Thus, to ignore the question
of the value or rate of exchange of money would make it
impossible to know whether a change actually occurred in the
ratio between money and property in the inventory descriptions of estates, or whether an increase took place in the
absolute value of these estates.

There are serious studies that have already resolved
some of the questions that come up in connection with this.
These works have dealt with such topics as the changes in the
value of the coins circulated in the Ottoman Empire; the
occasional devaluation of the dominant currency, Turkish
silver coins, as a result of the decrease in the amount of
precious metal they contained; the fluctuation of prices
caused by the monetary crisis in Europe in the sixteenth
and seventeenth centuries; and the disturbances in the central budget and measures taken by the state to stop inflation
and to hold the currency rate level.[10] Nevertheless, the
scholarship has as yet failed to establish price indexes for
all types of foodstuffs, for other essential commodities, or
for wages. Nor has the budget for a single family yet been
compiled. Depending on the initial archival material that
they were processing, individual authors have used various
methods of analysis. On the whole, however, undeniable advances in the research on the problem of the movement of
prices do permit a number of conclusions (albeit not definitive ones). Trends in the fluctuation of prices have been
explained by the general movement of prices of the European
market, a market in which the Ottoman Empire was also
involved.

Starting with a price index of 100 for 1489-90, the next
century saw nominal prices rise to 162. There followed the
20 years from 1585 to 1605, when the index shot up to 631.

(However, indexes based on the number of grams of silver
contained in the akçe show a much more limited rise, to 265.)
As noted by Barkan, who carried out these calculations,
there "was a clear disproportion between the growth of prices
and the fall in the real value of moneys, which must be
explained by other factors."[11] He has cited a number of
circumstances connected with the function of money as a means
of exchange and as a treasure--but these are questions that
have not yet really been studied. Barkan, in noting the
general condition of the empire, the wars that it conducted,
and the disruption of the central budget, has also attached
great significance to European commerce, which began to have
a one-sided influence on Ottoman exports as early as the end
of the sixteenth century and caused serious difficulties for
individual handicrafts.

An idea of the changes that took place in the seventeenth century and in the first decades of the eighteenth in
the ratio of the kuruş to the Venetian ducat, as well as in
the price of wheat in Edirne, is provided by the diagram composed by the Turkish scholar, H. Sahillioğlu[12] (fig. 4).

The curve that describes the movement of the price of
wheat in Edirne coincides with the curve for the price of
bread shown above for Vidin, Ruse, and Sofia. In this
period, these prices rose several times, with the two curves
peaking about 1730, after which the prices stayed at a fairly
constant level. These changes do not coincide with the
movement of the value of the Venetian ducat.

The eighteenth-century relationship between the kuruş
and the Venetian ducat is shown in fig. 5.[13] The depreciation of the kuruş went on throughout the whole century,
but the rate of that depreciation was quite slow and almost
uniform. For the first two decades of the century the rate
of depreciation ranged from 2.78 to 6.67%, and it did not
climb to a level of 10 or 11% until toward the end of the second decade of the century. From the mid-1730s to the mid-
1750s, it ranged from 22 to 30%. At the end of the 1770s, it
is true, a relatively major depreciation took place, from
about 40 to 70%, until in 1793 the rate of depreciation exceeded 150%. There is no doubt that there was a relationship
between this sharp end-of-the century devaluation and the
increased prices of several goods that can be observed at
that time, but limitations in the data prevent a determination of the quantitative extent of this correlation.

The conclusion that may be drawn from a comparison of
the movement of prices with changes in the rate of the kuruş
is that price fluctuations, particularly where foodstuffs
were concerned, cannot be explained by changes in the value
of coins. While the value of the currency changed gradually,

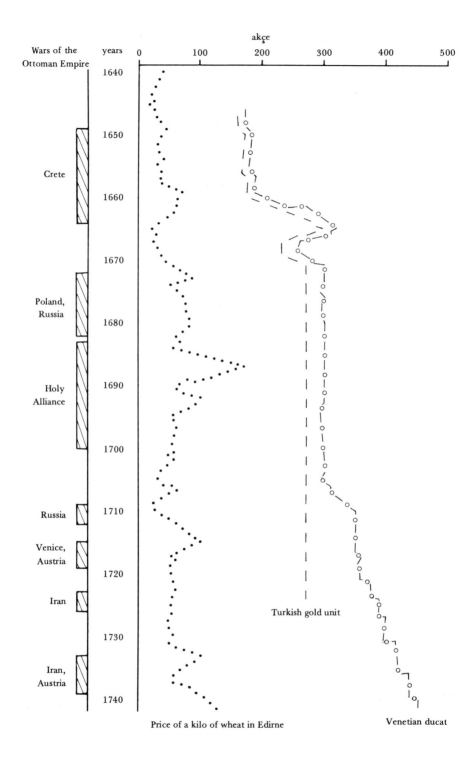

Fig. 4. Changes in the value of moneys according to H. Sahillioğlu

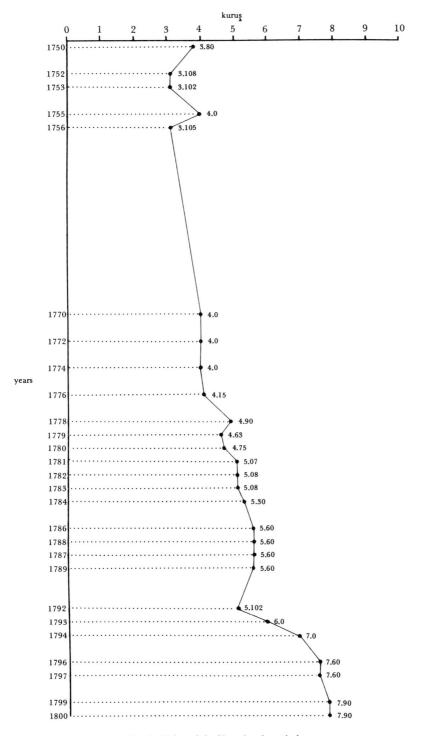

Fig. 5. Value of the Venetian ducat in kuruş

there were abrupt increases in the prices of some goods. It
can be stated, furthermore, that the greater part of the
eighteenth century was characterized by a relative stability
in the prices of those items included in the inventories of
estates. This trend was perhaps also due to the force of
tradition and the role of state regulation manifesting themselves most freely in the registration of estates and in the
sale and purchase of property. On the basis of the foregoing
discussion, therefore, one can confidently assert that
changes in the size of inheritances and different valuations
of the component elements of estates were not due to changes
in prices but rather to changes in the actual variety and
content of the estate or property under consideration. Let
us now examine the material status of the urban population
and its internal differentiation as based on the study of
inheritances and other property records.

Differentiation of the Urban
Population in the Eighteenth Century

9. PROPERTY STATUS
IN VIDIN, SOFIA, AND RUSE

The property status of the urban population is best reflected in the total value of the inheritances bequeathed by
individuals. This sum comprises all of the elements making up
an individual's property. It included, for example, such real
estate as houses, shops, workshops, inns, water mills, and
also land that was privately owned *(mülk)*, chiefly vineyards
and gardens. Also included were household articles and personal items such as clothing, bedding, covers, rugs, pots and
pans, weapons, jewelry, and decorations, and, finally, artisan goods and money.

Table 13 shows a breakdown, by ranges of assessed value,
of 2,179 inheritances in Vidin, Sofia, and Ruse in the eighteenth century. The largest part of the testators bequeathed
estates that fall into the lower value ranges. Almost three-
fourths of the bequeathed estates considered here had an
assessed value of up to 1,000 kuruş. Estates valued at from

147

TABLE 13

DISTRIBUTION OF 18TH-CENTURY INHERITANCES IN VIDIN, SOFIA, AND RUSE
(BY ASSESSED VALUE)

Assessed Value (in kuruş)	Vidin		Sofia		Ruse		Total	
	Number	Percentage	Number	Percentage	Number	Percentage	Number	Percentage
Up to 1,000	1,235	71.0	192	70.8	132	78.5	1,559	71.5
1,001-2,000	279	16.0	44	16.2	20	11.9	343	15.8
2,001-3,000	89	5.1	13	4.8	6	3.6	108	5.0
3,001-4,000	47	2.7	10	3.7	2	1.2	59	2.7
4,001-5,000	19	1.1	4	1.5	2	1.2	25	1.1
Over 5,000	71	4.1	8	3.0	6	3.6	85	3.9
Total	1,740	100.0	271	100.0	168	100.0	2,179	100.0

1,001 to 2,000 kuruş form the second most numerous group and
constitute 15.8% of the total number of the estates being
examined. Thus, these two groups take in most of the registered inheritances.

The groups of estates assessed at values higher than
2,000 kuruş represent a relatively small number of the inheritances examined, and as the assessment of the estates goes
up, the number of recorded instances progressively decreases.
In this respect estates valued at over 5,000 kuruş do not
represent an exception. That such inheritances seem to claim
a relatively higher share of the total number of recorded
cases results from the summary character of this grouping.
If these estates are broken into subgroups--of from 5,001 to
10,000 kuruş; 10,001 to 15,000 kuruş; 15,001 to 20,000 kuruş;
and over 20,001 kuruş--the number of inheritances that would
fall into any one of them would represent no more than 1% of
the total.

The distribution revealed by the table--that of a
limited number of estates assessed at a high value in contrast to the mass of the other inheritances--indicates an
advanced polarization in the property differentiation of the
urban population. This conclusion is supported by a concrete
analysis of the estates themselves; for the structure and the
valuation of these inheritances also reveal the social status
of the testator.

Since the first group, which includes estates whose assessments run a wide range of values up to 1,000 kuruş, takes
in the greatest number of estates, it is necessary to look at
the internal distribution of the inheritances it contains
(see table 14). The groups of estates valued at 500 kuruş or
below include about three-fourths of all of those assessed at
up to 1,000 kuruş in Vidin (74%) and Sofia (74.5%), and somewhat more than that in Ruse (86.3%). In the first three

TABLE 14

DISTRIBUTION OF 18TH-CENTURY INHERITANCES IN VIDIN, SOFIA, AND RUSE
(ASSESSED VALUE UP TO 1,000 KURUŞ)

Assessed Value	Vidin		Sofia		Ruse		Total	
	Number	Percentage	Number	Percentage	Number	Percentage	Number	Percentage
Up to 100 Kuruş	218	17.6	30	15.6	23	17.4	271	17.4
101-200	239	19.3	43	22.4	30	22.7	312	20.0
201-300	187	15.1	29	15.1	33	25.0	249	16.0
301-400	148	12.0	22	11.5	15	11.4	185	11.9
401-500	121	9.8	19	9.9	13	9.8	153	9.8
501-600	7	7.9	10	5.2	5	3.8	112	7.2
601-700	70	5.7	10	5.2	3	2.3	83	5.3
701-800	64	5.2	10	5.2	3	2.3	77	4.9
801-900	53	4.3	8	4.2	4	3.0	65	4.2
901-1,000	38	3.1	11	5.7	3	2.3	52	3.3
Total	1,235	100.0	192	100.0	132	100.0	1,559	100.0

groups (inheritances valued at up to 300 kuruş), the estates
are distributed almost evenly. For the others one can observe a gradual decrease in the incidence of recorded cases.

This progressive decrease in the number of instances
ceases at the point where the assessed value of estates
brings them into the next major category, in this case the
group assessed at from 1,001 to 2,000 kuruş (see table 13),
where again there is a significant concentration of estates.
Undoubtedly, the registration process itself played a certain
role in this uneven distribution. In classifying estates
into categories, the administrator employed certain general
indexes, and he inevitably rounded off his assessments of the
worth of an inheritance. In making such judgments, however,
he clearly had in mind a definite kind of property owner.

Despite differences in the number of registered inheritances, the distribution was very similar in all three
cities. Furthermore, only minor changes are apparent when
the distribution is examined in different decades of the
eighteenth century. In the second half of the eighteenth
century, there was a relative percentage decrease for all
three cities in the groups of estates appraised at lower
values, and a relative percentage increase in the groups of
estates in the higher assessment ranges. In this respect the
most indicative curve is that of Vidin, the city for which
the greater amount of information is available. As early as
the decade from 1730 to 1740 the percentage decrease sets in
for the group of estates valued at up to 100 kuruş. Over the
first five decades of the eighteenth century the percentage
claimed by this group comprises 35.6%, 52.9%, 30.6%, 19.3%,
and 9.5% of the total; and for 1770 and 1790, it falls to

only 3.2% and 1.9%. Although not so dramatically, the relative incidence of the next two groups of estates (incorpo-
rating inheritances valued up to 300 kuruş) also declines. At
the same time, beginning in the 1750s, there is a percentage
increase in the groups of estates assessed over 300 kuruş.
This increase is not pronounced for the groups of inheritances
valued up to 500 kuruş, but it becomes sharp for those assessed at from 1,001 to 2,000 kuruş. For the first half of
the century this group's relative share of the total comprises, respectively by decade, 8.5%, 2.9%, 5.8%, and 8.9%
of the total. For the second half of the century these figures increase, again by decade, to 15.9% 13.0%, 19.9%, 24.0%,
and 23.6%. The groups of estates valued at more than 2,000
kuruş also show a percentage increase. This statistical
pattern--an increase in the incidence of estates of high value
and a decrease in the incidence of estates in lower value
ranges--is a sign of the increased wealth of several categories of the urban population.

* * *

The figures just provided on the numerical breakdown of
inheritances demonstrate the existence of several groups of
property owners whose existence defined the socioeconomic
structure of the population. It is now necessary to examine
in detail and in a consistent manner the basic components of
an estate, so as to establish what might be called the property profile of each group. This analysis will follow in
separate discussions of houses, shops, and money, but first
it may be worthwhile to describe the typical components
of the estates that mirror the social characteristics of given
groups of the population.
    The estates in the group valued up to 100 kuruş consisted
basically of houses assessed at very low values. Houses
valued at up to 30 kuruş occur in half of these inheritances,
and by including cases where the house had an assessed value
of up to 50 kuruş one can account for three-fourths of them.
The household items mentioned in the inventories had little
worth. Occasionally, the estates falling into this group also
involved an insignificant amount of money.
    A few examples will serve to illustrate the kinds of
inheritance in question. An inhabitant of Ruse named Hasan
beşe, the son of Hüseyin, died in 1715 leaving an estate with
a total value of 81 kuruş. The estate consisted of a house
valued at 26 kuruş, household goods worth 25 kuruş, and 30
kuruş in cash.[1] An inhabitant of Sofia named Zulfikar, the
son of Mehmed, died in 1756 and bequeathed to his heirs a
house worth 33 kuruş and furnishings worth 35.8 kuruş.[2]
Another resident of Sofia, Hüseyin beşe, who died in 1762,

left a house valued at 35 kuruş and furnishings worth 28
kuruş.[3] Similar examples are available.

Vineyards were always in the inheritances contained in
this group and when they were, their assessed value did not
greatly differ from the amounts at which the houses were
evaluated. Unlike the vineyards contained in the estates of
other groups, the vineyards here had little value. Livestock
seems to have rarely been involved, and when it was, it was
usually a matter of only one or two animals.

Shops, too, were seldom part of these estates. The inheritance of shops occurred in less than 10% of the cases in
Vidin. In Sofia and Ruse, there were only isolated cases, and
these represented shops assessed at a low value. Furthermore,
the shopowners involved (as testators) usually lacked houses
of their own. When he died in 1753, for example, an inhabitant of Ruse named Ibrahim, the son of Abdullah, left an estate
worth 63 kuruş, consisting of a shop valued at 30 kuruş and
furnishings worth 33 kuruş.[4] Ahmed beşe, an inhabitant of
Vidin who died in 1731, did not have his own house, but owned
a barber's shop and one-twelfth share of a butcher's shop with
a total value of 15 kuruş.[5]

The increased worth of estates that fall into the group
of inheritances ranging between 101 and 500 kuruş in value
was due chiefly to higher house assessments or to the presence
of a larger amount of money. For example, let us dwell on
the subgrouping of estates whose values ranged from 401 to 500
kuruş (beyond this point, until we reach values of 1,000 kuruş
or more, there is a sharp decrease in the number of recorded
inheritances). The characteristic feature of these estates
is that the houses were now worth from 100 to 300 kuruş. In
Vidin such inheritances constitute 59% of the total, while
only 11% of the cases involve houses valued at less than
100 kuruş. Houses with an assessed value of over 400 kuruş
represent 14% of the total number of cases of this subgroup.
The highest house assessment was 450 kuruş.

Money was not as important as houses in raising the over-
all worth of the inheritances of this subgroup. Here, too,
as in the estates of lower value, vineyards and shops were
the exception rather than the rule. Of the 117 inhabitants
of Vidin who fall into this subgroup, there are only 20 cases
where the estate included shops. On the other hand, the
subgroup in question does present, as a new element, isolated
inheritances containing storehouses, inns, coffeehouses,
bathhouses, and shop inventories and merchandise.

The group of inheritances valued at between 1,000 and
2,000 kuruş is of particular interest, not only because it
includes a larger number of recorded inheritances, but also
because both the size and the content of these estates signify

a different type of testator. With his seemly residence and
premises for work, the testator of this group had the appearance of the materially secure citizen. The estates here have
more expensive houses, larger sums of money, and a considerable number of shops and workshops.

In the estates of this group, to be more specific, only
rarely were houses worth less than 100 kuruş. Houses priced
from 100 to 300 kuruş occur in 25% of the estates of this
group for Sofia, and in 36% of those for Vidin. More than
25% of the total number of houses included were appraised at
from 300 to 400 kuruş, and there are almost as many cases
involving houses worth over 400 kuruş (24% in Vidin and 28% in
Sofia). The maximum house assessment here was 1,500 kuruş.
The owner of this house was a certain Nikolcho of Sofia, an
inhabitant of the neighborhood called Elhac Hamza. When he
died in 1794, Nikolcho, in addition to his house, left his
heirs home furnishings worth 471 kuruş.[6]

This group also contains a higher incidence of owners
of two or more houses, whose properties had a fairly high
value. In 1709 an inhabitant of Ruse, the mason Todori, bequeathed to his heirs two houses valued at 110 and 300
kuruş.[7] Houses worth 110 and 400 kuruş were also included in
the estate of Zeyneb hatun, an inhabitant of Vidin who died
in 1758.

The same group of estates also contains a significantly
greater number of shops and workshops. For Vidin, for
example, shops are mentioned in 30% of the cases (and these
often included several shops), as are the shop's inventory,
its finished goods and in certain cases even its capital.
Molla Mehmed beşe of Vidin, who died in 1760, left an estate
worth 1,396 kuruş that consisted of two houses (valued at 500
and 80 kuruş), a shop with half a storehouse (100 kuruş),
one-half of another shop (50 kuruş), a vineyard (20 kuruş), a
leathermaking workshop (120 kuruş), beehives (80 kuruş),
capital (200 kuruş), and receivables in the form of money
that the testator had lent to various borrowers (79 kuruş).[8]
The 1794 estate of the Sofia grocer Molla Mustafa consisted
of a house worth 500 kuruş, various home furnishings worth
214 kuruş, 450 kuruş in cash, and merchandise in the grocery
shop valued at 372 kuruş.[9]

The estates valued at over 5,000 kuruş were those of
wealthy property owners, which is shown in both the variety
of their property and the high valuation of the individual
components of their estates.

The houses of this group of testators were usually worth
more than 500 kuruş. Only 12 of the 71 recorded cases of
estates for Vidin in this value range have houses valued
below 500 kuruş (but even so, three of the twelve testators

involved had left two houses each, the total worth of which
in each case exceeded 500 kuruş). For all three cities, this
group features an increased number of testators leaving two
or more houses. There were fourteen persons who left two
houses each and four who left three houses each. Several of
the houses included in this group were worth 3,000 kuruş--the
highest figures mentioned in the data being used here.

The presence of one or more shops was also widespread in
the inheritances valued over 5,000 kuruş. Another significant
element is the number of inns, storehouses, water mills,
coffee shops, and other buildings that had some commercial
purpose, each of which had a high value. Money also represented a big part of these inheritances, including significant
amounts in the form of receivables from the testator's
debtors.

To illustrate the great variety in size and in composition of the inheritances of rich testators, a detailed list is
provided in appendix 2. A study of that list suggests the
image of the persons who formed the propertied upper stratum
of the city. These individuals lived in expensive homes and
were also the owners of commercial property and of other real
estate, property that gave them economic power and weight in
society. They enjoyed considerable monetary resources and
put this money into circulation. As a result of their wealth,
they obtained positions wherein whole strata of the urban
population and the population of the surrounding villages
became dependent on them.

The social nature of this propertied urban elite can be
partially reconstructed. It was Muslim and, for some of the
individuals involved, the registers mentioned their titles
and duties in the Ottoman feudal hierarchy (as *alemdar*s or
standard-bearers, as *molla*s or senior members among the
doctors of Muslim religious law, as kethüdas, as military
officers, etc.). Such references and the size of the inheritances make it clear that the group in question was composed
of provincial representatives of the Ottoman ruling class.[10]
As a provincial elite, these individuals had a level of
wealth that could be matched by the wealth of individuals
from other social categories.

As a rule, wealthier non-Muslims used the services of
their ecclesiastical community organizations in the registration of estates, wills, and even property transfers; accordingly they are not well represented in the kadı registers.
Moreover, only a handful of the church and obshtina registers
of that time have been preserved, and data from such
sources can only be used as illustrations and examples. For
example, records have survived on several Greeks who
bequeathed their entire fortunes in the form of dowries and

wills. In 1790 the widow of Panayotis Benakis, who as a merchant and big landowner had been one of the most outstanding representatives of the Greek bourgeoisie in the Peloponnesus, gave a wealthy dowry to her daughter.[11] Its total worth is not shown, but the enumeration of its movable and real property speaks for itself. Together with luxurious home furnishings, clothing, embroideries, and jewelry (12 strings of pearls, 2 diamond necklaces, and strings of gold coins), the daughter received fifty-four orchards (half olive groves and half with mulberry and fig trees), sixty decares of vineyards, fifty decares in fields, the ownership of four villages, a tower with a fountain, two flour mills, two houses, seven shops situated in the market place, nineteen shops in other various places (some of them in a dilapidated condition), and half interest in a bakery.

The metropolitan of Monemvasia, Ignatios Tsamblakos, whose brother's son was married to the daughter of Benakis, was the descendant of a medieval aristocratic family. He took the metropolitanate in 1776, paying an annual fee of 30,000 akçe (about 250 kuruş) to the patriarch. (What he had paid to acquire the post in the first place is not known.) In his will of 1801, the metropolitan left 2,000 kuruş in cash to the patriarchate, 1,000 kuruş to the Greek schools in Monemvasia and Kalamata, and 1,000 kuruş to churches, monasteries, and the poor. He left his furniture and personal effects to his successor. [12]

In 1787 a certain Anthonios, the son of Griparis of the island of Siphnos, bequeathed to his two children and his wife several fields each, olive trees, a vineyard, and his shares in three ships and a boat. He divided his gold, silver, and pearls between his two children and he gave each of them three houses with everything inside. He left his daughter an iron pier and his wife a stairway that ran to the river. He distributed his cash (4,250 kuruş) as follows: 1,500 kuruş to his daughter; 1,000 kuruş to his son; 500 kuruş to his wife; and 1,250 kuruş to charities.[13]

On the same island in 1773, Maria, the daughter of Konstaninos Baos, married Petros Kamarasis and received as a dowry all kinds of home furnishings, vessels, utensils, clothing, fabrics for furnishing her new home, several houses, three shops, an olive orchard, a vineyard, three fields, fifty sheep, expensive jewelry, and 1,500 kuruş in cash.[14] Several decades later, in 1813, Maria's husband, Petros Kamarasis, made out his will in which he distributed money amounting to 35,000 kuruş ("20,000 of which I acquired by my own labor and work") in the following manner: 10,000 kuruş to his wife, 15,000 to nephews, and the remaining 10,000 to charities.[15] A year later his widow Maria provided her adopted niece with a dowry of 2,500 kuruş, several houses, orchards, vineyards, home furnishings, clothing, and numerous items of jewelry.[16]

These examples are of various representatives of the prosperous stratum of Greek society. Along with the metropolitan (who both by origin and by status was a member of the ruling feudal stratum), the individuals mentioned include big Greek landowners in the Peloponnesus (persons who also claimed to represent the Greek aristocracy), and elements of the rising commercial and shipbuilding bourgeoisie of the islands. Even the partial assessment of their wealth was sufficient to place the individuals named among the propertied elite in the Ottoman state.

An even more precise depiction of the social nature of those who left estates worth more than 5,000 kuruş can be obtained by comparing their estates with the inheritances left by artisans.

The profession of the deceased was seldom noted in the inventory descriptions of estates, and thus it is impossible to establish a link between profession and property status. However, insofar as the available records contain a few dozen known cases of artisans whose estates fell into the different groups, the possibility exists for comparing the artisans as a group with the urban elite already described.

To this end, a group of thirty artisan estates has been assembled using as a primary criterion the representation of several crafts in the person of one or two craftsmen each. An effort has also been made to include individuals with different material positions who represented the two basic ethnic components of the population, Bulgarians and Turks.[17] These artisan estates are grouped according to their total value as shown in table 15.

Analysis of the inheritances in question reveals a sharp difference in the value of the houses of the artisans and those of persons who left estates valued over 5,000 kuruş. Whereas the houses of most artisans were valued under 500 kuruş, and only in one or two cases reached 1,000 kuruş in value, this higher figure was the usual worth of the home of the urban propertied elite.[18]

The different social characteristics of the two groups are also apparent from the business properties of the estates. As might be expected, the Muslim elite owned business buildings of greater value and in greater numbers. Furthermore, these properties were often rented out rather than used for productive purposes by the owners themselves. The list provided in appendix 2 describes individual owners who possessed as many as eighteen to twenty shops each. But rather more typical were owners who had several shops and other commercial property.

TABLE 15

DISTRIBUTION OF THIRTY 18TH-CENTURY ARTISAN
ESTATES IN VIDIN, SOFIA, AND RUSE

Assessment in Kuruş	Number of Inheritances	Percentage
Up to 500	11	36.7
501-1,000	9	30.0
1,001-5,000	8	26.7
5,001-10,000	2	6.6
Total	30	100.0

Unlike these proprietors, only a few artisans owned commercial properties in addition to their own shops. However,
craftsmen did possess their artisan capital, and in their
estates this capital took the form of their shop's inventory,
tools, raw materials, and finished goods. The value of artisan capital varied widely, and a comparison of individuals
reveals a qualitative difference in their status. Thus, a
certain tailor named Pŭrvan, who left an estate worth 174.5
kuruş, lacked his own shop. His tools were assessed at 1.5
kuruş, and the estate inventory did not note any finished
goods or raw materials. Undoubtedly, Pŭrvan was one of those
craftsmen who worked with materials supplied entirely by their
clients. The abaçı Lazar, on the other hand, who worked in
basically the same branch of production as Pŭrvan, owned
artisan capital worth 1,171 kuruş--part of an estate worth
1,644.7 kuruş. This capital consisted of a stock of materials
and finished goods, aba, and aba clothing.[19] Similar differences existed among dyers, tanners, and other craftsmen. Two
of the dyers included in table 15 bequeathed estates that did
not contain finished goods and raw materials, while those of
another two dyers listed considerable amounts of these
items.[20] As these examples indicate, the ranks of the artisans included not only those who worked with material supplied by the customer, or who themselves went out to work in
the client's home (and who thus also depended on the orders
they received), but also artisans who enjoyed their own stock
of raw materials and finished goods. However, although they
had ceased to work only on demand, and although they produced
goods for nearby markets or for export, they were not really
set apart by wealth. The internal changes within artisan
production were only very slowly lifting individuals to a
higher material level, and it was still a rare occurrence for
an artisan to reach the plateau of the propertied elite.

In ethnic terms, there was no difference in the distribution of estates by value, with the exception of the propertied elite, where representatives of the Ottoman ruling class
predominated. Both Muslims and Christians were concentrated
in the groups of estates valued at up to 1,000 kuruş.

* * *

A comparison of the material status of the provincial
Ottoman feudal class and other parts of the urban population
can also be made on the basis of certain seventeenth-century
data (see table 16). Since it has been drawn from inheritance records, this information is similar in character to
that examined so far, and therefore, although expressed in
akçe rather than kuruş, permits a comparison with the eighteenth century. (On account of the great fluctuations in the
value of the akçe--which was withdrawn from circulation
toward the end of the seventeenth century--we have left the
totals in akçe. Comparisons, of course, thus become more
difficult, but at least this method avoids the inaccuracies
that would result from an attempt to convert the values.)[21]
This data has been drawn from registers (which Barkan has
published) of the estates of military personnel in Edirne
from 1545 to 1649, and also from the kadı registers of Vidin
and Ruse of the late seventeenth century (specifically for
the years 1686 to 1700).

It is clear from their size and value that the Edirne
estates were largely bequeathed by rich people, which was
natural when one bears in mind that they belonged to members
of the military-feudal stratum. Nearly three-fourths of
these estates had valuations of more than 100,000 akçe each.
Those individuals leaving the largest estates (over 500,000
akçe each) included senior military officers and persons
occupying administrative posts; however, there were also three
saddlers in the sultan's service, a school teacher, and
others. The houses in this group were usually valued at over
50,000 akçe, and in individual cases the value of the house
exceeded 200,000 akçes. Practically all of these estates
contained one or more shops, çiftliks, water mills, and other
farming property such as vineyards and orchards. Another
consistent element was large sums of money, usually more than
100,000 akçe and including some cases of sums over 500,000
akçe. These data illustrate the material wealth of one of
the basic strata of the Ottoman feudal class--the military.

In contrast to the breakdown of the estates in Edirne,
more than half of the inheritances in Vidin and Ruse had low
value--up to 50,000 akçe. These estates usually consisted of
a house valued at from 10,000 to 20,000 akçe, a vineyard or
orchard, a small amount of furniture, and, although more

TABLE 16

DISTRIBUTION OF CERTAIN 17TH-CENTURY
ESTATES IN EDIRNE, RUSE, AND VIDIN

Assessed Value of Estates (in akçe)	Edirne		Ruse		Vidin	
	Number	Percentage	Number	Percentage	Number	Percentage
Up to 50,000	21	13.9	24	58.6	15	62.5
51,000-100,000	21	13.9	7	17.0	6	25.0
101,000-500,000	80	53.0	9	22.0	3	12.5
Over 500,000	29	19.2	1	2.4	--	----
Total	151	100.0	41	100.0	24	100.0

SOURCES: Ö.L. Barkan, "Edirne Askerî Kassami'na Âit Tereke Defterleri
(1545-1659)," *Belgeler* 3, nos. 4-5 (1968): 1-479. NBKM, Oo, Vkr and Rkr,
R_3, R_4, R_2, S_{13}, S_{14}.

rarely, a small sum of money. Where the estates were worth
less than 20,000 akçe, the value of the house was usually below 5,000 akçe and the furnishings tended to be more uniform
and less costly. In Edirne, too, the estates bearing lower
assessments of from 20,000 to 50,000 akçe included houses
valued at 5,000 to 10,000 akçe, a small amount of furniture,
a vineyard, and a small sum of money.

Inheritances valued at over 50,000 akçe had costlier
homes, richer and more varied furniture, and a more significant amount of cash. On rare occasions these inheritances
also included artisan shops and workshops. Estates that surpassed 100,000 akçe in value took in houses worth more than
20,000 akçe. In Ruse, only one estate had a value exceeding
500,000 akçe, an inheritance left by a former ship captain
that totaled 1,216,680 akçe. The captain's house was worth
120,000 akçe. Aside from the house, the inventory listed a
water mill worth 120,000 akçe and three vineyards and four
orchards with a total worth of 360,000 akçe.

These data indicate a certain diversity of the social
characteristics of the rich layer of the population. Included
as testators here were not only representatives of the Ottoman
ruling class, but also individual artisans.

To judge by the value of the houses they owned, other
segments of the population also had a significant property
differentiation. Data on house assessments can thus be used
to differentiate the military-administrative layer from the
productive population (see table 17).

In Ruse and Vidin, where the data concerns the civil
population in general, one-third to one-half of the houses
were assessed at values under 5,000 akçe. Only the houses of

TABLE 17

DISTRIBUTION OF BEQUEATHED HOUSES
IN EDIRNE, RUSE, AND VIDIN (1686-1700)

Assessed Value (in akçe)	Edirne		Ruse		Vidin	
	Number	Percentage	Number	Percentage	Number	Percentage
Up to 5,000	35	25.1	10	28.5	10	55.5
5,001-10,000	15	10.8	4	11.5	3	16.7
10,001-20,000	22	15.8	8	23.0	3	16.7
20,001-30,000	19	13.7	10	28.5	2	11.1
Over 30,000	48	34.6	3	8.5	--	----
Total	139	100.0	35	100.0	18	100.0

wealthy members of the commercial and artisan layer of the population approximated the high values of the houses contained in the estates of the Ottoman ruling layer. For example, the house of the ship captain mentioned above was worth 120,000 akçe;[22] the house of Elhac Abdullah Çelebi bey was worth 42,500 akçe (as part of an estate that totaled 247,680 akçe);[23] and there was a female testator who bequeathed a house only one part of which was valued at 37,920 akçe (as part of an estate valued at 145,320 akçe).[24]

Additional confirmation for these findings can be found in an examination of data concerning houses that were sold in Sofia (see table 18). More than half of the houses in question had low values; only six-tenths of 1%--obviously the houses of the wealthy--had values of more than 30,000 akçe. Thus, for example, a merchant from Dubrovnik ceded to his co-owner Marko, the son of Stefan, the second half of his house for 24,000 akçe. It was a two-story house with a cellar and running water.[25] To cite another example, 20,000 akçe was the price of a house that the sons of Mustafa çelebi sold to Omer çelebi, a servitor of the sultan. (The brothers had inherited the house in question.)[26] In another case, prices of 27,000 and 30,000 akçe were paid by two other Turks for houses with winter and summer rooms, with a porch, a grain storage bin, and a livestock shed. An Armenian priest paid 20,000 akçe for another house.[27] The houses of the Ottoman military stratum, a third of which were assessed at more than 30,000 akçe, are in contrast to these small and medium-sized houses in Sofia, Vidin, and Ruse.

What has been said to this point about the characteristics of various layers of the urban population can be supple-

TABLE 18

DISTRIBUTION BY VALUE OF HOUSES
SOLD IN 17TH-CENTURY SOFIA

Value in akçe	Number	Percentage
Up to 5,000	112	65.8
5,001-10,000	40	23.7
10,001-20,000	13	7.6
20,001-30,000	4	2.3
Over 30,000	1	0.6
Total	170	100.0

SOURCE: NBKM, Oo, Skr, S_1, *bis*, S_{308}.

mented by a consideration of the percentage breakdown of the
major components in the estates of the three cities.   For
Ruse, houses constitute 15.4% of the total value of estates,
and for Vidin 10%.   For these two cities shops and workshops
constitute 5.2% and 1.4% (respectively) the total value of the
estates surveyed.   For agricultural properties (vineyards,
orchards, çiftliks, water mills), the respective figures are
15.8% and 5.9%, and for inventory and stock, .9% and .1%.
Cash (both cash on hand and amounts to be collected from
debtors) accounts for 9.5% of the value of the estates in
Ruse, and 17.3% in Vidin.   According to the results of the
data that Barkan has summarized, the distribution of separate
elements in the estates of the military figures in Edirne was
as follows: houses--9.9%, shops--3.8%, agricultural properties
--7.9%, commercial and artisan shop inventories--11.9%, and
cash on hand and cash loans due--19.2% and 21.1%.[28]   In
addition to these items, household goods and clothing made up
a relatively high share of the estates (14.6%).   Another essential element was slaves (2.9%).   The difference between
Edirne, on the one hand, and Ruse and Vidin on the other,
immediately strikes the eye.   Only isolated representatives
of the productive population came close to the position of
the sipahis, the Janissaries, and the other branches of the
provincial military and administrative layers.

                              * * *

    A further source of information on the social character-
istics of the different categories of testators is another
common element of inheritances--personal effects and home

furnishings. The variety of such items makes it necessary to
group them into the two broad categories just mentioned.
Personal effects include clothing, furs, fabrics, valuables,
and arms; home furnishings take in, among other things, utensils, rugs, bedding, and various kinds of other domestic
items. As well as indicating the value and the material from
which such items were made, the estate inventories describe
their actual physical condition. The documents, for example,
indicate whether items of clothing were new, worn out, frayed,
and so forth. When studied carefully, such descriptions
would permit an interesting portrait of various levels of
material status. The thousands of recorded cases describe an
incredible variety of contemporary clothing. The first goal
here is to compare, in value and type, the clothing used by
the representatives of the Ottoman urban elite in contrast to
that worn by artisans of various trades.

In 1768, for example, Esseid Mehmed Ağa of Vidin had a
rich and varied wardrobe with an assessed value of 582 kuruş.
It included fifteen undershirts, twenty-seven pairs of pants,
three thick woolen capotes made of broadcloth, one hooded felt
coat, one sleeved jacket made of broadcloth, one sleeveless
broadcloth jacket, three new broadcloth jackets, three short
zebun jackets, two white padded jackets, three broadcloth
overcoats, and four fur overcoats lined with broadcloth. He
also owned three furs.[29] Similar in assessed value (520
kuruş) was the clothing in the estate of a former military
officer in Vidin, Ismail Ağa. In this case, however, the
wardrobe was more varied. Probably as a result of his military service, Ismail's wardrobe included a number of furs and
other cold-weather items: two pairs of woolen gloves, five
shawls, nine padded jackets, one aba caftan from Baghdad, one
heavy caftan (described as old), another heavy caftan, two
fur caps, one hood, two sleeveless woolen jackets, one
sleeveless jacket made of broadcloth, one hooded felt cloak,
one short jacket with silver decorations, two sashes, two
belts, two shirts, and a great number of furs and skins (a
"Crimean" skin, a tiger skin, three weasel furs, a fur for
lining the overcoat, six other furs, and so forth). The
separate value of the furs and fabrics was 524 kuruş.[30]

For artisans, estates of varying values have been chosen
to determine the corresponding differences in their material
position, as reflected in personal effects, particularly in
clothing. Of the four dyers from Vidin whose wardrobes have
been examined, two left relatively small inheritances worth,
respectively, 377 kuruş and 479 kuruş.[31] The clerk who
registered the property of the estate of one of these artisans
paid no attention to the modest personal effects involved. In
the other case, the inventory listed only two fur overcoats

worth seven kuruş. The other two dyers, however, left estates
of much greater value (5,033 kuruş and 2,794 kuruş). These
estates contained clothing, valuables, furs, fabrics, and
other personal belongings whose value in each case exceeded
300 kuruş.[32] Each of the testators possessed several outer
garments: padded jackets, trousers made of coarse woolen cloth
or of broadcloth, sleeveless jackets made of both broadcloth
and wool, fur overcoats and other jackets, fur caps, fezzes,
hoods, and fur-lined aba coats. One of the dyers, whose name
was Ibrahim, even owned a sable overcoat. This itemization of
the estates of the two dyers in question reveals not only a
larger but a more varied wardrobe, which reflects the testators' taste for the kinds of expensive furs and fabrics worn
by the rich.

Significant differences also arise in the examination of
the personal effects of other artisans. A study of nine
artisans (Muslim and non-Muslim) who left estates worth up to
500 kuruş shows that in five of these inheritances the clerk
failed to mention personal effects. The records of the remaining four estates noted the presence of one or two overcoats, and a pair of pants or some other kind of outer gar-
ment. In most of these cases, moreover, the inventory
expressly states that the garments in question were old and
worn.[33] Estates valued at over 500 kuruş, however, usually
contained a larger amount of clothing, although the value of
these items was still not very large. In the estates of three
Vidin tanners who left inheritances worth 777, 798.5, and
905.5 kuruş, the wardrobes included were valued, respectively,
at 64 kuruş, 96 kuruş, and 32 kuruş. A Vidin goldsmith named
Dimcho left an estate totaling 833 kuruş that contained the
following wardrobe: three padded jackets (one was white,
another was multicolored, and the color of the third was not
indicated), one broadcloth caftan, one furred aba sleeveless
cloak, one short jacket, one fur overcoat, a shirt, pants,
another shirt, one sleeveless jacket, two waistbands, another
caftan, one bathrobe, and various cloths and other items.
The value of this wardrobe was 71 kuruş.[34]

Another seven artisans who left estates that were approximately equal in value (between 600 and 800 kuruş) owned
clothing that was quite different both in style and in worth.
Four men in Vidin--the mender Petko, the furrier Tomo, the
fishmonger Halil, and the shoemaker Osman beşe--possessed
wardrobes valued at about 20-30 kuruş.[35] As a rule, they consisted of one or two pairs of pants, one or two padded
jackets, fur caps or fezzes, boots, shoes, and one or two
furs. The other three artisans--the dyer Vel'o, the tailor
Konstantin, and the scale-maker Ibrahim--had wardrobes worth
less than 3 or 4 kuruş. Tailor Konstantin's estates did

contain over one hundred padded jackets, but these were
jackets of various sizes and obviously represented his shop
inventory. As recorded in the estate, his personal clothing
consisted of only an old padded broadcloth jacket, an old red
fur cap, an overcoat, and another two padded jackets.[36]
     The inheritances valued at 1,000 kuruş or above display
a greater variety in the clothing, more furs, and such other
personal effects as jewels and arms. However, no sharp
division seems to have existed between inheritances that
included these goods and the examples cited above.[37] The
value and the variety of the personal effects were greater for
those artisans who, in this respect, were by and large coming
to resemble the rich Ottoman notables.
     As the foregoing examples illustrate, estates worth a
few hundred kuruş had wardrobes that usually failed to go
beyond basic necessity. Only when the estate's value reached
a certain level, usually about 1,000 kuruş, did it feature a
greater variety of clothing and personal effects in general,
a variety expressed both in the types of items and their
value. This analysis, of course, is not sufficient to support
conclusions leading to a definite classification of the
testators in question, but that has not been the purpose here.
This discussion is meant simply to stress the gradualness of
the appearance of this type of differentiation as it was
reflected in inheritances and as it was expressed for various
types of testators.
     The presence in inheritances of arms, to continue, de-
serves special attention. Weapons were a highly individual-
istic item, in whose selection the owner had the opportunity
to reveal his tastes and to demonstrate his prosperity. In
this area, too, estate records provide sufficient material for
analysis. The firearms and other weapons involved differed
both in type and in value. For example, there were several
types of silver daggers, various silver pistols, swords
decorated with precious stones, and so forth. Of course,
some of the inheritances being examined here involved only
the arms obligatory for every military rank, but in other
cases there was a large number of various kinds of weapons,
some of which were true treasures in their standard of
workmanship.[38] The lower the value of the estate, the lower
the value of the weapons it contained. The arms of most of
the Muslim testators consisted of a dagger and a saber made
of ordinary steel. Richer Muslims occasionally owned fire-
arms--for example, a set of pistols or an unadorned gun.

                              * * *

     Home furnishings were also regularly mentioned in inher-
itance records. Using selected representatives of both the

Ottoman urban elite and of the artisans, an effort has been
made to assess the relative weight of these home furnishings
in the general value of estates. Where the Ottoman elite
was concerned, such items comprise from 0.4% to 5.7% of the
total value of the inheritances. For the artisans, on the
other hand, furnishings tend to constitute a much larger part
of inheritances: in six cases more than 10% of the estate's
value, in nine cases between 5 and 10%, and in twelve cases
up to 5% (but never less than 1%). When measured against
the moveable and immoveable property of an *ağa* (officer), the
value of the artisan's funishings seemed small, but for both
the ağa and the richer artisan, this item was a definite and
constant element that mirrored the level of their everyday
life. Among the household goods, the most valuable items
were usually copper or silver utensils and vessels, followed
in turn by bedroom items made of various materials.

Utensils and vessels can thus be taken as an important
sign of material prosperity. More so than other personal
effects, these items were retained and passed down from
generation to generation as part of a family's accumulated
treasures. As a rule, they were worth over 200 kuruş in those
estates whose total value was more than 10,000 kuruş. The
estates of the urban well to do, inheritances whose value
ranged from 1,000 to 5,000 kuruş, also included utensils of
considerable value, items usually worth between 50 to 100
kuruş and often more. Like clothing and arms, the value of
such items decreased with the decline in the total value of
the estate. In inheritances bearing the lowest assessed
values (up to 100 kuruş), vessels and utensils usually failed
to be worth more than 1-3 kuruş.

Let us now supplement the analysis of houses and shops
based on estate records with data on the purchase and sale
of real estate drawn from kadı registers. In addition to the
names of the persons involved in the transaction, these
documents give the value of the property and, in a number of
cases, also the number of rooms and the presence of auxiliary
structures. The information gathered and analyzed from such
records pertains to 2,697 houses and 1,404 shops and workshops
(see table 19).

The greater part of the houses (62.6%) had values ranging
up to 200 kuruş. One-fourth of the houses ranged in value
from 201 kuruş to 500 kuruş; the remainder (12.6% of the total) were valued over 500 kuruş.

The registers noted the date of sale or transfer of the
property, making it possible to examine the distribution by
periods (see table 20). A look within the separate groups
over various periods of the eighteenth century reveals
certain differences between the first and second half of that

TABLE 19

DISTRIBUTION OF HOUSES IN VIDIN, RUSE,
AND SOFIA IN THE 18TH CENTURY (BY VALUE)

Assessed Value (in kuruş)	Number	Percentage
Up to 100	1,052	39.0
101-200	636	23.6
201-300	345	12.8
301-400	203	7.5
401-500	122	4.5
501-1,000	243	9.0
Over 1,000	96	3.6
Total	2,697	100.0

century. Until roughly the year 1750 houses worth up to 200 kuruş make up more than three-fourths of the total, their relative incidence ranging between 80 and 90%. From 1751 to 1800, however, the incidence of such properties decreases to between 60 and 40%. At the same time, houses valued at from 201 to 500 kuruş tend to make up a greater relative share of the total, an increase even more pronounced for the group of houses valued from 401 to 500 kuruş. But the strongest increase occurs for the houses valued over 500 kuruş. In contrast to their 2-4% share of the total in the first half of the century, these houses come in the next fifty years to represent a percentage share ranging from 12.1 to 24.5%.

As suggested by these data, the outset of the eighteenth century saw a sharply defined property polarization. The situation forms a pyramid whose broad base is formed by the majority of houses and whose apex represents that small group of houses in the highest value ranges. Relatively speaking, this group of highly priced houses is very small, showing that any economic differentiation involved only a limited part of the population. But toward the middle of the century these compact groupings, one small and one large, start to break up. There now appear groups of houses falling into varied price ranges with each of these groups represented by a relatively large number of houses--unconditional statistical evidence of the advancement of property differentiation. With the appearance of intermediate categories in this portrait of social relations one can discern the formation of a

TABLE 20

SALE AND TRANSFER OF HOUSES
IN VIDIN, RUSE, AND SOFIA IN THE 18TH CENTURY

Assessed Value (in kuruş)	1700-1710		1711-1720		1721-1730		1731-1740		1741-1750		1751-1760	
	Number	Percentage	Number	Percentage	Number	Percentage	Number	Percentage	Number	Percentage	Number	Percentage
Up to 100	11	91.7	86	61.0	152	69.7	160	66.3	130	52.0	130	38.3
101-200	1	8.3	25	17.7	40	18.3	44	18.3	63	25.2	77	22.7
201-300	--	---	19	13.5	15	6.9	18	7.5	20	8.0	49	14.5
301-400	--	---	6	4.3	5	2.3	11	4.6	21	8.4	22	6.5
401-500	--	---	2	1.4	3	1.4	4	1.7	5	2.0	20	5.9
501-1,000	--	---	3	2.1	3	1.4	3	1.2	10	4.0	34	10.0
Over 1,000	--	---	--	---	--	---	1	0.4	1	0.4	7	2.1
Totals	12	100.0	141	100.0	218	100.0	241	100.0	250	100.0	339	100.0

Assessed Value (in kuruş)	1761-1770		1771-1780		1781-1790		1791-1800		Total	
	Number	Percentage	Number	Percentage	Number	Percentage	Number	Percentage	Number	Percentage
Up to 100	111	37.5	109	28.7	79	21.1	84	18.8	1,052	39.0
101-200	75	25.3	100	26.3	110	29.4	101	22.6	636	23.6
201-300	38	12.8	58	15.3	63	16.9	65	14.6	345	12.8
301-400	19	6.4	34	8.9	34	9.1	51	11.4	203	7.5
401-500	9	3.1	20	5.3	23	6.2	36	8.1	122	4.5
501-1,000	34	11.5	38	10.0	45	12.0	73	16.4	243	9.9
Over 1,000	10	3.4	21	---	20	5.3	36	8.1	96	3.6
Totals	296	100.0	380	100.0	374	100.0	446	100.0	2,697	100.0

relatively differentiated society. In the eighteenth century
the generally homogeneous property structure of the great bulk
of the population, typical of the medieval city, gave way to
an evolving property situation in which the development of
artisan and commercial activity was leading to an entire
ladder of different social categories. This is precisely the
value of table 20: using what is relatively speaking a conservative indicator, it demonstrates the emerging property
differentiation of the urban population in the eighteenth
century.

As noted above, many registers also provide both the
number of rooms in a house and the appurtenant structures.
Such descriptions have been gathered for 519 houses in Vidin,
Ruse, and Sofia (see table 21). The largest number of houses
considered here were one-roomed structures, which, when combined with two-roomed houses, account for more than three-
fourths of the houses in question. The remaining 25% of the
houses had three or more rooms. The same breakdown holds
true for the cities of Ruse and Vidin, except that for Ruse
there is a higher incidence of one-room houses (46.2%) than
for Vidin, and a somewhat lower incidence of houses with
three or more rooms.

When recording cases in the kadı registers, the clerk
usually included the courtyard (*havlu*) as a common feature.
It is interesting to note that in Ruse the clerk often noted
the presence of a covered yard (*hayat*), as well, a structure
that the Vidin registers do not include. Another difference
was that the Vidin registers record a kitchen (*matbah*) as a
common feature for any type of house. For Ruse, on the other
hand, the records very seldom note the presence of a kitchen.
Whether they concern estates or sales, the records of both
Vidin and Ruse frequently refer to orchards (*beoçe*), both
fruit tree (*müsmere*) orchards and others (*gayri müsmere*), and
to cellars (*mahzen*). In certain cases in Vidin the registers
employ various terms for designating such auxiliary and
external structures as livestock sheds (*ahur*), lean-tos
(*sayban, sayeban*), and granaries (*ambar*). Clerks rarely
noted such other features of domestic property as pantries
(*kiler*), halls (*sofa*), terraces (*çardak*), or dugouts. Also
rare was the description of such additional details as the
number of stories (*fokani ve tahtani*); the existence of
interior and external parts of a house (*dahiliyesi ve
hariciyesi*); the presence of stone foundations (*kâgir*); the
type of roof (whether of straw, planks or tiles); or the
presence of shutters (*kepenk*), foundations (*mayi*), and wells
(*pinar*).

The terms just cited were the ones used most often in
the sicils of the three cities for indicating the various

TABLE 21

DISTRIBUTION OF 18TH-CENTURY HOUSES IN VIDIN,
RUSE, AND SOFIA (BY NUMBER OF ROOMS)

Number of Rooms	Number of Houses	Percentage
One	230	44.3
Two	164	33.6
Three and four	87	16.8
Five and over	38	7.3
Total	519	100.0

elements of a house. It immediately has to be added, however, that an abundance of word forms was possible due to the presence in the documents of a great number of Arabic, Persian, and Turkish words. The Ottoman language was generally a rich one and was suitable for various word combinations. This whole area is a matter of considerable interest, and although this is not the place for an exhaustive discussion several examples may suffice to illustrate it.

Along with the basic term for designating a room--the Turkish word *oda*--some sicils (chiefly those of Ruse) also contain the Arabic word *beyt*, which has a dictionary meaning of "home," "house," and "heated room," to specify a room that contained a stove. Likewise frequently used, in the possessive case, was the term *oda evi*, which cannot be literally translated, but which can be taken to mean "the place of the room." The Turkish word *ev* ("house") was also employed in other combinations of the possessive case for specifying various parts of a house: for example, *kiler evi* (pantry), *as evi* (the place of the fire, fireplace), and, in the Sofia sicils, *sofa evi* (hall). The Vidin and Sofia sicils include additional combinations based on various attributes combined with the basic word "oda": for example, *soba odası* or *sobalı odası* (a room with a stove); *çardak odası* (the room with a door to the terrace); *kömür odası* (a coal bin); and so forth. Particularly in Sofia (and more rarely in Vidin), the word *soba* was replaced by *şitevi oda*--that is, a room for use in the winter as opposed to a summer room, called a *sayfi oda*. In the Ruse sicils, a covered yard was designated by the Arabic word *hayat*. In the records of Sofia, the word used was the Turkish term *yazlık* (although the intermediate combination *yazlık hayati* was also employed. For designating

the house itself, there was a uniform usage in the three
cities. From among the great number of possible words for
house or dwelling ("ev," "hane," *dar*, "beyt," *mesken*, and
menzil), only the Arabic word menzil was used. (The Persian
word "hane" was also employed, but only in combinations
describing some auxiliary buildings--*saman hane, kiyak hane*.

The descriptions of various houses are also of scholarly
interest. Such descriptions reflect local variations and
signs of varying levels of material culture, as can be seen
by several descriptions of houses in different price ranges
in the cities of Ruse, Sofia, and Vidin. One example concerns
the sale of a house involving a Muslim buyer and seller in the
Old Mosque quarter of Ruse. A one-story building with a
tiled roof, this house consisted of two rooms, a cellar, a
fruit orchard, and another orchard, and it commanded a purchase price of 130 kuruş.[39] Another Muslim home of practically the same value (120 kuruş), in Vidin, consisted of a
room with a stone stove and another room with a fireplace and
a courtyard.[40] In another example, a house in Sofia had considerably less value (65 kuruş), but it nevertheless comprised both inner and external sections, a feature normally
restricted to the more affluent properties. The inner part
of this home consisted of two rooms each with a stove, two
halls, and two covered courtyards. Its outer part had two
rooms with stoves, two halls, and a courtyard.[41] Among the
examples of low-priced houses is a particularly striking case
involving a transaction in Ruse between two Armenians, Agop
and Ovanes. The house in question was priced at 2,000 kuruş.
It had a two-story inner part. The upper floor contained
four rooms, all covered by a tiled roof. The lower floor was
composed of two stone cellars and opposite these cellars was
a bathroom, an oven, and a pantry. Two other rooms and
another cellar were also attached. The exterior part consisted of an upper level containing a room covered with a
tile roof; and on the lower level there was a cowshed, a lean-
to shed fronting the courtyard, a fruit orchard, and another
orchard.[42] Another example worth citing involved a highly
priced (1,725 kuruş) Christian house in Vidin. It had an
interior part with four rooms, a kitchen, and a courtyard,
and an external section containing two rooms, a cowshed, a
haybin, and a courtyard.[43]

The 519 houses for which descriptions are available
break down in roughly the same distribution as the total
group of 2,697 houses being considered here (see table 22).
More than half of these houses were priced below 200 kuruş,
and an additional 25% were valued at from 201 kuruş to 500
kuruş. Houses worth more than 500 kuruş account for 20.2% of
the total. The great majority of the houses priced below

TABLE 22

DISTRIBUTION BY ASSESSED VALUE OF 18TH-CENTURY
HOUSES DESCRIBED IN THE REGISTERS OF VIDIN, RUSE, AND SOFIA

Assessment in kuruş	Number	Percentage
Up to 100	165	31.8
101-200	114	22.0
201-300	68	13.1
301-400	38	7.3
401-500	29	5.6
501-1,000	66	12.7
Over 1,000	39	7.5
Total	519	100.0

200 kuruş were one-roomed. Thus, of all the houses valued up
to 100 kuruş, 77% were one-roomed dwellings, and only 18.2% of
the houses in this value range had two rooms. In the group of
houses priced at between 101 and 200 kuruş, the incidence of
two-roomed homes is twice as great (36%). Houses with two or
more rooms become increasingly prevalent as the amount of
the assessments increases. Thus, the group valued at between
201 and 400 kuruş consists chiefly of two-roomed and one-
roomed houses. This value range includes 33% of all the two-
roomed houses, and only 13% of those with one room. Close
to one-half of the houses worth between 401-500 kuruş had
three and four rooms, although the relative incidence of two-
roomed houses still remains high (34.5%). A similar pattern
holds true for homes valued at from 501 to 1,000 kuruş, where
three-fourths of the residences included had from two to four
rooms. Half of the houses valued at more than 1,000 kuruş
had five or more rooms. Comprising the remainder of this
group are chiefly houses of three and four rooms, with only an
insignificant number of two-roomed houses.
     The above tables thus make it clear that the large
majority of one-roomed houses fall into the groups assessed at
up to 200 kuruş, and that one-roomed houses are an exception
in the groups of houses valued at over 300 kuruş.
     The distribution of two-roomed houses differs from both
that of one-roomed houses and that of multiroomed houses.
Unlike the other types of homes, two-roomed houses are distributed almost evenly in all assessment ranges. This phenomenon is perhaps an indication that various strata of the
population preferred houses of this size. (The varying

values of two-roomed houses resulted from considerations of
construction, layout, and probably the size of the rooms
involved.)

Houses containing three and four rooms occur both below
and above the 500 kuruş breakoff point. In contrast to two-
roomed and multiroomed houses, these three and four-roomed
houses show a gradual increase in incidence in the groups
assessed at between 200 and 500 kuruş. The majority, however,
fall into the group of houses valued over 500 kuruş.

Multiroomed houses almost entirely fall into the assessment range of over 500 kuruş. Most were solidly constructed,
built on stone or brick foundations, and covered by tile
roofs. These residences contained both an exterior and an interior section, each of which was two storied, and it was
these houses that characteristically possessed such appurtenant structures as lean-tos, stables, grain bins, and such
other elements (though met more infrequently) as baths, ovens,
halls, terraces, and summer houses. An interesting example
of this type of dwelling was the Vidin home of Elhac Mustafa.
In addition to other features, this two-storied residence had
ten rooms in all and was worth 4,200 kuruş.[44]

The group of houses valued over 500 kuruş does include
some houses that had a smaller number of rooms. For example,
in 1794 a two-roomed house in Vidin cost 900 kuruş,[45] and in
1708 in Sofia a six-roomed house was priced at a mere 100
kuruş.[46] These were undoubtedly exceptions caused by the type
of construction and by the location. A house's value was very
much dependent on the construction material used, as can be
seen from two examples from Ruse. One involved a price of 8
kuruş for a one-roomed house with a covered courtyard and a
garden, but with a thatched roof.[47] The other house had absolutely identical features, but it had a wooden roof and was
priced at 30 kuruş.[48] Accordingly, various factors influenced
the worth of a house. However, in the final analysis the
determining criteria were the number of rooms and, at least to
a large extent, the type of construction.

The distribution, by number of rooms, of the houses for
which a description is available can also be used as a guide
to indicate the types of the rest of the houses that were presented in table 19. Assuming that the distribution of houses
in both groups (those with and without accompanying descriptions) is roughly the same, and keeping in mind that both
groups pertain to the same period (the eighteenth century),
it can be assumed that the majority of houses valued at up
to 200 kuruş were one-roomed dwellings. In this group from
one-half to three-fourths of the houses are of that type,
and only about one-fourth of the houses priced below 200 kuruş
possessed two rooms. The houses valued at from 201 to 400

kuruş are primarily two-roomed houses (which constitute between 40 and 60% of the houses of this group). The incidence
of one-roomed houses is small in houses valued at between 401
and 500 kuruş, and the incidence of two-roomed houses goes
down at the expense of the rapidly growing incidence of houses
containing three and four rooms (which comprise about half of
the houses of this group). Houses valued at more than 500
kuruş are chiefly dwellings of five rooms or more. However,
this group still contains a noteworthy number of two-roomed
houses, the incidence of which does not sharply decline
until house values reach more than 1,000 kuruş. Houses worth
more than 1,000 kuruş were exclusively dwellings containing
five or more rooms.

The distributions in question are almost identical for
all three cities (Vidin, Ruse, and Sofia). It should be
noted, however, that in Vidin there is a skew toward the
higher price ranges, as seen from a comparison of the data by
city (see table 23).

An interesting phenomenon revealed by table 23 is the
prevalence in Ruse of houses of lower values and (as compared
with Vidin) the relatively small number of high-priced houses.
An explanation for this apparently has to be sought in Ruse's
historical evolution. Both Ruse and Vidin were Danubian
cities located at two extremes of the Bulgarian hinterland
and both served as natural ports for that hinterland. Accordingly, the difference in the value of their houses cannot
be explained solely in terms of the economic factors that
shaped their development during the period under consideration. Rather, such economic factors should be seen as a more
general explanation for why and how, in the conditions of the
Ottoman state, it was possible and necessary for these two
points on the Danube to develop as cities and ports of
approximately equal size. But it is also true that the difference in house prices in the two cities was not a reflection
of the number of rooms. Accordingly, the reasons for this
phenomenon in all probability rested in the differing
historical character of the two cities. Vidin was the capital
of the medieval Bulgarian state and possessed a strong fortress wall. The housing that was preserved could not but act
as a model in the expansion of the city and in the constant
renovation of housing. Ruse, however, lacked this feature,
and it followed the natural course of a settlement undergoing rapid development as a result of its special geographical position as a junction linking (through Varna) the lands
beyond the Danube to Istanbul.

Such a conclusion is supported by the data for Sofia.
Like Ruse, the bulk of Sofia's houses were grouped in the
lowest price range (up to 100 kuruş). At the same time,

TABLE 23

PERCENTAGE DISTRIBUTION BY ASSESSMENT AND BY CITY OF
18TH-CENTURY HOUSES IN VIDIN, RUSE, AND SOFIA

Assessed Value (in kuruş)	Vidin	Ruse	Sofia
Up to 100	19.8	42.3	50.3
101-200	21.9	23.1	20.2
201-300	15.6	15.4	10.1
301-400	7.5	11.5	5.7
401-500	6.6	1.9	5.1
501-1,000	17.6	3.9	7.3
Over 1,000	11.0	1.9	1.3

however, Sofia had a higher incidence of homes priced over
500 kuruş than did Ruse (although not to the same extent as
did Vidin). The explanation of this distribution can be
found in the specific features of Sofia, a city that, in its
level of development, occupied an intermediary position between Vidin and Ruse. In comparison with Ruse, Sofia was an
old city; in significance, however, it was inferior to
Vidin.[49]

* * *

Shops and workshops, another item of inheritance, are
particularly revealing in what they can tell us about the
social characteristics of various layers of the population.
The eighteenth-century kadı registers being used here contain
information on some 1,404 shops and workshops. Of these cases,
220 involved sales, and the remainder were recorded as items
of inheritances.

Although an assessed value is indicated for all of these
shops and workshops, this figure sometimes represents a lump
sum for several shops, or the combined value of houses and
shops. Nevertheless, for nearly half the cases (803), the
value of the shop itself is specified, and these are the
shops and workshops that have been analyzed here (see table
24). These data have been studied in the aggregate, disregard-
ing the city in which the shops were located and combining
both sales and estates. Such an approach seemed permissible
because preliminary studies of the material failed to show
essential differences in the valuation or in the distribution
among the separate cities, or in these properties as items
of sale or inheritance.

TABLE 24

DISTRIBUTION BY ASSESSED VALUE OF SHOPS AND WORKSHOPS
IN 18TH-CENTURY VIDIN, RUSE, AND SOFIA

Assessed Value (in kuruş)	Number	Percentage
Up to 100	378	47.1
101-200	167	20.8
201-300	91	11.3
301-400	37	4.6
401-500	29	3.6
501-1,000	53	6.6
Over 1,000	48	6.0
Total	803	100.0

Nearly half of the shops are grouped at the lowest value range (to 100 kuruş). By including the next two value ranges, the bulk of the shops surveyed--about 80%--turn out to be worth less than 300 kuruş.[50] Only a relatively small percentage (12.6%) were priced higher than 500 kuruş. This distribution is of course similar to the distribution of houses. In that case, too, the majority of registrations involved houses valued at up to 300 kuruş, and only a small percentage of the houses had higher prices.

That shops and workshops were concentrated at the lower value ranges and were roughly equal in value was a sign of the continuing prevalence in the eighteenth century of a certain type of shop belonging to those artisans and merchants who remained subjected to the dominant equalizing regulation of their professions. This regulation was expressed both in fixed rates of profit and rents and in equal conditions of production and sale.

These minor differences that did exist in the distribution of shops might be the result of both the property differentiation that had occurred and of the different conditions in which a given handicraft was being practiced. To a certain extent this question can be clarified by an analysis of shops by type of production and by assessed value. Those records that do indicate type of shop testify to a rich and wide variety of crafts. Some forty different crafts are identified, and this number undoubtedly is not exhaustive, since the records fail to specify the type of many of the shops in question.

   A comparison, for the three cities, of several crafts
represented by a relatively large number of shops and workshops does not produce any particular difference in the assessed value of shops belonging to the artisans in different
fields. In the cases examined--which include coffee shops,
bakeries, groceries, tanneries, barbershops, butcher shops,
and harness-maker shops--the assessments were both low (up
to 100 kuruş) and high (over 500 kuruş). The same kind of
distribution holds true for those other crafts represented by
a smaller number of recorded cases. (One should also keep in
mind that the assessors, in appraising shops, took into
account both general conditions and, at least to some extent,
the equipment, for they assessed separately the specific
stock and the instruments.)
   But within a given handicraft, there did exist great
differences between the lowest and highest shop values. Some
of the higher priced coffehouses were anywhere from 30 to 100
times as valuable as those appraised at the lowest values.
Some bakeries bore prices from 20 to 100 times higher than
other bakeries; some tanneries were 50 times more valuable
than others; some harness-maker shops were 70 times more
costly than similar shops; some flour dealers had shops 30
times more costly than other flour dealers. For each of the
crafts enumerated above, there was some greater or lesser
differentiation in the values of shops. This suggests
great property differentiation within a given craft and is
evidence of the changes in the material position of persons working within the same economic activity.
   The distribution of shops among individual shopowners
adds to this emerging picture of property differentiation.
The 1,404 shops in question were owned by a total of 724
individuals, most of whom owned one or two shops each.
Nevertheless, a large number of the shops in question were
concentrated in the hands of a relatively small number of
proprietors who owned more than two shops each. Thus, 65
proprietors owned 3 to 4 shops each, 53 had from 5 to 10
shops each, and 8 owned more than 10 shops each. Of the 724
individuals in question, 126 persons (17.4% of the total)
owned more than 2 shops each, but this same number of persons
owned a total of 660 shops (47% of the total). This concentration of shop ownership is a convincing piece of evidence
for the interest that the propertied urban elite showed in
shops as a means for the profitable investment of their
monetary capital. But this was a coin with a reverse side.
It entailed the existence of a large number of direct producers who lacked ownership of the means of production and
were compelled to rent shops and workshops to work and to
survive. Finally, from the much greater concentration of the

ownership of shops (as opposed to the ownership of houses),
one can see that the development of monetary-commodity
relations, and of the city in general, in combination with
the rising demands of the market, were raising the significance of shops and workshops in urban economic life and were
making such properties an important source of monetary income.

Differentiation of the Urban
Population in the Eighteenth Century

10. MONEY AS A SIGN
OF PROPERTY DIFFERENTIATION

Money is one of the most frequently encountered elements
in the estates of both Muslims and non-Muslims, and of people
of different material status and professions. Money took
first place among the component parts of an estate; it played
more of a role than did the value of a house in determining
the over-all worth of an inheritance. In the first half of
the eighteenth century it constituted from 10 to 23% of the
total value of inheritances, and in the second half of the
century this figure rose to about 35% (reaching about 50% in
the decade of the 1750s). This trend can be seen from the
data from Vidin, which is the fullest available: in the decade
from 1710 to 1720, 13.3% of recorded inheritances was in
money; from 1721 to 1730, 18.2%; from 1731 to 1740, 21.2%;
from 1741 to 1750, 23.3%; from 1751 to 1760, 45.7%; from 1761
to 1770, 32.9%; from 1771 to 1780, 36.0%; from 1781 to 1790,

34.9%; and from 1791 to 1800, 32.8%. This money included not
only ready cash, but also loans that the testator had made
and his heirs could collect. There was also money due from a
surviving wife or husband. This last category included the
money that, under the şeriat, a husband had to assign to his
wife in the event of a divorce. (Since this money was bound
up by religious law with strictly governed personal relationships among members of a family, it will not be made part of
this study. It did not amount to more than 1 or 2% of the
total amount of the inheritance in different decades.)

Cash on hand is one of the most interesting components
of an inheritance, although the amounts involved did not
surpass loans that remained for collection. This item best
illustrates the character of the propertied urban elite that
had succeeded in accumulating sizable amounts of money. More
than half of the estates in Vidin that included ready cash in
amounts greater than 1,000 kuruş were bequeathed by ağas,
beys, and former military officers. Although the inventories
do not record the social position of the remaining testators
of this group, they do include a number of *hacıs* (*elhac*),[1]
definite evidence that they too belonged to the more prosperous stratum of the Muslim population. Of the whole group
of persons who left estates containing more than 1,000 kuruş
in cash, inheritance records describe only two as artisans.
The holders of larger sums of money, say over 3,000 kuruş
(there were nine such cases mentioned in the records), were
exclusively ağas and beys. A similar picture holds true for
Sofia and Ruse, where the small number of holders of ready
cash over 1,000 kuruş belonged almost entirely to the same
category of the population. Furthermore, as can be seen in
the data provided in appendix 2, there was high positive
correlation between large sums of ready cash and estates that
had a high total value. Thus, for example, the estate of
Ahmed ağa of Sofia, which had a total value of 27,845 kuruş,
contained 6,180 kuruş in ready cash. The estate of the Vidin
resident Mustafa ağa had a value of 15,477 kuruş, of which
5,849 kuruş was in cash. The estate of the *serdengeçti*
(high-ranking officer) Ibrahim ağa of Vidin contained 6,442
kuruş in cash. A particularly characteristic example from
Vidin--which is not contained in appendix 2 since it involves
an inheritance composed only of money--tells how in 1766
Ahmed ağa, the son of Elhac Mahmud ağa and a member of the
garrison of Vidin, left an inheritance totaling 101,529.5
kuruş. Of this amount, 40,000 was in cash, with an additional
20,000 or so realized through the sale of articles. The
remainder was in loans that had yet to be collected.[2]

Occasionally artisans and merchants were also among the

testators who bequeathed large amounts of money. In 1774,
for example, a dyer named Elhac Ali ağa, who had formerly
served on the Vidin defense force, left a total inheritance
of 20,254 kuruş. According to the inventory, this total included 950 kuruş from the sale of a house, about 100 from
the sale of various goods (coffee, butter, rice, and barley),
100 from other articles, 2,006 kuruş in cash on hand, and a
large sum of money to be collected.[3] The estate of Iakov,
the son of Ion of Vidin, was entirely in cash--3,715 kuruş.[4]

Money in loans owed to the testator predominates over
cash on hand in the estates that contained sums of money. It
is encountered more frequently and forms a greater part of the
value of the whole. This holds true for all three cities of
Vidin, Ruse, and Sofia, and for all decades of the eighteenth
century. Such moneys account for from 70 to 90% of the total
amount of money involved in inheritances. The amounts in
question were lent out for a variety of reasons: for production, for the acquisition of merchandise, for the payment of
taxes, for the purchase of tax-collecting contracts, or
monopolies, and so on. It would be impossible to establish
the exact amounts put to any of these various uses. In the
majority of cases the register notes the amount of the debt
against the name or names of the debtors, but does not record
the purpose for which the money was lent.

In more than 10% of the cases where debts were recorded,
however, the occupation of the debtor is also indicated. And,
in the material studied here, the debtor's occupation can be
determined in even more cases, since the documents occasionally state either that the debtor was the testator's partner
or that the debt of a given person arose from the joint ownership of a shop or of some other property or merchandise.[5] On
the basis of such information, one can conclude that the
debtors in question were also artisans or merchants.

Together with the debts of individual artisans, which
made up the majority of the cases in question, there were also
instances where a given person lent money to a group of
several members of the same guild or of various guilds. Thus,
Elhac Mustafa of Vidin was owed 808 kuruş from ten artisan
debtors: two goldsmiths, two coffeehouse keepers, one grocer,
one saddler, one cooper, and so forth.[6] The estate of Mustafa
beşe of Vidin enumerated the debts of eight artisans--barbers,
horseshoers, fishmongers, and so on--debts that totaled 754
kuruş.[7] Ahmed bey of Ruse, to cite another example, was owed
money by seven persons who represented various trades. Mehmed
effendi of Sofia had lent 1,478 kuruş to merchants and to two
soap boilers. In the same city the carter Todor, who died in
1756, was owed 262 kuruş by two other artisans, and a Chris-

tian named Georgi was owed 550 kuruş by a grocer and by a tavernkeeper.[8]

There were rarer cases where the debtor was a whole guild of merchants or artisans. The sum borrowed might have been used to pay the guild's obligations to the state or it was possible that the debt arose from the delivery of merchandise or to cover expenses arising from the needs of production. Vidin merchants owed 1,800 kuruş to Hassan ağa and another 750 kuruş to Elhac Ali, and the dyers' guild there owed 1,600 kuruş to the dyer Ibrahim. In all probability, this debt involved that member of the dyers' esnaf who handled the guild's commercial operations.

As these examples suggest, those who were in a position to lend money did not necessarily comprise only those individuals who fit the common image of the big lender.[9] The lenders here include persons who belonged to the same guild that they had just indebted. Clearly, the artisans mentioned above enjoyed a position different from that of the other members of their guild and from that of other representatives of the same branch of production.

Officials and representatives of the Ottoman ruling stratum occupied a unique place among those persons who had become indebted. In Sofia and Ruse there were relatively few cases of this sort, but the Vidin records listed more than eighty. Thus, in 1773, those who owed money to Ismail ağa of Vidin, an *emin* (commissary) of the army, included a certain Abdi paşa (for 2,770 kuruş), the *voyvoda*s (mayors) of two villages (for about 800 kuruş each), an alemdar (for 1,600 kuruş), and so on. Also indebted was the vilâyet deputy Omer ağa. His debt of 14,974 kuruş was in return for obligations undertaken for grain deliveries and for straw, for the purchase of the bedel tax, and for the maintenance of state communications (the menzils, postal stations).[10] Since Ismail ağa had himself borrowed some 38,000 kuruş, his net monetary inheritance totaled 3,400 kuruş.

The estate records frequently mention the names of ağas of the city and of neighboring villages, and of military and administrative officers who for various reasons resorted to the services of those who possessed large amounts of capital. In a similar example, the inventory of the estate of Ali ağa, the son of the *hamamcı* (public bathkeeper) of Vidin, whose monetary inheritance totaled 58,767 kuruş, listed forty-seven monetary loans to various ağas, alemdars, purchasers of the cizye tax, and (in two cases) Jews.[11] This type of loan clearly has to be seen as a mutual service that persons at the same level rendered to one another in close connection with the fiscal organization of the Ottoman state.

As well as in such arrangements between individuals,

ready money was used to serve the interests of the ruling
feudal system in other ways. For example, the population
itself often turned for help to those who possessed monetary
capital to pay obligations that had come due. Whole villages,
groups of peasants, and individuals all borrowed money to pay
their taxes to the state or the tax farmer who had received
the right to collect them. In 1778, for example, the kethüda
Ibri-zade Suleyman aga, the son of Ismail and a resident of
the Cami atik quarter of Ruse, left his heirs 13,180 kuruş
in loans to be collected from about twenty villages where
there were a number of persons who were his debtors.[12] In
1761, the residents of thirteen villages of the Sofia region
borrowed 1,242,789 akçe from Ahmed aga of Sofia, the *zâbit* or
police officer of the village of Boiana, to pay both regular
and extraordinary taxes such as the cizye, the avariz, the
nüzul,[13] the tax on sheep, and others.[14] The *kâtib* (clerk) of
Sofia, who died in 1751, had debtors in eleven villages who
had borrowed a total of 952,345 akçe. Many of the amounts due
for collection, as indicated in the inventory of his estate,
arose from his purchase of the right to collect the cizye
and the *bedel-i nüzul*.[15] The 1761 inventory of the estate of
Ahmed aga lists sixty-four loans, seventeen of which involved
villages. The remainder involved persons who had secured
their loans with receipts from the collection of taxes.[16]
The inventories record dozens of other cases where whole
villages borrowed money, evidence that such a practice was
quite widespread. The documents for Sofia at various times
record as debtors more than forty villages and more than
sixty individual villagers. In Vidin sixteen villages are
so listed, as well as private individuals, and that city's
records note thirty-nine loans to a group of persons covered
by the general term of reaya. Debtors in Ruse also included
several tens of villages. Furthermore, the sums borrowed
in such cases were quite high. In Sofia from 1771 to 1780
the debts of villages constituted 50.4% of all the money
that estate inventories list as being due for collection.
In the next decade this figure was 48.2%.

The progressive, absolute, and relative growth of
money as part of estates testifies to the presence of
advanced monetary and commodity relations in the urban
economy. The presence of some money in almost every estate,
and the great number of purely monetary inheritances, reveals
the wide involvement of the urban population in commodity
and monetary relations. The appearance of money among testators cannot be explained solely by their ownership of leased
real estate, or simply by official duties that they might have
held, for their trades or artisan activity were their basic
monetary sources. In the eighteenth century the urban economy

had reached that stage of development where whole layers of
the urban population had the opportunity to employ their own
monetary resources. Money was also playing an increasing
role in credit and moneylending operations that involved not
only peasants, but also representatives of ruling circles
who, for short-term purposes, sought the assistance of those
who possessed monetary capital. Those who participated in
credit operations came from all layers of the urban popula-
tion--individual artisans and merchants, persons with un-
stated professions, whole guilds, individual peasants and
whole villages, and representatives of the Ottoman ruling
class. In the eighteenth century money, either ready cash or
in loans, had become a major sign of wealth.

* * *

The comparison of the data drawn from sicils that record
eighteenth-century inheritances and property transfers in the
cities of Vidin, Sofia, and Ruse permits a number of conclusions about the material status and property differentiation
of the urban population.

The examination of a basic type of property--houses--
establishes that 87.4% of the houses examined here were
assessed at values below 500 kuruş. If houses valued up to
100 kuruş were those of the poor, and houses worth more than
1,000 kuruş belonged to the rich, then the sharp polarization
of the urban population becomes obvious, for there was a
limited group of persons whose houses were valued at several
thousand kuruş apiece. But in the second half of the eighteenth century there was a twofold increase in the number of
recorded instances involving houses of high value. Both this
phenomenon and the increase in houses in the middle value
range bear witness to an eighteenth-century growth in the
material status of the urban population. The gradual development of handicrafts and trade was more and more resulting in
the movement of individuals from the intermediate strata of
the population into the ranks of the propertied elite, a
stratum that until this point had been composed mainly of
persons drawn from the Muslim military and administrative
milieux. Throughout the course of the eighteenth century,
the composition of the prosperous layer of the population was
changing in all three cities under review.

The distribution of shops coincides with that of houses,
but here another feature comes up--the concentration of property: as the data reveal, 17.4% of the proprietors owned 47%
of the shops. And these proprietors included several dozen
individuals who owned five, ten, or more shops each.

These characteristics of property differentiation have
been supplemented by a comparison of the other components of

an inheritance. A consideration of vineyards, household
belongings, and clothing has permitted a more detailed study
of the essential differences in the material position of the
urban producer, of the small proprietor, and of the owners
of considerable real estate who left estates valued at more
than 5,000 kuruş.

Persons whose estates were below 100 kuruş formed the
lowest layer of the population. They owned only an insignificant amount of property and had no monetary means; these
were people who lived in constant need, and who lacked the
material means to apply their work. These were the urban
poor.

The group of urban residents whose inheritances were
worth from 1,000 to 2,000 kuruş enjoyed a different social
position. Their estates included significant real estate
of which the most notable element was shops (together with
their equipment and even finished production). The testators
here were urban citizens whose productive activity had
brought them sufficient material prosperity to be independent
and to support a standard of living equal to that of the rich
citizen.

The great part of the urban productive population rested
between these two groups. Some of these individuals owned
only a home, but others had both a home and shops, various
sums of money, vineyards, and so on. This property diversity
meant differing degrees of material security. In their
property some of these citizens approximated the status of
the rich, while others could not break out of poverty.

The group of urban residents whose estates were valued
at more than 5,000 kuruş formed the rich layer of the population in all three cities, and this element has already
been characterized in detail. One might also include in it
the majority of persons whose estates surpassed 2,000 kuruş
and who clearly approximated the status of rich citizens. But
a concrete analysis of the group of artisans of the three
cities and of the propertied elite has disclosed certain
basic differences in the character of these urban strata.

The propertied elite was almost exclusively members of
the Ottoman feudal class. Only isolated merchants and artisans, regardless of their ethnic affiliation, had a material
position that drew them close to the provincial Ottoman
military and administrative layer. Furthermore, having developed in a belated fashion, the emerging elements of the
local productive population could not help but be influenced
by the Ottoman feudal elite. The life style of the rich
Ottoman citizen left an imprint on the consciousness of both
the Muslim and non-Muslim urban stratum that was beginning
to acquire both property and social position. This was a

period when there was a certain drawing together of the
material status of individual representatives of the nascent
urban bourgeoisie with that of the Ottoman feudal class, a
period when certain features of the way of life of the Ottoman
rich permeated the way of life of the Christian notable. The
rising bourgeoisie thus tried to imitate the way of life of
the established urban elite, including even those aspects that
were feudal in character. In general way of life and of
dress, those members of eighteenth-century Bulgarian society
who were achieving prominence by virtue of their property and
their social position had not yet taken on the elements of
the Viennese life style--such things as chairs, candlesticks,
glassware, and china of Czech and Saxon manufacture--that were
to become so typical for Bulgarian (and Greek) merchants and
entrepreneurs during the first half of the nineteenth century.
But that was another period, when roles had changed, and when
the leading elements of socioeconomic life had become the
bourgeoisies of the empire's subjugated peoples.

PART TWO

NEW DIRECTIONS
IN THE DEVELOPMENT OF THE BALKAN CITY

Plate 14. A view of 19th-century Plovdiv and the bridge over the river Maritza. Courtesy of National Library, Plovdiv.

Plate 15. A sketch of Gabrovo by F. Kanitz from *La Bulgarie danubienne et le Balkan* (Paris, 1882).

11. THE PRIMITIVE ACCUMULATION OF CAPITAL

Transitional historical periods, when the disintegration of one socioeconomic formation is intertwined with the birth of another, are distinguished by an exceptional variety of developmental processes and by the appearance of aberrant forms depending on the many factors that affect these processes. For decades now, Marxist historical science has been studying problems involved in the transition from feudalism to capitalism. This scholarship has established the basic regularities and main stages of this transition, and defined the general chronological framework of the genesis of capitalism. Nevertheless, in a number of countries, an over-all clarification of the birth of capitalism in industry and in agriculture is still absent. This question has been a constant topic of vigorous discussion in the Soviet Union, whose historians have achieved remarkable successes in the study of both the feudal epoch and the era of capitalist development.[1]

187

Of late, an increasing number of historians and economists in the Balkan countries themselves have been focusing
their attention on the peculiarities of Balkan feudalism, its
disintegration, and the emergence and development of capitalist relations. Valuable studies have appeared and, as one
might expect, the more profound such studies have become, the
more their results have been accompanied by inevitable differences in opinion.[2]

It is perhaps superfluous to speak about a point of
departure in the study of the genesis of capitalism. Every
Marxist author attempts to apply the general theoretical
positions of Marxism and to give meaning to the factual material while simultaneously taking into account the chronological development and the dynamics of the processes being
examined, as well as certain peculiarities that might have
appeared as a result of the uneven development of productive
forces in different countries. For the sake of greater accuracy, however, one might recall the words of Marx that the
most general prerequisites of capitalist production are commodity circulation. Commodity production, which plays such an
important role within the framework of feudalism, has to reach
that state of development where there occurs a root change in
the position of the small producers: some of them rise to the
level of capitalist entrepreneurs while others become hired
laborers, for capitalist relations presuppose that two kinds
of commodity owner come into mutual contact. On the one hand,
there is the hired worker--the direct producer to whom feudal
society has to provide the chance to dispose of his own
personality so that he might become economically compelled to
sell his labor as a commodity. On the other hand, there is
the holder of money who concentrates in his hands the means
of production and the means of existence.[3]

This process was taking place in the very womb of feudal
society. For a long time after their initial emergence,
capitalist relations coexisted with feudal relations, which is
why every feudal society had some specific effect on the
development of capitalism. In retracing the history of capitalist relations in England, Marx made special note that the
emergence of these relations preceded serfdom's liquidation
(or the feudal dependence of one person to another) and also
preceded the weakening of guild restrictions.[4] In Russia, the
genesis of capitalism occurred when decaying serfdom was
reaching its most brutal forms wherein the dependence of one
person on another attained its fullest expression and came
closest to slavery (a situation in which all three types of
dependency--personal, land, and judicial--were concentrated in
the same hands).[5] In other countries too, the genesis of
capitalism reflected local peculiarities. Therefore, before
examining the emergence and development of capitalist rela-

tions in the Balkans, let us once again characterize those
several features of Balkan feudalism that affected this
process.

To begin with, in attempting to subsume under the same
law of regularity the development of feudalism in all countries, some authors have unconsciously been misled because the
best studied medieval society, at least until a certain point
in time, was that of Western Europe. And since personal
dependence reached its fullest expression there--both in the
relations among the representatives of the feudal class
itself, as based on hierarchy and vassalage, and in the relations between rural producers and the feudal class as a whole
--these authors have raised West European feudalism into a
norm. All differences with the accepted "classic" feudalism
of Western Europe have thereupon been characterized as specific peculiarities or deviations lacking any particular significance or only holding back the normal course of feudal
relations (as in the Ottoman Empire). It is the general
features that are studied as the true manifestations of
feudal relations. The absence, for example, of immunity
(i.e., of something typical in Western European feudalism, a
separate feudal law distinguished from the general state law)
has been taken as a divergence from the "authentic" feudal
society.

Two characteristic features of Ottoman society are
crucial in this discussion. First, there was the existence of
a powerful centralized state with a far-flung and highly
specialized administrative and fiscal apparatus; second, there
was significant urban development. Though accepted at first
glance, these considerations have not always received the
weight they deserve and have very often been insufficiently
considered in the concrete analysis of this or that aspect
of Ottoman feudalism.

The first and most critical consequence of strong state
power in the "only truly military state of the Middle Ages"[6]
concerns land relations. Without dwelling on the characteristics of all forms of land tenure in the Ottoman Empire, let
us note only that, unlike the *pomeshckik*, who by right of
ownership owned all of the land and could arbitrarily determine the type and size of peasant obligations, and unlike the
seignior who received rent in kind and cash from the direct
producers who lived within the boundaries of his holding, but
did not have the right to alter the conditions of land usage,
the overwhelming majority of Ottoman fief holders lacked basic
rights to the land. Fief holders in the Balkans received a
given type of revenue in an amount strictly determined by the
state. To a certain extent they enjoyed the right of control
and supervision over land cultivation but these functions too

were established by the state. The Ottoman fief (timar,
zeamet, and has), which was invariably obtained in return for
service (chiefly military), represented the acquisition of
certain fiscal rights over income from the land and, very
often as well, income from a nonagricultural source. In its
entirety, the rent that was received by the Ottoman holders of
such grants, and which was fixed and controlled by the financial organs of the state, constituted that part of the feudal
rent that was determined in a centralized manner.

Numerous registers reveal the determining role of the
state as the basic regulator and collector of feudal rent.
These registers state precisely the name and the size of tax
paid by each taxpayer as well as the revenues that went to the
benefit of every fief holder. This particular feature of
Ottoman feudalism, with its accompanying regulation of the
revenues designated for the benefit of fief holders, became
the source of sharp struggles over the distribution of rent
among the various strata of the Ottoman ruling class. This
struggle resulted in the total victory of the uppermost
level of that class--those who occupied the highest administrative posts. It was they who triumphed over the stratum of
military fief holders.

Since the state regulated their status, the great
majority of the population remained essentially state peasants
up to the eighteenth century. The state determined the size
of their obligations in cash and kind, doing so without regard
for the recipient--be it the treasury or an individual fief
holder. Indeed, the latter was often unable to find out the
location of the reayas from whom he received his income. As
several Bulgarian studies have shown, the specific kind of
peasant tenure, even vakıf tenure, made no difference in the
actual position of the peasant. The same was true for those
reayas who fulfilled various special duties (and whose
exploitation was carried out fully by the state).[7]

It is as difficult to establish the extent to which the
peasant in the period from the fifteenth to the eighteenth
century was a small-commodity producer connected with the
market as it is to determine the extent of property differentiation in the villages. In any event, what must be remem-
bered is that the peasants did not endure the kind of personal
dependency that would have seriously restricted their ability
to be their own masters.[8]

Having examined in detail the problem of the city in the
Ottoman feudal system in the first part of this study, the
discussion here will concentrate on certain unique features of
the role and the place of the city in the economic development
of the Balkans. As early as the fifteenth and sixteenth
centuries, the relatively developed urban economy assisted the

realization in the form of money of a large part of the feudal
receipts of the treasury and of the revenues received by the
holders of timars, zeamets, and has holdings. The development of Balkan cities thus freed contemporary Ottoman society
of that basic socioeconomic contradiction that was inherent in
the West--the contradiction between the natural character of
the economy and the consequent dearth of opportunities open to
feudal lords or to peasants to realize surpluses from feudal
rent and market production. Given the level of commodity
production in the Ottoman Empire, the existence of such major
centers of consumption as Istanbul, Edirne, Salonika, Athens,
Sarajevo, Serres, Plovdiv, and other cities created opportunities for the acquisition of cash surpluses through the
market. This possibility was perhaps one of the important
sources of the greater stability of feudal relations in the
Balkans. At a very early point this society created sufficiently favorable conditions for the expansion of commodity
production and for the development of capitalism.

Another question that arises in this connection is that
of the accumulation of capital. As suggested by much evidence, in the Ottoman Empire the accumulation of monetary
resources on a precapitalist basis came centuries before the
beginnings of capitalist relations. That a considerable
portion of feudal rent was rendered in cash already constituted an essential condition for the accumulation of money by
the feudal lords themselves--be they private individuals, the
sultan and his circle, or the state. And, as also shown by a
number of examples, part of the feudal rent paid in kind was
converted into cash through the sale, on both the domestic
market and (in part) on the foreign market, of revenues
received through the tithe. The purchase of the right to
collect taxes, as expressed in the mukataas system, also contributed to the accumulation and growth of moneylending capital in the Ottoman Empire. As early as the end of the fifteenth century and in the sixteenth century, transactions
worth millions of akçe were taking place in this area.
Enormous profits were also being made by moneylenders from
different backgrounds who financed tax farmers and other
officials.

Part of the monetary capital that had been amassed in the
empire found a secure and profitable application in the
development of mines, saltworks, and other enterprises that
the state ceded to purchasers. Urban real estate also
produced large profits for certain urban--chiefly feudal--
elements. The income from the leasing of ships, caravansaries,
inns, and public baths was also reaching significant proportions and constituted the foundation of the resources accumulating in the hands of part of the ruling Muslim stratum in
the city.

Joining this capital, which had feudal origins, was the commercial capital that arose on local soil. One facet of this capital was linked to the remnants of the Byzantine aristocracy and newly emergent Greek families who grouped around the patriarchate. Although they had lost the largest part of their wealth during the Turkish conquest, these circles, thanks to the posts they occupied and to the trade that they conducted under the protection of the patriarchate, again began to play an important role in the economic life of the empire. When in the second half of the seventeenth century they began to settle in the Danubian principalities, they discovered a new source of profits and wealth.

In addition to these Greeks, merchants from Dubrovnik significantly expanded their commercial operations in this period. Their trade in skins (raw and processed), wool, and other agricultural and craft goods took them into even the most remote corners of the Balkans. This commercial activity likewise broadened the sphere of commodity and monetary circulation.

A compact Jewish population, meanwhile, had taken shape in the busier centers of the empire and particularly in Salonika (from the end of the 15th century and in the 16th century). In their new country, the Jews continued their previous economic activities, either inaugurating or invigorating the development of a number of areas of production and trade. Thanks to their considerable capital, their business contacts, and their expertise, these Jews soon won for themselves a predominant position in Levantine commerce. Thanks to its Jews Salonika became one of the chief commercial cities in the eastern Mediterranean from the fifteenth to the seventeenth century.

In these same centuries, accordingly, commodity-monetary relations were developing. The significant accumulation of commercial and usury capital was being put into exchange, tax farming, and moneylending and was being directed into such other spheres of activity as production. A characteristic example concerns the organization of the production of woolen textiles in Salonika. The production involved practically the whole Jewish population (as small-scale commodity producers, big entrepreneurs, merchants, and others). The basic precondition, however, that assured the regular annual production of several thousand rolls of cloth, was the state's cession to Jewish merchants of a monopolistic right to purchase wool from a widespread territory. (The free sale of wool to other merchants in this region was permitted only after the Jews had made their purchases. This monopoly was tied to the circumstance that all of the wool production of Salonika was intended for the capital.)[9] Each successively higher level of economic organization, conse-

quently, continued to presuppose the creation of special
privileges and monopolistic rights over the supply of raw
materials and the assurance of a regular market. Such conditions would also be necessary for the development of manufacturing production in the most important textile branches
in the Balkans in the nineteenth century, despite the presence
by then of what was an extensive market.

Also at that time, it was becoming possible to secure--
in return for payment for the work involved--a considerable
part of the labor force needed for large building projects.
The use of free labor was also illustrated by the state's
need to establish certain norms for remunerating the labor
of the "worker" (*işçi*). Here, too, as with purchases and
sales, the government used state regulation.[10]

* * *

In the seventeenth and eighteenth centuries, the economic
development of the Balkans underwent a number of changes, and
the two centuries were characterized by the development of
productive forces. Property and social differences within
the population increased, and more capital accumulated in
the hands of new propertied strata of the subjugated peoples--
Greeks, Jews, Armenians, Bulgarians, Serbs, and others.
Throughout the whole Ottoman Empire and beyond, dozens of
fairs became popular as centers for the sale of goods produced
during the year by the local population. In these two
centuries as well, the Balkan Peninsula and the eastern Mediterranean became involved both in European maritime trade,
(the so-called Levantine trade) and in caravan trade with
Central Europe.

In the eighteenth century, as periods of peace became
longer, and as military operations were far removed from the
central parts of the Balkan Peninsula, changing trade patterns
became even more extensive. England, France, and Austria now
replaced Dubrovnik and Venice and acquired the command of
trade with the Ottoman Empire. In the wake of this shift
fundamental changes occurred in the role of local commercial
capital, which now became directly involved in European trade.
Groups of merchants from among the Balkan peoples appeared in
practically all of the most important cities of the Mediterranean area, in Central Europe, and, a little later, in
Russia. Closely connected with the merchants and producers
back home, and enjoying the protection of European states,
these businessmen gradually attained an almost total control
over the imports and exports of the Balkan Peninsula. At the
same time there was an increase in the production of those
artisan goods that were in demand on both the local and the
foreign market: goods produced from skins; woolen, cotton, and

silk fabrics; yarn; and raw wool. The production of grain and
other agricultural items also increased. All of these goods
were the object of an ever increasing legal and illegal trade.

The 1774 Treaty of Küçük Kajnarca provided an additional
impetus to local commercial capital, particularly by opening
the Black Sea to the trade of ships under a Russian flag.
More generally, the treaty encouraged the emerging local
bourgeoisies, especially those springing up among the Greek
and Bulgarian peoples. The settlements that now grew rapidly
on the Black Sea coast of southern Russia irresistibly lured
the Greek and Bulgarian population of the Balkan Peninsula.
Indeed, in this period representatives of these peoples
shaped the appearance and development of these settlements,
and the Greek mercantile fleet, sailing under a Russian flag,
underwent a true upsurge.

The result of this later eighteenth-century economic
development was the formation of a bourgeois class among the
individual Balkan peoples--Greeks, Bulgarians, and Serbs. As
they consolidated their economic position, these bourgeoisies
began to take an increasingly active part as leaders in the
affairs of their peoples, for it was at this time that
national self-consciousness was being born on the Balkans.
In the second half of the eighteenth century this idea ma-
tured, finding tangible expression in national programs in
which content reflected heightened ethnic self-awareness.
The young urban bourgeoisie, which consisted of different
propertied strata, came to bear this national identity.

During the same period, however, the ruling nationality
remained a stranger to the general growth of productive
forces. This phenomenon was one of the specific features of
that form of feudalism that placed its imprint on all aspects
of the social and political life of the Ottoman Empire. The
decline of the sipahis and of the entire Ottoman military-
fief system--a decline that had begun in the late sixteenth
century--failed to bring about the end of the feudal mode of
production; rather, without resulting in the creation of
new productive relations, it simply undercut the material
strength of Ottoman feudal domination. What happened was that
the elite of the Ottoman ruling class continued its search for
easier and more promising means of obtaining greater fiscal
returns and used any and all means to ascribe to themselves
real or purported talents to obtain higher administrative or
military posts. More generally, this elite found its major
stimulus in its increasingly interlocking relationship with
the state apparatus, and this linkage in turn produced its
full bureaucratization and its transformation into one of the
most parasitic of feudal classes.

It was this character of the Ottoman ruling class that

explains why, despite the increased Western interest in the
agricultural output of the Ottoman Empire and the growing
exports of cereal and other farm produce in the eighteenth
and early nineteenth centuries, the Ottoman Empire did not
develop estate agriculture with organized large-scale market
production and the new version of serfdom that was so typical
of Eastern Europe. When large-scale farming did appear in the
central and eastern parts of the Balkan Peninsula, it was
primarily the work of successful landlords of non-Muslim
origin, of persons outside the Turkish feudal class.
    In both the West and in Russia, the eighteenth century
saw the definitive formation either of strong nation-states
or of strong multinational states in which the ruling nation
set the pace of capitalist development. In the Ottoman
Empire, on the contrary, the bearers of new capitalist
relations sprang up from the ranks of the state's subjugated
peoples. It was thus under the difficult conditions of alien
rule that these peoples had to pass through the stages of
small-commodity production, of property differentiation, of
the gradual accumulation of capital, and of the development
of markets and fairs with all of their associated risks both
to give birth to indigenous entrepreneurs and merchants, and
more generally, to raise the over-all level of their social
and economic development. Thus, the contradictions between
productive forces and the relations of production were becoming intertwined with ethnic contradictions in such a way
that they imparted a uniquely sharp edge to these contradictions. Because of the religious norms prevalent in the
entire state system and the backwardness and rigidity of the
ruling class that held them, the state's giving in to the
demands of changing times could only be seen as a concession
to the non-Muslim population. As the gap grew between the
bourgeoisie's economic role and its lack of political rights,
and as the gap grew between its cultural level (which was the
fruit of both its constant contact with European culture and
its consistent efforts to develop secular education) and the
ignorance of the Ottoman rulers, it became far more difficult
to endure an alien yoke that followed methods inherited from
the period of the Turkish invasion. Even when discussing
purely economic questions, this specific feature of Balkan
development during the eighteenth and nineteenth centuries
must always be borne in mind.
    The attempt of Selim III (1789-1807) to lead the Ottoman
Empire out of the grave crisis that appeared in all spheres
of economic and political life in the late eighteenth century
ended in complete failure. Selim's reforms could not break
the vicious circle. They required a social base that the
empire's subject peoples already possessed to a greater or

lesser degree, but such an affiliation--even if concluded only
with the emerging middle classes--was unacceptable, for it
would have inevitably strengthened the movements for national
liberation and thus the drive toward fragmentation of the
empire.[11] This situation became further complicated after the
disastrous end of Selim's reforms, when the Turkish government
subjected the empire, both politically and economically, to
the large capitalist states of the West. These states
gradually turned the empire into their own special raw material reserve.

From the sixteenth to the eighteenth century, to sum up,
the other large states of Europe had seen the turn toward a
capitalist mode of production in which a part of the feudal
class accquired a bourgeois character. These states, despite
their essentially feudal character, had aided the consolidation of capitalism. In the Ottoman Empire, on the other hand,
the carriers of capitalist relations had to overcome the
hostility of the ruling class, and only in individual cases
did such emerging capitalists receive state support. In spite
of temporary efforts to reconcile the interests of the ruling
class and those of the national bourgeoisies, Ottoman
absolutism failed to find a solution to the grave crisis
that was besetting it.

* * *

Contemporary historians of the Balkan countries have
accepted the second half of the eighteenth century as the
period of the birth of capitalist relations. During the last
quarter of the eighteenth century and the first years of the
nineteenth, these relations, influenced by a number of factors, underwent both a qualitative and a quantitative
increase. However, debate has continued over the exact degree
of development in the eighteenth and nineteenth centuries in
both industry and agriculture, and in the interior of the
peninsula as well as the littoral and the islands. This discussion has been taking place in the historical literature of
all Balkan countries equally--Bulgaria, Yugoslavia, Albania,
Greece, and Turkey. In addition to the discussion on a
general theoretical level, there have also been vigorous
disputes on such specific topics as the nature of the productive activity of individual settlements, of various population
strata, and of different enterprises.[12] In Bulgarian historiography questions have also been raised over the primitive
accumulation of capital.[13]

Most historians have agreed that although large-scale
farming did exist, especially in the Pelopponesus and in the
western parts of the Balkans, most of the nineteenth-century
rural population was composed of small peasant farmers.[14]

But this general unanimity has ceased as soon as the discussion has turned to questions of the property and social differentiation of the rural population, the flight from the village, and peasant efforts to seek a livelihood through seasonal work. These phenomena were part of the agricultural scene throughout the nineteenth century and were produced not by expropriation (which, to the extent that it existed at all, played only an insignificant role here) but by a variety of causes. Crucial among these were the alien yoke and the socioeconomic oppression of the peasants by the disintegrating feudal state.

One essential reason for the difficult position of the Bulgarian peasants, which was also a factor in their flight from the village, was the relative shortage of land in agriculture. This land shortage was only partly the result of the peasant's own self-restraint in land utilization (a self-restraint produced by the peasant's failure to see the point of farming in the face of the government's exactions, and by the many difficulties that stood in the way of the cultivation of the so-called empty lands). A considerable part of the good land was held by the large Muslim population, which in certain regions lived in compact groups but which was generally dispersed throughout the country. The widespread Muslim population contributed to the sharpening of existing contradictions. Since, however, the Muslims had the same internal differentiation as did Bulgarian society, its presence did not alter the social structure of the village. The relative land shortage and social differentiation within the village led either to peasant demand for arable land or to a flight from the village and to the pauperization of some peasants. Moreover, the high rents paid by peasants willing to pay any price to find an outlet for their labor thwarted the emergence of large capitalist farms. Instead of managing çiftliks themselves, the large landowners preferred to carve up their land into small rental properties. Capital was more profitably invested in the trade in farm produce, in usury, and in share cropping than it was in organizing large-scale capitalist production. The absence of extensive large-scale farming was conceivably why the programs of the later Bulgarian revolutionaries did not include demands for an agrarian reform that would give land to peasants by expropriating it from large landowners.[15] Rather, these programs posed the question of a liquidation of that basic contradiction between peasants, who as commodity producers wanted to develop their farms on a plot of land, and a state whose tax system and whose tax farmers were draining rural vitality.[16]

The unending flow of peasants into the cities constantly

increased the manpower market. (Even in the cities these
workers could not find enough opportunities for their labor
and they overflowed into Central Europe, the Danubian
principalities, and Russia.) Meanwhile, this stratum of the
urban poor became a manpower source for the capitalist production that was developing in the nineteenth century in
urban industry. The existence of an urban poor who constituted a separate social layer and who pursued any and all
possibilities to find work even for low remuneration was
characteristic of the urban economy of the Balkans throughout
the whole of the nineteenth century.

(In examining the development of the Albanian movement
for national liberation, and in discussing the motive forces
of this movement, an Albanian historian has recently demonstrated that the Albanian lands had the same socioeconomic
trends observable in the central and eastern parts of the
Balkan Peninsula. True, the complexity of ideological
relations in Albania and the close links between the Albanian
Muslim elite and Ottoman authority hindered the political
struggle of the Albanians for liberation. However, these
circumstances did not change the deeper processes that were
at work within Albanian society and which followed the
general regularities of the other Balkan societies.)[17]

* * *

The emergence of capitalist relations acquired its sharp-
est focus in commerce and in industry, particularly in the
production and trade of textiles. The earliest bourgeoisie
in the Balkans, the Greeks, resulted from the growth of trade.
As a maritime and commercial people, the Greeks became the
necessary middlemen in the commerce of all European states
with the Ottoman Empire. Greek merchants rapidly displaced
the French in Levantine trade and came to control three-
fourths of this French commerce. The Greek colony in Marseilles grew into one of the richest in Europe, and the Greek
colonies in Italy and in the interior of Europe (in Russia,
Austria, and Germany) expanded and underwent a thorough
transformation. Ceasing to be inward-looking groups of
refugees and immigrants who had sought protection in face of
the invasions, they changed into true merchant colonies, and
a majority of their members even succeeded in acquiring the
protection of foreign governments.[18]

Greek merchant ships grew out of their limited role in
coastal transit to become a powerful mercantile fleet that
crossed not only the territorial waters of the Ottoman Empire
but all of the Mediterranean. According to a French consular
report of 1764, Hydra, Spetsai, and Psara (Ipsara)--islands
that were to gain fame during the Greek uprising--each had
its own fleet employing several thousand seamen. Hydra

had a fleet of 120 ships and large boats with a combined
capacity of 45,000 tons, employing 5,400 sailors and carrying
2,400 guns (merchant ships were armed against frequent pirate
attacks). The 60 ships of Spetsai had a total capacity of
19,500 tons, employed 2,700 sailors, and carried 900 guns.
Psara had 60 ships with a combined capacity of 25,500 tons.
Its ships carried 1,800 sailors and 720 guns. Other Greek
islands also possessed their own large commercial fleets. In
all, at that time the Greeks had some 615 ships with a total
capacity of 153,580 tons, and a work force of 37,526
sailors.[19]

Albeit possibly exaggerated, this report attests to both
the strong development of shipping and to a shipbuilding
industry that was equally well developed. Indeed, this was
the activity that had the earliest expansion of capitalist
enterprise. Hydra, which had become a focal point both for
shipowning activity and for commercial credit capital,
possessed, by the eve of the Greek uprising, some 80 large
ships and 800 second- and third-class vessels.[20] Such rich
shipowners as L. Kunduriotis earned clear profits amounting
to several hundred thousand kuruş a year, sufficient testimony
of how the shipowners represented the wealthiest and strongest
layer of the Greek bourgeoisie. This activity also involved
widespread use of hired labor and it was here that the earliest struggle between the newly emergent classes began. The
huge number of sailors represented wage labor. Although
sailors and seamen sometimes received a part of the profits,
this occurred only when piracy was rife and during the time
of the Continental Blockade, periods when practically all
trade was conducted by smuggling and involved great risks for
the crews, and accordingly, when more inducements were necessary to find a sufficient number of workers. (It should be
added that in the Greek fleet merchant activity and piracy
went hand in hand. Whenever the occasion was right, the guns
mounted for defense were used for pirate raids. This has
led some historians to assert that brigandage formed the basis
of the primitive accumulation of Greek commercial capital.[21])

The Greek merchant fleet acquired a predominant position
in the Mediterranean in the wake of the 1774 signing of the
Treaty of Küçük Kajnarca between the Russian and the Ottoman
empires. This treaty opened the Black Sea to European
commerce, allowed the Greeks to sail under the Russian flag,
and extended the privileges of some of the Aegean islands.[22]

The Greek colonies on the southern shore of Russia now
grew at an unparalleled rate, and Greek merchants took control
of practically the entire Black Sea trade of Russia. "The
majority of ships that called at the port of Odessa belonged
to Greek shipowners."[23] With the protection of Russia, these

Greeks ousted their European competitors from Western commerce
with the Ottoman Empire, and for a period of time they had
most of the imports and exports of the Balkans and the eastern
Mediterranean concentrated in their hands. It was no accident
that at the end of the eighteenth century voices of protest
were raised in England calling for the elimination, while
there was still time, of this new and dangerous competitor.

Although great distances separated the centers where
Greek commercial capitalists appeared and developed--the
Russian cities of Moscow, Nezhin, or Odessa; the Mediter-
ranean ports of Marseilles and Trieste; such cities of
Central Europe as Vienna or Leipzig; and various Aegean and
Balkan ports--these centers had a common bond: the role of
middleman the Greek commercial bourgeoisie played.

A number of other changes in Greek economic life accompanied the successes of Greeks as commercial intermediaries,
and, more generally, followed in the wake of the ever expanding involvement of the Balkans in European commercial
exchange. Agriculture became more and more tied to the foreign market. There was an increased cultivation of those
crops in demand on local and distant markets: foodstuffs
(olives, raisins, figs, olive oil, etc.), silk, wool, wine,
and tobacco. Individual islands specialized in the cultivation of these crops. Chios, for example, prospered from
the export of olive oil and silk, as did the Peloponnesus in
continental Greece. Those areas with a long history of the
manufacture of the traditional textiles--aba, yarn, and
braid--were now transformed into flourishing economic centers
and into centers of public and national affairs.[24]

As early as the nineteenth century, for example, European
contemporaries were focusing their attention on the small
settlement of Ambelakia in Thessaly, which in the previous
century had developed a cotton manufacture that involved the
settlement's whole population. Carried away by the ideas of
Utopian socialism, F. Boulanger, a disciple of Fourier,
contrasted his idealistic picture of the organization of
production in Ambelakia with the ruthlessly exploitive
character of Western European capitalism.[25]

It is the disputed question of the nature of Ambelakia's
production--whether it was capitalist or a true cooperative--
that raises the whole matter of the emergence and role of the
capitalist entrepreneur in textile production.[26] An analysis
of the capitalist textile producer will shed light on such
specific problems as that of the character of production in
Ambelakia and will introduce the complex issue of the primitive accumulation of capital in the Balkans.

* * *

A careful analysis of the abundant material pertaining to
individual capitalist entrepreneurs, who in the late eighteenth
and the first half of the nineteenth century set up organized
production, shows that textile production was undergoing the
process of the "genesis of the industrial capitalist." About
this capitalist, Marx wrote: "Doubtless many small guild-
masters, and yet more independent small artisans, or even
wage-labourers, transformed themselves into small capitalists
and (by gradually extending exploitation of wage-labour and
corresponding accumulation) into full-blown capitalists."[27]
This process was marked by its gradualness, but it was precisely this gradualness that characterized the genesis of the
capitalist even in the most rapidly developing branches of
textile production in the Balkans.

At the beginning of the nineteeth century, the minimum
prerequisites for capitalist relations were already generally
present and required only those decisive measures that would
expand their scope and impose them over the whole territory.
These emerging capitalist relations, however, did not encounter the set of circumstances that would hasten the transformation of the feudal mode of production into a capitalist one
that would shorten the period of transitional forms. Instead
they came into conflict with the existing feudal arrangements.
Thus, these nascent capitalist relations were restrained by
the activity of a state that had taken up the defense of the
feudal system as a whole. One of the most typical features
of the primitive accumulation of capital elsewhere was that
the process had, for those concerned, the full support of the
state. The individuals involved were presented with the huge
potentials of the state for the acquisition of resources from
within and from without the country itself. But instead of
enjoying these kinds of opportunities, the peoples inhabiting
the Ottoman Empire were exposed to colonial robbery. Furthermore, and perhaps to an even greater extent, both the state
itself and the feudal class subjected the bearers of new
capitalist relations to incredible larceny, to constant
extortion, and even to murder. It was for this reason that
capitalist relations could not take the upper hand and claim
a strong position in the economy of the Balkan countries
before their liberation from Ottoman rule.

This discussion of the nascence of capitalism and the
origins of workers and capitalists must necessarily deal with
the thorny question of the primitive accumulation of capital
in the Balkan lands. First of all, it should be recalled
that "primitive accumulation" was not a term created by Marx.
According to Marx, it was introduced to play a role similar
to that played by the concept of original sin in theology, to

explain the appearance of wealth and poverty at some point in
the distant past. Marx himself, furthermore, decisively
rejected any idealistic understanding of the concept itself
of "primitive accumulation"; rather, he demonstrated the role
of "conquest, enslavement, robbery, murder, briefly, force" in
actual history.[28]

Having chosen England as the classic capitalist country
for the analysis that would reveal the course of primitive
accumulation, Marx described the usurpation of landed property by the destruction of feudal land relations that made
possible the acquisition of the right to contemporary (i.e.,
bourgeois) private ownership of land that had previously
been subject solely to a feudal right. Clad in the form of a
law whose direct result was the creation of a proletarian
army placed outside this law, usurpation and force marked the
source of the mass of hired labor in England.

The other side of primitive accumulation--the concentration of huge amounts of capital--was also the sum total of
methods similarly based on the most brutal force exercised
under the cover of the state or by the state directly. Chief
among these methods were the colonial system, the slave trade,
the system of state debt and loans, the contemporary fiscal
system, and protectionism. Thanks to the plunder of colonies,
fortunes sprang up like mushrooms in the aftermath of a warm
shower, often without the investment of a single shilling.
Slave trade, another element of primitive accumulation, contributed to the concentration of incredible amounts of capital
during the early manufacturing stage of capitalism at a time
when, as Marx wrote, commerce still enjoyed hegemony over
industry.

Primitive accumulation had become a historical necessity
because the transformation of the "small guild-master, and yet
more independent small artisans, or even wage-labourers . . .
into small capitalists and then . . . [into] full-blown
capitalists"[29] was a very slow process, one that was not
responsive to the great demands of the developing world market. "The snail's pace of this method," wrote Marx, "corresponded in no wise with the commercial requirements of the
new world-market that the great discoveries of the end of the
fifteenth century created."[30]

More specifically, primitive accumulation occurred during
a period in the development of capitalist relations that was
characterized by the application of these special methods, and
ended with the domination of the capitalist mode of production in major countries. Therefore, as a historical step in
the development of the capitalist system, primitive accumulation did not occur at the same time as the emergence of
capitalist relations in different countries. As Marx himself

wrote, capitalist relations were born as early as the fourteenth and fifteenth centuries in the cities of the Mediterranean (i.e., in the Italian republics) and, though more
sporadically, in other European countries (and in Byzantium
as well, according to some authors). But Marx dated the true
start of the capitalist era from about the sixteenth century.[31] Marx certainly did not doubt that in such countries
as Italy there was a separation of the direct producer from
the means of production and that the accumulation of capital
there was just as much the result of theft as it was in England, but he did not include Italy in the countries that participated in the epoch of primitive accumulation. "The
different momenta of primitive accumulation," wrote Marx,

> distribute themselves now, more or less in chronological
> order, particularly over Spain, Portugal, Holland,
> France, and England. In England at the end of the seven-
> teenth century they [i.e., methods of primitive accumu-
> lation] arrive at a systematical combination, embracing
> the colonies, the national debt, the modern mode of
> taxation, and the protectionist system. These methods
> depend in part on brute force, e.g., the colonial system.
> But they all employ the power of the state, the con-
> centrated and organized force of society *to hasten . . .*
> *the process of transformation of the feudal mode of*
> *production into the capitalist mode and to shorten the*
> *transition.* [Emphasis added][32]

Primitive accumulation began with the application of a
number of coercive measures that within a short period of
time severed the link between the direct producer and the
land and compelled him, as Marx wrote, to shoulder the yoke
of hired slavery. This happened because the enormous needs
of the world market could not be satisfied either by the
commodity production of feudal society or by those rudiments
of capitalist production that had existed up to that point.
Accordingly, the view here is that primitive accumulation was
a historical category with a clearly established chronological
limit and with its own definite methods. It speeded up the
slow process of the genesis of capitalism and represented a
kind of "dawn of capitalism," a period when the capitalist
mode of production was being consolidated in the world's most
important countries, and hence became a universal socioeconomic formation.

    As a historical category, primitive accumulation thus
had a definite content that did not coincide simultaneously
or substantively with the capitalist relations that had
sprung up in different countries. It might be argued that
primitive accumulation was identical with the genesis of

capitalism in general. To accept that argument, however,
would mean that one would have to speak about it every time
that capitalist relations appeared and were consolidated in
this or that country, be it in the past or in the present (in
the period of the decline of the capitalist mode of production). As noted above, primitive accumulation was not (and
is not) that kind of ubiquitous phenomenon. Summarizing most
generally, primitive accumulation was a system of circumstances that came to life during the adolescent stage of
capitalism to quicken, by definite means and within given
boundaries, the establishment of the conditions necessary for
the consolidation of capitalist formation.

                              * * *

     It now remains to examine some general connections
between the genesis of capitalist relations in the Ottoman
state and the question of primitive accumulation.
     During the height of its power, the Ottoman Empire cre-
ated such a unilaterally favorable position for Western
merchants that it engendered the situation through which, by
the late nineteenth century, it would be transformed into a
dependent and semicolonial country. So bad did the situation
become that the only individuals who failed to receive monopolistic privileges and concessions were those who did not ask
for them. To cite but one example, the commercial treaty
signed in the 1830s between England and the Ottoman state
bore all the signs of a colonizer's act.[33]
     By the same token, it was the demand for tariffs and for
protectionism that acted as the first manifestation of the
awakened economic thought of both the subjugated Ottoman
population and of the more progressive Turkish public figures.
For decades during the nineteenth century such demands filled
the many newspapers and periodicals published in the Ottoman
Empire. But this public outcry proved unable to overcome the
parochialism and venality of the Turkish rulers. And it could
not subsequently overcome the connections between these
leaders and the foreign capital on which they were dependent.
     One element of primitive accumulation to which Marx
attached the utmost importance had to do with the general
fiscal policy of the state, its taxation system, and the
system of state debts and borrowing. Although there is no
need here to establish the parasitical nature of the Ottoman
tax system, especially the manner in which its taxes were
collected, it would be worthwhile once again to examine the
question of the target toward which state resources were
directed. Did not these resources in whole or in part flow
into the hands of the capitalist class? And did not these
resources thus serve, to some greater or lesser extent, capi-

talist development in the Ottoman Empire? The answer to both
questions is generally no. The resources that in various
ways were extracted from the peoples of the Ottoman Empire
were primarily used to satisfy the needs of the Ottoman feudal
elite and the central power. To all intents and purposes,
furthermore, these funds were spent without any application
to production. In most cases the emerging capitalists and
the representatives of the subjugated peoples were locked in
deep conflict with the Ottoman feudal system. The opening of
several state enterprises simply illustrates that possibilities for economic development were open to the Ottoman
government, but they were rarely exploited.

Actually, it was precisely the area of state finances
that, toward the middle of the nineteenth century, became the
chief target for the encroachments of the capitalist states of
the West. By the second half of the century the lion's share
of the moneys collected by the Ottoman state was passing
directly into the hands of these Western states, and their
governments had set up organs of their own to supervise the
collection of these funds. A similar fate met the loans
concluded by the Ottoman state. The "Ottoman debt" was nothing more than billions of francs bled from the whole population of the Ottoman Empire. Often extracted by force, these
huge amounts of money were concentrated in England, France,
and other countries that, in economic terms, had greatly out-
distanced the Ottoman Empire.

The Balkan provinces of the Ottoman Empire thus lacked
all of the methods of primitive accumulation as established
by Marx, and they lacked as well its basic result--the consolidation into a position of predominance of the capitalist
means of production. To speak, therefore, of primitive
accumulation in this case is to confuse that concept with the
simple appearance of capitalist relations. Rather than
"primitive accumulation" one would do better to use such
phrases as "the appearance of capitalist relations" or "the
genesis of capitalism" to describe, with the help of terminology taken from Marx, the accumulation of capital on a precapitalist basis and the stratification of small-commodity
producers. Inherent in every feudal society, these processes
inevitably led, at a certain state of development, to the
appearance of the most primitive forms of capitalist production.

To insist on the use of the phrase "primitive accumulation" to stress that theft forms the basis of the capitalist
activities of each and every entrepreneur and that all wealth
comes from draining the vitality of countless people (something that is indisputable) is thus simply to set up an
artificial barrier that hinders the discovery of the incredi-

ble variety of the forms and methods produced by socioeconomic
development and by the genesis of capitalism in particular.
To be sure, the variety of forms that marked the transition
from feudalism to capitalism in various countries have to be
studied on the basis of Marxist laws of economic development.
But this does not mean that those methods of primitive
accumulation noted by Marx for England and for other Western
European states should be held up as rigid models for each
and every country (especially those that in the middle of the
twentieth century have still failed to achieve mature capitalism).

The emergence and development of capitalist relations in
the Balkan countries under Ottoman rule proceeded under the
conditions of the existing world capitalist system. The
involvement of the Balkans in the European and world capitalist markets could not but have a strong effect on the socioeconomic processes that chiefly affected the Balkan peoples.
At the same time, these factors produced changes in the
Ottoman feudal system and state. Keeping all of this in mind,
the task here is to explore facts and processes--that is, the
variety of forms and methods of capitalist development--to
determine the characteristic features of the genesis and
consolidation of capitalist relations in the Balkans, a
process that had to take place in a complex and difficult
situation--that is, under the domination of a feudal system
that had a distrustful or hostile attitude to the new phenomena, and in a situation where it endured the consequences
of a world capitalist system that had already been established.

12. THE DEVELOPMENT OF HANDICRAFTS AND GUILDS

Capitalist industry in the Ottoman Empire blazed its way
primarily in the textile branches of production on the basis
of property and social differentiation of small-commodity producers. However, the differentiation of capitalist elements
took place more slowly in the Ottoman Empire than in the West,
and also unlike in the West, early capitalist enterprises in
the Ottoman Empire were intertwined with artisan workshops.
As is known, Marx related the entire history of capitalist
manufacture to the initial period of capitalism, the period of
simple cooperation when manufacture was still in a rudimentary
state.[1] About these "handicraft beginnings of manufacture,"
Marx wrote as follows with regard to the mode of production:
"manufacture . . . in its earliest stage is hardly to be distinguished from the handicraft trades of the guilds otherwise
than by the greater number of workmen simultaneously employed

by one and the same individual capital. The workshop of the
medieval master handicraftsman is simply enlarged".[2] Marx
repeatedly emphasized that the fundamental distinction
between the initial forms of capitalist industry and the
artisan workshops was a purely quantitative one.[3]

In the bourgeois historiography of the Balkan countries
the question of the appearance of the capitalist enterprises
among the artisans or the related matter of the decline of the
guild itself has not really been raised. To the extent that
such issues have been dealt with, they have been so only in
general terms of the total decline of the handicrafts and the
guilds that occurred in the nineteenth century from such
factors as European competition, a growing taxation burden,
and a changing way of life. Marxist historians, although they
have provided a clear interpretation of the role of the guild,
have not contributed toward the clarification of the guild's
historical development for a long time.

Most contemporary Bulgarian historians hold the view that
in the first half of the nineteenth century the craft guilds
in the Bulgarian lands either lost all their real importance
as an economic institution or, insofar as they retained a
certain position, that they hindered the country's capitalist
development. This idea has been expressed in the work of S.
Tsonev, whose study is otherwise exceptionally broad in scope.
In his work on the decline of the craft guild during the
Bulgarian Vŭzrazhdane, he has examined the process in question
chronologically. He has advanced the idea that the restrictive apparatus of the guilds quickly lost its real meaning,
and that the majority of the guild regulations that survived
had an advisory rather than an obligatory character.[4] Basically, Tsonev has concluded that toward the end of the eight-
teenth century the guilds had fallen into a constant state of
decay and that as early as the first half of the nineteenth
century they lost all of their significance. The continued
"authority" and "respect" accorded the esnafs was due to the
public functions that the guild performed in the nineteenth
century.

Handicrafts and guilds in Serbia, because of the different socioeconomic conditions that existed in Serbian lands and
the establishment early in the century of an autonomous
Serbian principality, had a somewhat different fate. The
Belgrade scholar N. Vučo has examined the nineteenth-century
history of these guilds and shown how in the second quarter of
the century the influx of Serbian craftsmen from Austria
reinvigorated these institutions. The Serbian guilds also
received the sanction of the state. It was only later that
they began to decline.[5]

Contemporary Turkish scholars, meanwhile, have been

dealing with the state of handicrafts in Anatolia, linking
their decline both to changes that were taking place in the
nineteenth-century Ottoman Empire and to the country's
general backwardness that came in the wake of the unequal
trade treaties with Western Europe. In his study on the
working class in Turkey, O. Sencer has also examined the conditions of capitalist development in the Ottoman Empire.[6]

* * *

Given this somewhat sparse historiographic background,
the main goals of this chapter will be to show the internal
changes that were taking place in the guild and the place of
the guild in the economic life of the Balkan provinces of the
Ottoman Empire in the first half of the nineteenth century,
then to determine the extent to which the guilds hindered the
development of capitalist relations in industry and to clarify
the relationship between entrepreneurs and guilds.

Since the preparation of aba and braid was one of the
oldest and most widespread of the handicrafts, and highly
important to the Balkan economy, the guilds involved in their
production will be our focus in this discussion. The centers
of aba and braid production were the most vigorous of the
Bulgarian National Revival and it was there that the first
manufacture and factory production appeared. Accordingly, any
weakening of the guilds would have taken its earliest and
fullest forms in these handicrafts. Changes in the guild
organization of these branches of production are most suitable
for study and analysis.

Aba-making was initially an exclusively urban handicraft,
and at first the abacıs usually worked on orders with material
supplied by their clients. With the growing division of labor
between the city and the village, however, and when a greater
specialization of handicrafts appeared in the cities, the aba
craft began a new stage of its development. The abacıs now
started to produce clothing with their own material, material
that they themselves did not prepare but that they purchased,
chiefly from peasants, gradually involving the peasants in
the productive life of the country. Market relations also
expanded, and the social division of labor deepened. Other
craftsmen (fullers, dyers, etc.) became specialized in cities
and villages in connection with the shaping of aba into
various kinds of clothing, and village weavers also appeared.
Meanwhile, the abacıs had ceased to rely solely on the local
market, and where circumstances permitted, were soon producing for fairs and for more distant markets. This, then, was
how aba-making generally evolved, although it reached different levels of development in various parts of the Balkan
Peninsula.

The Plovdiv area had the most highly developed aba pro-

duction in the Bulgarian lands, and one of its features was
the early combination of individually contracted work with
production meant for sale at fairs. As early as the mid-sixteenth century the aba made in Plovdiv enjoyed a wide popularity both inside and outside the country. In 1550, an
Italian traveler described Plovdiv as one of the principal
centers of wool and aba production in the Ottoman Empire:
"Here, at the time of the feast day of the Holy Trinity, merchants from all over Turkey gather, for this area is known
both for the finest wool in all of Turkey and for its abundance; the best aba of Turkey is made here, [and it] is
exported to Syria--to Damascus and as far as Aleppo."[7] The
Turkish government also took an interest in the aba production
of Plovdiv.[8] Probably as early as the sixteenth century, it
began to use Plovdiv aba for clothing for the army. Evliya
Çelebi, who visited Plovdiv in 1652, wrote in the most
flattering terms about the work of the abacıs, declaring that
they were "very good masters." He described the preparation
of various kinds of broadcloth--white, black, and other colors
--as a "specialty of this city."[9]

The rich Thracian valley constituted a raw material base
for the development of those economic activities involved in
the processing of agricultural goods.[10] The area's wool, for
example, for a long time fully met both local needs and the
constantly expanding export trade. In the fifteenth and
sixteenth centuries this trade was totally controlled by
merchants from Dubrovnik,[11] but in the seventeenth century it
passed into the hands of local merchants who were acting as
middlemen for Western European countries.[12] It was not until
the seventeenth century, when France increased its purchase of
wool from this area by 300 or 400%, that it became necessary
to look for wool in other parts of the country and in Wallachia and Moldavia.[13]

By the eighteenth century aba production in the city of
Plovdiv itself further expanded, but it was not able to meet
a demand that never ceased to grow. The supply of the
increasing Ottoman markets gradually came to include such
neighboring cities as Tatar Pazardzhik, Pirdop, and
Koprivshtitsa. In the early nineteenth century a new territorial specialization took shape in the aba-related trades.
Whereas the abacıs of Plovdiv dealt with the sewing of garments, and the artisans of the Rhodope villages wove the aba
itself, the settlements in the foothills of the Balkan
Mountains became the center of a newly independent craft,
braidmaking (*gaitandzhiistvo*).

The introduction of the iron-toothed wheel--the machine
used to prepare braid--in the second quarter of the nineteenth
century transformed gaitandzhiistvo into one of the most
important branches of the textile industry in the Bulgarian

lands, and this activity acted as a powerful lever for the economic upsurge of Kalofer, Karlovo, Sopot, and Kazanlŭk.[14] From the end of the eighteenth century on the entire region around Plovdiv functioned as a vast workshop that operated not so much for the local market as for the markets of the whole Ottoman Empire.[15]

Exactly how much of the aba made in Plovdiv and its district was exported cannot be determined. However, the names of many Plovdiv abacıs give evidence both that the basic part of the aba production was sold in such distant markets as Istanbul and Asia Minor and that from the eighteenth century on this trade was carried out not by outside merchants but by the local producers themselves. The sobriquets or nicknames of contemporary aba producers usually corresponded to the city where they sold their wares,[16] and as the records of the Plovdiv abacı guild and of the Plovdiv metropolitanate show, some of these handicraftsmen bore such names as "Brusali," "Amaskhali," "Izmirli," "Kaiserli," "Erzerumli" (with three partners), "Diarbekirli," and "Khalepli." There were also more general sobriquets such as "Arabistanli" and "Industanli."[17] To cite a more striking example, the books of the Plovdiv metropolitanate for the early 1780s recorded an act of dissolution of a company involved in trade with India that was breaking up after the death of one of the partners in Calcutta.[18] Numerous abacıs also traveled to Syria. Deeds have been preserved on the partition of the property of a late eighteenth-century abacı concern that had a permanent representative in Damascus and in a few other Syrian cities.[19] The ties of Plovdiv with these areas were so close that in the early nineteenth century a Syrian aba dealer settled in Plovdiv.[20] Some time later he became the chief master of the city's abacı guild and was re-elected for ten years, from 1811-20 (exceptional in the guild practice of the abacıs).[21] At about the same time, in 1817, the last testir or public celebration of the abacıs in Plovdiv occurred, a celebration that drew the participation of more than one thousand masters, journeymen, and apprentices from the city and from the surrounding areas.[22]

As these details illustrate, what chiefly characterized the economic development of the Plovdiv area in the seventeenth and eighteenth centuries was the gradual blossoming of the textile crafts and the trade in these goods that supplied the markets of the Ottoman Empire. The ranks of the small middlemen and artisans gave birth to new entrepreneurs who wended their way through the thicket of various feudal restrictions and came to link the most backward parts of the country with the markets of the entire empire. Large fairs began to become general marketing centers, attracting mer-

chants from all parts of the empire and from Europe as well.
Woolen goods continued to claim a leading place in commerce,
holding their own against the export of cotton, tobacco, hides,
and even cereals. Meanwhile, the growing Ottoman trade with
Western countries was also falling gradually into the hands of
local merchants--Greeks, Bulgarians, Jews, and Armenians.

The actual volume of aba production in the Plovdiv region
is suggested by documents of the 1830s on the fulfillment of
government contracts. As a rule, these contracts were joint
ones for Plovdiv and Tatar Pazardzhik (which was also known as
the center of a major fair and which sent a considerable
amount of aba to Istanbul, Asia Minor, and Syria).[23] Thus,
in the 1830s the Turkish government purchased from Plovdiv and
Tatar Pazardzhik 70,000 rolls of both finished garments and
rough aba produced in the Rhodope villages.[24]

This large-scale marketing by the abacıs in the Plovdiv region had an imprint on the character of their production. The greater part of the population was engaged in the
preparation of woolen goods. Assisted by women and children,
the masters, journeymen, and apprentices worked from dawn to
dusk in the spring and summer months. In the autumn, the
masters and journeymen set forth for the south in large
caravans. If the cities of Asia Minor were the destination,
their journey would last at least a month. When they reached
their destination, the abacıs set up shop, for not only did
they sell their finished goods, they now fashioned into
garments those items that they had brought along in a half-
finished condition. They also took their merchandise into
adjacent small cities, and would sell their goods on credit.
At the end of their stay they obtained their money and
returned home. Even in the wealthiest abacı families, during
the same autumn and winter months, the women, children, and
old people would be making sashes and knitted woolen stockings
that enjoyed a good market among the Turks and Arabs of Asia
Minor.[25]

The abacıs of Koprivshtitsa, a center of large-scale
livestock husbandry, were linked closely with those of Plovdiv. In the early eighteenth century the herds and flocks of
the people of Koprivshtitsa amounted to tens of thousands of
head of cattle and sheep.[26] At the end of the same century
Koprivshtitsa was thoroughly destroyed by *kircalı* bands,[27]
but in the first and second decades of the nineteenth century
it recovered rapidly because most of its capital had remained
intact. The chief investments of the people of Koprivshtitsa
outside the settlement were either flocks of sheep on pasture
in Thrace or artisan goods sent by caravans for sale in
Istanbul and Asia Minor.[28] The economy of Koprivshtitsa was
dominated by its trade in agrarian commodities and by the

close ties between artisan production and commercial capital.
Vasil Aprilov, a leading Bulgarian merchant and activist who
had settled in Russia, visited Koprivshtitsa in 1837 and wrote
that "the inhabitants, about 5,000 in number, are engaged in
large-scale sheep raising, and in the most important places of
Turkey, in Constantinople and other cities, they trade in wool,
from which they also fashion various handmade articles, which
they sell in different places."[29] Their earlier sheep raising
was the reason why the Bulgarian abacıs of Koprivshtitsa,
together with the Plovdiv aba producers, were some of the
first to begin to serve the markets of the Ottoman Empire.

Sliven was another major center of Bulgarian abadzhiistvo,
one that was widely known throughout the whole Ottoman Empire.
The varied industry of this city drew the attention of merchants from Rumelia, from the Arab lands, from Persia, and
even from Europe.[30] In the 1820s and 1830s Sliven's month-long
fair was regarded, along with that in Uzundzhovo, as "the largest fair in European Turkey." Sliven also possessed a special
inn used by merchants from Anatolia and Austria in aba
trade.[31]

The Turkish authorities began to pay particular attention
to the production of aba in Sliven in the late 1820s, after
the establishment of a regular army. They sent a special
representative from Istanbul who in 1848 concluded a contract
with local abacıs for the sewing of 10,000 uniforms for the
army.[32] This official took up permanent residence in Sliven
to assure the uninterrupted production and regular delivery of
the finished goods.[33] A number of measures were also taken
to guarantee the supply of raw wool for local production
from other parts of the country.

Sliven, like Plovdiv, thus became one of the principal
suppliers of aba and aba garments for the Turkish army. In
the early 1850s, together with Kotel, Sliven was delivering
to the government from sixty to eighty thousand rolls a
year.[34] All of this led to the establishment of the first
textile mill in the Balkan possessions of the Ottoman Empire,
a mill constructed in 1836 by D. Zheliazkov with state
subsidies.[35] At mid-century, Sliven was processing 320,000
kilograms of wool, of which 80,000 kilograms were processed
industrially and turned into about 650,000 meters of cloth.
An additional 60,000 kilograms of wool were being used to
make another kind of coarse woolen cloth known as *kebe*.[36]

Another sign of the importance that the government
attached to the wool craftsmen of Sliven is that it chose
several master abacıs from this city to be sent to relay
their experience to the artisans in Erzurum.[37] The success
of Sliven's aba was due to good quality workmanship, its
fine dyes, and several other attributes of the cloth that

mirrored the city's good water and other favorable climatic
conditions. As Aprilov had written earlier, "the inhabitants
of Sliven are engaged in trade with Asia, Austria and Wallachia; they deal in very important woolen products that they
color with red and yellow dyes in a manner that is unknown in
other places and even in Europe, thanks, it seems, to the
properties of the water."[38]

The detailed report of a Russian consul that in June 1831
was sent by the Asiatic Department of the Russian Ministry of
Foreign Affairs to the Department of Manufacture and Domestic
Trade also disclosed the great importance of Sliven's textile
production. The report recommended the introduction into
Russia of the production of aba and kebe since "the demand for
these two commodities . . . is incredibly great throughout
Turkey and particularly Anatolia, but it is being met very
poorly and insufficiently." As the consul added, "the broadcloth which is called aba and yağmurluk of a certain level of
quality is being made only in [Sliven], [Kotel] and in several
settlements in their vicinity."[39]

Aba-making in Kotel and Zheravna developed in close
connection with the textile industry in Sliven. The settlement of Kotel had sprung up as late as the seventeenth
century, but it very quickly became important thanks to its
livestock husbandry.[40] From the second half of the eighteenth
century on, the making of aba became a differentiated handicraft engaging not only the population of Kotel itself, but
also women from surrounding villages who wove aba cloth
during the winter. Women later began to arrive from the
Zagora region (in the southern Sredna Gora Mountains) and
were hired for thirty kuruş a month.[41] In the 1830s Kotel was
exporting aba chiefly to the Dobruja and to the Black Sea
coast, although the Turkish government annually received
20,000 pieces from there. Kotel's best wool, however, was
sent to Sliven.[42]

The development of aba-making in Zheravna, which was
located close to Kotel, was similar. This settlement was also
a center of livestock husbandry that expanded to such an
extent that the Turks began to call it *Küçük Filibe* (Little
Plovdiv).[43] Some *kehâya*s (heads of shepherds' associations)
owned flocks of 10,000 and even 30,000 sheep. Gradually, the
population began to process a certain part of the wool and to
produce aba for export. By the 1840s aba-making had grown to
the extent that Zheravna abacıs opened workshops not only in
Zheravna but also in the cities along the Danube, and masters
from Zheravna could also be found in Istanbul and Izmir. One-
third of the population was engaged in the production of
handicraft articles--clothing, footwear, and so on.[44]

Together with the areas of Plovdiv and Sliven, Samokov

became the third major aba-making center in the Bulgarian
lands. For the eighteenth century period of this aspect of
Samokov's history, the only sources that have been preserved
are the names of individual abacıs that were recorded in the
register of the metropolitanate. For the nineteenth century,
however, material is available in a local history of the area,
which reveals that by the middle of that century a massive
production of aba goods had been organized in the city. To
supply this industry the raw aba was brought from Rhodope
villages and from Panagiurishte, while braid was made in
Samokov itself.[45] From Panagiurishte alone Samokov abacıs
purchased about 100,000 arshin of aba.[46] According to K.
Jireček, the Samokov workshops clothed two Turkish armies.[47]
The Samokov artisans were able to prosper rapidly and to overcome the strong competition of the already established Plovidiv
abacıs because they worked for the western markets of the
Ottoman Empire, chiefly for Bosnia, from where merchants came
and purchased Samokov's aba goods.[48] In the middle of the
nineteenth century the Panagiurishte abacıs were also working
for the same market.

In northern Bulgaria, abadzhiistvo was most widespread in
Tŭrnovo and Shumen. In Tŭrnovo the aba was prepared in the
city itself, but in insufficient quantities, and additional
aba had to be transported from Kotel and Sliven.[49] In the
mid-nineteenth century, in the words of a contemporary, there
were "some 60-70 workshops not including those of the poor
masters who worked at home or in workshops with [only] one or
two journeymen and apprentices each."[50] The finished garments
were sent to Ruse, Shumen, Tŭrgovishte, Sevlievo, and markets
in the Dobruja. In the early nineteenth century, braidmaking also developed somewhat, but in the middle of the same
century it began to decline as a result of competition from
Gabrovo.[51]

With the concentration of large garrisons in Shumen
starting in the second half of the eighteenth century, Shumen
too saw favorable conditions for producing clothing for the
army. Aba was brought from Kotel, Sliven, and Zheravna.[52]
At the turn of the century, travelers found that Shumen had a
well-developed aba handicraft with a considerable division of
labor. "In this town," wrote J. Bocage, "there are spinning
workshops, filatures, and tanneries. . . . Large amounts of
Turkish clothing are sewn from aba here and are sent to Constantinople and the large cities of the empire."[53] In the
middle of the nineteenth century, the Greek consul in Varna,
A. Vretos, wrote that Shumen possessed two textile mills for
aba and carpets. The carpets, like other woolen goods, were
much-sought commodities in Asia Minor.[54]

The abadzhiistvo of Tŭrnovo and Shumen also went beyond

the boundaries of the local market, and part of what these
cities produced was sold at fairs. These abacıs, however, did
not have the flourishing development that characterized this
handicraft in the other regions.

In summary, in the first half of the nineteenth century,
aba handicraft in the Bulgarian lands had attained different
levels of development. There were abacıs who worked on order
in their own workshops, and others who had no such workshops
but went to sew garments in the houses of their customers.
Other abacıs, having satisfied local needs, began to sell part
of their merchandise at neighboring fairs. But the greatest
prosperity in the first half of the nineteenth century came to
those artisans who produced chiefly for mass sales at both
fairs and distant markets.

* * *

But if trade with distant markets was so decisive for the
development of the aba craft, was not this industry adversely
affected by the general economic decline in the nineteenth-
century Ottoman Empire caused by foreign competition? One
immediate answer to this important question is that the general decline of the handicrafts in the Ottoman Empire did not
affect the bases of aba production that quickly or directly.
There were several factors at work here. First, in the late
eighteenth and early nineteenth century, Ottoman crafts continued to hold their own in the face of foreign competition.
Second, the commodity involved--the aba itself--also helped
thwart the immediate effects of foreign competition.

The continued prosperity of the Balkan textile industry
is borne out by the data on the commerce that the European
states conducted with the Ottoman Empire at that time.[55]
France and England controlled practically all of the imports
and exports of Turkish textiles in this period. In the eighteenth century France had ranked first in the foreign trade of
the Ottoman Empire, with the core of its exports composed of
expensive fabrics that were sent to the Ottoman Empire in ever-
increasing quantities, until from the 1720s to the 1760s they
had increased fourfold.[56] In absolute figures, to be sure,
the volume of this trade was not very high. Nevertheless, on
the eve of the French Revolution, French exports to Istanbul
were estimated at 6.6 million francs, as opposed to Turkey's
exports to France, estimated at 3 million francs.[57] The
French Revolution, Napoleon's wars, the Continental Blockade,
and France's subsequent defeat disrupted these brisk commercial ties and led to the displacement of France by England. In
the 1830s, wool exports from the Balkan Peninsula to France
failed to reach even 1,000 bales a year, falling from 3,000
bales yearly in the second half of the eighteenth century.[58]

There are few sources on the eighteenth-century trade
between the Ottoman Empire and England, and one has to rely
on the findings of a Turkish researcher who has written that
"no cotton textiles in amounts worth mentioning were exported
from England to Turkey."[59] By the 1820s, however, as noted by
the traveler D. Urquart, British exports of cotton textiles
into Turkey were increasing at an incredibly brisk rate. In
1828 these imports were estimated to be worth 10,384 pounds
sterling, a sum that in four years was to increase tenfold (to
105,615 pounds sterling).[60]

Up to the end of the 1820s, therefore, industry in the
Balkan provinces of the Ottoman Empire had no really strong
competition from foreign goods. In the late eighteenth century even the cotton and silk industries (which were to fall
under the blows of foreign competition earlier than others)
were still not only meeting the basic needs of the country,
but were at least in part also producing for export.[61]

As the nineteenth century progressed, changes took place
in the trade of the Ottoman Empire. Raw materials started to
occupy an ever-increasing share of Ottoman exports, while
manufactured and industrial goods claimed a larger place in
its imports. Particularly deplorable in their consequences on
the state of Turkey's industry were the trade conventions of
1838 with England and France, treaties that prohibited the
establishment of internal monopolies and preserved low customs
duties (5%) on goods imported into Turkey.[62] If at that time
in the West the low overhead of large-scale capitalist industry displaced local cottage industry, the more so was this
true in the Ottoman Empire where a system of customs was
directed exclusively against local producers. This customs
system also included internal tariffs that were very high,
accounting for about 12% of the value of the goods. These
duties were collected in the form of *âmediýe*, *reftiye*,
mürüriye, *masdariye*, and other imports--and precisely in those
branches of production geared toward the larger market.[63]

Data published by the French Ministry of Agriculture
and Commerce from 1831 to 1851 and certain other information
as well illustrates the stronger penetration of French (and
other) commodities in Turkey after the 1830s (see table
25). Thus, France's exports to Turkey trebled, while its
imports increased by only one-third. At the same time,
British exports to Turkey more than trebled, and Britain was
increasingly displacing France. As shown by other sources,
the export of textile products from Britain to Turkey from
1825 to 1855 increased more than seven times over.[64]

Turkey was more and more becoming both a supplier of
foodstuffs and raw materials for the industry of European
countries and simultaneously "an open market for European
goods."[65] Foreign competition began to have a destructive

TABLE 25

TRADE OF FRANCE AND BRITAIN WITH THE OTTOMAN EMPIRE,
1831-1850

State	Years	Exports	Imports
		(To and from the Ottoman Empire, in francs)	
France	1831-36	16,600,000	15,000,000
	1841-45	47,500,000	19,500,000
Britain	1831	22,000,000	
	1850	78,000,000	

SOURCE: Mikhov, *Rapports consulaires français*, pp. 221-22.

effect on industry in the Ottoman state, particularly from
the 1830s on, when the industrial revolution in the West
entered its final stage. But rather than occurring suddenly,
the crisis gripped different handicrafts gradually.[66] Those
large cities and ports more directly connected with European
trade were the ones to suffer most. Greater vitality was
shown by those Balkan industries that served local markets,
especially in the regions located far from the major thoroughfares of the country, and by those branches of production that
were linked to the specific needs of the population.
    In the interior of Asia Minor, as well, aba and the
finished products of the abacis continued to find a market
that allowed this handicraft to retain its former importance.
Even in the 1850s, and in individual cases even later (such
as during the construction of the Suez Canal), the demand for
the coarse but durable Bulgarian cloaks, clothing, and stockings continued to nurture aba production, at least for a
time.[67] Meanwhile, the important domestic aba market in the
Bulgarian lands--largely composed of the rural population--
remained practically unchanged. These factors imparted
stability both to aba production and to the abacı guilds.[68]

* * *

    The oldest and most developed esnaf among the textile
crafts in Bulgaria was the guild of the Plovdiv aba-makers,
whose preserved registers date to 1685. There is every reason
to believe that the abacı guild in Plovdiv, as all craft
guilds in the Ottoman Empire, was marked by strict internal
discipline, an obligatory training period for apprentices and
journeymen, and the regulated distribution of raw materials
and output.

Toward the end of the eighteenth century and in the first half of the nineteenth century a number of new developments were recorded in the guild book of the Plovdiv abacis that illustrate the increased activity of the artisans and the gradual expansion of the guild's autonomy in resolving numerous questions in defense of its egalitarian principles. The analysis here shall examine those essential measures that were linked both to the regulation of production and to the application of equalizing principles, and can thus be taken as the most reliable indicators of how the guild's role was changing, particularly how relations developed and were shaped between the guild and capitalist entrepreneurs.

If information is summarized on newly appointed masters by decades, for example, an interesting picture emerges (see fig. 6). From 1685, the number of newly promoted masters constantly decreases (from 147 in the decade 1685-95 to 82 in the decade 1765-75). The occasionally slower rate of decrease and even a temporary rise of the curve (1705 to 1715 and 1725 to 1735) does not alter the basic downward trend, which precipitated a prolonged reduction in the number of masters until the end of the eighteenth century. The lowest point in the decrease was in the decade of 1765-75. Not a single master was promoted in 1768 or 1769; only two were promoted in 1770 and only one in 1771.[69] But toward the end of the eighteenth century and in the first decade of the nineteenth century the situation changed, and a sharp increase began in the number of newly promoted masters. This increase reaches its peak in the second decade of the nineteenth century, with 183 masters promoted from 1805 to 1815. It was precisely in this period of abaci upsurge, and specifically in 1817, that there occurred the largest gathering of abacis in Plovdiv, one involving more than 1,000 individuals. Soon after, however, in the 1820s, another downturn set in and continued at a much higher rate after the 1830s.

In all likelihood the growth and decline in the number of new masters was directly related to the development of the aba craft in neighboring Balkan cities. With every passing decade, the Plovdiv artisans had greater competition. This rivalry subsided only temporarily under the influence of the feudal strife that, at the turn of the century, caused the ruin of most of the Balkan Mountain settlements. By the second quarter of the nineteenth century, moreover, the activity of capitalist entrepreneurs also began to have an effect on the number of new masters.

More generally, however, conditions on the promotions of new masters should be regarded as the result of an effort to preserve the stability of the guild and the monopolistic position of its members. At the same time it was a sure sign of the increasing exploitation of the journeymen's labor.

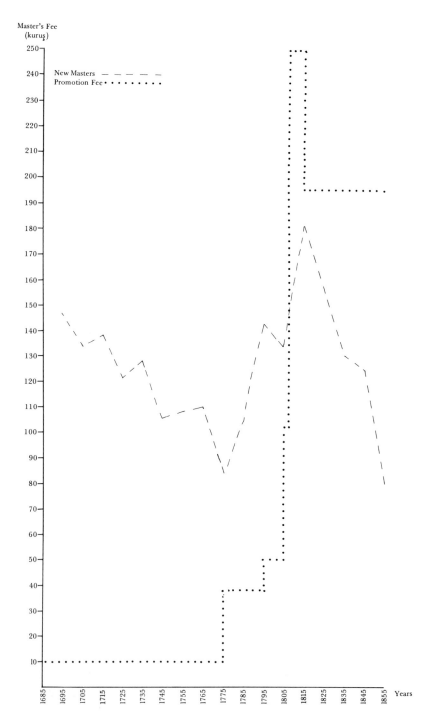

Master's Fee
(kuruş)

New Masters — — — — —
Promotion Fee • • • • • • • • •

Years

Fig. 6. Newly promoted masters of the abacı guild in Plovdiv, 1685-1855

Increases in the guild's entrance fee for masters and a
number of other regulatory provisions were signs that the
master craftsmen implemented a deliberate policy of regulating
the promotion of new masters. On his promotion every new
master had to pay an entrance fee into the guild treasury.
The size of the fee changed several times. From 1685 to 1773
it amounted to 10 kuruş, in 1773 it was raised to 40 kuruş,
and twenty years later it was increased to 50 kuruş. In 1805
the fee was again increased, to 100 kuruş, in 1807 to 250
kuruş, and in 1815 it was finally set at 200 kuruş.[70] The
devaluation of Turkish coins in the late eighteenth and in the
early nineteenth century undoubtedly affected the fee
increases,[71] but the greatest increases--those from 10 to 40
kuruş, from 50 to 100 kuruş, and from 100 to 250 kuruş--coin-
cided with the periods of strong decline in the number of
newly promoted masters (see fig. 6).

A number of measures of Plovdiv's abacı guild on the
regulation of production and exchange were also directed
toward controlling the growing competition. The arbitrary
opening of artisan workshops, for example, was prosecuted,
and by a decision of the 1706 general assembly of the guild,
the exercise of the aba craft without the agreement of the
guild itself was strictly forbidden. Violations of this rule
were punished not only by imposing the regular entrance fee,
but also with a fine of up to 200 kuruş.[72] At a time when
the normal receipts of the guild treasury rarely surpassed
200 kuruş, the size of this fine was itself sufficient
testimony to the strict character of the regulation in
question. (To cite comparative examples, in 1708 smaller
houses in Sofia were being sold for 25, 40, and 60 kuruş; and
for the care of orphans a judge of that time established a
daily expenditure of 2 akçe.)[73]

The defense of the corporate privileges of the masters
went even further when in 1789 the Plovdiv guild forbade journeymen from entering into partnerships with masters.[74] Until
that point such partnerships had not been rare.[75] In the same
year, moreover, the general assembly of the esnaf decided to
prohibit for two years any promotion of journeymen to masters.[76] The policy of the guild was directed toward increasing the length of training of journeymen, a measure that
created conditions for their exploitation as a hired labor
force.

A number of other late eighteenth-century regulations of
the Plovdiv abacı guild were also characteristic of the
rivalry between the artisans of this guild and the craftsmen
of neighboring settlements. The Plovdiv guild included dealers in canvas and also dyers, as well as makers of aba. A decision that the guild took in 1792 dealt explicitly with the

work of the dyers by establishing fixed and permanent prices
for the dyeing of wool, yarn, and canvas. A fine was to be
imposed on any master who sent merchandise for dyeing to Karlovo or Tatar Pazardzhik.[77] Clearly, this decision went far
beyond ordinary price fixing, but constituted an agreement
among masters of the several branches contained within a guild
in a particular city to eliminate competition from masters of
other cities. The guild's purview was thus being extended to
cover even nearby settlements.

A related but new agreement was reached in 1800. This
time the dyers of Karlovo and Kalofer came to Plovdiv and,
after negotiations with the Plovdiv dyers, obtained permission
to practice their craft as before, but only in their own settlements. This right fell to eighteen masters, with no one
else allowed to open a new workshop. The masters in question
were denied the right to receive merchandise or articles for
dyeing from the surrounding villages, and they were also forbidden from dyeing anything that belonged to inhabitants of
Plovdiv, even if the latter brought their goods to Karlovo and
Kalofer in person.[78]

All of this regulation mirrors the growth of competition
both among individual Plovdiv abacıs and, as soon as the
boundaries of the local market proved to be too narrow for the
guild's dyers, between Plovdiv artisans and the abacıs of
other Balkan settlements. The agreement between the abacıs
and dyers (who, to repeat, were members of the same guild in
Plovdiv) on the establishment of permanent prices meant a concession in favor of the abacıs, a concession they won in
return for their refusal to use the service of dyers in other
cities. It is important to note again that the esnaf's regulation went beyond the city itself to cover a surrounding
area.

* * *

These developments formed the background that explains
the famous ferman of 1773 of Sultan Mustafa III (1757-74),[79]
for this decree has to be regarded as an attempt by the central authorities to assist the guilds to retain their position
through the strict and state-supported application of regulatory provisions.

Such a motive permeates the ferman's very text. The
decree states how guild spokesmen who were descended from the
respected elders of the guilds had turned to the sultan with
the plea that he issue "a most exalted decree" forbidding the
opening of workshops by apprentices who had "not yet been
girded with a sash" and who had not sufficiently mastered the
craft or did not possess the necessary permit. On the basis
of this plea, the sultan decided to forbid local authorities,

via the ferman, to allow persons who lacked qualifications
and the required permit to open workshops:

> According to the fundamental rules in force since
> olden times among the tanners and other groups of arti-
> sans in the Ottoman possessions . . . the apprentices who
> have not yet been girded with a sash and who have not
> acquired the necessary experience [have no right to open
> a shop] and in this sense [the petitioners] beg for a
> sacred order that [for these individuals], as long as
> they are not sufficiently trained, have not been girded
> with a sash, and have not been supplied with the required
> permit, the opening of a shop and bench be prohibited
> and abolished. That is why I have decreed that upon
> receipt of my sacred order you make inquiries in accord-
> ance with its provisions and that you not permit the
> opening of a shop by him who is not girded with a sash
> and has no shop according to the customs that still in
> olden times were in force among artisans.

The ferman further enjoined local authorities from allowing
any external intervention when corporal punishment was being
meted out to the violators of the law.

The ferman was sent to all kadıs in the country. It was
registerd as well in a Greek translation with essentially
the same content but with the first part rendered more
concisely and with special emphasis on the exclusive power of
the guild leadership to render judgment (it could even apply
corporal punishment). The Greek text also had a more insist-
ent prohibition against outside intervention. [80]

The ferman of Mustafa III, therefore, did not mark the
start of a new organizational period in the life of the guilds
but was brought about by the complaints of guildsmen themselves, who were unable to implement the regulations that had
been established. The ferman ordered the Ottoman bureaucracy
to give full support to the application of those guild
decisions that sought to preserve the existing order. Thus,
state action was combined with the efforts of the overwhelming
majority of the guildsmen in the direction of guild consolidation. In the second half of the eighteenth century, the
restrictive measures of the guilds once again received state
approval, and it would be possible to cite a number of cases
involving the search for administrative protection against
the competition of artisans who opened shops without appropriate permission. [81]

* * *

How the guilds were thus trying to maintain their old
ways in the face of new challenges and pressures is even more

clearly expressed in an 1805 declaration of the Plovdiv
abacıs, a valuable and hitherto unstudied document.[82] The
preamble to the declaration reveals that abacı masters had
decided to lay down rules to regulate the way of life of the
guildsmen because the order established by the old masters was
being trampled upon. Traditions and laws were no longer being
observed and the guild was threatened with decay, a circumstance that dictated first of all that masters should act
together so as to avoid harming their common interests:
"Together, all masters--and the new and those who are to
follow--should have mutual solidarity and love and they should
not speak against each other and harm one another, be it here
in the motherland or abroad. . . ." Masters, furthermore,
should regularly participate in guild meetings. "When a
meeting [lonca] takes place, let no one ever speak out of
complaisance or flattery or ingratiatingly, but let everyone
speak what is right and what in God and in his soul he finds
proper. [T]he younger shall accept and take examples from
the older and shall not speak words that should not be uttered
nor bad words before the elder. . . ."

A separate provision specified the rate of admission
fees: "He who shall become a new master shall pay 50 kuruş
for [this promotion] if he is a native and 100 kuruş if he
is a stranger, and he must give 100 para to the çavuş as well.
No master from another nationality or another race shall be
admitted."[83]

The declaration also strictly defined the conditions
under which a partnership could be established, allowing such
partnerships only between masters of the same guild: "A
master who wants to become a partner can become a partner
only with another master of the guild, but he may not become
a partner, either openly or secretly, with a journeyman or
with someone else who is not a master of the same guild.
Only if he is the son of a master and [even in those cases
only] with the permission of the guild."

The spirit of equalizing regulation likewise shaped the
terms of the supply of raw materials and of commerce: "None
of the masters is permitted to go to the mountains or to
travel from inn to inn to buy aba, but let everyone wait in
his premises or in his workshop, and let those who sell it
[aba] bring it around as before. And let he who has purchased
aba give part of it to another master if he asks for it."
Somewhat later on the document states: "Let no master ruin
another's market by slandering his wares or by telling his
client that he himself is selling at a lower price."

The document's final two provisions concern journeymen
and apprentices. They had to work two years without pay and
an additional year at mutually agreed wages. Only then could

the pupil leave his master. It was strictly forbidden for one
master to entice apprentices away from another master. The
journeyman, moreover, was denied the right to buy material on
his own account, nor could a master buy it for him. The
provisions of the Plovdiv declaration were obligatory for all
masters, with infringements and concealment liable to punishment by the entire guild. This declaration was signed by all
masters and received the approval of the bishop of Plovdiv.

Elaborated as they were in detail, these rules clearly
reflect the fundamental principles on which the abacı guild
rested. Both the declaration's motives and its basic provisions were aimed at protecting the privileged position of
the masters. This was the spirit, for example, of the
decisions to impose a double entrance fee for outsiders, to
deny access to persons of another nationality, and to allow
a master's son to become a partner without having himself
been proclaimed a master. Violating the equalizing principles
was absolutely forbidden and the guild restricted the attempts
of masters to increase their income by methods contrary to
accepted guild practice--that is, lowering or raising the
prices of goods, enticing buyers, or increasing the duration of
the working period.[84] Similarly, all the words of respect for
the old masters had but one purpose--to preserve and protect
the position that had been achieved by the main core of the
abacı guild.

Although the aim of these decisions was to keep the guild
as closed as possible and to protect the privileged status of
the guild's masters, some of the provisions also reveal how
the guild gradually adapted itself to the activity of those
members who, by infringing the various regulations, had begun
to expand the scope of their operations. There was, for
example, the prohibition against entry into partnership with
journeymen. This decision was taken as early as 1789, and in
the 1805 declaration it was supplemented with several new
provisions (e.g., that masters had no right to buy either
merchandise or raw materials on behalf of their journeymen).
In addition, masters were forbidden from purchasing themselves
the aba they needed--that is, they could not buy unlimited
amounts of raw materials. Such measures had an even more
anticapitalist character than those discussed above, since
they were aimed at thwarting the spread of latent capitalist
production.

As suggested by such provisions, certain individuals of
the guild for certain periods of time left their workshops and
traveled about the country in search of raw materials that
were better, cheaper, and available in larger quantities.
These artisans were thus able to reap additional benefits,
which could be increased even more if the master turned a
journeyman into his partner. But because he lacked a master's

title and capital, such a journeyman partner was in a subordinate position, which involved a change only in the form of
his exploitation by a master. Entrusting the supervision of
the workshop to his journeyman and partner, the master was
able to deal with the organizational and commercial aspects of
his enterprise. In other words, he was taking the first steps
toward becoming an entrepreneur. It was the effort to
forestall the transformation of individual abacıs into
capitalists, and to stop such practices, which were undermin-
ing the equality of production and trade among guild members,
that lay behind some of the measures taken by the Plovdiv
abacı guild.

An assessment of these rules would not be complete, however, without considering that the sale of goods in distant
markets was neither restricted nor subject to regulation. In
this respect the only provision that had various practical
consequences in one's own area and beyond its boundaries was
the prohibition against slander of the shortcomings (i.e., in
the merchandise) of another master and against causing him
harm abroad. In the domestic market, such a measure protected
against unfair competition, but abroad it meant that there was
nothing to stand in the way of a master's ability to obtain
additional profits wherever and whenever he could.

To a certain extent, moreover, the decisions concerning
apprentices and journeymen had a contradictory character. On
the one hand, they were aimed at reducing the potential competition of journeymen and apprentices--the future masters--
by establishing strict rules for their admission and period of
training. On the other hand, by fixing the maximum wages of
journeymen while at the same time not limiting their number
and the arbitrary use of their labor, the guild made it
possible for individual artisans to be enriched by the capitalist exploitation of the labor of minors and hired workers.

In summary, despite the provisions restraining capitalist
trends in the guild, the 1805 declaration of the Plovdiv
abacıs opened the way for such tendencies to be manifested in
the commerce in aba goods in other regions of the Ottoman
Empire. As a result, monetary capital was accumulating in the
hands of some abacıs, the differentiation of their property
was increasing, and foreign market conditions were convincing
these incipient entrepreneurs to organize the kind of production that would yield a mass output of goods of a standard
type.

This early adaptation of the Plovdiv guild to the
requirements of trade with distant markets also appeared among
the craftsmen of Tatar Pazardzhik. There, the artisan producers for distant markets were allowed to produce in the
manner they desired, while persons working for the domestic

market were denied the right to introduce any innovations into
their work. A decree of the abacı guild of Tatar Pazardzhik
illustrates the acceptance of certain new norms for those
abacıs whose output was destined for outside markets. "Who-
ever goes to Anatolia," this decree states, "shall make his
wares properly [i.e., in conformity with the expectations of
purchasers in Asia Minor], but those who do not go are not
permitted to sew new kinds of clothing, they are to sew the
way it has been done since long ago. . . . Those who are to
go to Anatolia are not to be permitted to sell even a single
piece here."[85]

The abacıs and *gaitancıs* (braidmakers) of the city of
Karlovo followed a pattern similar to that of the Plovdiv
guildsmen, and their guild records also express the trends
that appear in the 1805 declaration of the Plovdiv abacıs.[86]
The preserved registers of the Karlovo aba-makers cover the
period after the 1830s, a period when the Karlovo guildsmen
continued to be dependent on those of Plovdiv.[87] At the same
time, however, this was one of the most interesting periods
in the history of the Karlovo artisans, the time when the use
of the mechanized iron-toothed wheel really took hold in the
production of braid. The introduction of this machine led to
great changes in the distribution both of labor and of
capital.

The development of the textile industries in Karlovo,
however, did not follow exactly the road blazed by the other
centers of abacı production, for this city was greatly
affected by the special economic relationships that had been
established at that time in the economically advanced regions
of southern Bulgaria. Economically linked with Plovdiv, the
Karlovo abacıs quickly experienced all of the good and bad
developments that affected this territory. After the turn-
of-the-century feudal strife, which disrupted economic life
primarily in small settlements like Karlovo that were located
on the southern slopes of the Balkan Mountains and were
difficult to defend, the abacı handicraft continued to grow,
but it now found itself dependent on the aba industry of
Plovdiv, Tatar Pazardzhik, and Sliven, where there were firmly
established traditions and secure markets. Accordingly, an
increasing part of Karlovo's population switched over from
making aba and aba clothing to the preparation of yarn and
braid. This shift was favored both by geographical conditions
and by the great demand for braid that followed upon the
expanding trade in woolen clothing and other commodities.[88]
The widespread acceptance of the machined wheel after the
1830s was also pivotal for the upsurge of braidmaking.[89]
With its introduction, braidmaking became, as a cottage
industry, the basic livelihood of the population of Karlovo.

Male gaitancis appeared who worked with metal machines,
although of a primitive kind. Meanwhile, the increased
output of braid in turn brought about a greater demand for
yarn. The local wool proved insufficient, and the artisans
were forced to obtain yarn and wool from nearby villages.[90]
This yarn was prepared by hand by women spinners whom the
machine owners gradually transformed into an army of intensely
exploited workers. A considerable stratification occurred,
with the women spinners standing in sharp contrast to the
small producers who were organized in the guild and owned
the machines.

The introduction of the metal braidmaking wheel also
altered the relationship between artisans in other handicrafts. Until its spread, the abacis played the central role
in Karlovo's textile industry. After the introduction of the
wheel, roles were switched, and the gaitancis came to dominate
the guild. Nevertheless, both groups of artisans continued
to be members of a common guild.[91]

The activity of this combined guild of abacis and gaitancis in Karlovo occurred during the period when practically all
of that city's output was destined for markets in Asia Minor.
Several decisions of a general meeting of the guild in the
1830s strictly regulated the manner in which yarn and raw
material were delivered to the gaitancis and abacis. Abacis
who used braid in their work were not permitted to search it
out or to buy it directly from gaitancis. Even more characteristic were the guild's decisions that established the
exact size of a roll of braid and prohibited the use of poor-
quality braid. At a general meeting on July 12, 1836, for
example, the guild explicitly forbade the purchase of lower
quality braid from Pirdop and its intermixture with that of
Karlovo. It is interesting to note that the guild promised
a reward to persons who exposed violators of this rule, while
intercession on their behalf was punished with a fine.[92]

These rules came several decades later than the 1805
declaration of the Plovdiv abacis, but they are permeated with
the same regulative spirit. The aba producers were forbidden
to obtain their own supply of braid direct from the workshops
located in the outskirts of Karlovo, and the gaitancis in
turn could not buy yarn without the guild's permission. Furthermore, the procapitalist tendency expressed in the provisions concerning the quality of the merchandise were formu-
lated here much more clearly than in the Plovdiv declaration.

In the space of less than a year there were three occasions in Karlovo when guildsmen at general meetings discussed
the specifications that braid was expected to meet. These
deliberations were required not so much because of the
interests of the state, and not so much by a desire to weaken

internal competition, as by the effort to produce standard
merchandise geared to the needs of wholesale trade. The
question of the quality and type of braid was raised precisely
in the period when machines were being used for its mass
production, and when Karlovo (together with Kalofer) began to
be transformed into one of the most important centers for
braid production in the Ottoman Empire.

The decisions in question, which brought the traditional
norms ("braid of 50 cubits") into line with the standard of
the braid made in Kalofer ("of 80 cubits"), provided both the
artisans and merchants of Karlovo with access to already
established markets.[93] This same consideration also explained
the simultaneous decision of the gaitancıs of Karlovo to prohibit any admixture of poor-quality yarns and braid that might
lower the quality of the Karlovo braid in comparison to that
of Kalofer.

Thus, those equalizing that seemed most old-fashioned
were actually the result of a new phenomenon--a large number
of braid producers engaged in wholesale trade.

* * *

The arrangements of the abacı guild in Zheravna, another
well-known aba center, were similar. Discovering that the
demand for their wares by merchants was constantly declining,
in the 1840s the elders of the guild called several general
meetings at which it was decided not only to regulate the
size and appearance of the goods, but also to introduce a
special marking or stamp.[94] Similar meetings followed. The
guild introduced technical innovations to raise the quality
and reputation of the merchandise and fought to attract
customers. In these activities the guild constituted a
collective body whose authority and competence encompassed
the widest range of possible problems of esnaf life--from
questions of production to the relations between masters
and journeymen in conditions of developed commodity relations.

The registers of the artisans in such other aba-producing
centers as Sliven, Kotel, and Samokov have not been preserved.
But, as can be seen from the information already provided and
from other sources, the abacı guilds also were important to
the economic and social life of these cities. It is safe to
assume that their activity did not appreciably differ from
that of the abacıs and gaitancıs of Plovdiv and of the centers
located on the southern slopes of the Balkan Mountains.

In the first half of the nineteenth century Gabrovo, in
northern Bulgaria, emerged as one of the most highly industrialized settlements in the country. Braidmaking, which was the
foundation of this city's textile industry, did not appear as
an independent branch of production until the 1830s. From the

very beginning, however, braid production took on a manufacturing character with both a division of labor and the
exploitation of hired workers. Nevertheless, there also
existed a guild whose rules of discipline were obeyed even by
such a master merchant and manufacturer as Ivan Palpazanov,
who after the 1878 liberation of Bulgaria was to become a
leading industrialist. Despite being the owner of a centralized manufacture, in the 1860s Palpazanov was not only a
formal member of the guild who observed a number of its
regulations; he also became a guild elder.[95]

                            * * *

     In the first half of the nineteenth century, therefore,
the guilds of the most developed branches of Bulgaria's urban
economy constituted a real force in urban economic life.
Admittedly, the various aba-producing centers had not all
reached the same level of development. There were centers in
which this artisan activity served only the local market and
the property differentiation of the craftsmen involved failed
to go beyond the emergence of wealthier elements among guild
members, but there were other areas where social differentiation was clearly marked and where even entrepreneurs appeared.
     The role of the guild differed in these cases, but in
the first half of the nineteenth century it had not become
what one historian has described as merely a "cover used by
the urban administration for fiscal purposes."[96] On the
contrary, the guild statutes and registers, only some of
which have been cited here, lead to the unmistakable conclusion that in the first half of the nineteenth century the
guilds continued to be an obligatory form of organization for
the commodity producers in Bulgarian lands. On the one hand,
in cities with a longstanding aba industry, the guilds
expanded the scope of their activity. From the end of the
eighteenth century, they included in their competence an
ever larger number of questions concerning the preparation and
sale of merchandise that earlier had fallen within the purview
of state regulation and control. On the other hand, in the
new branches of production that appeared in the first half
of the nineteenth century, even when they had a manufacturing
character, the guild organization also appeared as a historical necessity.
     The question arises as to whose interests this regulation
served. Or, to put it more indirectly, how does the considerable role of the guild in urban economic life in the first
half of the nineteenth century relate to the development of
capitalist relations?
     Naturally, all guild members were directly interested in
expanded trade, and the regulations in question, which took

the form of decisions of the general meetings of guildsmen,
mirrored the involvement of numerous abacıs and gaitancıs in
the wholesale business. But certainly the greatest interest
in this trade was shown by those guildsmen who had set up considerable production or who concentrated in their hands the
export of finished output. It was they who insisted on the
acceptance of provisions to establish standardized merchandise
--and thereupon used these rules for their own benefit.

The problem of the social differentiation of the guildsmen has not hitherto been the subject of a special study, in
terms of either the formation of a guild elite or its nature
and character. For this reason, new information drawn from
several registers and other sources will be used in discussing
these matters here.

As shown by a comparison of material drawn from the
existing records of the aba guilds of Plovdiv, Karlovo, Zheravna, Etropole, Teteven, Shumen, and other cities, there was
an essential difference between the position of the abacıs
working to meet the needs of the local market and those who
produced for outside markets. Contrary to expectations, the
stronger guilds were those connected with distant markets.
Though it was expressed in other ways as well, their greater
vitality primarily took the form of both more extensive and
more varied regulative activity.

Cash balances are also evidence (albeit indirect) of the
strength of a given guild. In Shumen, according to information for the period after the 1830s, the treasury of the
tailors' guild rarely contained more than 10,000-15,000 kuruş
in cash and in vouchers, while the coffer of the abacı guild
of Plovdiv contained some 200,000 kuruş.[97]

The matter of cash assets brings up another characteristic difference between guilds. While the funds of a guild of
masters linked with the local market were used for the usual
purposes appropriate for any guild (public needs included),
in organizations such as the abacı guild of Plovdiv the treasury became a financial and credit institution put at the
disposal of some twenty members. These masters received
regular credits of several thousand kuruş each, while a number
of other members of the same guild were encumbered for years
with debts of 100 or 200 kuruş that they were unable to
repay.[98]

Also noteworthy were the changes that took place in the
holding of guild offices. In Plovdiv in the seventeenth century and throughout the eighteenth century, the elders or
leaders of the guild were changed every year, and they seldom
repeated office. In the nineteenth century, however, several
persons remained at the head of the guild for four, five, and
sometimes even for ten years.[99]

Finally, the majority of abacıs in the Bulgarian settlements worked without assistance or, perhaps, from time to
time with one or two apprentices. But, as revealed by a
study of information concerning apprentices and journeymen
taken on by the abacıs in the cities specified above, from
the 1830s on there arose several masters with five, six, and
up to ten apprentices and journeymen (indeed, in some cases
even more).

In the first half of the nineteenth century, the aba
guild was thus undergoing the formation of a small elite,
consisting of persons who headed the organization as its
elders and who used the guild treasury to obtain sums that
were several times larger than those received by other
guildsmen. These masters employed apprentices and journeymen
in numbers far surpassing the number of assistants used by
other craftsmen.

There is no need to discuss all of the information
that is available in this regard. What has been said is
sufficient to establish that already in the first half of the
nineteenth century there was substantial differentiation
among the guildsmen. From among the ranks of the mass of
artisans there had emerged a handful of propertied individuals
who enjoyed considerable social prestige.

* * *

A description of the economic and other activities of
several of the prominent representatives of this elite will
help complete their social portrait. There was, for example,
Kiriak Menon of Plovdiv, an elder of that city's abacı guild
from 1811 to 1820 who was engaged in large-scale trade in aba
goods in Asia Minor.[100] Another Plovdiv guildsman was Stancho
Ivanov, who was an elder of the esnaf in 1840-41, and who
regularly drew several thousand kuruş from the guild's treasury to fund his operations. Ivanov organized a very large
manufacture of aba in the Rhodope villages and acted as a
middleman for the output of small producers, goods that he
sent chiefly to Syria. Ivanov owned a çiftlik near Plovdiv.[101] Another prominent member of the abacı guild was Argir
Koyumcoglu, the descendant of a well-known family of abacıs,
who as a guild spokesman is constantly mentioned in the
accounts of the treasury and in the documents of the Plovdiv
obshtina. He was a partner in the large "Koyumcoglu" commercial firm, which had its head office in Vienna.[102] To this
day his spacious house in Plovdiv, which has been preserved as
a historical monument and houses that city's ethnographic
museum, remains a striking building in its architectural
completeness. Konstantin Mandracioglu, a major exporter of

aba merchandise as far as India, left an estate in Calcutta over which litigation was to continue until the 1930s.[103]

Perhaps the most famous case of all is that of Atanas Gümüşgerdan, who until the 1830s signed all of the major documents of the abacı guild and of the Plovdiv obshtina as the first or as certainly one of the leading members of the guild. Gümüşgerdan rose to be the most successful merchant and manufacturer in Bulgaria. Hundreds of small-commodity producers in the Rhodope villages worked for him. His son-in-law, Toma Stefanu, was the first master of the abacı guild in Istanbul and had considerable sums involved in organizing production for the needs of the Turkish government.[104] The son of Atanas Gümüşgerdan, Mihalaki, became an extremely wealthy man, a large landowner and the proprietor of vast properties in the cities of Plovdiv, Tatar Pazardzhik, and Istanbul. He not only expanded the manufacture he had inherited from his father, but in 1848 he also founded a mill with several dozen workers.[105] This same Mihalaki Gümüşgerdan, though a notable of the city of Plovdiv, did not take direct part in the affairs of that city's abacı guild, but he closely watched the activity of the aba guild located in the area covered by his putting-out manufacture, and in the 1850s he became its elder.[106]

Hacı Simeonko of Shumen, a prominent abacı who in the 1840s signed documents as one of the leaders of the guild there, later founded the first factory in the city and had the first farm machines imported.[107] The father of Panteli Kisimov, a Bulgarian activist, was "one of the senior masters of the abacı guild in Tŭrnovo," and in the 1830s he set up a commercial and industrial concern for trade in aba goods and European textiles.[108] One contemporary noted that early in the nineteenth century in Tŭrnovo there were many master abacıs, *basmacıs*, (makers of cotton print), and other masters, each of whom had fifteen to twenty journeymen and apprentices. Such was Todor Basmadzhiiata, who had enough capital to buy outright the entire output of cotton prints in Tŭrnovo, a deal that earned him several tens of thousands of kuruş.[109] Atanas hacı Pavli from Plovdiv traveled every year to Izmir where he exported aba. In addition, he sold attar of roses in Vienna and Russia.[110]

This list could be expanded with the names of many other persons who to a greater or lesser extent were engaged in the same kind of activity. All of this evidence supports a conclusion that has been making itself quite clear--that it was basically a bourgeois elite that was taking shape in the guilds. Some of these bourgeois elements were distinguished mainly by their commercial activity and others by their organization of enterprises; in all cases, the individuals

involved possessed an undeniably capitalist character. For
it was precisely this differentiated upper layer of the
artisans that gradually seized control of and expanded all of
the units of textile production and drew together a number of
rural districts into a network of capitalist relations.

                              * * *

    A concluding point that requires some clarification
concerns why, in the face of the obstacles caused by a number
of guild restrictions, such leading capitalists not only
failed to abandon the guild themselves, but also did not
show any interest in seeing the institution wither and die.
    The explanation for this phenomenon rests, first, in the
kind of situation prevailing in the Ottoman Empire, and
second, in the specific character of the commodity produced
(particularly the aba). In the Ottoman Empire great obstacles
stood in the way of free capitalist development. Whereas in
the West the emerging urban bourgeoisie usually enjoyed
royal support for a time (insofar as absolutism in turn was
also interested in the support of the cities), the situation
in the Ottoman Empire was rather different. There, the
nascent bourgeoisies of the subjugated peoples could not
depend on the support of the Ottoman government, for--and
here was the rub--in their development these middle classes
had outstripped the ruling nationality whose interests the
Ottoman feudal state had to protect. The situation was
further complicated by the Porte's policy of opening the doors
to foreign capital in a period when, given the pell-mell
industrial development of the West, every emerging branch of
native capitalist industry needed serious protection.
    Guided, furthermore, by various fiscal and (as related
to the army) logistical interests, the government lent its
support only to the guilds. Thus, the local bourgeoisie had
to struggle against the guilds not only as an economic
institution, but also as an institution of the feudal state
that the Turkish monarchy sought to protect even as late as
the nineteenth century. Because the Balkan bourgeoisies were
politically oppressed, the antagonism between them and the
state deepened, hindering their open struggle against the
guilds. Furthermore, the emerging capitalist elements preferred to shelter themselves and their activity within the
guild, for when things were at their worst, they could at
least rely on the support that these institutions received
from the government. The guarantees that the guilds thus
offered encouraged the capitalist elements to seek the appropriate legal conditions and sanctions for their entrepreneurial activity within them.
    In addition, the opportunities that aba production and

trade in particular created for procapitalist activity were
essential to the adaptation of the bourgeois elements to the
esnaf. As already noted, the peculiarity of the aba as a
commodity that could find a market deep in the interior of
Asia Minor meant that in the first half of the nineteenth
century the general decline of the crafts in the Ottoman
Empire did not affect the work of the aba producers. Indeed,
at this time the acquisition of contracts to supply aba
clothes and cloaks to the constantly growing Turkish army and
police forces furnished even greater opportunities for this
textile craft. All of these market considerations lent
stability to the abacı guilds.

Meanwhile, production for distant markets imposed a
certain kind of manufacturing character on the work of the
abacıs. Half of the year there was intensive production,
which engaged all of the free hands of the family and of the
settlement; subsequently, the finished or semicut goods were
shipped by caravans to Asia Minor, where they were completed
and sold. This periodization of the work of the abacıs
presupposed a specific division of labor and at the same time
the availability of large quantities of raw material. Great
opportunities thus opened up for the investment of large
amounts of capital in the supply of raw material, in the
organization of the market, and later in production itself.
These possibilities represented the crucial element that
permitted the weakening of the contradiction between wholesale trade and the small-scale scope of artisan production
within a given guild. Distant marketing also allowed a number
of commodity producers to escape those regulative provisions
that continued to operate with full force mainly with regard
to the preparation of goods for the domestic market. A
unique merger of interests thus developed between the bulk
of the abacıs and the capitalist elements.

The hiring of journeymen and their rate of payment was
usually determined with the general agreement of all masters
or the board of the guild--a clear expression of guild
regulation. But if there were no firmly established single
system for payment, and in the absence of restrictions on the
number of apprentices and journeymen that every member of the
guild had the right to take on, individual masters were in a
position to apply their own system of payment and to enlarge
their workshops. In short, they could effectively ignore
the principle of equality in the conditions of production.

Nor, to cite another example, was the length of the working day subject to hard-and-fast regulations. In the first
half of the nineteenth century all of the prohibitions concerned only holidays and those days when the general meeting
was in session. But since every guildsman had a vineyard

and needed help here and in a number of other domestic chores, the use of apprentices and journeymen outside the workshop constituted a component part of their exploitation by the masters. All guildsmen profited by this exploitation regardless of the scope of their production.[111]

The restrictive provisions that bore on the technique of production and the introduction of technical improvements had a somewhat different character. The secret of a number of processes, particularly those connected with dyeing, was being protected even in the second half of the nineteenth century. Nevertheless, the course of several decades had seen the introduction of more modern combing machines, the metallic wheel, imported looms (or looms constructed after foreign models), and so on and none of these innovations had provoked counteraction by the guild authorities. It was not accidental that the only opposition recorded in mid-nineteenth century sources against the introduction of machines came not from the guilds, but from some women workers. Thus, in September 1851 female workers in Samokov, both Bulgarians and Turks, organized a protest demonstration and attempted to prevent the establishment of a factory equipped with imported machines.[112] The members of the textile guilds, on the contrary, were interested in the introduction of technical improvements in those labor operations involving the initial preparation of the raw material, the aba cloth and the yarn. And it was precisely these stages of production that first saw the employment of hired labor. In their attitude to hired labor the guilds had what came fairly close to a capitalist understanding.

Putting all of these considerations together, and given the general uncertainty that beset open industrial activity, it became more advantageous for the capitalist elements not to isolate themselves from their fellow guildsmen who constituted the great bulk of commodity producers. But while accommodating themselves to the guilds, these bourgeois elements simultaneously shaped some aspects of the guilds to the needs of large-scale commerce and production (albeit production based on lower capitalist forms). This phenomenon was clearly evident in the relationship established between various guilds and the capitalist entrepreneur Mihalaki Gümüşgerdan.

The economic activity of the abacı guilds thus came to reflect the changes that had taken place in Bulgarian society in the late eighteenth century and the first half of the nineteenth century. This activity was no longer the fruit of the regulative policy of the state, and no longer were economic operations a question of the imposition of rules by the central and local organs of power so as to assure

supplies to large centers of consumption. Free trade now
fully satisfied these needs, with both cities and villages
widely involved in the empire's market relations. Also,
economic relations were now the result of the initiative of
the guilds themselves and their members. The guildsmen
called general meetings at their own discretion, discussed
questions concerning the supply of raw material and terms
of sale, and specified the norms of production.

Furthermore, the increased economic role of the guilds--
which resulted not from a struggle against the Turkish rulers
but with their support of esnaf initiative--lent the craft
organization a public importance that it had not hitherto
possessed. This public role had nothing to do with the
nationality of their membership. Purely Christian, Greek,
or Bulgarian guilds had existed for centuries, but only
structural changes in artisan production itself could bring
about major changes in the role and place of the guilds in
public affairs. Naturally, in this respect the greatest
headway was won by those guilds connected with the most
advanced branches of production, those in which capitalist
relationships had taken the greatest strides. It was these
esnafs that began to participate in urban affairs, with
some even eventually leading their people's movement for
national autonomy or independence.

As part of the social and state system, guilds participated in urban self-government, and their increased public
role largely preceded and shaped the increased activities
that in the second and third quarters of the nineteenth
century characterized the Bulgarian obshtinas. (The situation was similar in other parts of the Balkan Peninsula
where there was a higher level of development). At the
same time, the *corbacis, dzakis,*[113] and other segments of
the local population who played semi-feudal roles or were
otherwise closely associated with the Ottoman state system--
and who had controlled the obshtinas for centuries--were now
being displaced by the new strata of the nascent bourgeois.
Although the shift in power was accompanied by social struggles
in many Balkan cities, this conflict took place with the
relative noninterference of the Turkish authorities, since
it was conducted in the name of, and under the banner of
the guilds.

All of this helps to explain why the role of the guilds
did not weaken in the first half of the nineteenth century,
and why, despite the presence there of highly developed
capitalist relations, they continued to be a leading factor
in economic life in the large cities of the Balkan Peninsula.

The Transition from Feudalism to Capitalism

13. THE CAPITALIST ENTREPRENEUR

In the nineteenth century the largest dispersed manufacture or putting-out industry on the Balkan Peninsula was that
conducted by the famous Gümüşgerdan firm. Access to the
exceedingly rich archives of this firm has permitted research
into the enterprise's varied activities and organization of
production, and has allowed its detailed study as a typical
Balkan business operation in the nineteenth century.

The distant genealogy of the Gümüşgerdans is unknown.[1]
In the sources the first mention of the name occurred in 1769,
when a certain hacı Georgi Gümüşgerdan appeared among the
master abacıs of Plovdiv as the one who, by decision of the
guild, handled the cash in the guild treasury.[2] By 1784 and
1786 hacı Georgi was signing as a witness to sales and as a
representative of the abacı guild on the receipt of cash
loans.[3] A document of 1794 notes that this apprentice had

become a master. Thus, hacı Georgi Gümüşgerdan gradually
became one of the active members of the abacı guild. In 1793
his nephew, Atanas, also became a master. For this promotion
Atanas paid twenty kuruş, half of the sum other abacıs had to
pay on becoming masters[4]--direct evidence that the father of
Atanas was likewise a master abacı, for it was only the sons
of master craftsmen who paid half of the fee fixed for
admission into their ranks.

The name of Atanas Gümüşgerdan later appears in the
register of the abacı guild and often in the records of the
Plovdiv metropolitanate. At first mentioned only sporadically, his name occurs more often after 1803 as a witness to
sales, wills, and contracts--that is, in roles that signified
his growing prestige both among the aba producers and with
the Greek obshtina in Plovdiv. In 1805 he was third of 129
masters to sign a statute of the abacı guild in Plovdiv. In
1813, he appeared as one of the trustees of a Greek school
that granted a loan of 10,332 kuruş to the abacı guild;[5] in
1815 he was the first to witness the will of a certain
Kalinik;[6] in 1818 he was the second of twenty-six signatories
to an agreement introducing strict procedures for the election
of representatives to the Plovdiv obshtina;[7] and in 1821 he
was the first of eighteen masters to sign a verified account
of the treasury of the abacı guild.[8] In this way the signature of Atanas Gümüşgerdan is found in various documents up
to 1836. Two years later, in 1838, he died.[9] In the will
made several months prior to his death, he left 15,000 kuruş
to charities, and 100,000 to his children. His real estate,
which he left to his sons, consisted of a house in Plovdiv and
two farms in the village of Dermendere (Pŭrvenets) with
orchards and meadows. Gümüşgerdan's inheritance of 115,000
kuruş represents the largest sum of all of the estates noted
in the records of the Plovdiv diocese.

Although he clearly started off as an ordinary member
of the abacı guild, during the early years of the nineteenth
century Atanas Gümüşgerdan came to enjoy considerable prestige
among the guild and local authorities, and toward the end of
his life he had become the owner of considerable real estate
and large amounts of cash.

The nature of his economic activity can be ascertained
from preserved ledgers that deal chiefly with his purchase of
rolls of aba cloth. In 1806, for example, Atanas bought
365 rolls of this material; in 1807 (on the basis of incomplete data), he bought 698 rolls; and 1809, 963 rolls; in 1815,
380 rolls; in 1816, 393 rolls; and in 1817, 217 rolls. He
paid on the average between 18 to 20 kuruş per roll.[10] He
acquired the bulk of this woolen cloth from neighboring villages as well as from the cities of Karlovo (50 rolls in 1800),

Salonika (12 rolls in 1816, 16 rolls in 1817), and other places.[11]

To be sure, this information by itself is too fragmentary to assess the nature of Gümüşgerdan's activity in the first decades of the century. Since, however, the amounts of aba he purchased could meet only the annual raw material requirements of a workshop employing one to three apprentices, it can be concluded that Gümüşgerdan's shop was a small-commodity operation. Other calculations tend to support the same conclusion. Thus, one roll contained from 14.5 to 15.5 arshin of aba [12] on the average, and in the best of circumstances not more than two sets of clothing could be sewn from one roll. A master working with one or two apprentices could turn out at most from three to four sets of clothing per day (and if they were decorated with braid, not more than two). It appears, therefore, that the rolls of aba purchased by Gümüşgerdan during these years went entirely to the sewing of clothes in his own shop.

Additional evidence for the small-scale character of Gümüşgerdan's initial output is that the guild register noted the promotion of only one of his pupils to the rank of master, and that was as late as 1808.[13] It would thus seem that for a long time Gümüşgerdan worked only with one or two apprentices, and that only when market conditions permitted him to expand his output did he promote one of his assistants.

But gradually Gümüşgerdan underwent a metamorphosis from petty producer to large-scale entrepreneur. Although the lack of sufficient sources unfortunately prevents a detailed study of this transformation, the process itself can be seen through his activities, which from the 1820s on became more varied and intense. The diversity of his economic pursuits illustrates how Gümüşgerdan increasingly separated himself from his artisan workshop.

Atanas Gümüşgerdan became one of those abacıs who already as small-commodity producers combined commercial with artisan activity. In explaining the origin of the byname "Gümüşgerdan" ("silver necklace"), a nineteenth-century writer suggested that Atanas received it when he, like other abacıs, went to Asia Minor to deal in aba goods.[14] But he did not limit himself only to the forms of commerce permitted by the guild. As told by the same writer, Atanas was once brought to a guild court by the masters of his esnaf who, enraged by their dispute with him, were about to throw him out of the window of the building where the meeting was being held. Gümüşgerdan was rescued, however, by two hacıs who were prominent members of the guild. The bad feelings arose, according to the author in question, because Gümüşgerdan, although he "was an abacı," was disliked by all members of the guild.

They regarded him as an "intriguer" and a "traitor."[15] In all
probability, the hostility of the other abacıs toward Gümüşgerdan was provoked by activities that violated guild rules
and impinged on artisan interests.

In addition to aba production, Gümüşgerdan also became
engaged in trade in groceries, agricultural items, and so on.
Raw wool took a leading place among the commodities in which
he dealt commercially. He sometimes supplied wool on credit.
For example, his records reveal that in September 1832, he
lent an amount of wool worth 5,162 kuruş, to be repaid by the
opening date of the Plovdiv fair.[16]

Another facet of Gümüşgerdan's activities that became
very important by the 1830s was usury and banking operations.
The sum of money he lent out rose from circa 30,000 kuruş in
1830-31 to 93,099 kuruş in 1837, and to 118,392 kuruş in
1838. (In 1839, the year after his death, Atanas's sons
granted loans amounting to 104,841 kuruş.) On his loans
Gümüşgerdan charged an interest rate of from 13 to 15%.[17]

But in addition to mentioning small and medium-sized
sums ranging from a few hundred to several thousand kuruş
lent at interest, Gümüşgerdan's ledgers also list large sums
that he obtained for himself under the same conditions. For
instance, they note that in July 1837, he received 61,400
kuruş and some time later repaid 37,700 kuruş of it. An entry
for 1838 recorded a sum of about 40,000 kuruş paid to another
person.[18] There are no grounds for believing that the movement of such sums was connected with the start of partnership
operations, since on several occasions Atanas paid 15%
interest on these accounts and repaid them promptly. Nor was
Atanas's receipt of such sums a sign of his usury activity,
since the interest that he paid on them equalled the interest
on the money he lent. These were sums, therefore, needed by
Gümüşgerdan to carry out some large-scale commercial deal or
in connection with some sudden opportunity to expand the
production of aba.

By the 1830s, then, Gümüşgerdan's activity went far beyond
the boundaries of the artisan's workshop. He was investing
capital in moneylending and commercial operations, and he
was attracting the capital of others for his own production.

The nineteenth-century writer mentioned above furnishes
other information suggestive of the varied ways in which
Gümüşgerdan acquired the funds that were so necessary for
any commercial activity or expanded production. Thus,
Gümüşgerdan gave one of his daughters as a wife to a rich tax
farmer, who in this author's words, "backed" his father-
in-law and helped him "to get out of a state of poverty."
No doubt Gümüşgerdan made wide use of the possibilities and
connections provided by his son-in-law in his commercial

activity, and particularly in terms of increasing both his
capital and his supply of raw wool.

Equally advantageous was the marriage of Gümüşgerdan's
second daughter. The son-in-law, though not so rich, had
the advantage of being the head of the abacı guild in
Akhŭchelebi. This family tie afforded Atanas the opportunity
to expand his operation by skillfully camouflaging it behind
the guild. The extent to which the craft guild in the first
half of the nineteenth century continued to be a necessary
cover for the entrepreneur and to offer definite advantages
can be seen from the efforts of one of Atanas's sons, who not
only enlarged his father's enterprise but also founded a mill,
to become the elder and head of the guild, goals he eventually achieved.

* * *

The earliest data that permit a clear and definite
characterization of the productive and entrepreneurial
activity of Atanas Gümüşgerdan and his sons concern the
years 1837-38.[19] The ledgers for those years list information on the processing of wool in the mountain villages in
the Plovdiv region. One of the ledgers bears the characteristic title: "1837. The Amount of Wool Allotted for Work in
the Mountains."[20] More specifically, the ledgers enumerate
the persons to whom wool had been given for making aba, the
amount of wool, and the sums paid to the individuals involved.
The amount of wool given to process one roll of aba varied,
depending on its quality, from 2.8 to 3 okka, and (chiefly)
from 3.2 to 3.4 okka.[21] The production of one roll of aba
from raw wool earned the person who made it from 2.2 to 4
kuruş. In all probability, the width of the roll and other
features were taken into consideration in determining the rate
of payment.[22] The money was not paid all at once. For these
reasons, it is difficult to establish exactly what persons
from different villages were paid for their work, and whether
their location made any difference. The wool was allotted in
small consignments, and for the years in question the ledgers
very rarely mention persons who received an order to process
more than twenty rolls of aba.

Summary data on the number of rolls of aba processed in
these years and the number of persons engaged in this work
is provided in table 26. As can be seen, in the years 1837,
1838, and 1839, peasants of nearly twenty villages produced
6,386, 12,935, and 10,131 rolls of aba for the Gümüşgerdans.

The interesting question arises here of whether the
Gümüşgerdans, both Atanas and his sons, were more truly merchants or producers in this period. By its very volume, their
production was much more extensive than that of other guild

TABLE 26

GÜMÜŞGERDAN ABA: PRODUCTION AND EMPLOYMENT, 1837-1839

Village	1837		1838		1839	
	Number of		Number of		Number of	
	Rolls	Workers	Rolls	Workers	Rolls	Workers
Liaskovo	948	57	2,063	147	913	70
Küçük'oy[a]	31	2	401	17	---	---
Orizovo	767	37	-----	---	---	---
Churekovo	150	16	-----	---	193	7
Goren Deven (D'ovlen)	746	32	467	24	62	3
Petvar	981	51	1,559	94	303	19
Nastan	140	8	260	9	63	2
Mugla	1,583	81	1,654	88	1,300	40
Mikhalkovo	926	56	1,166	71	875	55
Osikovo	114	10	30	2	---	---
Selcha	-----	--	185	10	---	---
Grokhotno (Grotna)	-----	--	775	38	522	27
G'ovren	-----	--	387	17	496	21
Iagodina (Balaban)	-----	--	1,653	56	1,232	67
Kesten (Kestendzhik)	-----	--	241	7	130	3
Kaindzhali[a]	-----	--	572	22	1,300	39
Trigrad	-----	--	1,522	42	2,377	173
Vodni Pad (Diustiukdere)[b]	-----	--	-----	---	419	6
Total	6,386	350	12,935	644	10,131	532

SOURCE: TsDIA, f. 161. For these years it cannot be determined whether wool was given to the same person on more than one occasion.

[a]These villages cannot be identified.
[b]The figure for the number of workers in this village is not exact, since 322 pieces of aba were received for distribution by one of Gümüşgerdan's agents (H. Mehmed).

masters who also used hired labor. By way of comparison, the Sliven mill of Dobri Zheliazkov, which was rather large for the Ottoman Empire and was built with state assistance, employed about 500 workers. In the 1860s it produced some 11,000 rolls of aba a year--that is, about the same as the Gümüşgerdans obtained in the late 1830s from the wool that they sent out for production in the villages.[23]

     The Rhodope region, where the Gümüşgerdans conducted
their putting-out operations, was a mountainous area with
underdeveloped farming. Its inhabitants raised sheep, and for
many years they had engaged in the production of woolen cloth.
The aba produced in this area enjoyed a good name and represented an important part of the region's exports. The bulk
of the Rhodope aba was purchased by Plovdiv abacıs, and from
the 1820s on part of this production went to meet the aba
requirements of the Turkish army.[24] It is perhaps this
circumstance that contributed to the cautious assessments that
exist in Bulgarian historical literature concerning the
activities of the Gümüşgerdans and the doubts that have been
raised as to the capitalist nature of their operations as
entrepreneurs and landowners. This reluctance has been
reinforced by certain sources indicating that in the second
half of the nineteenth century the Gümüşgerdans employed some
forced labor (*angariia*).
     Accordingly, to clarify the relations between the
Gümüşgerdans and the local producers is to characterize the
nature of productive relations and the class structure in one
of the most important regions of the country. As the biggest
state contractor, Gümüşgerdan had close economic and political
relations with the Turkish administration. But for determining the social nature of the persons engaged in the
Gümüşgerdans' production, it is the system of paying labor
rather than the political connection that has the greater
significance. In practically all cases, the ledgers of the
Gümüşgerdans contain the sums advanced and the accounts of
the office with the workers. But these payments were recorded
in a peculiar fashion: the account of the money paid out did
not coincide with the worth of the consignment of wool that
was allotted at the same time. Accordingly, this material
alone is not sufficient to clarify the nature of payment.
(It seems that once or twice a year a balance sheet was made
up for each person's account; unfortunately, the registers
and receipts for this particular period have not been
preserved.) Be that as it may, the regular advancement of
money reveals the constancy of the relationship between the
Gümüşgerdans and the workers.
     The year 1839 is the earliest for which there is specific
material to permit a clarification of the mode of payment used
by the Gümüşgerdans. There is a detailed report from that
year about a consignment of wool sent to be processed into
aba. There are not many such descriptions extant, and no
more than ten are included in all of the ledgers up to 1845.
Thus, it deserves detailed examination.
     In 1839, the document records, the Gümüşgerdans gave to
a certain Osman of the village of Kaindzhali 33 okka of wool
without the tare for the production of 12 rolls of aba for

which he received 12 kuruş in cash. Osman had wool from a
previous supply, and in the end he delivered a total of 25
rolls of aba, for which he received an additional 10 kuruş
in cash. But in the ledgers the production of the 25 rolls of
aba is entered against a figure of 45 kuruş.[25] It is clear
that the latter sum did not include the value of the wool
itself, for in those years the Gümüşgerdans were purchasing
wool for several kuruş per okka. The sum in question reflects
only the costs of the aba production, and in this sum the
Gümüşgerdans undoubtedly included the cost of wasted wool as
a wage expense. Thus, in 1839, 78,805 okka of wool without
the tare were sent to Osman in the village of Kaindzhali for
the production of 268 rolls of aba. Their production cost
the Gümüşgerdans 1,074 kuruş, of which 428.15 kuruş represented various expenses and 624.25 kuruş were paid for the
labor itself (257.20 kuruş in cash and 388.5 in receipts).[26]
These sums too failed to include the cost of the wool itself.
The payment by receipts illustrates that the Gümüşgerdans were
not loath to subjugate local producers by advancing sums. The
records for the year 1839 indicate that from the village in
question the Gümüşgerdans received a consignment of finished
production consisting of 385 rolls worth 1,149.20 kuruş.
A note on the ledger stated that "they have been made and
delivered against the payment of the debt of the village."[27]
The same kind of situation arose in 1840 when the village of
Trigrad supplied 913 rolls of aba.[28]

There is no doubt that a system of advances afforded
the Gümüşgerdans an opportunity to use the economic dependence
of rural artisans and producers to intensify their exploitation. But in such cases the procedure did not involve any
resale of the raw materials or the finished goods, and thus
there was no change in the basic nature of the relationship
between the Gümüşgerdans and the producers. It was simply
a question of reduced remuneration for the labor.

The only direct mention of the method of payment concerns
the village of Nastan. In November 1842, Mihalaki Gümüşgerdan,
one of Atanas's sons and successors, received 71 rolls of aba
for whose production 162 okka of wool had been provided.
Payment for the labor had been agreed upon at 1.20 kuruş
per okka, or 243 kuruş in all.[29] This was clearly a situation
where the owner of raw material and disposable capital stood
at one pole and the worker selling his labor as a commodity
stood at the other.

Also of considerable interest for clarifying the nature
of hired labor in the mid-nineteenth century are the specific
receipts and contracts between the Gümüşgerdans and the
various persons they employed. Unfortunately, the several
thousand such documents that have been inspected contain only

isolated receipts from workers who accepted orders to produce
aba. The documents for the years 1846 and 1849 will be cited
here since they are the only ones known that reflect the
mutual obligations of the entrepreneur and the worker engaged
in putting-out manufacture. The standard character of these
documents suggests that the economic relations they reveal
had been in existence for some time.

The first of these documents, drawn up in Greek, reads
as follows: "I, the undersigned, declare that I have received
525 okka of wool (of light color) to produce 150 rolls, and
also 150 kuruş in cash from Gogo, kehâya of çelebi Mihalaki
Gümüşgerdan, and so put my signature. February 15, 1846,
[signed] I, Vasil Kurtuglu of Shiroka Lŭka, so undertake."[30]
A second document is dated June 13, 1846, and is written in
Bulgarian. The signatory, Gogu çorbacı Radkooglu, received
1,400 kuruş for 1,200 okka of wool, undertaking to process
this wool in sizes of up to 4.5 rupe in width at 100 para
(i.e., 2.5 kuruş) per arshin. In addition to the signature
there is also a seal.[31]

Another document, again in Greek, was signed by three
individuals from the village of Büyük Palas (today the city
of Rudozem).[32] They received wool and 733.5 kuruş in cash
and in return undertook to produce the aba within thirty-one
days. If the aba did not meet the terms specified, the
individuals were to return the money. The document was signed
in the village of Chitak on February 8, 1859.

Yet another document, also in Greek, is essentially a
contract. After the customary expressions of obligation to
Mihalaki Gümüşgerdan, the document states that "receipt has
been made of the below-mentioned: wool 329 3/4 okka in 10
sacks [kuruş] 4,451 25/40; fleece 74 okka in 3 sacks [kuruş]
26; and received in cash 6,050 5/40 [kuruş] undertaking to process it into rolls of şayak cloth, the ware to be pure and good,
in accordance with his wish, and to have it delivered to him
in 61 days [and] by agreement the şayak cloth to be 4 rupe in
width at [4 15/40] kuruş and 4.5 rupe in width at [4 25/40]
kuruş and I so declare, April 24, 1859. Chitak." (Being
illiterate, the recipient Teodor Vŭlko empowered someone else
to sign on his behalf.)[33]

As these documents once again confirm, the wool remained
Gümüşgerdan's property through all the stages of production.
True, its worth was sometimes incorporated into the sum that
also included the payment for labor, thus making it appear
that a sale of the wool had taken place with the wages dis-
solved into the total sum. This, however, was only a monetary
procedure in which the cost of the raw material was included
in the workers' monetary obligation as security for the wool
they received. In paying for labor the only considerations

taken into account were that the merchandise had to correspond
to the terms specified and to be delivered within a fixed
period of time. The remuneration itself depended on the number of arshin contained in the roll of cloth produced. The
persons who worked for Gümüşgerdan, therefore, received
monetary payment in its pure form, the money often handed over
simultaneously with the supply of raw wool.

As to the rate of payment, there was a difference between
the rates specified and the amounts actually paid. This
difference arose because the Gümüşgerdans deducted the
cost of the wool ruined in the course of production from the
sums paid to the workers. In the example cited above for the
village of Nastan, the worker actually received 183 kuruş
instead of the 243 specified (which meant a rate of 1 kuruş
and 5 para per okka of wool instead of the 1 kuruş and 20 para
in the contract; or, put another way, 2 kuruş and 25 para
instead of the envisaged 3 kuruş and 18 para per roll of
finished aba).[34]

The system of payment held true in all cases, although
there were other rates of payment. These rates ranged from
3 to 4 kuruş, with no cases discovered involving the payment
of more than 4 kuruş per roll of aba.[35]

Thus the great bulk of the people who produced aba for
the Gümüşgerdans were artisan weavers who had been reduced to
the level of hired workers. There are 350 such workers
recorded in the ledgers for 1837, 644 in 1838, and 533 in
1839. But these figures are not quite exact. As will be
shown, these individuals included some artisans who in turn
hired other workers. On the other hand, there are numerous
instances where the same persons received wool several times
a year, and the total number of hired workers would have to be
reduced by several dozen cases per year. Although it leads to
a reduction in the absolute number of hired workers, awareness
of this contributes to a better understanding of the character
of this hired labor. Work for the Gümüşgerdans became routine
for much of the male population of the area, and the names of
the same men are encountered year after year. That they
regularly received wool from the Gümüşgerdans over the course
of many years convincingly demonstrates that this work was
a constant source of income. The sale of their labor became
for these individuals their basic means of existence.

In this respect another important point is the minimum
wage received by those who produced aba for the Gümüşgerdans.
Given the differences in the living conditions of the urban
and rural population, and given that information is available
on the prices of foodstuffs in the town markets, it seemed
appropriate to approach this question by comparing the
weavers with other permanent hired workers employed by the

Gümüşgerdans. Late in 1845, for example, the Gümüşgerdans
hired carters at wages of 300, 400, and 500 kuruş a year. [36]
They often employed hired carters since they needed their
own transport for a system of production involving the
transfer of wool and finished aba over great distances. The
same held true for woodcutters. Having their own forests, the
Gümüşgerdans required permanent workers to assure a regular
supply of building material and fuel for the mill, for the
dyehouses and for their own home. In 1847 they employed
four woodcutters, three of whom received 520 kuruş and one
of whom earned 600 kuruş per year. There was also one servant
woodcutter who was paid both in kind (wheat, vegetables, etc.)
and 250 kuruş in cash. [37] That same year the Gümüşgerdans'
gardener received 500 kuruş and their shepherds were paid
amounts ranging from 100 to 400 kuruş. [38] Examples have been
chosen here of seasonal workers whose situation resembled
the working conditions of the persons engaged in the production of aba. The rate of payment received by permanent hired
workers varied from 100-600 kuruş, but wages close to 500
kuruş prevailed.

In moving on to determine the sums received by those who
produced aba for the Gümüşgerdans, it must be admitted that
there are no accurate data on the annual output and payment.
Accordingly, the calculations here are approximate ones.
In the examples provided above, the *terzi* (tailor) Molla Ömer
received 80 kuruş, the person from Nastan 193 kuruş, Musta-
foglu Osman of Goren Deven received a total of 140 kuruş, and
Vasil Kurtoglu of Shiroka Lŭka received 150 kuruş. [39] Calculating the quantity of processed rolls of aba shows that
work was paid on an average of 50 to 100 kuruş for each consignment of raw wool.

This material, therefore, would set the rate of payment
of those workers who produced aba in the villages at about
one-third to one-half of the sums paid to the majority of the
Gümüşgerdans' permanent hired workers. In the villages where
domestic production of aba went along with continued farming,
this amount of payment was a sign that the transformation of
labor into a commodity had made considerable headway. The
people working for the Gümüşgerdans received in cash the basic
means of their livelihood in return for their labor.

This conclusion has taken into account the important
circumstance that in the eighteenth century and perhaps even
earlier spinning and weaving had become the population's
principal occupation in this mountainous and basically nonagricultural region. In other words, the emergence of these
crafts predated the onset of the Gümüşgerdan operation, and
the latter's relations with the workers have to be seen as
relations with small-commodity producers who had been around

for a long time. Furthermore, these relations were based on
the free purchase of labor, which was renewed continuously
from year to year.

                              * * *

    The increased activity of the Gümüşgerdans, meanwhile,
could not but give rise to the appearance of a considerable
number of middlemen. In the period that has just been
studied, the late 1830s, the ledgers do not isolate the
middlemen as a separate group. Starting in the mid-1840s,
however, permanent accounts were opened for such individuals,
who were listed in the ledgers by the use of the term "our
man."[40] These middlemen were trusted individuals who received
raw materials from the Gümüşgerdans for distribution not only
among workers but also to other local go-betweens. As the
hierarchy of middlemen became more complicated, the exploitation of the producers also increased. In some villages the
emergence of local middlemen from the ranks of the artisans
and village elders or muhtars, was completed by the late 1830s,
while in other villages the process was still going on. In
addition to artisans, the middlemen included corbascıs, hacıs,
and other local wealthy individuals who received wool in bulk
and then distributed it in small portions to village weavers
and abacıs. The abundance of middlemen between the capitalist
and the worker is one of the most characteristic features of
capitalist cottage production during the manufacturing stage
of industry's development. The middlemen, who lived in direct
proximity to the producers, could take into account all the
conditions of local work and were able to introduce more
intensive exploitation.
    The separation of a layer of middlemen from the rural
artisans, moreover, is a sign of the birth of the rudiments of
capitalism in the rural crafts themselves. Some of the
middlemen who dealt in aba production began to use hired
workers, and individual agents of the Gümüşgerdans themselves
became capitalist entrepreneurs, reducing the producers in
their own villages and even in neighboring settlements to a
state of dependence. This was the case, for example, of the
wealthy capitalist entrepreneur and agent of the Gümüşgerdans
in the Smolian area, A. Pangalov of Raikovo. So large and
impressive was his dwelling that it was chosen to house the
ethnographical museum of Smolian.

                              * * *

    When Marx wrote that "in manufacture, the revolution in
the mode of production begins with the labor-power," he did not
limit himself to describing only the nature of the exploitation
of labor; he also showed the evolutionary process of a whole

hierarchy of specialized workers on the basis of a deep division of labor within the manufacturing process.[41] Thus, along
with the nature of the manpower being used, the extent of
both the social and the technological division of labor
also becomes a fundamental criterion in determining the
essence of a given enterprise. Where the operation of the
Gümüşgerdans is concerned, unfortunately, material is not
available on the organization of the labor process itself--
that is, information that would immediately help to determine
the true character of their enterprise. Conclusions must
therefore be drawn on the basis of the analysis of the material presented above and by setting forth certain other
considerations.

To begin with, the production of aba as organized by
Atanas Gümüşgerdan should be regarded as a kind of putting-
out manufacture, with Atanas himself as the capitalist entrepreneur. And even if we accept that the majority of specific
operations were not differentiated into independent labor
processes--since the fundamental economic unit remained the
rural family that did the spinning, weaving, and possibly
other supplementary operations--the manufacturing character of
the Gümüşgerdans' operation is, in our opinion, beyond doubt.

Operating as a large-scale entrepreneur, Gümüşgerdan
adroitly took advantage of certain special features of the
aba production in the territory in which he operated. In the
1820s and 1830s the population of the Rhodopes annually
produced from 120,000 to 200,000 arshin of aba, and there
were cases where orders were received from the Turkish government for up to 1,000,000 arshin,[42] which meant the production
of 9,000 to 15,000 rolls a year. Thus, throughout this whole
region there existed a well-developed weaving industry connected
with the fulfillment of large contracts.

Without doubt, all of the transitional forms of the small
producer's dependence on the merchant and supplier were widespread before the advent of the Gümüşgerdans. Atanas
Gümüşgerdan apparently differed from the others only because
he was able to concentrate in his hands both the supply of
raw materials and the sale of the finished merchandise, thus
cutting the producer off from both materials and the market.
And in other ways too Atanas was not just an ordinary merchant
or even entrepreneur. He came to exploit hundreds of workers
under his direct control in addition to the large numbers of
workers involved in his putting-out operations. Working at
fixed rates of remuneration, these producers received wool
through the agents of the Gümüşgerdans and turned it into
aba. The relationships of dependency thus established lasted
for years.

The nature of these relationships might be defined in

the words of Marx: "It is no longer a mere accident,
that capitalist and labourer confront each other in the market
as buyer and seller. It is the process itself that inces-
santly hurls back the labourer on to the market as a vendor of
his labour-power. . . . Capitalist production, therefore, as
under its aspect of a continuous connected process, . . .
produces not only commodities, . . . but it also produces and
reproduces the capitalist relation, on the one side the capitalist, on the other the wage labourers."[43]

Very revealing in this sense is the situation of the
hired workers employed by the Gümüşgerdans in the 1840s.
Leaving aside temporary workers (mainly farm hands), whose
number in the first half of the nineteenth century cannot
be accurately established, the workers in question were those
who received wages and who would work for the Gümüşgerdans
throughout the whole year. The ledgers employed separate
accounts for such workers, with entries from some fifty to
sixty persons a year and sometimes even more. Although the
actual number fluctuated from month to month, it always
exceeded thirty.

As disclosed by an analysis of the composition of these
hired workers, there was, despite a considerable occupational
variety, a prevalence of persons in some way connected with
the textile production organized by the Gümüşgerdans. There
were three or four carters, four or five dyers, an accountant,
an overseer, a clerk, and so forth. There was a rather large
group of ten to fifteen servants, some of whom were actually
engaged in domestic work. The majority, however, were
unskilled laborers used for all kinds of work. Another large
group of ten to fifteen individuals comprised employees working in offices or as agents who maintained ties with rural
producers. Among the artisans whom the Gümüşgerdans hired
on a permanent basis, the most identifiable group was that
of the abacıs. Some of these craftsmen were employed in the
Gümüşgerdans' own centralized manufacture and others worked
in the villages. Other permanent employees included a mason,
a carpenter, a cook, a grocer, a few woodcutters, millers,
shepherds, gardeners, and so forth.[44]

The presence of such a permanent number of hired workers
signals the Gümüşgerdans' considerable concentration of
capital, thanks to which they were able to proceed toward the
organization of a capitalist enterprise of a different type.

Although information is lacking on the precise position
of these groups in the production process, the variety of
their job titles would suggest that in the early 1840s a
manufacturing division of labor existed in the Gümüşgerdan
enterprise. Buying wool in huge lots, the entrepreneurs
stored it in amounts sometimes reaching several tens of

thousands of okka in their warehouses in Tatar Pazardzhik,
Plovdiv, and Akhŭchelebi.[45] The presence of warehouses,
storehouses, and other buildings in these cities and in other
places located relatively far away from the centers of the
Gümüşgerdans' organized production indicates that some of the
preliminary operations in the grading and processing of wool
were differentiated from the basic labor process but were also
controlled by these entrepreneurs. The ledgers used to enter
the consignments of wool sent for production to mountain
villages invariably record its type, grade, and condition, a
categorization that in turn determined the manufacture of
different types of cloth (black, white, and gray aba, or
şayak). Thus, both territorially and technologically, the
initial operations connected with the preservation and preparation of the wool for further processing were differentiated
from the next stage in production. The village artisans were
provided with material that had already undergone initial
processing in another place.

    There is no need to dwell in great detail on the next
round of operations immediately preceding the weaving of the
wool itself, since their technique is known from the
literature (and in any event the archives would not permit a
study of these operations in the Gümüşgerdan enterprise).
The Gümüşgerdans quite probably engaged women who washed,
dried, carded, and graded the wool according to its color,
in the same way that these operations were handled in other
cities in the middle of the nineteenth century, and it was for
these kinds of initial operations that they began to introduce
hired labor earlier than in other parts of their production.
The accountant, clerk, overseer, and the other ten to fifteen
office employees, together with a few permanent general
workers, directed the work of the day laborers in all stages
of production, and particularly in the preparatory stages
(washing, carding, and grading the wool).

    Much the same kind of situation held true for some of the
final stages of production. From the early 1840s on, not
less than four or five master dyers were permanently employed
by the Gümüşgerdans.[46] These individuals could not dye all
of the aba produced, and judging by data from the 1850s and
1860s, part of the enormous amounts of pigments purchased by
the Gümüşgerdans was handed over, together with rolls of
finished aba, to artisan dyers in Plovdiv, Tatar Pazardzhik,
Karlovo, and Kalofer.[47] If the Gümüşgerdans had to resort to
the services of guild artisans and to whole guilds of dyers
even in the second half of the century when the dyeing
section of their own mill processed from 20,000 to 30,000
rolls of aba annually, then they must have had to do this to
an even greater extent in an earlier period when they were

still organizing their manufacture. Moreover, the fact that
the several dyers employed as permanent hired workers took
part in what was apparently a separate final stage of production has to be appreciated as another example of the differentiation of the labor process from the very beginning of the
Gümüşgerdan enterprise. To sum up, after the most elementary
sorting of the wool in centers where it was concentrated for
storage and distribution, the graded wool was sent for additional preliminary processing to the village of Dermendere.
This was the location of the largest number of hired workers,
and it was here that the preliminary processing was more
advanced and where the dyeing was done in a special workshop.
All of these circumstances indicate the introduction of a
manufacturing and territorial distribution of labor with the
establishment of definite relationships among separate
groups of workers.

In coming to this conclusion, it should once again be
stressed that the concentration of significant production and
capital in the same hands, when combined with a relatively
stable labor process, made possible the emergence of a large-
scale putting-out capitalist manufacture that continued to
exist over a long period of time without a centralized
enterprise. For the Gümüşgerdans to move on to the establishment of a mill, certain other factors were necessary, and
these will be studied in the next chapter.

It might be noted in passing, however, that in examining
forms of manufacture, Marx pointed out that capitalist
manufacture need not always be identified with a centralized
enterprise. When competition among the workers permits the
use of ruthless exploitation, capitalists would have nothing
against saving themselves the unnecessary expenses of factory
buildings and other overhead costs by putting out the work.[48]
It is precisely this kind of approach that explains the over-
all uniqueness of the Gümüşgerdans' manufacture of the late
1830s and early 1840s. Or as Lenin wrote, "the different
historical situation . . . modifies only the forms of the
manifestations of the same capitalist relations."[49]

* * *

The Gümüşgerdans' place and role in the textile industry
went far beyond the establishment of a putting-out manufacture. Taking into consideration the requirements of the
market, they also moved into various commercial operations to
meet--in return for a profit of course--the increased demand
for textiles. They likewise invested their capital in trade
in other goods where large, quick returns were possible.

On the commercial side of the Gümüşgerdan operation,
table 27 provides the combined amounts of aba produced

TABLE 27

FINISHED ROLLS OF ABA PRODUCED AND PURCHASED BY
THE GÜMÜŞGERDANS IN 1837-1845

Year	From Own Wool		Total Quantity of Aba Produced and Purchased,[a] in Rolls and Bales
	Delivered for Production of Aba (in rolls)	Aba Received	
1837	6,386[b]	-----	51,022 Rolls
1838	12,935	-----	------------
1839	10,131	6,537	------------
1840	3,232	6,241	------------
1841	3,377	1,753	------------
1842	3,344	5,542	------------
1843	2,038	2,599	------------
1844	351[c]	1,194[d]	2,298 Bales[e]
	3,566		(of 37,000 to 64,500 Rolls)
	935		3,022 Bales[f]
1845	1,235	5,577	(of 48,000 to
	9,836		84,600 Rolls)

SOURCE: TsDIA, f. 161, defters 9, 11, 23, 29.

[a]This rubric contains data wherein it cannot be accurately determined whether the figures pertained only to prepared or to purchased
rolls.
[b]All of these figures are based on material contained in defters
9 and 11 and pertain to the villages noted in table 26.
[c]The first number concerns the aba produced in the villages indicated in table 26. The second figure pertains to the production of
aba in other villages (Raikovo, Palas, Tekir, Uzundere, Pashmakli,
etc.) in late November and December, 1844 (see ibid., defter 29,
1-21). The third number is for the rolls delivered for production
in Akhǔchelebi (see ibid., defter 23, 96).
[d]Received from January to May, inclusive; and in November and
December (ibid., defter 11, 76-78; defter 23, 106).
[e]Ibid., defter 23, 1-9. It is possible that some of these bales
produced in Akhǔchelebi might have been sent there from other
places. The numbers in parentheses are based on calculations using
a figure of 16 to 28 rolls per bale. In another defter for 1845,
the author has discovered a figure for the amount of aba in rolls
(53,052 rolls).
[f]Ibid., defter 11, 86-88, 29-31.

and purchased from the end of the 1830s to the mid-1840s.
Up to 1839 the Gümüşgerdans themselves provided wool for the
manufacture of 6,000, 10,000, and even more than 12,000 rolls

of aba a year, but from 1840 to 1844 they supplied wool for
the production of only about 3,000 rolls a year. There is no
doubt about this reduction, for it is expressed as well in
documents not cited here on the expected receipt of finished
aba. It should also be noted that the supply of wool and the
receipt of aba were a continuous operation, and at the end of
the year production of aba contracted by the Gümüşgerdans
would still be going on.

From the end of 1844, however, the number of rolls of
finished aba again rose as new villages came to be involved
in the sphere of the Gümüşgerdan operations. As shown by the
table, in 1844 and 1845 several tens of thousands of rolls
were made (and in part probably purchased as well) in the
settlement of Akhücelebi. Since it cannot be determined what
part of this amount was produced by the Gümüşgerdans and what
was simply purchased, these data have been entered in separate
columns. Be that as it may, the figures show that in 1844
the firm had increased its entrepreneurial activity over the
1837-38 level. In 1845 the number of rolls of aba variously
produced in villages reached a total of 53,052.[50]

A comparison of the amount of aba that the Gümüşgerdans
sent to Istanbul with the data on the aba they themselves
produced can help establish the difference--that is, the
amount of aba they purchased for resale from small-scale
producers. Thus, in 1837 the Gümüşgerdans sent 47,071 rolls
to Istanbul, in 1838 53,765 rolls, in 1844 2,349 bales, and in
1845 3,147 bales.[51] Even in 1837 the Gümüşgerdans handled
many more rolls of finished aba than can be accounted for in
terms of the wool they supplied to their own producers.
Taking into account the subsequent data as well, it follows
that the Gümüşgerdans' own production failed to meet the
amount of aba they needed for trade by some 50,000 rolls. To
make up the difference it was natural that they would resort
to the purchase of the finished product of other producers,
small and large. The same thing happened in 1838, when the
Gümüşgerdans' own production represented only from one-fourth
to one-third of the number of rolls they sent to Istanbul.

For subsequent years data is unavailable on the
deliveries of aba to Istanbul, but direct references to the
purchase of finished merchandise have been found. From
1839 to 1842 the Gümüşgerdans bought only insignificant
amounts of aba. This decrease in the purchase of finished
rolls came sooner and was much sharper than the cutback in
their own production. The decrease in textile demand--and
the consequent drop in deliveries to Istanbul--led first
to the curtailment of the purchase of finished rolls and only
then to a cutback of the Gümüşgerdans' own manufactured output.

All of this supports the idea that the principal activity
of the Gümüşgerdans was the organization of their own production, which moreover, had acquired considerable stability.
The commercial purchase of the finished goods of other
producers played a secondary role and was primarily dependent
on market fluctuations. Nevertheless, having bought up raw
materials, and enjoying a market that could absorb enormous
quantities of finished goods, the Gümüşgerdans easily became
engaged in commercial activity that saw them purchase and
resell the production of small producers. This simply confirms the extent to which the Gümüşgerdans were typical representatives of industrial capitalism in its manufacturing
stage, a stage when commercial capital is closely intertwined
with industrial capital.

The continuous blending of commercial and industrial
activity in this period is reflected in practically every
individual operation of the Gümüşgerdans, and it is particularly well expressed in terms of the supply of raw materials.
Having met the needs of their own production of wool, the
Gümüşgerdans usually sold part of the surplus. From the sale
of wool they obtained a profit of one or two kuruş per
okka.[52] In addition their profit from the resale of a roll of
aba was not less than three kuruş.[53] In any event, such basically commercial operations did not earn the Gümüşgerdans the
profit that they drew from the sale of the aba they produced.
Even a rough calculation shows that the production of a roll
of aba cost them less than 15 or 16 kuruş,[54] but the Gümüşgerdans sold it at the same price--28 or 29 kuruş per
roll--at which they sold rolls purchased from small-scale
producers. Naturally, such factors as the length of the
turnover and fluctuation of market prices influenced the rate
of profit. The different profit rates, however, speak for
themselves in explaining the persistent effort of the Gümüşgerdans to expand their own production of aba.

* * *

Not all of the material on the Gümüşgerdans' exports necessary to study the influence of the market on the output of
their enterprise is available, but there is no doubt that
Istanbul and the Turkish government were the principal consumers of the Gümüşgerdans' production. This point leads to
the very important question of the role of state contracts in
the development of the textile industry in the Balkans. As
this topic has been dealt with in the preceding chapter (and
will be later on), it will be discussed here only to clarify
the nature of the relations between the Gümüşgerdans and the
Turkish government.

From a detailed nineteenth-century narrative account of

the Gümüşgerdans, it is clear, first, that Atanas was not
really involved in the fulfillment of contracts for the
Turkish government, and second, that Mihalaki Gümüşgerdan
and his brothers became involved in army procurement only
when their position on the open market in Istanbul became
difficult. Furthermore, they were enticed into state contracts by the considerable amount of capital that they
received in return--which they did not, however, invest in
production. They preferred to utilize the state's intervention as a supreme sanction for the rapacious methods they used
to exploit the population that worked for them.[55]

A recently discovered document clearly illustrates the
manner and the extent to which the Gümüşgerdans robbed the
rural producers. This document details the complaints of
the peasants of thirty-six villages in the Plovdiv area.
The peasants enumerated the work they had done, the payment
they were supposed to receive, the amount they actually got,
and the remainder still due after years of trying to get
their money.[56] N. Nemski, who uncovered this document, has
summed up some of the numbers involved. Thus, peasant
producers from fifteen villages had turned out considerable
amounts of şayak cloth, delivered in consignments using
different measures: 2,700 arshin, 3,567 *qubit*, and 127,411
alebiia.[57] For this amount of merchandise Mihalaki Gümüşgerdan paid only 635,054.2 kuruş, a sum far short of the
amount due. He arrived at this figure by paying prices that
were two to four times lower than the prices that had been
agreed upon and by alleging that considerable quantities of
the şayak cloth in question did not meet size specifications.
Furthermore, Gümüşgerdan exploited the inability of the
peasants to meet the established quota by forcing them to pay
for the amount they had failed to deliver. He also declared
a certain part of the merchandise to be wastage, a charge
against which the peasants were unable to protest.

Gümüşgerdan likewise shrewdly utilized the monopoly he
received during the Crimean War, which put all local wool at
his disposal. He had already learned to cheat peasants by
weighing raw wool being delivered for processing while it was
damp and then weighing finished cloth in terms of its dry
weight. The scholar who has looked into these matters has
shown how on one occasion Gümüşgerdan paid a fraudulent price
of only 79,133.20 kuruş for 9,012 okka of wool; and for
another 835.5 okka worth 13,779 kuruş he paid nothing at all.
In delivering wool to cottage weavers Gümüşgerdan often used
the blunt interference of Turkish police officials.

Another item of raw material whose supply involved sheer
robbery on the part of Gümüşgerdan was the roots of the dock
plant that were used as a pigment. Twenty-four villages once

complained that Gümüşgerdan had cheated them out of 56,332
kuruş in a transaction involving this item. Sums due for
the cartage of various goods were also left unpaid. At one
time, some peasants claimed 386,509 kuruş from Gümüşgerdan,
most of which had to do with the transport of rice and
textiles to Tekirdağ, but a considerable part was made up of
the transport cost of goods taken by carts or on horseback
to the mill in Dermendere, to other centers where Gümüşgerdan's
warehouses and shops were located, and to neighboring cities.
This cartage constituted a kind of forced labor, and any
attempt to protest against it was crushed by beating and other
punishments on the part of the Turkish police.

     This exploitation of the population on several occasions
produced open dissatisfaction. In 1856 the brother of
Mihalaki was killed, although the latter was actually the
target, and in 1865 a spontaneous rebellion broke out in the
Rhodopes. About 2,000 or more Christians and Muslims rose
with whatever weapons they could find and chased off Gümüşgerdan's men. The rebellion ended only after the forced
labor was discontinued and the peasants received compensation
for their work.[58]

     The grievances of the peasant producers were some of the
consequences of the association between the Gümüşgerdans and
the Turkish authorities. This relationship involved the tie-
in between the capitalist enterprise and state contracts.
From the documents it is evident that the production organized
by Atanas Gümüşgerdan was closely connected with the Istanbul
market. Part of the aba and şayak cloth that Gümüşgerdan
produced or purchased for resale was sold on the capital's
open market, but some of it also went into the preparation of
clothing for the army. This relationship must have already
existed for some time, since the documents speak of regular
monthly deliveries to Ottoman forces. Actually, the ledgers
indicate that at that time practically all the aba produced
and purchased by Gümüşgerdan was sent to Istanbul. In 1837,
Toma Stefanu, Atanas's son-in-law in Istanbul, received
47,071 rolls worth 1,334,573.25 kuruş, and in 1838 and the
first two months of 1839 he received 53,765 rolls worth
1,582,991.20 kuruş.[59]

     While the relations between Gümüşgerdan and the govern-
ment remained hidden, the name of Toma Stefanu loomed very
large. Stefanu's role was unique. He was not simply the
Istanbul agent of the Gümüşgerdans, nor was he simply a holder
of monetary capital who was on the lookout for profitable
investments in the business operations of his in-laws.
Stefanu was a man who had a considerable social position,
for he was the head of the abacı guild in Istanbul and the
leader of the first board of the capital's Bulgarian church

of St. Stefan.[60] As the head of the guild he was undoubtedly
in a position to influence the placement of orders for the
supply of aba to the "Khambar" (a building in Istanbul in
which about one thousand Bulgarian artisans gathered to make
clothing for the Turkish army).

In the correspondence between Stefanu and Gümüşgerdan,
the name of a certain Halil Paşa occurs often; it is also
mentioned in the ledger in references to bribes paid to other
Turkish officials--for it was through bribes that state
contracts were obtained. The annual statement for 1830,
for example, lists a bribe of 12,600 kuruş to Halil Paşa.[61]

Toma Stefanu, moreover, did not limit himself to the role
of a go-between, for he himself became a partner in the
Gümüşgerdan firm. Stefanu was one of those representatives
of the guild elite who sprang up at a time when the guilds
themselves were decaying and when guild functions served only
as a cover for capitalist relations. As can be seen from the
provisions of the contract between him and his in-laws, the
partnership was organized not only to assure a market for the
goods produced by the Gümüşgerdans; Stefanu also took part in
the firm's widespread commercial operations in the purchase
of aba, and he shared half of all the income and expenses.
The case of Stefanu is yet another example of the path taken
by a guildsman in becoming an entrepreneur.

There is no need to cite other documents to confirm the
obvious conclusion that state contracts were of paramount
importance for the aba production organized by the Gümüşgerdans. Their putting-out industry was dependent on deliveries to the state (although with the exception of the war
years the connection was made through the open market). In
this particular case, government contracts were the factor
that allowed the realization of a capitalist production whose
prerequisites already existed.

In June, 1848, Mihalaki Gümüşgerdan sent a letter of
thanks to the *vali* of Plovdiv in response to the latter's
salutations on the occasion of the opening of the firm's
textile mill in Dermendere. The vali had praised Mihalaki
for his efforts to expand the output of aba for the needs
of the army; at the same time insisting that 100,000 arshin
of a government order of 400,000 arshin be made in the mill.
Gümüşgerdan, expressing his profound gratitude for the
sympathy and assistance shown by the vali, promised that he
would not spare any effort to fulfill the state orders in
compliance with the contracts and to step up the mill's
output of aba.[62]

From this important document it follows, on the one hand,
that the transition to a mill, with its capacity for mass
production of goods of the same quality but at lower produc-

tion costs and with simplified control, was an inevitable
development for the textile industry and was conditioned
by the laws of economic development. On the other hand, the
Gümüşgerdans would not have decided to establish a mill without a permanent market guaranteed in advance, without, in
other words, government contracts and the support of Turkish
administrators.[63]

* * *

Any discussion of the Gümüşgerdans would be incomplete
if it were limited to one aspect of their many-sided activities. To describe fully the typical features of the capitalist entrepreneur of the nineteenth-century Ottoman Empire,
and to isolate some of the unique traits in the capitalist
development of the Balkans, requires an examination of all of
those areas in which capital was applied. The Gümüşgerdans,
for example, were also owners of large amounts of urban and
rural real estate, and they carried out commerce in agricultural goods. Every year they allocated a certain sum for
the purchase of property and livestock.[64]

Four inventories of the Gümüşgerdan property holdings
have been preserved, prepared in the years 1858, 1865, 1868,
and 1880. In the first three the enumeration of the property
is accompanied by an indication of the sum of rent that property produced. In the fourth inventory, which was drawn
up on the eve of Mihalaki Gümüşgerdan's death, the information
on rents is supplemented by the sums that had been spent
acquiring the urban and rural property in question. The
comparison of the data of the first three inventories with
the last one thus permits a determination of the size of
the capital investments in property. The list drawn up in
1880 to distribute property among the heirs of Mihalaki
Gümüşgerdan cites the sums originally paid for the property
(which was listed by name) and not the value of this property
in the year 1880. This inventory did not include the
property that Gümüşgerdan received as dowries and the property
that he personally used. His çiftlik, the mill, and other
property in Dermendere were in general not included; another
principle was followed in the distribution of these
properties among the heirs. Their absence, however, does not
lessen the importance of the inventory. On the contrary,
it shows in even better relief the nature of the Gümüşgerdans
as large-scale property owners who invested nearly 2.5
million kuruş in urban and rural real estate (see table 28).
The largest portion of this sum was used for the purchase
of urban real estate (62% of the total capital outlay),
but the sums invested in agricultural property, mostly in
fields, were also considerable (over 600,000 kuruş or 26%).

TABLE 28

THE REAL ESTATE OF M. GÜMÜŞGERDAN ACCORDING
TO A PROPERTY INVENTORY OF 1880

Type of Property	Purchase Price (in kuruş)	Percentage of Total Value of Property
Urban		
Inns	489,029	20.0
Houses	166,561	7.0
Workrooms	152,625	6.5
Shops	356,815	15.0
Storehouses	287,967	12.0
Courtyards	39,300	1.5
Total	1,492,297	62.0
Rural		
Fields	277,729	11.5
Meadows	58,975	2.5
Orchards	157,402	6.5
Çiftliks	37,875	1.5
Islands on Maritsa River	94,648	4.0
Total	626,629	26.0
Flour Mills	290,429	12.0
TOTAL	2,409,355	100.0

SOURCE: TsDIA, f. 161, 1b8, Testament of M. Gümüşgerdan.

Of particular importance were the mills that, together with
oil presses, yielded significant profits. The total sum of
the rent obtained by the Gümüşgerdans in the mid-nineteenth
century amounted to at least 180,000 kuruş a year.

As to urban property, as early as 1858 the Gümüşgerdans
concentrated in their hands 43 workrooms of varying values,
4 inns (3 in Plovdiv and 1 in Dermendere), 10 houses (8 in
Plovdiv and 2 in Istanbul), 45 shops and workshops (practically all in Plovdiv but a few in Istanbul, Dermendere,
and Tatar Pazardzhik), a public bathhouse in Plovdiv, a
casino in Istanbul, and 10 storehouses. Rent from this urban
real estate represented an important item in the Gümüşgerdans'

revenue. From the leasing of inns, workrooms, and houses, they obtained from 20 to 35% of their total rental income in different years. They rented the inns and workrooms either to several persons or to a single individual who in his turn would sublet them. In the majority of cases, the inns and workrooms were the places for work and trade of artisans and shopkeepers, as was the case with the 45 to 90 shops also owned by the Gümüşgerdans. There could hardly be a more reliable proof of the developing transfer of ownership of the means of production into the hands of a big capitalist.

The Gümüşgerdans obtained the greatest return from flour mills, about 30% of their entire rental income. In absolute terms, only the rent from the shops (which amounted to from 60,000 to 70,000 kuruş) exceeded that from mills. Their high rate of return was the reason why the flour mills occupied a leading place in the will of Mihalaki Gümüşgerdan.

As noted, the Gümüşgerdans also had considerable investments in land. In three years alone (from 1855 to 1858) they purchased 2,568 hectares of fields, 20.04 hectares of meadows, and 12.25 hectares of vineyards. At the same time they possessed 13,905 fruit trees. That agricultural rent made up only an insignificant percentage of the total rental income was due to most of the land not being leased but rather cultivated by the Gümüşgerdans themselves. The labor force used to farm this land consisted of day laborers whose ranks included numerous shepherds, cowherds, swineherds, grooms, gardeners, rice growers, and many cultivators.[65] The cultivators worked for weeks and sometimes for months every year and numbered between thirty and forty. Many people were also employed to cultivate the vineyards. It was a case, in other words, of agricultural production spread over several çiftliks and organized in a capitalist fashion.[66]

* * *

Finally, it is also necessary to analyze the relations between the Gümüşgerdans and the craft guilds located within their area of manufacture. In some cases these relations had to do with artisans and guilds in the rural areas of the Rhodopes, and in others with urban guilds.

The date of the emergence of the abacı guild in the Akhŭchelebi area is not known. After the Gümüşgerdans established their putting-out manufacture, the guild of the local Rhodope producers was the first organization with which they came into contact, and they used it to fulfill large orders. The links were permanent, and to emphasize how much the firm relied on this organization, Mihalaki Gümüşgerdan became head of the guild. Without much doubt, the abacı guild of Akhŭchelebi was completely under Gümüşgerdan's thumb.

More detailed information, however, is available on the

relations in the late 1840s and 1850s between the firm and the
dyers' guilds in Plovdiv, Karlovo, Kalofer, and Tatar Pazardzhik. As well as individual receipts, the archives contain
several contracts concluded between the Gümüşgerdans and
spokesmen of guilds in these cities. Sufficient information
is present in these records to study the volume of the fabrics
dyed, the amount of dyes used, the rate of payment of labor,
and other matters.[67] Insofar as the main concern here is the
relationship between a capitalist entrepreneur and a guild,
only portions of these documents will be discussed.

All of the contracts are practically identical, differing
only in the amounts they specify. Commonly, the guild leaders
who signed these contracts provided the person who placed the
order with a special sample, stamped with a seal. The contract itself listed the specifications that the guildmen had
to observe in dyeing the entire consignment. Thus, the first
clause of a contract with the Karlovo dyers dated July 27,
1854, reads as follows: "The şayak cloths which we are to dye
have to be done according to the contract and must not differ
from the sample which we have given to the highly esteemed
[purchasers], stamped by us, without having any spots and
dark patches." The third clause of the same contract states:
"We are to assure . . . that the şayak cloths should be so
saturated that they remain clear blue, as is the sample which
we gave with a stamp."

The contracts specified the dyes, the degree of satura-
tion, and so forth, and the guild was responsible for any
failure to meet the specifications, even to the point that it
undertook the obligation to pay the expenses of redyeing at
the Gümüşgerdan mill should this prove necessary. Thus, the
second paragraph of the contract in question stipulates: "If
spots appear in the şayak we have dyed and delivered, we
undertake to make them right ourselves, or to bear the
expenses and the right to make them good if these same gentle-
men wish to dye them anew and to correct them in their
factory." The guild undertook not to tolerate any falsifica-
tion of dyes, threatening its members with public censure
and fines. Paragraph four of the contract thus reads: "In
the dyeing of the şayak . . . pure blue dye has to be used, dye
which has not been used before, nor dye mixed with *bakami*
[a blue-dye substitute obtained from campeachy wood]; and no
other incorrect method should be used by us in the dyeing,
for, if such an infringement is discovered, let us be
punished by the guild by moral censure and a fine."[68]

For the work involved, the Gümüşgerdans paid 3 and 4
kuruş per okka. In addition the dyers were required to buy
from the Gümüşgerdans all the dye that they needed, clause
five of the contract stating: "Whatever amount of blue dye we

use for the şayak which we are to dye, we must obtain from the
highly esteemed M. and D. Gümüşgerdan at the price of 140
kuruş, without having the right to purchase a single dram
from anybody else."

In this manner, the regulations whose norms existed in
the guilds during the middle of the nineteenth century, and
whose infringement was punished with all of the authority
of the guild, were not an expression of guild equality. The
establishment of a single price for dyeing for all guildsmen
had nothing in common with the earlier regulations of the guild
or the state. Nor were these measures aimed at stepping up
the struggle against competition in order to preserve equality
among the artisans of a given guild in the production and sale
of their merchandise. Rather, they were designed to foster
the output of standard goods according to the orders placed
by big entrepreneurs. In its regulations and all of its
institutions, the guild emerged in this case only as a branch
of production supplementing the industrial enterprise of the
Gümüşgerdans. The guild proved most suitable for rallying the
efforts of the scattered artisans to meet the needs of the
capitalist who had placed the order.

* * *

The discussion so far has revolved around a capitalist
enterprise that produced the basic aba cloth. This area of
activity constituted the backbone of aba-related production
in a considerable part of the Bulgarian lands and the Balkan
provinces of the Ottoman state where livestock raising and
wool processing were developed. To put into better per-
spective the specific nature of the capitalist manufacture of
the Gümüşgerdans--which involved the preliminary processing
of the wool, the weaving of the cloth itself, and the dyeing
of the aba made by peasants--an examination will now be made
of another capitalist enterprise that dealt with the sewing
of aba clothing, the so-called Egyptian Company.

Information about this firm is contained in the memoirs
of Mikhail Madzharov, the son of the firm's founder.[69] The
memoirist, a prominent Bulgarian publicist, politician, and
man of culture, was himself for a certain period of time an
apprentice who worked together with the other apprentices and
journeymen. He also kept the firm's books, and as an abacı
he toured the country and visited Istanbul. The commercial
affairs of the firm often compelled him to travel to various
parts of the Balkan Peninsula and Egypt, where the firm had
representatives (hence the name of the enterprise). The
absence in Madzharov's memoirs of data on the volume of production and the amount of invested capital is fully compensated by his lively narrative concerning the relations among

the workers, between his father and the partners, and between
the enterprise and the guild. Madzharov himself described his
origins as "bourgeois," having in mind the period when his
father consolidated his material position (about the mid-
nineteenth century) and passed as one of the richest persons
in Koprivshtitsa. In Madzharov's words, his great-grandfather
was a priest with limited income, and his grandfather was an
artisan who produced and dealt in cotton fabrics and ker-
chiefs. For cotton he traveled to Serres and Salonika, leaving his wife to manage his workshop in his absence. In
describing the initial steps of his father as an abacı, Madzharov wrote that for a long time he lacked the means to
support his family.

But soon Madzharov was going to Pazardzhik to buy large
quantities of aba produced in the Rhodope villages. He
brought it back to Koprivshtitsa where he had it fashioned
into clothing. The clothes were cut by Madzharov himself,
and when the company was set up, by the other partners as
well. They worked, however, in their own homes, which they
had adapted for turning the aba into clothing and thick woolen
slippers. As a permanent work force, Madzharov hired ten to
fifteen apprentices and journeymen for monthly wages and food
three times a day. Even so, Madzharov had even larger
quantities made to order outside the workshop. The finished
merchandise was packed up in large sacks and in the autumn
was sent by caravans to the places where it was intended
for sale.

Up to and during the Crimean War, as long as Madzharov
worked alone, the finished merchandise was sold in Istanbul
where he had an office. That Madzharov himself resided in
the capital five or six months or more a year, and that the
merchandise sent there was accompanied by several journeymen
and apprentices, suggests that even prior to the establishment
of the Egyptian Company Madzharov maintained a workshop in
Istanbul.

His major clients were Egyptian merchants who traded with
Istanbul and often visited the city, which made it imperative
for Madzharov to organize an additional workshop in the
capital itself. Aba clothing varied in cut and it was
necessary to conform to the requirements of the different
merchants. Thus, the traveling abacıs took along not only
finished clothing but also a certain amount of aba cloth
together with several journeymen and apprentices to put the
final touches on the semifinished clothing where the merchandise was sold in Istanbul and Asia Minor.

Madzharov had long since been familiar with the potential
and requirements of the Egyptian market with which he was
thus closely connected prior to the foundation of the Egyptian

Company in the mid-1850s. And although the establishment of
the firm represented a new stage in his activity and signaled
the creation of new forms of production, the activities of
Madzharov had already become capitalist in nature. Indeed, by
the mid-1850s his transformation from an artisan into an
artisan-merchant and a capitalist had already been completed.
He exploited the labor of more than ten journeymen and
apprentices who worked for him on a permanent basis and
approximately the same number or perhaps even more people who
labored outside his workshop. In addition, Madzharov also
dealt in stockings, which he bought in large quantities from
women knitters.

It should be stressed, however, that Madzharov's entire
activity was still taking place within the framework of the
aba guild. His considerable output did not bring him into
collision with the guildsmen since, as has been indicated, the
very character of abacı production and trade presupposed the
application of only a limited amount of equalizing regulation.
Accordingly, medium-sized enterprises of a capitalist character grew up and became indistinguishable among the mass of
artisan workshops, differing from them only in terms of the
volume of production. Only when Madzharov's activity reached
the point where it began to affect the interests of the abacı
artisans more deeply did the guild declare itself against
him and proceed to the application of economic sanctions. And
this situation came about as a result of the activity of the
Egyptian Company.

Carefully watching the state of the market, Madzharov got
in touch with Doncho Palaveev, also a master abacı, and
founded an enterprise for the manufacture of aba goods and
their sale in Egypt. Since Madzharov invested the greater
part of the capital, he also received an additional 10% on
top of his corresponding share of the profits.

The establishment of the firm did not lead to any basic
changes in the organization of production in Koprivshtitsa
itself. As before, ten to fifteen journeymen and apprentices
worked at the home of each partner. The entire output,
together with merchandise manufactured outside the workshops
and quantities of stockings that had been purchased for
resale, was dispatched by caravans to Gelibolu and from there
by sea to Alexandria and Cairo.

In Istanbul, however, some modifications in production
did take place in connection with increased market demand.
Along with the office and the workshop in the Corapci Han
quarter, where several journeymen worked permanently, the
firm also resorted to the services of a Greek abacı. Every
week Madzharov gave this Greek abacı rolls of şayak cloth
and received ready-made clothing. About a dozen journey-

men were permanently employed in the workshop of the Greek
master.

In Cairo, where most of the merchandise made in Istanbul
was sold, the firm owned accommodations for Palaveev and the
journeymen, one shop for wholesale trade, and two retail
shops. The firm's direct trade with the population was not
that significant. Rather, it sold its ware to Arab and
Bokhara merchants and shopkeepers who dealt in both wholesale and retail trade. Palaveev settled down in Cairo. He
was responsible for the commerce in Egypt and the completion
of semifinished goods in Cairo, while Madzharov managed the
production and commerce in Koprivshtitsa and Istanbul.

Originally Alexandria was only a point of delivery where
two journeymen saw to the regular receipt and dispatch of the
merchandise. Soon, however, its importance as a new center
of production and trade increased, and ten permanent employees
came to be located there. With seasonal workers, the firm's
personnel in Alexandria then grew to between fifteen and
twenty persons. Changes in the status of the journeymen
accompanied this expansion of production. After a certain
period of time, the first two journeymen became partners. The
new partners, however, jointly received only one share of the
profits, though they also received an additional monthly
remuneration. The firm opened agencies in other towns as
well: Serres, Salonika, and Bursa. In these cities its permanent agents and middlemen purchased finished products from
local producers and sent them on to Egypt.

The Egyptian Company was clearly a capitalist enterprise
in both its production and commerce. It permanently employed
about one-hundred workers, and no less impressive was the number of those temporarily engaged for piecework or those from
whom the firm purchased finished products for resale. The
partners' relations were structured on a purely capitalist
basis. Madzharov received a percentage against the invested
capital in the enterprise. But since they had no capital, the
status of the two new partners (the former journeymen) to all
intents and purposes did not change after their incorporation
into the firm. They received part of the profits in Alexandria, but essentially they participated in the firm as masters
employed by Madzharov, for which they were paid monthly wages.
It was precisely for this reason that at the first chance they
left the firm, as Madzharov himself admitted, "dissatisfied
with their position in seeking higher profits."

The most important trait of Madzharov's enterprise was
that it linked all of its activity with the free market. In
the first stage of its existence, it sold its output to merchants in Istanbul. Later on, after the establishment of
the Egyptian Company, the firm expanded its commercial

and productive activities, and began to send the merchandise
directly to the places of demand without the mediation of
wholesale merchants. In neither case, moreover, was the
enterprise in any way linked with the Turkish government.

The character of the firm's production, however, did
not differ from artisan production. The workers were taken
on as journeymen, and for some time the capitalist proprietor
himself shared in the work. There was no centralized enterprise, and the organization of production failed to acquire
the stable forms observed in the Gümüşgerdans' manufacture.
The firm had several workshops in different centers with a
primitive division of labor that differed only slightly from
that used in artisan workshops.

For quite some time Madzharov's bond with the craft guild
was fairly close and strong. Although the subsequent activity
of the company produced a conflict that considerably weakened
this link, Madzharov nevertheless remained a member of the
guild until Bulgaria's liberation from Turkish rule. This
continuing relationship had purely economic motives as well
as being due to the public role of the guild (which was one
of the fundamental organs of self-government of the Bulgarian
people). The abacı guild in Koprivshtitsa owned a dyehouse
where all guildsmen dyed their aba. Throughout the whole
period of its activity the Egyptian Company also used the
guild's dyehouse.

The conflict mentioned between the company and the guild
in the early 1850s was brought about by the impact that the
company began to have on the market. Not only Madzharov and
Palaveev but all of the abacıs of the Koprivshtitsa guild
sold their wares in Istanbul. During this period Egyptian
merchants who came to the capital were the major purchasers
of these goods. When the Egyptian Company began to deliver
merchandise to Egypt, it diverted part of the merchants from
the Istanbul market, for they now could receive goods from
Madzharov and his partners in such cities as Alexandria and
Cairo. This circumstance could not but affect the market
in Istanbul, where the Koprivshtitsa abacıs continued to
export their wares.

To stop this trend, the guild employed all forms of
struggle, including the use of economic sanctions. On one
occasion the guild forbade the company from producing more
goods in Koprivshtitsa than before. This decision was
subsequently revoked, but the partners were thereupon compelled to transport their total output first to Istanbul and
from there to Egypt. In this way the guild attempted to
exercise control over the firm's production and trade. It
also tried to compel it to make up any shortfall in its
needs by purchases only from guild members. But the guild's

struggle ended in failure. The company won, acquiring the right to produce and to trade freely according to its potential, and the partners remained members of the guild.

The story of Madzharov is a vivid example of the transformation of an artisan into a capitalist, one whose variegated activities typify the entrepreneur combining both commerce and production, for Madzharov, like Gümüşgerdan, invested a considerable part of his capital in agriculture. He was one of the biggest stock raisers in Koprivshtitsa and he organized this work on capitalist principles.

The Egyptian Company is a case illustrating the establishment of capitalist relations in industry via the submission and unification of numerous artisans under the management of one or several capitalists. Particularly characteristic of the process of subordination are the relations of the company with the Greek abacı in Istanbul. By supplying him regularly with raw materials and buying up all of his finished output, the firm effectively transformed his workshop into one its own branches, thus tending toward its complete absorption.

In its capitalist development, however, the Egyptian Company did not reach the level of a centralized enterprise. This is what differentiates it from the Gümüşgerdans' enterprise.

The ultimate demise of the Egyptian Company was caused by European competition, which undermined the company's markets despite the existence of generally favorable conditions for its development. It was soon forced to use European broadcloth as well, but even this was of no avail. By the late 1860s the company had begun to decline, although it did continue to exist until Bulgaria's liberation in 1878.

* * *

Keeping in mind the comparison with the Madzharov enterprise, the material and social conditions that made it possible for the Gümüşgerdan manufacture to consolidate, expand, and act as the basis for the emergence of one of the earliest factories in the Balkans, must now be clarified.

It is first necessary once again to discuss the nature of the commodity involved. Aba cloth was the universally used fabric for clothing throughout practically the whole Ottoman Empire. The production of this cloth and the clothing made from it very early went beyond the limits of local markets and found opportunities for sale in Istanbul and throughout the Middle East, for these goods were purchased not only by Turkish merchants and consumers but by Arabs as well. By the end of the eighteenth century the production of aba had gradually acquired a manufacturing character in some areas. The great distance to the principal markets and the chance to go beyond the guild's regulations shaped the specific features of the production of aba and aba garments. For six months there would be an intensive sewing of clothing; during the rest of the year these goods would be transported to distant markets for sale (with finishing touches added at the destination). The need for more massive and intensive production made it imperative for the abacıs to resort to the employment of temporary labor on a scale that was restricted only by the potential of their capital. The employment of a labor force was carried out in a manner typical of artisan forms of production (i.e., the workers were taken on as journeymen).

Such intensive production of clothing, moreover, called for a preliminary supply of raw material--wool cloth. This need in turn presupposed a supply of aba made by village weavers and homespun wool in general, a supply that would regularly provide fixed quantities. Conditions were thus created for reshaping the old forms of the cottage weaving industry and the rural handicrafts, and for the emergence of manufacturing forms in the production of aba cloth itself.

Selling clothing at distant markets provided the abacı with an opportunity to expand their economic activity, taking advantage of the difference that existed between the local prices and those in faraway markets. While the abacı was engaged in marketing the aba clothing that had already been produced, his family continued to turn out goods for sale and to meeting their own needs. Starting as domestic production, this additional output--in woolen stockings for instance--soon came to augment the abacı's expanding commerce and growing profits.

All of this was still insufficient, however, for the emergence of a higher type of capitalist production, of scattered and centralized manufacture, and of factories. It was also necessary to obtain a permanent market for fixed amounts of merchandise. Greater security was also required in the face of growing foreign competition and the transformation of the Ottoman Empire into a source of raw materials for the various capitalist states. This security and stability could be achieved only through the system of state contracts, and it was precisely the establishment of an almost monopolistic and more or less stable position in the fulfillment of state contracts that made possible the appearance of the factory type of production set up by the Gümüşgerdans. The lack of such conditions prevented other similar enterprises, such as Madzharov's, not only from expanding their production but also from overcoming the primitive capitalist forms in which they continued to develop.

To attain this favored position, the Gümüşgerdans had to
ensure the benevolence of the Ottoman administration. They
tried to secure this support by any and all means--bribes,
various gifts, and so on. In addition, the more that economic
development led to the appearance of other centers of mass
aba production and the more intensive the penetration of
foreign capital into the Ottoman state became--the sharper
the external and internal competition--the more complex
became the methods used by the Gümüşgerdans to hold onto
their permanent market in the form of state contracts. They
stepped up bribes; they entered into business ties with the
representatives of the Turkish administration; and they drew
several senior officials into some of their operations. But
this description of the linkage between the Gümüşgerdans
and the administration would be incomplete if it also failed
to emphasize once again the ruthless exploitation of the
producers and the use of even open robbery that took place
with the full support of the Turkish authorities.

But notwithstanding their practically monopolistic
position in the market and the protection they received from
the state, and despite all of their opportunities for exploitation in aba production, the Gümüşgerdans did not put all of
their eggs into this basket. The absence in the Ottoman
Empire of the basic conditions for bourgeois accumulation
denied them those economic and social conditions necessary
for a steadily progressive development of the industrial forms
of production they had introduced. Therefore, they also
concentrated their capital in commercial operations, bought
vast tracts of land and urban real estate, and for decades
adhered to industrial forms already established in the 1830s.

* * *

The cases just examined in the different branches of
textile production are significant because they illustrate
general regularities in the development of entrepreneurial
capital and capitalist enterpreneurs in the Balkans. As
already indicated, historians have accepted the eighteenth
century as a period of fundamental changes in the socioeconomic structure of all peoples in the Ottoman Empire. In
terms of Greek society, too, Greek historiography, including
Marxist historiography, has defined this century as a period
of the consolidation of new social forces: a merchant estate
according to some, a true bourgeoisie according to others.[70]

Along with the development of capital involved in middleman commercial operations, and together with the involvement
of agriculture in the export trade, industry in Greece also
underwent a considerable growth, and in the eighteenth century
it entered the manufacturing stage. The favorable European

situation in the last decades of the century augmented an
intensive export of woolen and silk products and yarn--all of
which were produced throughout practically all of Greece.

This growing production also saw the emergence of specialized settlements with a well-advanced manufacturing
division of labor. Thus, settlements in the area of Zagora
(in Epirus) concentrated on the production of yağmurluks
(hooded felt cloaks) and other clothing much in demand by
large numbers of Greek sailors. Producers in Salonika were
some of the principal suppliers of woolen products to the
Turkish army. The commercial textile firms of Ioannina had
representatives throughout Europe, from Moscow to Venice. The
manufacture in Ambelakia (Thessaly) achieved a flourishing
state of development, supplying yarn to a number of big
enterprises in Austria, Germany, and even France.[71]

In the case of Ambelakia the Greek lands provide an
example of a unique form of the capitalist organization of
textile production, one involving a unification of several
capitalist entrepreneurs and commodity producers in the form
of an export-import association. The story of Ambelakia
has found a place in the literature if for no other reason
than the impact it made on the Western European market
through the production supplied by the association. For many
years it successfully competed with the capitalist production
of England, the most advanced industrial country of all.[72]

The true upsurge of Ambelakia took place in the second
half of the eighteenth century and in the early nineteenth
century. But even prior to this time the settlement, which
was entirely Christian, had well-developed handicrafts. The
transformation of Ambelakia into the most important textile
center in northern Greece was connected with the strong
development of Greek commercial capital as early as the
seventeenth century and the beginning of the eighteenth
century, a time when this capital started to seek application
in production.

Ambelakia became famous, however, on account of the
unsurpassed skill of its artisans in dyeing textiles. In the
late eighteenth century, twenty-four dyehouses were in operation, employed fully for the dyeing of cotton yarn and textiles. It seems that the process involved, adopted perhaps
from Asia Minor or elsewhere, used plant pigments that imparted
a unique red color to the yarn. All of the reports of Western
European consuls, travelers, and entrepreneurs concerned with
this matter were unanimous in this respect: the yarns dyed in
Ambelakia could not be matched in the European market. The
secret of the dyeing process was rigidly protected, although
there was such an interest in the technique that numerous
efforts were made to discover it. Thus, workers from

Ambelakia were invited to various Western enterprises. Finally, in the early nineteenth century the traveler F. Beaujour wrote that the French had succeeded in mastering this technique and were now using it in Montpellier. Beaujour's enthusiastic description of Ambelakia[73] is explicable when one bears in mind that, despite the great industrial progress of Manchester and the other English textile centers, the red-colored French textiles for a long time withstood English competition thanks to the dyers brought to France from Ambelakia and the discovery of the technology they employed.

According to the information furnished by various travelers the annual output of the yarn dyed in Ambelakia reached 3,000 bales, each weighing 250 pounds (125 kilograms). Many contemporaries wrote about exports in the range of 250,000 to 300,000 okka. These are impressive figures for a settlement of a few hundred houses.

As noted, Ambelakia specialized in the dyeing of cotton textiles, an activity related to the eighteenth-century expansion of cotton production in Thessaly and Thrace. This was the period when Serres became one of the great cotton growing areas in the Balkans. The cotton brought from these places, and that imported from Egypt and elsewhere, was made into yarn. According to contradictory information, from one thousand to two thousand dyers were engaged in dyeing this yarn in Ambelakia.

Another characteristic of Ambelakia was a production geared for distant markets, in this particular case for European markets in Austria and Germany. The dominating commercial purpose of the capital determined the organizational structure of the enterprise. In the 1780s several commercial companies or associations for export were set up, and they gradually took under their control the production and dyeing of cotton and yarn. The finished merchandise was transported to the nearby port of Karitsa (four hours from Ambelakia) from where it was carried by sea to Salonika, Smyrna, and Istanbul; or on land--in caravans of hundreds of mules, horses, and sometimes of camels--to Vienna, Leipzig, Dresden, and Hamburg.

In 1778 the associations merged under the leadership of the richest firm into a company that incorporated about eighty of the bigger merchants and several hundred masters. Some time later other associations sprang up. The merger and dissolution of the associations was linked with market fluctuations. Before it finally drove Ambelakia's yarn out of European markets in the 1820s, English competition on several occasions sharply disrupted the town's marketing with serious consequences for production itself. New markets were sought and a reorientation toward Asia Minor was considered,

and attempts were made to import machines for improving the
quality of the yarn.

Masters who participated in the associations by shares
did so individually or in groups that had formed to put
together the minimum rate of 5,000 kuruş needed for one share.
The bulk of the workers were excluded from participation in
the company. The system of payment was such that about half
of the total wages were paid after the marketing of the
merchandise.

In Ambelakia, furthermore, there was a close relationship
between the associations and municipal administrative authorities, a phenomenon also observable in the Bulgarian lands in
the third quarter of the nineteenth century. The same persons
and business circles that headed the associations--that is,
the richest merchants and entrepreneurs--dominated the ranks
of those municipal authorities who were responsible to the
Ottoman government for the collection of taxes. They thus
enjoyed full power over the population, since they used
association funds to pay taxes.

* * *

The introduction of a manufacturing division of labor
and organization also led to the development of other branches
of artisan production in the Greek lands. Some settlements
specialized in the manufacture of arms and gunpowder (e.g.,
Demiciana in the Peloponnesus). Ore mining was developed
mainly in the peninsula of Chalcidice, in whose area more
than three hundred villages and about ten small towns
formed a unique semiautonomous corporation known by the
name of "Mademochoria."

In this way continental Greece saw the emergence of a
strong stratum of bourgeoisie composed of capitalist entrepreneurs and organizers of scattered and centralized manufacture. This capitalist stratum was most directly connected
with industrial production. The general economic laws concerning the appearance and development of capitalist relations
in the textile crafts, which have been examined above, hold
equally valid for Greece. But it would be of even greater
interest to study how this process developed in another
truly powerful stratum of the Greek bourgeoisie, that of
the shipowners.

The specific aspects of the rise of Greek capital in
shipowning and shipbuilding have not as yet been studied.
However, the Greek scholar V. Kremmydas has been the first
to examine certain facets of capitalist organization in
this area on the basis of the archives of a large Greek
shipowner. This author's point of departure is that in the
mid-eighteenth century the Greek bourgeoisie took shape as a

class. On this basis he has studied the activities of the
family of Hacı Panayoti-Politi of Tsakonia (a region in the
Peloponnesus), summarizing the material in the form of several
tables equipped with a commentary.[74]

The author has first of all established that outsiders
had investments and shares in the ships owned by Panayoti.
For the period from 1792 to 1799, a period when the names of
investors began to appear in the ledgers, fifty-five investors
have been isolated who provided a total outlay of 63,672
kuruş. Of these investors, seven persons (whose investments
accounted for 38% of the total sum mentioned) were also
shipowners, an illustration of the extent to which large shipowners were interlocking their activities and interests and a
sign of how difficult it was "for the small capitalist to
increase his capital while working in the ranks of the already
established economic oligarchy."[75] Furthermore, nine of the
investors (including those providing the largest sums) were
Panayoti's close relatives. His brother had the biggest
investment, totalling 9,790 kuruş. The course of eight
years saw the investors repeatedly putting in shares of several tens of kuruş to about a hundred kuruş a year. Over
the whole period these came to total from a few hundred to
several thousand kuruş from each. The ledgers list sixteen
persons with investments of more than 1,000 kuruş each.

The number of investors that the author has described
as capitalists and the amount of their investments are shown
in table 29. The year 1795 saw a sharp decrease both in the
number of investments and in the total sum involved. There
was another significant decrease in investments in 1799, but
for that year the author has noted the appearance of the names
of some thirty new investors. On the basis of Panayoti's
archives, the author has concluded that the flourishing period
of their entrepreneurial operations occurred toward the
beginning of the nineteenth century, the period of Napoleon's
Continental Blockade, when Greek smuggling and shipbuilding
became very intense.

Another group of persons that the author has defined
rather tentatively were those with whom Panayoti invested some
of his own capital. These individuals were also shipowners--
although operating on a smaller scale of activity (ordinary
captains, etc.)--with whom Panayoti frequently entered into
association. In consideration of a fixed percentage or a
single payment, Panayoti participated in numerous individual
operations of various dimensions.

According to the author, Panayoti was "a big Greek
capitalist." He emerged and was active in the late eighteenth century and in the early nineteenth century, a period
when the capitalist development of Greek society was making

TABLE 29

INVESTMENTS IN THE SHIPOWNING ACTIVITY OF H. PANAYOTI,
1792-1799

Year	Number of Investors	Number of Investments	Total Investments (in kuruş)
1792	8	17	5,250
1793	9	18	5,340
1794	22	67	15,300
1795	17	29	7,750
1796	25	78	11,430
1797	32	111	12,460
1798*	--	---	------
1799	71	71	4,480

SOURCE: Kremmydas, "Opseis tes Tsakonikes Koinonias (1784-1821)," p.23.
  *The documents contain no information for 1798.

rapid headway. The great development of commercial capital in
Greece and the favorable concurrence of international circumstances provided a powerful impetus to this unique combination
of commercial capital with shipowning and shipbuilding. It
was in this sphere of activity that entrepreneurial capitalism
in Greece attained its greatest development.

The Transition from Feudalism to Capitalism

14. THE FIRST FACTORIES

The eventual and total bankruptcy of the solemnly proclaimed reforms of the Ottoman *Tanzimat* (c. 1839-78) explains why Balkan historiography has ignored the Porte's concurrent attempts to bring about some modernization of industry in the empire. In this regard historians have generally limited themselves to a discussion of the related efforts of Midhat Paşa as part of his overall reform activity in the Danubian vilâyet. But however insignificant such efforts appear when measured against what was happening in the rapidly developing industries of other states, they should not be overlooked in studying the concrete development of industry in the territories of the Ottoman state. Actually, the space of one or two decades saw state subsidies being used in the establishment of not less than fifteen factories built on a European model and using imported machinery.

Ottoman authorities, it is true, did not sufficiently
understand or consistently implement this kind of activity,
and as a result of the general ignorance and the rampant cor-
ruption and malfeasance of the ruling circles, a large number
of these enterprises soon went under.[1]

A broadcloth mill in Sliven was the first state industrial enterprise in the European domains of the empire. Its
appearance signaled a new stage in the evolution of the Balkan
textile industry, a transition from the manufacturing stage
to mechanized factory production.[2] (Beginning in the 1840s,
the period of transition was to continue for several decades.)
After the successful experiment with the opening of the Sliven
mill, the Turkish government proceeded with the opening of
several other mills for the production of broadcloth and
other textile products, thus also encouraging private initiative.

The mill in Sliven survived until the end of the century.
Its existence and prolonged operation pose a number of interesting questions for historians, questions that are the
initial concern of this chapter. An effort will also be made
to analyze the structure of the first private mill, one which
the Gümüşgerdans constructed in 1848 in the vicinity of
Plovdiv.[3] What is of particular significance in the study
of these factories is that they mirror the level of development of capitalist relations in the Bulgarian lands, which
at that time constituted the economically most advanced part
of the Balkan possessions of the empire.

These mills--the one in Sliven and the one near Plovdiv--
were the first true factories. Their buildings were specially
constructed for an industrial purpose; they had workers whose
numbers grew rapidly (from a few dozen to more than one
hundred); and they possessed machinery imported from Western
Europe. This factory production convincingly demonstrates
the irreversibility of the process of emerging capitalist
relations, which had begun in the eighteenth century. During
the first few decades of the nineteenth century this led to a
considerable growth in the number of capitalist enterprises
and amount of putting-out production, and to the appearance
of some centralized manufacture and factories. The lack of
sources has hitherto hindered the study of this important
stage in the economic development of the Balkan lands. The
analysis that follows is aimed at filling, insofar as possible,
this gap.

It might be noted here that historians have usually
argued that the Sliven and Plovdiv factories employed a work
force that consisted of convicts or of forced labor.[4] More
generally, and however strange it may seem, Balkan historians
have not used, even with the broadest caveats, the term

"working class" for this period. This has been true even
though these same historians have frequently mentioned Greek,
Bulgarian, Serbian, and other "bourgeoisies" as an independent
class and with a number of strata, including the "big industrial bourgeoisie." In the class analysis of Bulgarian
society, for instance, Bulgarian historians have usually
placed at the opposing pole of this bourgeoisie such social
groups as "ruined craftsmen," "proletarianized rural and urban
masses," the "lowest strata of society," and so on. When
the term "workers" has been cited, it has been employed only
to point out that in some branches of production growing
stratification was beginning to set journeymen and apprentices
apart from their masters as "workers." Even those authors who
have most sympathetically described the unfortunate life of
the numerous apprentices, journeymen, and others who toiled
in manufactories have ignored hired labor as a new class
phenomenon and as a class force.[5] Accordingly, another major
purpose of this chapter will be to clarify the nature of the
labor force engaged in the two mills in question. As Lenin
emphasized, the "degree of the spread of hired labor is
almost of the greatest importance in the problem of the
development of capitalism."[6]

* * *

     The first true factory in the Bulgarian lands and in the
Balkan provinces of the Ottoman Empire was built in Sliven
in 1836.[7] It was an event whose significance was immediately
understood by contemporaries. Konstantin Fotinov, for
example, a Bulgarian activist living and working in Smyrna,
greeted this development with delight in a work entitled
General Geography, which he published in 1843. Sliven, he
wrote, "has become truly worthy of fame because of the
broadcloth mill that its highly praiseworthy and memorable
citizen, the wise Mr. Dobri Zheliazkov has put into operation,
with the aid of the highly skilled G. Atanassio, the watchmaker; and let his name be immortal and praised forever by
all industrious Bulgarians."[8]
     That this was not empty patriotic adulation can be seen
from the great impression the mill made on foreigners. The
well-known traveler Ami Boué, who left the first description
of the mill almost immediately after its opening, viewed it
as having great importance as a serious attempt by the
Ottoman government to free itself from a dependence on the
import of high-quality fabrics and broadcloth in particular.[9]
Two decades later Sliven was visited by another traveler, who
stayed in the area for a longer time. For this visitor,
"the elegant buildings of the mill remind one of our
European comfort."[10]

It was not accidental that Sliven was the site of the
first Balkan factory. As early as the eighteenth century
such Sliven products as thick woolen blankets, rugs made of
goat's wool, and carpets were exported not only to Rumelia,
but also to Arab and Persian lands. Merchants from distant
parts of the empire gathered to do business at the month-long
Sliven fair. Writing in the mid-1830s, the Bulgarian activist
Aprilov reported that the inhabitants of Sliven (who numbered
about 20,000) "trade with Asia, Austria and Wallachia, have
important woolen products which they dye red and yellow [and
which are] unknown in other places, even in Europe."[11] It
was precisely the qualities of the Sliven aba that drew the
attention of the Turkish government, which, still failing to
meet its needs even after buying up almost all of the broadcloth made in Salonika and a large part of the aba produced
in Plovdiv, entrusted the Sliven voyvoda with organizing the
supply of aba from his part of the country as well. This
aba was needed for the reorganized Turkish army, which
required large quantities of standard material for the
uniforms of soldiers and officers. In 1827 the Sliven abacıs
Todor and Iordan signed a contract on behalf of other Sliven
producers with the manager of the military arsenal in Istanbul
for the supply of 10,000 pieces of aba cloth.[12] Only a few
years later Sliven, together with Kotel (in other words the
whole eastern Balkans), became involved in supplying the
Turkish government with 60,000 rolls of aba at 18.5 kuruş
per roll. On the insistence of the Porte, this amount was
increased to 80,000 rolls.[13] About the middle of the century,
Sliven was producing some 650,000 meters of cloth from about
250,000 okka of wool (320,513 kilograms).[14] On the average
each home processed about 10 okka of wool for its own needs
and used another 20-30 okka to make yarn or other goods for
sale.[15]

As noted, the Sliven voyvoda was the official entrusted
with the supply of aba for the Turkish army. The treasury
placed funds at his disposal and at the same time granted
him a personal monopoly in the purchase of both the necessary
amount of wool and the aba cloth whose supply had been contracted. From the scanty information available on this
subject, it is easier to study the misappropriations and
violence that befell the direct producers rather than the
manner of delivery of the aba produced. The voyvoda took advantage of his monopoly to buy an okka of wool at a price 40-50
para lower than the market price and to charge the abacıs a
price higher than the market one.[16] Furthermore, citing
his prerogatives in the supply of wool for state contracts,
the voyvoda even collected a special levy from abacıs who
procured their own wool. The voyvoda, moreover, paid lower

than market prices for the finished aba. At most, and regardless of its quality, he paid from 14 to 16 kuruş per roll of
aba. This situation enabled him to commit additional fraud
since he could then select the best aba for resale to merchants at 25 kuruş a roll while using cheap aba to make up the
resultant shortfall in the amount of aba that he had contracted
to deliver.[17] The voyvoda could easily prevent the abacıs
from trying to avoid being defrauded; he was in a position to
accuse them of smuggling or of failing to fulfill a state contract, charges that might result in fines and even in incar-
ceration.[18]

The misuse of authority aside, Sliven's intensified production for the domestic and foreign markets, and particularly
for the needs of the army, provided the backdrop against which
Dobri Zheliazkov began his manufacturing activity. Having
left Sliven during the mass emigration of its inhabitants in
the aftermath of the Russo-Turkish War of 1828-29, Zheliazkov settled in Ekarterinoslav (Dnepropetrovsk), where he
was able to observe that city's developing textile industry.
He copied designs of looms, spinning wheels, and carding
machines, and purchased machinery. In 1834, after his return
to Sliven, he set up in his home a workshop with a carding
machine driven by a horse.[19] The local authorities took an
interest in his work, prompted more by the quality and appearance of the broadcloth he produced than by its method of
production. For the needs of the court and the officer corps,
the Turkish government had been procuring broadcloth from
Salonika, where Jewish refugees from Spain had set up a considerable production as early as the sixteenth century. This
source, however, could no longer satisfy the government's
large demand, and expensive broadcloth from Western Europe
was coming to occupy an important place in Turkey's imports.
It was in order to curtail these imports that the Turkish
government became interested in Zheliazkov's activity. It
summoned him to the Porte, together with samples of the
broadcloth he had made from both local and Spanish wool.
Zheliazkov's workmanship was found satisfactory, and by a
ferman of 1835 he was entrusted with the "weaving and careful
making of fabrics" according to the samples presented.[20]

Little is known about the actual construction and equipment of the mill that subsequently appeared. Boué provided
some important information about its appearance, machinery,
and number of workers, but it was Zheliazkov's first biog-
rapher who originated the view that Zheliazkov went to
Belgium to procure machinery for the mill.[21] Zheliazkov himself was the owner or at least the director of the mill, but
"slandered and persecuted by the local authorities in Sliven,
he was expelled from the mill which fell into the hands of
inexperienced Turkish administrators and deteriorated."[22]

Certain documents that have been preserved in the Oriental Department of the Cyril and Methodius National Library
permit a more detailed review of the initial period in the
work of the mill, its character, the origin and type of its
machinery, and the production process itself. But what
initially requires clarification is the question of the place
of the mill in the Turkish state system and Zheliazkov's
exact role in its construction and management.

* * *

Zheliazkov's rights and duties are not clear from the
ferman that he received. The document expresses satisfaction
with the work he had been doing; it states that he would
exercise supervision over the proper fulfillment of a plan
for construction and production; and it also informed the
voyvoda of Sliven that Zheliazkov was "to transform everything
from words into deeds and to reveal to the workers such things
as they in point of fact do not know." [23] One may assume that
these words refer to the decision of the Turkish government to
open a mill in Sliven after being convinced by Zheliazkov
that this was possible and that factory-produced broadcloth
would be both cheaper and better than the sample submitted.

The first documents to permit a somewhat more definite
evaluation of Zheliazkov's activity and the structure of
the mill itself concern the year 1837. Two documents are
involved here: a report of an inspector specifically sent
by the Turkish government, the *barutcubaşı* Ovanes,[24] "a know-
ledgeable expert on the question of the manufacture of woolen
cloth"; and a memorandum addressed to the grand vizier with
a request for an allocation of funds for the implementation of
the proposals that Zheliazkov had made. On several occasions
these documents mention that all recommendations "have been
explained one by one to His Excellency Mehmed ağa and to the
chief master Dobri."[25] In subsequent documents Zheliazkov is
again referred to as "chief master."[26]

To be sure, this information is still too fragmentary to
delineate clearly the relations between Mehmed ağa and Zheliazkov, but on one point the documents are indisputable: from
the time of the mill's founding there is absolutely no indication that Zheliazkov was its owner. In 1839 he was summoned
again "so as to settle in a definite manner the conditions
and arrangements about the work of this mill,"[27] though again,
as always, in his capacity as "chief master of the newly
opened broadcloth mill in Sliven"--that is, as chief technolo-
gist, engineer, and organizer of the enterprise.

The question of Zheliazkov's role can be definitely
answered by considering the following facts. In connection
with a planned expansion and improvement of the mill, the
proposal to the Porte requesting the necessary credits

also suggested as manager of the mill a certain Niyazi
Paşa, a member of the state council, while Zheliazkov, the
"chief master," was to be awarded an order as a sign of
esteem and appreciation and was to receive a high salary.[28]
Over part of the next two decades the mill was successively
managed by a number of individuals. In 1842-43 the manager
was the *kapıcıbaşı* (military officer) Mustafa Kani Bey; in
1845, Ali Riza; he in turn was followed by Kani Bey, Salih
Bey, Dervis Bey, Esseid Mehmed, Salih, and Said Bey.[29]
Initial impressions notwithstanding, these individuals were
not simply officials (although in a few cases--Niyazi Paşa,
Dervis Bey--they were simultaneously appointed as the kay-
makams of Sliven). Rather, as the documents indicate on at
least two occasions, they seem to have received the mill
through a form of auction. Before the inspection of the
accounts and the actual transfer of the mill with its inventory there was a detailed stocktaking involving the local
administrative *meclis* (council) and the kadı by which all of
the accounts were certified. This report was then relayed to
the financial authorities in Istanbul. In the capital, the
financial details were entered into the books and orders
were issued concerning the granting of additional credits, if
needed, for the replacement of machinery and tools, the supply
of more wool, and the introduction of various improvements.
These credits for the mill were transferred from the tax
returns of various sancaks and the budget of the military
department, which thus paid for the aba it received.[30] The
sum for which the mill was ceded to the individuals mentioned
above is not indicated, and one also cannot determine the profits they earned.

Zheliazkov was the "chief master" or "director" of the
mill. The importance that the Turkish government attached to
this post can be seen from the size of his salary, which was
fixed at 2,500 kuruş a month.[31] (This sum, it might be noted,
corresponded to the salary received by the kaymakam of
Sliven.)[32] Zheliazkov's annual salary of about 30,000 kuruş
constituted a small capital, equaling as it did the annual
profits of a medium-sized Bulgarian commercial enterprise.[33]

In the Istanbul archives the Turkish scholar Mehmed
Genç has discovered the Turkish translation of a memorandum
by Zheliazkov dated April 8, 1840, perhaps the only preserved
document from his hand.[34] The Turkish translator of the
memorandum used the word "director" to specify Zheliazkov's
post: "In connection with the improvement of the broadcloth
mill situated in Sliven which has your august support and
assistance, and of which I am the director, I take the
liberty of setting forth in detail for you the need for
certain materials. . . . As a traveler, I, your obedient

servant, visited Germany and the various regions of Russia,
carefully examining the broadcloth mills there, and I decided
to follow their model in setting up a small factory in my
homeland; and in the course of ten years I have labored and
made every effort to collect the knowledge necessary for this,
being aware that a lot of thought was required. . . ." What
this passage suggests is that Zheliazkov had considered the
idea of founding a mill for many years but went ahead only
after solid preparations.

The document also contains other information on the start
of Zheliazkov's manufacturing activity, concerning the broadcloth made during the 1840s and the conditions that he felt
would make effective industrial activity possible. Most
revealing in this respect is the following passage: "In
general the founders of such useful mills in Europe for 8,
10 and 12 years require, for their exploitation, only definite
rights and privileges and the condition that no other person
be permitted to set up such a mill; [and their governments],
acting with foresight, indeed grant certain privileges to
these persons. Had I enjoyed such privileges, I would have
freed myself of the initial losses."

* * *

Another set of questions that can in part be clarified
concerns the general appearance of the mill and the basic
steps in its construction. Boué reported that the main building had two stories with twenty-four windows on each floor.
In addition, there were separate accommodations for the senior
staff and other separate structures housing the smithy, the
forge, the foundry, the carpentry shop, the dyehouse and the
mechanic's shop.[35]
Encouraged by the successful construction of the mill,
the favorable assessment its work received from the inspector
sent to the mill, and the good quality of the broadcloth it
was producing, local authorities--and, as can be inferred
from other documents, Zheliazkov as well--decided as early as
1839 to propose the construction of an extension to the mill.
Actually, this request envisaged the construction of a
second and even larger factory.[36] Information concerning
the new building and its adjoining structures was recorded in
the correspondence that was generated on this question.[37]
The new factory building--which at that time was the
sole structure of its kind in the Balkans--was 102 arshin
long, 20 wide, and 14 high.[38] Its walls had a thinkness of
1 arshin and 10 inches, and its foundation had a raw brick
border one-half arshin in width. The structure was constructed
of stone and mortar, and its preliminary design envisaged one
hundred iron-barred windows.[39] The design also included

offices for administrative purposes, for the manager and, in
all likelihood, the chief master. These premises were to be
built to the left side of the mill and they consisted of two
"European" rooms (i.e., rooms with European-style furniture),
a coffee room, a bath and a toilet, and a few other rooms
whose purpose was not described. Five rooms in a separate
building were allocated for the workers and journeymen, and
for offices. The factory and its adjacent structures were
surrounded by a wall 408 arshin long, 3 arshin wide, and 4 1/2
arshin high. According to calculations made by a Bulgarian
writer in 1901, the enclosed space of the mill had an area of
about 15,500 square meters, which included a built-up floor
space of 3,920 square meters.[40]

* * *

Unfortunately, records have not survived on the funds
spent on construction; nor has the ledger recording the
expenses incurred for building materials and for the wages
paid to the construction workers been found. It has been
generally argued that forced labor was used to build the
factory. However, individual references to sums spent on the
building cast some doubt on that conclusion, and it can be
assumed that paid labor was used for at least a certain and
not insignificant part of the construction.

Such a conclusion finds support in an account submitted
on January 19, 1843, for the construction of the drying
shop.[41] The construction of this shop cost 80,000 kuruş and
its equipment cost 59,000 kuruş, for a total cost of 139,000
kuruş. The various features of the shop itself partially
explain this very high cost. (It was a solid building with
three stories. The bottom floor was designed for winter drying and contained a large stove; the middle floor was used
as a weaving section; and the top floor was set aside for the
drying of wool in the summer.) Even so, the sum involved
seemed too high even for the administrator of the mill, Mustafa Kani. In trying to justify the cost, he wrote: "In view
of the fact that the price of lumber and manpower has gone up
in comparison with last year, and [because] the ground turned
out to be stoney, the sum expended on the building, despite
all efforts, exceeded the estimate."[42]

Notwithstanding a suspicion that misappropriations might
have indeed been a big factor here (and Mustafa Kani did find
it necessary to add at the end of his report that "there have
been no misappropriations"), his arguments deserve attention;
in listing the causes of the cost overrun in the form of
arguments that higher fiscal authorities could accept as
plausible, Mustafa Kani attached primary importance to the
rise in the cost of labor. His mention of the ground turning

out to be rocky points in the same direction, for it suggests
that it was thus necessary to use a larger amount of manpower
than had been expected, requiring higher expenditures. Had
the construction been carried out by forced labor, the work
would have continued until the completion of the project without the need to report such cost details to higher authorities. In other words, the quoted passage unambiguously
testifies to the use of paid labor in the mill's construction.

* * *

As already noted, information is lacking on the specific
items of expenditure for the construction and equipping of the
mill. The accounts of Mustafa Kani Bey do, however, reveal
the total sum involved in the construction of the second
factory building. Against the sum of 1,051,531 kuruş spent
"on the construction of the building mentioned together with
the expenditure on the purchase of the necessary equipment,"
he entered a sum of 1,047,007 kuruş and 11 para, which had
been received in 1841 and 1842 from the tax collector and the
kaymakam's office of Tŭrnovo. The remainder--4,524 kuruş and
9 para--was entered in the books as a debt payable by the
government.[43]
A sum of this size--about 1,000,000 kuruş--had already
been mentioned in the memorandum requesting an extension of
the mill. It was to pay for the building, the necessary
installations, other unspecified expenditures, and wool. In
order to avoid adding this quite sizable sum as a supplementary expenditure for the state treasury, it was decided to
reduce by 1,500,000 kuruş the amount that the military department had budgeted for cloth for uniforms.[44] These figures
have been cited here since they are the only indication we
have for evaluating, and then only in a most general way, both
the funds spent by the government to clothe the regular army,
and indirectly, the savings that it anticipated as a result
of the construction of the Sliven mill (as a means to avoid
the use of merchants in the supply of broadcloth from abroad).

* * *

Much fuller information has survived on the furnishing of
the first building with machinery and on the technological
process it employed.[45] The wool was loosened up on a scutching machine and was then teased on the first four carding
machines. Three of these machines were made and purchased
in Russia and the fourth had been brought from Russia earlier
by Zheliazkov. The yarn was twisted on seven coarse spinning
machines and on twelve fine spinning machines. The first
seven machines had forty spindles each. Two of them had been
imported from Russia and the other five had been constructed

by Sliven mechanics using models that had been supplied. Of
the twelve fine spinning machines, nine had sixty spindles
each, two had forty spindles, and one had twenty spindles. It
was the twenty-spindle machine that Zheliazkov had brought
back from Russia. Two of the sixty-spindle machines had also
been ordered in Russia, and were used as models to build the
others. There were an additional eight looms about whose
origins there is no information. The machines owned by
Zheliazkov and installed in the mill were valued at 20,000
kuruş, a sum that was entered as a debt owed to him by the
state. (It is not known whether the state paid him this
amount, and its failure to settle this debt was perhaps the
reason for Zheliazkov's complaints.) A sum of 211,500 kuruş
was paid for the equipment supplied from Russia and an additional 36,000 kuruş worth of supplementary machinery was
ordered at the time of the mill's inspection.[46] The machines
were driven by water and by hand.

In the late 1840s various types of machinery and equipment worth about 50,000 kuruş were imported from England.
Unfortunately, information has not survived about the kind of
equipment involved (except that it was delivered in thirteen
large crates). The mill was later equipped with Jacquard
looms, but it is impossible to say when or how many.

The inspector sent from Istanbul, who made an inventory
of the machines, compared the method of production at the
Sliven mill with the process employed at English mills he
had visited earlier to became acquainted with the textile
industry. His report noted that the mill had been built
after an English plan, but that "it lacks some equipment."
Accordingly, and also as a result of certain less-than-
perfect processes, the broadcloth it produced was coarse and
with an insufficient cover of nap. The main problem, however,
was what the inspector described as the poor quality of the
wool.

The raw wool received by the mill had to be cleaned
by hand so as to remove dry excrement and rough hairs. But
this was not sufficient. What was required was the organization of a supply of high quality wool. To this end the
inspector recommended that mill employees be sent to purchase
wool in areas where good sheep were raised. In any case,
after the preliminary selection, the wool was sorted into
three grades for three kinds of broadcloth, with the finest
set aside for the uniforms of officers and the rest for
soldiers. Wool unusable for broadcloth was to be used for
making carpets and rugs, or set aside for resale. The
inspector calculated that each one-hundred okka of wool
supplied yielded only thirty okka of wool suitable for the
mill. But even after the wool had undergone a preliminary

grading, the broadcloth produced was still no match for English broadcloth, for the latter employed Spanish wool. The inspector thus also concluded that Merino sheep should be imported, arguing that in three or four years hybrid sheep producing a Spanish type of wool would be available.

The report went on to describe in considerable detail the cleaning of the wool that had been sorted. The wool was first kept in a mixture of urine and manure for twenty-four hours, after which it was washed in running water. The wool was then placed in a sack and the water squeezed out. At this point the wool was spread about until it dried off, whereupon it was passed from hand to hand and beaten with a stick. However, as the inspector noted, the workers made the mistake of dyeing the wool before it had been thoroughly cleaned.

After this initial processing the wool was scutched. But, in the inspector's opinion, the scutching machine used in the mill was not a convenient one. Although it removed the impurities, it did not fluff up the wool. The inspector thus recommended the construction of a new scutching machine on an English model. Such a machine, he noted, would also render unnecessary the manual handling of the wool at this stage.

In order to impart greater elasticity and smoothness to the wool, it was then greased. The greased wool was rapidly combed into slivers in the carding machines without being torn.

The carding machines were similar to those the inspector had seen in England, and in his opinion they had no deficiencies. The machines for spinning both fine and thick thread were also like those used in English factories. They too functioned well, although they were driven by child labor rather than by steam. The sole defect in the spinning process was that it twisted the thread too much, leaving yarn that was too thick, and in turn broadcloth that was uneven and had a visible weft. The thread, according to the inspector, should not be twisted so much. (This recommendation demonstrates great powers of observation since for each centimeter of warp there were twelve twists and six to seven twists for the weft.) In addition, the inspector believed that the amount of wool fed into the carding machines should be reduced to 130 dirhem for ordinary wool and to between 80 and 90 dirhem for curly wool. The fundamental defect of the weaving department, where the looms themselves operated "as they should," was that the weaving was too loose. Since close weaving produced a smoother cloth, the reeds should be increased from 3,200 to 4,400 dents. The inspector's final recommendations had to do with the shrinking of the broadcloth, its fulling, and various operations outside of the mill itself.

Except for a few remarks on the use of child labor, this otherwise detailed report says nothing about the kind of power used to operate the machines. It mentions only the placement of a "large wheel" on the southern side of the new building, which was turned by water that passed by underground channels through the basement of the mill. The wheel itself had a diameter of eight meters. The driving mechanism of the first factory building had functioned completely independently, and it also used a "large wheel" that drove the carding machines.

Although it cannot be determined whether all of the inspector's recommendations were considered, it is known that in the same year the former voyvoda of Sliven and Zheliazkov were summoned to Istanbul. The question of the continued operation of the mill was submitted to the Supreme Council, which decreed that 200,000 kuruş be granted to the "chief master" and that he be assisted in the supply of wool.[47] This sum was actually spent on mill equipment. In an account of the sums and inventory of the mill transferred by the late director Kani Bey to Ali Riza, reference was made to an item recorded as follows: "Received as capital--200,000 transferred [to Kani Bey] from D. Zheliazkov, 200,000 by cession from the Sliven kaza."[48]

The authorities also took into account some of the inspector's recommendations designed to assure the mill's supply of high-grade wool. With the question of Spanish wool left to the future, in 1837 50,000 kuruş were released to purchase good local wool--8,000 okka from Edirne and Dimotika and their environs, and 12,000 okka from the sancak of Silistra, from Babadag, Balchik, and other places.[49] A special person was entrusted with the purchase of the wool. One of Sliven's biggest inns, the "Tas Han," was converted into a storehouse for the finished aba and wool, and 5,349 kuruş were spent to repair the building.[50]

A subsequent *irade* (rescript) of 1842 ordered that the Sliven mill use Spanish wool to manufacture broadcloth for officers' uniforms.[51] An undated document that can be assigned to the years around mid-century indicates that the mill had indeed obtained a flock of sheep yielding Spanish-type wool. This state-owned flock numbered 8,956 Merino sheep, 9,119 ordinary white sheep, and 748 black sheep.[52] The flock was adequate for the mill's needs. As noted, the mill used about 20,000 okka of wool during the initial period of its existence. After the reconstruction of the mill, its capacity actually doubled, and in 1842 the amount of Spanish wool used in the mill amounted to 20,351.5 okka.[53] But a flock of 9,000 Merino sheep with an average yield of five or six okka per head could easily meet the mill's ex-

panded requirements, in addition to providing an annual
surplus of some 10,000 okka.

On the basis of the amount of wool it used, one can estimate the mill's volume with greater certainty. (Specific
information on output has been preserved only for the year
1851, when the mill delivered 48,696.5 arshin of broadcloth to
the warehouse.[54] When he took over the mill in 1850, Said
Bey had fixed the amount of obligatory delivery at 50,000
arshin of broadcloth).[55] To produce cloth that at that time
was from 60 to 70 centimeters wide required about 400-450
grams of fully processed wool for each meter of aba and not
less than 300-320 grams for a meter of broadcloth. Thus,
20,000 okka of wool, of which more than one-third would be
discarded at the first grading, and which would be cut in half
again during actual production, could yield about 50,000
arshin of broadcloth. This rough calculation simply confirms
that from the very foundation of the mill its annual production of broadcloth was always about 50,000 arshin. By the
1850s, its increased output included the production of
several types of broadcloth, of which it seems that the best
grade alone--the one using Spanish wool--amounted to 50,000
arshin.[56]

The fragmentary data that are available do not permit
definite conclusions concerning the actual value of this aba
and broadcloth. The information on the cost of an arshin of
broadcloth is contradictory. In 1847, the value of one arshin
of broadcloth produced at a newly founded mill in Izmid was
set at 21 kuruş. The government departments concerned with
these matters asked the sultan to equalize broadcloth prices,
suggesting that the price of Sliven broadcloth (and that
produced in another state factory in Beykoz) be reduced from
24 kuruş to 21 kuruş.[57] A detailed report of 1851, which
mentions the total amount of the broadcloth produced, contains a calculation showing that on reaching the warehouse
the wool was valued at 17 kuruş per arshin and that the
"cost price" was fixed at 16 kuruş and 39.5 para.[58] One can
assume that the difference between 17 and 24 kuruş represented the amount entered as "revenue" of the treasury, after
which the treasury entered the whole account with its debits
and credits in the military department's budget, which now
had to transfer the appropriate sums to the mill and the
treasury.[59]

* * *

A search of the Ottoman documents contained in the
oriental department of the Cyril and Methodius National
Library has failed to locate information on the composition
of the mill's work force. But an idea of the total number of

workers and the factory's working regime can be constructed
on the basis of such sources as Zheliazkov's memorandum
mentioned above, Boué, and several other travelers' accounts
from the second half of the century. In the early 1840s, the
mill employed eighty Bulgarian workers and two masters, in all
likelihood Czechs from Moravia.[60] This number refers only to
those individuals who worked in the factory itself. It seems
too small, however, given the number of machines then in use.
For example, each scutching machine required three persons,
each combing machine needed one operator, an eighty-spindle
spinning machine required at least four persons, and each loom
needed about ten persons. Furthermore, a substantial number
of workers was needed to carry out auxiliary operations
around the machines. And, of course, there were many workers
engaged in cleaning and sorting the wool, or in ironing and
dyeing the finished output, and there was the auxiliary technical and clerical staff as well.[61] A Turkish document
records that every spinning wheel that twisted the thread was
driven by two children. At the opening of the mill six such
spinning wheels were delivered, and a seventh arrived later.[62]

In his 1840 memorandum Zheliazkov wrote: "The local
workers whom I engaged were novices, and I had to train all of
them from the very beginning. On the other hand, owing to the
existing fear about taking up state work, it was only through
the payment of fairly high wages, the provision of food and
the payment of their cizye, and by other additional measures,
that [this] fear . . . was overcome; and now it is clear to
everyone that everything is proceeding in a correct and legal
manner. In this way I succeeded in attracting the workers
needed, but since they were beginners most of the goods we
produced were defective."[63]

This passage leaves no doubt that the workers did not
consist of soldiers or of forced labor, and that, speaking
in the most general terms, working conditions in the mill were
similar to those in any other private capitalist factory or
manufacture. In other words, the mill exploited the labor
of hired workers who even included children.[64]

Although the place of origin of the workers cannot be
determined, it might be noted that the mill was set up in a
city very well-known for its textile production. Even in the
late 1850s, long after the opening of the mill, intensive production continued on about 2,000 individual looms scattered
about the city. The mill thus emerged, as contemporaries
correctly wrote, "in one of the most industrialized cities
of the whole Empire."[65] Practically all contemporary
observers shared this assessment of mid-nineteenth century
Sliven. Of course, this is not to say that Sliven was the
center of a developed factory production. The point is only

that the city contained an important textile production whose
output went beyond the local framework and drew the broadest
kind of public and state recognition.

The mill appeared as the result of the economic development of a city that contained all of the prerequisites for the
emergence of higher forms of capitalist production: a sufficient hired-labor reserve; the presence of capital in amounts
at least sufficient to permit the start of factory activity;
considerable technical advancement in the construction and
repair of a number of technical installations; and the lack
of much or even any opposition on the part of strong guild
organizations.[66] All of these conditions were present in
Sliven in the 1830s.

Only one source contains information about the rate of
wages. According to Boué, an ordinary worker received an
average of 75 francs a year, or at the current rate of
exchange, about 500 kuruş, a sum not much higher than the pay
received by artisan carpet weavers (35 kuruş a month).[67]
The only comment in the Turkish documents about the payment
of the workers is a summarized total of 14,301 kuruş for 1842,
a sum entered as an "obligation to the factory workers."[68]
How many people and how many working hours figured into this
sum cannot be reconstructed, but the term used by the account-
ant--"factory workers"--speaks for itself as to the nature
of the manpower used.

That the mill drew favorable comments and was constantly
improving its machinery and production, when combined with
the absence of any suggestion about a special regime for the
workers, demonstrates that in its external appearance,
machinery, and technical and organization structure the
Sliven factory did not differ from contemporary European
enterprises. This enterprise met the contemporary criteria
of factory industry.

* * *

Another interesting Balkan enterprise was the private
textile factory founded by the Gümüşgerdan brothers in the
vicinity of Plovdiv about ten years after the opening of the
Sliven mill. The Gümüşgerdan mill serves as vivid proof of
the culmination of the differentiation taking place in the
late eighteenth century and early nineteenth century among
the small-commodity producers. As shown in the preceding
chapter, the founders of this mill had emerged from among the
ranks of small aba producers in Plovdiv. Until the 1878
liberation of Bulgaria their mill continued to operate as a
thriving capitalist enterprise.

The location of the mill was an apt one. It was situated
close to Plovdiv and also in close proximity to the Rhodopes

on the deep-flowing Dermendere River and in the neighborhood
of the well-organized farm run by the Gümüşgerdan family. As
indicated by the firm's annual financial statement, the mill's
first building was erected in 1847.[69] Machines were ordered
from Austria, and they were mounted by two specialists from
the same country. The contract covering the assembly of the
machinery specified a time limit of 42 to 50 days and envisaged a payment of 400 kuruş each for the two installers, and
a daily wage of 10 kuruş for other repairs.[70] One of the
installers remained on in a paid position to train local master workers in the operation of the machinery.[71]

The nature of these first machines is not clear. However, the machinery did include an imported spinning machine
with sixty-four spindles, as revealed by an order placed by
the Gümüşgerdans early in 1848 with local mechanics in Plovdiv
to construct a second spinning machine copying the imported
one. The contract drawn up in Greek between the Gümüşgerdans
and the Plovdiv master mechanic Atanas Milushev listed the
specifications the machine was expected to meet. Thus, it
was to run smoothly and to be as easy to operate as the
machine from Vienna so that even the smallest irregularity
might be avoided. The machine had to be completed and
delivered within fifty-one days. If this deadline were not
met, or if the machine proved more difficult to work with
than the Vienna machine, the contract obligated the master
mechanic to return the advance together with two percent
interest. A sum of 1,000 kuruş was advanced to cover the cost
of both labor and materials.[72]

In early 1853 the Gümüşgerdans overhauled and enlarged
their mill, and in the 1860s they imported new machines--a
press from Brno for cutting the aba and spinning machines
from Vienna. At the same time a second building was constructed to serve as a warehouse and for administration.[73]

The basement of the factory building itself was used
to sort wool and to pack the finished cloth into rolls and
bales. Eight combing machines of the "Brun" type were
installed on the ground floor. The next floor housed the
spinning machines--twelve for fine yarn and two, with sixty-
four spindles each, for thick yarn. The same floor also
contained fourteen mechanical looms.[74] Placed outside the
engine room was a wooden driving wheel six meters in diameter.
The minimum capacity of the driving mechanism used for the
two wheels of the fulling machines was twenty-five horsepower
even in the months of July and August (when the level of water
was especially low in the channel used to provide water to
turn the wheels). Though this technical description of the
mill dates from the 1860s, there is every reason to believe
that the situation was similar in previous years. The 1860s
saw only the replacement of hand looms with mechanical ones.

The mill had several departments connected with the preparatory and final stages of production--dyeing, carding, and fulling. It is impossible to establish, however, the extent to which these departments were auxiliary to the mill and the extent to which they played a separate role in the Gümüşgerdans' putting-out manufacture. In any case, it was the needs of this earlier production that brought into being the dyeing department, the carding section, and the fulling operation, and these in turn served as the starting point for the establishment of the mill. Moreover, these operations were the reason why large amounts of aba made elsewhere were concentrated in the village of Dermendere. This total amount of aba surpassed several times over the amount made at the mill.

The mill's capacity, or rather its expected capacity, may be judged by a letter dated July 16, 1848, from Mihalaki Gümüşgerdan to the vali of Plovdiv. In this letter Gümüş-gerdan thanked the vali for his expression of congratulations on the opening of the mill; he promised to carry out the vali's instruction to use the mill to produce 100,000 arshin of şayak out of a total of 400,000 arshin that the firm had contracted to supply the government.[75] Taking into consideration that a weaver working a hand loom could turn out an average of 6 to 8 arshin during a 14 to 16 hour working day (or 10 arshin of cloth at the most), one can calculate that a mechanical loom could turn out at least 4 or 5 times as much, particularly if operated by several workers in different shifts. That is, the mechanical loom could produce between about 25 to 30 arshin of cloth per day, or about 9,000 arshin in 10 months.

There is also fragmentary information concerning the mill's output two or three years after its establishment, but prior to its complete overhaul in 1853, which involved the construction of a new building[76] (see table 30). The figures do not include the mill's total output, but only that part of the wool produced into aba and the number of rolls of aba sold.[77] During these years the mill also produced şayak cloth as well as several hundred rolls of lining.[78] There is no accurate information on the quantities of these items.

In addition to providing a more or less valid idea of the mill's aba production, the above figures, when compared with other information, can be used to calculate the profit rate realized by the Gümüşgerdans. In 1853 81,583.50 kuruş were paid for wool purchased and delivered to the mill, while 18,559.32 kuruş were paid out in the form of wages and other expenses. In composing the tally sheet for this consignment of wool, and in particular to balance the bookkeeping operation, a profit of 22,507.63 kuruş was included.[79] In this case, therefore, the profit margin of the Gümüşgerdans

TABLE 30

ABA PRODUCTION IN THE GÜMÜŞGERDAN MILL IN 1851 AND 1853

Year	Amount of Wool Supplied (in okkas)	Price of Wool per Okka (in kuruş)	Amount of Aba Sold (in rolls)	Cost per Roll (in kuruş)
1851	6,097	8	2,064	33.75
1853	8,795	7.5 to 12.5	1,849	45

SOURCE: TsDIA, defter 104, pp. 44, 47, 70-71.

amounted to 22.5%. This rate was not especially high for that
time and place, but it fluctuated within the range of profits
obtained about the middle of the century by the well-known
Bulgarian commercial firms of the Minchoglus (24%) and the
Tŭpchileshtovs (30%).[80]

* * *

The earliest information about workers employed at the
Gümüşgerdan mill dates back to the year 1847, when the following individuals took up work "at the machine": Ivan Panagiu-
rets (at 300 kuruş a year); Boiko Kurtev, also of Panagiurishte, a fuller (750 kuruş a year); Ivan Slivnaliia, a carder
(5 kuruş per day); Panaiot Peshtimaldzhiia, a weaver (5 kuruş
per day); Dimitŭr Masurdzhiia (5 kuruş per day); Atanas
Kalemdzhiia (60 kuruş a month); Ivan Hastardzhiia, a lining
weaver (a daily wage of 7 kuruş); Petŭr Lazarov, another
lining weaver (400 kuruş a year); and others.[81] A little
later, in 1848 and 1849, Haralambi Kalemdzhiia began work at
350 kuruş a month; as did Ayram Dolapchiia, together with his
child (100 kuruş a month); and Petŭr of Melnik who worked "at
the machine" as of January, 1849 (at 400 kuruş a year, with
an increase to 600 kuruş in May of the same year).[82]
       Although such information cannot of course really
describe the overall composition of the mill's work force, it
can be used to establish the daily wage rate of the factory
workers. A comparison of their wage rate with the wages of
the workers employed in 1847 by the Gümüşgerdans to carry out
other tasks yields the results shown in table 31.
       This data suggests that the average monthly wage for hired
workers employed by the Gümüşgerdans was 67 kuruş, with most
cases between 55 and 67 kuruş. There was no difference between
these wages and the average wages received by the factory
workers. But if we examine, in contrast to the over-all

TABLE 31

WAGES PAID IN 1847 TO WORKERS HIRED BY THE GÜMÜŞGERDANS

Month	Number of Workers	Amount Paid to All Workers (in kuruş)	Average Wage per Worker
January	38	2,040.30	54
February	38	1,328.20	35
March	44	3,627.10	82
April	42	3,290	78
May	28	1,017	36
June	55	3,244	59
July	40	2,424	61
August	44	2,508	57
September	36	2,684	75
October	53	3,958	75
November	42	4,849	115
December	--	3,786	---

SOURCE: TsDIA, f. 161, defter 42, pp. 58-72. The data for December, 1847, is drawn from ibid., defter 51, pp. 1-49, 281-282.

average, the actual rate of the wages paid to the different categories of workers, however fragmentary the information, it can be seen that the majority of workers at the mill received from 60 to 80 kuruş a month, or from 600 to 800 kuruş annually. At the higher end the big exception was the specialist who came from Austria and received 2,640 kuruş a year, more than three times as much as the factory average.

Among the hired hands who worked in other parts of the Gümüşgerdan operations, only skilled masters such as dyers, abacıs, and millers received wages similar to those of the workers at the mill, between 600 to 800 kuruş a year and up. The wages of all other workers fluctuated. The wages of shepherds and carters ranged from 100 to 400 kuruş a year; the wages of carpenters, gardeners, and woodcutters fluctuated from 400 to 600 kuruş; and the wages of harvesters and unskilled laborers used as farm hands ranged from 2.5 to 3 kuruş a day, with the same wages paid for work in vineyards.[83] The lower pay of those factory workers hired to work "at the machine"--300 and 400 kuruş--can be explained by this work being regarded as light and in all probability entrusted to minors and often to small children.[84]

The wages of the factory and other workers might usefully

be compared with the salaries received during roughly the
same years by certain administrative functionaries and by the
personnel of the state saltpeter workshop in Razgrad. In 1844
the following monthly salaries were paid in the kaymakam's
office in Sliven: for the kaymakam himself, 2,500 kuruş (i.e.,
a salary 35 to 50 times the average wage of a factory worker);
for the accountant, 500 kuruş (7-10 times as large); for the
secretary, 400 kuruş (6-8 times as large); for the clerk, 150
kuruş (2-3 times as large); for the mail clerk, 150 kuruş
(2-3 times as large); for the mailman, 75 kuruş (equal to the
monthly wages of a factory worker).[85] (Such were the salaries
not only in Sliven, but also in Iambol and even for the postal
officials of the village of Ichera. In this village the postman received 80 kuruş a month, probably because his route was
longer.) Meanwhile, the monthly salaries and wages paid in
1843 to the workers and employees, all of whom were Muslims,
of the state saltpeter workshop in Razgrad ranged as follows:
the senior administrator, 1,000 kuruş; the clerk, 250 kuruş;
the overseer, 750 kuruş; and 12 workers who received 80
kuruş each (a total of 960 kuruş).[86]

This comparison illustrates the characteristically low
level of the workers' wages. The average monthly wages of
master specialists and skilled workers in the Gümüşgerdans'
mill and manufactory corresponded to the lowest paid job in
the civil service, the postman. Or, to put it another way,
ordinary clerks and secretaries received salaries that ranged
from two to eight times higher than wages received by workers.
Even the individual who was brought from abroad and employed
as the technical manager of the Gümüşgerdan mill received only
220 kuruş a month, which was not even half the size of the
salary paid to the secretary in the kaymakam's office.

But a true picture of the real purchasing power of the
workers' wages can be obtained by examining these amounts
against the current prices of the goods they needed most. In
the early 1850s in Plovdiv, and also in the area where the
Gümüşgerdans operated, the grocery store prices of such
staple products (in kuruş per okka) were as follows: bread--
1.20 kuruş; wheat--1 kuruş; rice--2.25 to 3.50 kuruş; meat--
2 to 4 kuruş; dried meat and sausage--4 kuruş; butter--7 kuruş;
soap--5 kuruş; apples--1 kuruş; candles--7.50 kuruş; and nails
--6.25 kuruş.[87] The current cost of other essential commodities can be seen in deductions made by the Gümüşgerdans in
workers' wages when the firm supplied such items. Thus, for
shoes supplied to workers the firm withheld from 15 to 20
kuruş. (The shoes provided to the foreign specialist were
more expensive, 35 kuruş. He also received 3 shirts at 20
kuruş each.) In terms of other commodities, a pair of slippers sold at 3.5 kuruş;[88] a sheep could be bought for 36-38
kuruş; and a horse sold for between 600 and 1,200 kuruş.[89]

Putting it all together, with his monthly wage of 70-80
kuruş the better paid worker could buy bread, a little dried
meat, and some other foodstuffs--hardly enough to feed a medium-sized family--and the daily wage of 2-3 kuruş received by
other workers doomed them to a chronic hunger. (It was for
this reason that both the Sliven and the Gümüşgerdan mills
often provided their workers with meals.)

* * *

The terms on which the workers were hired at the Gümüşgerdan mill can be seen from a contract signed by three
weavers on October 5, 1848. Following a general statement of
the workers' obligations, the contract lists the more specific
responsibilities and privileges of both parties. The first
clause notes that the three individuals were starting work
as master weavers. If, however, the occasion arose where
there was not enough weaving to be done, the employer had the
right to assign other tasks. By the second clause the workers
promised diligently to carry out the tasks assigned to them.
In the event that they failed to perform their duties properly
and caused a loss for the employer, they would have no right
to complain or to leave his employ. The third clause fixed
the rate of pay at 70 kuruş a month while again reiterating
that the workers could not leave the factory unless compelling
reasons required the employer to let them go. The fourth
clause noted that food was to be provided at the employer's
expense, the same food furnished to all workers. If the three
weavers did not like the food, they would be allowed to eat
outside the factory but at their own expense. According to
the fifth clause, their holidays were to be the same as those
of the other workers, and this same clause stipulated that
during the winter months the three weavers would work during
the evening hours by artificial light. The final clause noted
that the workers could not be assigned to another job without
the permission of the employer or his assistants.[90]
This contract is an important source, illustrating as it
does a number of aspects of the workers' position in one of
the first textile mills on the Balkan Peninsula. Particularly
striking are the efforts of the Gümüşgerdans to assure the
uninterrupted exploitation of their work force. In addition,
the provision that workers were to do whatever work was
assigned to them is a sign that the firm was still not sufficiently sure that it could maintain the simultaneous operation
of all the departments of the factory. In the event, for
example, of an accidental stoppage of the machinery, the
Gümüşgerdans wanted to retain the possibility of transferring
labor to do work at other points of the production process.
The wool, for instance, arrived in large consignments, and
its cleaning, sorting, and combing required a great deal of

labor. In order to carry out these operations more quickly,
particularly when other parts of the mill needed raw materials,
it was useful to be able to transfer workers from other
sections.

No less categorical were the stipulations concerning the
weavers' obligations to carry out their appointed tasks. The
Gümüşgerdans preferred to have workers who mastered that part
of the mill's operations to which they had been assigned.
This required that they stay in the same place for a long time.
A similar thrust was contained in that clause of the contract
stating that the workers would not be transferred to some
other job without the permission of the employers or their
deputies. The diverse entrepreneurial activities of the
Gümüşgerdans offered all sorts of opportunities for the
use of dyers, weavers, and spinners outside the mill itself,
and it was against the arbitrary abandonment of work in the
mill that the stipulation was directed.

One is also impressed by the several provisions in the
contract whereby the firm tried to control turnover. The
workers were thus forbidden from freely leaving their work,
even if the firm had been guilty of causing physical damage or
loss. Retaining the right to release workers if it considered
them unsuited, the firm sought to protect itself against all
other kinds of abandonment. A shortage of manpower did not
dictate this provision, for in addition to the factory
workers the Gümüşgerdans employed several dozen other hired
hands who formed a reliable pool of labor from which they
could meet sudden needs. Rather, they were trying to avoid
the loss of those workers whose departure would disrupt
production. They also wanted to hold onto for as long as
possible that new category of worker--the skilled worker--who
had mastered an operation to perfection. It was not accidental that one of the two technicians called from Austria was
retained, with a pay several times higher than the wages of
other workers, to train others in operating the machines.
The provision that all workers celebrate the same holidays
also shows a similar effort to assure an uninterrupted and
regular factory operation.

The contract contained no provision concerning the length
of the working day, and it is clear that this matter raised no
major problems. Work was done here as it was traditionally
done throughout the country, from dawn to dusk. But the working day must have been rather prolonged if it was necessary
to obtain the workers' preliminary agreement to work in the
winter by artificial light.

An important condition specified in the contract was the
provision of food as an element of pay. As has already been
indicated, wages were so low that it was difficult for the

workers to feed their families on this income alone. Furthermore, and as will be shown below, the majority of the hired
workers at the mill and in the different sections of the manufacture were persons who had come from distant places where
they had left families and parents who also depended on their
small earnings.

These circumstances were carefully taken into account by
the Gümüşgerdans who, though paying very low wages, also
provided free meals to their workers both to retain them and
to demand in return the maximum amount of work. Meals and
food were an important material stimulus that played an
essential role in procuring a steady stream of labor for the
mill and the manufacture. Furthermore, the establishment of
a common kitchen and the supply of necessary foodstuffs did
not involve any special problems or expenditures. The Gümüşgerdans owned several farms in the village of Dermendere and
in its environs and they had their own flour mills, oil
presses, and large herds of cattle and flocks of sheep.

As the foregoing discussion makes clear, the Gümüşgerdan
work force represented a group of hired workers who took up
with the firm as a result of fixed contractual relations.
These workers were hired for specific tasks inside the mill
(or outside it) and received pay in the form of a daily or
monthly wage. The written agreements concluded at the time of
hiring were a characteristic capitalistic device in the
purchase and sale of labor, and their use shows that the
Gümüşgerdans had a relatively developed system of recruitment
and considerable experience in hiring labor.

Although there are really no grounds for speaking of the
creation of generations of factory workers, it should be
stressed that at the Gümüşgerdan mill an awareness did appear
among workers that toil in the factory was becoming their
inevitable fate. One of the workers, Avram, who worked with
the water wheel, brought his son along to train him in the
comparatively easy operation of the wheel, for which he
received an increased salary (100 kuruş a month). It might
also be noted that the names of the majority of those in
the Gümüşgerdan ledgers appear for years in a row--another
sign that they had become permanent factory workers.

* * *

During the 1850s the mill employed fifty-seven workers
and an administrative staff of three (manager, clerk, and
overseer). In addition, there were two technicians, in all
probability Czechs, who were hired for several years to see
to the correct use of the machines brought in from Austria.
Four men worked at the coarse-yarn machine, and seven with
the fine-yarn machine. The other machines were staffed accord-

ing to the count of the yarn: no. 5 (five workers), no. 4
(three workers), and no. 3 (two workers). There were six
warpers (*kalemcis*) and eight bobbin winders (*masurcis*) for
preparing the weft. There were eight carders and twelve
thread makers.[91] (Not included here were the several dozen
workers engaged in sorting wool or working in the fulling
department.)

An analysis of the list of mill workers on a name-by-name
basis supports the conclusion that the workers in the mill were
without exception hired workers employed in return for pay
and food. The firm's ledgers show this fact quite clearly
and the documents make no mention whatsoever about the use
of convict labor.[92] It can thus be stated without reservation
that the Gümüşgerdan mill was a true and typical private
capitalist enterprise.

An examination of the workers' places of origin produces
a picture that raises more general questions concerning the
movement of the population (see table 32). Of the fifty-seven
employees mentioned above, only eight had village origins
(and five of these eight individuals came from the village
of Dermendere itself, while the other three sprang from nearby
villages). This fact is extremely interesting, for it persuasively demonstrates that the mill was oriented toward the city
and not toward the village. Contrary to the widespread
historiographical view, the mill drew its workers from urban
and not rural residents.

For most of the workers, their native cities were loca-
tions of developed textile production. Already in the eighteenth century, for example, Pirdop had become a famous center
of cotton production, and Plovdiv and Tatar Pazardzhik were
well known for their aba production as far back as the seventeenth century. Panagiurishte and Karlovo were also textile
centers, and in the first half of the nineteenth century they
were exporting merchandise to distant markets in Asia Minor.
Before its late eighteenth-century decline, Melnik was likewise a major commercial and producing center whose prosperous
firms sent representatives to Italy and Austria.

Full information has not been preserved on the place of
origin of the Gümüşgerdans' other eighty-eight hired workers,
who were partly connected with the mill and partly with the
manufacture, but for the sake of greater completeness, let us
provide this information as well. The ledgers record the
origins of twenty of fifty-one dyers. Of these twenty,
fourteen came from localities with advanced textile production
(five from Kalofer, three from Sopot, three from Samokov,
etc.), and six from nearby villages. Practically all of the
twenty or so hired farm hands had village origins. The two
blacksmiths were from Kuistendil and the cooks were from

TABLE 32

ORIGIN OF EMPLOYEES OF THE GÜMÜŞGERDAN FACTORY IN THE 1850s

	Number of Workers
Cities	
Pirdop	16
Plovdiv	10
Tatar Pazardzhik	7
Asenovgrad	6
Panagiurishte	2
Melnik	2
Karlovo	1
Peshtera	1
Villages	
Dermendere	5
Chepelare	1
Belovo	1
Unknown Village	1
Not Stated	4
Total	57

SOURCE: TsDIA, f. 161, defter 177, pp. 40-41.

Kiustendil and Asenovgrad.[93] Obviously, workers of rural
origin constituted an insignificant minority among the hired
labor in the mill and in the dyeing section. In terms of the
mill itself (for which the data are complete), such workers
make up a mere 13% of the work force.
    The question arises as to how to explain this movement
of workers away from centers of production (i.e., cities) as
early as the first half of the nineteenth century. Without
having put the question in such a way (for their lack of
documents kept them from talking about the composition of the
workers in the manufacture and the mill), some historians who
have written about the Gümüşgerdans have used the rural location of the mill deep in the Rhodopes as an argument that the
capitalists sought to invest their capital far from the large
centers where the guilds were strong and might restrict
private enterprise. Though pegged to the Gümüşgerdan mill,
this generalization has been expanded to cover all of the manufacture and factory industry that existed in the Bulgarian

lands. It thereby ignored the fact that, save for the Gümüş-gerdan mill, not a single other factory or centralized manu-factory was founded outside of urban centers.

There were specific reasons why the Gümüşgerdan mill was constructed in a village. For more than ten years before the opening of the mill Dermendere had been the principal base of the large putting-out manufacture that the Gümüşgerdans organized in the Rhodopes, and this village was the location of their large hereditary çiftlik. It had abundant running water, which was necessary both for the different processes involved in aba making and for driving power. These reasons were sufficient to convince these shrewd capitalists to con-struct their mill in the most economically advantageous location.

But to dispel any possible doubt about this matter, it can also be noted that the area where the Gümüşgerdans' put-ting-out manufacture and mill were located did have a guild organization. At a point when the mill had been in operation for a whole year (February, 1849), Mihalaki Gümüşgerdan received a collective address from the abacı guild in the Akhŭchelebi district signed by twenty-eight Bulgarians and ninety-eight Turks. In this address the guild wanted to thank Gümüşgerdan for his attitude toward the abacıs. They added that they had received the money for the şayak they had made for the army on work orders Gümüşgerdan had provided them.[94]

This is new evidence not only of the resignation with which the guild approached capitalist activity in a territory it controlled, but also a new argument in favor of the thesis that in the middle of the nineteenth century the guild, with all of its regulations and institutions, had in many cases begun to function as a productive branch supplementing the activity of the industrial enterprise, be it manufacture or factory. (A similar relationship was established between guilds and the state saltpeter workshop in Razgrad.) There are no grounds, therefore, for claiming that the guilds, despite their reservations with respect to the bigger capital-ist enterprises, could have an effect on the choice of a mill's location.

* * *

During the first half of the nineteenth century, to sum-marize, certain branches of the Balkan textile industry were at the peak of their development. The entire able-bodied population--men, women, and children--on both sides of the Balkan Mountains, in the Sredna Gora Mountains, and in the Rhodope Mountains, as well as in many areas of Greece, was involved in the production of woolen textiles, and it was the strong growth of this industry that led to the emergence of

a considerable manufacturing production and the first factories in the Bulgarian lands.

The various aspects of these enterprises studied here
have a much broader significance. They show that capitalist
relations in industry had passed from one stage to another;
from one level of productive forces to a new, higher one; from
a lower degree of capitalist exploitation to a higher one.
This process, however, neither reached the necessary scope nor
attained the degree of strength that would have corresponded
to the real potential that lay before it. The reasons for
this failure varied.

As early as the second quarter of the nineteenth century,
and perhaps even earlier, Balkan cities possessed available
free manpower as a result of the constant influx of semiprole-
tarianized elements from the villages. This labor market
expanded constantly since those who constituted it were unable
to find sufficient opportunities for the application of their
work. As a stratum of urban poverty, this labor reserve
became the source that nourished capitalist relations even in
their rudimentary forms in whole branches of the textile
industry (while that industry was still taking place in artisan workshops and in conditions where the guilds still prevailed). Moreover, the existence of an adequate market of
hired labor helps account for the fact that no shortage of
manpower was felt even when, for a short period of time during
the second quarter of the nineteenth century, the textile
industry was undergoing a great upsurge. The influx of
workers to the manufactories and mills in the first half of
the century was caused not by the ruin of small-commodity
producers in the same branches, but by the flow into a thriving industry of elements of the urban poor who had not been
involved in small-scale production. This explains why those
industrial settlements that have usually been cited as
examples of flourishing artisan production experienced a considerable social stratification even long before the Crimean
War. In short, it was not the shortage of free hired labor
that hindered capitalist development in the Balkan provinces
of the Ottoman Empire.

Entrepreneurial efforts to found factories involved the
expenditure of considerable funds. The founder of the first
broadcloth mill, Zheliazkov, lacked the necessary capital and
had to lay his plans before the government, which in turn was
interested in finding cheap broadcloth for the army. This
turn of events was perhaps inevitable, given that the construction of the Sliven mill and its equipment cost more than
one million kuruş. A considerable part of the local Sliven
capital, though regarded as enormous, was actually far from
being that big when seen in context. The process of the

genesis of the Balkan industrial capitalist, although it had
reached the point of capitalist production where the accumulation of monetary capital should have been more rapid and been
employing noneconomic methods to pile up major fortunes,
failed to experience these developments for a number of reasons.

But this was only one aspect of the over-all failure of
Balkan industrial capitalism to achieve its full potential
for, after all, the establishment of smaller factories and
centralized manufactures required less capital, amounts that
Balkan entrepreneurs possessed. Here we come up against the
simple reluctance of the representatives of this bourgeoisie
to get involved in factory activity. Given the general
insecurity in the Ottoman Empire, they preferred to retain
the possibility of an easier transfer of their capital from
one sphere into another. They wanted to be able to mobilize
their funds at the slightest danger and, if necessary, even
take them out of production and out of the country. This
phenomenon was part and parcel of the inhibiting influence
of Ottoman rule on Balkan capitalist development. Even when
the strong demand for certain goods favored the emergence of
industrial enterprises of a higher type, the capitalists
obviously preferred such lower forms of production as putting-
out manufacture.

A typical example in this respect was Mihalaki Gümüşgerdan, who actually set up a mill although it did not occupy
a predominant place in the firm's production. Gümüşgerdan
continued to invest capital in a great variety of fields--
in commerce, in the acquisition of urban and rural real estate,
and in the maintenance of a widespread putting-out operation
that involved the population of dozens of villages and whole
urban guilds.

The mill, moreover, was set up only when Gümüşgerdan
succeeded, through the intercession of the Plovdiv vali, in
securing a contract for the regular supply of about 40,000
arshin of aba. In this case the advantages of the factory
mode of production were obvious for a capitalist such as
Gümüşgerdan. But on the other hand, without a permanent
market guaranteed in advance, without government orders, without the support of the Turkish administration, the Gümüşgerdans too would not have decided to set up their mill.

In closing, it is also important to stress that the
emergence and development of capitalist relations was a slow
and painful process. The relentless laws of expanded production pushed the capitalist entrepreneurs toward the application of constantly improved forms of production. The conditions in the Ottoman Empire, however, led them to move forward in the organization of their enterprises only after they

obtained the appropriate support from Ottoman authorities.
It is not necessary here to describe in detail the effect on
capitalist activity of the onerous regime of the decaying
Ottoman feudal system. Generally speaking, it was lack of
security that was one of the greatest obstacles to larger and
more permanent investments in industry. The words of Engels
about the incompatability of Ottoman rule and the capitalist
system are well known.[95] In this case Engels had in mind the
major precondition for capitalist accumulation, namely an
elementary security for the capitalists (the majority of whom
were non-Turks) and for their property as well. It was
precisely this security that was lacking in the "sick man of
Europe."

Plate 16. A 19th-century painting of the castle of Belgrade.
Courtesy of Municipal Library of Belgrade.

Plate 17. The state textile factory in Sliven. Reprinted
from F. Kanitz, *Donau-Bulgarien und der Balkan* (Leipzig, 1879).

Plate 18. The fortress of Ruse. Reprinted from *Donau Ansichten nach dem Laufe des Donaustromes* (Vienna, 1862).

Plate 19. The fortress of Vidin. Reprinted from *Donau Ansichten nach dem Laufe des Donaustromes* (Vienna, 1862).

Demographic Character
in the Nineteenth Century

15. THE POPULATION
OF THE BALKAN PROVINCES

In the early nineteenth century there began the successful struggle of the subjected Balkan peoples of the Ottoman Empire to win
their liberation. The Serbian uprising of 1804, although it ended
in failure several years later, eventually led to the formation of
what was at first a semiautonomous and then a fully autonomous principality. Starting in 1821, the Greek uprising lasted about eight
years, and an independent Greek state resulted from the Russo-Turkish War of 1828-29. Meanwhile, in the Balkan provinces that remained under Ottoman rule, the movement for national liberation was
also assuming significant proportions. This compelled the Turkish
authorities to devise and to implement a series of reforms.

The period from the late 1830s to the 1878 liberation of Bulgaria thus came to be known as the *Tanzimat* ("period of reforms").
These reforms involved both the administrative reorganization of
the Balkan provinces and many changes in the taxation system. These
changes in turn presupposed a new registration of the taxable popu-

lation, and in the second quarter of the nineteenth century
censuses were conducted throughout the empire. (Simultaneous
censuses also took place in Serbia and Greece.)

It is the data contained in these censuses that have
been used here in an analysis of the demographic composition
and development of the nineteenth century Balkan cities.
(This analysis has retained the terminology used in the documents themselves for classifying the population by religion
and, when the documents permit, by ethnic affiliation).

* * *

The 1831 census was the first general count of the population of the Ottoman Empire. It was carried out, however,
solely for fiscal purposes, and covered males only. But it
was not only the exclusion of women that kept this census
from an accurate count of the population, for it also failed
to employ a uniform system in collecting information. The
character of the registration itself played a role in this
respect. Religious profession provided the basis on which
the population was divided into major groups, a practice
that has frustrated attempts to determine its true ethnic
structure. The division of the population by age was also
not uniform. The Muslim population was divided into those
able and unable to work in three age groups: from one to
sixteen, from sixteen to forty, and forty and over. But the
sixteen-year-old breakoff point was tenuous, and children of
twelve, thirteen, and fourteen were often included in the
second group. There was a similar lack of system in the enumeration of non-Muslims, and it is difficult to know how accurately the nomadic population of Yuruks, Vlachs, and others
were counted. Naturally, the methods in question produced
great inaccuracies.

Census returns in the Ottoman Empire were not published
at the time they were taken, nor, except for individual registers, have they been preserved in the archives. One such
defter has been published by a Turkish historian along with
a brief commentary.[1] The material in this defter was broken
down by kazas, 137 in all, with additional information on another 10 nahiyes and 9 cities. For greater clarity, the data
for the kazas in question has been regrouped and summarized
here according to a geographical principle to conform to the
new vilâyet structure introduced in the middle of the nineteenth century, and specifically the vilâyets of Edirne,
Danube, Salonika, and Bitolj (see table 33). In several other
vilâyets (Bosnia, for example), where the implementation of
the Tanzimat reforms was opposed by local authorities and
feudal lords, it was not until 1851 that a census was taken.
These later data have been combined with the 1831 results in
table 33.[2]

TABLE 33

THE MALE POPULATION OF THE BALKANS
(Censuses of 1831 and 1851)

Vilâyet	Christians	Muslims	Gypsies	Jews	Armenians	Others	Total
Danube	306,534	159,308	11,603	417	-----	-----	477,862
Edirne	247,666	158,249	11,298	2,128	1,787	593	421,721
Salonika	127,200	100,249	7,047	5,915	-----	-----	240,411
Bitolj	120,582	81,736	4,682	1,163	24	35	208,222
Bosnia*	263,587	175,177	4,640	1,074	-----	-----	444,478
TOTAL	1,065,569	674,719	39,270	10,697	1,811	628	1,792,694

SOURCE: Karal, *Osmanlı Imparatorluğunda ilk nüfus sayımı 1831*, pp. 196-201; and Pejanović, *Stanovništvo Bosne i Hercegovine*, pp. 29-31.   *Data for 1851

The 1831 census included the male population in its entirety, since the defter counted both the non-Muslims exempt from the cizye (the minors, elders, and the disabled) and the Muslims exempt from military obligations. In most areas the percentage of non-Muslims exempt from taxes ranged from 20 to 40% (children formed most of those excluded). For the Muslim population, the division was between those liable for and those exempt from military duty, and the breakdown between the two groups was about the same as it was for the non-Muslim population, since most of the Muslim population was freed from military duty and was obligated to pay a tax instead. The basic contingent of military personnel was quartered in fortresses and in garrison cities.

The results of the census of 1831 came to the attention of the official representatives of foreign states in Istanbul and in a year or two appeared in the press. They served as the basis for calculating the Ottoman Empire's population.

In the census tables composed by contemporaries, the size of the population in the European possessions of the Ottoman state was put at between nine and ten million.[3] When these contemporaries wished to be more specific, they sought the assistance of diplomatic agents and others who possessed data on the taxable inhabitants of individual kazas and settlements, and who, through direct observation, could compile detailed tables.[4]

Although most heavily concentrated in the vilâyet of Salonika, the Muslims everywhere represented a large part of the population, as can be seen in table 34, which shows the percentage distribution of the population by religion according to the results of the 1831 census (and for the vilâyet of

Bosnia, the 1851 census). In the territory of the Danubian
vilâyet, there were twice as many Christians as Muslims. Although an accurate comparison is impossible, it should be
noted that in the sixteenth century the ratio of non-Muslims
to Muslims in the Balkan provinces of the Ottoman Empire had
been about four to one. In the first half of the nineteenth
century, however, the Muslims had come to constitute more than
one-third of the population in each of the vilâyets. Obviously, changes had taken place in the religious composition of
the population in favor of the Muslims.

TABLE 34

DISTRIBUTION BY RELIGION OF THE MALE POPULATION OF THE BALKANS
(Censuses of 1831 and 1851)

Vilâyet	Christians	Muslims	Gypsies	Jews	Armenians	Others	Total
			(In percentages)				
Danube	64.15	33.33	2.43	0.09	-----	-----	100.0
Edirne	58.73	37.53	2.68	0.50	0.42	0.14	100.0
Salonika	52.91	41.70	2.93	2.46	-----	-----	100.0
Bitolj	57.91	39.25	2.25	0.56	0.01	0.02	100.0
Bosnia	59.30	39.41	1.04	0.25	-----	-----	100.0

SOURCE: Karal, *Osmanlı İmparatorluğunda ilk nüfus sayımı 1831*, pp. 196-201;
and Pejanović, *Stanovništvo Bosne i Hercegovine*, pp. 29-31.

Table 35 lists the full data from the 1831 census on
the population of those kazas with more than 10,000 male residents. The most populous kazas were those of Sofia, Ruse, and
Vidin in the Danubian vilâyet; Plovdiv, Edirne, and Komotinē
in the vilâyet of Edirne; Bitolj itself in the vilâyet of
Bitolj; and Salonika and Serres in the vilâyet of Salonika.
For thirty-one of the kazas the census returns noted the number of migrants who were practicing a trade in a place away
from their homes. The Ottoman administration provided these
individuals with documents for movement, on the basis of which
the enumerators put them in the category of *yabançis*--outside
or migrant artisans and merchants. In the majority of kazas
the number of Christian migrants ranged from .5% to 4%. The
greatest movement of migrants seems to be in the direction of
the Salonika area, where they reached 25-30% of the total
male population, a figure that held true for both Muslims and
Christians. The movement of Muslims was strongest in the direction of Salonika, Serres, Veroia, and several other adjacent cities. Since the 1831 census did not state the occupations of the original population, it is impossible to determine the exact ratio between the local and migrant producers,
but the percentage figures noted above do reveal a consider-

TABLE 35

KAZAS OF BALKAN VILÂYETS WITH MALE POPULATIONS OF OVER 10,000
(Census of 1831)

Kaza	Christians	Muslims	Gypsies	Jews	Armenians	Others	Total
Danubian Vilâyet							
Ruse	7,196	16,165	1,437	-----	-----	-----	24,708
Svishtov	5,760	3,897	629	-----	-----	-----	10,286
Nikopol	8,598	3,893	1,190	-----	-----	-----	13,681
Lovech	-----	12,404	-----	-----	-----	-----	12,404
Vidin and several other kazas[a]	24,846	6,695	1,289	-----	-----	-----	32,830
Svŭrlig and other kazas	23,954	-----	420	-----	-----	-----	24,374
Vratsa	14,282	1,463	262	-----	-----	-----	16,007
Niš	18,313	1,862	575	178	-----	-----	20,928
Sofia	39,692	4,161	886	-----	-----	-----	44,739
Konitsa (Doniche)	11,642	4,317	-----	-----	-----	-----	15,959
Samokov	11,973	816	111	94	-----	-----	12,994
Kiustendil	14,070	1,853	232	145	-----	-----	16,300
Berkovitsa	13,549	1,125	382	-----	-----	-----	15,056
Štip	9,826	6,920	-----	-----	-----	-----	16,746
Kumanovo	10,819	2,276	-----	-----	-----	-----	13,095
Kratovo and other kazas[b]	21,068	4,749	627	-----	-----	-----	26,444
Vilâyet of Edirne							
Tekirdağ	7,727	3,773	57	-----	-----	-----	11,557
Gelibolu	6,613	4,179	-----	-----	-----	-----	10,792
Uzŭnköprü	8,886	1,929	-----	-----	-----	-----	10,815
Edirne	10,042	10,174	-----	-----	-----	-----	20,216
Edirne (city)	6,722	8,313	750	1,541	1,443	25	18,794
Akhŭchelebi	4,107	6,080	-----	-----	-----	-----	10,187
Kazanlŭk	8,097	7,195	748	-----	-----	-----	16,040
Stara Zagora	12,782	5,586	-----	-----	-----	-----	18,368
Didymoteikhon (Dimotika)	10,852	7,525	-----	-----	-----	-----	18,377
Komotine	5,339	30,517	1,712	-----	-----	-----	37,568
Yenice Karasu	2,540	7,582	1,273	-----	-----	-----	11,395
Khaskovo and other kazas	10,118	9,941	633	-----	-----	-----	20,692
Plovdiv	45,650	10,920	2,021	344	344	568	58,847
Tatarpazar	13,206	1,935	3,653	119	-----	-----	18,913
Vilâyet of Salonika							
Drama	3,077	8,618	1,007	-----	-----	-----	12,702
Tikvesh	6,104	4,454	-----	-----	-----	-----	10,558
Nevrokop	8,620	10,417	739	-----	-----	-----	19,776
Timur Hisar	6,611	3,229	494	-----	-----	-----	10,334
Zuhna	10,017	2,867	642	-----	-----	-----	13,526
Serres	16,606	4,459	1,761	248	-----	-----	23,074
Salonika	21,669	12,368	511	5,667	-----	-----	40,215
Yenice Vardar	4,766	6,811	-----	-----	-----	-----	11,577
Veroia	11,052	1,680	-----	-----	-----	-----	12,732
Avret Hisar	6,949	3,176	322	-----	-----	-----	10,457
Vilâyet of Bitolj							
Bitolj	24,550	6,723	705	1,163	-----	-----	33,141
Florina	5,253	5,596	365	-----	-----	-----	11,214
Veles	12,718	4,767	390	-----	-----	-----	17,875
Prilep	14,489	3,683	450	-----	-----	-----	18,622
Kostur	16,124	3,921	335	-----	-----	-----	20,380
Prizren and other kazas	2,857	9,488	366	-----	-----	35	12,746
Tetovo	8,043	11,766	472	-----	-----	-----	20,281

SOURCE: Karal, *Osmanlı Imparatorluğunda ilk nüfus sayımı 1831*, pp. 197-201.

[a] Including Lom, Akchar, and Belogradchik   [b] Including Vranja, Egridere, Palanka

able movement of manpower on the Balkan Peninsula. This migration was not regular in terms of timing or the areas affected, since varying circumstances dictated long- or short-
term migration to different settlements, but it was the product of socioeconomic forces that affected the Christian and
Muslim populations equally.

Understanding this movement would require a study of
the changes in the structure of land relations that occurred
in the eighteenth and the early nineteenth century. As well
as being the result of the classic laws of economic development common for every country, this situation was also influenced by factors connected with the decline of the military
fief-holding system and the abolition of the sipahi institution, and with the relatively limited spread of large-scale
landowning. The cluster of socioeconomic circumstances that
gave rise to long- or short-term migration (either within or
without the country) also brought about a flow from the countryside to the cities. Many migrants settled on the outskirts
of cities and continued to do farming work; others joined the
ranks of journeymen and apprentices who were increasingly becoming a permanent layer of hired labor; and others, although
not many, entered the urban economy as artisans recognized by
the craft guilds.

* * *

A revealing illustration of this process occurred in
the town of Lom, a case that can be studied thanks to the
preservation of an 1844-45 register of that settlement's Bulgarian population.[5] Actually, this population lived in the
varoš of the city, that is, in its new and entirely Bulgarian
section. The register in question enumerated the Bulgarian
houses and their owners (363 persons), their occupations,
annual incomes, and the taxes they paid.

A contemporary report published in 1856 in *Tsarigradski
vestnik* (*Constantinople Herald*) confirmed these figures and
disclosed the origin of Lom's Bulgarian population. After
pointing out that the Turkish part of the city consisted of
1,000 houses and the Bulgarian part of 500 houses, the report
stated: "Our city, though existing since olden times, used
to be very small, and only in the last ten years or so has it
begun to grow with Bulgarians who come and settle [here] from
nearby towns and villages."[6] Thus, the recent and the primarily peasant origins of the Bulgarians of Lom were obvious.
These immigrants did not immediately settle in the city. At
first they lived and worked in the outskirts, where they
bought land. Gradually, as they acquired property and social
status, they moved closer to the city center.

Nevertheless, a fairly sizable number of the settlers
continued to engage in farming. Of the total of 363 persons

entered in the register noted above, 76 were the owners of
larger or smaller pieces of land from which they earned their
living. Since there were also 50 *irgat*s (farmhands), about
35% of the male population of working age in the varoš of Lom
was engaged in farming. But this new Bulgarian population
did include individuals who worked in a variety of other occupations and who received varying amounts of income (see
table 36). True, about 60% fell into the two lowest income
ranges shown here, of up to 200 kuruş and from 201 to 300
kuruş. These income ranges included all of the farmhands,
all journeymen and apprentices, workers, various servants and
unskilled laborers, and all fishermen, sailors, and carters,
as well as many of the independent farmers and artisans.
Nearly half of the farmers (47%) and 20% of the artisans were
registered as receiving incomes equal to those of an irgat or
journeymen. The low-income category also took in some minor
state employees such as postmen (of whom there were four),
with salaries of 50 kuruş. The bulk of the artisans and half
of those described as merchants fell into the income range of
from 301 to 1,000 kuruş.

    Although on the whole they were not very high, the in-
comes of Lom's Bulgarian population did not exclude an internal social polarization within the community. Of the four
persons with incomes over 2,000 kuruş, three were merchants
and one was an artisan. Two of the merchants were grocers
who conducted their business in their own shops. One of them,
Todor, the son of Petko, owned two other shops from which he
received 400 kuruş in rent; a still for making brandy, which
brought an income of 250 kuruş; fourteen dönüm of vineyard
yielding 210 kuruş; two meadows producing twenty-one cart-
loads of hay and recorded as yielding a revenue of 210 kuruş;
and beehives that earned him 100 kuruş a year. The total income from Todor's other activities was 1,170 kuruş, and when
added to the 2,000 kuruş in income from his grocery store, he
had, in all, an income of 3,170 kuruş.[7] The other grocer,
Tseko, the son of Vŭlo, possessed only five dönüm of vineyard, which earned him 75 kuruş, a meadow from which he obtained 100 kuruş worth of hay, and a mare. He too earned
2,000 kuruş from his grocery.[8] The third businessman was
Kamen, the son of Stano, described as being engaged in "tavern and innkeeping" in his own "shop." He possessed three
fields bringing in 304 kuruş, sixty milch ewes that yielded
an income of 840 kuruş, forty rams and barren sheep (140 kuruş), a milch cow (25 kuruş), two mares (60 kuruş), two stills
(500 kuruş), and a vineyard of six dönüm (90 kuruş). In all,
these properties produced 1,959 kuruş in income.[9]

    The only artisan with an income of over 2,000 kuruş was
named Stan Keremidchiiata ("the Tiler"). (There is no way of

TABLE 36

DISTRIBUTION OF THE POPULATION OF THE VAROŠ OF LOM IN 1844-1845 BY OCCUPATION AND BY INCOME

Occupation	Yearly Income (in kuruş)												Total			
	Up to 200	201-300	301-400	401-600	601-800	801-1,000	1,001-1,500	1,501-2,000	2,001-2,500	2,501-3,000	3,001-4,000	Not Indicated	Independent	Journeymen servants	Others	Total
Farmers	21	15	7	15	7	4	5	2	--	--	--	--	76	--	--	123
Farmhands	37	10	--	--	--	--	--	--	--	--	--	--	--	47	--	
Artisans	6	9	4	25	10	6	10	2	1	--	--	2	75	--	--	103
Journeymen	22	4	--	1	--	--	--	--	--	--	--	1	--	28	--	
Fishermen, sailors	16	1	--	--	--	--	--	--	--	--	--	--	17	--	--	41
Assistant fishermen	17	7	--	--	--	--	--	--	--	--	--	--	--	24	--	
Merchants	2	1	1	4	2	8	9	2	1	--	2	1	33	--	--	63
Carters	8	4	--	--	--	--	--	--	--	--	--	--	12	--	--	
Servants, workers	15	3	--	--	--	--	--	--	--	--	--	--	--	18	--	
Minor officials	--	6	--	--	2	--	--	--	--	--	--	--	--	--	8	33
Poor, sick*	9	--	--	--	--	--	--	--	--	--	--	--	--	--	9	
Unknown, priests†	2	--	--	--	--	--	--	--	--	--	--	14	--	--	16	
TOTAL	155	60	12	45	21	18	24	6	1	1	2	18	213	117	33	363

SOURCE: NBKM, Oo, Lom, 20/7. *"Poor and sick" were those with no property and no regular income. They had to rely on others. Only two individuals in this group had vineyards, one having an indicated income of 30 kuruş, the other with a registered income of 60 kuruş. Ibid., ℓ. 13b, 45b. †Besides individuals whose profession was not noted or was unclear, this category includes three priests. The entry for one of these priests noted that "since the respondent lacks any property, he fares as a priest." The two other priests, however, did own property. One had a shop that earned him a yearly rent of 120 kuruş; the other owned ten dönüm of vineyard, which produced a yearly income of 150 kuruş. Ibid., ℓ. 5a, 5b, 7a.

determining whether he was the father of the innkeeper just
mentioned.) Stan Keremidchiiata was the largest owner of
urban real estate among the Bulgarians in the varoš of Lom.
His sources of income included the tilemaking shop in which he
himself worked; and rents from a tavern and inn (130 kuruş),
and from two grocery stores (250 and 500 kuruş). He also
earned income from two brandy stills (750 kuruş), and he had
ten dönüm of vineyard (150 kuruş). His total income amounted
to 2,770 kuruş, of which 1,000 represented the revenue from
his tilemaking shop.[10] The register, however, mentioned the
name of "Stan" on several other occasions as the owner of
other shops not entered in the enumeration of his personal
property: a grocer's shop with a rental income of 120 kuruş
and two tilemaking shops with rents of 150 and 300 kuruş.[11]

Undoubtedly, all of the individuals in question to some
significant extent used permanent and part-time hired labor
for the cultivation of their vineyards or fields, for rearing
livestock, for running their stills, or for work in their
shops, workshops, and taverns. However, this group did not
include a single entrepreneur or founder of either putting-
out or centralized manufacture, or a single individual who
had established strong production ties with urban and rural
producers. Although the subsequent careers of these individuals cannot be studied, there is sufficient information in
the register to conclude that the path to enrichment was the
same for all; the differences consisted only in the degree of
prosperity reached by these individual representatives of the
nascent Bulgarian bourgeoisie. The first step in the rise of
individuals from amidst the small-commodity producing artisans
and farmers--that is, their rise to a higher level of property
differentiation--was the possession of slightly more stores,
of slightly more fields, and of slightly more urban real
estate.

In general, Lom in the 1840s was a small urban settlement that engaged in little true commerce, but was a typical
market town for a farming area. True, its port had begun to
develop, providing work for a number of hands, but Lom was
still far from being the commercial center that it was to become in the second half of the nineteenth century when it
handled much of the imports and exports for the whole of
northwestern Bulgaria. Industry--the major factor producing
social transformation--was still at a low level of development
and had not yet reached even the manufacturing stage. Lom,
however, was one of those cities that was to undergo a rapid
transformation. It had taken only several decades for the
appearance, together with the citadel and the port district
with its stalls, of a new part of the city, a varoš with a

compact Bulgarian population drawn from the neighboring villages. And such was how Lom was described by travelers in
the 1830s. "Lom is a market place," wrote on visitor, "The
Turks deal partly with livestock trade, with small-scale
grocery stores, with fishing; and in part, like the Bulgarians, they are occupied with farming. Basically, the latter
are engaged in viticulture and livestock breeding and they
should be regarded as belonging to the propertied class. There
are artisans both among the Turks and the Bulgarians--dyers,
tailors, bootmakers, coopers, bakers and goldsmiths. The
weekly market takes place on Sunday, but [in fact] begins
Saturday afternoon and ends Sunday at lunchtime. The products
offered on the market are mostly fruit, wheat, oats, corn,
livestock, honey, wax, lard, wool, timber, and other kinds of
farm produce."[12] Many of the small urban settlements on the
Balkan Peninsula at the end of the eighteenth and in the
first half of the nineteenth century were similar in appearance and course of development.

* * *

By the second half of the nineteenth century, interest
in the size of the population of the Ottoman Empire was increasing, for in this period the renewed movement of the Balkan peoples for national liberation had put on the agenda the
question of the future state structure of that part of the
Balkans still under Ottoman rule. Austria and Russia, the
states most interested in Balkan affairs, assigned certain
persons the task of developing demographic information on
the Balkan provinces, and these individuals received all
sorts of confidential material. Some of them were sent as
agents to tour the Balkan Peninsula, and they made extensive
use of information collected by British, French, Russian, and
other travelers and historians.

For each vilâyet of the Balkans there were authors of
various origins who, on the basis of material collected by
them personally or by others, prepared surveys on the size of
the population by kazas and settlements. In 1865, for example, a contemporary published in Belgrade a book on Bosnia
and Hercegovina with a description of that region's population, and in the late 1870s the book was reissued in a revised version containing new data.[13] Extracts from the reports of Russian, Austrian, and other consuls in Mostar and
Sarajevo, as well as from official censuses, were printed in
various European publications and were used to compile comprehensive demographic statistics for the same region.[14]

The most famous traveler was Felix Kanitz, who in the
second half of the nineteenth century repeatedly visited the
Balkans. Thanks to its serious informative content and to

the presence of concrete demographic information, his book, *Donau-Bulgarien und der Balkan*, was quickly translated into several languages.[15]

In Russia, meanwhile, the need for detailed population data became particularly acute on the eve of and during the Russo-Turkish War of 1877-78. In 1877 in Bucharest the staff of the Russian army published several volumes that, as well as citing current laws, contained data on the size of the population of Bulgaria drawn from official Turkish sources, from diocesan sources, from local councils (obshtinas), and from other sources as well.[16] Published at the same time were the works of a number of Russian scholars and translations of European works, all of which dealt with the composition of the population of the Ottoman Empire.[17]

Although there were these published contemporary sources, they often contained divergent and even contradictory information, for obvious reasons. It was difficult to collect statistical information in a backward country where the population was not only ethnically complex, but also where both the Turkish administration and the local population looked with general distrust on this kind of activity on the part of foreigners. This, in conjunction with the frequent political goals of such studies, led to the publication of all sorts of conflicting information. Other factors that hindered the depiction of the true demographic situation involved the level of professional training and good faith of individual authors, and their excessive trust or hostility toward the different ethnic groups that supplied information.

The confused state of demographic knowledge about the Balkans became even more entangled in the 1860s and 1870s, when the renewed eastern crisis offered the national bourgeoisies in the Balkans realistic prospects for their peoples' right to claim a place in the sun. Despite brilliant argumentation, an attempt to buttress national aspirations by the use of an historical argument that glorified the past grandeur of Balkan medieval empires failed to produce the desired results either for Greece or for Serbia. Indeed, even some regions that had revolted were not included in their liberated territories. As a result, the Greek and Serbian middle classes turned their attention to more realistic arguments--the purported ethnic affiliation of the population. The Bulgarian bourgeoisie followed the same course. Thus, European authors could now also make use of (and sometimes be misled by) the organized services of such national institutions as state bodies, churches, and community councils. The publishing arms of these groups likewise encouraged the collection of demographic information, and local cultural activists composed demographic lists, which they published or passed on to interested circles in European states.

By that time, however, demographic science had progressed enough to be dissatisfied with partial and haphazardly
compiled data. What primarily interested the professional
observers were official sources, and the census results that
the Ottoman administration published in the so-called *salnames*
or yearly statistical registers became the major object of
intensive study. Now, wherever possible, both travelers and
the various authors of books on the Ottoman Empire and the
Balkan countries adhered to official Turkish statistics.
Turkish authorities carefully controlled the publication of
census returns, however, and there were numerous cases where
they arbitrarily inflated the number of Muslims.[18] As Kanitz
wrote: "If one adds up the figures at which the patriotically
[inspired] Turks, Serbs, Bulgarians, Greeks, Tsintsars, Albanians, and Armenians estimate their numbers, then Turkey
would represent a country with the densest population of all
the European states. It is perfectly well known, though,
that this is far from being the case."[19]

To overcome the shortcomings of the official census
returns and of some lacunae (e.g., the absence of data on
women and children), certain contemporary authors tried to
establish the total number of the population by coefficients
that they devised for calculating the missing components.
Such coefficients were employed by the Russian scholar V.
Teplov, who in 1877 published one of the most comprehensive
population studies of the Balkans, one that dealt with a considerable part of this region of the Ottoman Empire. For his
sources Teplov used the published data of the Turkish salnames
of 1874 and 1877, as well as information drawn from Kanitz,
from the church, from obshtinas, from lists compiled by other
contemporaries, and from personal observations--all of which
he subjected to statistical processing. But although Teplov
was a conscientious scholar, his attempt to establish the
population of part of the Balkan domains of the Ottoman Empire
is not satisfactory, for his coefficients are arbitrary and
unconvincing. Though natural and necessary in the case of
incomplete data, the use of coefficients must follow a careful consideration of all the circumstances and a thorough
critical analysis of the raw data. On the whole Teplov successfully accomplished his tasks of showing the ratio between
Muslims and non-Muslims on the basis of Turkish official information and, on the basis of special inquiries, of showing
the ethnic distribution of the non-Muslim population in a
number of areas. But his total figures on the population
are arbitrary, and they fail to convey its true size. For
example, after giving the size of the taxable male population
of the kaza of Ruse in accordance with the salname as 21,057

non-Muslims and 24,293 Muslims, Teplov went on to calculate
the absolute number of inhabitants by multiplying the number
of households (after Kanitz) by 6 for the non-Muslim households (14,028 households) and by 4.8 for the Muslim households
(15,482 households). He thus obtained the following results:
84,168 non-Muslims and 76,044 Muslims.[20] But for Tǔrnovo,
Teplov multiplied 5,844 Muslim households by a coefficient of
5 and obtained 29,220 Muslims. At the same time he estimated
the number of non-Muslims there at a 93,329, which means that,
having started with a figure of 10,483 non-Muslim households,
he had to use a coefficient of 9.37.[21] Both the absolute
figures thus obtained for Ruse and Tǔrnovo, and the arbitrary
use of coefficients (which were different every time), cast
doubt on Teplov's final calculations. (Teplov has been discussed in detail, since his work possessed much greater merit
than did those of other authors.)[22]

* * *

In the second half of the nineteenth century, official
census returns were published in the salnames, which, however,
did not contain all the information recorded in the original
schedules. It was perhaps for this reason that the salnames
lacked uniformity in their method of presenting the material
by means of various columns and categories. Furthermore, the
salnames contained a number of transcription and printing errors. But despite their incompleteness and inaccuracies, the
salnames have been used here--at least for their more important information--since the material they contain has remained
unknown or has been insufficiently used in research. To the
extent that certain nineteenth century authors utilized this
data, they used only the totals for larger administrative
units or for the entire peninsula instead of for individual
kazas and cities.

Data from the salnames is summarized in table ·37, which
shows the male population in the Balkan provinces of the Otto--
man state mostly for the year 1871-1872, a year in which the
censuses coincided for the majority of vilayêts. A comparison
between this information and the census returns for the 1830s[23]
shows that there had been a considerable population increase
over these forty years: a growth of about 100% for the Danubian vilâyet, of 50% for the vilâyets of Edirne and Salonika,
and of close to 50% for the vilâyet of Bosnia. The particularly strong increase of the Muslim population in the Danubian
vilâyet, a threefold growth, was to a large extent due to the
settlement of Circassians and Tartars transferred there from
Russia.

Owing to the practical impossibility of listing full
salname data for all settlements (the material is simply too

TABLE 37

MALE POPULATION OF THE BALKAN VILÂYETS
(Salnames, chiefly for 1871-1872)

Vilâyets	Males
Danube[a]	1,034,390
Ioannina	718,077
Edirne	667,757
Bosnia	621,229
Salonika[b]	396,727

SOURCE: Salnames preserved in the State Library
in Istanbul. More specific citations are given
in the tables analyzing the data by vilâyets.

[a]For 1869-70   [b]For 1882

voluminous), the population of individual vilâyets has been
broken down only into sancaks. Tables 38 and 39 contain data
from the salname of 1873-74 for individual sancaks of the Danubian vilâyet. The sancak of Ruse had the largest population,
followed by the sancaks of Vidin and Tŭrnovo. These sancaks

TABLE 38

URBAN AND RURAL MALE POPULATION OF THE DANUBIAN VILÂYET
BY SANCAKS (SALNAME OF 1873-1874)

Sancaks	Cities			Villages			Total	
	Number	Male Population	Per-centage	Number	Male Population	Per-centage	Male Population	Per-centage
Ruse	10	54,032	18.8	840	233,987	81.2	288,019	100.0
Vidin	7	36,767	19.0	456	156,969	81.0	193,736	100.0
Tŭrnovo	10	28,993	14.2	396	162,680	85.8	189,673	100.0
Sofia	11	28,676	16.1	706	149,781	83.9	178,457	100.0
Tulcea	10	20,844	18.7	262	90,652	81.3	111,496	100.0
Varna	5	13,697	23.2	400	45,287	76.8	58,984	100.0
Total	53	181,009	17.8	3,060	839,356	82.2	1,020,365	100.0

SOURCE: NBKM, Oo, Salname-i Tuna vilâyet-i, Ruscuk, 017.

also contained the largest number of villages. The ethnic
composition of the population (see table 39) was strongly
mixed, with almost 50% more Christians than Muslims. Muslims
tended to be less numerous in the western part of the vilâyet.
The more easterly the sancak, the higher the percentage
of Muslim, with the highest such concentration occurring
in the sancak of Varna. In absolute figures, however,
the largest number of Muslims lived in the sancak of Ruse.

TABLE 39

THE MUSLIM AND NON-MUSLIM POPULATION OF THE DANUBIAN VILÂYET
BY SANCAK (SALNAME OF 1873-1874)

| | Muslims | | | | Non-Muslims | | | | Total | | | |
Sancaks	House-holds	Per-centage	Popu-lation	Per-centage	House-holds	Per-centage	Popu-lation	Per-centage	House-holds	Per-centage	Popu-lation	Per-centage
Ruse	------	----	167,156	58.0	------	----	120,863	42.0	------	------	288,019	100.0
Vidin	12,457	22.7	37,657	19.4	42,416	77.3	156,079	80.6	54,873	100.0	193,736	100.0
Tŭrnovo	22,366	40.7	75,085	39.6	32,526	59.3	114,588	60.4	54,892	100.0	189,673	100.0
Sofia	10,116	19.2	24,443	13.7	42,459	80.8	154,014	86.3	52,575	100.0	178,457	100.0
Tulcea	17,406	60.0	67,238	60.3	11,591	40.0	44,258	39.7	28,997	100.0	111,496	100.0
Varna	17,905	78.1	43,187	73.2	5,011	21.9	15,797	26.8	22,916	100.0	58,984	100.0
Total	------	----	414,766	40.7	------	----	605,599	59.3	------	------	1,020,365	100.0

SOURCE: NBKM, Oo, Salname-i Tuna vilâyet-i, Ruscuk, 017.

The urban population ranged from 14.2 to 23.2% of the
total population of the sancaks (see table 38), with the highest urban percentages occurring in the sancaks of Varna and
Vidin. Since the number of cities in both sancaks was relatively small (five in the Varna sancak, and seven in Vidin),
the urban population was concentrated in individual cities.
In the sancak of Varna, for example, this population was concentrated chiefly in the cities of Varna and Bazargic, and
represented about one-third of the total population of their
respective kazas. Urban population in the other kazas and
cities in the sancak of Varna failed to exceed 10 or 15% of
the total, and in some cases was even less than 10%.
    Sancaks differed greatly in both number and size of
their villages. The sancak of Tŭrnovo stood first in relative
size of its villages, followed by the sancaks of Vidin and
Tulcea. At the opposite end of the pole were Varna and Sofia,
where the average size of villages was two to three times
smaller than in other sancaks. According to the census of
1874-75, the total population of the Danubian vilâyet had decreased by 64,341 since 1873-74.[24]
    A breakdown by sancak will not be provided for the
vilâyet of Ioannina for 1871-72. According to the salname
data of 1871-72, this vilâyet's population included 467,128
Christians (65.1%), and 250,949 Muslims (34.9%).[25]

    Salname data for 1871-72 on various categories of the
population of the sancaks of the vilâyet of Edirne is shown
in table 40. The sancak of Plovdiv had the largest population of this vilâyet, followed by Edirne. The smallest sancak, Tekirdağ, had a population that was four to six times
smaller than the first two. In all of the sancaks here, the
ratio of the two basic components of the population, Muslims
and non-Muslims, was approximately the same, with the Muslim
element comprising from 30.4 to 40.2% of the total.

TABLE 40

MALE POPULATION OF THE VILÂYET OF EDIRNE BY SANCAK AND BY RELIGION
(SALNAME DATA FOR 1871-1872)

Sancaks	Non-Muslims		Muslims		Gypsies		Total	
	Number	Per-centage	Number	Per-centage	Number	Per-centage	Number	Per-centage
Plovdiv	171,350	61.2	108,794	38.8	-----	---	280,144	100.0
Edirne	122,412	67.6	57,921	32.0	763	0.4	181,096	100.0
Sliven	49,287	57.1	35,557	41.2	1,496	1.7	86,360	100.0
Gelibolu	40,229	57.2	30,155	42.8	-----	---	70,384	100.0
Tekirdağ	34,175	68.7	15,110	30.4	488	0.9	49,773	100.0
Total	417,453	62.5	247,557	37.1	2,747	0.4	667,757	100.0

SOURCE: Istanbul, Belediye kütüphanesi, Salname-i Edirne, 13/2, pp. 141-51.

    According to a salname issued four years later (in 1875-
76), the population of the vilâyet of Edirne had increased to
806,707. Unlike the previous salname of 1871-72, it furnished
greater details on the individual components of the population:
280,050 Muslims; 468,987 Greeks and Bulgarians (instead of
listing just "Christians"); 22,688 Muslim Gypsies; 4,614 non-
Muslim Gypsies; 8,274 Jews; 8,100 Armenians; and 6,114 Roman
Catholics.[26] (The sharp increase in the number of Gypsies was
because the previous salname had not listed Muslim Gypsies--
those shown as Gypsies were actually the non-Muslim Gypsies.)
    It was more difficult to take censuses in Bosnia, and
such counts as there were took place more irregularly than in
other Balkan provinces. As one Yugoslav authority notes, the
Bosnian material published in 1865 was not the result of a
fresh census. For many regions the data presented was approximate and inaccurate.[27] But the author in question was himself unable to use salname data from the census of 1871; he
utilized only general figures taken from O. Blau's work. Furthermore, despite his fundamental criticisms, he cited the
1865 data in detail.
    Cited here, then, is demographic material for the vilâ-
yet of Bosnia according to the salname of 1871-72 (see table

41). Over the vilâyet as a whole there was a practically
even breakdown of Muslims and non-Muslims, although Muslims
predominated in the sancaks of Novi Pazar, Sarajevo, and Zvornik, and non-Muslims were in majority in Banja Luka. Adher-
ents of the Eastern Orthodox church comprised from 27.1 to
50% of the non-Muslim population. Roman Catholics were centered in Travnik and Hercegovina.

The material on the vilâyet of Bosnia for 1865 permits
some comparisons. Then the total population numbered 639,425
males, including 296,774 Orthodox Christians (46.4%), 128,960
Roman Catholics (20.2%), 209,814 Muslims (32.8%), and 3,877
Jews (0.6%).[28] The 1871 count indicates a considerable decrease in population, especially in the sancaks of Banja Luka,
Bihac, Sarajevo, and Zvornik. The Bosnian uprising of the

TABLE 41

THE MALE POPULATION OF THE VILÂYET OF BOSNIA
BY RELIGION AND BY SANCAK (SALNAME OF 1871-1872)

Sancaks	Muslims		Eastern Orthodox		Jews	
	Number	Per-centage	Number	Per-centage	Number	Per-centage
Zvornik	63,661	51.3	46,767	37.7	126	0.1
Travnik	43,487	47.0	25,095	27.1	157	0.2
Banja Luka	29,902	33.3	44,923	50.0	23	0.0
Bihac	45,186	53.3	37,117	43.8	---	---
Novi Pazar	52,626	62.7	30,575	36.4	40	0.1
Hercegovina	39,472	48.2	23,492	28.7	---	---
Sarajevo	35,188	55.1	18,343	28.7	959	1.5
Total	309,522	49.8	226,312	36.5	1,305	0.2

Sancaks	Gypsies		Roman Catholics		Total	
	Number	Per-centage	Number	Per-centage	Number	Per-centage
Zvornik	1,964	1.5	11,663	9.4	124,181	100.0
Travnik	658	0.7	23,161	25.0	92,558	100.0
Banja Luka	589	0.6	14,426	16.1	89,863	100.0
Bihac	400	0.4	2,098	2.5	84,801	100.0
Novi Pazar	742	0.8	------	----	83,983	100.0
Hercegovina	676	0.8	18,289	22.3	81,929	100.0
Sarajevo	677	1.0	8,747	13.7	63,914	100.0
Total	5,706	0.9	78,384	12.6	621,229	100.0

SOURCE: Istanbul, Belediye kütüphanesi, Salname-i, Bosnia, 9/6,
pp. 134-35.

1850s and 1860s accounted only partially for the difference in
question. It was mostly a question of certain inaccuracies in
the census data. In making this point, the Yugoslav expert
mentioned calculated the increase in the population as shown
by the census of 1851 and that of 1865 at about 33%, an annual
growth of 2.22%. He has considered this figure to be unreal-
istic, since the highest rate of growth Bosnia was later to
experience under Austrian rule was 1.6%. There had, however,
been a certain increase as a result of the resettlement of
about 20,000 Muslims from Serbia.

For Bosnia, the salname of 1874-75 has little value for
comparative purposes, since part of its material was simply
transferred from earlier salnames with only minor corrections.
In the final analysis, according to official data for the
period from 1851 to 1876 (25 years), the population of Bosnia
went up by 200,000, an increase that implies an approximate
annual rate of growth of 0.8%. Bearing in mind that these
decades were filled with uprisings and rebellions, and that
the highest rate of growth was about 1.5%, the increase in
question seems realistic. By sancak, the percentage of Eastern Orthodox Christians varied from 32.6 to 46.6%, and the
percentage of Muslims ranged from 32.6 to 51.9%, and Roman
Catholics fluctuated from 14.97 to 20.17%.[29]

Salname information on the vilâyet of Salonika has been
preserved only for a later date (see table 42). In this vilâyet, too, the population was thoroughly intermixed in terms
of religion, but with Christians predominating in the two
largest sancaks.

TABLE 42

MALE POPULATION OF THE VILÂYET OF SALONIKA BY RELIGION
AND BY SANCAK (SALNAME DATA FOR ABOUT 1882)

Sancak	Muslims		Christians		Total	
	Number	Per-centage	Number	Per-centage	Number	Per-centage
Salonika	90,079	40.8	130,604	59.2	220,683	100.0
Serres	52,146	38.7	82,675	61.3	134,821	100.0
Drama	33,301	80.8	7,922	19.2	41,223	100.0
Total	175,526	44.2	221,201	55.8	396,727	100.0

SOURCE: Istanbul, Belediye kütüphanesi, Salname-i Selânik,
27/7, p. 172.

Demographic Character
in the Nineteenth Century

16. CITIES IN GREECE AND SERBIA

The first census in Greece was taken in 1828 by the newly
formed Greek government at the request of England, France,
and Russia. The grave situation facing Greece in the aftermath of its liberation hardly permitted a precise count.
Nevertheless, the published results of this census reveal
the basic changes in the composition of the population that
occurred during the prolonged war for liberation from 1821
to 1828 (see table 43).

During the war, the population decreased by 185,365 persons. About three-fourths of this loss were Greeks who had
either been killed in the fighting or who had fled from Greece.
The Turks, who had numbered about 10% of the population, to
all intents and purposes abandoned Greece and resettled in
various parts of the Ottoman state.

In 1836 the Greek government began to conduct regular
censuses, setting up a special department to carry out this

TABLE 43

POPULATION OF GREECE, 1821 and 1828

Area	1821			1828		
	Christians	Muslims	Total	Christians	Muslims	Total
Continental Greece	247,850	20,865	268,715	172,850	11,450	184,300
Peloponnesus	450,000	42,750	500,750	400,000	------	400,000
The Islands	169,300	------	169,300	169,100	------	169,100
TOTAL	875,150	63,615	938,765	741,950	11,450	753,400

SOURCE: *Apographe tou plethysmou kata ten 27 Oktobriou 1907*, 1:9.

task. Up to 1845, information on the size of the population
was published annually. Afterward, a census was taken at fixed
intervals. On the basis of these censuses, one can determine
the movement of the population of Greece from 1839 to 1879
(see table 44).

The liberated regions of Greece were, generally speaking,
sparsely populated. It was only by about 1845 that Greece
overcame the population loss suffered during the war, thanks
both to the influx of Greeks from outside the kingdom and to
natural growth. By 1848 the population had increased by 30%
over the 1828 figure. The growth of the population, particularly in the second half of the nineteenth century, was not so
much a matter of natural increase as of immigration of Greeks
from outside the kingdom--chiefly to Athens, Piraeus, and
Phthiotis.

Throughout the whole nineteenth century, however, the
density of the population per square kilometer stayed low.
The density of only 19.76 persons in 1821 rose to 23.08 in
1861, to 29.04 in 1864 (after the annexation of the Ionian
Islands), and to 34.39 in 1881 (after the acquisition of Thessaly).[1]

As revealed by the censuses of 1861, 1870, and 1879, the
male-female ratio was in favor of males--108 to 100. This
ratio held true for all age groups. The male population was
smaller than the female population only on certain islands that
had experienced a great emigration.

The censuses of 1870 and 1879 also permit certain findings concerning the age structure of the population of Greece
(see table 45). On comparing the age characteristics of the

TABLE 44

MOVEMENT OF THE POPULATION OF GREECE, 1839 TO 1879

District	1839	1842	1845	1848	1853	1856	1861	1870	1879
Attica	42,542	47,113	57,644	58,019	65,101	67,879	82,284	97,971	141,338
Boeotia	25,838	27,884	30,767	30,852	29,706	29,630	33,740	38,833	44,026
Phthiotis	32,929	36,252	41,664	43,016	45,842	49,906	57,857	61,487	76,855
Phocis	30,192	31,743	35,894	37,661	43,855	42,028	44,434	46,934	51,585
Acarnania and Aetolia	58,283	61,331	68,214	69,584	71,228	73,506	82,899	88,675	103,649
Evritania	21,546	23,259	25,543	27,129	30,037	30,135	26,493	33,018	34,795
Achaea	69,753	65,604	81,249	81,818	87,435	90,354	92,109	98,495	115,580
Elis	35,140	34,011	36,316	34,484	37,549	40,237	46,140	51,066	65,752
Argolis	59,817	64,016	70,873	70,785	74,864	78,322	75,501	85,017	87,593
Corinth	30,508	30,883	34,592	32,589	33,624	35,014	37,409	42,803	48,488
Arcadia	100,604	100,443	111,387	116,105	124,099	126,550	113,719	131,740	148,600
Messenia	43,877	46,075	53,699	54,766	56,797	57,175	67,670	75,504	90,869
Triphylia	35,727	37,557	43,526	42,118	43,203	44,096	49,511	54,913	64,891
Lacedaemon (Sparta)	40,023	40,376	45,673	47,470	48,848	51,841	57,670	65,354	74,761
Laconia	35,258	35,650	36,265	38,379	37,998	38,752	38,876	40,497	46,335
Euboea	51,583	56,238	62,896	65,543	66,169	68,813	72,368	82,541	95,136
Cyclades	110,153	114,570	124,234	136,413	139,172	138,379	118,130	123,299	132,020
Ionian Islands	------	------	------	------	------	------	------	218,879	231,174
Serving in the army and navy	------	------	------	------	------	------	------	20,868	25,703
TOTAL	823,773	853,005	960,236	986,731	1,035,527	1,062,627	1,096,810	1,457,894	1,679,470

SOURCE: *Apographe tou plethysmou kata ten 27 Oktobriou 1907*, 1:72-73.

population by sex, one can note a slight increase in the number of male children in the age range of 0 to 15. In terms
of the 15 to 25 age bracket, however, there is a sharp decrease in the number of males. Generally speaking, children
up to 5 years old constituted one-seventh, children up to age
15 two-fifths, and children from age 15 to 20 one-tenth of
the total population.

TABLE 45

AGE STRUCTURE OF THE POPULATION OF GREECE
(Censuses of 1870 and 1879)

Age Range	Males				Females			
	Census		Increase		Census		Increase	
	1870	1879	Number	Per 100 Persons	1870	1879	Number	Per 100 Persons
0-15	238,312	340,550	57,238	20.20	264,661	308,285	43,624	16.48
15-60	407,934	469,642	61,708	15.13	400,656	448,371	47,715	11.91
Over 60	42,059	44,610	2,551	6.07	38,398	41,852	3,454	8.99
Total	733,305	854,802	121,497	16.84	703,715	798,508	94,793	13.47
Not established	20,871	26,150	5,279	25.29	3	10	7	23.33
TOTAL	754,176	880,952	126,776	16.81	703,718	798,518	94,800	13.47

SOURCE: *Statistiki tes Hellados, plethysmos 1879*, p. 30.

The occupational distribution of the population of Greece
was recorded in the census of 1879. This census characterized
about one million persons as being without a real occupation
(women, students, etc.). The remainder of the population whose
occupations were shown is analyzed in table 46.

This breakdown shows half of the population exclusively
engaged in agriculture. These peasants had a difficult position, for they had not received land in the aftermath of
Greece's liberation. In 1830 some 100,000 families lacked
their own land. State land, which constituted about 720,000
hectares and was chiefly that of Turks who had fled, was rented
out. Agrarian reform did not come until 1871, and even then
it was a partial measure. Usurers lorded it over the villages.

Among the artisans the most numerous element (6.1%) was
the combined group of construction workers. Also considerable
was the group of persons registered as "workers." Sailors,
another part of the hired labor force, numbered about half as
many as the "workers."

Generally speaking, it was only toward the end of the
nineteenth century that a more intensive capitalist development
began in Greece. Until then, for example, the country lacked
good transportation: up to the end of the century there were

only 1,864 kilometers of highway and a single railroad line
running 8 kilometers. Shipping, of course, was an exception,
and in this area Greece had made significant headway.

TABLE 46

OCCUPATIONAL DISTRIBUTION OF THE POPULATION OF GREECE
(Census of 1879)

Profession	Number	Percentage of Total Known[a]
Farmers	254,491	48.05
Artisans	77,304	14.59
Merchants	34,133	6.44
Workers	42,966	8.11
Officials	51,313	9.73
Seamen	16,157	3.05
Seamen abroad	5,180	0.98
Clerics	7,952	1.50
Free professionals	9,634	1.82
Military reservists	1,265	0.25
Active military servicemen	18,521	3.50
Naval seamen	2,002	0.38
Others	8,631	1.60
TOTAL	529,749	100.00

SOURCE: *Statistiki tes Hellados, plethysmos 1879*, pp. 32-33.

[a]Excludes also the 1,000,000 or so individuals characterized
by the census as being without a definite occupation.

The 1879 census counted 335,159 buildings in Greece. Of
these structures, 316,300 were residences and the remainder
consisted for the most part of workshops, schools, and churches.
There were 1.13 families or an average of 5.23 persons per
house for the country as a whole. This indicates that housing
was lagging behind the growth of the population, since the
census of 1870 had shown an average of 4.60 inhabitants per
house.[2]

* * *

The growth of the population of Serbia from 1833 to 1868
is shown in table 47. In this period, the population of Serbia

TABLE 47

MOVEMENT OF THE POPULATION OF SERBIA, 1833-1868

Year	Christians	Muslims	Total
1833	673,632	4,560	678,192
1834	696,610	4,690	701,300
1835	716,409	4,820	721,229
1836	739,736	4,950	744,686
1837	762,427	5,080	767,507
1838	785,009	5,210	790,219
1839	806,956	5,340	812,296
1840	823,417	5,478	828,895
1841	835,894	5,554	841,448
1842	842,011	5,630	847,641
1843	853,839	5,706	859,545
1844	874,111	5,782	879,893
1845	891,783	5,859	897,642
1846	907,225	5,936	913,160[a]
1847	922,625	6,023	928,648
1848	936,363	6,110	942,473
1849	940,216	6,197	946,413
1850	950,610	6,283	956,893
1851	963,013	6,370	969,383
1852	979,166	6,458	985,624
1853	983,464	6,545	990,009
1854	992,289	6,632	998,919[a]
1855	1,011,424	6,708	1,018,132
1856	1,032,228	6,784	1,039,012
1857	1,053,763	6,860	1,060,623
1858	1,074,190	6,936	1,081,126
1859	1,093,868	7,011	1,100,879
1860	1,103,621	7,090	1,110,711
1861	1,111,472	7,174	1,118,646
1862	1,117,375	6,245	1,123,620
1863	1,130,111	6,294	1,138,405[a]
1864	1,149,811	6,360	1,156,171
1865	1,178,645	6,430	1,185,095[a]
1866	1,209,078	6,498	1,215,576
1867	1,231,513	6,580	1,238,093
1868	1,247,843	6,660	1,254,503

SOURCE: *Državopis Srbije* 3 (Belgrade, 1886):107.   [a]The
totals do not represent the exact sum of Christians and
Muslims. This is the manner in which the figures are given in
the original.

almost doubled. The average annual growth was highest in the
period from 1833 to 1837 (with an average increase of 17,759
per year) and in the years from 1863 to 1867 (with an average
annual increase of 20,280). From 1846 to 1866, the coefficient
of growth in different districts ranged from 679 per 100,000 to
2,657 per 100,000. The highest average annual growth took
place in the districts of Belgrade, Knjaževac, and Aleksinac.
The non-Christian population was very small. In the first half
of the nineteenth century it comprised only .7% of the total
and by the 1860s had decreased to .5%.

The Serbian census of 1866 contained information on the
male-female ratio and on the number of houses (see table 48).
Males were only slightly more numerous, and only in Belgrade
did they enjoy a marked preponderance. In Serbia as a whole
there was an average of 6 persons per house; this density
rose to between 7 and 8 per house in the districts of Valevo,
Knjaževac, Šabac, and Belgrade.

TABLE 48

THE MALE-FEMALE BREAKDOWN OF THE POPULATION OF SERBIA
AND THE NUMBER OF HOUSES, 1866

District	Number of Houses	Population Males	Per-centage	Females	Per-centage	Total
Belgrade	3,454	14,447	58.8	10,135	41.2	24,612
Topčidere	24	111	71.2	45	28.8	156
Aleksinac	7,844	24,671	51.3	23,465	48.7	48,136
Belgradsko	9,730	33,043	51.7	30,837	48.3	63,880
Valevo	10,691	43,177	51.7	40,306	48.3	83,483
Knjaževac	7,713	28,136	51.1	26,943	48.9	55,079
Kragujevac	16,145	50,983	51.9	47,158	48.1	98,141
Krajna	13,269	36,021	51.2	34,272	48.8	70,293
Kruševac	10,864	34,749	51.5	32,690	48.5	67,439
Podrinski	7,225	24,623	50.4	24,204	49.6	48,827
Požarevac	29,011	72,885	51.8	67,716	48.2	140,601
Rudnik	7,649	24,070	50.7	23,397	49.3	47,467
Smederevo	10,303	30,934	51.5	29,143	48.5	60,077
Užice	15,042	52,794	50.6	51,583	49.4	104,377
Crnorečkski	9,614	27,559	51.7	25,725	48.3	53,284
Čačak	10,761	29,869	51.5	28,168	48.5	58,037
Šabac	10,022	37,677	51.2	35,942	48.8	73,619
Ćuprija	9,611	28,585	51.2	27,299	48.8	55,884
Jagodina	12,084	31,856	51.2	30,328	48.8	62,184
Total	201,056	626,220	51.5	589,356	48.5	1,215,576

SOURCE: *Državopis Srbije* 3:100.

* * *

Nineteenth-century censuses in Greece and Serbia also captured demographic material on the urban network in both countries, including some material on the occupational composition of the urban population.

The growth of the urban population in Greece in the second quarter of the nineteenth century is expressed in table 49. The population grew in all cities with the exception of the island cities of Hydra, Argostolion, Zante, and one city of central Greece, Kranidion. The port cities had the greatest increase: Piraeus (300%), Argos (250%), and Patras (66%). Athens, the capital city, doubled its population.

Established norms have been used here to group these cities by the size of their population (see table 50). It is true that different authors classify nineteenth century European cities in various ways, and some writers do so by taking into account the dynamics of a city's development throughout the whole century. One German scholar, for example, has proposed that a European "small" city would characteristically have had a threefold increase of its population over the century, while the "large" city would have had a fivefold increase. Thus, for 1815 this writer has established a population of 5,000 residents as the lower limit for the "small" city, a criterion that increases to 10,000 residents for about the year 1870, and to 15,000 residents for about the year 1925.[3]

Here, such gradations can be used only as a general orientation. Despite the progress of statistical studies and the accepted division of cities into categories of "small," "medium," and "large," for the nineteenth-century unanimity of opinion exists only for the differentiation of large cities (i.e., with over 100,000 inhabitants), and in part for the category of medium-sized cities (over 20,000 or, sometimes, over 50,000 inhabitants). The lower limit suggested above for the small city (10,000 residents for the 1870s) does not mean that settlements with a smaller population would be excluded from this category. For Germany, to cite the example of a different area, historians have introduced the category of the "rural city" with a population of from 2,000 to 5,000 inhabitants, with cities whose populations surpassed 5,000 recognized as "small cities."[4]

In the period from the 1850s to the 1870s, about 85% of all the cities of Greece fell into the category of small cities (see table 50). It is true that in the 1870s there was a decline in the percentage of such cities, but this decrease was not significant. Practically the entire urban network of Greece was composed of cities whose development remained static over the course of the whole century. Cities whose size was sufficient to make them "medium" in the fifteenth and sixteenth centuries now joined the class of small cities. Furthermore,

TABLE 49

MOVEMENT OF THE URBAN POPULATION OF GREECE
FROM THE 1850s THROUGH THE 1870s

| City | Census | | | | |
	1853	1856	1861	1870	1879
Athens	30,590	30,969	41,298	44,510	65,499
Agrinion	4,081	266	3,886	4,273	5,218
Salona	4,160	3,953	4,394	4,463	4,667
Argos	9,275	10,351	9,157	8,981	9,861
Gargaliani	------	------	1,959	2,251	3,397
Hermoupolis	19,981	16,830	18,511	20,996	21,540
Gition	1,422	1,594	1,681	1,991	2,720
Hydra	12,572	13,008	9,592	7,380	6,446
Kalamata	3,942	4,526	6,292	6,327	8,109
Karpenision (Carpenisi)	1,508	1,443	1,409	1,437	1,727
Corinth	------	------	1,636	1,862	2,619
Kranidion	7,689	6,574	6,639	7,185	5,628
Kiparissia	2,269	2,708	3,212	2,959	3,754
Lamia	3,001	3,376	4,685	4,873	5,506
Laurium (Lavreion)	------	------	------	------	4,706
Lebadeia	3,347	2,841	3,149	4,067	4,524
Megara	2,916	3,208	3,460	4,023	5,348
Mesolongion (Missolonghi)	5,067	4,890	6,059	5,714	6,324
Messene	3,597	3,692	4,790	5,397	5,853
Nauplia (Navplion)	3,435	4,260	6,024	3,958	4,598
Patras	15,854	15,131	18,342	16,641	25,494
Piraeus	5,434	6,057	6,452	10,963	21,618
Pyrgos	3,502	3,875	4,520	6,140	8,788
Sparta	1,129	1,634	2,024	2,699	3,595
Tripolis	6,600	7,271	7,292	7,020	10,057
Philiatra	2,652	2,701	3,720	4,183	5,632
Chalcis	5,317	4,086	4,585	6,447	6,877
Egion	2,690	2,581	3,525	3,936	5,311
Egina	2,716	2,791	2,859	1,773	2,917
[a]Argostolion	------	------	------	8,106	7,871
[a]Zante (Zakynthos)	------	------	------	17,516	16,250
[a]Corfu (Kerkyra)	------	------	------	15,452	16,741
[a]Leukas	------	------	------	2,065	3,434

SOURCE: *Apographe tou plethysmou kata ten Oktobriou 1907*, p.
104.   [a]Cities of the Ionian Islands that were joined to
Greece in 1864.

in the course of the thirty-year period from the 1850s to the
1870s, at least 80% of the cities belonged to the group of
cities with less than 10,000 people.

   For a half century following the liberation of Greece
only one city belonged to the category of medium-sized cities,
and only in the 1870s did the number of such cities increase
to four. In addition to Athens, this group included the rapidly developing port of the capital, Piraeus, and the cities
of Patras and Hermoupolis. Of the cities of the interior only
Tripolis, which was located in the center of the Peloponnesus,
grew significantly, in this case by almost doubling its population.

TABLE 50

DISTRIBUTION OF GREEK CITIES BY SIZE OF POPULATION
FROM THE 1850s THROUGH THE 1870s

Year of Census	Number of Inhabitants						Total	
	Up to 10,000		10,000-20,000		Over 20,000			
	Number of Cities	Per-centage	Number of Cities	Per-centage	Number of Cities	Per-centage	Number of Cities	Per-centage
1853	22	84.6	3	11.5	1	3.9	26	100.0
1856	21	80.7	4	15.4	1	3.9	26	100.0
1861	25	85.2	2	7.2	1	3.6	28	100.0
1870	24	85.6	2	7.2	2	7.2	28	100.0
1879	24	82.8	1	3.4	4	13.8	29	100.0

SOURCE: *Apographe tou plethysmou kata ten 27 Oktobriou 1907*, p. 104.

   In 1879 Athens itself had a population of 63,374 residents (excluding soldiers) and 15,209 families. Its population
represented 3.83% of the total population of the country.[5] The
average size of the Athenian family was 4.17 persons. The city
had 17,316 houses. Of these residences, 3,661 were owner-
occupied, and the remainder were rental dwellings. Eighty-
three homes were under construction. Commercial and business
property included 599 various food shops and stores, 598 artisan workshops, 350 commercial establishments, 399 clothing and
footwear workshops and stores, 288 taverns, 161 coffeehouses,
126 hotels and inns, 112 tobacco shops, 77 barbershops, 30
pharmacies, 24 offices for clerical purposes, and 60 cultural
establishments. The occupational distribution of the population of Athens in 1879 is shown in table 51.

   Lagging urban development was even more marked in Serbia,
where only the capital city of Belgrade stood out in terms of
the relative size of its population. The other Serbian cities
fell into the category of the smallest-sized cities, those

TABLE 51

OCCUPATIONAL DISTRIBUTION OF THE POPULATION
OF ATHENS ACCORDING TO THE CENSUS OF 1879

Occupation	Number of Individuals
Artisans	5,552
Merchants	3,815
Farmers	758
Large Proprietors	1,167
Workers	3,258
Servants	6,594
Free Professions	760
Clerics	163
Officials	1,382
Active Military Service	305
Teachers	617
Others	991

SOURCE: *Statistiki tes Hellados plethysmos 1879*,
p.54. The census indicated the profession of
34,278 individuals.

with a population of less than 10,000 inhabitants (see
tables 52 and 53).

The cities of Serbia might appropriately be compared in
detail with the cities of the contiguous Danubian vilâyet.
As such a comparison shows immediately, Belgrade's experience
as the capital of a country for half a century had a significant impact on its development. The size of Belgrade was
unmatched by any city of the Danubian vilâyet. It contained
more than 22.4% of Serbia's male population--twice the combined populations (12.6%) of Ruse and Shumen, the largest
cities of the Danubian vilâyet. On the other hand, there was
a significant difference in the size of other Serbian cities.
They all belonged to the smallest category, containing less
than 10,000 inhabitants. Although more numerous than the
cities of the Danubian vilâyet (37 versus 31), these Serbian
cities had a total population of 50,000 males in contrast
to the 65,000 males in cities of a similar character in the
Danubian vilâyet. The Serbian city that belonged to the category of the smallest cities had an average number of 1,351
males, while in the Danubian vilâyet the average population

TABLE 52

THE URBAN POPULATION OF SERBIA ACCORDING
TO THE CENSUS OF 1866

Cities	Number of Houses	Number of Inhabitants per House	Males		Females		Total	
			Number	Percentage	Number	Percentage	Number	Percentage
Aleksinac	898	4.4	2,065	52.2	1,889	47.8	3,954	100.0
Belgrade	3,478	7.1	14,588	58.9	10,180	41.1	24,768	100.0
Valevo	690	4.4	1,911	62.3	1,155	37.7	3,066	100.0
Zaecar	835	4.6	2,101	54.4	1,759	45.6	3,860	100.0
Kragujevac	1,404	4.5	3,861	60.5	2,525	39.5	6,386	100.0
Knjaževac	711	4.3	1,595	52.2	1,462	47.8	3,057	100.0
Kruševac	832	3.6	1,615	53.4	1,407	46.6	3,022	100.0
Milanovac	212	4.0	506	59.0	352	41.0	858	100.0
Negotin	984	4.4	2,388	55.2	1,937	44.8	4,325	100.0
Požarevac	1,481	4.7	3,903	56.5	3,006	43.5	6,909	100.0
Smederevo	1,134	4.5	2,906	56.7	2,216	43.3	5,122	100.0
Užice	694	4.6	1,741	55.0	1,422	45.0	3,163	100.0
Čačak	607	3.2	1,099	57.2	823	42.8	1,922	100.0
Šabac	959	6.8	3,662	56.2	2,854	43.8	6,516	100.0
Ćuprija	529	4.6	1,276	52.3	1,163	47.7	2,439	100.0
Jagodina	1,084	4.1	2,378	53.7	2,051	46.3	4,429	100.0
Aranjelovac	187	4.1	473	62.1	289	37.9	762	100.0
Banja	328	5.1	878	52.5	794	47.5	1,672	100.0
Grocka	295	4.7	759	54.3	640	45.7	1,399	100.0
Gradište	532	4.7	1,305	51.8	1,214	48.2	2,519	100.0
Ivanica	247	4.6	601	52.4	547	47.6	1,148	100.0
Karanovac	523	3.6	1,038	55.5	833	44.5	1,871	100.0
Majdanpek	238	4.3	574	56.1	450	43.9	1,024	100.0
Mitrovica	46	5.4	141	57.1	106	42.9	247	100.0
Milanovac	301	4.0	604	50.0	603	50.0	1,207	100.0
Obrenovac	256	5.1	751	57.2	562	42.8	1,313	100.0
Požega	130	3.9	274	54.2	232	45.8	506	100.0
Palanka	315	4.3	746	54.7	619	45.3	1,365	100.0
Paraćin	918	4.7	2,284	53.1	2,018	46.9	4,302	100.0
Raška	57	4.0	121	53.1	107	46.9	228	100.0
Rača	198	4.4	516	59.4	353	40.6	869	100.0
Svilajnac	851	4.7	2,085	52.0	1,924	48.0	4,009	100.0
Trstenik	188	3.8	368	52.1	339	47.9	707	100.0
Ub	243	8.1	1,198	60.5	781	39.5	1,979	100.0
Loznica	488	4.2	1,101	54.0	938	46.0	2,039	100.0
Krupane	144	4.2	319	53.0	283	47.0	602	100.0
Kladovo	335	4.4	765	51.7	715	48.3	1,480	100.0
Lešnica	178	5.0	459	51.9	425	48.1	884	100.0

SOURCE: *Državopis Srbije* 3:103

of a city of this category was 2,092 males. By including Belgrade for Serbia and Shumen and Ruse for the Danubian vilâyet,
the average size of the male taxable population was 1,709 persons in a Serbian city and 3,577 in the cities of the Danubian
vilâyet. This difference was produced by the general conditions
of socioeconomic development of the Principality of Serbia and
northern Bulgaria. In the previous century the growth of the
urban network in Serbia had been a weaker one, and the appearance and development of the Serbian bourgeoisie followed a different path of development than was true in Bulgaria.

TABLE 53

DISTRIBUTION OF SERBIAN CITIES BY SIZE OF
POPULATION IN 1866

Categories of Urban Size by Number of Inhabitants	Cities		Population	
	Number	Percent	Size	Percent
Up to 10,000	37	97.4	91,160	78.6
From 10,001-20,000	--	----	-------	-----
Over 20,001	1	2.6	24,768	21.4
Total	38	100.0	115,928	100.0

SOURCE: *Državopis Srbije* 3:103.

*Demographic Character
in the Nineteenth Century*

17. THE ETHNIC COMPOSITION
OF THE DANUBIAN VILÂYET

The Oriental Department of the Cyril and Methodius National
Library in Sofia possesses a comparatively rich archive on the
cities of the Danubian vilâyet. The documents therein concern
the 1860s and 1870s. It was at that time that the government
introduced printed forms that brought unification to the assessment and taxation system. The preserved documents of this kind
include both permits to exercise a craft and receipts for the
payment of income and property taxes (as well as lists of the
population drawn up during the census taken in 1866 and in
following years).

The guild tezkeres or permits, which were issued after
payment of the appropriate levy, were of two kinds: those
granted to local persons and those issued to migrants (the
yabancıs). Using several columns and boxes, these permits
listed name and surname, domicile, present residence, address,
year, profession, income, and tax.

340

The property tax receipts covered a six-year period.
They had columns for recording information both on the property
owner (name and surname, the general number and volume of the
individual's entry in the register of vital statistics, and
domicile and present residence), and for the property itself
(type; entry number in the general registry; its space or size
in dönüm, *lekh*, and arshin; the assessment in kuruş; and the
income, tax, and location of the property). In addition, these
documents recorded all ownership changes that resulted from
property sales. The annual tax installments were entered at
the very bottom.
      An examination of all of the collections of such receipts
in the Oriental Department has shown that its holdings pertain
solely to the Danubian vilâyet and, more precisely, to the
cities located in the eastern half of that territory. (Only
isolated documents of this kind have been encountered for
cities of southern Bulgaria and elsewhere.) Thus, the cities
for which the available information permits comprehensive study
are Shumen, Provadiia, Varna, Silistra, Bazargic, Medgidia,
Constanţa, Babadag, Macin, and Tulcea. The data drawn from the
documents in question on occupational tax obligations and on
property status concern some 15,000 inhabitants of these cities
--a figure sufficiently large to be used as the basis for extensive analysis.
      True, not all of the documents for the cities in question
have been preserved, and part of those extant are in poor condition, with many pages missing. Hence, the records cover only
part of the urban population. Although there is much data for
some of the cities, for others it is extremely scanty, which
has hindered their individual description. Some problems have
had to be examined on the basis of unavoidably selective data,
and their analysis has been susceptible to the errors inherent
in such an approach. The extent to which this material is
representative of the total population remains questionable.
      A related problem has arisen out of the inevitable errors
of the registration itself. For example, some of the figures
in the initial schedules were rounded off, and receipts and
permits do not reflect exact incomes as might have been determined on the basis of the ledgers of the individuals concerned.
That is, rather than list exact incomes, the Turkish administration used a scale of income ranges, and individuals were
entered according to categories. To a certain extent, this
method of registration has eased analysis, since the income
categories involved were applied with the knowledge and cooperation of the population itself. They can thereby serve as
an indication of income differentiation as actually perceived.
      Other kinds of information--on real estate within the
boundaries of given settlements, on land, and on taxes in the

Danubian vilâyet in the late 1860s--were gathered by specially
created commissions. After relevant training, members of these
commissions went around to each house and, using detailed
schedules, recorded data on the age, the year of marriage, the
occupation, the income, and the property of each person. This
name-by-name information on the occupations and on the urban
real estate of the population was not complete. Nevertheless, the summaries of these parts of the census were included in a statistical table of the vilâyet for the year
1866. This document has also been extensively analyzed and
will be treated first.

This *Table of the Taxes and of the Population*[1] of the
Danubian vilâyet contains exhaustive information on the size
of the taxable population of the cities of the vilâyet, on the
general value of real estate, and on the totals of registered
taxable incomes. It should be stressed that a strict distinction has been made here between the information published
for public use in the salnames[2]--and from which contemporary
travelers and authors obtained material--and the raw data collected during the censuses and contained in such documents as
the *Table*, which had a strictly practical purpose. It has been
primarily the latter type of source that has been examined here.
A comparison between the two kinds of documentation leads un-
questionably to the conclusion that the informative value of
the documents drawn up for fiscal purposes is much greater:
first, because of the greater accuracy of the data recorded
therein; and second, because they incorporate more extensive
information in their various columns and subcolumns. For
example, in the *Table of the Taxes and of the Population* there
are nine columns containing material on the size of the urban
population, its ethnic composition, and its property status.
Despite its rich content, however, it is difficult to use this
source for purely demographic studies since, given the fiscal
purposes of the table, it failed to indicate the number of
women and children and other population material collected
during the actual census, and recorded only in the initial
schedules. On the other hand, some of these partially preserved schedules have been located in the Oriental Department
and have been used to assemble information concerning several
thousand people. This material pertains to the population of
five mahalles of the city of Bazargic, two mahalles of Tŭrnovo,
and three of Svishtov, and it gives the number of all members
of the households of both sexes, their dates of birth and of
wedlock, their occupations, and property status. On the basis
of this information, an attempt has been made here to establish
the male-female ratio of the population, its age structure,
family status, and the number of children in a family.

* * *

The Danubian vilâyet, which was set up during the administrative reform of 1864, consisted of seven sancaks: Ruse,
Vidin, Niš, Sofia, Tŭrnovo, Varna, and Tulcea. These districts
were subdivided into forty-seven kazas and about ten nahiyes.[3]

By sancak, the vilâyet included the following cities:

Ruse: Ruse, Shumen, Razgrad, Tŭrgovishte, Novi Pazar
        (Yenipazar), Pleven, Svishtov, Nikopol, Silistra,
        Turtucaia
Vidin: Vidin, Lom, Oriakhovo (Rakhovo), Vratsa, Berkovitsa,
        Belogradchik, Kula (Adlye)
Niš: Niš, Pirot (Schirkoy), Vranja, Leskovac, Prokuplje,
        Kuršumlija, Trŭn (Iznebol)
Sofia: Sofia, Kiustendil, Samokov, Dupnitsa (now Stanke
        Dimitrov), Radomir, Zlatitsa (Izladi), Orkhanie
        (earlier Samundzhievo, now Botevgrad), Ikhtiman,
        Etropole, Teteven, Gorna Dzhumaia (now Blagoevgrad)[4]
Tŭrnovo: Tŭrnovo, Sevlievo, Gabrovo, Lovech, Omurtag (Osman
        pazar), Gorna Oriakhovitsa (Rakovitsa), Elena,
        Drianovo, Triavna, Kotel (Kazan)
Tulcea: Tulcea, Sulina, Babadag, Macin, Constanţa, Mahmudie,
        Medgidia, Hirşova, Isaccea, Kiliya (Chilia-Nouă)
Varna: Varna, Provadiia, Bazargic, Mangalia

There are certain differences in the number of cities given by
the salname of 1873-74 and the data in the table, although
both were prepared on the basis of data drawn from the same
census. The table omitted the entire Niš sancak.

Reports in the newspaper *Dunav* on the progress of the
registration indicated that the census of the Niš sancak was
planned to be on an equal footing with the others. On December
1, 1865, the newspaper reported an estimate of the time it
would take to carry out a census of the real estate and the
population in all of the cities of the Danubian vilâyet. The
same count in the cities of the Ruse sancak had taken four
months to complete. "Allowing four months for the registration
of each sancak," the commentator noted, "it is believed that
the registration of the sancaks of Tŭrnovo, Varna, Tulcea,
Vidin, Niš, and Sofia will last for two years."[5] The writer
even thought that the census might be completed earlier, since
the other sancaks were smaller than that of Ruse.

Early in the following year, in addition to traveling
teams of enumerators, the government appointed permanent officials and clerks to carry on with the registration of the property and population in all the sancaks of the Danubian vilâyet,
the sancak of Niš included.[6] More than three years later the
paper *Dunav* noted that "the registration of the cities in the

Danubian vilâyet was carried out some time ago" and that a
royal decree had arrived ordering officials to proceed to the
registration of the property and the population in "the villages of the seven sancaks."[7]   Five years after that, in
October, 1874, the newspaper published, in Bulgarian and Turkish, a "Statistical Table of Residents in the Danubian Territory" on the total size of the population in the Danubian
vilâyet (for Muslims and for Christians), but without breaking
down this population by settlements or even by sancaks. A note
accompanying this table stated that the statistics had been
collected from two consecutive stages of the census. The first
stage had covered 47 cities, 8 nahiyes, and 1,352 villages;
the second stage had taken in 8 nahiyes and 1,708 villages.[8]
The 8 nahiyes listed in the earlier *Table of the Taxes and of
the Population* were Liaskovets and Chertovets (both villages);[9]
Gorna Oriakhovitsa (a city); Bebrovo (a village); and Elena,
Trîavna, Drianovo, Gorna Dzhumaia, and Etropole (all cities).[10]
     The analysis of the cities of the Danubian vilâyet will
start with the *Table of Taxes and of the Population*, since it
is the most detailed document available (see table 54). For
the cities not included in the table, material has been drawn
from the 1873 salname (see table 55). Table 56 shows the distribution of these cities in terms of the size of their taxable
population using the criteria discussed above. Since the data
represent the taxable population only, it is difficult to
state the actual size of the population. Speaking very
generally, the boundary for the first group (5,000 taxable
households) would imply a total population of at least 10,000
to 12,000 inhabitants.
     It might be noted that the first category includes practi-
cally all of the mountain cities of the central and western
parts of the Balkan Mountains, the Danubian ports (with the
exception of the larger Danubian cities such as Ruse, Vidin,
and Svishtov), and most of the cities in the Dobruja. Despite
the first category comprising the great majority of the vilâyet's cities (70%), the settlements here take in less than
half of the taxable male population (40.4%). Two-thirds of
all the settlements in the first category are concentrated in
a subgrouping of cities with taxable populations of between
1,000 and 3,000 persons.
     Of the cities in the second category, half of the settle-
ments included had between 6,500 and 7,500 taxable inhabitants.
These cities were the district centers of Varna, Vidin,Tŭrnovo,
Sofia, and the two cities of Pleven and Vratsa, which were
emerging as district centers. It was due precisely to the
nature of these cities that the second category, although it
contains only one-fourth of the vilâyet's cities, accounts for
almost half of the total taxable population.

TABLE 54

SIZE AND ETHNO-RELIGIOUS COMPOSITION OF THE TAXABLE POPULATION OF 45 CITIES OF THE DANUBIAN VILÂYET ACCORDING TO THE
Table of the Taxes and the Population
(CENSUS OF 1866)

City	Total Number of Taxable Inhabitants	Bulgarians	Muslims	Muslim Migrants	Muslim Gypsies	Non-Muslim Gypsies	Armenians	Jews	Catholics And Others
Ruse	10,338	3,885	5,355	-----	128	105	378	487	-----
Shumen	10,060	4,062	5,173	-----	119	---	481	223	-----
Pleven	7,793	3,684	3,513	-----	247	162	---	187	-----
Vidin	7,664	2,610	3,954	-----	208	271	---	621	-----
Varna	7,537	3,732	2,169	885	101	---	596	54	-----
Sofia	6,770	2,544	2,618	-----	238	35	---	1,355	-----
Tŭrnovo	6,529	4,242	2,168	-----	65	54	---	-----	-----
Vratsa	6,524	4,774	1,564	-----	50	8	---	128	-----
Svishtov	6,063	3,463	2,295	-----	159	146	---	-----	-----
Samokov	5,663	3,732	1,434	-----	220	---	---	227	-----
Bazargic	5,648	653	1,838	2,738	210	15	192	2	-----
Tulcea	5,477	1,565	280	289	9	32	155	430	2,717
Lovech	5,043	1,826	3,039	-----	123	55	---	-----	-----
Razgrad	5,026	1,380	3,400	-----	99	90	---	57	-----
Tŭrgovishte	4,812	1,671	3,026	-----	83	31	---	1	-----
Sevlievo	3,962	2,707	1,146	-----	109	---	---	---	-----
Silistra	3,787	1,133	2,351	-----	84	---	132	87	-----
Dupnitsa	3,529	1,341	1,616	-----	175	---	---	397	-----
Kiustendil	3,398	1,284	1,471	115	163	---	---	365	-----
Gabrovo	3,307	3,232	------	-----	45	30	---	-----	-----
Lom	3,013	1,738	1,051	-----	62	20	---	142	-----
Berkovitsa	2,932	1,676	1,017	-----	11	9	---	116	-----
Nikopol	2,855	148	2,550	-----	99	58	---	-----	-----
Turtucaia	2,437	1,383	1,018	-----	21	15	---	-----	-----
Omurtag	2,432	458	1,830	-----	144	---	---	-----	-----
Etropole	2,376	1,728	598	-----	50	---	---	-----	-----
Balchik	2,164	482	1,155	421	100	---	6	-----	-----
Medgidia	2,112	14	------	2,021	59	---	3	15	-----
Gorna Oriakhovitsa	2,066	1,732	158	-----	116	60	---	-----	-----
Babadag	2,035	411	1,200	188	44	---	131	61	-----
Kula	2,021	1,242	758	-----	---	21	---	-----	-----
Gorna Dzhumaia	1,866	753	1,012	-----	101	---	---	-----	-----
Macin	1,488	270	600	18	17	---	2	8	573
Oriakhovo	1,380	694	684	-----	---	---	---	2	-----
Drianovo	1,362	1,300	------	-----	31	31	---	-----	-----
Ikhtiman	1,335	892	358	-----	85	---	---	-----	-----
Provadiia	1,318	309	775	163	3	---	14	54	-----
Zlatitsa	1,305	218	990	-----	97	---	---	-----	-----
Triavna	1,172	1,118	------	-----	---	54	---	-----	-----
Elena	1,149	966	------	-----	---	183	---	-----	-----
Orkhanie	1,050	773	183	41	53	---	---	-----	-----
Radomir	906	500	349	46	11	---	---	-----	-----
Belogradchik	641	202	416	-----	23	---	---	-----	-----
Sulina	345	182	23	-----	---	---	9	22	109
Mangalia	314	21	183	100	10	---	---	-----	-----
Total	161,004	72,730	65,320	7,025	3,875	1,485	2,099	5,071	3,399

SOURCE: NBKM, Oo, Cetvel-i mizan-i vergi ve nüfus, Rs 98/8

Thanks to their larger taxable populations, the cities
of Ruse and Shumen form a category of their own. The fact
cannot be ignored, however, that the Danubian vilâyet lacked
a city whose population was far greater than all the others.
Although for a certain period of time Ruse and Shumen headed
the urban network of the vilâyet, they were not substantially
larger than the other cities.

TABLE 55

NUMBER OF HOUSES AND SIZE OF THE POPULATION OF EIGHT
CITIES OF THE DANUBIAN VILÂYET
(Salname of 1873)

City	Houses	Number of People	Non-Muslims		Muslims	
			Houses	People	Houses	People
Novi Pazar	389	1,030	114	340	275	690
Teteven	884	2,182	884	2,182	---	-----
Kotel	1,033	2,853	970	2,540	63	313
Constanţa	575	1,228	32	146	543	1,082
Mahmudie	226	1,054	120	544	106	510
Isaccea	418	1,704	155	633	263	1,071
Hîrşova	389	1,546	122	419	267	1,127
Kiliya	302	701	231	538	71	163
TOTAL	4,216	12,298	2,628	7,342	1,588	4,956

SOURCE: NBKM, Salname-i Tuna vilayeti, Ruse, 017, pp. 121, 235, 265,
273, 275, 281, 283.

TABLE 56

DISTRIBUTION OF CITIES OF THE DANUBIAN VILÂYET BY CATEGORIES
IN TERMS OF THE SIZE OF THEIR TAXABLE POPULATION

	Cities		Taxable Population	
Categories	Number	Percent	Number	Percent
Up to 5,000	31	68.9	64,869	40.4
From 5,001 to 10,000	12	26.7	75,737	47.0
Over 10,001	2	4.4	20,398	12.6
Total	45	100.0	161,004	100.0

SOURCE: NBKM, Oo, Cetvel-i mizan-i vergi ve nüfus, Rs 98/8.

Basic trends in the development of cities of the Danubian vilâyet would be much easier to trace if data were available from several successive censuses; unfortunately, such information is lacking. All that can be used to determine certain directions in this urban growth are some figures included by exception in the *Table of the Taxes and of the Population* and described by that document as being from something called the "Old Registration." The date of the census to which this Old Registration pertains cannot be determined, although the earliest possible date would have been 1831. The figures from the Old Registration included in the table are arranged in summary columns similar to those used for the 1866 census, but the absence of reliable information on the date of this material means that calculations cannot be carried out on the interesting question of the growth of the urban population. The discussion will be limited to noting certain general trends in the growth of cities in the Danubian vilâyet (see tables 56 and 57). (It should be noted that table 57 excludes a few cities for which data was lacking in the Old Registration--Bazargic, Radomir, Ikhtiman, Orkhanie, Babadag, Medgidia, and Tulcea.)

TABLE 57

DISTRIBUTION OF CITIES OF THE DANUBIAN VILÂYET
ACCORDING TO THE OLD REGISTRATION

Cities by Size of Taxable Population	Cities		Taxable Population	
	Number	Percent	Number	Percent
Up to 5,000	30	79.0	62,917	55.5
From 5,001 to 10,000	8	21.0	50,523	44.5
Over 10,001	--	-----	-------	-----
Total	38	100.0	113,400	100.0

Source: NBKM, Oo, Cetvel-i mizan-i vergi ve nüfus, Rs 98/8

Keeping the same division of cities used above, Shumen and Ruse now fall into the second or middle category. With 7,434 inhabitants according to the Old Registration, Ruse does not particularly stand apart from the cities of Sofia (6,481) and Vidin (6,095). Only Shumen stands out with 9,263 inhabitants. These examples suggest that the growth of the cities of the Danubian vilâyet was gradual and even, being subject to the

natural socioeconomic development of this part of the Balkan
Peninsula, an area that experienced a strong outside influence
only with the transformation of the Danube into an important
European commercial artery from the 1830s on.

Although it did not become the leading city of the vilâyet, Shumen grew into one of the area's relatively larger
cities as the main point in the fortification system directed
against Russia in the northwestern part of the Ottoman Empire.
Within a short time this city saw the construction of bastions,
barracks, and a military hospital. It housed a large garrison
as well. The transformation of Shumen into a prominent military center inevitably entailed a number of demographical
changes. The need for expanded handicraft and manufacturing
production and for a larger commercial network made Shumen an
attractive target for the surrounding population, which flowed
to the city in large numbers. But conditioned as it was by
such specific factors, Shumen's population growth soon reached
its ceiling, and the relative growth of the city can be seen
to have slowed down in the period between the two censuses.
(It grew by only 797 persons as compared with increases of
2,500 to 3,000 persons in Ruse, Varna, and Pleven, and an
increase of more than 1,500 persons in Vidin.)

Ruse is another example of the importance of specific
factors for the growth of a city. It sufficed for this city
to be proclaimed the administrative center of the Danubian
vilâyet--and to enjoy the concentration of the various services
connected with this role--for it to undergo substantial demographic changes. Ruse began to grow rapidly, outstripping
other cities, Shumen included. In this case the same laws of
development were at work as those that can turn a capital into
a country's largest city.

A different kind of breakdown also holds true for the
other two urban categories when the data from the Old Registration is compared to that of the census of 1866. For seven
cities, it is true, information from the Old Registration is
lacking. But, judging by their size under the later census,
these seven cities would have fallen into the first or smallest
category. On the basis of the Old Registration, therefore, the
the second category comprised only the district centers (Varna
excluded) and such larger cities as Shumen, Pleven, Vratsa, and
Svishtov. According to the census of the 1860s, this category
takes in an additional six cities--Varna, Tulcea, Razgrad,
Samokov, Bazargic, and Lovech.

Finally, it is worthwhile to note that the distribution
of the urban population according to the three categories of
urban size undergoes a turnabout in tables 56 and 57. In table
57, which was based on the Old Registration, the population
predominates in small cities, that is, those with up to 5,000
taxable inhabitants. But in table 56, which was based on the

1866 census, the majority of the population is concentrated in cities with more than 5,000 taxable inhabitants.

                                    * * *

    Another question that can be discussed on the basis of the comparatively exhaustive data contained in the *Table of the Taxes and of the Population* concerns the ethnic composition of the cities of the Danubian vilâyet (see table 58). For clarity, the entire territory of the vilâyet has been divided into its western, central, and eastern parts in accordance with the currently accepted economic and geographical regionalization of northern Bulgaria.[11] A subcategory for the eastern part has been formed from those cities of the Dobruja for which information is available.

    Even the most cursory glance at the *Table of the Taxes and the Population* is sufficient to show a highly intermixed urban population. This intermixture was chiefly of Bulgarians and Turks, insofar as the latter represented the basic component of the Muslim population.

    Five cities--Gabrovo, Drianovo, Elena, Triavna, and Gorna Oriakhovitsa--can be taken as purely Bulgarian, for these cities lacked noteworthy numbers of other ethnic groups and their Bulgarian taxable residents made up more than 80% of their population. These settlements were small highland towns of the Balkan Mountains that comprised 11% of the urban settlements listed in the table but which took in only 5% of the taxable population. Cities that were to the same extent purely Muslim included Nikopol, Mangalia, Bazargic, and Medgidia. This group constituted 9% of the number of cities and included about 6% of the taxable population. The high percentage of Muslims in the last two cities was due to strong concentrations of Muslim settlers from the Crimea and the Caucasus.

    Analysis of the material provided in the Old Registration does not indicate any significant general differences over the two censuses. The comparison, however, does reveal a perceptible increase of Bulgarians in Gabrovo and Gorna Oriakhovitsa, the absence of such an increase in Drianovo and Triavna, and a decrease of Bulgarians in Elena. These nineteenth-century changes were linked with the migration of the population from highland areas to the developing manufacturing and commercial centers both inside and outside the country. Somewhat different was the situation in cities where a Muslim population had been prevalent at the time of the Old Registration (Nikopol, Mangalia, Provadiia, Balchik, and Belogradchik). On the basis of the later census, the last three cities move from the category of cities containing a Muslim preponderance of more than 80% to the category of cities whose population was truly mixed. This development was due to the insignificant increase (and, as in Belogradchik, in some cases even the decrease) of Muslims

TABLE 58

THE ETHNIC STRUCTURE OF THE URBAN POPULATION ACCORDING TO THE
Table of the Taxes and the Population (CENSUS OF 1866)

Region According to the Current Regionalization and City	Bulgarians	Muslims	Muslim Migrants	Muslim Gypsies	Non-Muslim Gypsies	Armenians	Jews	Catholics and Others	Total
NORTHWEST									
Vidin	34.1	51.6	--	2.7	3.5	--	8.1	--	100.0
Vratsa	73.2	24.0	--	0.7	0.1	--	2.0	--	100.0
Lom	57.7	34.9	--	2.1	0.6	--	4.7	--	100.0
Berkovitsa	57.1	34.7	--	3.9	0.3	--	4.0	--	100.0
Oriakhovo	50.3	49.6	--	--	--	--	0.1	--	100.0
Belogradchik	31.5	64.9	--	3.6	--	--	--	--	100.0
Kula	61.5	37.5	--	--	1.0	--	--	--	100.0
Sofia	37.6	38.7	--	3.5	0.5	--	19.7	--	100.0
Kiustendil	37.8	43.3	3.4	4.8	--	--	10.7	--	100.0
Samokov	65.9	25.3	--	3.9	--	--	4.9	--	100.0
Dupnitsa	38.0	45.8	--	4.9	--	--	11.3	--	100.0
Radomir	55.2	38.5	15.1	1.2	--	--	--	--	100.0
Ikhtiman	66.8	26.8	--	6.4	--	--	--	--	100.0
Gorna Dzhumaia	40.4	54.2	--	5.4	--	--	--	--	100.0
NORTH CENTRAL									
Pleven	47.3	45.1	--	3.2	2.0	--	2.4	--	100.0
Tŭrnovo	65.0	33.2	--	1.0	0.8	--	--	--	100.0
Svishtov	57.1	37.9	--	2.6	2.4	--	--	--	100.0
Lovech	36.2	60.3	--	2.4	1.1	--	--	--	100.0
Sevlievo	68.3	28.9	--	2.8	--	--	--	--	100.0
Gabrovo	97.7	--	--	1.4	0.9	--	--	--	100.0
Nikopol	5.2	89.3	--	3.5	2.0	--	--	--	100.0
Etropole	72.7	25.2	--	2.1	--	--	--	--	100.0
Gorna Oriakhovitsa	83.9	7.6	--	5.6	2.9	--	--	--	100.0
Drianovo	95.4	--	--	2.3	2.3	--	--	--	100.0
Triavna	95.4	--	--	--	4.6	--	--	--	100.0
Orkhanie	73.6	17.4	3.9	5.1	--	--	--	--	100.0
Zlatitsa	16.7	75.9	--	7.4	--	--	--	--	100.0
Elena	84.1	--	--	--	15.9	--	--	--	100.0
NORTHEAST									
Ruse	37.6	51.8	--	1.2	1.0	3.7	4.7	--	100.0
Shumen	40.4	51.4	--	1.2	--	4.8	2.2	--	100.0
Varna	49.5	28.8	11.8	1.3	--	7.9	0.7	--	100.0
Razgrad	27.5	67.6	--	2.0	1.8	--	1.1	--	100.0
Silistra	29.9	62.1	--	2.2	--	3.5	2.3	--	100.0
Turtucaia	56.8	41.8	--	0.5	--	--	0.9	--	100.0
Balchik	22.3	53.4	19.4	4.6	--	0.3	--	--	100.0
Provadiia	23.4	58.8	12.4	0.2	--	1.1	4.1	--	100.0
Omurtag	18.8	75.3	--	5.9	--	--	--	--	100.0
Tŭrgovishte	34.7	62.9	--	1.8	0.6	--	--	--	100.0
Bazargic	11.6	32.5	48.5	3.7	0.3	3.4	0.1	--	100.0
(OTHER CITIES IN THE DOBRUJA)									
Tulcea	28.6	5.1	5.3	0.2	0.6	2.8	7.9	49.5	100.0
Sulina	52.8	6.7	--	--	--	2.6	6.4	31.5	100.0
Babadag	20.2	59.0	9.2	2.2	--	6.4	3.0	--	100.0
Macin	18.1	40.4	1.2	1.1	--	0.1	0.5	32.6	100.0
Medgidia	0.7	--	95.7	2.8	--	0.1	0.7	--	100.0
Mangalia	6.7	58.3	31.8	3.2	--	--	--	--	100.0
Total	45.2	40.6	4.4	2.4	0.9	1.3	3.1	2.1	100.0

SOURCE: NBKM, Oo, Cetvel-i mizan-i vergi ve nüfus, Rs 98/8.

at the same time as Bulgarians were increasing in numbers.

More generally, however, the retention over the two censuses of practically the same small number of "pure settlements" convincingly confirms the extremely restricted spread
of ethnically homogeneous cities in the Danubian vilâyet. Bulgarians lived for decades and even centuries in cities containing greater or lesser numbers of Muslims and other ethnic
groups. Without wishing to enter into the realm of social
psychology, one can consider this as an essential element in
the development of a Bulgarian ethnic awareness that avoided
any special emphasis on national egoism and exclusiveness.

Noting the demographic relationship between Bulgarians
and Turks that generally characterized the cities of the Danubian vilâyet, it is difficult to establish any kind of further
broad differentiation. However, certain specific features of
the ethnic distribution of the urban population can be pointed
out. Fifteen settlements, including the centers of sancaks
and the larger cities of the vilâyet (Ruse, Shumen, Vidin, Varna,
Pleven, Sofia, and Svishtov), had minimal differences in percentages of Bulgarians and Turks (or Muslims in general)--a
difference of less than 20% in either direction. Among the
twenty-one other settlements with a difference between the two
groups greater than 20%, one can notice a certain geographic
differentiation. As a rule, Bulgarians were more than 20% more
numerous in north central and northwestern areas (and specifically in Tŭrnovo, Sevlievo, Vratsa, Berkovitsa, Kula, Lom, and
in the Samokov-Orkhanie area). Turks were predominant in the
eastern parts of the vilâyet, in the region between the Balkan
Mountains and the Danube--Omurtag, Tŭrgovishte, Razgrad, and
Silistra, as well as in Provadiia and Balchik. The tentative-
ness, however, of this geographical distribution can be judged
both by the fact that settlements with a higher percentage domination of combined Muslim and Turkish population were also located more to the west (Lovech, Zlatitsa, Belogradchik) and
also in Tulcea, as well as by the absolute figures of the two
components of the population, which were high in all three economic and geographical areas.

Table 59 illustrates what has just been said about the
distribution of Bulgarians and Muslims and the ratio between
them in the cities of the vilâyet. On the whole, the Bulgarians
were evenly distributed over the three areas with an insignificant deviation of about 8%. For the Muslim population the
deviation of from 18 to 21% between the northeast and other
areas undoubtedly reflects the greater concentration of Turks
in some cities of the eastern region, but the relatively high
percentage of Muslims in the other two areas shows that there
was generally an even distribution of Turks in the vilâyet.

The difference in the relative percentage of Bulgarians

and Muslims is greatest between the cities along the Danube and
those in the Balkan Mountains and in the region just to the
north, the so-called *Predbalkan*.[12] The Danubian cities include Ruse, Vidin, Svishtov, Silistra, Lom, Nikopol, Turtucaia,
and Oriakhovo. The Predbalkan cities are Tŭrnovo, Vratsa,
Lovech, Sevlievo, Gabrovo, Drianovo, Triavna, Elena, Orkhanie,
Belogradchik, Omurtag, and Tŭrgovishte. The cities of the
Balkan Mountains include Berkovitsa, Etropole, Teteven, Kotel,
and an added settlement, Zlatitsa.

TABLE 59

PERCENTAGE DISTRIBUTION OF THE URBAN POPULATION
OF THE DANUBIAN VILÂYET BY REGIONS
(CENSUS OF 1866)

Region	Bulgarians	Muslims	Migrants
Northwestern	32.9	28.0	2.3
North Central	37.3	25.5	0.6
Northeastern			
(and the Dobruja)	29.8	46.5	97.1
Total	100.0	100.0	100.0

SOURCE: NBKM, Oo, Cetvel-i mizan-i vergi ve nüfus, Rs 98/8.

In the Danubian cities Bulgarians comprised 51.31% of the
population, and in the cities of the Predbalkan and the Balkan
Mountains they represented 61.34%. The predominance of Bulgarians was so marked that there is really no doubt as to the
Bulgarian character of the cities of the Predbalkan and the
Balkan Mountains. The prevalence of Muslims in the cities
along the Danube is also undisputed, though it was not so
strongly expressed.

However, a more detailed examination of the population
ratio city by city shows that four out of the eight Danubian
cities (Lom, Svishtov, Oriakhovo, and Turtucaia) had a predominant Bulgarian population, while five out of the sixteen cities in the Predbalkan and Balkan Mountains had a predominance
of Muslims (Lovech, Zlatitsa, Omurtag, Tŭrgovishte, and Belogradchik). In other words, regardless of the over-all ratio,
there was an interpenetration of the two components of the population in practically all cities in the geographical regions
indicated. This trend becomes even more obvious when absolute

figures are studied. Thus, there were 15,054 Bulgarian males
and 19,258 Muslim males in the Danubian cities, while in the
Predbalkan and the Balkan Mountains the number of Bulgarian
males was 28,623 and the number of Muslim males was 16,135.

* * *

To speak of Bulgarians and Turks, however, is not to exclude the presence in these cities of other smaller ethnic
groups whose exact number is impossible to determine. The administrators of the Danubian vilâyet were aware of these
groups. The general table of the census results published in
the newspaper *Dunav* was equipped by the editors with an ex-
planatory note as to what should be understood by "Muslims"
and what by "Christians."[13] "Muslims," the note indicated,
would include indigenous Muslims (as opposed to the settlers),
Tatars, Nogays, Circassians, Albanians, Bosnians, Kurds, and
Muslim and Tatar Gypsies. "Christians" included Greeks, Bulgarians, Gagauzes, Bulgarian-Shops, Bulgarian-Albanians, Mol-
davians, Wallachians, Orthodox Armenians, Roman Catholic Armenians, Italians, Frenchmen, Englishmen, Hungarians, Serbs,
Germans, and several groups of Cossacks.

But this breakdown was only partly used in the *Table of
the Taxes and of the Population*. In the column for Muslims,
indigenous Muslims were distinguished from Muslim settlers and
Muslim Gypsies. In the column for Christians, the table indicated separate numbers for Bulgarians, Armenians, and an
aggregate group of Catholics and Other Nationalities. This
grouping most likely comprised a few Europeans and perhaps
some local inhabitants who had become foreign subjects as
well as the more numerous Wallachian-Moldavian and other Balkan populations, Roman Catholics of all nationalities, Bulgarians included, and finally, the Cossack groups that had
settled in eastern Bulgaria and the Dobruja.[14]

What column included the Greeks is not clear. The raw
census material of the data originally collected did not en-
visage a separate column for Greeks, and in the *Table of the
Taxes and of the Population* there was no summary data on the
Greek population as there was for Armenians and Jews. The reports in the *Dunav* on the census of the population of the
cities in the sancak of Ruse and of ten or so cities in other
sancaks failed to distinguish separate groups of Greeks. Thus,
after all of this it seems very strange that in the general
census returns published in *Dunav* there was a separate column
for Greeks listed immediately after the column for Bulgarians.
The column for Greeks stated a total of 7,655 persons, which
was obtained by adding two other figures: 3,523 and 4,132.[15]

A careful examination of the *Table of the Taxes and of
the Population* uncovered only a single note pertaining to

Greeks, a reference stating that in Varna there were "3,532
Greeks and 662 Bulgarians." It should be assumed that this
note was made later, after the final census tabulations had
been completed, since the enumerators and the fiscal agents
failed to take this figure into consideration in composing the
official data on the population and in determining the taxes.
The figures in the note, furthermore, do not tally with the
number of Varna's Christian population either generally or when
considered separately. According to the Old Registration, the
Christian population of Varna comprised 2,032 Bulgarians and
596 Armenians. In both cases these results are quite different
from the information contained in the note. For Varna there
were no other columns given for other Christians--Orthodox or
Catholic--or for other nationalities, and thus there is no
reason to believe that the figures in the note involved some
kind of combination with other non-Muslim elements.

It follows that in the registration itself the enumerator
did not deem it necessary to differentiate between Bulgarians
and Greeks, and that he lumped them together in the column for
Bulgarians as was done for the scattered small groups of Greeks
in other urban settlements of the vilâyet. Only where there
was a more compact Greek population, as there was in Varna, did
its spokesman request, or so it seems, at least a note to be
made to reflect the existence of the Greeks as a separate ethnic
group. (It may be assumed, furthermore, that the figure cited
above represented the total of the Greeks in the entire sancak
of Varna.)

The presence of Greeks in the category of Bulgarians does
not alter what has been said so far about the ratio between the
Bulgarians and the Turks, since the largest group of Greeks was
located in the cities of the Black Sea coast. Further on, in
dealing with concrete material on the socioeconomic situation
of the individual cities, an attempt will be made to establish
the relative percentage of Greeks on the basis of more reliable information.

A Jewish taxable population was present in various numbers in half of the cities of the vilâyet. Twelve cities had
up to 100 Jewish taxable residents, 6 cities had between 100
and 300 and 5 cities had between 300 and 600. The city with
the largest number of Jews was Sofia, where there were 1,355,
or 20% of the taxable population. The distribution of the
Jewish population by cities shows the largest concentration of
Jews in the western part of the vilâyet: Sofia, Kiustendil,
Samokov, Dupnitsa, Vratsa, Berkovitsa, Lom, and Vidin. Elsewhere, there was a relatively compact Jewish population in such
large cities as Ruse, Shumen, and Varna.

This pattern of Jewish settlement can possibly be explained by the route of Jewish migration. The old Jewish com-

munities that existed in medieval Bulgarian cities from Roman
and Byzantine times absorbed some of the Jews fleeing from
Spain, but the majority of the refugees settled in the southern
parts of the Balkan Peninsula, primarily in Istanbul, Salonika,
and Edirne. In the north--i.e., the Danubian vilâyet--the
picture began to change with the eighteenth century settlement
of Jews from Central Europe and especially from Austria.
These migrants enlarged the Jewish colonies in the cities along
the Balkan thoroughfares: the Istanbul road and the Danube.
Thus, considerable numbers of Jews came to reside in the large
cities along these thoroughfares that were situated close to
Austria (i.e., Sofia and Vidin).[16]

An Armenian population was present in only half as many
cities as contained Jews (13 as opposed to 24). Unlike the
Jews, Armenians were concentrated in the cities of the eastern
parts of the vilâyet (Shumen, Ruse, Varna, Bazargic, Silistra,
Tulcea, and Babadag). Some of the Armenian colonies, the
sources reveal, also had their origins in the early Middle Ages.
For example, it has been shown that an Armenian population
lived in Varna and Provadiia even prior to their conquest by
the Turks.[17] It seems, however, that the large number of Armenians in this part of the Danubian vilâyet was a more recent
phenomenon and the result of the direct economic link between
Istanbul and Varna, and, through the latter port, with eastern
Bulgaria, the Dobruja, and Wallachia. The economic upsurge of
this area and the appearance of several permanent fairs attracted a considerable number of Armenian merchants--whose
names are met in the registers of Varna and Bazargic.

Gypsies were present in practically all cities, regardless
of whether the predominant population was Bulgarian or Turkish.
Both Muslim and non-Muslim Gypsies formed a compact group ranging in size from several tens of taxable males to between 200
and 250. Muslim Gypsies were the more numerous--3,875 persons
(or 2.4% of the total population) as opposed to the 1,485
Christian Gypsies (or .9% of the population).

Finally, according to the *Table of the Taxes and of the
Population*, 12 cities contained Muslim settlers. These settlers
numbered 7,025 in all (or 4.4% of the total taxable population).
The majority lived in two cities, Bazargic and Medgidia, each
of which contained more than 2,000 settlers. Varna had about
1,000.

*   *   *

As the foregoing survey makes clear, the ethnic components
of the populations of the Danubian vilâyet were thoroughly
intermixed throughout the whole territory. A large Bulgarian
taxable population lived together with a large Muslim and Turkish one. The population of a number of cities also included

other ethnic elements--Greeks, Jews, and Armenians. In absolute figures, the Bulgarian urban taxable population in the Danubian vilâyet was larger than the whole taxable population in either Serbia or Greece--areas equal to the vilâyet in size. This phenomenon resulted from the advanced stratification of agriculture in northern Bulgaria, the intensive growth of cities, and their role in the socioeconomic life of the area. Furthermore, the existence of a large Muslim urban taxable population--large both in relation to the Bulgarian population and in absolute numbers--is unambiguous evidence that analogous processes of social stratification and migration were also at work among the vilâyet's Muslims, though not with the same intensity.

Additional confirmation of this point comes from a comparison of the ratio of Bulgarians and Turks over the two censuses (see table 60). The earlier registration shows that the Muslim taxable population was 3.6% larger than the Bulgarian. This numerical superiority holds true both in the small settlements--those with a taxable population of up to 5,000 (indeed, it is even more marked here at 4.5%)--and in the larger settlements--those with between 5,000 and 10,000 male inhabitants (where it stands at 2.8%). In the census of 1866, however, the ratio changed in favor of the Bulgarian taxable population, which then had a 4.6% edge over the Muslim population. In other words, the taxable Bulgarian urban population underwent an absolute increase that was twice as large as the corresponding increase in the Muslim population. In the small cities this growth in absolute numbers was not very large. It was biggest in the cities with a population of between 5,000 and 10,000 inhabitants, and there was an increase in the next category as well. A similar thing happened with the Muslim taxable population, where the table also shows a definite drift away from the small cities and an over-all increase in the absolute size of the Muslim population in those cities with between 5,000 and 10,000 taxable inhabitants. So despite its percentage decrease in comparison with the Bulgarian urban population, the Muslim community in the cities also grew in absolute numbers.

The trend toward increase was common for the entire ethnic spectrum of the urban population in the Danubian vilâyet, with certain differences in the rates of growth of the individual ethnic groups. Furthermore, as noted above, population movement affected the various categories of cities in different ways. While there was a general standstill or even decrease in the size of the population of the small cities, the bigger cities had a relatively larger population increase. What essentially was involved here were migrations and other phenomena dictated by socioeconomic development--which will be discussed below.

TABLE 60

THE BULGARIAN AND MUSLIM COMPONENTS OF THE URBAN POPULATION
OF THE DANUBIAN VILÂYET (OLD REGISTRATION [n.d.]
AN THE CENSUS OF 1866)

Cities, by size of taxable population	Number		Ethnic Breakdown					
			Bulgarians		Muslims*		Others	
	Cities	Residents	Number	Per-centage	Number	Per-centage	Number	Per-centage
Old Registration								
Up to 5,000	30	62,917	28,627	45.2	31,290	49.8	3,000	5.0
5,001-10,000	8	50,523	22,413	44.4	23,881	47.2	4,229	8.4
Over 10,001	--	--	--	--	--	--	--	--
Total	38	113,440	51,040	45.0	55,171	48.6	7,229	6.4
Census of 1866								
Up to 5,000	31	64,869	30,578	47.1	26,518	40.9	7,773	12.0
5,001-10,000	12	75,737	34,205	45.2	28,272	37.3	13,260	17.5
Over 10,001	2	20,398	7,947	39.0	10,530	51.6	1,921	9.4
Total	45	161,004	72,730	45.2	65,320	40.6	22,954	14.2

SOURCE: NBKM, Oo, Cetvel-i mizan-i vergi ve nüfus Rs 98/8. *In order to examine the
movement of the local population, Muslim settlers from the Caucasus and the Crimea have not
been included here.

* * *

To continue for the moment with the demographical analysis
per se, certain other data contained in the original schedules
drawn up for the 1866 census permit observations on the composition of the household and the family, and on age structure
in the Danubian vilâyet. Material is available on 998 households in the cities of Bazargic, Svishtov, and Tŭrnovo. Table
61 shows the breakdown and the size of these households by
urban mahalles. It should be noted that the enumerators took
the census by houses but at the same time listed the data for
each household separately. In all cases the number of households tallies with the number of houses--which indicates an
identity between household and house.

The households contained 4,509 persons or 9.9% of the
total population of the cities in question. There is an over-
all average of 4.5 members per household, except in the two
mahalles of Tŭrnovo (where it is below 4 persons). An explanation for this deviation might be sought in general socioeconomic causes, which produced a drift from the Balkan mountain regions. The smaller average size of the households in
Tŭrnovo and their larger size in Bazargic was most likely connected with the settlement in the Dobruja of colonists from
the Crimea and the Caucasus. Nearly all of the households,
957 (or 95.9%), consisted only of persons related to each

TABLE 61

DISTRIBUTION OF 998 HOUSEHOLDS BY MAHALLES IN THE CITIES OF BAZARGIC,
SVISHTOV AND TŬRNOVO ON THE BASIS OF RAW
CENSUS DATA FOR THE CENSUS OF 1866

City, Mahalle	Number of Households	Total Number of Household Members	Average Number of Members per Household
BAZARGIC			
Hacı Bayram	28	163	5.8
Terzi bazirgan	72	342	4.7
Cami atik	67	392	5.8
Tabakhane	146	636	4.3
Saray	197	850	4.3
Total	510	2,383	4.7
SVISHTOV			
Nova dzhamiia	95	439	4.6
Ihsaniye Banya	76	347	4.6
Pop Mikho	100	542	5.4
Total	271	1,328	4.9
TŬRNOVO			
Haydar	81	295	3.5
(name not readable)	136	503	3.7
Total	217	798	3.7
TOTALS	998	4,509	4.5

SOURCE: Calculations made by the author using census records and the
records of permits issued in Bazargic, Svishtov, and Tŭrnovo in the
1860s and preserved in NBKM, Oo.

other--parents, children, brothers, sisters, spouses, aunts,
nephews, and so on. The households comprising both related
and unrelated persons are considerably fewer in number (14, or
a mere 1.4% of the total). These were chiefly households that
included servants. In the Hacı Bayram mahalle of the city of
Bazargic, for example, the household of the settler Abdula the
innkeeper consisted of two families, one of which was that of
his servant who, together with his wife and son, was incorpo-

rated into his master's household. In the Cami atik ward of
the same city, the household of Stefan, the son of Kapriel, a
dry-goods dealer, had eighteen members, among whom there was an
unmarried woman servant. In the Tabakhane mahalle of Bazargic,
the household of Selim, the son of Muhiyedin, included a widowed
servant in addition to Selim's own family and that of his married brother. There are other cases that show that servants,
married or not, were included in the households of their masters. The households that comprised both related and unrelated members also involved three composed of the families of
landlords and those of their tenants.

Among the heads of the households being studied here there
were 38 women. All of these women were widows who in most
cases lived with small or unmarried children or with mothers,
daughters, or sisters who were also widowed or otherwise unmarried, but in some cases these women lived completely alone.
There were three cases in the Ihsaniye Banya ward of Svishtov
where a widowed mother was the head of the family although she
lived with married daughters and sons-in-law. In one such case
the mother lived with five sons, but she was nevertheless regarded as head of the household.

In terms of the nuclear family (i.e., parents and unmarried children), the 998 households in question represented
1,125 families, whose members totaled 4,241 persons. Making
up the difference (268 persons) between this group and the
total number of household members were those individuals who
were remnants of other families or who constituted one-member
households. In the former case, these were usually widowed
mothers and mothers-in-law who lived with their married children, unmarried brothers and sisters of the spouses, nephews
and nieces, and so on--in other words, members of the extended
family.

There are 27 one-member households (i.e., 2.7% of the
total). As a rule these households involved widows or unmarried
and unattached men.

In examining such families it is necessary to differentiate them by the nature and degree of kinship. In all, there
were 188 families that included relatives other than parents
and children. The greater part of these families (90, i.e.,
48.4%) included widowed mothers and mothers-in-law, the exact
relationship depending on who was the head of the household.
Next came families that included unmarried brothers and sisters,
there being 33 such households (i.e., 17.5%). Relatively less
numerous were those households (25 or 13.3%) that included
grandmothers, fathers-in-law, brothers-in-law, and sisters-in-
law. Finally, 29 families (15.4%) included either other
relatives or several of the relatives already mentioned (e.g.,
a mother and a widowed sister, a father and a widowed grand-

father). This reveals that the family, irrespective of its
ethnic composition, consisted chiefly of parents and children,
the few exceptions including such close relatives as grand-
parents and unmarried brothers and sisters.

Because the registers listed information on both men and
women, the male-female ratio can be determined as well. To establish this ratio full data have been used for fifteen cities
of the Danubian vilâyet (see table 62). The data show that
an excess of men over women--an average ratio of 1,000 men to
956 women--was characteristic of the population of all of the
cities listed. Comparatively large deviations from the mean
ratio are noticeable for Ruse and Silistra, where the number of
women and men was almost equal, and for the cities of Gabrovo,
Razgrad, and Turtucaia, where the excess of men was considerably higher than the average.

TABLE 62

THE MALE-FEMALE BREAKDOWN OF THE POPULATION
OF FIFTEEN CITIES OF THE DANUBIAN VILÂYET
IN THE MID-1860s

City	Total Population	Males	Females	Females per 1,000 Males
Ruse	20,644	10,338	10,306	997
Razgrad	9,723	5,026	4,697	935
Shumen	19,814	10,060	9,754	970
Pleven	15,296	7,793	7,503	963
Silistra	7,546	3,787	3,759	993
Nikopol	5,580	2,855	2,725	954
Svishtov	11,915	6,063	5,852	965
Tŭrgovishte	9,438	4,812	4,626	961
Turtucaia	4,687	2,437	2,250	923
Novi Pazar	1,717	881	836	949
Tŭrnovo	12,884	6,529	6,355	973
Sevlievo	7,690	3,962	3,728	941
Lovech	9,843	5,043	4,800	952
Gabrovo	6,349	3,307	3,042	920
Omurtag	4,762	2,432	2,330	958
Total	147,888	75,325	72,563	956

SOURCE: *Dunav*, October 17, 1865 (preliminary results of
the census).

The significance of the partial registers of the population of certain mahalles as cited above becomes even more apparent when we compare their information with the data just provided (see table 63), for this comparison shows that the ratio between men and women is approximately the same both according to the full data for the fifteen cities and the more limited information available for certain mahalles in the cities of Bazargic, Svishtov, and Tŭrnovo.

TABLE 63

THE MALE-FEMALE BREAKDOWN OF THE POPULATION
OF TEN MAHALLES IN THE CITIES
OF BAZARGIC, SVISHTOV, AND TŬRNOVO
IN THE MID-1860s

City	Total Population	Males	Females	Females per 1,000 Males
Bazargic	1,643	848	795	938
Svishtov	1,321	672	649	966
Tŭrnovo	795	402	393	978
Total	3,759	1,922	1,837	956

SOURCE: Calculations made by the author using census records and the records of permits issued in Bazargic, Svishtov, and Tŭrnovo in the 1860s and preserved in NBKM, Oo.

The excess of men over women held equally true for the two basic components of the population, Bulgarians and Turks. Factors behind this phenomenon include the lack of compulsory military service and the restricted character of emigration, that is, factors that otherwise would have taken away certain layers of the male population.

Data have also been collected on age structure for 3,760 persons, 1,922 men and 1,838 women, who resided in the ten mahalles in question in the cities of Bazargic, Svishtov, and Tŭrnovo. In table 64 this sample is distributed into three basic age groups. The largest number of both males and females are in the age range from 15 to 49 years, the group that would have included the most active part of the population in production and in socioeconomic life. The group that ranks next

in size is the younger generation. On an average for the three
cities covered, this group forms 36% of the male population and
37% of the female population. Least numerous is the age group
over 50 years of age, which is 15.7% of the male population of
the 10 mahalles and 16.7% of the female population. This breakdown reveals a progressive age structure, one very favorable
to the socioeconomic development of the area in question. It
would be interesting to study the changes in the proportion of
these groups over time, but the lack of data for earlier periods
prevents that kind of analysis.

TABLE 64

AGE STRUCTURE OF THE POPULATION OF THREE CITIES OF THE
DANUBIAN VILÂYET IN 1866

Age Group	BAZARGIC		TŬRNOVO		SVISHTOV		TOTAL	
	Males	Females	Males	Females	Males	Females	Males	Females
0-14	38.2	37.8	31.3	31.3	36.0	39.4	36.0	37.0
15-49	46.0	47.2	53.5	52.7	48.1	41.5	48.3	46.3
50 and Over	15.8	15.0	15.2	16.0	15.9	19.1	15.7	16.7
Total	100.0	100.0	100.0	100.0	100.0	100.0	100.0	100.0

SOURCE: Calculations made by the author using census records and the records of
permits issued in Bazargic, Svishtov, and Tŭrnovo in the 1860s and preserved in
NBKM, Oo.

The ratio between married and single people is also
interesting (see table 65). The data are limited to persons
over the age of 16, although marriages were concluded at a
younger age. The table makes it clear that single persons were
more numerous among the male population (30.9%), and that the
percentage of single men was highest in Svishtov and lowest in
Tŭrnovo. The percentage of unmarried women was considerably
lower, averaging 14.7% for all 3 cities. In all, married women
represented over 82% and married men from 65 to 72% of the total
The average age at marriage was directly linked with
family status. For the men in the 10 mahalles being studied,
this age fluctuated from 26 to 31 years; for women it ranged
from age 15 to 21. But marriages were concluded even before
the age of 14. The number of girls who married at an early age
was larger. In all 10 mahalles the documents note 78 girls who
married before reaching the age of 14--22 below the age of 10.
Marriages contracted over the age of 50 were predominantly
second marriages, and were more frequent for men than for
women. In this study group there were 62 who had second

marriages, and 31 women. The reason for the second marriage--divorce or death of the first spouse--is not shown in the records.

TABLE 65

THE PERCENTAGE OF MARRIED AND UNMARRIED MEN AND WOMEN
IN TEN MAHALLES IN THE CITIES
OF BAZARGIC, SVISHTOV, AND TŬRNOVO
IN THE MID-1860s

City	Women		Men	
	Married	Unmarried	Married	Unmarried
Bazargic	88.0	12.0	70.1	29.2
Svishtov	84.2	15.8	65.6	34.4
Tŭrnovo	82.4	17.6	72.4	27.6

SOURCE: Based on calculations made by the author using census records and the records of permits issued in Bazargic, Svishtov, and Tŭrnovo in the 1860s and preserved in NBKM, Oo.

Contrary to the general view that polygamy was widespread among the Muslim population, the material studied here reveals the opposite to have been true--it mentions only two cases of men who had two wives each.

Material is also available on the number of widows and widowers--31 men and 273 women in the population of the ten mahalles. The great difference between the number of widows and widowers is to a large extent due to the manner of registration adopted by the enumerators. They recorded as widows and widowers only those who had not remarried. Since the number of second marriages was much larger among men than among women, there was a great difference in the number of widows and widowers enumerated.

It is more difficult to study the question of the number of children. The principal difficulty springs from the character of the Ottoman legislation under which only males over a fixed age were subject to taxation, and that the nontaxable population was usually not covered in censuses taken for fiscal purposes. As a result there is no reliable data whatsoever on the number of children. Accordingly, the full data on the number of children up through the age of 15 have been drawn from the registers for the 10 mahalles (see table 66).

The over-all ratio for the 10 mahalles is 939 girls per 1,000
boys, that is, a ratio that comes close to the over-all ratio
of males and females in the age groups over 14 years.   In
Bazargic there were an average of 1.8 children per household,
in Svishtov 1.9, and in Tŭrnovo 1.2 children.   For the 10 mahalles as a whole, there were 1.7 children per household.

TABLE 66

FAMILY SIZE IN TEN MAHALLES IN THE CITIES OF BAZARGIC,
SVISHTOV, AND TŬRNOVO, MID-1860s

| City | Number of Families per Number of Children | | | | | | | |
	1	2	3	4	5	6	7 and Over	Total
Bazargic	168	143	96	58	17	6	8	496
Svishtov	71	66	48	33	27	9	5	259
Tŭrnovo	66	63	31	6	6	1	-	173

SOURCE: Calculations made by the author using census records
and the records of permits issued in Bazargic, Svishtov, and
Tŭrnovo in the 1860s and preserved in NBKM, Oo.

The question of the average number of children per family
rather than per household is also interesting (see table 67).
The data here are not limited to children up to age 15 inclusive, as for households, but include all the unmarried
children in the family.   The majority of families (81.1%)
limited themselves to 1, 2, or 3 children.   Families with a
single child constituted one third of the families with unmarried children, and those with 2 children formed 29.3%.
Put together, families with 1 and 2 children comprised 62.2%--
that is, families of this size were characteristic.   Families
with 3 children were 18.9%, and those having 4 children, 10.4%;
the percentage of families with 5 or more children was 8.5%.
The archival material also contains information on adopted
children and stepchildren.   There were 38 adopted children in
the 10 mahalles, and 74 stepchildren.   It is interesting to
note that more than half (17 out of 31) of the families with
adopted children had their own children as well.
Summing up, the data analyzed here leave us with an
urban demographic portrait characterized by a not very large
family size (below 5 members), by a slight predominance of the
male population, and by a progressive age structure.   These

demographic phenomena held pretty much the same for both the Bulgarian and the Turkish populations.

TABLE 67

THE NUMBER OF CHILDREN IN THE MAHALLES IN THE CITIES
OF BAZARGIC, SVISHTOV, AND TŬRNOVO
IN THE MID-1860s

City	Boys		Girls		Total	
	Number	Per-centage	Number	Per-centage	Number	Per-centage
Bazargic	493	52.2	451	47.8	944	100.0
Svishtov	258	49.9	259	50.1	517	100.0
Tŭrnovo	141	52.6	127	47.4	268	100.0

SOURCE: Calculations made by the author using census records and the records of permits issued in Bazargic, Svishtov, and Tŭrnovo in the 1860s and preserved in NBKM, Oo.

*Demographic Character
in the Nineteenth Century*

18. MIGRATION IN THE NORTHEASTERN BALKAN PENINSULA, 1860-1880

Although migrations are of great scholarly interest in clarifying the stratification of the population and of many other processes in the Balkan city and village, no serious studies have been undertaken on this question. The greatest obstacle has been the lack of sources suitable for statistical analysis. For this reason, an effort has been made to search the archives of the Oriental Department of the National Library in Sofia for the so-called yabançı tezkeres, permits to exercise a handicraft or trade, which the government issued to outsiders who arrived in a new place of residence.

The information gathered from such sources concerns a significant number of people--1,957 in all. These individuals had either a definite occupation or worked as general laborers and came from various parts of the Balkan Peninsula to seek employment in northeastern Bulgaria and in the Dobruja.[1]

Part of the documents in question are annual records, but

others cover a six-year period of time. In such cases the bio-
graphical information has been drawn for the first year or for
the year falling closest to that year. The great bulk of the
data used here pertains to the years 1868-70. For certain
cities, it is true, the registers for these years have been
lost but partial registers have been preserved for the following one or two years (1871, 1872). These have been used
as well, since the influx of outside labor was not accidental
or ephemeral--something that happened only in a given year--
but was rather a continuous process. Furthermore, this method
involves no real danger of exaggerating the number of migrants,
since specific care has been taken to assure that the same individual has not been accidentally counted twice.[2] Only in two
or three cases has the same individual been counted more than
once, and only where in a subsequent year this person appeared
in a new status (e.g., instead of being an apprentice or journeyman, he had become an independent tradesman). Accordingly,
the assembled data cover a single stream of people who over the
course of up to four years arrived as migrants to work in a new
setting. This group represents of course only part of all of
the migrants to the region in question and it is impossible to
determine its exact percentage of this total.

The admittedly incomplete data used here show that, in
the years 1868-72, migrants seem to have composed an average
of about 6% of the population of the nine cities included in
table 68. To judge by the numeration of registers that were
drawn up but have not survived, there were undoubtedly more
such settlers. It is also noteworthy that in Constanţa and
Bazargic--two cities for which the information is more ex-
haustive--the number of migrants reached 14.5% and 33%, respectively.

The material assembled here can be broken down by the
region of origin of the migrants, establishing these regions on
the basis of relevant socioeconomic considerations (see table
69). One group is thus formed of persons from the area of the
Balkan Mountains, a territory that would take in the settlements
located in the foothills of the eastern and central regions of
this range--Kotel, Sliven, Omurtag, Tŭrnovo, Gabrovo, and other
smaller settlements. Another group is composed of persons from
Thrace, particularly from the Plovdiv region, from Kazanlŭk,
Edirne, Kirklareli, and Burnar Hisar; it includes a small number of individuals from the Black Sea littoral. A third group
is formed of migrants from Macedonia, which for these purposes
would also include individuals from Kiustendil and its environs.
A special grouping has been used for the inhabitants of northeastern Bulgaria and the Dobruja who sought a livelihood outside of their own settlements but still within the boundaries
of this region (and to the extent that they were not accepted

as permanent residents in their new location but continued to
be registered as migrants). Breaking down the data thus by region of origin makes it possible to establish and discuss certain migration processes.

TABLE 68

NATIVE RESIDENTS AND MIGRANTS IN NINE CITIES OF NORTHEASTERN
BULGARIA AND THE DOBRUJA, 1868-1872

City	Native Residents			Number of Known Migrants	Per- centage
	Muslims	Non-Muslims	Total		
Varna	4,382	3,155	7,537	150	2.0
Provadiia	377	941	1,318	101	7.7
Bazargic	981	4,383	5,364	781	14.5
Silistra	1,325	1,892	3,217	181	5.6
Medgidia	--	2,624	2,624	48	1.8
Constanţa	146	1,082	1,228	407	33.1
Babadag	1,131	2,555	3,686	116	3.1
Tulcea	4,517	589	5,106	95	1.8
Macin	1,371	1,195	2,566	78	3.0
Total	14,230	18,416	32,646	1,957	6.0

SOURCE: The data for Varna and Provadiia are taken from information contained in the *Table of the Taxes and of the Population* of the Danubian
Vilâyet of 1872 (NBKM, Oo, Rs 98/8). For the other cities data have
been assembled from 1873 material from the same archive published by V.
Todorov-Khindalov, "Dobrudzha v minaloto spored turski ofitsialni iztochnitsi," *Godishnik na Sofiiskata narodna biblioteka, 1926-1928* (1931), pp.
210-73. On the number of migrants in the nine cities, the numbers cited
are based on calculations made by the author of the present work on the
basis of the tezkeres of these cities as contained in NBKM, Oo.

Concerning table 69, however, it is necessary to note
that the indicated ethnic distribution of migrants cannot be
entirely exact.[3] Among those described as Muslims, the most
numerous were the Turks, but the number of Albanians was not
small, especially among those migrants who came from Macedonia.
The category of "others" includes seventy-seven Greeks and
covers those individuals whom the texts explicitly call Greek
or whose names leave no doubt that they were. But the number
of Greeks was undoubtedly larger than what is suggested here.
The category of "others" also takes in twenty-one Armenians,
twenty-four Jews, several Germans, Czechs, Frenchmen, and a
group of Romanians whose exact number cannot be established.
For about ten migrants the ethnic origin is unclear.
A more concrete idea of the place of origin of migrants

TABLE 69

REGION OF ORIGIN AND ETHNIC COMPOSITION OF MIGRANTS OF NINE
CITIES OF NORTHEASTERN BULGARIA AND THE DOBRUJA, 1868-1872

Place of Origin	Bulgarians		Muslims		Others		Total	
	Number	Per-centage	Number	Per-centage	Number	Per-centage	Number	Per-centage
Balkan Mountains								
Stara Planina	618	90.8	62	9.1	1	0.1	681	100.0
Thrace	366	80.6	56	12.3	32	7.1	454	100.0
Macedonia	193	64.3	104	34.7	3	1.0	300	100.0
Northeastern Bulgaria and the Dobruja	203	62.5	76	23.4	46	14.1	325	100.0
Elsewhere	59	29.9	49	24.9	89	45.2	197	100.0
Total	1,439	73.5	347	17.7	171	8.8	1,957	100.0

SOURCE: Based on calculations of the author using material contained in tezkeres of nine cities of
northeastern Bulgaria and the Dobruja.

can be obtained by a specific listing of those settlements that
produced groups of more than twenty migrants each (see table
70). The first conclusion that can be drawn from table 70 is
that the largest migration were individuals from Tŭrnovo and
the district surrounding it. This region was the place of
origin for three times as many migrants as its closest rivals.
A second finding is that migration from settlements of the
central and eastern regions of the Balkan Mountains was several times as large as that from the regions mentioned. (This
is not to say that migration in general from other places was
smaller; it only demonstrates that the mountain area sent more
migrants to northeastern Bulgaria and the Dobruja than did
Thrace, Macedonia, etc.) In part this phenomenon rested on the
major economic links between the Dobruja and the eastern part
of the Balkan Peninsula and specifically on the economic community that had been created between them in large-scale stock
raising on the Dobruja plain and in the development in the
mountain settlements of the crafts connected with this animal
husbandry. However, if it were only a question of this
factor, then the proportion of those seeking work from Tŭrnovo
on the one hand, and from Sliven or Kotel on the other, would
have been reversed, since the Kotel area had much deeper and
more enduring links with the Dobruja than did the Tŭrnovo area.
Furthermore, the number of migrants coming from such distant
areas as Tetovo and Ohrid, from such Thracian plain cities as
Plovdiv and Kazanlŭk, from Gabrovo, and from the cities of
eastern Thrace was close to the number of migrants who came
from the eastern part of the Balkan range. It is obvious,
therefore, that in addition to revealing specific phenomena
such as was the case with Tŭrnovo, the migration reflects other

general factors that held true for all settlements regardless of whether they were situated in the mountains or in the plains.

TABLE 70

SETTLEMENTS AND DISTRICTS THAT WERE THE PLACE OF ORIGIN OF AT LEAST
TWENTY MIGRANTS TO NORTHEASTERN BULGARIA
AND THE DOBRUJA, 1868-1872

Settlement	Bulgarians			Muslims			Others	Total
	From the City	From the District	Total	From the City	From the District	Total		
Türnovo	145	72	217	7	16	23	1	241
Sliven	39	52	91	1	1	2	--	93
Plovdiv	13	62	75	2	6	8	--	83
Ormutag	23	46	69	5	8	13	--	82
Kotel	75	6	81	--	--	--	--	81
Tetovo	27	2	29	43	5	48	--	77
Kazanlŭk	32	39	71	3	2	5	--	76
Gabrovo	24	43	67	--	--	--	--	67
Ohrid	42	--	42	5	--	5	--	47
Kirklareli	41	4	45	--	--	--	--	45
Bunar Hisar	16	19	35	--	--	--	--	35
Shumen	23	6	29	2	--	2	3	34
Edirne	8	14	22	7	--	7	4	33
Prizren	--	--	--	31	2	33	--	33
Stara Zagora	23	8	31	--	--	--	1	32
Sevlievo	7	13	20	1	8	9	--	29
Silistra	1	18	19	--	5	5	3	27
Pomorie	4	--	4	--	--	--	21	25
Tulcea	11	4	15	1	--	1	9	25
Bitolj	22	2	24	--	--	--	--	24
Ioannina	2	--	2	--	14	14	8	24
Skopje	19	3	22	--	--	--	1	23
Kiustendil	7	15	22	--	--	--	--	22
Wallachia*	--	--	8	--	--	--	13	21
Varna	3	4	7	2	2	4	10	21
Ticha†	--	21	21	--	--	--	--	21
Lovech	--	8	8	1	11	12	--	20
Bazargic	10	6	16	1	1	2	2	20
Palanka	19	1	20	--	--	--	--	20

SOURCE: Calculations made by the author using tezkeres for 1868-1872, as contained in NBKM, Oo. *A district in Romania. †A village.

* * *

An examination of the occupations of the migrants will help clarify both the essential nature and some of the causes of the migration to northeastern Bulgaria and the Dobruja. The distribution of the migrants by occupation, both as a whole and in terms of region of origin, is presented in table 71. In the table the category of "hired labor" takes in only individuals explicitly described as amele (workers), or registered as servants, porters, and apprentices without a designated trade. Other apprentices and journeymen are included with independent commodity producers in Handicrafts and Commerce,

TABLE 71

BREAKDOWN BY OCCUPATION AND BY PLACE OF ORIGIN OF MIGRANTS TO NINE CITIES OF NORTHEASTERN BULGARIA AND THE DOBRUJA, 1868-1870

Region of Origin	Stara Planina				Thrace				Macedonia			
Type of Occupation	From Cities	From the District	Total	Percentage	From Cities	From the District	Total	Percentage	From Cities	From the District	Total	Percentage
Handicrafts	169	48	217	32	110	25	135	30	157	31	188	63
Commerce	43	24	67	10	25	8	33	7	16	--	16	5
Agriculture	98	129	227	33	52	45	97	21	31	3	34	11
†Hired labor	45	114	159	23	61	117	178	39	35	22	57	19
Officials	--	--	--	--	5	2	7	2	2	--	2	1
Not known	--	--	11	2	--	--	4	1	--	--	3	1
Total			681	100			454	100			300	100

Region of Origin	Northeastern Bulgaria and the Dobruja				*Elsewhere	
Type of Occupation	From the Cities	From the District	Total	Percentage	Total	Percentage
Handicrafts	60	86	146	45	95	48
Commerce	39	21	60	18	50	25
Agriculture	11	8	19	6	18	9
†Hired labor	32	56	88	27	31	16
Officials	2	4	6	2	3	2
Not known	--	--	6	2	--	--
Total			325	100	197	100

SOURCE: Calculations of the author based on the tezkeres for 1868-1870 contained in NBKM, Oo. *For the individuals in this category, the recorded place-of-origin was usually a general one: "Wallachia," "Moldavia," "Greece," "Anatolia," etc. Thus, this group cannot be differentiated into urban or rural origins. †As noted in the text, this classification includes only those individuals described by the documents as being "workers" or who were hired workers without a definite occupation. Otherwise, artisans and journeymen are included under "Commerce"; and cultivators and other hired farmhands are included under "Agriculture."

and some land cultivators are included in the category of Agriculture. In terms of their actual social position, however,
all of these individuals should also be considered as hired
labor.
     Artisans formed the largest element among the migrants,
totaling 781 persons or 40% of the total. However, certain
differences in the percentage breakdown of artisan migrants
from different areas deserve attention. Whereas the Balkan
Mountains and Thrace contributed roughly the same percentage
of artisans (respectively, 32% and 30%), and although northeastern Bulgaria itself had a very high percentage of such
migrants (45%), it was Macedonia that sent a truly striking
percentage of artisans (63%). Among these artisans the most
numerous were masons (54 persons), followed by bakers (49 individuals), and *boza* (millet beer) makers (42). The other ten
or so crafts included in this group from Macedonia were represented by one or two persons each, with the exception of
weapon-makers (8 persons), coffeehouse keepers (6), and
tailors (4). Obviously, the mass of the artisan migrants
from Macedonia to northeastern Bulgaria consisted of craftsmen
whose trade required no workshops, capital, or any kind of
relatively expensive equipment. In this regard most of the
bakers were no exception, since half of them (26 out of 49)
were apprentices and journeymen who assisted master bakers.
     Among the artisan migrants from the Balkan Mountains,
masons were again the most numerous (68 persons), followed
directly by abacıs (61) and tailors (35). Here, too, other
crafts were represented by only a few persons each, but these
individuals did range over about twice as many crafts as were
practiced by migrants from Macedonia. A similar pattern holds
true for migrants from Thrace, with the difference that brickmakers (51) came first, followed by bakers (29).
     The artisan migrants from northeastern Bulgaria and the
Dobruja were not so strongly differentiated into compact groups
of individuals practicing a certain craft. Nevertheless, here
again tailors, abacıs, masons, and bakers were the most numerous, each group comprising from 10 to 20 persons. Another
peculiarity was that even though this area yielded a smaller
total number of artisans, the migrants included practiced the
greatest variety of trades--36 as opposed to the 25-26 for the
Balkan Mountains and Thrace and the 16 crafts represented by
the artisans from Macedonia. Furthermore, only in northeastern
Bulgaria and the Dobruja were there more artisan migrants with
rural rather than urban origins.
     Summing up, there existed among the artisan migrants
specific types of craftsmen present in such numbers that they
characterized the over-all occupational content of the migration
in question (at least among craftsmen practicing a definite

trade). The mason was such a craftsman among the migrants from
all of the regions indicated. In some cases the mason was
joined by the baker, and in other cases by the abacı and the
tailor. All of these individuals were seeking elsewhere a
livelihood that their native region had failed to provide.

                                * * *

     Let us dwell in greater detail on the migration from the
Tŭrnovo area, the area that produced the largest absolute number of migrant artisans. The ranks of these craftsmen were
dominated by abacıs and tailors (40% of the total). But did
the abacıs included in this group who possessed yabancı tezkeres coincide to some extent with those who annually carried
their goods to near and distant markets and who might have
been coming to the Dobruja in much the same way as the Plovdiv abacıs traveled to markets in Anatolia and elsewhere?
An answer to this question is provided by some indirect data
on the distribution of craftsmen by income. A document for
Tŭrnovo for 1868-69 records the registration of 292 persons
that had moved into that city from surrounding villages and
from the nearby settlements of Triavna, Elena, Gabrovo, Sevlievo,
Drianovo, Lovech, and Troian.[4] Three-fourths of these individuals had low incomes, and they augmented the number of low-
paid artisans and artisan helpers already in Tŭrnovo.[5] As the
largest city in the area, Tŭrnovo had become a sort of reser-
voir for the excess labor of the countryside and of neighboring settlements of the Balkan Mountains. Coming to Tŭrnovo
made it easier for this labor force to learn about existing
demand elsewhere and to move to areas where there were better
opportunities to find work.
     Not enjoying the same number of state contracts as did
their counterparts in other Bulgarian cities, the abacıs of
Tŭrnovo began to sense a growing stagnation in the demand for
aba goods in the city itself and had to turn their attention
to other markets. The Dobruja offered certain opportunities,
which they hastened to pursue. As amply demonstrated by such
things as the construction of the Ruse-Varna railroad, the
growth of the Bazargic fair, and the brisk traffic of the
Danubian ports, the Dobruja had a constantly growing economic
importance that attracted manpower from different branches of
production and trade.
     Naturally, the leading position among the migrants to the
Dobruja was taken by master builders and construction workers,
but opportunities also opened up for the employment of abacıs
and tailors in meeting the needs of both the local population
and the army of incoming artisans. Similar opportunities arose
for bakers, but since that trade required a certain amount of
capital (for the supply of flour and maintenance of a bakery),

the majority were actually bakers' apprentices and journeymen
(though they did include some master bakers who carried out
subsidiary roles in the shops of local bakers, such as preparing
the dough, serving at the counter, and putting the bread in the
ovens).[6]   In these respects the abacıs and the tailors were in
a better position, for they could work with material supplied
by their clients. With their tape measures and needles they
easily moved from settlement to settlement. Of a total of 158
of these abacıs and tailors, half had recorded incomes of 500
kuruş and another fourth had incomes up to 1,000 kuruş; that is,
three-fourths of these master craftsmen had incomes comparable
to various categories of apprentices and journeymen. Put another way, independent abacıs and tailors who received such
incomes did not essentially differ from the hired labor in the
same branch of production. There were, however, masters who
had incomes of 1,500 kuruş or more. This group consisted of
23 persons, almost all of whom were abacıs, and included 2
persons with incomes of 2,000 and 4,000 kuruş. It can only be
assumed that in their resettlement the latter masters had brought
along a few journeymen and apprentices. Furthermore, there is
not much doubt that these abacıs produced goods for sale at
more distant markets.

     Based on the foregoing discussion, it can be said that
most of the resettlement of abacıs and tailors from Tŭrnovo to
the Dobruja was connected both with the heightened competition
in the city of Tŭrnovo itself--resulting from the limited market
for aba goods and the influx of village artisans--and with the
opportunities that existed in the Dobruja.

                              * * *

     Among the over-all body of migrants being studied here,
the 266 persons engaged in commercial activities were the
smallest (11.5%) of the occupational groups. One-third of this
group was made up of grocers, and there were roughly equal numbers of tavernkeepers, innkeepers, dry-goods dealers, and those
described in the documents as "merchants." This kind of internal breakdown and the presence of many small dry-goods dealers
and itinerant peddlers among the so-called merchants indicates
that there were few true merchant businessmen here. The status
of most of these "merchants" was essentially similar to that
of the artisans.

     An analysis of the place of origin of those migrants en-
gaged in agricultural pursuits discloses differences both in
the numbers involved and in the kind of work done by migrants
from different regions. As might be expected, the most numerous group of the migrants in agriculture (more than half) came
from the Balkan Mountains where farming was difficult, followed
by agriculturalists from Thrace (who made up about 25% of the

total). More than half of the migrant agriculturalists from
the mountains were a combined group of shepherds (129 persons),
gardeners (49), and reapers (42). Among those coming from
Thrace, reapers were the most numerous (38 persons), followed
by cultivators (19), and shepherds (16). From Macedonia, which
produced the smallest number of migrants engaged in agriculture,
the largest group were cultivators (22), followed by shepherds
(8). About half of all migrants engaged in agriculture came
from cities rather than villages, and the comparatively few
agriculturalists from Macedonia were entirely of urban origin,
further reinforcing the finding that Balkan cities were taking
in a large part of the superfluous manpower in the villages.
While looking for agricultural work elsewhere, many of these
migrants continued to practice their farming related activities
from the cities in which they settled.

It has already been pointed out that the category of hired
labor takes in persons recorded in the documents as being "hired
workers" (who were comparatively few in number, 21 in all),
servants (111) and apprentices for whom a specific occupation
was not cited (349). The breakdown of this group by place of
origin fails to yield any noteworthy patterns save that it
represented a constant 20 to 40% of the migrants from all
regions. But if we add to the hired labor category persons
engaged in agriculture who with scant exceptions were also
wage earners, and assistants who worked with artisans and
traders (i.e., the apprentices, journeymen, and servants--
which together constituted 33.5% of the artisans and 27.5% of
the commercial category), who albeit somewhat conditionally
can also be regarded as wage earners, then hired labor turns
out to be the predominant element among the migrants to northeastern Bulgaria and the Dobruja.

It is difficult to draw broad conclusions on the basis of
the rather limited material used here. But to open the pages
of Bulgaria's preliberation press, particularly the pages of
the newspaper *Dunav*, is to find dozens of reports and announcements that suggest the reasons and motives that prompted the
movement of manpower to the area in question: news about the
construction of buildings and bridges; announcements on the
search for manpower in connection with railroad construction
(work that attracted hired labor from various parts of the
country); complaints about the unemployed who had flooded the
larger cities and had been reduced to beggary; reports on the
opening of various workshops, factories, and enterprises, some
of which (such as the "Şerket" transport company) employed
several hundred people; reports about the widespread construction of wharves and of both state-owned and private
shipyards in Ruse.[7] When taken together, all of this infor-
mation--even when simply given as a list--explains both the

accumulation of hired labor in the cities and the movement
of manpower about the country. There is really no additional
proof needed that in the 1860s a new class force had emerged
on the historical stage.[8]

* * *

Of considerable interest for determining the social
nature of the migrants to northeastern Bulgaria and the
Dobruja is the analysis of the income they received (as presented in tables 72 to 76). Thus, 59% of the independent
artisans had an income of 500 kuruş or below; 27.5% had an
income of between 500 and 1,000 kuruş; and 13.5% earned
over 1,000 kuruş (see table 72). On the basis of their incomes, a majority of the independent artisans corresponded
to the position of journeymen and apprentices, three-fourths
of whom had incomes of approximately 500 kuruş or below.
More succinctly, most of the larger distinguishable groups
of artisans were poor.

True, a large group of bakers, several of the abacıs,
and isolated individuals in other crafts are encountered among
the middle-income and more well-to-do artisans (i.e., those
earning over 1,000 kuruş). The bakers who earned higher incomes included a certain Anastas (the son of Yorgi of Ioannina), who settled in Constanţa and had an income of 1,650 kuruş; Yorgi (the son of Stati or Pirot), who worked in Varna
and had an income of 2,000 kuruş; Ivancho (the son of Khristo
of Ohrid), who settled in Bazargic and earned an income of
2,000 kuruş; and Onas (the son of Artin of Van), who established himself in Varna where he earned an income of 3,000 kuruş.[9] The two abacıs with relatively high incomes included
Doncho (the son of Vŭrban of Kotel), who worked in Bazargic
and who had an income of 2,000 kuruş, and Kristofor (of Kazanlŭk), who worked in Constanţa where he earned 3,500 kuruş.[10]
The tobacco dealer with an income of 3,000 kuruş was Panaiot
Dipolat (of Cephalonia), who came to work in Constanţa.[11] A
more well-to-do tailor was Garo (the son of Onik of Tulcea),
who worked in Varna and had an income of 2,000 kuruş.[12] In
Constanţa there was a scale maker named Edem aga (the son of
Saaddedin of Ioannina), who earned income of 2,000 kuruş.[13]
Shoemakers earning the best incomes included Sava (the son of
Yeremi, a Greek subject from Cephalonia), who settled in Cons-
tanţa and made an income of 2,000 kuruş; Hacı Akop (the son
of Ovanes of Kayseri), who worked in Varna and earned 1,500
kuruş; and Franci (the son of Rodrig of Austria), who worked
in Babadag for an income of 1,000 kuruş.[14] The best paid ma-
sons were Azmanko (the son of Iliia of Tetovo), who worked in
Varna and received 2,000 kuruş; Yanaki (the son of a Varna
Greek named Zafir), who settled in Bazargic and earned 1,500

TABLE 72

DISTRIBUTION BY INCOME OF MIGRANT ARTISANS IN NORTHEASTERN BULGARIA AND THE DOBRUJA, 1868–1870 (IN KURUŞ)

Craftsmen	Independent — Income Range									Working As Hired Labor — Income Range								Unknown	Total
	Number	To 250	251–500	501–750	751–1,000	1,001–1,250	1,251–1,500	1,501–2,000	Over 2,000	Number	To 150	151–250	251–500	501–750	751–1,000	1,001–1,250	1,251–1,500		
Masons	91	26	45	9	8	--	2	1	--	47	--	13	31	1	1	--	--	1	138
Bakers	56	--	14	11	8	--	19	3	1	53	--	7	25	16	4	--	--	1	109
Abaqıs	46	--	17	1	7	14	5	1	1	35	--	10	12	3	10	--	--	--	81
Tailors	23	6	9	2	4	1	1	--	--	55	2	10	25	11	6	--	--	1	78
Brickmakers	43	2	23	8	8	--	2	--	--	9	--	1	6	--	2	--	--	--	52
Bozamakers	40	21	15	4	--	--	--	--	--	3	1	1	1	--	--	--	--	--	43
Shoemakers	26	2	13	8	1	--	1	1	--	4	--	2	1	1	--	--	--	--	30
Coffeehouse keepers	24	5	11	6	2	--	--	--	--	8	--	4	3	--	1	--	1	--	32
Ironsmiths	16	5	3	2	2	--	2	--	--	6	--	2	3	1	--	--	--	--	22
Cooks	12	1	4	4	2	--	1	--	--	5	--	2	2	1	--	--	--	--	17
Carters	13	1	6	--	4	--	2	--	--	1	--	--	--	--	1	--	--	--	14
Tobacconists	9	2	4	2	--	--	--	--	1	5	--	1	3	--	--	--	--	--	14
Water carriers	9	1	7	--	1	--	--	--	--	--	--	--	--	--	--	--	--	--	9
Ax makers	3	--	2	--	1	--	--	--	--	5	--	--	--	--	--	--	--	--	8
Gunsmiths	3	--	2	1	--	--	--	--	--	5	1	2	--	--	--	--	--	--	8
Coppersmiths	5	--	4	1	--	--	--	--	--	2	--	2	--	--	--	--	--	--	7
Weavers (goat hair)	2	--	--	--	1	--	--	--	--	5	--	--	1	--	--	--	--	--	7
Barbers	6	--	3	2	1	--	--	--	--	1	--	--	--	4	--	--	--	--	7
Tinsmiths	5	4	--	2	--	--	--	--	--	1	--	1	--	1	--	--	--	--	6
Furriers	5	1	3	--	1	--	--	--	--	1	--	--	--	1	--	--	--	--	6
Stone-cutters	6	--	5	1	--	--	--	--	--	1	--	--	--	--	--	--	--	--	6
Dyers	4	--	--	4	--	--	--	--	--	1	--	--	1	--	--	--	--	--	5
Fishermen	5	2	3	--	--	--	--	--	--	--	--	--	--	--	--	--	--	--	5
Halva-makers	4	3	1	--	--	--	--	--	--	1	1	1	--	--	--	--	--	--	5
Potters	2	1	1	--	1	--	--	--	--	2	--	1	1	--	--	--	--	--	4
Woodworkers	4	1	2	--	--	1	--	--	--	--	--	--	--	--	--	--	--	--	4
Boilermakers	3	--	3	--	--	--	--	--	--	--	--	--	--	--	--	--	--	--	3
Tanners	3	--	3	--	--	--	--	--	--	--	--	--	--	--	--	--	--	--	3
Butchers	1	--	--	1	--	--	--	--	--	2	--	--	2	--	--	--	--	--	3
Saddlers	3	--	--	3	--	--	--	--	--	--	--	--	--	--	--	--	--	--	3
Goldsmiths	--	--	--	--	--	--	--	--	--	3	--	--	1	--	--	--	--	--	3
Watchmakers	--	--	--	--	--	--	--	--	--	3	--	1	2	1	--	--	--	--	3
Bath attendants	3	--	1	1	--	--	1	--	--	2	--	--	--	--	1	--	--	--	3
Others	41	6	12	5	10	1	3	4	--	2	--	--	1	--	--	--	1	--	43
Total	516	89	217	74	67	16	40	10	3	265	5	60	127	40	28	--	2	3	781

SOURCE: Calculations of the author based on the tezkeres of nine cities of northeastern Bulgaria and the Dobruja.

kuruş; and Dimitŭr (the son of Krustiu of Palanka), who worked
in Varna for 1,500 kuruş.[15] Two high-income oar makers were
both Greeks: Yani (the son of Yorgi of the district of
Bandurma), who settled in Constanţa and earned an income of
2,000 kuruş; and Dimitri (the son of Yani of Nussebŭr), who
worked in Varna and received 1,500 kuruş.[16]

    These names have been given to provide a clearer idea of
the more well-to-do artisans. It can be assumed that these
individuals included some entrepreneurs who hired additional
assistants for expanded artisan workshops or for small-scale
capitalist enterprises. In general terms the number of apprentices and journeymen, particularly among masons, bakers, and
tailors, averages out at two per each independent artisan. But
since most artisans received low incomes and could hardly have
employed supplementary manpower, the distribution of the journeymen and apprentices would not have been an even one--some
masters had a number of assistants while the great majority
had none.

    Let us also examine those engaged in commercial activity,
most of whom combined with the artisans to form the stratum of
independent commodity producers in the city (see table 73).
The table makes it clear that four kinds of persons shaped the
character of this category: grocers; dry-goods dealers;
tavern-keepers (together with innkeepers, casino operators, and
restaurateurs); and the "merchants" proper (to whom one could
join carters, shopkeepers, and poultry dealers). Here again
there was quite a sizeable group of people with incomes of 500
kuruş or below, but unlike the artisans, these individuals numbered only 30% of the total. Falling into this low-income
group were half of the tavernkeepers, practically all of the
carters, poultry dealers, and used-goods dealers, one third of
the "merchants" (chiefly peddlers), and a rather small group of
grocers. Thus, in terms of the character of its activity, this
low-income group was composed of the distributors of foreign
goods, petty retailers of wares brought from wholesale importers, neighborhood grocers, and tavernkeepers.

    Examples of the more well-to-do individuals in the com-
mercial sector were the money changer Yahudi (the son of Isak
of Ruse), who worked in Constanţa and made an income of 3,000
kuruş; the merchant Kristodor (of Iaşi district), who settled
in Constanţa where he earned an income of 3,000 kuruş; the merchant Khristo Despot (of Brăila), who also worked in Constanţa
but for an income of 6,000 kuruş; and Stefan (the son of Ivancho of Tŭrnovo), who as a commission agent in Varna earned an
income of 3,000 kuruş.[17] Three big merchants who settled in
Constanţa and had registered incomes of 15,000 kuruş were the
Austrian subject Janko (the son of Nestor of Kolomyya); the
Prussian subject and grain dealer Ernest (the son of Roy of
Vienna); and Christian Joseph of Danzig.[18] What is extremely

TABLE 73

DISTRIBUTION BY INCOME (IN KURUS) OF MIGRANTS IN THE COMMERCIAL SECTION (INDEPENDENT AND WORKING AS HIRED LABOR) IN NORTHEASTERN BULGARIA AND THE DOBRUJA, 1868-1870

Types of Activity	Number	Independent Income Range										
		To 250	251-500	501-750	751-1,000	1,001-1,250	1,251-1,500	1,501-2,000	2,001-3,000	3,001-4,000	4,001-6,000	6,001-15,000
Grocers	50	--	8	8	13	4	8	8	1	--	--	--
Dry goods dealers	26	--	2	2	3	--	15	1	--	3	--	--
Merchants	30	2	8	2	8	1	3	--	2	--	1	3
Tavern keepers	22	6	6	6	-	1	1	2	--	--	--	--
Innkeepers	7	--	2	2	1	--	--	2	--	--	--	--
Carters	10	--	8	--	2	--	--	--	--	--	--	--
Poultry dealers	5	--	4	--	1	--	--	--	--	--	--	--
Secondhand goods dealers	3	1	2	--	--	--	--	--	--	--	--	--
Shopkeepers	3	--	1	2	--	--	--	--	--	--	--	--
Fancy goods dealers	1	--	1	--	--	--	--	--	--	--	--	--
Casino operators & restaurateurs	3	--	1	1	--	--	--	1	--	--	--	--
Workers in foreign companies	--	--	--	--	--	--	--	--	--	--	--	--
Dealers in construction materials	1	--	--	--	--	--	--	1	--	--	--	--
Money changers	1	--	--	--	--	--	--	--	1	--	--	--
Total	162	9	43	23	28	6	27	15	4	3	1	3

Types of Activity	Number	Engaged as Hired Labor Income Range							Total
		To 250	251-500	501-750	751-1,000	1,001-1,250	1,251-1,500	1,501-3,000	Not Stated	
Grocers	27	7	14	4	2	--	--	--	--	77
Dry goods dealers	9	4	1	3	1	--	--	--	--	35
Merchants	5	1	2	--	--	--	1	--	1	35
Tavern keepers	12	--	4	4	2	--	--	--	1	34
Innkeepers	6	1	--	1	4	--	--	--	--	13
Carters	--	--	--	--	--	--	--	--	--	10
Poultry dealers	--	--	--	--	--	--	--	--	--	5
Secondhand goods dealers	1	--	--	--	--	--	--	--	--	4
Shopkeepers	--	--	--	--	--	--	--	--	--	3
Fancy goods dealers	2	--	--	--	--	--	--	--	--	3
Casino operators & restaurateurs	--	--	--	--	--	--	--	--	--	3
Workers in foreign companies	2	--	--	--	1	--	--	1	--	2
Dealers in construction materials	--	--	--	--	--	--	--	--	--	1
Money changers	--	--	--	--	--	--	--	--	--	1
Total	64	14	24	12	10	--	1	1	2	226

SOURCE: Calculations of the author based on the tezkeres for 1868-1870, contained in NBKM, Oo.

noteworthy in this admittedly fragmentary information is that
until now documents have not been discovered that show local
merchants earning incomes as high as those received by these
foreign businessmen.

The big grain dealer--indeed, the big merchant generally
--had a registered income that was from five to seven times
higher than that of the well-to-do grocer and tavernkeeper,
and about four times larger than the income of the dry-goods
dealer.[19] It is between the income of the rich merchant and
that of the itinerant peddler (whose incomes stood at about
1,000 kuruş) that one should seek the average merchant.

A study of the income distribution of migrants engaged
in agricultural activities also permits certain conclusions
(see table 74). Of this group, 35% had incomes up to 200 kuruş, and another 40% fell into the income range of from 200-
500 kuruş. In other words, three-fourths of all those migrants engaged in agricultural work were poor and fell into
the same position as the bulk of the apprentices and journeymen (and, indeed, the lowest-paid artisans). The majority of
the remaining 25%, moreover, earned incomes of between 500 and
750 kuruş--their position was not much better. The presence
of a few millers, gardeners, and one shepherd who received
higher incomes emphasizes not so much the property as the
social differentiation between this handful and the great
majority of the other shepherds, harvesters, gardeners, cultivators, and others.

Of hired labor, 85% had incomes of up to 500 kuruş (see
table 75). Within this group, however, no one received less
than 200 kuruş, which was the amount received by some of the
seasonal workers, shepherds, and harvesters. In the same
vein, the number of persons with incomes of between 200 and
250 kuruş was smaller among the group of hired labor (26.5%)
than it was for the group of farmhands (35%).

It might be noted briefly that the group of state employees was composed of a few fieldkeepers, chief shepherds,
criers, and çavuşeş (all with incomes of from 250 to 500 kuruş); two teachers, one in Tulcea (Nasko, the son of Izar of
the kaza of Tulcea, with an income of 400 kuruş) and the other
in Babadag (Stoian, the son of Papageridi of the village of
Shipka, with an income of 250 kuruş); and three *kileçis* (grain
weighers) from Pomorie and Nessebǔr who worked in Constanţa
for incomes of 1,000 and 1,500 kuruş. With the exception of
the last three individuals, the other state employees can also
be counted as part of the stratum of the poor, a stratum that,
as has been shown, formed the absolute majority of the migrants to northeastern Bulgaria and the Dobruja.[20]

A summary income distribution of the various groups of
migrants is contained in table 76.

TABLE 74

DISTRIBUTION BY INCOME (IN KURUŞ) OF MIGRANTS ENGAGED IN AGRICULTURAL ACTIVITIES
IN NORTHEASTERN BULGARIA AND THE DOBRUJA, 1868-1870

Type of Activity							Income Range									
	To 150	151-200	201-250	251-300	301-400	401-500	501-600	601-700	701-750	751-800	801-900	900-1,000	1,001-1,250	1,251-1,500	1,501-2,000	Total
Shepherds	10	3	28	5	21	43	26	14	1	10	-	7	-	1	-	169
Harvesters	32	36	7	1	--	3	1	--	-	--	-	-	-	-	-	80
Truck gardeners	--	--	5	1	11	20	2	1	5	--	1	5	2	1	-	54
Cultivators	--	--	4	1	3	31	--	1	9	--	-	-	-	-	-	49
Cheese-makers	--	2	2	2	5	--	--	--	--	--	-	-	-	-	-	11
Day-workers	--	--	1	-	--	6	--	--	2	--	-	-	-	-	-	9
Millers	--	--	2	-	--	1	--	2	--	--	-	-	-	1	2	8
Farm workers	--	1	4	-	2	--	--	--	--	--	1	1	-	-	-	9
Viticulturists	--	--	--	-	--	1	--	--	1	--	-	1	-	-	-	3
Farmhands	--	--	2	-	--	--	--	--	--	--	-	-	-	-	-	2
Cowherds	--	--	--	-	--	1	--	--	--	--	-	-	-	-	-	1
Total	42	42	55	10	42	106	29	18	18	10	2	14	2	3	2	395

SOURCE: Calculations of the author based on the tezkeres for 1868-1870, NBKM, Oo.

TABLE 75

DISTRIBUTION BY INCOME (IN KURUŞ) OF MIGRANTS WORKING AS HIRED
LABOR IN NORTHEASTERN BULGARIA AND THE DOBRUJA, 1868-1870

Type of Hired Labor	Income Range													Total
	To 150	150-200	201-250	251-300	301-400	401-500	501-600	601-700	701-750	751-800	801-900	901-1,000	Over 1,000	
Apprentices	--	22	50	28	76	109	52	6	-	5	-	3	2	353
Servants	--	1	34	14	16	36	1	-	2	-	-	-	-	104
Porters	--	3	16	1	--	2	--	-	1	-	-	1	-	24
Hired workers	--	1	8	--	5	7	--	-	-	-	-	-	-	21
State employees	--	--	1	2	2	4	--	-	1	-	-	1	-	11
Total	--	27	109	45	99	158	53	6	4	5	-	5	2	513

SOURCE: Calculations of the author of data drawn from the tezkeres contained in NBKM, Oo.

TABLE 76

DISTRIBUTION BY INCOME OF MIGRANTS IN NORTHEASTERN BULGARIA
AND THE DOBRUJA, 1868-1870

Occupations	Income Ranges (in kuruş)				
	Up to 250	251-500	501-1,000	1,001-1,500	Over 1,501
Artisans	17.0	42.0	27.5	11.0	2.5
Merchants	5.5	26.0	31.5	20.5	16.5
Servants in merchant establishments*	22.0	37.5	34.5	1.5	1.5
Journeymen, apprentices†	24.5	48.0	25.5	0.8	--
Agriculturalists	35.0	40.0	23.5	1.5	--
Hired Workers	26.5	59.0	14.0	0.5	--

SOURCE: Based on calculations of the author of data drawn from the tezkeres contained
in NBKM, Oo. *Includes two individuals (3%) whose income was not stated. †Includes
three individuals (1.2%) whose income was not stated.

* * *

In summary, the short-term and long-term ebb and flow of
the working population--that is, an internal migration--was one
of the significant phenomena of the socioeconomic life of the
Balkan possessions of the Ottoman Empire in the second half of
the nineteenth century. This process was intimately connected
with the constant drift of the rural population to the cities
and with the formation in most of these cities of a differentiated stratum of the urban poor. Based on the analysis here of
data on northeastern Bulgaria and the Dobruja, material that is
admittedly incomplete, migrants appear to have been a constitu-
ent part of the urban poor amounting to an average of about 6%
of the entire urban population. These migrants came from many
different parts of the Balkans. Being chiefly of urban origin,

they settled once again and remained in cities, although this did not necessarily exclude the possibility of their moving to and from work in the surrounding district.[21] The migration was chiefly of skilled manpower, mainly artisans, but from a social point of view, most migrants, despite their occupations, consisted of low-paid persons.

Plate 20. An overview of Sparta. Reprinted from O. M.
Stackelberg, *La Grèce; vues pittoresques et topographiques*
(Paris, 1834).

Plate 21. A sketch of late 19th-century Kavalla by the Rev. W.
C. Bourchier. Courtesy of Gennadion Library, Athens.

Plate 22. The interior yard of a Greek house in early 19th-century Athens. Reprinted from O. M. Stackelberg, *La Grèce; vues pittoresques et topographiques* (Paris, 1834).

Plate 23. A sketch of late 19th-century Volos by the Rev. W. C. Bourchier. Courtesy of Gennadion Library, Athens.

Plates 24 and 25. *Above*, the early 19th-century watchtower in Triavna; *below*, 19th-century houses in Plovdiv. Photos by Christo Yonkov.

Occupations and
Incomes in the Danubian Vilâyet

19. POPULATION
DISTRIBUTION BY OCCUPATION

To reveal the occupational distribution of the urban
population of the Danubian vilâyet, use has been made of material drawn from artisan tezkeres and from tax receipts.[1]
These receipts were drawn up to cover a six-year period and
indicate both the income from the occupation being practiced
and the tax levied on that income, with the entry being made
annually by the appropriate clerk. The data that is available
covers 6,124 persons whose incomes are known for the years
1868-70. Since, however, the records do not show the occupation of 287 of these individuals, the sample used here to
study occupational patterns is composed of 5,837 persons.
These individuals can be grouped into several broad categories
according to the general character of the occupations they
practiced (see table 77).

The first three groups take in persons whose activities
placed them in handicrafts, commerce or agriculture, irrespec-

tive of their social status. The only internal differentiation
applied here--that between independent and hired work (i.e.,
journeymen and apprentices)--is not a matter of our interpretation, but reflects distinctions made in the documents. Furthermore, by grouping journeymen and apprentices separately,
though without divorcing them from their respective area of
economic activity, a better foundation is provided for a comparative analysis of the different types of livelihood. The
group of state employees does not include all types of civil
servants--only those subject to taxation. A separate cate-
gory--"general workers"--comprises general laborers, servants,
apprentices without a specified profession, porters, and water
carriers.

TABLE 77

OCCUPATIONAL DISTRIBUTION OF A STUDY GROUP OF THE TAXABLE POPULATION
OF TEN CITIES OF THE DANUBIAN VILÂYET IN THE 1860s

Occupation	Independent		Hired Workers		Total	
	Number	Percentage	Number	Percentage	Number	Percentage
Artisans	2,235	61.6	613	27.7	2,848	48.8
Merchants	848	23.4	140	6.3	988	16.9
Agriculturalists	455	12.6	706	31.9	1,161	19.9
State employees	86	2.4	---	----	86	1.5
General laborers	-----	----	754	34.1	754	12.9
Total	3,624	100.0	2,213	100.0	5,837	100.0

SOURCE: Tezkeres and tax receipts contained in NBKM, Oo, for 1866-1868.

In order to determine the general occupational distribution of the urban population, the data assembled here have
been considered in their totality. Insofar as possible, special
features in the development of a particular occupation by
cities are also examined by establishing the frequency of given
types of occupations represented in these individual cities.
Due to skews in the data, however, it has not been possible to
analyze them for each and every city. As can be seen from
table 78, which compares the sample against the results of the
census of 1866, the information is fullest for four cities--
Provadiia, Bazargic, Silistra, and Constanṭa. As far as the
other cities are concerned, the available material covers only
a small portion of the total population, and it would be prob-
lematic to attempt to draw their general occupational characteristics on the basis of such small samples. On the other
hand, even though the available data for these cities are too
scanty to permit a separate analysis, this information--which
involves more than 1,000 individuals--retains its value in the
aggregate, and it has been used for this purpose. Table 79

shows the distribution of the aggregate data by occupation and
by city.

TABLE 78

OCCUPATIONAL DISTRIBUTION OF THE TAXABLE
POPULATION OF THE URBAN DANUBIAN VILÂYET
(BY CITY AND BY PERCENTAGE)

City	Total Size of the Taxable Population, Census of 1866	Population Documented in Tezkeres and Tax Receipts	
		Number	Percentage
Bazargic	5,648	2,555	45.2
Provadiia	1,318	509	38.6
Silistra	3,787	1,188	31.4
Constanţa	1,228	473	38.5
Varna	7,537	531	7.0
Macin	1,488	97	6.5
Babadag	2,035	130	6.4
Shumen	10,060	453	4.5
Medgidia	2,112	85	4.0
Tulcea	5,477	103	1.9
Total	40,690	6,124	15.1

SOURCE: On the total size of the population, see NBKM, Oo,
Rs 98/8.

    A study of the occupational distribution is also ham-
pered because historiography has not yet established a
firm occupational categorization for the nineteenth-century
Balkans. Thus, there is no basis for comparison, and by necessity the data being used here have to serve as the point of
departure.
    To ease the problem somewhat, the analysis will start
with Bazargic and Silistra, whose varying occupational patterns
can act as models for discussing the situation in other cities
in the area. To a great extent, for example, Bazargic preserved
its agrarian character, whereas Silistra became a markedly
artisan and commercial city. The handicrafts in Silistra engaged the labor of 64.5% of the sample being studied here, and
the combined group of artisans and traders accounted for more
than three-fourths (81.8%) of it. In Bazargic, on the other
hand, individuals in these occupations comprised little more
than half of that city's total (56.7%). Looked at another way,

TABLE 79

OCCUPATIONAL DISTRIBUTION OF THE TAXABLE POPULATION OF
TEN CITIES OF THE DANUBIAN VILAYET IN THE 1860s

City	Handicrafts		Commerce		Agriculture		Hired Work		State Employee		Not Known		Total	
	Number	Percentage	Number	Percentage	Number	Percentage	Number	Percentage	Number	Percentage	Number	Percentage	Number	Percentage
Provadiia	179	35.2	72	14.1	123	24.2	65	12.8	6	1.2	64	12.5	509	100.0
Bazargic	1,057	41.5	387	15.2	620	24.3	428	16.8	10	0.1	53	2.1	2,555	100.0
Silistra	767	64.5	206	17.3	115	9.7	20	1.7	25	2.1	55	4.7	1,188	100.0
Constanța	166	35.1	116	24.5	52	11.0	122	25.8	8	1.7	9	1.9	473	100.0
Varna	221	41.5	69	13.0	102	19.2	59	11.1	16	3.1	64	12.1	531	100.0
Shumen	264	58.3	66	14.6	70	15.4	3	0.7	15	3.3	35	7.7	453	100.0
Babadag	58	44.7	23	17.6	18	13.8	27	20.8	3	2.3	1	0.8	130	100.0
Tulcea	52	50.5	21	20.4	16	15.5	11	10.7	2	1.9	1	1.0	103	100.0
Macin	50	51.5	23	23.7	6	6.2	12	12.4	1	1.0	5	5.2	97	100.0
Medgidia	34	40.0	5	5.9	39	45.9	7	8.2	--	--	--	----	85	100.0
Total	2,848	46.4	988	16.2	1,161	19.0	754	12.3	86	1.4	287	4.7	6,124	100.0

SOURCE: Based on material contained in tezkeres and tax receipts, NBKM, Oo.

in Bazargic those engaged in agriculture accounted for one-
fourth of the sample. This relatively high percentage, when
considered in conjunction with the fact that the majority of
Bazargic's hired laborers (16.8%) were also farm hands, clearly
demonstrates the agrarian character of Bazargic as opposed to
Silistra (where only 9.7% of the sample were engaged in agriculture and only 1.7% were hired laborers). Or, to put it in
yet another way, of all the persons engaged in agriculture in
the total sample for all cities, more than half (both independent and hired workers) were in Bazargic.

To a certain extent these essential differences in the
general occupational distribution of the two cities were mirrored in patterns of handicraft activity (see table 80).[2] This
breakdown of kindred groups of artisans by cities shows that
the trades connected with clothing and footwear account for
one-fourth of the artisans included in the sample for both
Bazargic and Silistra. Furthermore, a closer examination of
some of the individual crafts (old-style tailors, shoemakers,
and tanners) covered by the general groupings also indicates a
similar breakdown for the two cities. It requires a very attentive study of specific artisan activities to see the differences that did exist between Bazargic and Silistra. Thus,
in Silistra, modern tailoring (called *terziistvo* in Bulgarian),
which followed European styles and usually used European cloth,
seems to have been displacing the older abacı craft. In Bazargic, on the other hand, there were still equal proportions of
abacıs and terzis. There were other and stronger differences
related to trades connected with Bazargic's strongly developed
livestock husbandry, crafts such as leather tanning and the
making of leather articles. For Bazargic, for example, there
are seventy-three sole-leather makers and tanners as opposed to
eleven for Silistra. The artisans who made soft leather peasant
sandals and slippers are also far more numerous for Bazargic.

A distinctive feature of the two cities was the large
number of persons engaged in transport, which illustrates the
heightened role of these centers in the commercial life of the
southern Dobruja. The *araba*, the peasant's wagon, continued to
be a basic means of transport, as evidenced by the concentration
of a large number of *arabacıs* (carters) in Bazargic, the chief
distribution point to the interior of goods received from Silistra and elsewhere. Their beautifully crafted carts were highly
sought after for transport purposes, and some were exported
as far as Braşov. In Silistra, the transport workers also
included boatmen. Their large number was a sign that in addition to meeting local needs, they also used the Danube to
ship merchandise from and especially to the interior.

The analysis of the available material produces certain
other variations in patterns of handicraft activity that resulted

TABLE 80

DISTRIBUTION BY CITY OF KINDRED GROUPS OF HANDICRAFTS IN TEN CITIES OF
THE DANUBIAN VILÂYET IN THE 1860s

Groupings of Handicraft Activity	Bazargic		Provadiia		Constanţa		Silistra		Varna		Macin	
	Number	Percentage	Number	Percentage	Number	Percentage	Number	Percentage	Number	Percentage	Number	Percentage
Clothing & shoes	265	25.1	62	34.6	11	6.6	192	25.0	28	12.7	15	30.0
Preparation of food	121	11.4	15	8.4	92	55.5	140	18.3	63	28.5	15	30.0
Construction	114	10.8	20	11.2	40	24.1	48	6.3	49	22.2	3	6.0
Boating, fishing	1	0.1	1	0.6	2	1.2	78	10.2	6	2.7	4	8.0
Transport	376	35.6	21	11.7	3	1.8	111	14.5	21	9.5	1	2.0
Ironworking, tinsmithing	42	4.0	25	14.0	5	3.0	57	7.4	15	6.8	10	20.0
Hygiene	52	4.9	11	6.1	8	4.8	72	9.4	8	3.6	2	4.0
Other community services	76	7.2	20	11.2	5	3.0	49	6.3	17	7.7	--	---
Unknown, other	10	0.9	4	2.2	--	---	20	2.6	14	6.3	--	---
Total	1,057	100.0	179	100.0	166	100.0	767	100.0	221	100.0	50	100.0

Groupings of Handicraft Activity	Babadag		Shumen		Medgidia		Tulcea		Total	
	Number	Percentage	Number	Percentage	Number	Percentage	Number	Percentage	Number	Percentage
Clothing & shoes	20	34.5	78	29.5	3	10.0	14	25.0	688	24.2
Preparation of food	13	22.4	28	10.6	19	63.3	8	14.3	514	18.0
Construction	6	10.3	25	9.5	2	6.7	20	35.7	327	11.5
Boating, fishing	--	---	1	0.4	1	3.3	2	3.6	96	3.4
Transport	1	1.7	23	8.7	2	6.7	--	---	559	19.6
Ironworking, tinsmithing	10	17.2	36	13.6	2	6.7	2	3.6	204	7.2
Hygiene	1	1.7	19	7.2	--	---	5	8.9	178	6.3
Other community services	4	7.0	52	19.7	1	3.3	5	8.9	229	8.0
Unknown, other	3	5.2	2	0.8	--	---	--	---	53	1.8
Total	58	100.0	264	100.0	30	100.0	56	100.0	2848	100.0

SOURCE: Material contained in tezkeres and tax receipts, NBKM, Oo.

from the differing nature and degree of development of the two
cities. A typical example was the presence in Silistra of many
more sweetmakers, coffeehouse keepers, pharmacists, bath keepers
and masseurs--occupations that presupposed urban life of long
standing--as well as *tufekci*s or gunsmiths, who were among the
most highly specialized artisans. Bazargic, on the other hand,
had an impressively large number of butchers in comparison with
other cities. Furthermore, this city was also characterized by
an influx of more construction workers (masons and brickmakers),
a phenomenon connected with the increased building prompted by
an upsurge in the second half of the nineteenth century. An
explanation for Bazargic's relatively large number of registered
musicians (*çalgıcıs* or pipers) can be found in that city's
annual fair, which attracted numerous people from the surrounding villages.

However incomplete this description of Bazargic and Silistra, it does make possible a better comparative examination
of occupational patterns in other cities.

For the two inland cities of Shumen and Provadiia, for
example, there were relatively large groups of kindred handicraftsmen in clothing and footwear production and in iron-
smithery and tinsmithing (see table 80). About one-third of
the craftsmen in the sample drawn from these cities worked on
shoes and clothing. Among the artisans engaged in the preparation of goods, the bakers were the largest group. Another
noteworthy feature in the occupational pattern of these cities
was the high percentage of construction workers. Other handicrafts connected with transport, hygiene, and other communal
services are relatively evenly distributed in all the cities
noted. There are differences, but they are too minor to allow
an assertion of any definite occupational pattern.

Nevertheless, in attempting an over-all comparison of the
occupational structure of other cities with Bazargic and Silistra, there are several generalizations to be made. Like Bazargic, for example, Provadiia retained its agrarian character;
without taking into account hired labor, it had about the same
percentage of individuals engaged in agricultural work (see
table 79). With regard to its handicraft activities a predominant role was played by artisans who either cured leather
or produced leather articles. The pattern that emerges
from a consideration of both cities, therefore, is one of a
close relationship between different fields of economic activity.

In Varna, the distribution of the individual crafts suggests a developed artisan and commercial city. Although table
79 gives the impression that the percentage of artisans and
merchants here was lower than in Silistra or Shumen, for example, this apparent discrepancy is due to Varna's considerable
stratum of hired labor. With its heterogeneous composition,

this element of the urban population, which played an essential role in the social characterization of Varna, lent different nuances to that city's occupational structure.

As shown in table 79, Constanţa has the largest percentage share of merchants, one-fourth of the city's entire taxable population, or 11.8% of the total number of individuals engaged in commercial activities in the ten cities. Constanţa's agricultural component was relatively small. To cite another case, three-fourths of that part of the taxable population of Shumen for which data are avaiable was occupied in artisan and commercial work, a preponderance that likewise determined the character of that city. A number of handicrafts there were linked with servicing Shumen's garrison. Among the other cities Medgidia stands out as predominantly agricultural.

In moving on to study the ratio of independent artisans to hired workers, one can observe in the ten cities a predominance of crafts without any or with a very small number of assistants (see table 81). Whole groups of trades such as fishing, boating, and other transport-related activities--which account for about one-fourth of the independent tradesmen contained in the sample--involve no hired labor at all. Among the more compact groups of other tradesmen, only among bakers, tailors, and tanners is there a high percentage of hired labor. But in these fields too the ratio of independent tradesmen to hired workers is only one to one. In other fields, the hired labor force constitutes less than 40% of the total number of persons engaged in these activities. More specifically, hired labor accounts for 38.8% of the abacis, 32.8% of the cobblers, 34.1% of the masons, 33.3% of the barbers, 23.7% of the coffeehouse keepers, 21.1% of the slipper makers, 16.7% of the shoemakers, and so on down the line.

TABLE 81

INDEPENDENT MASTERS AND HIRED WORKERS BY TRADE IN TEN
CITIES OF THE DANUBIAN VILĂYET IN THE 1860s

Groupings of Trades	Independent Masters		Hired Workers		Total	
	Number	Percentage	Number	Percentage	Number	Percentage
Clothing & shoes	462	67.2	226	32.8	688	100.0
Preparation of food	350	68.1	164	31.9	514	100.0
Construction	238	72.8	89	27.2	327	100.0
Boating, fishing	96	100.0	---	----	96	100.0
Transport	556	99.5	3	0.5	559	100.0
Ironworking, tinsmithing	159	77.9	45	22.1	204	100.0
Hygiene	139	78.1	39	21.9	178	100.0
Other community services	182	79.5	47	20.5	229	100.0
Unknown, other	53	100.0	---	----	53	100.0
Total	2,235	78.5	613	21.5	2,848	100.0

SOURCE: Material contained in tezkeres and tax receipts, NBKM, Oo.

As this material illustrates, the artisans in this region generally took on only a restricted number of hired workers and assistants. Of course, the figures used here are average numbers, and it is quite possible that individual artisans might have had several journeymen and apprentices; however, one cannot but be impressed by the fact that, based on these figures, there was one hired worker for about every four artisans (or, to put it differently, that at least three-fourths of the artisans lacked even a single apprentice). The one-to-one ratio in the case of bakers and tailors simply reflects the nature of the activity in question, for this was work that required assistance. Only the poor baker might be without the almost indispensable hired helper, and only if he could rely on the assistance of a member of his family. Similarly, the tailor seeking to raise the level of his work by making clothes to measure could hardly fare without an apprentice to carry out the unskilled work.

In their status, therefore, the bulk of the artisans stood out as bearers of the small-commodity mode of artisan production, one of the signs of which is the absence of a large number of hired workers in the shop. Naturally (as will be shown below), what has been said does not exclude the presence of an artisan elite that had become a bourgeoisie.

The total sample includes 988 individuals registered as engaged in commercial activity, 848 independent and 140 hired workers. In all, this group takes in at least thirty different types of commercial activity (see table 82). Actually, commercial specialization was more complex than the table suggests, since 150 of the persons in question were registered not by their specific activity but simply by the general character of their occupations as "merchants" and "shopkeepers." Undoubtedly, such registration resulted from the clerk's failure to be precise, but at the same time the terminology used did bear elements of social characterization. Thus, "shopkeepers" were individuals engaged in petty trade, keepers of small stores, booths and so on. A "merchant," on the other hand, was a person who possessed a sufficient amount of accumulated goods and a store or shop large enough to merit an unqualified distinction for tax purposes as a *tüccar* or "merchant" distinguished from other tradesmen. It was not by chance that the majority of "shopkeepers" in the group being studied were concentrated in Bazargic, whose fair drew customers from the entire surrounding area. Generally speaking, the "merchants" are evenly distributed in Silistra, Constanţa, Varna, Bazargic, and Macin.

The prevailing localization in a city of a certain type of commercial activity can, as in the case of artisans, be used to provide a more definite idea of the character of the cities concerned. For example, all of the port cities had casinos. At the time these casinos were drinking establish-

ments offering better services than taverns, plus entertainment
(cabaret singers and, in some cases, women of easy virtue from
abroad). A casino operator in Varna was named Leonardo, the
son of Dionysius.[3] Casino keepers in Constanţa included Ivancho of Ohrid and Khristo Balaban.[4] The property receipts of
that city indicate the presence of yet another casino operator
and tavernkeeper, the Muslim Nusred Paşa.[5] There were six casino operators in Silistra (including one Muslim, three Bulgarians, and two Jews).[6] There was a Muslim casino keeper in
Lom,[7] and a Greek in Bazargic.[8]

TABLE 82

DISTRIBUTION OF INDIVIDUALS ENGAGED IN COMMERCIAL ACTIVITIES IN TEN
CITIES OF THE DANUBIAN VILÂYET IN THE 1860s

Type of Activity	Independent		Hired		Total	
	Number	Percentage	Number	Percentage	Number	Percentage
Grocers	220	80.6	53	19.4	273	100.0
Dealers in cloth	25	75.7	8	24.3	33	100.0
Dealers in flour	18	100.0	--	----	18	100.0
Dealers in second-hand goods	34	100.0	--	----	34	100.0
Haberdashers	28	93.3	2	6.7	30	100.0
Cattle dealers	17	100.0	--	----	17	100.0
Shopkeepers	82	95.4	4	4.6	86	100.0
Casino operators	4	57.2	3	42.8	7	100.0
Commission agents	19	100.0	--	----	19	100.0
Tavern keepers	47	77.1	14	22.9	61	100.0
Itinerant merchants (kurdzhii)	18	85.7	3	14.3	21	100.0
Dry-goods dealers	104	91.2	10	8.8	114	100.0
Entertainers at fairs	4	100.0	--	----	4	100.0
Stallkeepers	27	100.0	--	----	27	100.0
Wholesale dealers	5	100.0	--	----	5	100.0
Dealers in tobacco	33	82.5	7	17.5	40	100.0
Dealers in wool	3	100.0	--	----	3	100.0
Dealers in wood	3	100.0	--	----	3	100.0
Dealers in grain	3	100.0	--	----	3	100.0
Dealers in horses	35	100.0	--	----	35	100.0
Dealers in poultry and eggs	20	100.0	--	----	20	100.0
Dealers in shoes	7	35.0	13	65.0	20	100.0
Dealers in fruits	5	100.0	--	----	5	100.0
Merchants	60	80.0	15	20.0	75	100.0
Innkeepers	15	68.2	7	31.8	22	100.0
Others	7	87.5	1	12.5	8	100.0
Not stated	5	100.0	--	----	5	100.0
Total	848	85.8	140	14.2	988	100.0

SOURCE: Material contained in tezkeres and tax receipts, NBKM, Oo.

Another commercial occupation that turns up for the ports of Silistra and Varna is that of commission agent. For Varna, which sent large quantities of chickens and eggs to Istanbul, there is also a considerable group of poultry dealers (18), indicating the definite interest that food exporters had in this particular commodity. The commercial sector of Constanţa, a rising port city of the central and northern Dobruja, includes wholesale dealers (the *toptancıs*) and grain dealers set apart by their high incomes. For Bazargic, a center of agricultural production and trade, the commercial part of the population takes in a group of 18 flour dealers. For this city there is also a significant number of cattle, sheep, and horse dealers (Bazargic being the location of 36 of the 52 businessmen of this kind contained in the sample), and the same holds true for Shumen and Silistra. Practically all of the innkeepers in the sample (12 out of a total of 15) were centered in Bazargic. Perhaps on account of the town's high number of inns, the number of tavernkeepers in Bazargic was small, but this phenomenon may also be explained by the predominantly Muslim character of the city and its district, which in addition accounted for the concentration (during the fair) of a large number of sweet shops. The largest incidence of tavernkeepers occurs in Silistra and Shumen. Generally speaking, tobacco dealers, itinerant peddlers, and dealers in secondhand goods are evenly distributed over most of the cities.

The most numerous groups, composed of grocers and dry goods and cloth dealers, are concentrated, as might be expected, in Bazargic (on account of the fair) and in Silistra.[9] This occupational concentration reveals how Silistra was functioning as a depot for goods being sent to the interior of the Dobruja.

The use of hired labor by persons engaged in commercial activities cannot be taken as a sign of an individual's changing social position save as an exception, since the distribution of hired labor contained in the sample (see table 82) is more a matter of the nature of given fields of activity than of social stratification. The highest percentage of hired labor occurs in the trade in shoes, slippers, and so forth--that is, work that normally required clerks and salesmen. For other occupations--for example, innkeepers, casino operators, tavernkeepers, grocers, and dealers in cloth, hired labor was a matter of the ordinary and inevitable assistants and servants.

Finally, individuals engaged in agriculture constitute one-fifth of the total number of persons for whom information is available. In itself, this figure is not a low one and could be taken as a sign of the continuing agricultural nature of cities of the Danubian vilâyet. But such a sweeping statement would be wrong. By examining the actual occupations of these individuals (as shown in table 83) by city, it would be

more correct to say that only certain cities retained an agricultural character.

TABLE 83

DISTRIBUTION OF INDIVIDUALS ENGAGED IN AGRICULTURE
IN TEN CITIES OF THE DANUBIAN VILÂYET IN THE 1860s

Type of Activity	Number	Percentage
Independent Workers		
Farmers	67	5.8
Farmers and carters	54	4.6
Shepherds	220	19.0
Cowherds	11	1.0
Dairymen	11	1.0
Gardeners	79	6.8
Viticulturists	13	1.1
Total	455	39.3
Hired Workers		
Harvesters	80	6.9
Farm workers	69	6.0
Cultivators	553	47.8
Farmhands	4	----
Total	706	60.7
TOTAL	1,161	100.0

SOURCE: Material contained in tezkeres and tax receipts,
NBKM, Oo.

Of the total group of persons engaged in agricultural
work, only 5.8% were farmers who worked the land. To this group
might be added seasonal hired hands doing harvesting (6.9%) and
the combined group of farm laborers (6%). In other words, those
engaged in farming in the true sense of the word account for
19% of the total sample. There is an almost equal number of
shepherds (19%), whose case is rather special, since three-
fourths of them were registered in Bazargic and in Medgidia.
Since the Dobruja was an area of intensive sheep husbandry that
drew shepherds and shepherds' associations from distant regions,
even from abroad (Wallachia, Moldavia, and Hungary), it was
natural that a considerable stratum of shepherds should take
shape in the cities of the interior. Some of the shepherds

there were the owners of huge flocks, while others were individuals who simply tended flocks of sheep brought to the Dobruja to graze.

The so-called cultivators (*chapadzhii*), who number 553 individuals, form the bulk of the persons registered as being engaged in agricultural work. This impressive number is evidence of the area's widespread labor-intensive cultivation (as in vineyards, for example), which required the use of an almost permanent hired labor force. Viticulture was a source of additional income for a considerable part of the urban population of this region.

The breakdown in this category between hired labor and independent agriculturalists is a telling one, and the numbers here are much more revealing in terms of social status than was the case with artisans and merchants. There is no doubt that the "farmers" possessed the land they cultivated. The registering clerk, however, failed to note whether the land was encumbered with debts, and whether, in order to meet the needs of his family, the farmer had to cultivate land in addition to his own.

Even more obscure in these respects is the group of "farmers and arabacis" (or carters). This designation has been retained as it appears in the documents, since it points out one of the channels through which the rural population moved into the cities. What was required to be registered as a carter was a wagon, horses, and members of the household who were not needed to work the land. Although there is no doubt that the carting work itself (*arabacilik*) was the critical factor in the activity of most of the cases in question, carters have been included here among agricultural workers in order both to reveal, as much as possible (and albeit indirectly), the division of labor in agriculture, and to distinguish those carters who retained a continuing link with the land from those who had clearly become part of the urban population.

The shepherds and cowherds are the most difficult to analyze in terms of social status. Undoubtedly, some of these individuals, if not the majority, were actually hired workers, but in view of the nature of sheep raising in the Dobruja, it has seemed preferable not to dispute their status as independent workers. This approach reduces the possibility of error. Here, therefore, the hired labor force among those engaged in agricultural work embodies the smallest possible number of cases, and yet they still amount to 60.8% of the total number. This high percentage of hired laborers is a very telling comment on the character of agriculture and its subordinate role in the urban economy.

There are some unique aspects in the residential patterns of the larger and more definite groups included in the agri-

cultural professions. As already noted, the shepherds were
settled chiefly in Bazargic, as were all of the dairymen, 81.6%
of the "farmers and carters," and one-fourth of the farmers
(24%). Also resident in this city were practically all of the
harvesters (95%) and half of the cultivators (53.8%). These
figures tend to reaffirm the view that Bazargic was a city with
a definite agricultural character. Provadiia had a similar
character, and the same agricultural groups were present, though
in relatively smaller percentages. The farmers in Provadiia,
for example, amounted to 53.5% of the agricultural workers in
the city. The presence of viticulturists in Provadiia was one
difference between it and Bazargic, and in this respect Provadiia resembled Varna. In the latter city, where the majority
of viticulturists studied here were settled, there were also
compact groups of harvesters, farmhands, and gardeners--occu-
pational patterns that suggest the crops were usually farmed
intensively.

Having examined the three basic urban occupational
groups, an effort will now be made to clarify the character of
the group we have called general laborers or workers. Table
84 shows how the persons included in this group fall into two
basic categories: genuine common laborers with a specific
work designation, and the children and youths whom the documents describe as apprentices. The category comprises
various kinds of servants (most of whom were described by the
clerk as being *hizmetkâr*), porters (mainly stevedores), the
sakas who carried water buckets to homes and shops, and those
recorded in the documents under the designation of "workers"
by a term used even now in the Turkish language.

The second broad category comprises only apprentices.
The question arises as to whether there are sufficient grounds
to consider these apprentices together with common laborers.
Taking into account the thoroughness of the registration that
was carried out, it has been decided not to ignore the probably
conscious procedure on the part of the clerks not to enter a
specific occupation for the rather large number of apprentices.
It is possible that this method of registration either reflected
a distinction that was to some extent made between those who
had mastered a craft and those who had not, or was a way of
satisfying master craftsmen (by including their sons in the
category of individuals with an established occupation). Even
assuming that it was fully possible that a larger or smaller
part of the "apprentices" with no indicated occupation actually
worked in artisan and merchant shops and workshops, and had
real prospects of ultimately becoming independent masters and
merchants, in no way alters the inferences drawn here. In professional terms, these "apprentices" appropriately belong in
the category of unspecified occupations and are thus excluded

from the concrete analysis of the various crafts and commerce. In social terms they fall into the same category as does hired labor, and for these reasons they have been treated here together with hired workers. The importance of this group rests precisely in its social nature, for its presence and its numbers definitely show how the ranks of hired labor contained quite a layer of persons who at an early age were seeking work and regardless of their professions became simply "apprentices."

TABLE 84

CATEGORIES OF GENERAL LABORERS

Categories of General Laborers	Number	Percentage
Artisans	465	61.8
Servants	188	25.0
Porters	49	6.5
Waterbearers	13	1.6
Workers	39	5.1
Total	754	100.0

SOURCE: Tezkeres and tax receipts contained in NBKM, Oo, for 1866-1868.

The extent to which hired labor was used in various activities can be seen in table 85. Of the total sample, the hired labor used in artisan production, in commerce, in agriculture, and as common laborers, amounts to 2,213 persons (i.e., 37.8% of the sample and, by inference, more than one-third of the taxable urban population). They include all those workers who supported themselves and their families with the wages obtained in return for their freely given labor. The nature of this group as a true hired-labor force is beyond dispute. However, no attempt has been made here to establish the presence and number of hired workers in capitalist enterprises per se, since there is no way of determining the number and type of such enterprises in the first place. In any event, it has been considered more significant to distinguish this group in general social terms. A comparison of its material position with that of other groups--as will be attempted in the following chapter-- permits a better classification of the urban population by incomes as well as by occupations and allows some general con-

clusions concerning the standard of living of contemporary urban society.

TABLE 85

HIRED WORKERS BY OCCUPATIONAL FIELD
(NUMBER AND PERCENTAGE)

Area	Number	Percentage of Total
Handicrafts	613	27.7
Commerce	140	6.3
Agriculture	706	31.9
General Labor	754	34.1
Total	2,213	100.0

SOURCE: Tezkeres and tax receipts contained in NBKM, Oo,
for 1866-1868.

* * *

The assembled archival material also makes possible an
analysis of the occupational distribution of the taxable population by ethnic and ethnic-religious affiliation. As can be
seen from table 86, on the basis of the data used here, more
than half of the artisans, merchants, and farmers are Muslims
(respectively, Muslims are 57%, 52.6%, and 55.4% of the
total number of individuals in these fields). As might be expected, Muslims furthermore thoroughly dominate the ranks of
state employees (71.7%). Only in the hired labor category are
non-Muslims in the majority (56%).

But occupational patterns are perhaps better examined
through an analysis of their internal breakdown within the
framework of a given ethnic-religious group. Both Muslims (consisting mainly of Turks but including some Muslim settlers,
etc.) and the basic group of non-Muslims (made up of Bulgarians
as the major element but including a small number of Greeks,
Wallachians, and "Christians"), are distributed in roughly the
same way over handicrafts, trade, and agriculture. For both
groups the bulk are artisans--48.4% of the Muslims (Turks,
1,582 out of 3,261) and 42.9% of the non-Muslims (Bulgarians,
1,047 out of 2,443). Agriculture accounts for about one-fifth
of the representation of both nationalities, and the percentages
of those engaged in trade stand, respectively, at 15.6% and
14.8%.

Three-fourths of the Armenians and Jews contained in the

sample were engaged in handicrafts and commerce. While for the
Jews there is a ratio of one merchant to each artisan, for the
Armenians there are two artisans to each merchant. Also noteworthy is the relatively high percentage of state employees
among the Armenians, whereas for the Jews there is a slightly
higher percentage of hired labor.

TABLE 86

OCCUPATIONAL DISTRIBUTION OF TEN CITIES OF THE DANUBIAN VILÂYET
IN THE 1860s (BY ETHNIC AFFILIATION)

	Non-Muslims		Muslims		Armenians		Jews		Total	
	Number	Percentage	Number	Percentage	Number	Percentage	Number	Percentage	Number	Percentage
Occupation only										
Handicrafts	1,047	37.9	1,582	57.0	86	3.1	55	2.0	2,770	100.0
Commerce	362	37.4	508	52.6	40	4.1	57	5.9	967	100.0
Agriculture	507	43.9	640	55.4	3	0.3	4	0.4	1,154	100.0
Hired work	403	54.1	326	43.7	7	1.0	9	1.2	745	100.0
State employees	19	23.4	58	71.7	3	3.7	1	1.2	81	100.0
Not stated	105	37.3	147	52.4	22	7.8	7	2.5	281	100.0
Total	2,443	40.7	3,261	54.4	161	2.7	133	2.2	5,998	100.0
Social position										
Artisans	697	28.4	1,358	41.6	64	39.7	47	36.1	2,166	36.1
Traders	263	10.8	474	14.5	36	22.4	55	40.6	828	13.8
Agricul-turists	290	11.9	161	5.0	--	----	--	----	451	7.5
Hired workers	1,069	43.8	1,063	32.6	36	22.4	23	17.3	2,191	36.5
State employees	19	0.8	58	1.8	3	1.9	1	0.8	81	1.4
Not stated	105	4.3	147	4.5	22	13.6	7	5.2	281	4.7
Total	2,443	100.0	3,261	100.0	161	100.0	133	100.0	5,998	100.0

SOURCE: Material contained in tezkeres and tax receipts, NBKM, Oo.

The data just discussed incorporate both those working
independently and as hired labor in each of the areas of handicrafts, commerce, and agriculture. Also interesting is the
breakdown of these two categories for the different ethnic
groups. Thus, the percentage of hired labor among the artisans
and merchants is highest for the basic group of non-Muslims,
the Bulgarians (33.4%). Looked at another way, Bulgarians account for 57.9% of the total number of all hired workers in
artisan fields, and 71.3% of the total number of hired persons
working in commerce.

As can be seen from the second part of table 86, the
occupational breakdown changes when the categories are regrouped
to take into account the individual's actual social position
(thus, for example, the apprentices and journeymen who fell
into the artisan category in the first part of the table are
now made part of the hired labor category). To begin with,
there is a great increase in the percentage of hired workers
generally. For the basic non-Muslim grouping (again, chiefly

Bulgarians), hired labor now represents the largest group,
1,069 persons or 43.8% of the total. In the case of Muslims,
independent artisans retain their numerical superiority (41.6%),
but the hired labor force that heretofore had ranked fourth is
now in second place with 32.6% of the total. This higher over-
all percentage of hired workers among the Muslims in the second
part of the table comes about by virtue of the inclusion here
as hired workers of three-fourths of the group of Muslims engaged in agriculture as shown in part 1 of the table. The percentage of hired labor also increases considerably among the
Armenians, accounting for almost one-fourth of their total number (22.4%).[10]

*Occupations and
Incomes in the Danubian Vilâyet*

20. CATEGORIZATION
OF THE POPULATION BY INCOME

In grouping the urban population by income, those engaged
in their own business--that is, independent masters, merchants,
farmers, etc.--(including salaried state employees) have been
considered separately from those working as hired labor. Since
the historiography has not yet established any criteria for
the distribution of the population by income, such a categorization has been made part of this study (in the hope that these
categories will be found to be more generally applicable for
Balkan studies).

Individuals working on their own behalf have been grouped
into four income ranges: those earning up to 500 kuruş a year;
those making between 501 and 1,000 kuruş; those earning between
1,001 and 2,000 kuruş; and those earning over 2,000 kuruş (see
table 87).[1]

The great majority of those working on their own behalf
(81.6%) fall into the first two income ranges (i.e., those

earning up to 1,000 kuruş). These two groups include almost
all of the independent agriculturalists (92.2%) and persons
whose occupations were not stated (92%), as well as the great
bulk of artisans (85%) and state employees (86%). The percentage of merchants represented in these lower income categories
is comparatively lower, standing at 6.28%. When the two income
ranges--up to 500 kuruş and 501 to 1,000 kuruş--are considered
separately, a different breakdown results, although both ranges
include approximately the same number of persons. Whereas more
than half of the agriculturalists and state employees fall into
the first category (with incomes of up to 500 kuruş), a higher
percentage of artisans and merchants occurs in the second income range (from 501 to 1,000 kuruş).

TABLE 87

DISTRIBUTION BY INCOME RANGE OF INDIVIDUALS ENGAGED IN OWN BUSINESS OR AS SALARIED STATE EMPLOYEES
IN TEN CITIES OF THE DANUBIAN VILÂYET IN THE 1860s (IN KURUŞ)

Fields of Activity	Up to 500		501–1,000		1,001–2,000		Over 2,000		Not Stated		Total	
	Number	Percentage	Number	Percentage	Number	Percentage	Number	Percentage	Number	Percentage	Number	Percentage
Handicrafts	877	39.2	1,023	45.8	288	12.9	29	1.3	18	0.8	2,335	100.0
Trade	209	24.6	324	38.2	218	25.7	88	10.4	9	1.1	848	100.0
Agriculture	262	57.7	157	34.5	22	4.8	2	0.4	12	2.6	455	100.0
State employees	46	53.5	28	32.5	10	11.6	1	1.2	1	1.2	86	100.0
Not stated; other	163	56.8	101	35.2	16	5.6	1	0.3	6	2.1	287	100.0
Total	1,557	39.8	1,633	41.8	554	14.2	121	3.0	46	1.2	3,911	100.0

SOURCE: Tezkeres and tax receipts contained in NBKM, Oo.

    The artisan and merchants who fall into the first two
income ranges come from practically all types of handicrafts
and branches of commerce. Including only those trades represented by more than 50 individuals, for example, those in that
part of the sample whose income was below 1,000 kuruş would include the following:

        carters (93.9%)[2]   tilers (84.5%)
        draymen (90.5%)[3]   tailors (83.8%)
        shoemakers (90.9%)   ironsmiths (77.6%)
        furriers (90.7%)   butchers (74.6%)
        barbers (90.5%)   bakers (66.7%)
        masons (89.5%)   abacıs (59.6%)
        coffeehouse keepers (88.7%)

In fifteen fields out of a total of 26 represented here, the
majority of those engaged in commercial activities also fall
into the two lower income ranges. Thus, these income categories comprise most of the tavernkeepers, haberdashers, tobacco dealers, "shopkeepers,"[4] and grocers, as well as all
stallkeepers and dealers in secondhand goods.
    The income range of 1,001 to 2,000 kuruş shows a consider-

ably smaller incidence (14.2%) of individuals engaged in their
own business or working as salaried state employees. Of the
artisans included here, the abacıs form a considerably large
group (38.6% of the abacıs fall into this range), as do tanners
and bakers (one-third of both groups fall into this income
range). At this level there exists a marked income differentiation of artisans who are also represented in definite and large
groups in the income range of up to 1,000 kuruş.

Only a very small percentage of artisans is found in the
highest income range (over 2,000 kuruş). Such artisans are
distributed over about ten crafts, each of which is represented
by one or two cases. In this income range merchants have a 10
to 1 superiority over other occupations, persuasive if indirect
evidence of the basic difference between the position of the
artisans in this group and those who earned lower incomes.
Standing out among the merchants included in the highest income
range are dry-goods dealers, grocers, textile dealers[5] (this
income range accounts for 40% of their total number) and "merchants"[6] (one-third of their number is included here).

The analysis of the income distribution of hired labor
results in the formation of three basic income ranges: up to
500 kuruş, from 501 to 1,000 kuruş, and over 1,000 kuruş (see
table 88). The greatest incidence occurs in the first range,
which takes in about three-fourths (73.1%) of all the hired
workers considered, but the actual percentage representation
of the workers who fall into this range varies for different

TABLE 88

DISTRIBUTION BY INCOME OF HIRED WORKERS IN TEN CITIES OF THE DANUBIAN VILÂYET, 1860s
(IN KURUŞ)

Fields of Activity	Up to 500				501–1,000			
	To 250		251–500		501–750		751–1,000	
	Number	Percentage	Number	Percentage	Number	Percentage	Number	Percentage
Handicrafts	140	22.8	248	40.5	108	17.6	73	11.9
Trade	19	13.6	64	45.7	33	23.6	18	12.9
Agriculture	129	18.3	396	56.1	99	14.0	65	9.2
General labor	177	23.5	446	59.1	98	13.0	23	3.0
Total	465	21.0	1,154	52.1	338	15.3	179	8.1

	Over 1,000		Not Stated		Total	
	Number	Percentage	Number	Percentage	Number	Percentage
Handicrafts	28	4.6	16	2.6	613	100.0
Trade	3	2.1	3	2.1	140	100.0
Agriculture	15	2.1	2	0.3	706	100.0
General labor	5	0.7	5	0.7	754	100.0
Total	51	2.3	16	1.2	2,213	100.0

SOURCE: Tezkeres and tax receipts contained in NBKM, Oo.

types of hired work. The largest element here is general laborers (82.6% of whom are accounted for here), a natural result
given the low pay they received. This income range also takes
in the majority (74.4%) of the hired workers in agriculture.
Although there is a considerably lower incidence here of hired
labor engaged in artisan production (63.3%), and of hired workers employed in commerce (59.3%), the bulk of these workers
also fall into the lowest income range.

The first income range has also been broken down into two
subgroups: up to 250 kuruş, and from 251 kuruş to 500 kuruş.
The over-all percentage of the hired workers who fall into the
first subgroup is not a small one (21%), and these workers represent all fields of activity. They include agricultural
workers, common laborers, and hired workers in handicrafts and
commerce. That the percentage representation of the different
kinds of hired workers in this subgroup coincides comparatively
well with the general percentage breakdown of hired workers as
a whole suggests the presence of a stable group of very low-
paid workers in all fields.

On the basis of the foregoing discussion, it is now possible to characterize in a more definite manner the composition
and position of different income groups of the population. Thus,
individuals whose registered income was below 500 kuruş can only
be regarded as the low-income group of the population. This
conclusion finds support in the great majority of the hired
workers studied here having incomes in this range. Furthermore,
registered incomes in the range of 501 to 1,000 kuruş can also
be regarded as low. Only when we reach the plateau of incomes
of from 1,000 to 2,000 kuruş can we speak, at least conditionally, of a middle-income level. Larger incomes--that is, those
over 2,000 kuruş a year--put their recipients into the relatively high income groups of the population.

This kind of categorization becomes more convincing with
the examination of specific cases from the various income groups.
For this reason, a name-by-name list has been included here as
appendix 3 (albeit due to practical considerations the list
contains only individuals in the high income category), noting
the name, occupation, place of residence and ethnic affiliation.
It would be superfluous to discuss these cases in detail here,
but several of the more characteristic features of the internal
breakdown of this high-income group do warrant comment. Particularly noteworthy, for example, is the considerable gap that
existed between the incomes of a dozen or so of the businessmen and the remainder of persons on the list. In the documents
most of the individuals in question were designated simply
as "merchants", for in view of the large volume of their
commercial activities the clerk saw no need to add a more spe-

cific description of the goods in which they dealt. Similarly,
one individual was registered as simply a "wholesaler," with no
indication of the commodities involved. As to the remainder
of the individuals listed, there is a noteworthy group of dry
goods and textile dealers (also wholesalers), a stratum of grocers, and several other individual representatives of different
branches of commerce and handicrafts.

An examination of the place of residence of the individuals on the list underscores the differences between the cities
of Bazargic and Constanţa.[7] Many of the high-income "merchants"
and grain exporters were residents of Constanţa. For Bazargic,
on the other hand, the high-income recipients tended to be innkeepers, livestock dealers, and dealers in hides and leather
products.

A study of the list also discloses certain trends in terms
of ethnic and ethnic-religious affiliation. Thus, for example,
the number of Armenians increases dramatically in the higher
registered incomes. The highest incomes, however, belong
by and large to foreign nationals (a telling illustration
of the kind of domestic system that could not guarantee the
security of the persons and property of the citizens of the
Ottoman Empire). In percentage terms the Muslims on the list
hold their own vis-à-vis other ethnic groups, whereas Bulgarians
tend to occur less frequently in this high-income category.

* * *

Differentiating the population by income groups becomes
very complex if one wants to add a descriptive social content
to the quantitative indices that have been used here. Additional information is required to answer such questions as
the real value or purchasing power of the income received, the
basic urban subsistence wage, the amount necessary to maintain
a standard of living corresponding to social standing, and so
on. A full-fledged discussion of these questions is not possible here, among other reasons because of the limited state of
the historiography. There is, however, information in a variety
of sources--local records, travelers' accounts, and official
data--that permits an examination of some of the matters raised
above. In view of the basic data used here being dominated by
persons with low incomes who represent the large layer of the
urban poor (which was composed of hired workers, low-paid artisans, agriculturalists eking out a livelihood, and so on), this
effort will focus on the material status of those living at the
low and middle levels of society.

Information is available for teaching, one of the most
respected professions in nineteenth-century Bulgarian society.
Community councils or obshtinas bore the expenses of teachers'
salaries, using funds collected by means of voluntary contri-

butions. For this reason, only teachers who had already established their reputation and who were sought after by a number of obshtinas could expect to receive salaries several times
higher than those paid to ordinary teachers. Additional details
on the status of teachers and their salaries are found in the
correspondence of Naiden Gerov, an influential Bulgarian who in
the third quarter of the nineteenth century served as Russian
consul in Plovdiv. Prior to entering Russian service, Gerov
had himself been a teacher for a long time, and he did all he
could to improve the lot of Bulgarian educators. In late 1872
Gerov wrote to Evlogi Georgiev, a rich Bulgarian merchant in
Rumania, about the state of the schools in Karlovo, criticizing
the manner in which members of the city's obshtina went about
hiring teachers. Through Georgiev, a native of Karlovo who
maintained his connections there, Gerov advised the obshtina
"not to do as they had done so far, to have teachers...who received 500 and 1,000 [kuruş] and who do not know a thing, but
to engage worthier teachers."[8] At the same time a wealthy obshtina could pay a salary of several thousand kuruş to a well-
known secondary school teacher. Gerov himself once offered the
Russian-educated Bulgarian Todor Burmov from 10,000 to 12,000
kuruş to become a teacher in Plovdiv.[9] In Khaskovo and Koprivshtitsa, too, the community councils were willing to pay a
salary of 5,000 kuruş to a good teacher.[10] The teacher, however, could never be sure of receiving all of this amount, since
on the first suitable occasion the obshtinas would find a way
to avoid paying the negotiated salary. They did so even with
the pay of such long-standing teachers as Bot'o Petkov (the
father of the Bulgarian poet and revolutionary Khristo Botev),
who once complained to Gerov how the people of Kalofer had low-
ered his pay to 1,500 kuruş.[11]

Another case where more detailed information is available
on material status and standard of living concerns workers in
Samokov. In 1848 and 1849 the French mining engineers A. Daux
and F. Le Play visited Samokov and gathered information on the
family budget of a Bulgarian ironsmith employed at a local iron
foundry. Their published observations are quite informative
and interesting.

After describing the population of Samokov as consisting
chiefly both of workers attached to the various metalworking
shops and enterprises and of farm laborers connected with the
cultivation of the land of big Turkish landowners, they wrote:
"In principle the workers are voluntarily bound to the owners
of the enterprise and for a fixed period of time, but in reality
they are people obligated to work for them for life. Their
actual bond to the employer is as a result of some kind of debt,
often an inherited one, which prevents a worker from changing
employers until it is paid off."[12] It was in this manner that

the French authors explained the relationships between workers
and proprietors that lasted for generations. The worker who
was the object of special study by the two Frenchmen was described as being both a day laborer and a property owner (a
house and garden). But the fact that his employer furnished
him with food during the working period and with other assistance in kind brought this ironsmith closer to the status of
the domestic worker. His debt to the Turkish employer was small
enough that it could have been immediately paid off with the
family's available cash along with a valuable necklace it
possessed made of silver coins. Under the influence of established customs, however, the debt was retained as an expression
of the good relations between the worker and the employer.

In terms of other basic information, Daux and Le Play
pointed out that this worker and his family belonged to the
"race" of Bulgarian Slavs and sprang from a stock that had
been employed for many generations in metalworking. The family
consisted of five members: the worker Georgi, age thirty-seven,
head of the family, married for thirteen years; Sofia, his wife,
age thirty-two; Stanko, the eldest son, age twelve; Mariora, a
daughter, age ten; and Dimitŭr, the second son, age two. They
professed the Eastern Orthodox faith, but religious instruction
and religious sentiment were weak. Conjugal morals were described as "good." The children did not attend school and could
neither read nor write. Their health was found to be good.
(For the French observers, the whole population had a healthy
appearance. Rheumatism and fevers were the principal diseases.
Treatment was usually based on folk medicine, but the workers
of the iron foundry were attended to by a physician who practiced in Samokov at the employer's expense.)

Also extraordinarily interesting are the travelers' observations on the material position and way of life of the
Samokov workers. Among other things, Daux and Le Play argued
that the family in question was an example of how the poorest
workers of Samokov lived better than workers in the richest
industrial cities in Western countries, although the latter
received wages that were ten times higher. The Frenchmen found
a partial explanation for this better life in the fact that the
employer supplied the workers with food and allowed them to
raise their own livestock and to engage from time to time in
farming. For six months of the year Georgi worked in the
foundry, and only in the summer was he assigned to do other
jobs. He had ninety-six holidays a year. His house had
twenty-seven square meters of floor space. A stable for
the cow and a grain bin made up the ground floor. Two meters
above and accessible by an external staircase were the rooms
used by the family: a kitchen, a bedroom, and another room.

The two Frenchmen also added a description of how the

workers' permanent state of dependence was established. The
first big loan was granted at the time of wedlock and was used
for building a house, and for all intents and purposes it could
never be repaid. Sickness and old age were other causes of
debt, which weighed heavily on the children who inherited it.

    After a somewhat idealistic discussion of the patriarchal
customs that continued to exist, Daux and Le Play used a table
to provide detailed figures on the state of the family's finances and its means of existence, starting with a breakdown
of its net worth:

Property (excluding furniture and clothing   *(in francs)*
  House   141.60
  Fruit orchard attached to house--4½ ares   40.00
  Domestic animals (cow, 64 francs;
    6 hens, 3 turkeys, 10 francs)   74.00
  Garden tools, etc.   21.56

Cash   136.20
  In cash on hand and that lent
   out at no interest--68.10 francs
  In silver coins of wife's necklace,
  68.10 francs

Total value, property and cash   413.36

Debts
  To the employer   104.40
  (Remainder of debt arising from 261
   francs loaned at time of marriage)
  To various merchants   35.20

    The French observers then enumerated the family's income
and expenses. Since its members cultivated land owned by the
employer, the family received much of its remuneration for
its labor in foodstuffs, firewood, material for repairing the
house, and so on. The head of the family himself put 40 days
a year in this farm work and 170 days in his major occupation
in the workshop. The husband worked 44 days on the family's
own agricultural pursuits, the spouse 315 days, and the children 56 working days. As calculated by Daux and Le Play, the
family's total income broke down as follows:

Income from the property   *(in francs)*
  In kind   66.48
  In cash   22.95

Income from labor   *(in kind)*   *(in cash)*
  Father   72.6   192.95
  All family members   114.64   192.95

Finally, the French engineers calculated the family's yearly expenses, taking into account such details as the amount of food consumed and its cost per kilogram:

Consumed
  Bread, 924 kg.; olives, 38 kg.; dairy products, 351 kg.;
  meat and fish, 172 kg.; vegetables and fruits, 448 kg.
Total cost
  132.71 francs. *Of which, in cash:* 99.74 francs.
Expenses
  House, 16.07 francs; clothing, 62.09 francs; for moral
  (chiefly religious) and health needs, 31.69 francs. Of
  this last amount, 14.00 francs were for the church; the
  employer paid 2.26 francs for the doctor.
Other expenses
  Savings for the year, 14.55 francs; taxes, 5.50 francs; interest paid on the loan from the employer (5%), 5.22 francs;
  interest paid for purchases made on credit (20% for loans
  outstanding for a year), 7.01 francs.

The observations of the two Frenchmen have been cited here in detail since their account was the first case where exhaustive data was provided on the budget of a worker's family in the mid-nineteenth century Balkans. Expanded in this fashion, this information discloses such things as the importance of different kinds of revenue in the total income of a family, the relationship between this income and the value of the property, and the relative weight of daily expenses in the life of an urban and specifically a worker's family.

Only such detailed material on specific cases is complete enough to illustrate the various facets of the situation in which direct producers had to live and work, and makes it possible to reconstruct a realistic portrait of working conditions and the living standard in the Balkan lands. As to factory workers per se, the Gümüşgerdan archive is the only extant source that, with its clarity and fullness, throws light on the working conditions of persons employed in a capitalist enterprise for a prolonged period of time.

Some useful information on daily wage rates was published in official Istanbul newspapers around the middle of the nineteenth century. In 1848, according to this source, a master mason had a fixed wage of 13 kuruş a day, a journeyman 12 kuruş, a mason in charge of construction 15 kuruş, and a joiner from 12 to 14 kuruş. Many master builders with various related specialized skills (plasterers, makers of lead domes, painters, etc.) received from 11 to 13 kuruş a day. Common laborers earned from 5 to 8 kuruş a day, and porters 7 kuruş. These wages were laid down by the state to halt wage increases.[13]

But nine years later, when the same newspaper once again published the wages of construction workers, there had been an
increase of 3 kuruş for masons (now at 16 kuruş), 5 kuruş for
painter-plasterers and stonemasons (now at 18 kuruş), and 2
kuruş for common laborers (now 8-10 kuruş).[14]

It is not known exactly how many days a year these builders and others actually worked, but even at their busiest they
could hardly have worked more than 200 days, that is, a full
8 months. Even assuming that they worked 250 days a year, which
roughly equaled a farmer's working days,[15] they could not
have received more than 200 to 300 kuruş a month (at the higher
wage mentioned above). These then were the wages of artisans
and of those who lacked particularly high qualifications but
for whom there was a strong demand, especially for construction
in the capital.[16]

* * *

Finally, a more in-depth analysis of incomes is possible
through a comparison of individuals in different occupations
and of different nationalities by the use of yet another index,
their average income. This approach is aided by dispersion
analysis, which furnishes an alternative answer to the question
of whether or not there existed a cause and effect relationship between the variables studied (without, however, permitting
a quantitative analysis of this link). Thus, a study of the
incomes of non-Muslims classified as independent businessmen,
tradesmen, or agriculturalists (or as salaried state employees)
reveals that individuals in the commercial sector have the
highest average annual income, 1,251 kuruş. The average incomes of all other occupational subgroups fall below the general mean of this study group as a whole (i.e., independent or
salaried non-Muslims): the average annual income of the artisans is 679.2 kuruş, of state employees 625 kuruş, and of agriculturalists 499.1 kuruş. As this calculation demonstrates,
there are essential and nonaccidental differences among the
average incomes of the occupational groups in question. Put
more positively, the occupational variable exercises the critical influence on average income.

A similar situation holds true for Muslims and Armenians.
Here too, those in the commercial sector receive the highest
average income. Only for Jews classified as independent are
the divergences among average incomes of artisans, merchants,
and farmers insignificant. However, these results are undoubtedly due to the smallness of the sample.

As to the hired workers engaged in handicrafts, commerce
or agriculture, or who had no fixed occupation, there are significant differences in average income only for the ethnic
subgroups of non-Muslims and Muslims. For both Christians and

Muslims, hired workers in commerce have the highest average
annual incomes, followed by those engaged in agriculture.
Hired workers with no fixed occupation received the lowest
average income.

Of particular interest here is also the question of average income measured in terms of the ethnic variable. Analysis reveals that the average income of Armenian and Muslim artisans is higher than the general mean, whereas Jewish and Bulgarian artisans have average incomes below the general mean. Differences in average income among the various nationalities classified as independent agriculturalists or as salaried state employees are insignificant. The same holds true for the hired labor that worked in artisan and agricultural production, as well as in the sphere of commerce.

Occupations and
Incomes in the Danubian Vilâyet

21. THE BAZARGIC FAIR

Archival material on the Bazargic fair in the 1860s provides
a more concrete idea of the specific role played by representatives of various nationalities engaged in retail or wholesale
trade in the part of the Balkans being examined here. One of
the unique documents preserved in the Oriental Department of
the Cyril and Methodius National Library in Sofia is a register
of the property--shops, smaller buildings, and vacant lots--
located in the fair grounds of the city of Bazargic.[1] Twenty-
four sheets, each with ten separate columns list information
dated May 23, 1870 (though there are some subsequent entries
adding more precise details). Some of the columns recorded
the type and location of the property, the name of the owner,
its assessed worth, the revenue it produced, and the tax assessment. Other columns recorded such technical information
as the numeration of the property and the entry number for the
government's tax account; some were left blank.

   This information is interesting in several respects, but
perhaps most of all because Balkan historiography has never
yet been able to use such a document, which captures the basic
character of a whole fair as measured by the composition of
those who did business there.[2] True, comparatively full information about the famous Uzundzhovo fair can be found in the
reports of Naiden Gerov, the Bulgarian who in the third quarter
of the nineteenth century served as the Russian consul in Plovdiv,[3] but he dealt in round figures (at least for the number
of shops). Although he described the kinds of goods sold by
various shops, he did not do so in a way that would permit an
analysis of the proprietors involved. Furthermore, the Bazargic register possesses the added advantage that the shops listed
bear a statement of their assessed worth. In assessing shops
to set the tax rate, the governmental commission involved naturally had to consider current market prices, the special features of the structures (size, material, attachments), and especially the revenue realized from the sale of the merchandise
in which their proprietors dealt. The several hundred owners
involved, moreover, many of whom had strong public influence,
would certainly have taken the opportunity to dispute assessments they considered too high.[4]

   The fair itself was made up of several çarşıs--rows of
shops that almost always dealt in the same or kindred goods.[5]
As listed in the register, the Bazargic fair had the following
çarşıs:

Recreational	Large dealers in dry goods
Saddlers (in two places)	Dealers in dry goods[8]
Toptancıs (i.e., wholesalers)	Kerosene dealers
Slipper makers (in two places)	Abacıs
Salt dealers	Cutlers
Grocers[6]	Tobacconists
Tavernkeepers	Dealers in fancy goods
"Braşov goods"[7]	Sweetmakers
Furriers	

* * *

   The register notes only a few shops appraised at a particularly high value, the text explaining that the structures
involved possessed certain special features. Thus, the document mentions a "shop without an extension" valued at 12,500
kuruş (the highest individual assessment in the register).
Three assessments of 20,000 kuruş were each explained with the
comment that it was three shops taken together. Such comments
lead one to assume that assessments were generally made for
single premises and that they took into account the real or
supposed income from the shop's annual turnover.

The total assessed value of the entire fair's property--
748 shops, sheds, and other larger or smaller structures--
amounts to 2,113,850 kuruş. The distribution of these properties by range of assessed value and by çarşı is shown in table
89. These property assessments can also be equated to business investments on the part of their proprietors. A subsequent table (table 90) shows the breakdown of these investments by çarşı and ethnic affiliation of the property owners.
A third table (table 91) is used to break down these investments by çarşı in terms of their proprietors' place of origin.
In addition, a detailed list of the names of all of the larger
shop owners has been given in appendix 4, showing their type
of business, nationality, place of origin, and property holdings. Given this detailed information, there is no need to
describe the individual çarşıs.[9]

The material shows that at the beginning of the 1870s the
Bazargic fair was a fairly developed operation that saw wholesale and retail trade taking place in both domestic and imported
goods. True, the fair served the specific needs of the population of the Bazargic area and of the Dobruja more than those
of the country as a whole. Accordingly, most of its shops
dealt in imported merchandise: dry-goods shops offering imported textiles, grocery shops whose merchandise included such
imported items as coffee, sugar, and tea, the "Braşov" shops
that also sold imported wares, outlets for fancy goods, and so
on. Such shops made up nearly half the fair. Most of these
business properties were small retail shops, but they did include a few dozen essentially wholesale outlets bearing a high
assessment--for example, there were forty-five dry-goods outlets worth over 5,000 kuruş--from which both local merchants
from Bazargic and itinerant peddlers purchased their yearly
stock of goods.

Conversely, none of the shops seems to have dealt in
local goods earmarked for export. There was only a small number of abacı shops, which may indicate that the fair was not visited
by foreign merchants interested in this kind of merchandise
(despite the proximity of the wool-producing Kotel part of the
Balkan Mountains). With only three furrier shops the trade in
fur and leather articles was also rather small. It is possible that trade in these goods and in livestock was conducted
mainly at the slightly earlier fair held in the nearby city of
Tŭrgovishte. Leather articles were somewhat better represented by the saddler's shops. These outlets, almost all
of which were valued below 3,000 kuruş, furnished the population with saddles, reins, and other leather items for
the carts and draft animals that practically every family
possessed. Leather articles were also sold by the even larger
çarşıs of the slipper makers. Slippers were the basic type of

TABLE 89

DISTRIBUTION BY ÇARŞI AND BY RANGE OF ASSESSED VALUE OF BUSINESS PROPERTIES
AT THE BAZARGIC FAIR IN 1870
(IN KURUŞ)

Çarşıs	Ranges of Assessed Worth												Total Number	Total Assessed Value Per Çarşı
	Up to 1,000	1,001- 1,500	1,501- 2,000	2,001- 2,500	2,501- 3,000	3,001- 3,500	3,501- 4,000	4,001- 4,500	4,501- 5,000	5,001- 5,500	5,501- 6,000	Over 6,000		
Recreational	--	1	--	9	--	1	--	--	--	--	--	--	11	27,500
Saddlers	22	6	--	7	10	--	1	--	--	--	--	--	46	82,500
Toptancıs	--	17	--	3	--	--	--	--	9	--	--	--	29	78,000
Slipper makers	34	10	1	3	12	5	14	--	12	--	1	--	92	238,000
Salt dealers	--	--	3	5	10	--	--	--	--	--	--	--	18	48,500
Grocers	35	13	33	5	12	7	13	--	3	--	--	--	121	246,850
Tavern keepers	9	2	3	1	--	1	6	--	3	--	--	.9*	34	123,000
Braşov goods	--	9	10	5	2	6	3	--	11	1	--	--	47	145,500
Furriers	--	--	1	--	2	--	--	--	--	--	--	--	3	8,000
Large dealers in dry goods	--	--	6	--	7	4	2	1	5	--	--	--	25	84,000
Dealers in dry goods	17	28	13	7	14	6	36	--	25	1	13	1	161	526,500
Kerosene dealers	--	--	--	1	--	--	1	2	6	--	1	--	11	51,500
Abacıs	--	--	--	--	--	--	--	--	7	--	--	--	7	35,000
Cutlers	6	--	--	1	12	10	--	1	11	--	--	1†	42	150,000
Tobacconists	--	--	--	10	5	2	9	2	4	3	--	--	35	129,000
Dealers in fancy goods	--	--	16	4	--	--	--	--	--	--	--	1	21	49,500
Sweet makers	4	2	20	10	5	--	--	--	--	--	--	--	41	78,500
Bakers	--	--	--	1	1	1	--	--	--	--	--	--	3	9,000
Coffeeshop keepers	--	--	--	1	--	--	--	--	--	--	--	--	1	2,500
Total	127	88	106	73	92	43	85	6	96	5	15	12	743	2,113,850

SOURCE: NBKM, Oo, Tolbukhin (Bazargic), Meclis-i idare-i kaza, resm-i tapu, May 23, 1870. *Three of these nine were assessed at 20,000 kuruş each. †Assessed at 12,500 kuruş.

footwear, particularly for the area's large and compact Turkish population. The other çarşıs had an essentially similar economic role--to meet the growing needs of a local population that was more and more part of a market economy.

There was thus an entire çarşı of kerosene dealers. The kerosene shops were all assessed at over 4,000 kuruş, which suggests that they did a considerable volume of business. Kerosene lighting, as can be inferred, was becoming rather widespread in the interior of the country.

It is unfortunate that the register fails to mention the origin of the merchandise sold at the fair. The only indication of definite commercial relations with the outside world is the existence of the separate Braşov çarşı. The Braşov-produced wooden articles for household use (chests, carts, etc.), as well as the textiles imported through that city, must have arrived in large quantities if they were able to give their name to some fifty shops.

The register lists a total of 210 different proprietors, including 72 Bulgarians, 96 Turks, 29 Armenians, and 12 Jews. Expressed in percentages, Bulgarians make up 34% of the total, the Turks 46%, the Armenians 14%, and the Jews 6%. But it is the relative assessed value of their property holdings--in other words, the size of their business investments--that indicates the true role played at the fair by representatives of various nationalities (see table 90). In this respect Bulgarian investments account for 42% of the total (838,350 kuruş), Turkish holdings 36.5% (772,650 kuruş), Armenian investments 18.5% (383,850 kuruş), and Jewish holdings 3% (69,000 kuruş).

The nature of the Bulgarian investment capital here is interesting. If there are certain grounds for believing that some of the Turkish capital invested in fair property might have still been coming from feudal or semifeudal sources, this possibility did not exist for the Bulgarians. Their capital was connected chiefly with new economic endeavors that developed rapidly and extensively in the nineteenth century. This relationship is shown both by the distribution of investments by ethnic affiliation of proprietors and by the breakdown of these proprietors by their place of origin.

The distribution of investments by ethnic affiliation also illustrates how owners from different ethnic groups had a preference for certain economic activities. Very characteristic in this regard are the çarşıs that dealt in dry goods. For this major component of the fair, Armenians surpass all other ethnic groups both in the absolute amount of the capital involved and in the relative size of their investments (such shops account for 64% of their capital as opposed to the 22% of the Turkish and 21% of the Bulgarian investment). The small Turkish lead over Bulgarian capital[10] becomes more significant

TABLE 90

DISTRIBUTION BY ÇARŞI AND BY ETHNIC AFFILIATION
OF OWNERS OF CAPITAL INVESTED IN SHOPS
AT THE BAZARGIC FAIR IN 1870
(IN KURUŞ)

Çarşı	From Bulgarians	From Turks	From Armenians	From Jews	Total
Recreational	7,500	20,000	-------	------	27,500
Saddlers	-------	73,500	-------	9,000	82,500
Toptançıs	25,000	33,000	5,000	15,000	78,000
Slipper makers	57,500	101,000	73,500	6,000	238,000
Salt dealers	24,000	24,500	-------	------	48,500
Grocers	138,350	101,150	7,350	------	246,850
Tavern keepers	105,000	12,000	6,000	------	123,000
Braşov goods	121,500	24,000	-------	------	145,500
Furriers	-------	-------	8,000	------	8,000
Large dealers in dry goods	-------	57,500	27,000	------	84,500
Dealers in dry goods	188,000	108,000	226,500	4,000	526,500
Kerosene dealers	29,000	7,500	10,000	5,000	51,500
Abacıs	35,000	-------	-------	------	35,000
Cutlers	125,000	25,000	-------	------	150,000
Tobacconists	26,000	74,000	12,500	16,500	129,000
Dealers in fancy goods	-------	42,000	-------	7,500	49,500
Sweet makers	-------	64,500	8,000	6,000	78,500
Bakers	6,500	2,500	-------	------	9,000
Coffee house keepers	-------	2,500	-------	------	2,500
Total	888,350	772,650	383,850	69,000	2,113,850

SOURCE: NBKM, Oo, Tolbukhin (Bazargic), Meclis-i idare-i kaza,
resmi-i tapu, May 23, 1870.

when the related çarşı for fine goods is considered in conjunction with dry-goods shops. These results are explainable,
given the complicated route that Bulgarian commercial capital
had to travel to penetrate trade in imported textiles and fancy
goods. For a long time trade in these goods--which were major

import items in the Ottoman Empire--had been monopolized by representatives of the European states and by Jews living in the empire; later, Armenians, Greeks, and Turks also became actively involved. Bulgarians, on the other hand, were slow in gaining a role in this trade. Thus, even in trade conducted in an inland region located far from the major commercial centers, the commercial strata of other peoples still predominated, and Bulgarians, despite their considerable participation in this area of commerce, continued to lag behind Armenians and Turks.

For the grocers' çarşıs, however, the Bulgarians had to a large extent succeeded in taking the upper hand. It seems that Bulgarian commercial capital was predominant in imported goods only when it could depend on a particularly favorable concurrence of circumstances. This was the case with the shops dealing in goods from Braşov, which housed a large Bulgarian colony. A similar picture held true in a new area of trade, kerosene supply. The Bulgarians had more investments in this activity than the representatives of all other ethnic groups taken together.

As for trade in local goods, Turks contested the leading role of Bulgarians, thanks to their significant investments in the çarşıs dealing in slippers and saddlery. The çarşıs dealing in recreational items and sweets were predominantly Turkish properties, as were the larger part of the çarşıs of tobacconists and toptancıs. Armenians also had a lot of money tied up in the slipper-makers' çarşıs and somewhat less in the tobacconists' and others. Bulgarians, however, held total control of the çarşıs of the tavernkeepers and furriers, and it was because of these holdings that Bulgarians surpassed representatives of other ethnic goods in the total sum of capital invested in fair properties. Bulgarians also had money invested in çarşıs for salt, slippers, wholesale goods, and tobacco. The few abacı shops were in Bulgarian hands.

* * *

Table 91 distributes the investments in fair properties in terms of the proprietors' places of origin. As can be seen, Bazargic itself accounts for nearly 30% of the total investments involved. Next in line comes Shumen with 13% of the total investments, followed by Varna (8%), Silistra (7.5%), and Istanbul (7%). Taken together, the other 18 localities account for 18% of the investments (18% is also the amount of the investments made by owners whose places of origin are not stated or clear).

This breakdown reconfirms the finding that the Bazargic fair was largely of local significance, engaging primarily the capital of merchants and other investors drawn from a relatively

TABLE 91

DISTRIBUTION BY PROPRIETORS' PLACE OF ORIGIN AND BY ÇARŞI OF CAPITAL INVESTED IN SHOPS AT THE BAZARGIC FAIR IN 1870 (IN KURUŞ)

Çarşı / City	Recreational	Saddlers	Toptancıs	Slipper makers	Salt dealers	Grocers	Tavern keepers	Braşov goods	Furriers	Dry goods Large dealers	Dealers
Bazargic	------	56,000	25,500	92,000	16,000	27,000	41,000	42,000	------	27,000	167,000
Shumen	10,000	15,000	25,000	91,000	------	4,000	------	2,500	8,000	10,500	87,500
Varna	------	------	------	------	2,500	65,500	18,000	------	------	------	40,000
Silistra	------	------	------	39,500	30,000	------	------	67,000	------	------	------
Istanbul	------	------	5,000	------	------	15,850	------	------	------	25,000	29,500
Balchik	------	------	------	------	------	------	20,000	------	------	------	18,000
Razgrad	------	------	------	------	------	29,000	24,000	------	------	------	------
Ruse	------	9,000	10,000	------	------	------	------	------	------	------	4,000
Türgovishte	------	------	------	------	------	4,000	------	------	------	------	8,000
Türnovo	2,500	------	------	------	------	------	------	7,500	------	------	------
Liaskovets	------	------	------	------	------	------	------	26,500	------	------	------
Pobeda*	------	------	------	------	------	17,000	------	------	------	------	4,500
Oreshak†	------	------	------	------	------	------	20,000	------	------	------	------
Tulcea	------	------	------	------	------	------	------	------	------	------	------
Medgidia	------	------	------	------	------	10,000	------	------	------	------	3,000
Didymoteikhon	------	------	------	------	------	------	------	------	------	------	12,000
Burgas	------	------	------	------	------	------	------	------	------	------	10,000
Edirne	------	------	------	------	------	------	------	------	------	------	------
Kotel	------	------	------	------	------	7,500	------	------	------	------	------
Obrochishto**	------	------	------	------	------	6,000	------	------	------	------	------
Niš	5,000	------	------	------	------	------	------	------	------	------	------
Bitolj	------	------	------	------	------	4,000	------	------	------	------	------
Pleven	------	------	4,500	------	------	------	------	------	------	------	------
Not stated or unclear	10,000	2,500	11,000	15,500	------	57,000	------	------	------	22,000	143,000
Total	27,500	82,500	78,000	238,000	48,500	246,850	123,000	145,000	8,000	84,500	526,500

Çarşı / City	Kerosene dealers	Abacıs	Cutlers	Tobacconists	Fancy goods dealers	Sweet makers	Coffee shop keepers & bakers	Total
Bazargic	10,000	------	40,000	25,500	11,000	21,500	5,500	607,000
Shumen	10,000	------	------	5,000	------	2,000	------	270,500
Varna	------	------	------	34,000	------	------	2,500	162,500
Silistra	------	20,000	------	------	------	------	------	156,500
Istanbul	2,500	------	25,000	------	31,000	14,000	------	147,850
Balchik	------	------	22,500	------	------	------	3,500	64,000
Razgrad	------	------	------	------	------	------	------	53,000
Ruse	------	------	------	13,500	------	6,000	------	42,500
Türgovishte	------	------	------	------	------	27,000	------	39,000
Türnovo	19,000	------	------	------	------	------	------	29,000
Liaskovets	------	------	------	------	------	------	------	26,500
Pobeda*	------	------	------	------	------	------	------	21,500
Oreshak†	------	------	------	------	------	------	------	20,000
Tulcea	------	15,000	------	------	------	------	------	15,000
Medgidia	------	------	------	------	------	------	------	13,000
Didymoteikhon	------	------	------	------	------	------	------	12,000
Burgas	------	------	------	------	------	------	------	10,000
Edirne	------	------	------	------	7,500	------	------	7,500
Kotel	------	------	------	------	------	------	------	7,500
Obrochishto**	------	------	------	------	------	------	------	6,000
Niš	------	------	------	------	------	------	------	5,000
Bitolj	------	------	------	------	------	------	------	4,000
Pleven	------	------	------	------	------	------	------	1,500
Not stated or unclear	10,000	------	62,500	51,000	------	8,000	------	392,500
Total	51,500	35,000	150,000	129,000	49,500	78,500	11,500	2,113,850

SOURCE: NBKM, Oo, Tolbukhin (Bazargic), Meclis-i idare-i kaza, resm-i tapu, May 23, 1870. *Then called Gelincik, village in the area of Tolbukhin. †Then called Cevizli, village in the area of Varna. **Then called Teke, village in the area of Balchik.

restricted territory with the city of Bazargic as its center.
The same conclusion finds support in the decisive preponderance
of investments shown in the table, made by proprietors who resided in the interior of the country as opposed to those who
came from port cities. Even assuming that the investments from
Varna, Balchik, Silistra, and Ruse did not simply reflect their
proximity (which was the decisive factor), but rather their
intermediary role as important ports, these cities, together
with Istanbul and all the other ports, account for only about
30% of the investments, that is, an amount equal to the sum
contributed by Bazargic alone.

Differences existed not only in the volume of investments,
but also in their distribution by commercial activity. Such a
relationship is most difficult to establish for Bazargic itself,
since all of the large and small merchants and producers in
that city tried to take part in the fair regardless of their
area of activity. But even for this city one can note certain
areas of the fair with a prevailing amount of local capital
investment. Bazargic proprietors, for example, have an undisputed predominance in the saddlers' çarşı, for they account for
68% of the total capital invested in this type of shop. The
dry-goods çarşıs represent another significant concentration
of Bazargic activity: here this city's proprietors account
for 32% of the capital, twice as much as the following group
(proprietors from Shumen). Bazargic also stands far out in
front in the tavernkeepers' çarşı, where this source represents
33.5% of the total capital invested (as opposed to 19.5% for
its closest rival), and in the cutlers' çarşı, where the investments of Bazargic proprietors account for 27% of the total
(with the closest other group claiming 17% of the total). For
another two çarşıs, those of the toptancıs and slipper makers,
Bazargic investment is equal to that originating in Shumen.
When combined, the investments from Bazargic and Shumen account
for 80% of the total in the slipper makers' çarşı and 64% of
the total in the çarşı of the toptancıs. Bazargic investments
are much smaller in the other çarşıs.

As is true for Bazargic proprietors, business investors
from Shumen are also well represented in the çarşış for
leather goods (the saddlers, the slipper makers, and a few
furriers), as well as in shops for dry goods.

The commercial investments of proprietors from Varna fall
chiefly into the çarşıs for grocers and tobacconists. For
the former, Varna investors far outdistance proprietors from
Razgrad, Bazargic, and Istanbul. The relative participation
of property owners from Bazargic and Ruse is more marked in
the tobacconist shops.

The çarşı for Braşov goods is dominated by merchants from
Silistra, a city that was the nearest reception point on the
Danube for merchandise being sent to this area from Braşov.

Besides Silistrians, local merchants from Bazargic and persons
from Tŭrnovo and Liaskovets, which throughout the nineteenth
century had sent many migrants to Braşov were also participants.

The salt-dealers' outlets were essentially monopolized
by proprietors from Istanbul, but there was a certain amount
of activity here by merchants from Silistra, another place
where salt was imported. A large percentage of the salt dealers
came from Bazargic, individuals who were buyers and middlemen
in the trade in a product that was in great demand for that
area's developed livestock husbandry.

The largest number of investors in the çarşı of kerosene
dealers were from Tŭrnovo, with proprietors from this city
furnishing as much business investment as merchants from Bazargic and Shumen put together. The role of merchants from Tŭrnovo in this area was probably linked with the import of pe-
troleum from Romania, a country with which the people of Tŭrnovo had developed strong commercial ties.

This picture of the fair would be incomplete without a
discussion of the proprietors themselves, a discussion that is
also necessary for determining the precise character of the
commercial investments involved. For this reason data have
been summarized on proprietors who owned fair property valued
at 10,000 kuruş or more (see appendix 4).   Although the cutoff
point is an arbitrary one, it does make it possible to isolate
the well-to-do proprietors, both merchants and producers.   In
most cases these individuals were persons who maintained shops
at the fair or who rented them out to others since they also
possessed their own workshops, shops, and storehouses in their
principal place of residence.

An analysis of the list shows that about 50% of the Bulgarian and Armenian proprietors account for about 80% of all
of the investment capital contributed by property owners of
those nationalities. The coincidence of these two elements--
the number of wealthy proprietors among the Bulgarians and the
Armenians and the amount of their property investments--reveals
the predictable socioeconomic differentiation of more prosperous elements as measured by their participation in the fair.
There was no difference among the largest proprietors themselves in terms of the size of their holdings, for the upper
ranges of investment also coincide. Thus, two Bulgarians and
an Armenian each possessed fair property worth 50,000 kuruş,
three Armenians and one Bulgarian each had properties worth
30,000 kuruş, and another four Bulgarians and an Armenian each
possessed fair property valued at higher than 20,000 kuruş.

A somewhat different situation holds for Turkish proprietors. There were a smaller number of wealthier property owners
but about 16% of the proprietors account for 75% of all Turkish
holdings. Most of the Turks taking part in the fair were small
producers and merchants, and they were spread about the çarşıs

with a few persons in each. In sharp contrast, however, stood
a group of ·about ten proprietors distinguished by both the
large size of their holdings and by the nature of their activity.
Half of the wealthier Turks owned several shops each in various
çarşıs. Molla Bekir, whose property was assessed at four times
the value of the biggest Bulgarian or Armenian proprietor's,
was a typical representative of the Turkish propertied elite.
His property holdings totaled 206,500 kuruş, and by renting
out his premises at the fair he obtained considerable income.
Other large Turkish proprietors fit the same model. The impressive total value of their property resulted not so much
from the possession of highly valued individual shops, but from
their control of about a hundred sheds and stalls.

Here we have the basic difference between the largest
investors of Turkish origin and the Bulgarians and Armenians.
Among the latter there was only one Armenian from Bazargic,
Artin, the son of Kirkor, who had property worth 50,000 kuruş
and for whom everything said about Molla Bekir and the other
large Turkish investors would also be true. Unlike the Turks
and the one Armenian, who by and large dealt in rental income,
the other large proprietors among the Bulgarians and Armenians
were simply businessmen.

* * *

In summary, the Bazargic fair was an operation involving
disparate groups: local small commodity producers and merchants, more prosperous suppliers and merchants from neighboring cities, some successful tavernkeepers who were trying
to branch out into other activities, and about ten individuals
of various nationalities who invested considerable amounts of
capital in fair properties. The great bulk of the fair's customers were peasants who purchased goods directly or, subsequently, through the smaller or bigger suppliers from Bazargic
itself.

A report from Bazargic after the closing of the fair in
1872, published in the Istanbul newspaper *Turtsiia*, described
the relationship between the merchants and the peasant consumers. The merchants had been greatly alarmed by a four-month
drought that might have meant that the peasants would be unable
to pay their debts. The rains came, however, and the merchants
could rest assured. But despite the assurances that the fair
had been a success, the correspondent did not fail to note an
essential difference between that year's fair and the one held
the previous year: "The absence of the peasants." As described
by the correspondent, merchants who had been lending money had
been unable for the past four years to collect these debts,
and they were now refusing to grant further loans. This re-

fusal made it impossible for the peasants to make purchases at
the fair as they had done in previous years.[11] As suggested
by this report, the peasants were indeed one of the fair's
major customers. The merchants participating in the fair depended on them, and sold them much of their goods on credit.

* * *

Finally, one might want to compare the Bazargic fair with
the one held in Uzundzhovo, situated in southern Bulgaria along
the main thoroughfare linking Istanbul to Central Europe and
also connected with the Aegean and Greece by the Maritsa and
Arda rivers. Naiden Gerov, the Russian consul in Plovdiv, divided the outlets of the Uzundzhovo fair into three categories:
those trading in imported goods, those trading in local goods,
and those trading in both. The first category comprised 200
outlets for furs (with a total assessed worth of 100,000 kuruş),
210 shops for European cotton textiles (with a total value of
about 2,000,000 kuruş),[12] 32 shops for broadcloth (valued,
according to the worth of their merchandise, from 100,000 to
400,000 kuruş), and 40 shops for grocery items such as coffee,
tea, sugar, and so on (worth from 120,000 to 450,000 kuruş).
The Uzundzhovo fair thus comprised 482 shops dealing in imported goods, valued at between 2,320,000 and 2,950,000 kuruş.
     The çarşıs offering local goods consisted of 56 shops
for aba goods, either rolls of cloth or clothing (valued at
1,400,000 kuruş), 60 shops for woolen braid (valued at 2,000,000
kuruş), 67 shops for silk fabrics and cord (900,000 kuruş),
12 shops for bags made of goat's wool (200,000 kuruş), 6 shops
for Pirot carpets (about 25,000 kuruş), 5 shops for copper
vessels (800,000 kuruş), and an indeterminate number of tobacconists selling up to 50,000 okka of tobacco worth 750,000
kuruş (with the value of the shops themselves undetermined).
In all, there were more than 206 shops trading in local goods
and jointly valued at more than 5,325,000 kuruş. The 28 hardware shops--assessed at 700,000 kuruş--dealt in both local and
imported goods.[13]
     Unlike the Bazargic fair, therefore, the Uzundzhovo fair
had a pronounced emphasis on trade in local commodities. The
outlets dealing in local goods were at least two times more
valuable than those engaged in the sale of imported merchandise. This fact, combined with the difference in the size of
the property values, illustrates the clear contrast between
the character of a national fair of the mid-nineteenth century
with a local and more restricted fair of the same period. In
ways that were simply not evident in Bazargic, the well-known
fairs of southern Bulgaria of the eighteenth century and first
half of the nineteenth century had foreign and local merchants

converging by caravans to exchange their goods and carry them off, the foreigners going either to Istanbul or Salonika, or overland to Central Europe, while local merchants shipped their goods to warehouses in Plovdiv, Sliven, and Tatar Pazardzhik.

Occupations and
Incomes in the Danubian Vilâyet

22. URBAN REAL ESTATE

Census information on the total value of urban real estate
and on its owners can supplement the general description of the
Balkan city that has been attempted in the preceding chapters.
Of the two kinds of data used here, the first comprises the
general totals of the assessed value of all taxable urban real
estate including cultivated and uncultivated urban plots of
land in the cities of the Danubian vilâyet. This material,
when combined with other data on the amount of dönüm of agricultural property, on the number of houses and other covered
buildings, and on the amount of rents that were collected, permits a comparative analysis of the cities in question. The
second kind of data analyzed here--information listed on a
name-by-name basis for the property of some 4,500 urban resi-
dents--has been used to determine the types of contemporary
houses and commercial properties.
    Let us examine first the total value of urban real estate

in the various cities of the vilâyet as based on the 1866 census (see table 92). If these data were arranged in terms of

TABLE 92

REAL ESTATE ASSESSMENTS AND RENTS IN THE CITIES
OF THE DANUBIAN VILÂYET
(CENSUS OF 1866)

| City | Real Estate | | | |
	Total Value	Rents	Value per Taxable Resident	Rent per Taxable Resident
Ruse	48,345,540	1,006,830	4676.5	97.4
Shumen	29,636,475	544,790	2946.0	54.2
Razgrad	17,014,905	134,340	3385.0	26.7
Tŭrgovishte	11,909,935	197,065	2475.0	41.0
Svishtov	28,187,050	212,185	4649.0	35.0
Pleven	34,444,514	201,380	4419.9	25.8
Nikopol	6,507,450	86,640	2279.3	30.8
Silistra	14,791,676	199,180	3905.9	52.6
Turtucaia	7,102,900	54,975	2914.6	22.6
Varna	44,985,762	1,472,791	5968.6	195.4
Provadiia	3,350,905	61,590	2542.4	46.7
Balchik	9,912,256	599,520	4582.8	277.0
Mangalia	900,481	14,080	2867.8	44.8
Bazargic	12,984,968	278,908	2299.0	49.4
Tŭrnovo	23,963,550	322,041	3670.3	49.3
Sevlievo	11,936,625	33,535	3012.7	8.5
Lovech	10,901,975	133,901	2161.8	26.6
Gabrovo	9,803,025	39,315	2964.3	11.9
Omurtag	6,050,425	21,661	2487.8	8.9
Vidin	23,888,850	602,430	3117.0	78.6
Lom	8,222,325	142,175	2728.9	47.2
Oriakhovo	2,631,875	52,055	1907.3	37.7
Vratsa	15,094,350	80,425	2313.6	12.3
Berkovitsa	3,355,150	46,400	1144.3	15.8
Belogradchik	1,388,275	11,840	2165.7	18.5
Kula	4,077,200	10,575	2017.4	5.2
Sofia	10,498,775	249,570	1550.7	36.9
Kiustendil	5,096,950	83,010	1499.9	24.4
Samokov	9,916,125	140,180	1751.0	24.8
Dupnitsa	5,126,875	86,995	1448.7	24.6
Radomir	1,513,175	12,795	1670.1	14.1
Zlatitsa	2,484,025	2,355	1903.6	1.8
Ikhtiman	2,828,400	4,925	2118.7	3.7
Orkhanie	2,099,475	4,250	1999.5	4.0
Total	430,957,242	7,144,707	3087.8	51.2

SOURCE: NBKM, Oo, Cetvel-i mizan-i vergi ve nüfus, Rs 98/8.

the total value of urban real estate on a city-by-city basis,
there would result a ladder of cities whose lowest rung would
correspond to a total real-estate value of about 1,000,000
kuruş and whose top rung would represent about 50,000,000 kuruş.
Breaking down the data in this way reveals characteristic differences among cities in terms of the absolute value of their
real estate. Also, one can distinguish several groupings of
cities.

Although only in Mangalia does the value of the property
fall below 1,000,000 kuruş, 18 cities are in the range of total
property values between 1,000,000 and 10,000,000 kuruş, or
52.8% of the total number of cities involved. They are Provadiia, Oriakhovo, Berkovitsa, Belogradchik, Radomir, Zlatitsa,
Ikhtiman, Orkhanie, Kula, Nikopol, Turtucaia, Balchik, Gabrovo,
Omurtag, Lom, Kiustendil, Samokov, and Dupnitsa. These cities
were either situated on the slopes of the Balkan Mountains or
were ports.

Eight cities (or 23.4% of the total) had real estate
valued at between 10,000,000 and 20,000,000 kuruş: Sofia,
Tŭrgovishte, Silistra, Bazargic, Sevlievo, Lovech, Razgrad, and
Vratsa. The cities whose total property assessment ranged
between 20,000,000 and 30,000,000 kuruş were Tŭrnovo, Vidin,
Shumen, and Svishtov (11.8%). Three cities (9%)--Pleven, Varna,
and Ruse--fall into the range of over 30,000,000 kuruş. The
last two groups take in the centers of sancaks.

A distribution based on property value per taxable resident produces results that generally coincide with the breakdown described above. On this per capita basis, real-estate
value fluctuates from 1,100 to 5,000 kuruş, and only for Varna
does it reach almost 6,000 kuruş. Balchik also shows up among
the cities with a high per capita property assessment. What
explains these relatively high values for Varna and Balchik
was the special development of the port cities, which produced
a greater demand for business construction and especially for
costly commercial warehouses, the *mağazas*.

What has been said is also supported by the distribution
of total rental income per taxable resident. Most of the cities
where per capita rental income is over 50 kuruş are ports:
Ruse (97.4 kuruş), Vidin (78.6 kuruş), Silistra (52.6 kuruş),
and again, Varna (195.4 kuruş) and Balchik (277 kuruş), which
in this respect far surpass the other cities. The one city
here that is not a port is Shumen (54.2 kuruş).

* * *

A closer examination of urban real estate is possible
through the analysis of other data that are available on a
name-by-name basis for several thousand property owners. These
data pertain to eleven cities in all. (For the six cities

for which there is an overlap with the material just discussed
--Varna, Shumen, Silistra, Bazargic, Lom, and Provadiia--the
information on individual property owners represents anywhere
from 20% to more than 60% of their total real-estate value).[1]
The urban property listed in these individual records has been
grouped into several categories by type (see table 93). The
column for "Houses" includes all properties termed as such in
the documents regardless of the actual property assessment.
Furthermore, to be as precise as possible in what is included
here, the dwellings called *zemliks* and *odas* in the registers
have been placed in the column for "Others." In most cases
odas were special buildings containing several rooms and meant
to accommodate unskilled workers and seasonal laborers, and
considering these buildings apart from houses does not really
invalidate a determination of the breakdown by value of different kinds of urban property. The same is true for the zemlik
--the Slavic term used in Turkish documents--a dwelling of
little actual value that was dug out of the earth. "Agricultural Property" includes vineyards, fields, orchards, and un-
sown land; "Commercial Property," artisan and merchant shops,
as well as such properties as bakeries, coffeehouses, taverns, inns, storehouses, and mills. The column for "Other
Property" encompasses courtyards, vacant lots, stables, several bathhouses, and the zemliks and odas mentioned above.
        Certain differences arise from the comparison of indi-
vidual cities. Whereas in Shumen houses account for 71.1% of
the total value of property, in Varna they constitute only
28.8%; and, conversely, the value of commercial properties in
Varna is nearly three times larger than it is in Shumen. The
relative share of agricultural land values in both cities is
equal. An even larger percentage of the value of commercial
property can be observed in Constanţa. For the remaining
cities--Silistra, Lom, Provadiia, and Bazargic--there are only
slight deviations in one direction or another from the over-all
mean percentage of house values in terms of the total value of
urban property, but there are certain differences in the relative percentage of their other types of property. Such differences will be discussed as part of the following individual
analysis of different types of property, starting with houses.

                              * * *

        The assessment of houses and other real estate, as well
as the determination of what constituted the taxable revenue
of that property, was entrusted to specially trained officials
of the Turkish administration. These assessors were guided by
accepted rules; otherwise, each time the assessors produced an
arbitrarily low assessment they would have provoked the opposition of higher state authorities, whereas assessments that
were too high would have led to complaints. Since such a trans-

TABLE 93

DISTRIBUTION OF REAL ESTATE IN ELEVEN CITIES OF THE
DANUBIAN VILÂYET, CENSUS OF 1866
(IN KURUŞ)

City	Houses		Type of Real Estate — Agricultural Property		Commercial Property		Other Property		Total	
	Value	Percentage	Value	Percentage	Value	Percentage	Value	Percentage	Value	Percentage
Varna	2,598,780	29.5	754,545	8.6	4,934,972	56.0	519,725	5.9	8,808,022	100.0
Shumen	8,166,125	71.1	924,980	8.1	2,253,975	19.6	136,875	1.2	11,482,655	100.0
Silistra	4,874,300	53.4	990,560	10.9	2,917,725	32.0	336,025	3.7	9,118,610	100.0
Bazargic	1,751,850	46.1	305,990	0.8	1,551,800	40.8	192,975	5.1	3,802,615	100.0
Lom	1,883,745	52.8	3,000	0.1	1,610,675	45.1	71,450	2.0	3,568,870	100.0
Constanţa	350,500	25.2	------	---	1,010,650	72.7	29,250	2.1	1,390,400	100.0
Provadiia	396,425	49.8	100,855	12.7	276,750	34.8	21,300	2.7	795,330	100.0
Tulcea	548,800	43.0	75,040	5.9	638,750	50.0	14,600	1.1	1,277,190	100.0
Macin	44,250	27.3	17,625	10.8	91,000	56.0	9,600	5.9	162,475	100.0
Bababag	157,575	31.5	74,210	14.8	213,900	42.7	55,075	11.0	500,760	100.0
Medgidia	73,000	24.0	------	---	229,300	75.4	1,750	0.6	304,050	100.0
Total	20,846,050	50.5	3,246,805	7.9	15,729,497	38.2	1,388,625	3.4	41,210,977	100.0

SOURCE: NBKM, Oo, Cetvel-i mizan-i vergi ve nüfus, Rs 98/8.

action would be subject to taxes and duties, it can be assumed
that a purchase price registered at the time of a sale was
closest to the assessment as entered in the tax records. Thus,
to examine houses more closely, it has seemed appropriate to
use certain other documents, specifically the records on house
purchases in Ruse as recorded in the kadı registers of that
city (the sole such registers preserved for this region).[2]

The records of house sales suggest that assessment principally involved the number of rooms, the presence of additional
structures in the courtyard, and various other conveniences or
additions (such as baths, pantries, or a fountain). However
difficult it may be to draw distinctions on the basis of such
data, an effort will be made to indicate the differences that
occur in the transition from one assessment range to another.

In examining the material from Ruse it turns out that
among the houses assessed and sold at prices ranging from a
few hundred to 2,000 kuruş are those containing two rooms and
a courtyard, and sometimes a kitchen or cellar. Where a higher
value is involved--up to 5,000 kuruş--the houses usually have
three and four rooms. The incidence of such cases gradually
rises, and houses with three and four rooms constitute almost
half of all of the houses whose purchase price was between
4,000 and 5,000 kuruş. Meanwhile, all the two-roomed houses
sold at these higher prices always included kitchens, cellars,
or a covered courtyard.

More than one-third of the total number of houses priced
at from 5,000 to 6,000 kuruş continue to be houses of two rooms
with two additional features (a cellar and a kitchen; a cellar
and a pantry, etc.).

Some cases of higher selling prices might also be mentioned. In 1860, for example, a four-room house with a courtyard, cellar, kitchen, stable, and hayloft was sold for 6,700
kuruş;[3] in 1869 a two-room house with a courtyard and kitchen
was sold, together with a coffeeshop and a confectionary shop,
for 10,000 kuruş.[4] Priced at 16,500 kuruş was a two-story
house with a courtyard. The top floor contained four rooms
and a kitchen, and the lower story had a shop, storeroom, and
a place for straw.[5] In 1870 a house with a cellar, four rooms,
a guest room, a kitchen, and an inner part containing an additional five rooms, a pantry, a kitchen, and a courtyard,
sold for 35,000 kuruş.[6] In 1869, 68,000 kuruş was paid to
purchase a large two-story residence. The upper floor had six
rooms and a pantry and the ground floor contained four rooms,
a kitchen, a pantry, a bathroom with a dressing room, a storeroom with another room attached, a terrace, a kitchen, a storeroom for wood, a fountain, and an orchard. In addition there
was another wing with two rooms upstairs and three rooms down-
stairs, a stable, a place for straw, a grain bin, a room for
carts, and a courtyard.[7]

Among all the documents drawn from the kadı registers and tax receipts there are only two with notes about the size of the house. These data are included here by way of illustration. One item concerns a certain Nedelcho of Silistra, the son of Nedelcho, who owned a house worth 8,250 kuruş. Nedelcho sold four parts of the house and kept another (valued at 1,900 kuruş) for himself. A note written in Bulgarian on the back of the tax receipt names the four buyers. One of them was a certain Georgi who bought an area "144 [square] arshin, 8 wide and 18 long." Another was a man named Gospodin, who also bought 144 square arshin. The third buyer was Mino, who purchased 91 square arshin (7 by 13 arshin), and the last was Vlaicho, who purchased an area of 104 square arshin. Per square arshin, the assessed value of the house was 15.3 kuruş. In all, Nedelcho sold 483 square arshin of space for 6,300 kuruş, an average of 13 kuruş per square arshin. For the part he retained, the assessed value was 18 kuruş per square arshin.[8]

The second example concerns an ironsmith of Silistra named Rusi, the son of Iorgaki. He owned a house valued at 1,000 kuruş for which he received 125 kuruş in rent. Later he sold parts of the house for 750 kuruş. The back of the document in question contains, in Bulgarian, the following note: "The house of Rusi--12 arshin long, 2.5 arshin wide. The part fronting the street is 17 arshin long and 1 arshin wide."[9] It is difficult to know whether these 47 square arshins comprised the entire space of the house or whether they represented the part that was sold for 750 kuruş. Depending on this consideration, the average value per square arshin was either 16 or 21 kuruş.

The examples provided above indicate that houses valued at 5,000 kuruş or above had many rooms, various service areas, and adjoining structures. Houses valued at between 2,000 and 5,000 kuruş had between three and four rooms, or they had two rooms and some other addition. Houses valued below 2,000 kuruş usually had two rooms and a courtyard. The amount of square arshin served as the basis of the assessment.

Based on the admittedly limited number of property transfers where the property is described, and the relationship between the type and value of the houses, tax receipts have been used to group 4,144 houses by their assessed value range (see table 94).

The 4,144 houses belonged to 3,532 owners. Only 15% of the individuals for whom information is available lived in rented houses. Of course, the number of people without their own homes was actually larger, since individuals without real estate were not recorded in the documents.

As suggested by these data, houses worth up to 5,000 kuruş made up the basic part of available housing, with such properties representing 71.4% of the total number of houses included in the sample. In terms of value, however, they comprise 36.1% of the total. Among the houses priced below 5,000 kuruş, the largest subgroup is made up of the houses worth between 2,000 and 5,000 kuruş.

TABLE 94

DISTRIBUTION OF A GROUP OF 4,144 HOUSES BY PRICE RANGE
(IN KURUŞ)

Price Range	Number of Houses	Total Value	Percentage of Total Number	Percentage of Total Value
Up to 1,000	636	526,020	15.3	2.5
1,001-2,000	742	1,286,855	17.9	6.2
2,001-5,000	1,582	5,710,075	38.2	27.4
5,001-10,000	780	5,741,050	18.8	27.5
Over 10,000	404	7,582,050	9.8	36.4
Total	4,144	20,846,050	100.0	100.0

To relate housing to the property and social characteristics of the urban population, a breakdown has been provided on the average value of houses by occupational categories (see table 95). The average value of the houses of general workers and hired artisans stands at about 850 kuruş lower than the value of farmers' houses, and about 1,400-1,500 kuruş below the value of the houses of independent artisans and government employees. Using an average valuation of 15 kuruş per square arshin, these differences would imply some 40 to 70 square meters in living space. The houses of merchants have an average value twice as high as artisans' homes. There are also differences among these occupational groups in terms of the ownership of more than one house. In the case of artisans, 11.6% of the houses were owned by individuals already registered once before as homeowners; for merchants, on the other hand, the incidence of such cases rises to 21.6%--that is, nearly twice as much--while the incidence of 5% for farmers is only half as much as for artisans. For government employees, the incidence of ownership of more than one house is 14.5%.

Several noteworthy differences also crop up in the study of the ethnic variable (see table 96). As implied by the breakdown of the material, the local Bulgarian and Turkish population, which jointly comprised 85% of the total population, possessed housing on the average less valuable than the residences owned by the not very large groups of Greeks, Armenians, and Jews.

TABLE 95

DISTRIBUTION OF A GROUP OF 4,144 HOUSES
BY OCCUPATION OF OWNER

Occupation	Number of Persons	Number of Houses	Total Value	Average Value per House
Artisans	824	932	4,461,200	4,787
Agriculturalists	218	229	972,250	4,246
Merchants	207	264	2,490,950	9,435
Hired artisans	100	113	379,950	3,362
General workers	23	23	78,600	3,417
Government employees	207	242	1,181,500	4,882
Not stated	1,953	2,341	11,281,600	4,814
Total	3,523	4,144	20,846,050	5,030

TABLE 96

DISTRIBUTION OF A GROUP OF 4,144 HOUSES
BY ETHNIC IDENTITY OF OWNER

Ethnic Group	Number of Houses	Value of Houses Kuruş	Percentage	Average Value of House
Turks	2,577	11,002,870	52.8	4,269
Bulgarians	1,118	6,787,230	32.5	6,070
Greeks	143	1,340,750	6.4	9,376
Jews	74	567,650	2.7	7,671
Armenians	62	556,250	2.7	8,971
Others	117	344,350	1.7	2,943
Not stated	53	246,950	1.2	4,656
Total	4,144	20,846,050	100.0	5,030

For the Bulgarians and Turks the lower average value is due to
the greater incidence of houses having lower and average-size
assessments. The smaller number of cases involving Greeks,
Armenians, and Jews undoubtedly creates an atypical represen-

tation. But it is likewise true that the higher average value
of their homes resulted also from the presence of rich merchants and middlemen who, attracted by the region's favorable
economic climate, came to the Danubian vilâyet as temporary or
permanent residents. For example, there was a merchant in Provadiia named Sarkis, the son of Garabet. Sarkis bought two
houses, one of which cost 14,000 kuruş and the other 3,500
kuruş.[10] Dimitri Paspali, the second director of the Ottoman
bank, who owned property worth 93,000 kuruş, possessed four
houses in Varna worth a total of 31,000 kuruş.[11] Also located
in Varna was the house of the wife of a Greek subject from
Piraeus worth 22,000 kuruş, and the house of Luxandra, a daughter of a big merchant named Todor efendi, was worth 40,000
kuruş.[12] A merchant from Constanţa named Sarkis, the son of
Balaban, owned four houses with a combined worth of 33,500
kuruş.[13] Other examples could be cited.

When combined with the examples of persons who owned
several houses that they rented, these cases show that expensive
houses belonged to those who possessed property of a very great
value, usually over 50,000 kuruş. This category of the population included members of all of the ethnic groups living in
the Danubian vilâyet (see appendix 5).

* * *

Although data on the value of houses are useful, it is
information on shops, workshops, and other business premises
that best reveals the property and social differentiation of
the urban population. The analysis here will begin with shops,
which have been divided into three groups: "Artisans," "Commercial," and "Not stated" (see table 97). The latter are included in the distribution since they make up more than half
of the total.

As was true with houses, the bulk of the shops are concentrated in the value ranges up to 5,000 kuruş. Three-fourths
of the shops whose type is not known fall into this grouping,
as does an even greater percentage of artisan shops. Only
about 50% of the merchants' shops fall into the grouping valued
below 5,000 kuruş. In the group assessed at up to 2,000 kuruş
in value, the relative incidence of merchant shops is only half
as large as that of artisan shops. But a turnabout occurs at
the higher value ranges. In the group assessed at between
5,001 and 10,000 kuruş, the relative incidence of commercial
shops is twice that of artisan shops, and in the next range
(between 10,001 and 15,000 kuruş) it is five times as large.

In terms of the shops represented here in larger numbers,
footwear outlets rank rather low in their average assessed
value. For one-third of them, the average value is 2,821 kuruş.
The shops of the kunduracıs, shoemakers who produced a thick

TABLE 97

DISTRIBUTION OF SHOPS BY TYPE AND RANGE OF ASSESSED VALUE
(IN KURUŞ)

	Commercial	Artisan	Not Stated	Total
To 2,000				
Number	34	169	310	513
Value	40,800	260,850	412,625	714,275
Percentage of total number	13.2	29.1	34.1	29.3
Percentage of total value	2.1	10.6	10.5	8.6
2,001-5,000				
Number	105	306	379	790
Value	428,650	1,125,775	1,467,125	3,021,550
Percentage of total number	40.3	52.7	41.6	45.1
Percentage of total value	21.9	45.9	37.1	36.2
5,001-10,000				
Number	70	81	161	312
Value	615,500	624,625	1,157,225	2,397,350
Percentage of total number	26.7	13.9	17.7	17.8
Percentage of total value	31.1	26.0	29.4	28.7
10,001-15,000				
Number	34	14	42	90
Value	444,000	191,000	532,500	1,167,500
Percentage of total number	13.2	2.4	4.6	5.2
Percentage of total value	22.7	7.9	13.5	14.0
Over 15,000				
Number	17	11	18	46
Value	434,550	235,050	373,000	1,042,600
Percentage of total number	6.6	1.9	2.0	2.9
Percentage of total value	22.2	9.6	9.5	12.5
Total				
Number	260	581	910	1,751
Value	1,963,500	2,447,300	3,942,475	8,343,275
Percentage of total number	100.0	100.0	100.0	100.0
Percentage of total value	100.0	100.0	100.0	100.0

SOURCE: Calculations of the author as based on data contained in tezkeres
and tax receipts preserved in NBKM, Oo.

leather shoe averaged 2,100 kuruş, and those of cobblers or
kurpacıs 2,300 kuruş. The shops of slipper makers, on the
other hand, have a higher-than-average assessed value (almost
4,000 kuruş).

Shops belonging to pharmacists (23 cases) and tailors
(58) have average values of about 3,500 kuruş. Abacı shops
have a considerably higher average value of about 6,000 kuruş,
although it should be noted that there are only 13 such shops
in the sample.

Shops having assessed values of more than 5,000 kuruş
include the following: coffeehouses (85 cases), with an average
value of 5,846 kuruş; groceries (114), with an average value
of 6,556 kuruş; taverns (64), with an average value of 8,109
kuruş: bakeries (67), with an average value of 9,500 kuruş;
and dry-goods shops for the wholesale of cloth (about 10), with
an average value of 11,161 kuruş.

The distribution of shops by the owners' ethnic identity
reveals certain other noteworthy patterns. In the general number of commercial shops, there are twice as many Bulgarian as
there are Turkish establishments; however, the average assessment of the Bulgarian shops is 6,427 kuruş, while for Turkish
shops, 7,730 kuruş. Of the 64 taverns included, 38 were
owned by Bulgarians, 3 by Jews, 1 by an Armenian, 5 by Greeks,
and the remainder by Christians whose nationality cannot be
determined. For the 85 coffeeshops, on the other hand, 6 were
vakif possessions, 57 were owned by Turks, only 14 by Bulgarians, and the remaining 8 by Armenians, Greeks, and a Jew.

Table 98 presents in greater detail the distribution of
bakeries by city. The values listed here include the equipment
contained in these shops. The number of bakeries is larger
for such larger cities as Varna, Shumen, and Bazargic. That
no bakeries are indicated for Tulcea and Provadiia is due to
lacunae in the available data.

Unlike other shops, bakeries are distributed in a fairly
uniform manner in terms of their assessed value. Thus, there
are 14 bakeries (20.9% of the total) assessed at between 2,001
and 5,000 kuruş, 19 (28.4%) between 5,001 and 10,000 kuruş,
and the same number between 10,001 and 15,000 kuruş. The number of bakeries assessed at the lowest (to 2,000 kuruş) and
highest values (over 15,000 kuruş) is relatively smaller than
is true for other kinds of shops. There are 7 in the first
group and 8 in the second.

According to the material used, the upper limit of bakery
assessment is 25,000 kuruş. The owners of these bakeries were
the tobacco merchant Todor efendi, a Greek from Varna, and
Süleyman ağa, son of Mustafa, also of Varna. Respectively,
they received rents of 2,500 kuruş and 3,750 kuruş from these

bakeries.[14]   A bakery in Bazargic worth 23,000 kuruş was owned
by Sakir Ekyybu and Abdulla, the sons of Hüseyin Bey of the
village of Kara Bey.   In Varna a certain Hassan, the son of
Arif, owned two bakeries valued at 20,000 and 15,000 kuruş.
In Silistra there was another single owner of two bakeries,
Mestan Bey, the son of Mehmed ağa.   His bakeries were worth
16,000 and 15,000 kuruş.   Also included among those valued
over 15,000 kuruş were two bakeries that were vakif property.
One of them was in Varna and was valued at 20,000 kuruş; the
other was the vakıf property of a church in Silistra and was
worth 22,500 kuruş.

TABLE 98

DISTRIBUTION OF A GROUP OF SIXTY-SEVEN BAKERIES BY CITY

City	Number of Proprietors	Number of Bakeries	Value		
			Kuruş	Percentage of Total Amount	Average Value per Proprietor
Varna	17	20	247,000	38.8	14,529
Shumen	17	17	113,000	17.7	6,647
Silistra	6	7	85,500	13.5	14,250
Bazargic	13	11	91,500	14.4	7,038
Lom	7	8	66,250	10.3	9,464
Constanţa	1	1	12,000	1.9	12,000
Provadiia	--	--	-------	----	------
Tulcea	--	--	-------	----	------
Macin	1	1	13,000	2.0	13,000
Babadag	1	1	1,500	0.3	1,500
Medgidia	1	1	6,500	1.1	6,500
Total	64	67	636,250	100.0	9,940

SOURCE: Calculations of the author from data contained in
tezkeres and tax receipts preserved in NBKM, Oo.

Muslims dominate the ranks of the owners of bakeries,
numbering 41, or 64%, of the total number of proprietors.
The combined value of the shops owned by Muslims represents
65.7% of the total value of the bakeries being considered.

* * *

Another kind of commercial property for which data are
available is the storage facility called the mağaza, examples
of which can still be seen in many Balkan cities. Such
warehouses were one of the surest signs of the economic advancement and prosperity of Balkan cities during the nineteenth
century. Up to almost the end of the eighteenth century (and
even later in some regions), merchants had used the storage
facilities of such public buildings as inns and bezistans.
Now, however, they were building mağazas, basically private
warehouses constructed along contemporary lines. Single and
multistoried mağazas were large structures built of stone and
brick, with iron doors and shuttered windows, and usually with
deep basements and large lofts. Apart from its practical purpose, the mağaza was the outward expression of the merchant's
economic power. Accordingly, its design took into account not
only volume requirements but also the desire for an archi-
tecturally impressive façade. The mağazas thus lend a special
appearance to a city's commercial district.

The data available for the mağazas, although they are not
exhaustive for all eleven cities under review, are very revealing (see table 99). Analysis makes it possible to establish
certain regularities in the distribution of mağazas by city,
by their owners' ethnic affiliation, and by range of assessed
value. Three-fourths of those for which data are available are
concentrated in the cities of Varna, Lom, Constanţa, and Shumen. Three of these cities were ports, and given the contemporary character of commerce, which saw the greater part of goods
being shipped by water, it was natural that they would have
more mağazas. Nor is it accidental that one-fourth of all of
the warehouses studied here were located in Varna, the area's
largest port on the Black Sea. (The relatively smaller number
of mağazas indicated for Constanţa is due to the limited information available for that city.)

The presence of a greater number of warehouses also holds
true for the Danubian ports, in particular for Lom. Thanks to
the transformation of the Danube into a vital artery linking
Central Europe with the Ottoman Empire, Lom in the first half
of the nineteenth century grew into an important transit port
for all of western Bulgaria. At the same time it was increasingly becoming a focal point for the export of grain along the
Danube, and this vigorous trade compelled the big exporters to
construct numerous warehouses.

For the lower reaches of the Danube, even the scanty
information available for Tulcea points to the presence of a
considerable number of mağazas, something explained by this
city's role as an important commercial junction in the northeastern part of the Ottoman Empire. Silistra, which is located
between Constanţa and Tulcea and close to Ruse, the chief city

of the Danubian vilâyet, seems to have played a more limited
role, serving only part of the Dobruja and the Bazargic fair.
Although it was the second largest city in the Danubian vilâyet,
Shumen, which was located in the interior, falls behind neighboring Varna in terms of the number, size, and value of its
mağazas.

TABLE 99

DISTRIBUTION OF A GROUP OF 347 MAĞAZAS BY CITY

City	Number of Proprietors	Number of Mağazas	Value (in kuruş)	Percentage of Mağazas to Total	Average Value per Proprietor	Average Value per Mağaza
Varna	49	85	2,670,497	24.5	54,499	31,417
Shumen	40	53	265,525	15.3	6,638	5,009
Silistra	22	27	218,800	7.7	9,945	8,103
Bazargic	8	10	53,000	2.9	6,625	5,300
Lom	33	93	696,250	26.8	21,098	7,487
Constanţa	9	35	477,600	10.1	53,067	13,645
Provadiia	1	8	54,250	2.3	54,250	6,781
Tulcea	12	23	270,250	6.6	22,521	11,750
Macin	1	1	15,000	0.3	15,000	15,000
Babadag	1	2	38,000	0.6	38,000	19,000
Medgidia	5	10	79,300	2.9	15,860	17,930
Total	181	347	4,838,472	100.0	26,732	13,944

The varying roles played by port cities and those in the
interior in terms of commercial turnover are reflected not only
in the numerical distribution of warehouses, but also in their
assessed value. The mağazas in the port cities of Varna and
Constanţa have the highest average assessed value. Next in
line come those of Tulcea and Silistra. Because it was still
developing, Lom lacked storage facilities as large and as valuable as those in Varna, and the average assessment of its warehouses is lower.

The higher value of the warehouses in the port cities
becomes clearer when one considers that for all of the mağazas
for which data are available, 35.4% have assessed values between
1,000 and 5,000 kuruş, and 28.4% between 5,000 and 10,000 kuruş.
When combined with the warehouses assessed at up to 1,000 kuruş,
another 6.3%, the relative share of the mağazas valued below
10,000 kuruş totals 70.2%. Thus, the majority of all the mağazas
bear a much lower assessment than the warehouses in Varna and
Constanţa. The average assessed value of the warehouses in the
cities of the interior is lower than the average in the port
cities. For Shumen the average value is six times lower than
in Varna, and more than twice as low as in Constanţa.

The difference between the port cities and those of the
interior is also seen in the distribution of warehouses owners

in terms of their mağazas' value. In Shumen three-fourths of
these proprietors had warehouses in the low assessment range--
up to 5,000 kuruş. (Indeed, one-fourth have warehouses in the
lowest value range--up to 1,000 kuruş.) Only 2.5% of the mağaza
proprietors of Shumen are in the highest value range--up to
100,000 kuruş. For Bazargic, half of all the proprietors fall
into the range of mağazas valued below 5,000 kuruş. The remainder are grouped in higher categories, but most of them have
warehouses valued at no more than 30,000 kuruş. For Varna, on
the contrary, only 20.4% of the proprietors possess mağazas
valued below 10,000 kuruş, and nearly half of the remaining
80% have warehouses in the higher value ranges, 50,000 kuruş
and more. A similar picture holds true for Constanţa, where
88.9% of the proprietors possess warehouses valued over 10,000
kuruş (55.6% of these were valued at from 10,000 to 30,000
kuruş). For the cities of Lom and Tulcea, finally, one can
note a relatively equal incidence of proprietors whose warehouses bear either higher or low assessments.

Distribution of these proprietors by ethnic affiliation
is shown in table 100. Turks are the most numerous of these
proprietors (58.6%), and far outstrip Bulgarian owners. The
percentage breakdown is not the same for each city (see table
99). For Varna, 38 of the 49 owners are Turks, 4 Bulgarians,
5 Greeks, and 2 Armenians. For Lom, 28 of the proprietors are
Turks, and the other 5, Jews. For Tulcea, however, the mağaza
proprietors do not include Turks. Of the 12 proprietors, 7 are
Bulgarians, 2 Greeks, 2 Christians, and the affiliation of one
owner is not clear. For Shumen, there are roughly equal numbers of Turkish and Bulgarian proprietors. For Constanţa and
Silistra, various nationalities are also represented, although
in similar numbers.

TABLE 100

DISTRIBUTION OF MAĞAZA PROPRIETORS BY ETHNIC AFFILIATION

Ethnic Group	Proprietors Number	Per-centage	Number	Mağazas Value (kuruş)	Per-centage of total	Average Value per Proprietor	Average Value per Mağaza
Turks	106	58.6	214	2,621,322	54.2	24,729	12,249
Bulgarians	40	22.1	59	568,050	11.7	14,201	9,628
Jews	10	5.5	18	281,000	5.8	28,100	15,611
Armenians	6	3.3	6	81,000	1.7	13,500	13,500
Others	19	10.5	50	1,287,100	26.6	67,742	25,742
Total	181	100.0	347	4,838,472	100.0	26,732	13,944

It is impossible not to note the place taken by Greeks among the owners of mağazas (included in the table under "Others"). Whereas owners among other nationalities have one to two mağazas, the Greek proprietors own an average of four each. Even more striking is the difference in the value of their properties. On the average, the warehouses owned by Greeks are five times as valuable as those of the Bulgarians or Armenians.

From a list of warehouse owners included as appendix 6, it can be seen that 91.2% owning mağazas valued at over 50,000 kuruş were residents of port cities. The largest number is for Varna, with 17 such cases; there are 3 for Constanţa and Lom, and 1 for Tulcea. Half of these owners are Turks, and more than one-fourth are Greeks. Only two are Bulgarians. There is also 1 Jew and 1 Romanian in this group.

* * *

The inns for which information is available are from five cities: Bazargic (with 12 inns), Lom (10), Silistra (5), Varna (3), and Shumen (3). The assessed worth of these inns shows that they were commercial properties with fairly high values. Of the 33 inns, 17 (52%) bear assessments of over 15,000 kuruş. Their total assessed value amounts to 716,500 kuruş, or 87% of the total value (824,000 kuruş) of the 33 inns in the sample. The most valuable inns are those in Shumen, where the average assessed value stands at 59,000 kuruş. Next in line come the inns of Varna, with an average value of 57,667 kuruş, followed by the much lower average of the inns in Bazargic (20,250 kuruş), Silistra (13,300 kuruş), and Lom (7,600 kuruş).

The inns are distributed among 32 owners who represent practically all of the nationalities living in the area, though non-Muslims predominate. The owners include 11 Bulgarians, 3 Christians whose nationality is not clear, 2 Greeks, 2 Armenians, 1 Jew, and 13 Turks. Bulgarians own inns bearing the highest assessed value (30,455 kuruş), and those owned by Turks average 17,154 kuruş. The ownership of inns was one of the intermediary steps through which representatives of the rural elite penetrated urban life, a phenomenon indicated by, among other things, the higher percentage of Bulgarians among their proprietors.

* * *

An analysis of available material for flour mills reveals the clear distinction between the capitalist enterprise and the ordinary water- or wind-driven mill. Of a total of 48 flour mills, 18 have assessments over 15,000 kuruş. Whereas the average value of the ordinary water mill is between 5,000 and 15,000 to 20,000 kuruş, the mills equipped with steam

boilers (the *ateş değirmen* or "fire mills") are valued at
100,000 or 200,000 kuruş. From a number of reports published
in the newspaper *Dunav*, it is evident that the Bulgarian public
regarded the construction of such mills as a major event, a
true sign of progress. The owners of two mills, both located
in Varna, valued at 200,000 kuruş were the British subject
Sherno and the wife of the former *çauş*, Hacı Ali ağa. The latter
turned her mill into a vakif endowment. Two other mills worth
100,000 kuruş each belonged to Turks: Hasan, the son of Arif,
and the brothers Hasan and Risa Bey and their sister, all inhabitants of Varna. These individuals leased their mills in
return for a rent of 9,000 kuruş each. [15]
     The majority of the other mills considered here were
located along the Danube and particularly in Silistra. Their
owners were mainly Turks, some of whom leased these properties
to others. Among the non-Muslim owners were several Silistra
Bulgarians: Ivan, the son of Stan (whose mill was assessed at
28,000 kuruş), Andon, the son of Todor (25,000 kuruş), Georgi,
the son of Stoian (16,600 kuruş), and Iovan, the son of Dimitŭr
(10,000 kuruş). Another millowner in Silistra was a Greek
named Manasis, the son of Alexi. In addition to a mill worth
15,000 kuruş and a share in another mill assessed at 3,000
kuruş, Manasis owned a third, enlarged mill worth 25,000 kuruş.
In Constanţa, an Armenian named Manuk, the son of Matus, owned
a horse-driven mill worth 20,000 kuruş. In Bazargic, a certain
Encho, the son of Kolche, owned a mill worth 20,000 kuruş, and
Petri, the son of Ivan, was the owner of a mill worth 10,000
kuruş in Tulcea.

                              * * *

     Data are also available on other commercial properties
that, though represented by a smaller number of cases, bear
high assessments. First among this group are bathhouses, of
which there are six. Among their owners was a certain Varna
resident, Askery bey, the son of Hasan bey, whose bathhouse was
worth 200,000 kuruş and brought in some 20,000 kuruş in rent.
Other bathhouse owners include: in Silistra, Mestan bey, the
son of Mehmed ağa (whose bathhouse was worth 70,000 kuruş); in
Bazargic, Ahmed bey and Sarikoglu Ahmed ağa (55,000 and 32,500
kuruş); in Silistra, Hasan, the son of Mehmed (20,000 kuruş);
and in Lom, Fatme Hatun, the daughter of Ismail (15,000 kuruş).
All of their bathhouses were used as rental properties.
     The *salhanes* or slaughterhouses for which there is infor-
mation were Turkish properties. There are two in Shumen, valued
at 18,000 kuruş each, and another two in Varna and Silistra,
valued at 80,000 and 70,000 kuruş. The owners of these slaugh-
terhouses also used them to earn rental income.
     The spread of casinos was an interesting phenomenon in

the Balkans at that time. Of the casinos for which material
is available, one located in Constanţa had the highest assessed
value, 80,000 kuruş. The several casinos in Silistra were
worth 25,000, 13,000, 10,000, 7,500, and 3,500 kuruş: and those
in Bazargic and Lom 20,000 and 11,000 kuruş. Casino owners included a Bulgarian grocer named Kostandi, the son of Kalcho,
and Strati, the son of Todor, of Silistra. In Bazargic and
Silistra, Greeks named Apostili and Anastas owned casinos, and
in Constanţa, Silistra, and Lom, Turks owned casinos.

As shown by the foregoing discussion of various urban
properties, the propertied elite concentrated in its hands not
so much residential structures as a wide variety of commercial
and business property. In addition, that these commercial
properties found tenants able to pay a high rent shows that the
productive strata of the urban population also possessed considerable amounts of monetary capital.

* * *

Agricultural property occupied a special place in urban
real estate. It included vineyards, fields, and orchards. Of
these, the vineyard was the basic type of agricultural property
in the city (see table 101). Thus, on the average, vineyards
account for three-fourths of the total value of all agricultural
property being analyzed here. For the cities for which relatively more information is available, the percentage representation of vineyards tends to be even higher. An exception in
this regard is Bazargic, where the value of fields comprises
70.6% of the total value of agricultural property. Provadiia
is also a partial exception, but its vineyards, despite a
smaller percentage, are nevertheless more valuable than fields.

TABLE 101

DISTRIBUTION OF URBAN AGRICULTURAL PROPERTY
IN CITIES OF THE DANUBIAN VILÂYET IN THE 1860s

City	Vineyards Value (kuruş)	Percentage	Fields Value (kuruş)	Percentage	Orchards Value (kuruş)	Percentage	Total Value (kuruş)	Percentage
Silistra	836,090	84.4	127,820	12.9	29,650	2.7	990,560	100.0
Shumen	745,505	80.6	158,450	17.1	21,025	2.3	924,980	100.0
Varna	631,340	83.7	76,395	10.1	46,810	6.2	754,545	100.0
Bazargic	89,605	29.3	215,985	70.6	400	0.1	305,990	100.0
Provadiia	53,070	52.6	37,335	37.0	10,450	10.4	100,855	100.0
Tulcea	16,475	22.0	37,815	50.4	20,750	27.6	75,040	100.0
Babadag	46,925	63.2	22,710	30.6	4,575	6.2	74,210	100.0
Macin	6,050	34.3	11,575	65.7	------	----	17,625	100.0
Lom	-------	----	-------	----	3,000	100.0	3,000	100.0
Total	2,425,060	74.7	688,085	21.2	133,660	4.1	3,246,805	100.0

SOURCE: Calculations of the author based on tezkeres and tax receipts contained in NBKM, Oo.

All parts of the urban population owned vineyards. For
some, owning vineyards was the crowning mark of their status
of a prosperous person; for the majority of artisans and merchants owning a vineyard was simply one of the activities of
guildsmen. In any event, for most urban residents a vineyard was an important souce of additional income, and for some
it was the only source. On the basis of the data used here,
the occupation of half of the vineyard owners can be established
(see table 102).

TABLE 102

DISTRIBUTION OF VINEYARD OWNERS BY OCCUPATION

Occupation of Proprietor	Number	Value (kuruş)	Percentage of Total Proprietors	Percentage of Total Vineyard Value
Artisans	994	663,820	29.2	27.4
Agricul- turalists	218	136,050	6.4	5.6
Merchants	309	310,790	9.0	12.8
General workers	16	7,750	0.5	0.3
Hired artisans	145	58,810	4.3	2.4
Hired workers in commerce	8	3,875	0.2	0.2
Government employees	198	107,230	5.8	4.4
Not stated	1,522	1,136,735	44.6	46.9
Total	3,410	2,425,060	100.0	100.0

SOURCE: Calculations of the author based on tezkeres and tax
receipts contained in NBKM, Oo.

Since the ownership of vineyards was an important mark
of social status, a more detailed examination shall be made of
the information available for Varna, Provadiia, Silistra, and
Bazargic. For Varna there is information available on 357
persons who owned vineyards (see table 103). They include 211
Muslims (15 of whom were settlers), 124 non-Muslims, 14 Armenians, 1 Serb, 1 German, and 6 individuals whose nationality
is unclear. (There are roughly 15 incomplete files.) In 143
cases the records indicate that the proprietor involved owned
additional property--usually only a house, or a house and one
or more shops or storehouses. The vineyard appears as the only
piece of property for 214 individuals. It should not be

assumed, however, that all of these persons lacked their own
residences, since 79 of them were from various villages (Kes-
trich, Goliama, Frangia, Malka Frangia, etc.) situated around
Varna. Since they were not residents of the city, they did not
own houses there; they simply acquired vineyards within Varna's
territory. These were individuals who were becoming increasingly connected with the urban economy, where they exchanged
the yield from their vineyards in return for cash.

TABLE 103

DISTRIBUTION OF VINEYARD OWNERS IN VARNA

Assessment Range (kuruş)	Total Number	Proprietors				
		Muslims	Non-Muslims	Armenians	Not Clear	Various
Up to 500	88	72	12	3	1	-
501-1,000	89	50	32	3	4	-
1,001-1,500	67	37	27	3	-	-
1,501-2,000	48	22	24	2	-	-
2,001-2,500	18	8	7	2	-	1*
2,501-3,000	12	7	4	1	-	-
3,001-4,000	13	5	8	-	-	-
4,001-5,000	7	2	5	-	-	-
5,001-6,000	5	1	3	-	-	-
6,001-7,000	3	1	2	-	-	-
7,001-8,000	5	5	-	-	-	-
Over 10,000	2	1	-	-	1	1†
Total	357	211	124	14	6	2

SOURCE: Calculations of the author based on tezkeres and tax receipts
contained in NBKM, Oo.   *A Serb.   †A German.

It is difficult to assess whether owning vineyards was
a primary or supplementary source of income for those individuals for whom vineyards appear as their only property.
As already noted, for 79 persons vineyards were directly
linked with the urban economy. For the others, only indirect conclusions are possible. The basic occupations of
40 Muslims and non-Muslims are indicated in the records.
There are one or two persons each representing a variety of
crafts (masons, barbers, shoemakers, boatmen, etc.), hired
workers (cultivators, vineyard watchmen), and others, including
government employees, priests, merchants, and a consul. It is
clear that to these persons vineyards were an additional source
of income or a component part of their varied property holdings.
There is also no doubt about the role of vineyards for those
individuals who also possessed shops or storehouses. Of 55

such individuals, 51 were rentiers with yearly incomes of from
1,500 to 20,000 kuruş a year. It is interesting to note that,
with the exception of two Bulgarian partners, all of the others
who leased out the property they owned were Turks.

As to the remainder of those individuals for whom vineyards were sole property holdings, some conclusions are possible based on the size of their vineyards. Using 50 vineyards,
it can be calculated that one dönüm of vineyard was worth 400
kuruş.[16] It can be supposed, therefore, that only in those
cases where the vineyard was valued at over 2,000 kuruş (i.e.,
over 5 dönüm) could it serve as the only source of livelihood.[17]
Accordingly, this discussion will dwell in greater detail on
the owners of vineyards valued over 2,000 kuruş.

These owners fall into two groups--49 persons for whom
vineyards were the sole property, and 16 individuals who had
income from other property as well. Of the second group, 12
were Turks and 4 non-Muslims. One of the latter was the German
consul Keberle who had vineyards valued at 10,150 kuruş. The
others include an Armenian with vineyards worth 2,650 kuruş and
a house worth 30,000 kuruş, a Bulgarian tailor named Georgi,
the son of Ivan, who had vineyards worth 4,100 kuruş, and a
Greek merchant named Pandeli, the son of Stratiyadi, who owned
vineyards valued at 5,500 kuruş and other property worth 85,040
kuruş. Of the 12 Turks, only 2 lacked rental incomes; the other
10 were rentiers and owners of property of varying values from
which they drew considerable revenue--from 1,500 to 13,000
kuruş a year.

The tax accounts for the other 49 persons indicate no
other property except the vineyards (and in some cases a house
and individual fields). Of this group only 12 persons had
houses in the city; another 17 were inhabitants of villages in
the locality (Krestich and Goliama Frangia). The remainder
probably lived in rented houses in Varna. In addition, the
records indicate that 7 of these individuals were migrants.

Accordingly, of the 65 persons in Varna who owned vineyards worth more than 2,000 kuruş, about 50 were in all probability viticulturists, or generally speaking, people for whom
vineyard cultivation was their principal occupation. There
is no doubt that there were similar cases among those who owned
vineyards worth less than 2,000 kuruş. No firm boundary, however, can be fixed between viticulturists and the vineyard
owners who used such property as a source of supplementary income.

For Provadiia, data are available on the property status
of 93 persons, practically all of whom owned vineyards. The
general trend in Provadiia was a close association between
viticulture and farming. Thirty-one individuals who owned
fields were also owners of vineyards, whose value was higher

than that of the vineyards held by the remaining 63 artisans
and merchants. This indicates that as a rule only the combination of fields and vineyards could secure a livelihood in
purely agricultural work. Additional evidence lies in the size
of arable land. Only ten persons had fields over 50 dönüm.
Among these, only 5 had land between 85 and 140 dönüm, requiring additional labor and implying a higher social status.
The other 5 persons owned about 50 dönüm of land each. The
remaining 20 or so individuals possessed lesser amounts of land,
very often only several dönüm and one or two vineyards. The
situation in Silistra and Bazargic was similar to that in Varna
and Provadiia.

* * *

In examining the place of the city in the Danubian vilâyet,
our point of departure has been the position expressed by Lenin
that "the domination of the city over village (in an economic,
political, intellectual, and every other sense) is a general
and inevitable phenomenon in all countries with commodity production and with capitalism."[18] What is involved here is first
the great material resources of the city; second, the differentiation of a bourgeoisie that strives to impose not only new
economic relationships, but also a new way of life and culture;
and third, the considerable polarization of the population, a
process strengthened by the constant arrival of massive numbers
of hired workers from the villages.

The material analyzed here shows that in the territory
of the Danubian vilâyet the development of commodity-money and
market relations had reached the stage where they were producing
the appearance in small cities of both regular weekly markets
to serve the surrounding rural population and district fairs
that brought the immediate producer and the consumer into contact with the big merchants involved in import and export trade.
During the nineteenth century such local fairs became a regular
feature of Balkan life. Although they did not entirely dis-
place the large fairs of the eighteenth and nineteenth centuries, which were held periodically to meet the requirements
of wholesale trade for a large part of the Balkans, they undoubtedly limited their role.

Furthermore, the data examined in the past several chapters concern a decade or so of relative tranquillity in the
economic life of the Ottoman Empire, dealing as they do with
the period between two major crises that shook the empire in
1861 and 1873 (the latter was a financial crisis that sharply
disrupted the imperial budget and finally prompted the declaration of financial bankruptcy in 1875). The value of the
material is enhanced because it provides a picture of the material position, occupational distribution, and social differ-

entiation of the urban population at a time of relative economic
equilibrium.

This was a time when the Ottoman feudal elite had become
or was becoming transformed into what was chiefly an urban
stratum of rentiers. No longer the dominant socioeconomic
force in the city it had been in past centuries, this layer
had been displaced by the bourgeoisie of the subjugated peoples.
In its initial stage of development the Bulgarian bourgeoisie,
which was chiefly a commercial middle class, served the Ottoman
feudal state. The most important of the early Bulgarian merchants were those tax farmers who acquired control of the profitable business of supplying Istanbul with meat (which came
primarily from the Bulgarian lands situated near the capital).
The rich and propertied Bulgarians who began to stand apart
from the general milieu and play a certain independent economic role emerged primarily from among the ranks of these
cattle dealers and sheep tax farmers. Istanbul became their
chief place of business and of profits. The livestock suppliers, who applied their wealth and experience to other
economic areas as well, remained the leading element of the
Bulgarian commercial bourgeoisie well into the first half of
the nineteenth century. But as the Bulgarian lands became
more directly involved in European trade, the situation
began to change, and a new layer of prosperous merchants
was formed--Bulgarians, who at first acted as agents and
middlemen of foreign commercial firms, but later became
heads of their own commercial enterprises. For a time the
commercial penetration of the big Western states in the
Balkans in general, and in the Bulgarian lands in particular,
had a positive impact on local production and did not thwart
its growing volume.

Foreign trade activities, such as the opening of Austrian
shipping on the Danube, markedly contributed to the economic
quickening of the Danubian ports and their hinterland. By the
eve of the Crimean War, however, foreign trade began to work
against the Bulgarian economy. Foreign imports began to exceed
the exports of agricultural goods, which, moreover, were sold
on the European market at very low prices. The Bulgarian lands
were increasingly being transformed into an appendage of the
big European states, one whose function was to provide raw
materials. Nevertheless, the continuing potential of the domestic market rescued Bulgarian industrial production from an
immediate crisis.

Meanwhile, from about the end of the eighteenth century
on, the upsurge of artisan production, particularly in textiles,
led to the differentiation of yet another stratum--the entre-
preneurs--who organized putting-out and centralized manufactories, businessmen who turned the textile production of

whole districts into a prosperous livelihood indeed. These
entrepreneurs encouraged production with their introduction of
the iron-toothed wheel and other technical improvements, and
with their use of water-driven machinery. This classification
of the Bulgarian bourgeoisie is to a large extent a conditional
one. For about a century and a half there was a great deal of
overlap in the activities of different strata of the Bulgarian
middle class. But in general terms the three groups mentioned,
together with the group of small artisans and merchants, as
well as the proletarianized mass, formed the structure of Bulgarian urban society in the 1860s.

    This structure was outwardly expressed in social and class
relations. At that time and place, societal interaction and
conflict were manifested in great relief in the activities of
the Bulgarian obshtinas. Earlier, during the classical Ottoman
period, the role of the obshtinas had mainly consisted of being
responsible for the collection and regular payment of taxes.
From the end of the eighteenth century, however, the obshtinas
began to expand their activity, more and more becoming organs
of self-government. And as they acquired an ever increasing
function in economic and cultural life, the obshtinas became
the focus of sharp struggles between the representatives of
the new commercial and industrial bourgeoisie (as supported by
the guilds) and the traditional middlemen between the Ottoman
authorities and the population. It was in this complex situation, still under the domination of an alien feudal state system, that new social forces emerged and developed.

CONCLUSION

Urban settlements were already fairly widespread in the Balkans during the early period of Ottoman rule, the fifteenth and sixteenth centuries. This should not be explained in a one-sided fashion, however. Several of the factors that suggest the extent to which the establishment of Ottoman rule imposed new conditions on the economic reality of the peninsula are as follows: the elimination of the various political and economic barriers represented by the scattered medieval Balkan States and Byzantium; the loss by the Italian republics of those commercial privileges that had economically stifled Byzantium; the abolition of the feudal privileges of the individual rulers and princes; and the establishment of relative tranquillity in the Balkans once military operations had moved on to other areas. As a result of these and other factors, the development of the urban economy in all parts of the Balkans was now influenced by the gradual growth of internal commerce and the con-

solidation of economic ties both among neighboring areas and
between the interior and such major centers of consumption as
Istanbul, Edirne, and Salonika.

But if the Ottoman impact on the development of the Balkan
city was thus manifest, this is not to say, as some have claimed,
that Ottoman rule (or any other such rule) was capable of "organizing" such a large number of cities, or even only the largest
among them.   Actually, urban life was an essential feature of
the feudal period in Asia Minor and the Balkans irrespective
of the vicissitudes in the political fate of their states
(Byzantium, Bulgaria, Serbia and, ultimately, the Ottoman Empire).
These territories enjoyed a tradition and a continuity of urban
life that were centuries old and that themselves were to have
a decisive effect on the Ottoman social system that emerged in
the Balkans in the aftermath of the conquest.   Indeed, the
existing urban tradition contributed to the consolidation of
Ottoman feudalism, which in its turn continued to foster the
development of urban life.

That changes took place in the ethnic composition of the
Balkans is no argument for underrating or trying to deny that
an urban culture existed in this region before the Turkish invasion.   As shown here, the overwhelming majority of Balkan
cities preserved the non-Muslim character of their population.
At the same time, however, the fact that in parts of the Balkans a considerable Turkish stratum appeared as part of the
taxable--that is, the productive--urban population persuasively
illustrates how the ruling nationality cannot be approached
merely in terms of the formation in cities of a feudal or administrative elite.   A Turkish and Muslim ethnic element became
an enduring component of the urban population.   It is precisely
this that requires the study of the character and role of the
economic, social, cultural, religious, and other institutions
of the urban population as a whole regardless of what ethnic
element might have been predominant in a given period.

Furthermore, the examination of data on the socioeconomic
structure of the city, market and state regulation, and handicrafts and the esnafs has shown that it was primarily the
Ottoman state that established the public norms within whose
framework artisan production developed and the guilds operated.
It has remained impossible, however, to resolve such questions
as the emergence of the guilds in the Balkan lands, their
original structure, and the extent of their presence throughout
these territories.

Another question that has eluded a definitive answer is
the extent to which restrictive provisions hindered social
differentiation within the guilds from the fifteenth to the
seventeenth century.   In general terms it is safe to assume
that the dominance of state-equalizing regulation meant that

social stratification could not take place very quickly among
the artisans. But this question can and has been looked at in
another way--by taking into account the broader public significance of the guild's activity. In Ottoman society, the restricted independence of the guild, which distinguished it so
fundamentally from the European guilds, became one of its
major advantages. Given the existence of alien rule, the fact
that guilds enjoyed state sanction and protection created real
conditions for the development of artisan production by the
subject peoples of the Ottoman Empire. This governmental
attitude lent a public significance to the labor of non-
Turkish artisans that made it possible for them to increase
their role in the economic and social life of the cities.

The study of data on inheritances and property transfers
in the eighteenth century in the cities of Vidin, Ruse, and
Sofia has permitted a number of insights into the material
status and differentiation of the urban population. Thus, the
analysis of the value of houses--the basic component of inherit-
ances--has shown that 87.4% of these houses were worth less
than 500 kuruş. Having defined houses worth less than 100
kuruş as those of the poor (39%), and those worth over 1,000
kuruş as belonging to the rich (3.6%), the sharp polarization
of the urban population became obvious (as shown, for example,
by the distinctly limited group of persons with houses valued
at several thousand kuruş or more).

A comparison by periods, moreover, has revealed that in
the second half of the eighteenth century there was a doubling
in the number of high-priced houses. This phenomenon, as well
as the appearance of new intermediate categories, has been
cited as evidence of an eighteenth-century growth in the material prosperity of the urban population. The gradual development of handicrafts and commerce increasingly raised artisans
and merchants to the level of the propertied elite, hitherto
chiefly made up of the Muslim military and administrative stratum. In short, in the course of the century, changes were
taking place in the social composition of the urban well-to-do,
which now included some artisans and merchants (without regard
to their ethnic affiliation).

The analysis of shops has revealed a distribution similar
to that for houses, but here another characteristic feature
emerged: the concentration of property. Moreover, the study
of property differentiation has been augmented by looking at
other components of inheritances--such property as vineyards,
furniture, and clothing, which have thrown light on essential
differences in the material position of various urban groups--
artisan producers, small proprietors, and the owners of real
estate and inheritances valued at more than 5,000 kuruş.

A comparative analysis of the inheritances of a group of

artisans with one of representatives of the propertied elite--
both drawn from the cities of Ruse, Vidin, and Sofia--has also
illustrated marked differences in the role played by money as
an element of property. Though it constituted a good portion of
the inheritances of both groups, it was this element that first
and foremost distinguished the truly wealthy status of the urban
elite.

This comparison, the analysis of the other data, and the
study of inheritances in terms of their over-all value has revealed the existence of several different categories in the
urban population. Persons leaving inheritances valued at less
than 100 kuruş formed the lower layer of the urban population.
With insignificant property and no money, these individuals
were in constant need, and lacked even the means to earn a living. Radically different was the situation of those who were
able to leave inheritances worth between 1,000 and 2,000 kuruş.
Not only was their real estate more valuable, it was also more
varied. What particularly set this group apart was the ownership of a shop, in many cases together with its supplies and
inventory. As a result of their artisan or commercial activity, the persons in this group had reached that level of material prosperity that enabled them to be independent and
maintain the standard of living of the well-to-do urbanite.

Their varying amounts of property placed the major part
of the urban productive population between these two categories.
Some owned only a house; others also possessed shops, different
amounts of money, a vineyard, and so on--and the property variety meant different levels of material security. Some of
these individuals came close to the status of the well-to-do,
but others remained in a state of virtual poverty. In any
event, the property characteristics of these intermediate
groups have been used to define the mean of the urban standard of living. The group that left inheritances valued at
more than 5,000 kuruş represented the wealthiest element of
the three cities studied. Those in question included provincial representatives of the Ottoman ruling class and
individual artisans and merchants.

During the eighteenth century, numerous changes occurred
in the economic development of the Balkans. The growth of
productive forces led both to greater material and social
inequality within the population and to the accumulation
of increasingly larger amounts of capital in the hands of the
subjugated peoples--Greeks, Jews, Armenians, Bulgarians, Serbs,
and others. Many Balkan fairs gained wide popularity throughout the Ottoman Empire and beyond as centers for the sale of
the annual production of whole districts. In the eighteenth
century, furthermore, the Balkan Peninsula and the eastern
Mediterranean became involved in European commerce both by sea

(the so-called Levantine trade) and by land through the caravan trade with Central Europe.

One result of this economic development was the emergence, by the end of the eighteenth century, of bourgeois classes among the individual Balkan peoples--the Greeks, Bulgarians, and Serbs. As they consolidated themselves economically, these bourgeoisies began to play an ever more active role in their peoples' national affairs and local administration. At the same time, however, the ruling nationality remained aloof from the general development of productive forces. This peculiar feature of Ottoman feudalism put its imprint on all facets of the empire's social and political life. The decline of the sipahi institution (the Turkish military fief system), which had already begun at the end of the sixteenth century, did not spell the disintegration of the feudal mode of production; rather, without creating new productive relations, it only undermined the material bases of Ottoman feudal domination. The elite of the Ottoman ruling class now directed its major efforts to the easiest and surest ways it could find to obtain greater revenues--the acquisition of higher administrative or military posts. In other words, the fundamental stimulus of this class became its ever closer links with the state apparatus, which resulted in its almost total bureaucratization. It thus became transformed into one of the most parasitic of classes, one that was antithetical to economic development. This understanding of the character of the Ottoman ruling class perhaps also helps explain why, despite the increased Western interest in the agricultural production of the Ottoman Empire and the growing demand for cereals and other farm produce that appeared in the eighteenth and the beginning of the nineteenth centuries, the Balkans lacked the widespread development of organized large-scale estate agriculture based on the "second version" of serfdom that was so typical of Eastern Europe generally.

While in the eighteenth-century West and in Russia strong single-nation or multinational states had already taken shape in which the ruling nation developed capitalist relations, in the Ottoman Empire the subjugated peoples themselves were the bearers of the new economic orientation. There was another difference, too. In the other large European states at that time, the capitalist mode of production swept up part of the feudal class, which now joined the bourgeoisie, and the state, despite its feudal essence, lent essential support to the consolidation of the new relations. In the Ottoman Empire, on the other hand, the emerging capitalists had to overcome the general hostility of the ruling elite, and only in individual cases did these entrepreneurs receive state support. In general, Ottoman absolutism failed, even through a temporary

conciliation of the interests of the ruling class with those of
the national bourgeoisies, to find a solution to the grave
crisis into which the empire had fallen.

As in most countries, capitalist production in the Ottoman Empire made its first breakthrough in branches of the textile industry, doing so through the property and social differentiation of small-commodity producers. The differentiation
of these capitalist elements proceeded at a slower rate in the
Ottoman Empire than it did in the West, and early forms of
capitalist enterprise were more intertwined with artisan workshops. The study of the branches of the textile industry located in the economically most advanced areas of the Balkans
has demonstrated the gradual expansion of textile crafts and
the trade related to these activities, which was tied to the
opening of a growing number of markets outside the Balkans and
to increasing state requirements for clothing the army. New
entrepreneurs sprang up from among those small middlemen and
craftsmen who managed to make their way through various restrictions and set up numerous manufacturing enterprises whose
production involved the work of the population of whole cities
and hundreds of villages. During the spring and summer the
master, journeymen, and apprentices, helped by women and children, worked from early in the morning until late in the evening. In the autumn the master and some journeymen set off in
large caravans for the south. It was precisely those branches
of textile production geared for mass sales at fairs and for
the more distant markets that flourished the most in the first
half of the nineteenth century.

During the same half century, guilds in the most developed
branches of the urban economy continued to constitute a real
force in urban economic life throughout most of the Balkans.
The guilds remained an obligatory form of organization for
commodity producers. But during this period they expanded
their activity, including in their purview many matters concerning the production and sale of their wares, which earlier
had fallen within the scope of state regulation and control.
Even those new branches of production that emerged in the nineteenth century and had an essentially manufacturing character
possessed a guild form of organization.

But whose interests did guild regulation serve? And how
does the role of the guild in the urban economic life in the
first half of the nineteenth century relate to the development
of capitalist relations? These questions have been examined
by means of a social analysis of the composition and activities
of the guilds. More specifically, to determine the social
characteristics of the guild elite, it became necessary to
clarify the productive activities of its most outstanding representatives in a number of cities. This analysis has shown

that the guild elite then taking shape consisted of bourgeois
elements. Some of these individuals were distinguished by
their commercial activity, and others were predominantly active
as entrepreneurs in the organization of production. In any
case, this new element was undeniably capitalist, and it was
this guild elite that gradually seized control of all units of
textile production, expanded this production, and linked a
number of rural areas together in capitalist relationships.

Very interesting was the failure of the new capitalist
elements to show an interest in the destruction of the guilds;
indeed, they themselves continued to hold guild membership. As
discussed, explanations for this phenomenon have to be sought
in two areas: first, in the general conditions of economic
life in the Ottoman Empire; and second, in the specific character of the commodity produced. As noted, not only was it
difficult for capitalist development to make headway in the
Ottoman Empire, the Turkish government continued to support
guilds in pursuit of various interests (fiscal, logistical,
etc.). The national bourgeoisies of the subjugated peoples,
therefore, had to struggle against the guilds not only as an
economic institution, but as an establishment of the feudal
state protected by the Turkish monarchy even as late as the
nineteenth century. At the same time, however, the opportunities that the guildsmen of the textile esnafs created for capitalist activities also played an essential role in the adaptation of the bourgeoisie to the guilds. It was this capitalist activity--which even showed up in the regulatory efforts of
the guilds--that permitted the weakening of the contradiction
between production and wholesale trade on the one hand, and
the character of small-scale artisan production on the other.
While they adapted to the guilds, the capitalist elements also
succeeded in adapting the guilds to the needs of the wholesale
trade and capitalist production (or at least production based
on lower capitalist forms).

Other favorable conditions were necessary for the emergence of a higher type of capitalist production, of centralized
manufacture, and true capitalist enterprises. What was required
most of all was the assurance of a permanent market for definite
amounts of goods--one that at that time and place could be
achieved only by government contracts. Thus, it was the creation of an almost monopolistic and lasting position in the
fulfillment of state orders that made possible the appearance
of factory-type enterprises set up by the Gümüşgerdans. In
the absence of similar conditions, other firms could not make
the transition from small-scale to factory production.

But despite their near monopoly of the market and the
protection they received from the Turkish government, and
notwithstanding all the opportunities they enjoyed to exploit
and defraud producers, the Gümüşgerdans did not limit them-

selves to industrial activity. They invested vast amounts of
their capital in the purchase of real estate, in commercial
deals, moneylending operations, and so on. In other words,
they did not avail themselves of the economic and social conditions for a steady and progressive growth of the industrial
production they had established. For whole decades they retained the kind of production they had set up in the 1830s and
1840s.

Evidenced here is the reluctance of Balkan bourgeoisie to engage in factory activity. Given the general insecurity within the Ottoman Empire, representatives of this class
preferred to hold onto the chance to move their capital more
readily from one activity to another. Indeed, if it were necessary, at the least hint of danger they wanted to be in a position to take their capital out of production entirely and
even out of the country. Even when the intensified demand for
certain goods favored the appearance of a higher type of capitalist production, most of the capitalists expressed an obvious
preference for such lower forms of industry as putting-out
manufacture. Sufficiently indicative in this respect are the
examples of Gümüşgerdan, who set up a mill that failed to
occupy the central place in his production and that could
be established in Sliven only with the assistance of the
state. It is important to emphasize once again that in
the Balkans the emergence and development of capitalist relations was a slow and difficult process.

The classification of Balkan cities from the 1830s to the
1870s, based on official census data, has shown that the area
possessed a considerable number of small and medium-sized
cities. In this respect the Danubian vilâyet differed from
the states of Serbia and Greece, which had a less developed
urban network, and whose urban population was smaller both in
absolute and relative terms. On the other hand, the capital
cities of Serbia and Greece had several times as many inhabitants as the other cities in those countries; whereas in the
Danubian vilâyet there was no city that stood out so dramatically in terms of the size of its population.

In ethnic composition, the cities of the Danubian vilâyet
were characterized by an extensive intermixture of the basic
non-Muslim and Muslim groups (Bulgarians and Turks), as well
as less numerous ethnic elements such as Greeks, Vlachs, Jews,
and Armenians. Ethnically homogeneous cities were few and far
between. For all areas of the Balkans there was a trend toward increasing urban populations, but differences did exist
in rates of growth in different areas and for different groups.
Furthermore, the population movement of both Muslims and non-
Muslims was contributing to the growth of larger cities at a
time when the size of small cities was remaining static.

At the same time, internal migration had become one of

the characteristic phenomena of the socioeconomic life of the
Balkan domains of the Ottoman Empire. This migration was
closely linked to the constant flow of the rural population to
the cities and to the formation of a stratum of urban poor in
most of them. As early as the first half of the nineteenth
century, the percentage of registered artisans, merchants, and
workers who had migrated from other places fluctuated from
0.5% to 4% of the population. In the 1860s, as revealed by
data for northeastern Bulgaria and the Dobruja, these mi-
grants--who swelled the ranks of the urban poor--comprised
an average of 6% of the total urban population (a figure based
on incomplete information).

The movement of manpower toward the northeastern part of
the peninsula included migrants from various parts of the Balkans and other Ottoman territories and particularly from the
Balkan Mountains, Thrace, Macedonia, the Greek-populated lands
and islands, Wallachia, Moldavia, and even Anatolia. Predominantly of an urban origin, these migrants again settled and
remained in cities. Their urban domicile, however, did not
exclude their working in the surrounding countryside.

One of the explanations for the flow of such a large
number of people to northeastern Bulgaria has been sought in
the several factors that made this region attractive for migrants. There was, for example, the growth of the Bazargic
fair, which attracted artisans, shopkeepers, and merchants
from many places. They set up their business in permanent
sheds and shops in a specially designated location. The fair
itself was a sure sign of the growing commercial volume of the
area and of the Dobruja's attractiveness, which drew not only
the urban poor but those who could bring along relatively large
amounts of capital.

The migration included skilled manpower, primarily artisans. But in social terms the great bulk of the migrants of
most of the occupational groups involved were in low-income
categories and had earnings that did not surpass those of assistants in the same fields, be they journeymen, apprentices,
or common laborers.

Finally, an analysis of data on the distribution of the
urban population by occupation and means of livelihood, as well
as the classification of the urban society by income, has revealed how the cities of the Danubian vilâyet stood out as
centers of artisan production and commerce. These fields represented over 60% of the urban population. Moreover, the greater
part of that urban element engaged in agriculture and livestock
husbandry was composed of individuals with other primary occupations. Most of these individuals were hired hands used to
cultivate the widespread vineyards that served as an additional
source of livelihood for many of the urban population.

The artisans, for their part, employed only a small amount of hired auxiliary labor--evidence of the small-commodity character of their production. The same conclusion finds additional support in the earnings of the artisans. Of the sample studied, 44% earned only as much as did hired workers, less than 500 kuruş a year. And if 750 kuruş is accepted as the breakoff point between low and medium incomes, another 20% of artisans would fall into the low-income group.

In the sample analyzed here, there were only an insignificant number of artisans in the high-income group. Only one-third of the merchants fell into this grouping, and just two of those engaged in agricultural work.

On the other hand, by this time the urban propertied elite consisted not only of representatives of the Ottoman ruling class, but economically successful members of the Bulgarian, Greek, Armenian, and Jewish bourgeoisies.

But standing in contrast to the bulk of the commodity producers, merchants, and proprietors was a stratum of the urban poor composed chiefly of hired workers without a definite occupation and of those low-paid apprentices and journeymen who possessed little or no property. To a very large extent this property and social differentiation of the urban population explains the depth of the social conflicts that furnished an even greater impetus to the nineteenth-century movements of the Balkan peoples to attain their national freedom.

APPENDIXES

Appendix 1

Cities and their Feudal Revenues, ca. 1526-28

City	Revenue (akçe)	Type of Holding	Comment
Sancak of Gelibolu			
Gelibolu Malgara	55,000		
Sancak of Vize			
Ereğli	116,668	vakıf	
Silivri	85,070	vakıf	
Hayrabolu	65,000	zeamet	
Derkos	53,276	vakıf	
Vize	25,000	miriliva's has	
Babaeski	24,360	of a sipahi	

City	Revenue (akçe)	Type of Holding	Comment
Kirklareli	23,785	miriliva's has	
Çorlu	20,000	of two sipahis	
Lüleburgaz	18,350	of two sipahis	
Inces	10,060	vakıf	
Sancak of Silistra			
Silistra	117,831	miriliva's has	
Varna	61,134	vakıf	
Kiliya	60,025	sultan's has	
Pomorie	59,134	sultan's has	
Nessebŭr	44,760	miriliva's has	
Provadiia	25,390	miriliva's has	
Hirşova	15,429	miriliva's has	in 1569-70, 32,100 akçe
Aitos	13,750	pasa's has	in 1528-29, 14,496 akçe
Karnobat	13,128	miriliva's has	
Sancak of Nikopol			
Nikopol	230,686	miriliva's has	
Ruse	81,893	sultan's has	95,725 akçe*
Svishtov	64,448	sultan's has	
Tŭrnovo	62,359	defterdar's has	66,741 akçe; pasa's has*
Vratsa	42,553	sultan's has	53,162 akçe*
Lovech	30,972	of a subaşı	34,280 akçe; pasa's has*
Shumen	20,690	sultan's has	1556, 22,137 akçe
Sancak of Vidin			
Vidin	224,011	miriliva's has	1509-10, 173,537 akçe
Bania	5,611	miriliva's has	
Svŭrlig	1,833	miriliva's has	
Sancak of Chirmen			
Rodoschuk	67,720	vakıf	
Nova Zagora	32,185	miriliva's has	
Eynebazar	18,076	miriliva's has	
Khaskovo	17,085	miriliva's has	
Chirpan	12,509	zeamet	
Chirmen	11,134	miriliva's has	
Kazanlŭk	15,485	miriliva's has	

City	Revenue (akçe)	Type of Holding	Comment
Sancak of Sofia			
Sofia	175,523	sultan's has	
Samokov	98,201	sultan's has	
Breznik	96,417	sultan's has	37,045 akçe*
Chiprovtsi	47,553	sultan's has	
Pirot	8,524	of a defterdar	
Ikhtiman	5,231	vakıf	
Berkovitsa	4,882	of a kethüda	
Sancak of Kiustendil			
Kratovo	100,428	sultan's has	
Štip	56,630	miriliva's has	
Melnik	54,096	pasa's has	
Strumica	35,731	miriliva's has	
Radomir	30,060	of a subaşı	
Dupnitsa	23,430	sultan's has	
Kiustendil	21,373	miriliva's has	
Vranja	21,372	of a senior military officer	
Nugeric	20,391	of a subaşı	
Sancak of Smederevo			
Rudnik	213,769	sultan's has	
Smederevo	120,115	miriliva's has	
Jejne	80,000	sultan's has	
Niš	71,058	miriliva's has	
Belgrade	40,000	miriliva's has	
Užice	15,806	miriliva's has	
Kojludža	10,000	miriliva's has	
Hram	5,000	miriliva's has	
Golubac	4,500	miriliva's has	
Resava	500	miriliva's has	
Sancak of Kruševac			
Zaplanina	203,969	sultan's has	1528-29, 203,910 akçe
Kruševac	65,784	miriliva's has	
Leskovac	34,310	miriliva's has	
Prokuplje	26,445	miriliva's has	
Bolvan	17,081	zeamet	
Planina	9,491	sultan's has	

City	Revenue (akçe)	Type of Holding	Comment
Sancak of Vučitrn			
Priština	59,551	sultan's has	1527, 65,801 akçe; 1487, 26,204 akçe
Vučitrn	18,918	miriliva's has	1544-45, 20,132 akçe
Trepča	10,024	sultan's has	1544-45, 207,769 akçe
Novo Brdo	10,262	sultan's has	1527, 3,983,785 akçe
Sancak of Prizren			
Prizren	74,068	miriliva's has	
Foča	25,868	miriliva's has	
Trgovište	24,733	miriliva's has	
Sancak of Bosnia			
Novi Pazar	88,666	sultan's has	1488, 32,369 akçe
Sarajevo	80,688	miriliva's has	1488, 42,241 akçe
Olovo	77,711	sultan's has	1488, 80,491 akçe
Konica	50,507	sultan's has	
Višegrad	39,591	miriliva's has	1485, 24,279 akçe
Sancak of Zvornik			
Srebrenica	477,032	sultan's has	(including profits from the mine)
Zvornik	64,440	sultan's has; & miriliva's has	
Brevenik (?)	6,629	miriliva's has	
Sancak of Hercegovina			
Foča	41,560	miriliva's has	1519, 12,254 akçe
Goražde	27,891	of a subaşı	1519, 34,692 akçe; miriliva's has
Prepolje	17,773	miriliva's has	1477-78, 29,512 akçe
Blagaj	9,658	miriliva's has	
Mostar	8,521	miriliva's has	1519, 10,281 akçe
Novi	8,421	miriliva's has	1519, 9,501 akçe

City	Revenue (akçe)	Type of Holding	Comment
Sancak of Elbasani			
Durrës	255,932	sultan's has	
Elbasani	44,208	miriliva's has	
Sancak of Vlona			
Vlona	1,554,888	sultan's has	1506, 878,355 akçe
Kanina	51,796	timar	
Berati	51,280	miriliva's has	1506-07, 65,915 akçe
Delvinë	19,887	miriliva's has	1506-07, 19,798 akçe
Gjinokastër	17,850	of a subaşı	1506-07, 25,726 akçe
Përmet	13,232	subaşı's timar	1506-07, 16,478 akçe
Skrapari	13,407	of a subaşı	1506-07, 13,560 akçe
Sancak of Shkodër			
Peć	31,368	miriliva's has	1485, 30,001 akçe
Shkodër	31,328	miriliva's has	1485, 28,100 akçe
Podgorica (Titograd)	17,112	miriliva's has	
Sancak of Karliili (Preveza)			
Leukas	26,221	miriliva's has	
Angelokastron	21,002	miriliva's has	
Vonica	18,484	miriliva's has	
Sancak of Trikkala			
Navpaktos	212,837	sultan's has	1520, 213,830 akçe
Trikkala	131,019	miriliva's has	1520, 131,019 akçe
Larissa	113,079	miriliva's has	
Padražik	107,293	sultan's has	1569-70, 94,800 akçe
Fener	60,495	of a subaşı	

City	Revenue (akçe)	Type of Holding	Comment
Domokos	60,393	paşa's has	1569-70, 80,423 akçe
Agrafa	42,994	zeamet	1520, 48,994 akçe; pasa's has
Çatalca	39,912	paşa's has	1520, 239,912 akçe; sultan's has
Elasona	38,021	paşa's has	1520, 38,021 akçe
Sancak of Ioannina			
Arta	235,777	sultan's has	1579-80, 105,000 akçe
Ioannina	139,550	miriliva's has	1579-80, 165,000 akçe
Aidonat	40,208	miriliva's has	
Rogos	31,825	zeamet	
Kónitsa	21,012	of a subaşı	
Rinasa	20,110	miriliva's has	
Sancak of Florina			
Florina	36,494	of a subaşı	
Sancak of Agribos			
Thebes	167,595	paşa's has	
Athens	157,931	paşa's has	
Lamia	129,275	paşa's has	
Salona	69,774	paşa's has	
Euboea	65,038	miriliva's has	
Lebadeia	45,892	paşa's has	
Kizilhisar	37,100	for the military of the fortress	
Modoniče	35,000	miriliva's has	
Sancak of Morea			
Kóronē	162,081	sultan's has	1583, 110,000 akçe
Motoni	136,907	sultan's has	1571-72, 123,269 akçe
Patras	133,032	sultan's has	1571-72, 203,547 akçe
Mizestre	105,539	miriliva's has	1583, 113,250 akçe

City	Revenue (akçe)	Type of Holding	Comment
Corinth	62,470	for the military of the fortress	27,151 akçe;* miriliva's has
Karitena	40,968	of a subaşı	1571-72, 20,027 akçe; miriliva's has
Argos	36,831	paşa's has	1571-72, 7,885 akçe
Holumiče	33,011	sultan's has	1571-72, 27,064 akçe
Pylos	28,964	sultan's has	1571-72, 29,436 akçe
Kalavrita	24,717	of a subaşı	20,806 akçe*
Vanika	4,400	for the military of the fortress	
Sancak of Paşa			
Salonika	3,149,659	sultan's has	3,506,762 akçe*
Edirne	1,807,892	sultan's has	1519, 1,746,900 akçe
Plovdiv	1,321,891	sultan's has; and of a paşa	
Skopje	372,258	sultan's has	928,288 akçe*
Serres	188,301	sultan's has	1519, 100,397 akçe
Sidero-kapsa	155,817	sultan's has	
Kostur	125,604	sultan's has	1519, 73,888 akçe; zeamet
Bitolj	106,226	sultan's has	261,325 akçe*
Enec	90,667	vakıf	1492, 72,590 akçe
Prilep	76,977	zeamet	1476-77, 79,614 akçe
Komotinē	69,365	zeamet	1519, 68,514 akçe
Ergene	64,371	vakıf	1484, 37,108 akçe
Veroia	55,219	zeamet	1519, 96,606 akçe
Nevrokop	54,708	zeamet	1519, 51,509 akçe
Serfiçe	52,251	zeamet	1519, 83,713 akçe
Drama	51,374	paşa's has	1519, 51,374 akçe
Zuhna	49,950	of a subaşı	1519, 56,928 akçe; zeamet
Stara Zagora	49,098	of a subaşı	
Ipsala	45,579	paşa's has	49,279 akçe*
Demir-hisar	40,360	sultan's has	1519, 27,625 akçe
Didymotei-khon	39,057	sultan's has and vakıf	

City	Revenue (akçe)	Type of Holding	Comment
Veles	31,500	of a subaşı	1476-77, 32,684 akçe; 1544-45, 30,523 akçe
Ferecik	28,000	vezir's has	1529, 22,755 akçe
Tetovo	24,158	zeamet	1476-77, 46,604 akçe
Yenice Vardar	20,000	zeamet	1519, 49,822 akçe
Hrupište	18,569	has of a bey	1519, 16,509 akçe
Tatar Pazardzhik	18,250	has of a beyler-beyi	
Kičevo	17,836	of a subaşı	1544-45, 28,881 akçe
Voden	15,213	zeamet	1519, 34,417 akçe
Yenice Karasu	15,000	paşa's has	1519, 37,804 akçe
Biglişta	13,630	has of a bey	1519, 10,030 akçe
Avret Hisar	12,297	sultan's has	1519, 12,051 akçe
Elkhovo	11,741	zeamet	9,041 akçe*
Korçë	9,111	paşa's has	
Sancak of Ohrid			
Ohrid	54,954	miriliva's has	1613-14, 25,353 akçe
Krujë	8,279	miriliva's has	

SOURCE: Compiled on the basis of data contained in Gökbilgin, "Kanunî Sultan Süleyman," pp. 252-66.

*The year is not known.

Appendix 2

Testators with Estates Valued at More than 5,000 Kuruş in Ruse, Sofia, and Vidin, 1700-1800

Year	Testator	Total Value of Estate [Estate]	Houses: Number, Value [Houses]	Shops: Number, Value [Shops]	Landed Property, Value [Land]	Income-Producing Properties: Type, Value [Income Property]	Money [Money]	Other Property: Value [Other]
Ruse								
1700	Bakie, daughter of Elhac Mahmud	5,369	------	------	------	400--çiftlik; 500--watermill	250	4,219
1738	Elhac Ahmed ağa, son of Elhac Ibrahim	9,916	------	2--500	------	250--çiftlik	8,202	964
1779	Ibrizade Süleyman, ağa, son of Ismail-kethüda	31,235	2,000^a	1--50	75	1,030--çiftlik; 545--2 watermills	15,233	12,302
1786	Elhac Musa ağa, son of Ibrahim çelebi	29,799	2--930	5--250	42; 187	15,000--1 1/2 inns and 21 shops; 700--1/2 watermill	11,172	2,218
Sofia								
1772	Mehmed beşe, son of Abdulrahman-bazarbaşi	5,013	1--300	------	30	------	1,169	3,514
1792	Hasan ağa, son of Osman-kethüda	6,454	1--2,000	------	------	------	1,844	2,610
1800	Esseid Hüseyin ağa, son of Elhac Ahmed ağa	18,967	1--1,500	------	30	------	------	17,437
1786	Esseid Elhac Ahmed, son of Esseid Elhac Mehmed	13,535	1--500	1--200	------	------	7,535	5,300
1778	Esseid Elhac Abubekir, son of Mehmed ağa-müfti	21,124	2--3,233	21--2,577	------	3,500--2 mills; 1,100--mill and coffee-houses	10,213	501

Year	Testator	[Estate]	[Houses]	[Shops]	[Land]	[Income Property]	[Money]	[Other]
1777	Mehmed ağa, son of Said Ibrahim-serdengeçti	7,542	1--1,000	------	------	------	2,386	4,156
1762	Ahmed ağa, son of Mustafa ağa-zabitin	27,845	1--100	------	------	3,400--6 mills	16,630	6,815
1751	Mehmed, son of Mustafa kâtibin	8,689	1--140	------	69	------	8,080	------

Vidin

Year	Testator	[Estate]	[Houses]	[Shops]	[Land]	[Income Property]	[Money]	[Other]
1720	Kara Halil Çavuş ağa, son of Elhac Ali	11,742	1--500	18--3,750	75;45	2,250--bathhouse; 300--mill	1,500	3,322
1746	Abubekir beşe, son of Abdullah	7,006	1--50	7--500	------	------	------	6,456
1748	Elhac Mehmed ağa, son of Halil	11,417	2--1,200	------	20;40	------	7,033	3,124
1753	Elhac Ömer beşe, son of Mustafa	5,553	1--300	4--400	------	------	4,397	456
1759	Elhac Abubekir, son of Salih	5,189	1--150	------	------	------	4,767	272
1759	Derviş Ahmed, son of Şeyfullah	7,233	1--100	------	------	------	3,255	2,978
1761	Elhac Ömer	5,007	1--450	1--50	30	------	3,127	1,350
1762	Karamani Elhac Mustafa	11,000	2--650	------	------	------	8,348	2,002
1763	Hemamcizade Ali ağa	58,676	1--1,000	1--120	25;10	800--çiftlik with 2 shops and 2 mills	35,555	21,966
1771	Rafye hatun	12,560	1--1,305	4--1,066	------	------	2,245	7,144
1762	Mustafa beşe, son of Abdullah	16,564	3--840	------	15	------	13,683	2,026
1762	Ibrahim ağa	18,113	1/2--600	------	300	------	14,525	2,688
1748	Ibrahim, son of Abdullah	5,937	1--450	------	------	------	3,839	1,648
1772	Esseid Elhac Mehmed ağa	10,372	1/2--1,500	------	------	------	5,482	3,390
1772	Elhac Ahmed	6,000	2--1,160	------	------	------	3,960	880
----	Küçük Elhac Ali beşe, son of Abdullah	16,388	2--1,000	1--400	50	150--mill	12,417	2,371

Year	Testator	[Estate]	[Houses]	[Shops]	[Land]	[Income Property]	[Money]	[Other]
1767	Elhac Mustafa, son of Musi	23,321	3--1,400	1--100	------	700--inn	18,504	2,617
1770	Halil beşe, son of Hasan	5,333	1--300	------	85;45	57--1/2 of a slaughterhouse	2,854	1,992
1769	Elhac Hasan-âlemdar	5,028	1--1,202	1 1/2--703	------	------	2,304	819
1771	Elhac Hüseyin beşe, son of Mehmed	13,881	1--400	1/2--436	22	1,088--çiftlik	11,445	926
1770	Arnaut Hüseyin beşe, son of Tahir	6,941	2--1,220	------	------	------	2,418	2,867
1771	Esseid Elhac Mehmed ağa, son of Ali	20,448	1--1,350; and 3 shops	3--930	------	1,000--mill	------	16,168
1771	Süleyman beşe	7,254	1--800	------	60;15	550--2 mills; 150--1/2 çiftlik	4,633	1,046
1771	Ummegelsum hatun, daughter of Elhac Mehmed	11,489	1/2--500	------	15;55	------	6,145	4,774
1771	Mustafa ağa, son of Ibrahim	15,477	3--949	2--684	622	------	9,823	3,399
1762	Rafie hatun, daughter of Elhac ağa	13,021	1--210	------	20	100--part of mill	11,803	888
1773	Ismail, son of Osman ağa	41,389	1--1,800	------	341	------	22,087	17,161
1772	Elhac Ömer ağa, son of Abdullah	8,785	2 1/2--1,600	2--250	150;120	40--çiftlik	1,005	5,620
1773	Topal Memiş ağa, son of Hasan	22,410	1--3,101	------	279	------	4,228	14,802
1774	Elhac Ibrahim ağa serdengeçti	52,316	1--1,500	3--4,808	1,050	500--mill; 3,500--bath; 15,500--inn; 672--2 storehouses; 100--çiftlik	6,826	17,905
1776	Elhac Süleyman ağa	28,296	1--1,500	5--600	200	3,000--3 inns	18,112	4,884
1770	Balcioğlu Arif ağa	15,451	2--1,916	------	35	100--çiftlik	4,865	8,535
1776	Elhac Hüseyin ağa, son of Abdullah	8,452	1--800	------	150;110	------	6,331	1,061
1778	Ismail ağa, son of Ibrahim	6,249	1--1,440	------	240;270	------	1,226	3,073
1778	Elhac Mehmed ağa, son of Ali	5,261	1--305	------	100;33	------	3,173	1,650

Year	Testator	[Estate]	[Houses]	[Shops]	[Land]	[Income Property]	[Money]	[Other]
1778	Molla Mustafa, son of Osman	6,064	2--2,300	-------	36	-------	721	3,007
1780	Kara Ahmed beşe	5,879	-------	1--300	-----	-------	4,327	1,252
1780	Elhac Hüseyin, son of Ömer-âlemdar	5,623	1½--500	1½--500	30	-------	3,771	822
1786	Fatme hatun, daughter of Elhac Mustafa	5,690	-------	12--4,135	520;35	-------	-------	1,000
1786	Elhac Ömer beşe, son of Hanci Abubekir	9,601	½--250	3--200	100	500--çiftlik	4,999	3,552
1787	Hamza, son of Elhac Abubekir	10,710	-------	3--1,443	-----	-------	6,537	2,730
1783	Hasan beşe, tanner	5,997	1--400	9--1,750	71	800	1,891	1,085
1782	Ismail, son of Abdullah-âlemdar	6,076	1--1,000	-------	-----	-------	4,807	269
1784	Mehmed Emin efendi, son of Ali	20,475	1--2,250	-------	1,000	-------	13,400	3,825
1788	Ali ağa, son of Mehmed	5,962	2--270	2--260	-----	-------	2,340	3,092
1787	Bosnak Ahmed ağa	19,557	2--1,250	1--250	500	-------	16,793	834
1789	Süleyman beşe, son of Mustafa	14,260	2--1,733	-------	-----	-------	5,008	7,519
1780	Elhac Mehmed ağa, son of Elhac Ahmed ağa	46,069	2--6,000	1--1,000	150	-------	31,687	7,232
1780	Numan ağa, son of Halil	7,210	1--2,250	-------	-----	-------	1,380	3,580
1787	Esseid Elhac Ahmed	13,535	2--1,000	-------	-----	2--1,100	9,650	1,785
1789	Ibrahim beşe, son of Abdullah, decorator	5,033	1--600	1--43	250	-------	1,771	2,369
1789	Fena, son of Ismail-âlemdar	5,221	1--646	-------	-----	-------	2,702	1,873
1791	Elhac Mehmed ağa, son of Ibrahim	13,849	1--500	7½--2,150	-----	-------	10,649	550
1793	Seyd Mustafa ağa, son of Elhac Hasan ağa	15,811	1--900	19--7,542	691	2,000--buildings	885	3,793
1794	Elhac Salih, son of Abdullah-âlemdar	9,539	½--300	5--650	25	500--mill; 200--çiftlik; 400--storehouse	6,151	1,313
1794	Elhac Feyzullah, son of Abubekir	23,360	1--500	-------	300	2,000 mill	18,929	631

Year	Testator	[Estate]	[Houses]	[Shops]	[Land]	[Income Property]	[Money]	[Other]
1793	Abubekir ağa, son of Salih ağa	22,329	¹/₂--2,000	3--2,706	1,100	4,601--4 mills; 2,500--buildings at Smurdan village	2,178	7,244
1794	İbrahim-âlemdar	5,147	1--300	------	------	------	1,606	3,241
1794	Elhac Mehmed ağa	12,332	3--1,761	------	------	------	9,752	819
1794	İsmail ağa	22,000	2--600	4--1,900	------	3,000--¹/₂ mill	14,450	2,050
1794	Hatice hatun, daughter of İbrahim	5,342	1--2,500	------	------	------	------	2,842
1794	Elhac Abdullah ağa	6,533	1--500	------	------	------	3,137	2,896
1792	Hüseyin beşe, son of Salih	10,145	1--500	------	------	500--mill	6,382	2,763
1793	Memiş ağa, son of Yüsuf	11,583	1--3,550	------	2,600	------	2,197	3,236
1795	Esseid Molla Ahmed, son of İbrahim	6,961	1--800	3--550	------	------	4,723	888
1796	Hacı Risto, son of Mancho	5,230	1--600	------	------	------	1,144	3,486
1795	Vellieddin efendi	11,729	1--500	1--500	------	1,500--2 mills	3,500	5,729
1795	Nefise hatun, daughter of Abdullah	8,658	1--2,000	------	71	------	855	5,732
1795	Salih ağa, son of Elhac Ahmed	5,106	1--1,500	------	600;1,000	------	820	1,186
1762	Hacı Ömer, son of Osman	12,882	1--900	1--250	20	------	8,021	3,691

SOURCE: NBKM, Oo, Rkr, R5, R36, R8, R9; Skr, S17, S21, S26, S25, S173, S311/7, S23; Vkr, S62, S40, S81, S55, S41, S52, S63, S61, S74, S37, S307, S71, S159a, S11, S77, S310, S169, S82, S70, S65, S19, S59, S48, S79, S68, S6, S160, S69, S167. The total value of the estate and the assessment of individual parts thereof are given here as recorded in the registers. The column for 'monetary sums' includes both cash on hand and loans due for collection. Owing to errors in additions, the column for "Other Types of Property" has been calculated by the author.

aThere is no number shown in cases of the ownership of parts of property.

Appendix 3

Individuals with Incomes above 2,000 Kuruş

Annual Income (in kuruş)	Profession	Name	Residence
60,000	Merchant	(French national, former bishop)[1]	Constanţa
20,000	Merchant	Paleologi Chirlesto	Constanţa
20,000	Grain dealer	"mosyo" Kanaki[2]	Constanţa
15,000	Merchant	Yanko, son of Nestor	Constanţa[3]
15,000	Merchant	Christian Joseph	Constanţa[4]
15,000	Grain dealer	Ernest, son of Roy	Constanţa[5]
12,000	Merchant	Andon, son of Gudi	Constanţa
6,000	Merchant	Hristo Despot	Constanţa[6]
6,000	Merchant	Despot Orezi	Constanţa
6,000	Merchant	Hacioğlu, son of Tomazi	Constanţa[7]

Annual Income (in kuruş)	Profession	Name	Residence
6,000	Wholesaler	Solomonaki	Constanța
5,000	Merchant	Pandeli, son of Stratiiadi	Varna
5,000	Merchant	Mehmed ağa, son of Riza efendi	Silistra
5,000	Bathhouse keeper	Arif ağa, son of Ömer	Shumen
4,000	Merchant	Ohanes, son of Kirkor	Silistra
4,000	Merchant	Tseko Yani	Silistra
4,000	Merchant	"mosyo" Karidiya	Constanța
4,000	Merchant	Kapudan Yani Makri	Constanța
4,000	Wholesaler in dry goods	Kevork ağa	Constanța[8]
4,000	Wholesaler	Simonaki	Constanța
4,000	Dealer in dry goods	Nikolcho, son of Stan	Babdag[9]
4,000	Clothier	Tekfur Garabetoğlu	Provadiia
4,000	Merchant	Hafiz Hasan efendi, son of Mustafa	Bazargic
4,000	Drover	Tatar Mehmed, son of Ali	Babdag
4,000	Horse trader	Hasan Mustafa	Bazargic
4,000	Slippermaker	Telioğlu Bekir, son of Ömer	Bazargic
4,000	Casino keeper	Khristo Balaban	Constanța
3,500	Clothier	Isak, son of Haron, millet vekili[10]	Silistra
3,500	Clothier	Bohor, son of Isak	Silistra
3,500	Clothier	Hacı Artin, son of Hamparsun	Silistra
3,500	Clothier	Garabet, son of Ovanes	Silistra
3,500	Dealer in dry goods	Iliia, son of Stavri	Constanța[11]
3,500	Abacı	Hristohor	Constanța[12]
3,000	Merchant	İslâm efendi	Constanța
3,000	Merchant	Habiodula ağa	Constanța
3,000	Merchant	Hristohor	Constanța[13]
3,000	Merchant	Tusun ağa zair Memiş efendi	Silistra
3,000	Merchant	Hacı Mestan ağa, son of Süleyman	Silistra
3,000	Merchant	Dedeoğlu ağa	Silistra
3,000	Merchant and farmer	Araslan, son of Kurti	Silistra
3,000	Merchant	Pencho, son of Georgi	Macin

Annual Income (in kuruş)	Profession	Name	Residence
3,000	Merchant	Bekir efendi, son of Mümin	Varna
3,000	Merchant	Hacı Hasan, son of Isa	Bazargic
3,000	Dealer in dry goods	Hacı Ahmed, son of Idris	Bazargic
3,000	Dealer in dry goods	Ohanes, son of David	Bazargic
3,000	Dealer in dry goods	Artin, son of Kapriel	Bazargic
3,000	Dealer in dry goods	Ohanes, son of Kapriel	Bazargic
3,000	Dealer in dry goods	Said Tahir	Bazargic
3,000	Dealer in dry goods	Panaiot	Constanţa
3,000	Dealer in dry goods	Prekoim(?)	Constanţa
3,000	Clothier	Hacı Mardiros, son of Garabet	Silistra
3,000	Dealer in sole leather	Abullâtif, son-in-law of Hacı Ahmed	Bazargic
3,000	Dealer in sole leather	Murtaza, son of Behinşah	Bazargic
3,000	Dealer in sole leather	Mirza, son of Bahtişah	Bazargic
3,000	Tanner's apprentice	Cafer, son of Abdullah	Bazargic
3,000	Bootmaker	Cevazoğlu Mehmed, son of Halil	Bazargic
3,000	Master tanner	Hacı Hüseyin ağa, son of Ismail	Shumen
3,000	Grocer	[a Turk, name illegible]	Silistra
3,000	Grocer	Mehmedoğlu, son of Ömer	Silistra
3,000	Grocer	Seve, son of Tufan	Silistra
3,000	Grocer	Gelioğlu Hafiz Mehmed, son of Ömer	Bazargic
3,000	Grocer	Bekir, son of Abdulrahman	Bazargic
3,000	Grocer	Hasan, son of Abdulkerim	Bazargic
3,000	Grocer	Hafiz Mehmedoğlu Mustafa	Provadiia
3,000	Grocer	Ismail, son of Halil	Shumen
3,000	Innkeeper	Cenat, son of Abdullah	Bazargic
3,000	Innkeeper	Zai, son of Abdullah	Bazargic
3,000	Innkeeper	Vladi, son of Stoian	Bazargic

Annual Income (in kuruş)	Profession	Name	Residence
3,000	Innkeeper	Zheliazoğlu Radi	Shumen
3,000	Casino keeper	Ivan, son of Tahman	Constanţa
3,000	Tobacco dealer	Panaiot, son of Dipolat	Constanţa[14]
3,000	"Servant" for a foreign company	Panbar Ebiuril[15]	Constanţa[16]
3,000	Money-changer	Yahudi, son of Isak	Constanţa[17]
3,000	Goldsmith	Pŭrvan, son of Petri	Silistra
3,000	Dealer in salt	Kurd Alioğlu haci Ömer, son of Süleyman	Silistra
3,000	Porter	Molla Ismail, son of Ömer	Bazargic[18]
3,000	Peddler	Ismail, son of Mehmed	Bazargic
3,000	Shopkeeper	Hacı Alemdar Kara Rustem, son of Mustafa	Provadiia
3,000	Baker	Onasi, son of Artin	Varna
3,000	Dealer in grapes	Müezzinoğlu Edhem ağa, son of Mustafa	Varna
2,500	Merchant	Dulko, son of Ivan	Silistra
2,500	Merchant	Murad, brother of Hairiet	Varna
2,500	Dealer in dry goods	Bekli Hasan ağa	Bazargic
2,500	Dealer in dry goods	Garabet, son of David	Bazargic
2,500	Tailor and dealer in dry goods	Hacı Garabet, son of Mariar	Bazargic
2,500	Dealer in dry goods	Papazoğlu Kirkor, son of Garabet	Provadiia
2,500	Clothier	Abraham, son of Agop	Silistra
2,500	Clothier	Matus, son of Hamparsun	Silistra
2,500	Clothier	Nagotoz, son of Ohanes	Silistra
2,500	Ironmonger	Negutunmuz, son of Ohanes	Silistra
2,500	Dealer in fancy goods	Magurdich, son of David	Bazargic
2,500	Dealer in leather	Abdulfetah, son of Emin	Bazargic
2,500	Dealer in leather	Tosunoğlu Süleyman, son of Halil	Bazargic
2,500	Dealer in sole leather	Namik, son of Hacı Mehmed	Shumen
2,500	Master musician	Ismail, son of Hüseyin	Shumen

Annual Income (in kuruş)	Profession	Name	Residence
2,500	Journeyman tanner	Hasan, son of Hacı Hafiz	Shumen
2,500	Journeyman shoemaker	Ali, son of Hacı Hafiz Ali	Shumen
2,500	Journeyman mutafçi	Ali	Shumen
2,500	Master tanner	Hasan, son of Mehmed	Varna
2,500	Slippermaker	Hacı Isağlu, son of Salih	Bazargic
2,500	Grocer	[a Turk, name illegible]	Bazargic
2,500	Grocer	H. Ahmed, son of Hasan	Bazargic
2,500	Grocer	Mehmed ağa, son of Sadulah	Silistra[19]
2,500	Grocer	Theohari, son of Karayani	Constanţa[20]
2,500	Grocer	Mehmed, son of Hacı Cok	Provadiia
2,500	Grocer	Zlati, son of Yorgi	Shumen
2,500	Baker	Manto, son of Manto	Silistra
2,500	Head cook	Hacı Ismail, son of Mehmed	Constanţa[21]
2,500	Ironsmith	Petko, son of Georgi	Shumen[22]
2,500	Farrier	Ömer, son of Hacı Nizan Mustafa	Provadiia
2,500	Farrier	Hacı Zekeriya, son of Osman	Bazargic
2,500	Potter	Ömeroğlu Mustafa	Bazargic
2,500	Potter	Küçük Ali, son of Osman	Bazargic
2,500	Master cooper	Delioğlu Osman, son of Abdullah	Bazargic
2,500	Cooper	[a Turk]	Silistra
2,500	Dealer in tallow	Alis, son of Mustafa	Provadiia
2,500	Drover	Petri, son of Yorgi	Silistra
2,500	Shepherd	Zlati, son of Zhelez	Shumen
2,500	Viticulturist	Boiadi Andon, son of Mihal	Provadiia
2,500	"Master"	Hüseyin, son of Receb	Shumen
2,500	?	Halil, son of Hacı Hasan	Bazargic

SOURCE: Data compiled from tezkeres and tax receipts for ten cities as contained in NBKM, Oo.

1. No name given. See NBKM, Oo, f. 171, ed. 1238, ℓ. 13.

2. From the French "monsieur."
3. Origins in Kolomyya, Galicia; an Austrian national.
4. From Danzig, a Prussian national.
5. From Vienna, an Austrian national.
6. Originally from Brăila.
7. A Greek subject.
8. Originally from Istanbul.
9. Origins in Shumen.
10. That is, a representative of the population in local administrative organs. In the following year the size of his income was revised by the fiscal authorities, being reduced to 2,000 kuruş. It is this lower sum that has been used in the calculations based on the documents in question.
11. Origins in the island of Cephalonia.
12. Originally from Kazanlŭk.
13. Originally from the village of Zherevna.
14. Originally from the island of Cephalonia.
15. NBKM, Oo, f. 171, ed. 1235, ℓ. 7.
16. A French subject originally from Toulon.
17. Originally from Ruse.
18. Originally from Razgrad.
19. At first he was a tobacco dealer and a grocer with an income of 4,000 kuruş. Later he became only a grocer, his income being revised downwards to 2,500 kuruş.
20. Originally from Nessebŭr.
21. Originally from Burgas.
22. Originally from Tŭrnovo.

Appendix 4

Shopowners at the Bazargic Fair, 1870

Name	Permanent Residence	Amounts Invested Area	Sum (in kuruş)	Number of Shops
Armenians				
Mardiros, son of Garabet	Burgas	Dry goods	10,000	3
Sarkis Sarkisoğlu	Varna	Dry goods	10,500	3
Yako, son of Artin bey	Shumen	Dry goods	11,000	2
Bedros, son of Artin	Istanbul	Dry goods	12,000	2
Hacı Ohanes, son of Oniyan	Bazargic	Dry goods	12,000	5
Magurdich Stepanoğlu	Shumen	Slippers	12,000	3

Name	Permanent Residence	Amounts Invested Area	Sum (in kuruş)	Number of Shops
Stepan, son of Ohanes	Unknown	Dry goods	12,000	4
Sarkiz Topsakaloğlu	Silistra	Slippers	16,000	3
Hacı Ohanes Lalaoğlu	Unknown	Slippers	16,500	7
Hacı Ohanes, son of Stepan	Unknown	Dry goods	17,500	13
Artin, son of Kirkor	Bazargic	Dry goods	21,500	6
		Tobacco	12,500	5
		Kerosene	10,000	2
		Taverns	6,000	3
Kapriel Topsakaloğlu	Silistra	Slippers	23,500	5
Hacı Garabet Kehayoğlu	Shumen	Dry goods	32,000	6
Hachik, son of Mardiros	Unknown	Dry goods	32,000	7
Hacı Kevork, son of Kapriel	Unknown	Dry goods	35,000	10
		TOTAL	302,000	89

Bulgarians

Name	Permanent Residence	Amounts Invested Area	Sum (in kuruş)	Number of Shops
Zhelez, son of Papa Georgi	Bazargic	Dry goods	10,000	3
Hacı Yanko, son of Vicho	Unknown	Kerosene	10,000	2
Petko, son of Stoian	Medgidia	Groceries	10,000	3
Zlati, son of Filip	Gelindjik	Groceries	10,500	3
Hacı Pavli, son of Milush	Liaskovets	Flour	9,000	2
Stefcho	Liaskovets	Flour	7,000	2
[Hacı Pavli and Stefcho in partnership]		Flour	3,500	1
Todor, son of Mincho	Bazargic	Dry goods	12,000	2
Ivan, son of Radi	Unknown	Cutlery	12,000	3
Ivan, son of Doicho	Unknown	Groceries	13,000	3
Ivan Dzhumalioğlu	Balchik	Cutlery	13,500	4
Daskal, son of Dimitŭr	Unknown	Cutlery	15,000	5

Name	Permanent Residence	Amounts Invested Area	Sum (in kuruş)	Number of Shops
Hacı Yanko, son of Flori	Unknown	Cutlery	15,000	3
Raicho, son of Tanas	Silistra	Flour	15,000	3
Nikolcho Kŭrtevich	Tulcea	Abacı	15,000	3
Parush (?)	Varna	Dry goods	15,000	3
Hristaki (?)	Varna	Dry goods	15,000	3
Parashkev Paskalioğlu	Varna	Groceries	15,000	4
Parush, son of Yorgi	Varna	Tobacco	5,500	3
Maria, daughter of Yorgi	Varna	Tobacco	11,000	2
Yorgi, son of Chaulanoğlu	Bazargic	Dry goods	17,000	3
Hacı Yorgi, son of Parashkev	Unknown	Dry goods	9,000	6
Todor, son of Ivan	Unknown	Flour	8,000	4
		Cutlery	17,500	2
Vasil, son of Rusi	Balchik	Dry goods	8,000	2
Raicho, son of Rusi	Balchik	Dry goods	10,000	2
Kolyu, son of Hacı Kostaki	Shumen	Dry goods	18,000	3
Manol Baltadzhioğlu	Unknown	Dry goods	18,000	3
Todor, son of Khristo	Shumen	Slippers	19,000	6
Ivancho Beshoğlu	Shumen	Slippers	19,000	6
Nedo, son of Iovcho	Tŭrnovo	Kerosene	19,000	4
Yorgi, son of Yorgi	Silistra	Abacı	20,000	4
Sakuzli Yorgi	Bazargic	Taverns	20,000	3
Todor, son of Dimitŭr	Djevizli	Taverns	20,000	3
Petŭr, son of Staniu	Balchik	Taverns	20,000	3
Topal Lefteroğlu Yanko	Varna	Groceries	21,000	3
Gancho, son of Radul	Bazargic	Cutlery	23,500	6
Petŭr, son of Veliu	Shumen	Slippers	23,500	6

| Name | Permanent Residence | Amounts Invested | | Number of Shops |
		Area	Sum (in kuruş)	
Baltadzhioğlu Ivan, son of Yorgi	Bazargic	Cutlery	12,000	3
		Dry goods	12,000	3
Hacı Vasil, son of Ivan	Bazargic	Dry goods	15,000	3
Atanas, son of Khristo	Silistra	"Braşov" goods	52,000	11
Aleksi, son of Khristo	Razgrad	Groceries	36,000	13
		Taverns	24,000	6
		TOTAL	819,000	178
Turks				
Osman, son of Mehmed	Bazargic	Groceries	10,000	5
Nurizade Hasan ağa	Unknown	Groceries	10,000	10
Civred efendi	Ruse	Tobacco	10,000	2
Hacı Osman, son of Mehmed	Silistra	Slippers	10,500	3
Kibriz, son of Mehmed	Dimotika	Dry goods	12,000	3
Mehmed çavuş	Varna	Groceries	12,000	3
Bacemioğlu Hasan, son of Hüseyin	Unknown	Tobacco	12,500	5
Hacı Mehmed, son of Idrisa	Unknown	Tobacco	13,000	3
Molla Yakub, son of Hacı Emin	Gelindjik	Dry goods	3,000	2
		Groceries	13,500	7
Ibrahim Yazci, son of Ali	Varna	Taverns	12,000	11
		Kerosene	2,500	1
[Ibrahim Yazci in partnership with Avram]		Groceries	9,500	11
Seid efendi, set- tler, in part- nership with Arslan	Bazargic	Dry goods	13,500	3
		Groceries	12,000	6
Hüseyin efendi, son of Ahmed	Bazargic	Groceries	5,000	5
		"Braşov" goods	6,000	4
		Salt	8,500	3
		Recreational	7,500	3

| Name | Permanent Residence | Amounts Invested | | Number of Shops |
		Area	Sum (in kuruş)	
Grasie, daughter of Arslan	Shumen	Dry goods	22,000	8
		Leather goods	6,000	2
Sipahizade hacı Necib efendi, son of Süleyman	Istanbul	Dry goods	22,500	7
		Groceries	8,500	3
		Cutlery	15,000	3
Beyleroğlu Agiya, son of Servie	Istanbul	Cutlery	10,000	8
		Fine goods	31,000	15
		Coffee	2,500	1
		Halva	14,000	7
Molla Bekir, son of hacı Mehmed	Bazargic	Fine goods	11,000	5
		Dry goods	79,000	48
		"Braşov" goods	18,000	8
		Salt	7,500	3
		Halva	15,000	7
		Slippers	52,000	29
Hatice, spouse of Molla Bekir		Slippers	7,000	7
		Dry goods	10,000	9
Rakibe, spouse of Molla Bekir		Slippers	5,000	3
Aise, daughter of Molla Bekir		Slippers	2,000	2
		TOTAL	521,000	265

SOURCE: NBKM, Oo, T-n, Meclis-i idare-i kaza, I resm-i tapu,
ℓ. V. 1870.

Appendix 5

*Owners of Two or More Houses
in Ten Cities of the Danubian Vilâyet, 1860-70*

Name	City	Total Value of Property (kuruş)	Value of Houses (kuruş)
Temistokli	Varna	20,000	10,000; 10,000
Mustafa efendi, son of Mehmed, first *kâtibin*	Varna	29,450	10,000; 8,000
Tseko, son of Zheliaz, shepherd	Shumen	30,325	19,000; 11,000
Dimitŭr, son of Ivan, tailor	Shumen	39,500	15,000; 11,000
Trakoğlu Dimitro, son of Kozma	Varna	40,000	35,000; 5,000
Sarkis, son of Balaban, merchant	Constanţa	46,500	20,000; 6,000; 5,000; 2,500

Name	City	Total Value of Property (kuruş)	Value of Houses (kuruş)
H. Mehmed, son of Mustafa of Burgas	Varna	58,550	25,000; 13,000
Mehmed ağa, son of Abdulla	Varna	60,175	30,000; 14,000
Velichko, son of Dimitŭr, grocer	Shumen	62,850	30,500; 22,000; 3,000
Dimitri, son of Stancho, grocer	Shumen	66,375	35,000; 15,000
Dimitraki from Debur, innkeeper	Shumen	70,250	30,000; 28,000
Vasilaki, son of Petre, grocer	Shumen	74,975	26,000; 9,000
Lâtif efendi, son of Yakub	Varna	79,600	30,000; 7,000
Toparlakoğlu Mehmed efendi	Varna	81,475	25,000; 2,500
Hafuz Eyyub, son of Ismail	Varna	86,750	35,000; 21,000; 5,000
Hacı Ahmed ağa with his children, from Lom	Lom	89,500	16,000; 2,500; 2,000
Süleyman ağa, son of Mustafa	Varna	89,825	15,000; 4,000; 3,000
Mehmed efendi, son of Ali	Lom	92,000	3,500; 2,500
Dimitri Paspali, second director of the Ottoman Bank	Varna	93,000	15,000; 6,000 5,000; 5,000
Ahmed ağa, son of Hacı Ömer	Lom	107,450	14,000; 6,500; 5,500
Mustafa efendi, son of Ali of Sivas	Varna	135,750	30,000; 23,500
Hüseyin, son of Mehmed Emin	Varna	136,450	50,000; 12,000; 10,000
Aleksander Sotiru Bela	Constanţa	138,600	20,000; 6,500
Todor efendi, tobacco merchant	Varna	170,750	60,000; 3,000
Hacı Emin ağa Zade Hüseyin ağa	Constanţa	240,500	20,000; 20,000; 15,000
Dikidjioğlu Stanko, owner	Shumen	252,575	100,000; 50,000
Miltiadi, merchant	Constanţa	396,000	80,000; 24,000
Askeri bey, son of Hasan bey	Varna	674,525	60,000; 30,000

SOURCE: Tezkeres and tax receipts contained in NBKM, Oo.

Appendix 6

Owners of Mağazas
Valued at over 50,000 Kuruş, 1866-70

Name	City	Number of Mağazas	Total Value (kuruş)
Aleksandra, daughter of Todori, a Greek subject	Varna	6	350,000
Salil paşa, son of Mehmed paşa	Varna	3	300,000
Askeri bey, son of Hasan bey	Varna	7	274,500
Miltiadi, Greek merchant from Negraponti	Constanţa	10	238,000
Nikolaidi Bazirgan	Varna	4	190,000
[name unreadable, a Turk]	Varna	3	120,000
Ali efendi and Mahmud efendi, sons of Abdi ağa	Lom	14	103,500

Name	City	Number of Mağazas	Total Value (kuruş)
Tahsin paşa, mutasarrif of Benghazi	Varna	1	100,000
Mehmed Ali bey, son of Halil paşa	Varna	1	100,000
Halile hanim, wife of mutasarrif of Benghazi	Varna	1	100,000
Fatma, wife of Mehmed Emin paşa, former müdür zaptiye	Varna	1	100,000
Dikidjioğlu Stanko, storehouse keeper	Shumen	5	100,000
Hacı Emin ağa, son of Hüseyin ağa, merchant	Constanţa	10	81,000
Aleksandru Sotiru Belcha	Constanţa	5	76,100
Stefanaki, son of Todoraki	Tulcea	5	73,750
Mustafa efendi, son of Ali of Sivas	Varna	3	65,000
Tütünci Todor efendi	Varna	3	65,000
Dimitri Papali, second director of the Ottoman Bank	Varna	2	62,000
Yuda, son of Mois	Lom	2	62,000
Hüseyin, son of Mehmed Emin	Varna	3	60,000
Luksandra, daughter of Todor	Varna	1	60,000
Süleyman efendi, son of Hasan ağa of Shumen	Varna	1	55,000
Veliko, son of Khristo; and Kosta, son of Atanas	Varna	2	55,000
Mehmed and Hasan, sons of Ibrahim	Lom	5	55,000
Ibis Zaim, son of Mehmed Ali	Provadiia	8	54,250
Pandeli, son of Strati	Varna	2	52,000

SOURCE: Tezkeres and tax receipts contained in NBKM, Oo, for the years 1866-1870.

NOTES

ABBREVIATIONS

AN SSSR   Akademiia nauk SSSR

APP   *Arkhiv za poselishtni prouchvaniia*

BAN   Bŭlgarska akademiia na naukite

BIA   Bŭlgarski istoricheski arkhiv

Br.   Broi

ed.   edinitsa

f.   fond

GIBH   *Godišnjak istorijskog društva Bosne i Hercegovine*

GINI   *Glasnik na Institutot za nacionalna istorija*

GSUIF   *Godishnik na Sofiiskiia universitet: Istoriko-filologicheski fakultet*

I,BA   Istanbul, Başvekâlet Arşivi

IBID   *Izvestiia na Bŭlgarsko istorichesko druzhestvo*

IC   *Istorijske časopis*

IFM   *Iktisat Fakultesi Mecmuası*

493

IG	*Istorijski glasnik*	Rkr	Rusenski kadiiski
IP	*Istoricheski pregled*		registŭr
IVAD	*Izvestiia na Varnenskoto*	S	Selishta
	arkheologichesko	SBID	*Spisanie na Bŭlgar-*
	druzhestvo		*skoto ikonomichesko*
IZII	*Izvestiia na Instituta*		*druzhestvo*
	za istoriia	Skr	Sofiiski kadiiski
l.	list		registŭr
NBKM	Narodna biblioteka	SNU	*Sbornik za narodni*
	Kiril i Metodi		*umotvoreniia*
NTA	Novopridobiti turski	TsDIA	Tsentralen dŭrzhaven
	arkhivi		istoricheski arkhiv
OAK	Orientalska arkhivna	VB	*La Ville balkanique*
	kolektsiia		*XVe-XIXe ss.*
Oo	Orientalski otdel	Vkr	Vidinski kadiiski
PSBK	*Periodichesko spisanie*		registŭr
	na Bŭlgarskoto		
	knizhovno druzhestvo		

Introduction

1. Some 500,000 archival units are preserved in the
Oriental Department (Oo) of the Cyril and Methodius National
Library of Sofia (NBKM). Unfortunately, not all of the records have had appropriate processing, but about 120,000 units
are available. They are arranged into archival funds (f.) and
into several collections. The 319 funds are identified by the
name of the relevant inhabited locality, with documents chronologically classified. There are also three separate collections: the Eastern Archival Collection (OAK), Newly Obtained Turkish Archives (NTA), and Settlements (S). *Defters*
(registrarial records) and the *sicil*s (*kadı* registers) form
yet another separate collection. Work with the funds of the
Oo is facilitated by card indexes and inventory books. Documents are described in the inventories in groups according to
the classification scheme, and those of the collections with a
résumé of their contents. A place and subject-thematic index
has been developed for the OAK. For more detailed information
about the establishment and development of the Oo, see B.
Nedkov, "Orientalistika v Sofiiskata narodna biblioteka,"
Godishnik na Bŭlgarski bibliografski institut 1 (1948):3-15;
idem, "Orientalskiiat otdel na Dŭrzhavna biblioteka 'V.
Kolarov'," IP 10, no. 2 (1954):115-20.
2. A kadı was a Muslim judge; ferman a decree issued in
the name of the sultan; berat a charter for the possession of
land or for assumption of a salaried post; and buyrultu a
written order.
3. Besides the sicils for these three cities, the Oo

houses several sicils for the cities of Bazargic (also known
as Hadzhioglu Bazardzhik, Dobrich, and today Tolbukhin) and
Silistra, but they are of a later time. For the sixteenth
century, see also H. Duda and G. Galabov, *Die Protokollbücher
des Kadiamtes Sofia*.

    4. TsDIA, f. Gümüşgerdan no. 161. Also see P. Panaio-
tov, "Arkhivniiat fond 'Gümüşgerdan'," IP 12, no. 2 (1956):
115-16. Of the 408 defters in the fund, 395 are in Greek, 11
in Turkish, and 2 in Bulgarian. About 16,000 of the documents
represent payrolls and receipts for wages and salaries, contracts for hired labor, contracts for the supply of goods,
correspondence with banks, and documents of all sorts of property and financial questions. The correspondence consists of
16,900 letters: 13,000 in Greek, 2,500 in Turkish, 750 in
French, 450 in Bulgarian, 170 in Armenian and Hebrew, and 40
in German and Italian.

Chapter 1

    1. The following two collections of articles have ex-
tensive bibliographies and references to the classics of Marx-
ism-Leninism: *Obshchee i osobennoe v istoricheskom razvitii
stran Vostoka: Materialy diskussii ob obshchestvennykh forma-
tsiiakh na Vostoke* (Moscow, 1966); and *Recherches internationales à la lumière du marxisme*, nos. 57-58 (January-April,
1967), a special issue entitled "Premières sociétés de classes
et le mode de production asiatique."

    2. S. Divitçioğlu, "Modèle économique de la société
ottomane (les XIVe et XVe s.)," *La Pensée*, n.s., no. 144
(1969), pp. 41-60; and "Essai de modèles économiques à partir
du M.P.A.," *Recherches internationales à la lumière du marxisme*, nos. 57-58 (January-April 1967) pp. 277-93.

    3. H. Antoniadis-Bibicou, "Byzance et le mode de pro-
duction asiatique," *La Pensée*, no. 129 (October 1966), pp. 47-
72.

    4. Z. V. Udal'tsova, *Sovetskoe vizantinovedenie za 50
let*, p. 195.

    5. M. Ia. Siuziumov, "O roli zakonomernostei, faktorov,
tendentsii i sluchaionostei pri perekhode ot rabovladel'che-
skogo stroia k feodal'nomy v vizantiiskom gorode," *Antichnaia
drevnost'i srednie veka*, no. 3 (1965), pp. 5-16; idem, "Vizantiiskii gorod (seredina VII--seredina IX v.)," *Vizantiiskii
vremennik* 27 (1967):38-70.

    6. A. P. Kazhdan, "Vizantiiskie goroda v VII-XI vv.,"
Sovetskaia arkheologiia 21 (1954):164-88.

    7. B. T. Gorianov, *Pozdnevizantiiskii feodalizm*,
pp. 245-47.

    8. Udal'tsova, *Sovetsko vizantinovedenie*, p. 212, where
the views of the author and of A. P. Kazhdan and M. Ia.

Siusiumov are summarized.

9. *Vizantiiskaia kniga Eparkha*, trans. M. Ia. Siuziumov (Moscow, 1962), p. 296; E. Kirsten, "Die byzantinische Stadt," *Berichte zum XI. byzantinische Kongress* (Munich, 1958).

10. *Istoriia vizantii* 3 (Moscow, 1967):113.

11. More comprehensive publications are now appearing on the late medieval Bulgarian city. See S. Lishev, *Bulgarskiiat srednovekoven grad*. On the medieval cities in Yugoslavia see R. Stefanović, *Bibliografija radova srednjevekovnih gradova Srbije, Zeti, Bosne i Hercegovine* (Belgrade, 1963); A. Deroko, *Srednjevekovni gradovi u Srbiji, Crnoj Gori i Makedonji* (Belgrade, 1950).

12. H. A. R. Gibb and H. Bowen, *Islamic Society and the West*, vol. 1, part 1, pp. 276 ff.

13. One of the latest works in this field is the monograph of I. M. Lapidus, *Muslim Cities in the Later Middle Ages*, which is devoted to the social and political life of the Muslim city in the Mamluk Empire up to the beginning of the sixteenth century. The book is equipped with an extensive bibliography. See also the report of K. Karpat entitled "The Background of Ottoman Concept of City and Urbanity," read at the Second Conference on the Balkan City, Venice, May 1971 and the other materials of this conference, published in *Structures sociales et développement culturel des villes sud-est européennes et adriatiques aux XVIIᵉ-XVIIIᵉ ss.* (Bucharest, 1975), pp. 323-40.

14. In addition to the works already mentioned, see *La Ville*, vols. 6-7 (1954-55) of *Recueils de la Société Jean Bodin*, containing articles on the institutions and economic life of Muslim cities by Georges Marçais, Claude Cahen, and Ö. L. Barkan.

15. See V. A. Gordlevskii, "Gosudarstvo sel'dzhukidov Maloi Azii," in idem, *Izbrannye sochineniia* 1:153-58.

16. A medrese was a higher school for the study of Muslim law and various religious and scholarly disciplines.

17. The zaviye was a small cloister with a hostel.

18. The term taifa was used to denote the concept of a professional group.

19. Cited by H. İnalcık, "The Foundations of the Ottoman Economic-Social System in Cities," VB, p. 21.

20. Ibid., pp. 17-24.

21. Gordlevskii, "Gosudarstvo sel'dzhukidov Maloi Azii," pp. 276-86.

22. Authors are not unanimous on how this merger of the Futuwwa and the guilds came about. Some believe that the Futuwwa absorbed the guilds; others believe that the guilds only adopted the aims and ceremonies of the Futuwwa. See the numerous documents in A. Gölpinarli, "Islâm ve Türk Illerinde

Fütüvvet ve Teşkilâtı ve Kaynakları," IFM 9, nos. 1-4 (1949-50):3-354; C. Cahen, "Mouvements et organisations populaires dans les villes de l'Asie musulmane au Moyen Âge: Milices et associations de Foutouwwa," *La Ville*, 7 (1955):273-285; and Fr. Taeschner, "Futuwwa," *Encyclopedia of Islam*, new ed. (Leiden, 1965).

Chapter 2

1. K. Jíreček, *Istoriia Bolgar*, p. 572.
2. Ibid., p. 461.
3. V. N. Zlatarski, *Nova politicheska i sotsialna istoriia na Bŭlgariia i Balkanskiia poluostrov*, p. 15.
4. Ibid., p. 6.
5. BAN, Institut za istoriia, *Istoriia na Bŭlgariia*, 2nd ed., 1:270.
6. Ibid., p. 278.
7. AN SSSR, Institut slavianovedeniia, *Istoriia Bolgarii*, 1 (Moscow, 1954):172.
8. N. Todorov, "Po niakoi vŭprosi na balkanskiia grad prez XV-XVIII vv.," IP 18, no. 1 (1962), pp. 32-58; idem, "Quelques aspects de la structure ethnique de la ville médiévale balkanique," pp. 39-45; and Z. Pliakov, "Za demografskiia oblik na bŭlgarskiia grad prez XV-sredata na XVII v.," IP 24, no. 5 (1968):29-47.
9. The results of Yugoslav historical studies on the socioeconomic development of all lands forming part of today's Yugoslavia are concisely provided in *Istorija naroda Jugoslavije*, vol. 2 (Belgrade, 1960). This work also indicates the relevant literature and sources. On the general impact and consequences of the establishment of Turkish rule see, in particular, B. Djurdjev, "Osnovi problemi srpske istorije u periodu turske vlasti nad našim narodima," IG, nos. 3-4 (1950); idem, "O uticaju turske vladavine na razvitak nåsih naroda," GIBH, vol. 2 (1950); N. Filipović, "Pogled na osmanski feudalizam," ibid., vol. 4 (1952); H. Šabanović, "Organizacija turske uprave u Srbiji u XV i XVI vijeku," IG, nos. 3-4 (1955); and A. Handžić, "Zvornik u drugoj polovini u XV i XVI vijeku, GIBH 18 (1970):141-96.
10. Valuable material can be found in GIBH and *Prilozi za orijentalnu filologiju u istoriju jugoslovenskih naroda pod turskom vladavinom*; see also H. Šabanović, *Bosanski pašaluk*, and M. Hadžijahić, *Neki problemi bosanske privredne historije predkapitalističkog perioda*.
11. O. Zirojević, *Carigradski drum ot Beograda do Sofije (1459-1683)*, contains an extensive bibliography.
12. A. E. Vakalopoulos, *Historia tou neou Hellenismou*, pp. 62-98.

---

13. Ibid., pp. 64, 71, 74 passim.

14. T. Papadopoulos, *Social and Historical Data on Population (1570-1881)*.

15. General works on the history of Albania (e.g., *Historia e Shqipërise*, vol. 1; and K. Frasheri, *Istoriia Albanii* [Tirana, 1959]) contain separate chapters providing general assessments of the total decline and destruction of Albanian cities as a result of the Turkish invasion. See also Gr. Arsh, I. G. Senkevich, and N. D. Smirnova, *Kratkaia istoriia Albanii* (Moscow, 1965). Though devoted to more contemporary questions and to different kinds of topics, some other works also contain information on the question of the city; see, e.g., S. N. Naçi, *Pashallëku i Shkodrës nën sundimin e bushatllive në gjysmën e dytë të shekullittë XVIII (1757-1796)* (Tirana, 1964). This work has also been published in French in *Studia albanica* 3, no. 1 (1966):123-44.

16. Z. Shkodra, "Qytetet shqiptare gjatë dy shekujvë të parë të sundimit turk," *Ekonomia popullore* 10, no. 5 (1963): 66.

17. Ibid., pp. 75 ff.

18. Ö. L. Barkan, "Quelques observations sur l'organisation économique et sociale des villes ottomanes des XVIe et XVIIe siècles," *La Ville*, vol. 7 of Recueils de la Société Jean Bodin, p. 291.

19. Ibid., pp. 290-94.

20. Ö. L. Barkan, "Osmanlı İmparatorluğunda bir iskân ve kolonizasyon metodu olarak sürgünler," IFM, vol. 11 (1949-50); 13 (1951-52):56-79; 15 (1953-54):209-37.

21. At the First Congress of Balkan Studies in Sofia in 1966, H. İnalcık and Ö. L. Barkan stressed the necessity of unified efforts by the scholars of the Balkan countries for the objective and scholarly elucidation of the socioeconomic and political history of the Balkan peoples (see *Actes du premier congrès international des études balkaniques et sud-est européennes* 1:119-20; and 3:86-87). In his paper presented at the second conference on the Balkan city in Venice in 1971, K. Karpat drew a decisive distinction between the pre-Ottoman Muslim city and the cities of the Ottoman Empire. See his report entitled "The Background of Ottoman Concept of City and Urbanity," *Structures sociales et développement culturel des villes sud-est européennes et adriatiques* (Bucharest, 1975), pp. 323-40.

22. To define the city as a separate category requires not only the use of judicial criteria but also a consideration of the status of the urban population itself. The latter topic is dealt with in chap. 4, "Some Trends in Urban Growth," where a study is made of the conditions encountered by the people coming to the cities, as those conditions are recorded

in Ottoman legislation and in kadı registers.

    23. The languages of the local population preserve the names and categorization of settlements regardless of the official changes that occurred. It was not rare for a settlement simultaneously to bear a name in two and even three languages. In some cases the designation of a settlement in one language as a village and in another as city produces additional complications in the classification of cities even where one might have hoped to use the easiest indication--the designation adopted by the administrative authorities.

    24. For example, in vol. 2 of *Turski izvori za bŭlgarskata istoriia, cep. XV-XVI v.*, ed. N. Todorov and B. Nedlov (which contains 15th-century timar registers), one finds indicated as nefs settlements noted in the recapitulation as being cities (Tŭrnovo, Nikopol, Shumen, etc.) (see pp. 161, 165, 199). On p. 361, however, Trŭn, although in the recapitulation indicated as a village, is also shown as a nefs.

    25. The word "şehir" is of old Persian origin. It passed into the Ottoman Turkish language through Arabic, which influenced its pronunciation. In modern Persian the word is pronounced şahir.

    26. In addition to the word "kale," another Arabic word for fortress is *hisar*. In Ottoman Turkish, this word was as a rule not used independently, but was often encountered as the second component of the names of some settlements: Avret Hisar (today's Kilkis, also known as Kukush), Demir Hisar (also called Timur Hisar, today's Siderokastron), Alaca Hisar (today's Kruševac), and so on.

    27. In the Muslim west the same term "kasaba" denoted the highest part of the city where the city governor resided and which was separated from the other part of the city by a fortress wall.

    28. H. Šabanović, *Katastarski popisi Beograda i okoline 1476-1566*, vol. 1 of idem, *Turski izvori za istoriju Beograda*, p. xxvii.

    29. O. Zirojević, "Palanka," in VB, pp. 173-80. The hayduts were bandits or brigands.

    30. Cf. idem, *Carigradski drum*, pp. 109, 110, 114. Using examples, this work provides descriptions and the concrete characteristics of the palanka (see pp. 119-20, 149-51, 155, 158, 164 passim.

    31. Madrica in Bosnia was a village in the first half of the 15th century, a marketplace in 1548, and in 1620 a kasaba. Although these dates do not indicate the exact time the change took place, they do give an indication of the evolution of this settlement (see Šabanović, *Bosanski pašaluk*, p. 202).

    32. Handžić ("Zvornik u drugoj polovini u XV i XVI vijeku," p. 170, n. 140) points out that in the lists of 1533

and 1548 for Zvornik one encounters *der kala-i Izvornik, der nefs-i Izvornik*, and *der varoš-i Izvornik*.

33. *Turski izvori*, 2:161-297.

34. For a graphic presentation of the administrative divisions and the demographic situation in the early 16th-century Balkans, see *Atlas po bŭlgarska istoriia* (Sofia, 1963), p. 25.

35. The first registrations of the population also mentioned other administrative divisions, for example the vilâ-yet. The vilâyet was an administrative unit larger than the nahiye. After the administrative reform undertaken in the second half of the 19th century, this term again acquired widespread usage in denoting the largest administrative unit. The vilâyet was headed by a *subaşi* or a *voyvoda* (a term borrowed from the Slavs).

36. See chap. 3.

37. A has was a possession of the sultan or of members of his family that was the official allotment provided to an important official during his term of office.

38. T. Gökbilgin, *XV-XVI ıncı asırlarda Edirne ve Paşa livâsı, vakıflar, mülkler, mukataalar*, p. 11. Following the organization of the army, the Rumelian beylerbeylik was divided into a left and a right wing. The right wing (*sağ kol*) included the area north of the Maritsa River and the left wing (*sol kol*) the area south of the Maritsa, the coast of the Aegean, Salonika, and the Peloponnesus. After the mid-16th century, the lands in the direction of Bosnia and Hungary formed a middle wing (*orta kol*). As a beylerbeyi sancak, the Paşa Sancak followed the above organization of the army, but unlike the other one had two beylerbeyis.

39. D. Šopova, "Koga Skopje bilo centar na sandžak vo periodot od padanjeto pod turska vlast do krajot na XVI v.," GINI 1 (1957):89-97.

40. H. İnalcık, *Hicrî 835 Tarihli Sûret-i Defter-i Sancak-i Arvanid*.

41. For details, see the basic work on this question, Šabanović, *Bosanski pašaluk*.

42. Ibid., p. 52.

43. Barkan calculates the population of a certain number of 16th-century cities in Asia Minor and in the Balkans by accepting the coefficient of five for the composition of a household and by adding 20 percent for the nonproducing population of Istanbul and 10 percent for other cities. He notes that this coefficient and percentages are regrettably based only on assumptions (see Barkan, "Quelques observations," p. 293, n.1.).

44. For the different viewpoints on this question, see R. Mols, *Introduction à la démographie historique des villes*

d'Europe du XVIe au XVIIIe s., 2:38-43.

45. N. Todorov, "Za demografskoto sŭstoianie na Balkanskiia poluostrov prez XV-XVI vv.," *Godishnik na Sof. univ.:
Filos.-istor. fak.*, 1-3, no. 2 (1959-60):202. The terms in
quotation marks indicate changes in the number of households
as noted in each subsequent registration.

46. Following the first publications of Turkish authors
and of the Ottomanists of the Balkan countries, the information in Ottoman registers that indicates the size of settlements has also been used in other works and in the surveys of
national histories.

47. On economic aspects of the city, see chaps. 8-10,
this volume.

48. Mols, *Introduction à la démographie*, 2:39.

49. Ö. L. Barkan and E. H. Ayverdi, *Istanbul vakıfları-
tahrîr defteri 953 (1546) tarihi*, pp. xiv-xvi.

50. In the 16th century there was an increase in the
number of large cities. Venice had 130,000 inhabitants in
1540, 160,000 in 1563, and 170,000 in 1576, but in 1577 on
account of the plague the number dropped to 120,000. Naples,
one of the biggest cities of 16th-century Europe, had a population that reached 200,000 at the end of that century. End-
of-the-century Paris was also a city of 200,000. At the same
time Lübeck, Hamburg, Augsburg, and Nuremberg each had some
20,000 inhabitants; only Cologne among the German cities surpassed 30,000. London in 1545 had 80,000 inhabitants, and by
1582 this number had grown to 120,000. In 1550 Florence had
60,000 inhabitants and Lisbon 65,000 (Mols, *Introduction à la
démographie*, 2:47; and M. Reinhard, A. Armengaud, and J. Dupaquier, *Histoire générale de la population mondiale*, pp. 117-
21).

51. Reinhard et al., *Histoire générale*, p. 120.

52. A. I. Kopanev, "Naselenie Russkogo gosudarstva v
XVI veke," *Istoricheskie zapiski* 64 (1959):233-54.

53. Mols, *Introduction à la démographie*, 2:45, n. 7.

54. See the travelers' accounts published by P. Matković
in "Putovanja po Balkanskom poluotoku XVI vijeka," *Rad Jugosl.
Akademije znanosti i umjetnosti*, vols. 56 (1881), 57 (1882),
74 (1887), 122 (1892), 124 (1895), 129 (1896), 130 (1897), and
136 (1898), and also the travel notes published by the same
author in *Starine*, vol. 10 (1878) and vol. 12 (1890). See
also K. Jíreček, "Stari pŭteshestviia po Bŭlgariia ot XV-
XVIII v.," PSBK, vols. 3-7 (1882-84); B. Tsvetkova "Materiali
za selishtata i stroitelstvoto v bŭlgarskite zemi prez XV-XVI
v.," *Izvestiia na Inst. po gradoustroistvo i arkhitektura*,
vols. 7-8 (1955). The Institute of Balkan Studies of the
Bulgarian Academy of Sciences and the press of the National
Council of the Fatherland Front are publishing a series of the

most interesting travel accounts for the Balkans. Several
books have already appeared. Without pretending that we have
provided an exhaustive list of published sources, let us
simply add that the Genadion Library in Athens possesses one
of the fullest collections of books by travelers to the Balkan
Peninsula.

55. Matković, "Putovanja," vol. 129 (1896):9.

56. *Dnevnikŭt na Khans Dernshvam za pŭtuvaneto mu do
Tsarigrad prez 1553-1555 g.*, trans. Mariia Kiselincheva, pp.
38, 187, 192.

57. O. Zirojević, "Rajnold Lubenau o Beogradu i Srbiji
1587 godine," *Godišnjak grada Beograda* 13 (1966):54.

58. For such information gathered for Sofia, see Tsvetkova, "Materiali za selishtata," pp. 480-88.

59. In substantiating several conclusions we are using
the abundant factual material explored by Zirojević in his
Carigradski drum.

60. The devşirme was the so-called blood tax, the forced
collection of Christian youth to serve in the Janissary corps.

61. Zirojević, *Carigradski drum*, pp. 130-31.

62. Ibid., pp. 154, 155.

63. Ibid., pp. 133-34.

64. This total number of households results from an
approximate calculation. For the 27 villages for which information is lacking, we have used the calculated average size of
a household for the villages in the given section of the road.

65. Müstahfızes were the mounted guard of a fortress.

66. Azaps were the rank and file of a fortress garrison.

67. Topçus were the artillerists.

68. Armatoles were locally recruited armed guards.

69. Zirojević, *Carigradski drum*, pp. 121-27.

Chapter 3

1. Ö. L. Barkan, "Osmanlı Imparatorluğunda bir iskân ve
kolonizasyon metodu olarak sürgünler," IFM, vol. 11 (1949-50),
vol. 13 (1951-52), vol. 15 (1953-54); T. Gökbilgin, *Rumeli'de
Yürükler, Tatarlar ve Evlâdi Fâtihan*.

2. See *Turski izvori za bŭlgarskata istoriia, cep. XV-
XVI v.*, ed. N. Todorov and B. Nedkov, 2:55-103 passim.

3. H. A. Gibbons, *The Foundation of the Ottoman Empire*,
pp. 80-81.

4. J. Hammer, *Histoire de l'Empire ottoman* (Paris,
1840), 2:196-97.

5. N. Jorga, *Byzance après Byzance*.

6. R. Grousset, *L'Empire de Levant*, pp. 609-10.

7. M. F. Köprülü, *Les Origines de l'Empire ottoman*; J.
Hakkı, J. Uzunçarsılıoğlu, *Anadolu Beylikleri ve Akkoyunlu
Karakoyunlu devletleri* (Ankara, 1937); M. Akdağ, "Osmanlı

Imparatorluğunun kuruluş ve inkişafı devrinde Türkiyenin Iktisadî Vaziyetî," *Belleten*, vol. 13 (1949), vol. 45 (1950); H.
İnalcık, "L'Empire ottoman," in *Actes du premier congrès international des études balkaniques et sud-est européennes*
3:75-104.
    8. Barkan, "Osmanlı Imparatorluğunda bir iskân" (1949-
50) pp. 524-29.
    9. Gökbilgin, *Rumeli'de de Yürükler*, pp. 55, 71, 80-81,
84 ff.
    10. We shall not dwell here on the question of the ori-
gin and the exact time of the settlement of other Turkic
tribes. Although historians have repeatedly used the information on these other tribes contained in chronicles and in
manuscripts, they have not resolved the basic questions. In
addition to the literature already mentioned, see also M.
Drinov, "Istoricheskoto osvetlenie vŭrkhu statistikata na
narodnostite v iztochnata chast na Bŭlgarskoto kniazhestvo,"
PSBK, 7 (1884):1-24; 8(1885):68-75.
    11. On these matters there is an abundant literature in
various languages. Attempts have even been made to estimate
the number of seized Christian children. In Hammer's opinion
this number reached half a million. See J. Hammer, *Geschichte
des osmanischen Reiches* 1:98.
    12. Naturally, in presenting the Constantinople Patri-
archate with such rights, the Ottoman state was also guided by
other considerations: to deepen the contradictions between
the Eastern Orthodox peoples and the Western church and to
work against the intensification of the liberation movement of
the Balkan peoples in connection with the wars that the Catholic states were conducting against the Ottoman Empire.
    13. H. İnalcık has prepared a table indicating, by
sancak, the number of Christian sipahis (where the number was
more than 10): Trikala--36; Skoplje, Tetovo, and others--50;
Kicevo, Prilep--36; Vucitrn--27; Vidin; etc. See H. İnalcık,
"Od Stefana Dušana do Osmanskog carstva," *Prilozi za orijentalnu filologiju i istoriju*, 3-4 (1952-53):40 ff. See also
idem, *Hicrî 835 Tarihli Sûret-i Defter-i Sancak-i Arvanid*,
pp. 15 ff.; and B. Tsvetkova, "Novye dannye o khristianakh-
spakhiakh na Balkansom poluostrove v period turetskogo gospodstva," *Vizantiiskii vremennik* 13 (1958):184-97.
    14. N. Todorov, "Za demografskoto sŭstoianie na Balkan-
skiia poluostrov prez xv-xvi v.," *Godishnik na Sof. univ.:
Filos.-istor. fak.*, 1-3, bk. 2 (1959-60):223-24.
    15. S. Dimitrov, "Demografski otnosheniia i pronikvane
na isliama v Zapadnite Rodopi i dolinata na Mesta prez XV-XVII
vv.," *Rodopski sbornik* 1 (1965):63-114.
    16. See the special study by A. Handžić, "O islamizaciji
u severoistočnoj Bosni u XV i XVI vijeki," *Prilozi za*

orijentalnu filologiju 16-17 (1966-67):1-48.

17. S. Skendi, "Crypto-Christianity in the Balkan Area
under the Ottomans," *Slavic Review* 26, no. 2 (1967):226-46;
and see the author's comments on the same subject in *Actes du
premier congrès international des études balkaniques et sud-
est européennes* 3 (1969):563-65; see also K. Kyrris, "L'Importance sociale de la conversion (volontaire ou non) d'une
section des classes dirigeantes de Chypre à l'Islam pendant
les premiers siècles de l'occupation turque--fin du XVIIe s.,"
ibid., pp. 437-62.

18. This form of violence was not softened by the passing centuries. The tragic murder of the French and German
consuls in Salonika in 1876 is well known. In a statement
submitted in the middle of the 19th century to Grand Vizier
Reşid Paşa, Aleksandŭr Ekzarkh pointed to the abduction of
women with the connivance of local authorities as one of the
greatest abuses: "On the other hand, if one of these police-
men wants to marry one of these beautiful maidens, he turns
to the *bülükbaşı* [small unit commander] and tells him: 'Sir
I want at any cost to make this girl Moslem and then take her
for a wife. She does not want it, but parents do not want it
either. For God's sake, what should I do?'

"'You son of a bitch,' the *bülükbaşı* replies, 'abduct
her!'" (see N. Todorov, *Polozhenieto na Bŭlgarskiia narod pod
tursko robstvo* [Sofia, 1953], p. 165).

19. The data about the number of voynuks is confirmed by
many other sources. For example, their number in the sancaks
known for a high concentration of reayas of special designation did not exceed 1,000; in 1467 in Smederevo there were
720 voynuks (217 voynuks and 503 auxiliary *yamak*s); in the
early 16th century in Kruševac they reached 1,000; and in the
Vidin area there were 231 voynuks (see İnalcık, "Od Stefana
Dušana," pp. 35-36).

20. Müsellems were a regular cavalry force paid on a
salary basis.

21. Barkan, "Osmanlı Imparatorluğunda bir iskân," 15
(1953-54):235-36. In another place Barkan calculates the
entire population with a special designation of 26,239 persons
in Asia Minor and 12,464 in the "right wing" of the beylerbeylik of Rumelia.

22. Cebelis were the armed forces that a sipahi had to
raise for running the fief in the event of military operations.

23. Ö. L. Barkan and E. H. Ayverdi, *Istanbul vakıfları
tahrîr defteri 953 (1546) tarihi*, pp. xiv-xvi.

24. The term Istanbul did not at that time take in all
parts of the present city. Until the 1930s, Istanbul referred
only to the old part of the city, built on the peninsula

formed by the southern shore of the Golden Horn and the Sea of Marmara and separated from the mainland by the powerful fortress wall defending the city from all invasions. The Galata was situated on the northern shore of the Golden Horn and beyond it was Pera, the district for foreign colonies. These three sections--Istanbul, Galata, and Pera--together bore the name of "Konstantiniye" in Ottoman Turkish documents, "Constantinople" in Greek and western European languages, and "Tsarigrad" in Bulgarian and other Slavic languages. On the opposite (Asiatic) shore was located Üsküdar (Scutari), which essentially constituted a separate city.

25. This data can be found in the monograph of R. Mantran, *Istanbul dans la seconde moitié du XVIIe siècle*, pp. 42-47. The subsequent description of Istanbul is based on this work (pp. 49-64).

Chapter 4

1. The number of Jews expelled from Spain has not been accurately established. Approximately 300,000 persons were involved in a movement that took them to Portugal, France, Italy, and North Africa. From these points a considerable number moved on and resettled in the Ottoman Empire. It is believed that originally about 40,000 Jews settled in Turkey, and that soon thereafter their number was doubled by Jews who arrived a little later from Sicily and Portugal. See J. Loeb, "Le Nombre des juifs de Castille et d'Espagne au Moyen Âge," *Revue des études juives*, no. 14 (1887), pp. 160 ff.; M. Q. Franco, *Essai sur l'histoire des Israélites de l'Empire ottoman*, pp. 21-23, 29-31; J. S. Emmanuel, *Histoire des Israélites de Salonique* 1:46, 57-61, 133, 266; and A. Iosifov-Bokhachek, *Grad Nikopol prez vekovete*, pp. 82 ff.

2. T. Gökbilgin, "Kanunî Sultan Süleyman," p. 263.

3. NBKM, Oo, Sn 16/35.

4. T. Gökbilgin, *XV-XVI ıncı asırlarda Edirne ve Paşa livâsı, vakıflar, mülkler, mukataalar*, p. 60.

5. A document contained in the Oriental Department indicates that about a century later (around 1617) the Jewish population of Edirne had considerably declined: the number of mahalles had fallen to 3 and there were now only 4 households. This decrease occurred because Istanbul had by now definitely replaced Edirne in political significance and Istanbul and Salonika had emerged as the centers of economic life in the eastern Mediterranean. In all probability, part of Edirne's Jewish population moved to these cities, where they increased the size of the existing Jewish colonies (NBKM, Oo, *Ciziyedar* 1026--Edirne).

6. It was not until the 18th century that life expectancy began to rise; but even then infant mortality ran from

20 to 50%. See R. Mols, *Introduction à la démographie historique des villes d'Europe du XVIe au XVIIIe s.*, 2:313 ff.
    7. Over the comparatively short period of 30 to 40
years, London, Rome, Toulouse, Jena, and other cities (for
all of which we know the exact mortality rate) decreased in
population by several tens of thousands. Only an influx of
people from the outside made it possible for these cities to
overcome the high mortality rate and to grow (see ibid.,
2:366-68).
    8. Ibid., 2:333 ff. Mols cites a number of descrip-
tions by contemporaries, including the view expressed by
J. J. Rousseau.
    9. Ö. L. Barkan, "Türk Yapı ve Yapı Malzemesi Tarihi
için Kaynakları," IFM 17, nos. 1-4 (1955-56):20.
    10. G. Gŭlŭbov, *Turski izvori za istoriiata na pravoto
v bŭlgarskite zemi* 1:23.
    11. Ibid., p. 249. An analogous provision held true
for Nikopol, with the one exception that it specified remuneration: "And if someone's reaya does not do farming, and
if he has a craft that he performs or if he engages in carting, fishing, or hired work, then, if he is a Muslim, he is
to give his sipahi 50 akçe *bedel-i öşr*; and, if he is a kâfir,
he will give 62 akçe. And furthermore, if he is a Muslim he
will give 22 akçe *resm-i çift*; if he is a kâfir, he will give
25 akçe ispence" (the ispence was levied on non-Muslim men and
women who had reached the age of maturity; the *bedel-i öşr* was
an equivalent to the tithe; and the *resm-i çift* was an agricultural tax). See Ö. L. Barkan, *Kanunlar*, vol. 1 of *XV ve
XVI-ıncı asırlarda Osmanlı Imparatorluğunda ziraî ekonominin
hukukî ve malî esasları*, p. 271.
    12. Barkan, *Kanunlar*, pp. 61, 271, 288, 390; Gŭlŭbov,
Turski izvori, 1:99. In this period one can observe certain
fluctuations in the size of the çift bozan, but the rate remained close to the figures indicated.
    13. A mut was a dry measure equaling between 400 and 500
kilograms.
    14. Barkan, *Kanunlar*, p. 390; Gŭlŭbov, *Turski izvori*,
1:23.
    15. Gŭlŭbov, *Turski izvori*, 1:24.
    16. Barkan, *Kanunlar*, p. 61. "From the reaya who works
as a coppersmith or as a merchant in another vilâyet and who
returns home once a year or once every two years, and who with
this earns his full livelihood [i.e., his income came only
from this trade], from such a reaya must be taken 150 akçe
levandiye [instead of the 75 akçe if he practiced his trade in
the village]." (The first bracketed remark is Barkan's, the
second is the author's. The levandiye was a monetary tax paid
by peasants engaged in seasonal work).

17. Barkan, *Kanunlar*, pp. 2-3, 24 ff.

18. A. F. Miller has furnished a characterization of the Ottoman ruling class that is perfectly clear: "The ruling class was composed not simply of feudal lords, but of feudal lords as warriors for whom, as was usual in every feudal society, the exploitation of the peasantry--the receipt of rents from the land and the appropriation of surplus production--served as a supplementary source of enrichment, more precisely as a means of 'feeding.' What was fundamental for them was the conquest of new territories and their direct plunder" (see "Turtsiia," *Sovetskaia istoricheskaia entsiklopediia* 14 [Moscow, 1973]:560). Patrimonial estates were not created until the 17th and 18th centuries.

19. Barkan, *Kanunlar*, pp. 2-3, 7-9, 234, 271, 273, 288; Gŭlŭbov, *Turski izvori*, 1:99 and 159.

20. H. Duda and G. Galabov, *Die Protokollbücher des Kadiamtes Sofia*, docs. 938, 276, 287, 940, 352.

21. For example, the brothers Dimitŭr and Stoian, sons of Petko, sold their house in the village of Zhitene in the region of Sofia to Mehmed-beşe, the son of Abdulah, for 4,000 akçe. The price of the house indicates that it corresponded to a medium-sized urban house of the kind then being sold in Sofia. In another case, the priest Nikola, a resident of the village of Dragostintsi, sold his house in the village of Vrŭbnitsa. Todor, the son of Iliia, of the village of Filipovtsi, sold his house to Mustafa Çelebi for 2,600 akçe. A resident of Sofia, Suche, the son of Tovcho, sold his vineyard in the village of Konevitsa. See ibid., docs. 390, 432, 109, 1129. Other instances of the buying and selling of shops, vineyards, etc., are provided below.

22. Khr. Gandev, "Pronikvaneto i ukrepvaneto na bŭlgarite vŭv Vidin kŭm kraiia na XVII i prez XVIII v.," *Izvestiia na Etnografskiia institut i muzei* 4 (1961):8.

23. NBKM, Oo, Rkr, R_2, ℓ. 18b.

24. Ibid., ℓ. 108a-II.

25. Ibid., R_3, ℓ. 15-I; R_4, ℓ. 11a-II; ℓ. 14b-IV, etc.

26. The derogatory connotation of the concept of "reaya" as a name for the subject non-Muslim population did not take hold in the Ottoman Empire until the 18th century. Before that time the term had a societal meaning. See I. Kabrda, "Raia," *Izvestiia na istoricheskoto druzhestvo* 14-15 (1937): 172.

27. Gŭlŭbov, *Turski izvori*, 1:146. There did exist, however, certain differences in the land obligations of the urban and village resident. In and of itself, the land tax was the same for both, since it was based on the principle that the determining element was the land itself. A city dweller, however, paid it only in the case where his çiftlik

was on timar land. If it was on *mülk* (personal property) or
vakıf land (land endowed for religious or benevolent purposes), then the system of tax obligation was different;
specifically, the difference rested in the fact that the city
dweller did not pay the çift bozan tax and could freely
transfer his land (see ibid., p. 49).
    28. Ibid., p. 51.

Chapter 5

    1. The title "vezir" was given to beylerbeyis or those
of equal rank; a subaşı was the head of the 16th century
vilâyet; a vakıf was a trust established with a land grant to
support a pious foundation.
    2. In such cases the sancakbeyis received receipts from
a specified type of tax and in amounts that did not exceed
several tens of thousands of akçe. Thus, for example, the
sancakbeyi of Vlona was alloted only the *bad-i hava* tax (an
extraordinary tax that the sultan's administration collected
for the benefit of the feudal lord in return for the payer's
judicial immunity); and in Plovdiv the part of the urban
receipts alloted to the has holding of Ayas Paşa amounted to
30,000 akçe, whereas the sultan's has totaled 1,290,000 akçe
(see T. Gökbilgin, "Kanunî Sultan Süleyman Devri başlarında
Rumeli eyaleti livaları, şehir ve kasabaları," *Belletin* 20
(1956):263, n. 31).
    3. The mir-i alem was the sultan's standard keeper.
    4. Gökbilgin, "Kanunî Sultan Süleyman," p. 266, n. 52.
    5. A. Handžić, "Zvornik u drugoj polovini u XV i XVI
vijeku," GIBH 18 (1970):149.
    6. Gökbilgin, "Kanunî Sultan Süleyman," p. 264, n. 39.
The distribution of cities with high receipts indicates that
the larger feudal appropriations were not divided into timars.
Among the cities listed there are only isolated cases of the
fragmentation of has holdings into timars. During the time
of Mehmed II in the 15th century, to cite one such example,
the city of Zuhna, with its revenue of 50,000 akçe, was one
of the has holdings of Mehmed Paşa; but in the second quarter
of the 16th century the receipts of this city covered several
zeamets and timars.
    7. I. H. Uzunçarşılı, *Osmanlı tarihi* 3, pt. 2:331-32;
Z. Karamursal, *Osmanlı mâlî tarihi hakkında tetkikler*, pp.
152-62.
    8. Ö. L. Barkan, "Osmanlı Imparatorluğu bütçelerine
dair notlar," IFM 17, nos. 1-4 (1955-56):195.
    9. Ö. L. Barkan, "H. 933-934 (M. 1527-1528) Mâlî yılına
âit bütçe örneği," IFM 15, nos. 1-4 (1953-54):251-329.
    10. Ibid., pp. 255, 257.
    11. On the mukataas, see T. Gökbilgin, *XV-XVI ıncı*

asırlarda Edirne ve Paşa livâsı, vakıflar, mülkler, mukataa-lar, pp. 87 ff; and V. Mutafchieva, "Otkupuvaneto na dŭrzhav-nite prikhodi v Osmanskata imperiia prez XV-XVII v. i razvi-tieto na parichnite otnosheniia," IP 16, no. 1 (1960):41 ff.

12. Gökbilgin, *XV-XVI ıncı asırlarda Edirne,* pp. 125-33; Mutafchieva, "Otkupuvaneto," pp. 50-51; Barkan, "Osmanlı Imparatorluğu bütçelerine dair notlar," pp. 206, 210, 242.

13. In 1668-69 the cizye reached 107,013,358 akçe. To this amount should be added the following sums: 16,730,380 akçe from the cizye on the Gypsies of Rumelia; 16,406,220 from the Christians of Wallachia; 4,200,000 from the Christians of Bogdan (Moldavia); 1,430,000 akçe from the foreign Christians in the area of Salonika; 17,090,940 from the Armenians scat-tered about Rumelia and Anatolia; and 874,000 from the Jews in Istanbul (see Barkan, "Osmanlı Imparatorluğu bütçelerine dair notlar," pp. 225 ff).

14. *Turski izvori za bŭlgarskata istoriia, cep. XV-XVI v.,* ed. N. Todorov and B. Nedkov, vol. 2.

15. For the bad-i hava tax see n. 2; the resm-i huk was a tax in money levied on pig owners; the niyabet was an ex-traordinary tax levied on the reaya for defense of the region. The revenue from this tax was divided between the feudal lord and the sancakbeyi.

16. The Istanbul kile was equal to 25.656 kg for wheat and flour, and to 22.25 kg for barley. In the provinces the kile was a varying measure of dry weight.

17. *Turski izvori,* 2:57, 67, 73, 431, 457.

18. Ibid., pp. 73, 75.

19. Ibid., pp. 117, 119.

20. Gökbilgin, "Kanunî Sultan Süleyman," p. 269, n. 270.

21. Ibid., p. 282, n. 160.

22. Ibid., n. 161.

23. M. Sokoloski, "Prilog kon proučuvanjeto na tursko-osmanskiot feudalen sistem so poseben osvrt na Makedonija vo XV i XVI vek," GINI 2, no. 1 (1958):157-228; and idem, "Le Développement de quelques villes dans le sud des Balkans au XVe et XVIe siècles," *Balkanica* 1 (1970):81-106.

24. Over a period of not quite fifty years the proceeds from the ispence in relation to the total receipts of Veles ranged from 13.6% to 32.3%; in the middle of the 15th century in Tetovo this item represented one-third of the city's re-ceipts, but twenty years later only 10.8%. This tax had about the same relative weight in Kostur and Prilep (respectively, 20.4% and 12.5%).

25. Barkan, "Tahiri demografi araştırmaları ve osmanlı tarihi," *Tarihi Mecmuası* 10 (1953):25-26.

26. Handžić, "Zvornik v drugoj," pp. 183-84. A dönüm eventually came to equal 919.3 square meters. As an older

unit of square measure, the dönüm referred to a plot of land
40 steps long and 40 steps wide, the step or pace being recorded as an "average step."
27. NBKM, Oo, Sn. 16/35.

Chapter 6

1. See, e.g., *Turski izvori za istoriiata na pravoto v
bŭlgarskite zemi* 1:11-102.
2. Ö. L. Barkan, "XV Asrın sonunda bazı büyük
şehirlerinde eşya ve yiyecek fiyatlarının tesbit ve teftişi
hususlarını tanzim eden kanunlar," *Tarih vesikaları* 1, no. 5
(1942):326-40.
3. Ibid., p. 328.
4. A. S. Tveritinova, *Kniga zakonov sultana Selima I*
(Moscow, 1979).
5. H. A. R. Gibb and H. Bowen, *Islamic Society and the
West* 1:107-37; R. Mantran, *Istanbul dans la seconde moitié du
XVIIe s.*; and for a more detailed account see I. H. Uzunçarşılı, *Osmanlı devletinin Merkez ve Bahriye teşkilâtı*.
6. The kadıasker was a chief military judge whose administration was in charge of justice and education and was
guided by the laws of Islam.
7. The descriptions concerning Istanbul are based on
the works of Uzunçarşılı and Mantran.
8. L. Güçer, "XVIII yüzyıl ortalarında Istanbul un
iasesı için lüzumlu hububatın temini meselesı," IFM 11, nos.
1-4 (1949-50), 397-416; Sp. Asdrahas, "Aux Balkans du XVe s.,
producteurs directs et marché," *Etudes balkaniques*, no. 3
(1970), pp. 36-69.
9. Mantran, *Istanbul*, p. 192.
10. Barkan, "XV Asrın sonunda," p. 336.
11. *Dnevnikŭt na Khans Dernshvam za pŭtuvaneto mu do
Tsarigrad prez 1553-1555 g.*, trans M. Kiselincheva, p. 68.
12. The Oriental Department of the National Library in
Sofia contains a list of 17th-century celepkeşans that should
be published in the series of Turkish sources on Bulgarian
history. See B. Cvetkova, "Les Celeps et leur rôle dans la
vie économique des Balkans à l'époque ottomane (XVe-XVIIIe
s.)," in *Studies in the Economic History of the Middle East
from the Rise of Islam to the Present Day*, ed. M. H. Cook,
pp. 172-93.
13. Mantran, *Istanbul*, p. 196.
14. Gŭlŭbov, *Turski izvori*, 1:26.
15. H. Hadžibegić, "Kanum-nama sultana Sulejmana
Zakondavca," *Glasnik zemaljskog muzeja u Sarajevu* 4-5 (1950):
324; M. Sokoloski, "Pet zakoni za pazarnite taksi i ušurot
od vremeto na Sulejman Veličestveni," GINI, no. 1 (1958), pp.
304-5 ff.

16. Barkan, "XV Asrın sonunda," p. 330.

17. The dirhem was an Ottoman measure of weight equal to 3.148 g.

18. Barkan, "XV Asrın sonunda," p. 329.

19. Ibid., p. 336. Similar regulations are encountered in the laws pertaining to various cities.

20. Ibid., p. 331.

21. Ibid., p. 339.

22. Ibid., pp. 333, 334.

23. Ibid., p. 336.

24. Ibid., pp. 333, 334.

25. Ibid., pp. 332, 333, 335.

26. Ibid., pp. 336, 337, 338, 340.

27. Ibid., pp. 335, 337.

28. Ibid., p. 339.

29. Ibid., pp. 336, 338.

30. Ibid., p. 340.

31. Ibid., pp. 337, 338.

32. An arshin was a measure of length equaling 28", 71.1 cm.

33. Barkan, "XV Asrın sonunda," p. 332.

Chapter 7

1. Esnaf is the plural of *sinif*, a word of Arabic origin that has the literal meaning of "kind," "part," or "class." In the Ottoman-Turkish language it meant a corporative organization as well as the people belonging to such an organization--artisans and merchants. In Arab countries this term was not used for designating a guild organization. There, the word used was *hirfa* (which is also met in Ottoman-Turkish documents). The term *taifa*, which was introduced in the 13th century and was finally confirmed in the 17th century, became generally widespread for denoting a guild.

2. We do not know the organization of artisans in the Balkan Slavic countries in the Middle Ages and our knowledge of the late Byzantine guild is very scanty. At the time they were forming their state, and for a while thereafter, the Ottoman Turks lacked guilds.

3. Z. Shkodra, "Nouvelles données sur la législation des esnafs (corporation) en Albanie pendant les siècles XVI-XIX," in *Conférence des études albanologiques de l'Université d'Etat de Tirana*, pp. 15-24.

4. M. Apostolidis and A. Peev, "Kondika na Plovdivskiia abadzhiiski esnaf," *Godishnik na Nar. biblioteka i muzeia v Plovdiv*, 1-2 (1931):1-170; 3 (1932):1-186.

5. K. Marx and F. Engels, *The German Ideology* (New York, 1960), p. 12.

6. Ibid., p. 937.

7. J. Sauvaget, *Introduction à l'histoire de l'Orient musulman*, p. 85.

8. L. Massignon, "Le Corps de métier et la cité islamique," *Revue internationale de la sociologie* 28 (1920):473 ff.; F. Köprülü, *Les Origines de l'Empire ottoman*, pp. 34-78.

9. V. A. Gordlevskii, "Dervishi akhi Evrana i tsekhi v Turtsii," *Izvestiia Akademii nauk SSSR* (1927), pp. 1183-88; idem, "Gosudarstvo Sel'dzhukidov Maloi Azii," *Izvrannye sochineniia* 1:103 ff.

10. A. Gölpinarlı, "Islâm ve Türk Illerinde Fütüvvet ve Teşkilâti ve Kaynakları," IFM 11, nos. 1-4 (1949-50):3-354. This work contains a detailed résumé in French.

11. B. Lewis, "The Islamic Guilds," *Economic History Review* 8, no. 1 (1937):20-37.

12. Köprülü, *Les Origines de l'Empire ottoman*, pp. 64-78, 115; Gölpinarlı, "Islâm ve Türk Illerinde Fütüvvet"; Afet İnan, *Aperçu général sur l'histoire économique de l'Empire turc-ottoman*; Barkan, "Quelques Observations sur l'organisation économique et sociale des ville ottomanes des XVIe et XVIIe siècles," *La Ville*, 7 (1955):302-10.

13. M. Apostolidis, a resident of Plovdiv and a very productive author, has published in Bulgarian translation the oldest guild code of the Bulgarian lands (see M. Apostolidis and A. Peev, "Kondika na plovdivskiia abadzhiiski esnaf"). Apostolidis has also collected all of his studies concerning Plovdiv in one volume titled *He tes Philippoupoleos historia*. Artisan production and trade are also discussed in the following works: E. Vourazeli-Marinakou, *Hai en Thrake syntechniae ton Hellenon kata ten Tourkokratian*; M. Ath. Kalinderis, *Hai syntechniae tes Kozanes epi Tourkokratias*; K. M. Apostolidis, "Kodikes Anatolikes Thrakes," *Thrakika* 18 (1943):93-160; M. Sarantis, "Kodikes tes Episkopes Metron kai Athyra," *Thrakika* 15 (1934):163-78; idem, "Thrakikoi kodikes," *Thrakika* 10 (1938):122-36. See the bibliography on various types of Greek institutions under the rule of the Turks in the studies of N. Pantazopoulos on the development of Greek law and community councils, *Neon Hellenon syssomatoseis kata ten Tourkokratian*; idem, *Ekklesia kai dikaion eis ten Chersoneson tou Haimou epi Tourkokratias*. For a bibliography of Greek literature on individual settlements, on toponymy, and on onomastics, see D. Vayiakakos, *Schediasma peri ton toponymikon kai anthroponymikon spoudon en Helladi 1833-1962*.

14. A. Vakalopoulos, *Historia tou neou Hellenismou* 1:307-14; A. Hadzimichali, "Aspects de l'organisation économique des Grecs dans l'Empire ottoman," in *L'Hellénisme contemporain: Le cinq-centième anniversaire de la prise de Constantinople*, pp. 261-78.

15. T. Djordjevic, *Arhivska gradja za zanate i esnafe u Srbiji od drugog estanka do esnafske uredbe 1847 g.*; H.

Kreševljaković, "Gradska privreda i esnafi u Bosni i Hercegovini (od 1463 do 1851)," GIBH, vol. 1 (1949). On the guild
organization in 19th-century Serbia see N. Vučo, "Položaj
kalfe i šegrt a udoba raspada esnafa u Srbiji," IC 3 (1951):
39-80; idem, *Raspadanje esnafa u Srbiji*, 2 vols. (Belgrade,
1954-58).

16. Shkodra, "Nouvelles données," pp. 3-13.

17. I. Sakŭzov, *Bulgarische Wirtschaftsgeschichte*, pp.
237-40; P. Tishkov, *Prinos kŭm istoriiata na Bŭlgarskoto
esnafstvo* (Sofia, 1911); idem, *Istoriia na nasheto zanaiatchiistvo do Osvobozhdenieto ni*; K. Stoianov, "Bŭlgarskite
esnafi prez turskoto robstvo," *Godishnik na Vissheto tŭrgovsko
uchilishte vŭv Varna*, vol. 16 (1943); Kh. Khinkov, *Stopanski
faktori na Bŭlgarskoto Vŭzrazhdane*.

18. B. Tsonev, *Spomenna kniga na Sofiiskiia kroiashki
esnaf po sluchai 100-godishniia mu iubilei* (Sofia, 1907), pp.
31-38.

19. S. Tsonev, "Kŭm vŭprosa za razlozhenieto na esnafskata organizatsiia u nas prez epokhata na Vŭzrazhdaneto,"
Trudove na Visshiia institut za narodno stopanstvo 1 (1956):
1-56; N. Todorov, "Za niakoi promeni v kharaktera na tsekhovata organizatsiia v nas prez XVIII i pŭrvata polovina na
XIX v.," IP 14, no. 4 (1958):62-63; idem, "Iz sotsialno-
ikonomicheskiia zhivot na Sofiia prez XVI-XVII vv.," IZII 14-
15 (1964):215-33. Several of the works of B. Tsvetkova contain information on the spread of craft production in the
Bulgarian lands.

20. İnalcık, "L'Empire ottoman," *Actes du premier congrès international des études balkaniques et sud-est européennes* 3:86-87.

21. I. Sakŭzov believes that the production of hides
"as an independent branch [of production] of great national
economic significance emerged only after the settlement of
the Turks" (see I. Sakŭzov, "Razvitieto na gradskiia zhivot i
na zanaiatite v Bŭlgariia prez XVIII i XIX vv.," *Bŭlgariia
1000 godini*, p. 694).

22. I. Sakŭzov, *Stopanskite vrŭzki mezhdu Dubrovnik i
bŭlgarskite zemi prez XVI i XVII stoletiia*, pp. 114, 149.

23. D. Roller, *Dubrovački zanati u XV i XVI stoljeću*,
pp. 143, 150.

24. Sakŭzov, *Stopanskite vrŭzki*, pp. 116 ff.

25. P. Matković, "Putovanji po Balkanskom poluotoko XVI
vijeka," *Rad. Jugosl. Akademije znanosti i umjetnost* 57
(1882):102-4; 124 (1895):85-86.

26. G. Gŭlŭbov, "Osmanoturski izvori za istoriiata na
Sofiia, pt. 2: Sudebni dokumenti ot XVI v.," *Serdika* 6, nos.
3-4 (1942):87-88.

27. Ibid.

28. A. Refik, *Türk idaresinde Bulgaristan (973-1255)*, p. 29 (doc. 40).

29. H. Duda and G. Galabov, *Die Protokollbücher des Kadiamtes Sofia*, p. 469 (doc. 470).

30. Ibid., pp. 179-80 (doc. 660).

31. Ibid., pp. 146-47 (doc. 558).

32. Ibid., p. 278 (doc. 143).

33. P. Dinekov, *Sofiiski knizhovnitsi prez XVI v.*, vol. 1: *Pop Peio*, pp. 58 ff.

34. Duda and Galabov, *Die Protokollbücher*, p. 177 (doc. 654).

35. NBKM, Oo, Sofia, 26/8.

36. Duda and Galabov, *Die Protokollbücher*, p. 215 (doc. 765).

37. NBKM, Oo, Rkr, R_2, ℓ. 96a.

38. Duda and Galabov, *Die Protokollbücher*, p. 215 (doc. 765); p. 114 (doc. 470).

39. Ibid., p. 35 (doc. 114).

40. Ibid., p. 71 (doc. 275).

41. Refik, *Türk idaresinde Bulgaristan*, pp. 16-17 (doc. 18).

42. NBKM, Oo, Rkr, R_2, ℓ. 69a-1.

43. Ibid., R_3, ℓ. 4b-IV.

44. Ibid., R_3, ℓ. 79a-1. One such decision apparently involved one of the first elections of the head of the coopers' guild. On February 7, 1657, a number of Muslim master coopers appeared at the court of the şeriat in Ruse. Declaring that until that moment they had not had an ustabaşı, they had gathered and unanimously elected a certain Esseid Emin for that position. They wanted him to be equipped with a decision of the court that would obligate him to look into their affairs (ibid., R_1, ℓ. 4b-IV).

45. On this question there is a great deal of literature. For recent works see B. Tsvetkova, *Izvŭnrednite danŭtsi i dŭrzhavni povinnosti v bŭlgarskite zemi pod turska vlast*; V. Mutafchieva, "K voprosu o feodal'noi rente v Osmanskoi imperiii XVII-XVIII v. (Prinuditel'nye vykupy)," *Kratkie soobshcheniia Instituta slavianovedeniia AN SSSR* 24 (1958): 90-99.

46. Duda and Galabov, *Die Protokollbücher*, p. 330 (doc. 1085).

47. NBKM, Oo, Kiustendil, April, 1684. The kuruş was a monetary unit introduced in the 17th century.

48. Ibid., Skr, S_1 *bis*, ℓ. 87-II.

49. M. Andreev and D. Angelov, *Istoriia na bŭlgarskata feodalna dŭrzhava i pravo*, pp. 330-33.

50. Ibid., pp. 329, 331.

51. Gŭlŭbov, "Osmanoturski izvori," pp. 112-14.

52. V. Ganev, "Istoricheskoto razvitie na tŭrgovskoto
pravo," *God. na Sof. univ.: Iurid. fak.* 12 (1921):27-32;
Andreev and Angelov, *Istoriia na bŭlgarskata*, pp. 139-41, 166-
68. Unfortunately, sources have not been preserved that would
make possible an interpretation of the organization of artisan
production in Bulgaria prior to its capture by the Turkish
conquerors. We will note only that if a developed guild system had existed, it could not have but been reflected in the
practice of the Ottoman state. Indicative in this regard was
the state of ore mining in Bulgarian lands, which began to
develop in connection with the settlement of Saxons in the
14th century, and until the 17th century it continued on the
basis of old Saxon laws and organization. The Turkish law-
makers tried to ensure the regular delivery of ore for the
state through control and the strict observance of the distribution of production that had been established earlier (see
G. Koniarov, *Prinos kŭm istoriiata na rudarstvoto i metalurgi-
iata v Bŭlgariia*, pp. 29, 34, 57). Having analyzed the legislative sources of the Serbian state and the Ottoman Empire
that pertain to the extraction and processing of ore, Serbian
historians reached the same conclusion (see M. Begović,
"Tragovi našeg srednjevekovnog prava u turskim, pravnim spo-
menicima," IC 3 [1952]:67-85).

Chapter 8

1. H. İnalcık, "Documents on the Economic and Social
History of Turkey in the 15th century," *Revue de la Faculté
des sciences économiques de l'Université d'Istanbul*, nos. 1-4
(October 1953-July 1955), pp. 44-48; Ö. L. Barkan, "Edirne
Askerî Kassamı'na Âit Tereke Defterleri (1545-1659)," *Belgeler*
3, nos. 5-6 (1968):1-479; N. Todorov, "La Différenciation de
la population urbaine au XVIIIe s. d'après des registres de
cadis de Vidin, Sofia et Ruse," VB, pp. 45-62.
2. For more details, see the legislative texts of inheritance laws according to the şeriat and Byzantine law collected in: M. G. Caravokyro, *Le Droit successoral en Turquie
ab intestat et par testament codifié d'après le Chéri et le
droit byzantin*; cf. also the collection of Ottoman legislative
acts in: Aristarchi Bey, *Législation ottomane ou recueil des
lois, règlements, ordonnances, traités, capitulations et
autres documents officiels de l'Empire ottoman*, vol. 1, and
G. Joung, *Corps de droit ottoman*, vol. 1.
3. NBKM, Oo, Rkr, R_6, ℓ. 3a-I.
4. An okka was a measure of weight from 100 to 400
dirhem. In Istanbul an okka equaled 400 dirhem or 1,282 kg.
5. NBKM, Oo, Vkr, S_{305}, ℓ. 23a-IV.
6. Ibid., S_{63}, ℓ. 41b-II. A para was a monetary unit
introduced in the 17th century.

7. Ibid., S_8, ℓ. 18b-I.

8. Ibid., R_{51}, R_{38}, R_{37}, R_8, R_{35}; Vkr, S_{38}, S_{10}, S_9, $S_{25}a$, S_{63}, S_{71}; Skr, $S_{312/7}$, S_{16}, S_{21}. In most cases the prices were written on the inside cover of the sicils.

9. Ibid., Skr, S_{269}, $S_{312/8}$, S_{309}, $S_{312/3}$, $S_{312/5}$, S_{20}, $S_{312/7}$, S_{17}, S_{16}, S_{26}, S_{25}, S_{174}, S_{30} bis, S_{27}; Rkr, R_{167}, R_{38}, R_{37}, R_8, R_{10}; Vkr, S_{13}, S_{38}, S_{40}, S_{42}, S_{59}, S_{167}, S_{69}.

10. On the state of financial affairs from the 15th through the 17th centuries, see the works by Ö. L. Barkan and H. Sahillioğlu that examine the movement of prices in Istanbul and Edirne, the state of the budget, and the financial difficulties in the Ottoman Empire in this period: Barkan, "XV Asrın sonunda bazı büyük şehirlerde eşya ve yiyecek fiyatlarının tesbit ve teftişi hususlarını tanzim eden kanunlar, *Tarih vesikaları* 1, no. 5 (1942):326-40; idem, "XVI Asrın ikinci yarısında Türkiye'de fiyat hareketleri," *Belleten* 34, no. 136 (1970):577-607, which summarizes the results of all previous work on this question, citations to the greater part of which are also included in: H. Sahillioğlu, "XVII Asrın Ilk Yarısında Istanbul'da Tedavüldeki Sikkelerin Râicı," *Belgeler* 1, no. 2 (1964):227-33. Sahillioğlu's doctoral dissertation is devoted to the evolution of coinage in the Ottoman Empire in the 16th century, but to date it has not been published. N. Svoronos has done detailed research on market prices and the currency rate in Salonika (*Le Commerce de Salonique au XVIII siècle*), and V. Vinaver has carried out a study on the monies and prices existing in the period from the 16th through the 18th centuries in lands now composing Yugoslavia (*Pregled istorije novca Jugoslovenskim zemljama, XVI-XVIII v.*).

11. Barkan, "XVI Asrın ikinci," p. 571. In the absence of other kinds of data, Barkan compares over various years differences in the budgets of the kitchens of certain *imaret*s (charitable establishments). Other conditions remaining stable, these differences are ascribed to price changes in the the works of V. Vinaver and N. Svoronos, as developed by Sp.

12. This figure is published with the permission of Sahillioğlu, to whom the author would like to express his gratitude.

13. The figure has been drawn on the basis of data on the ratio between the kuruş and the Venetian ducat in the works of V. Vinaver and N. Svoronos, as developed by Sp. Asdrachas (who was kind enough to place this information at our disposal).

Chapter 9

1. NBKM, Oo, Rkr, R_{51}, ℓ. 15a-III.
2. Ibid., Skr, $S_{312/3}$, ℓ. 21b-I.

3. Ibid., S_{21}, p. 129-II; see also Vkr, S_{10}, p. 31-II;
S_{36}, p. 28-II; etc.
4. Ibid., Rkr, R_{37}, ℓ. 48a-III.
5. Ibid., Vkr, S_{42}, p. 18-II.
6. Ibid., Skr, S_{23}, p. 159-I.
7. Ibid., Rkr, R_5, p. 1-II.
8. Ibid., Vkr, S_{44}, p. 1-I.
9. Ibid., Skr, S_{23}, p. 125-I.
10. The kadı registers do not record the estates of the
highest officials. However, on the basis of information provided by Mehmed Genc of the Economics faculty of Istanbul University (where he has been working on several problems of the
economic development of the Ottoman Empire in the 19th century), it can be concluded that the value of the estates of such
dignitaries usually surpassed 100,000 kuruş. Thus, for example, the estate of Mehmed Paşa, *vali* or provincial governor
of Karaman, amounted to 532,383 kuruş in specie (Istanbul,
Başvekâlet Arşivi, Kamil Kepeci, no. 2449 (L1179), 1766 [I,
BA]). The estate of Ahmed Paşa of Amasya (Çanik) consisted of
103,464 kuruş in coins, a house, thirty-two shops, a çiftlik
and livestock (ibid., Cevdet Maliye Defterleri, no. 17964 [La
1193], 1774). One of the largest inheritances was that of
Cebarzade Mustafa, mutasarrıf of Borok, which was valued at
1,900,000 kuruş (ibid., Maliye Defterleri, no. 9741 [s. 108-
109], [15 Ca ii96], 1782).
11. S. V. Kougeas, *Ho Metropolites Monembasias kai Kalamatas Ignatios ho Tzablakos (1776-1802) kai tina peri autou
engrapha*, pp. 147-50.
12. Ibid., pp. 146, 162-63.
13. Akademia Athenon, *Mnemeia tes Hellenikes historias*
3, pt. 1:214-18.
14. Ibid., pp. 389-91.
15. Ibid., pp. 444-46. Part of the money that Kamarasis
gave for charitable purposes was to be used to free "the
people of Siphnos for three years from the sum demanded
by the bishop."
16. Ibid., pp. 401-2.
17. Four dyers, 2 grocers, 2 clothes menders, 2 candle-
makers, 2 tanners, 2 furriers, 2 gunsmiths, 2 barbers, 1 coop-
ersmith, 1 goldsmith, 1 tailor, 1 abacı, 1 silk dealer, 1
stonemason, 1 fur-cap maker, 1 shoemaker, 1 scalemaker, 1
fishmonger, 1 watchmaker, 1 butcher--i.e., 20 crafts in all.
18. Of all the cases where the registers note the artisan profession of the testator, only four individuals left
houses valued at more than 1,000 kuruş: the watchmaker Osman
beşe, the son of Mustafa, who left an estate valued at 1,395
kuruş (NBKM, Oo, Vkr, S_{159a}, p. 12-I); the goldsmith Huseyin
beşe, the son of Abdullah, whose estate totaled 2,095 kuruş

(ibid., S_{310}, p. 64-I); the fishmonger Osman beşe, the son of Ali, whose inheritance was worth 1,566 kuruş (ibid., S_{70}, p. 85-II); and the tanner Sandul, the son of Georgi, whose estate was valued at 1,480 kuruş (ibid., S_{192}, p. 70-II).

19. NBKM, Oo, Vkr, S_{49}, p. 60-II.

20. Ibid., S_{63}, p. 15-I; S_{79}, p. 92-I; S_{70}, p. 86-II; S_{59}, p. 123-II.

21. For a general idea of the equivalency one might use the ratio of 120 akçe to the kuruş. Thus, estates valued at from 101,000-500,000 akçe would be roughly equivalent to those in table 13 that fell into the 1,000-5,000 kuruş value range. The considerable number of Edirne estates valued at over 500,000 akçe would likewise roughly correspond to the highest range of table 13--over 5,000 kuruş.

22. NBKM, Oo, Rkr, R_2, ℓ. 7b-II.

23. Ibid., R_3, ℓ. 21-I.

24. Ibid., R_2, ℓ. 44b-I.

25. H. Duda and G. Galabov, *Die Protokollbücher des Kadiamtes Sofia*, p. 153 (doc. 581).

26. Ibid., p. 254 (doc. 877).

27. Ibid., pp. 292, 302 (docs. 983, 112).

28. O. L. Barkan, "Edirne Askerî Kassami'na Âit Tereke Defterleri (1545-1659)," *Belgeler* (Ankara) 3:472.

29. NBKM, Oo, Vkr, S_{307}, p. 98-II.

30. Ibid., S_{71}, p. 120-III.

31. Ibid., S_{70}, p. 86-II; S_{63}, p. 15-I.

32. Ibid., S_{59}, p. 123-II; S_{79}, p. 92-I.

33. Ibid., Rkr, R_5, ℓ. 7b-I; Vkr, S_6, p. 19-II; S_{160}, p. 40-III; S_{74}, p. 7-III; S_{69}, p. 59-I; Rkr, R_3, ℓ. 8b-II; Vkr, S_{65}, p. 65-II; S_{71}, p. 34-II; S_{18}, p. 46-IV.

34. Ibid., Vkr, S_{167}, p. 100-II; S_{169}, p. 53-I; S_{70}, p. 82-II; S_{79}, p. 77-II.

35. Ibid., S_{70}, p. 81-I; p. 141-III; S_{59}, p. 5-IV; S_{74}, p. 55-II.

36. Ibid., S_{69}, p. 32-I; S_{74}, p. 34-II; S_{65}, p. 135-II.

37. Ibid., S_{167}, p. 70-II; S_{49}, p. 60-I; S_{310}, p. 60-II; S_{64}, p. 117-I; S_{44}, p. 58-II; S_{79}, p. 153-III.

38. Ibid., S_{63}, p. 105-I; S_6, p. 149-II; S_{68}, p. 42-II, S_{37}, p. 138-I; S_{68}, pp. 207-I ff.

39. Ibid., Rkr, R_{38}, ℓ. 138-II.

40. Ibid., Vkr, S_{169}, p. 5-I.

41. Ibid., Skr, S_4, p. 9-III.

42. Ibid., Rkr, R_8, ℓ. 9a-II.

43. Ibid., Vkr, S_{169}, p. 9-III.

44. Ibid., S_{167}, p. 9-I.

45. Ibid., p. 15-II.

46. Ibid., Skr, S_4, p. 33-III.

47. Ibid., Rkr, R_2, ℓ. 43b-II.

48. Ibid., ℓ. 42b-III.

49. The architecture of houses has been treated in a
general way on the basis of information of a more recent date.
Scholars have sought to establish territorial differences, but
they have not assembled enough material to permit a study of
the evolution of house construction over time. See T. Zlatev,
Bŭlgarskiiat grad prez epokhata na Vŭzrazhdaneto and G.
Kozhukharov, *Bŭlgarskata kŭshta prez pet stoletiia.*

50. The ecclesiastical municipal community in Moshople
sold a shop left by someone who died without heirs for 250
kuruş and described it as "a small workshop." It sold another two workshops in Istanbul for 700 kuruş. See D. S.
Guinis, *Perigramma historias tou meta-Byzantinou dikaeou*, pp.
187-88, 277.

Chapter 10

1. A hacı was one who had made a pilgrimage to Mecca;
the article "elhac" was placed before the name as a title of
respect.

2. NBKM, Oo, Vkr, S_{74}, p. 131-II.

3. Ibid., S_{11}, p. 68-II.

4. Ibid., S_6, p. 248-III.

5. Ibid., S_{40}, p. 89-I; S_{63}, p. 174-II; S_{107}, p. 4-I;
S_{65}, pp. 149-III ff.

6. Ibid., S_{63}, p. 4-I.

7. Ibid., p. 70-I.

8. Ibid., Skr, $S_{312/9}$, ℓ. 5b-I; S_{30} *bis*, p. 149-II;
$S_{312/2}$, ℓ. 2a-II.

9. Those who possessed such liquid monetary resources
tried to find a profitable outlet for it by lending it out at
interest, by engaging in various kinds of business deals and,
most of all, by purchasing property from which they could receive a regular rent.

10. NBKM, Oo, Vkr, S_{71}, p. 120-II.

11. Ibid., S_{63}, p. 7-I.

12. Ibid., Rkr, R_8, ℓ. 88a-I. Among the villages mentioned were Kostendzha (3,648 kuruş) and Albanovo (352 kuruş).

13. The nüzul was an extraordinary tax introduced in the
16th century and imposed on the non-Muslim population in the
form of the collection of foodstuffs to feed the army in the
field. Like the avarız it later became a tax paid in money.

14. NBKM, Oo, Skr, S_{21}, p. 133-II.

15. Ibid., S_{17}, p. 28-II. The villages included: Stolnik (239,280 akçe), Iskrets (51,285 akçe), Rakovitsa (63,000
akçe), Batanovtsi (159,730 akçe), Zlatusha (89,940 akçe),
Kamenitsa (78,060 akçe), Draganovtsi (34,776 akçe), a settlement whose name is illegible (94,980 akçe), another settlement whose name is illegible (67,734 akçe), etc.

16. Ibid., S_{21}, p. 133-II. The villages were: Aldomi-
rovtsi (25,200 akçe); Shiakovtsi (12,975 akçe); Belitsa (750
akçe); Khanche (1,920 akçe); Poduene (105,861 akçe); a village
whose name is illegible (82,980 akçe); Stolnik (239,902
akçe); Boiana (406,260 akçe); Kokorsko (98,280 akçe); Bunar
chiflik (42,183 akçe); a village whose name is illegible
(49,140 akçe); Iardzhilovtsi (101,940 akçe); Kurilo (16,656
akçe); Obelia (60,891 akçe); Irukovtsi (45,276 akçe), a
village whose name is illegible (2,160 akçe), and another
village whose name is illegible (3,360 akçe).

Chapter 11

1. See the material in *Teoreticheskie i istoriografi-
cheski problemy genezisa kapitalizma* and *Perekhod ot feodalizma k kapitalizmu v Rossii*.
2. These recent works are all listed in the relevant
sections of national bibliographies.
3. K. Marx, *Capital*, ed. F. Engels, trans. Samuel Moore
and Edward Aveling, 1:714.
4. Ibid., p. 727.
5. V. I. Lenin, *Polnoe sobranye sochinenii*, 39:70.
6. Institut Marksa-Engel'sa-Lenina, *Arkhiv Marksa i
Engel'sa*, 6, *Khronologicheskie vypiski*, 2:189.
7. See B. Tsvetkova, "Prinos kŭm izuchavaneto na turskiia feodalizŭm v bŭlgarskite zemi, chap. 2: Zavisimoto
naselenie i negovata borba protiv turskiia feodalen gnet,"
IZII 5 (1954):115-74; and V. Mutafchieva, "Kategoriite feo-
dalno zavisimo naselenie v nashite zemi pod turska vlast prez
XV-XVI v.," IZII 9 (1960):57-90; and idem, "Feodalnata renta,
prisvoiavana ot lenniia dŭrzhatel v Osmanskata imperiia,"
ibid. 7 (1957):163-204.
8. On the advanced social division of labor in the
villages and the opportunities for movement on the part of
rural producers, see pp. 71-75.
9. J. S. Emmanuel, *Histoire des Israélites de Salonique*
1:20.
10. Ö. L. Barkan, *Kanunlar*, vol. 1 of *XV ve XVI ıncı
asırlarda Osmanlı İmparatorluğunda ziraî ekonominin hukukî ve
malî esasları*, pp. 28, 96, 330.
11. A. F. Miller, *Mustafa-pasha Bairaktar*, pp. 98-118.
12. On the Greek bourgeoisie, which was more advanced in
its development than the bourgeoisies of other Balkan peoples,
see such works as N. Svoronos, *Le Commerce de Salonique au
XVIIIᵉ s.*; S. Maximos, *He auge tou Hellenikou kapitalismou*; G.
Kordatos, *Historia tes neoteres Helladas*.
13. For various viewpoints on this question see Zhak
Natan, "Kŭm vŭprosa za pŭrvonachalnoto natrupvane na kapitala
v Bŭlgariia," IZII 1-2 (1954):13-46; idem, *Stopanska istoriia*

na Bŭlgariia, pp. 206-20; D. Kosev, "Kŭm iziasniavane na niakoi problemi ot istoriiata na Bŭlgariia prez XVIII i nachaloto na XIX v.," IP 12, no. 3 (1956):13-46; Kh. Khristov, "Niakoi problemi na prekhoda ot feodalizma kŭm kapitalizma v istoriiata na Bŭlgariia," ibid. 17, no. 3 (1961):102; and N. Todorov, "Po niakoi vŭprosi za ikonomicheskoto razvitie i za zarazhdaneto na kapitalizma v bŭlgarskite zemi pod tursko vladichestvo," ibid. 17, no. 6 (1961):87-105.

14. For the views of Bulgarian authors on this point, see D. Kosev, *Lektsii po nova bŭlgarska istoriia*, pp. 52, 62 ff; S. Dimitrov, "Za klasovoto razsloenie sred selianite v Severoiztochna Bŭlgariia prez 70-te godini na XIX v.," IZII 8 (1960):226-71; Kh. Gandev, *Aprilskoto vŭstanie*, p. 18; N. Todorov, "Novi danni za agrarnite otnosheniia u nas prez 60-te godini na XIX v.," IP 14, no. 5 (1958):102-13.

15. This problem has also been examined by the Soviet historian S. A. Nikitin. In studying a proposal of the Bulgarian liberal bourgeoisie for the state structure of Bulgaria drafted at the end of 1876, he looked at two clauses that dealt with agrarian relations. As Nikitin stressed: "No political program worked out in Bulgaria at that time or earlier contained a single word on agrarian relations. Not only the programs of the bourgeoisie but also those of the revolutionary democrats were silent about (these questions)" (see S. A. Nikitin, "Neopublikovannye proekt gosudarstvennogo ustroistva Bolgarii," *Slavianskii arkhiv: Sbornik statei i materialov*, p. 136). The two clauses in question read as follows: ". . . 21. Since the special incomes from the vakıf properties are to enter the sum of the incomes that the government shall take from the districts, the vakıf properties, like the other immovable properties, are to become the inalienable property of those who hold them. 22. All lands that do not belong to private individuals are to become the property of districts" (ibid., p. 130). What was meant by "the other immovable properties" is unclear, but in another document that was submitted to the 1876 Constantinople Conference as a petition from the side of the Bulgarians, and was composed in French, the two points were combined in one clause and permit an understanding of the phrase in question. This clause reads as follows: "The vakıf possessions as well as the other immovable properties are to become the real and full property of their holders, and the *mahlul* [an open inheritance that went to the treasury in the absence of legal heirs] is to be abolished, since the special incomes of the vakıfs shall (henceforth) be included in the yearly revenues that the Sublime Porte shall collect from this province" (AVPR, f. Kantseliariia, 1876, d. 33, 11. 221-27). The basic demand was for the liquidation of the vakıf land fund and of the feudal rights of the state over peasant lands. The agrarian program

of the Bulgarian revolutionary movement has been recently examined in detail by the Soviet historian V. D. Konobeev. He
has stressed that the determining issue to the Bulgarian revolutionaries was the state's ownership of the land. See V.
D. Konobeev, *Bŭlgarskoto natsionalno-osvoboditelno dvizhenie:
Ideologiia, programa, razvitie* (Sofia, 1972), pp. 368-437.
 16. Gandev, *Aprilskoto vŭstanie*, pp. 19-21.
 17. S. Pollo, "Traits distinctifs fondamentaux du mouvement national albanais," paper read at the II Congrès international des études balkaniques, Athens, 1970.
 18. Maximos, *He auge tou Hellenikou kapitalismou*, pp.
15-39.
 19. F. Pouqueville, *Voyage dans la Grèce* 6:194-97; I.
Konstantinides, *Karavia, kapetanaioi kai syntronautai, 1800-
1830*, p. 385.
 20. Kordatos, *Historia tes neoteres Helladas* 1:282.
 21. Ibid., p. 280.
 22. E. Druzhina, *Kuichuk-Kainardzhiiskii mir 1774 goda.*
 23. A. V. Fadeev, "Grecheskoe natsional'no-osvoboditel'-
noe dvizhenie i russkoe obshchestvo pervykh desiatiletii XIX
veka," *Novaia i noveishaia istoriia*, no. 3 (1964), p. 45.
 24. Braid and cord--*gaitan* in Bulgarian--was used to
decorate various types of clothing.
 25. F. Boulanger, *Ambelakia ou les associations et les
municipalités hélleniques avec documents confirmatifs recueillis et mis en ordre.*
 26. H. P. Georgiou, *Historia kai synetairismos ton
Ambelakion*; G. Kordatos, *Ta Ambelakia kai ho mythos yia ton
synetairismo tous*; K. Koukkidis, *To pneuma tou synergatismou
ton neoteron Hellenon kai ta Ambelakia: Ho protos synetairismos tou kosmou.*
 27. Marx, *Capital*, 1:750.
 28. Ibid., p. 714.
 29. Ibid., p. 750.
 30. Ibid.
 31. Ibid., p. 715.
 32. Ibid., p. 751.
 33. Oya Koymen, "The Imperialism of Free Trade: The
Ottoman Empire," paper read at the V International Congress
of Economic History, Leningrad, 1970.

Chapter 12

 1. As used here, the word "manufacture" describes a
form of capitalist production based on an internal division of
labor wherein the work itself is done by hand.
 2. K. Marx, *Capital*, ed. F. Engels, trans. Samuel Moore
and Edward Aveling, 1:322, 335.
 3. Ibid., 1:322.

4. S. Tsonev, *Kŭm vŭprosa za razlozhenieto na esnaf-skite organizatsii u na prez perioda na Vŭzrazhdaneto*, p. 53.

5. N. Vučo, *Raspadanje esnafa u Srbiji* 1:8-88.

6. O. Sencer, *Türkiye'de işçi sınıfı*, pp. 24-106; Ö. C. Sarç, "Tanzimat ve sanayimiz," in *Tanzimat* 1:434-39.

7. P. Matković, "Dva italijanska putopisa po Balkanskom poluotoku iz XVI vijeka," *Starine* 10 (1878):211.

8. A. Refik, *Türk idaresinde Bulgaristan (973-1255)*, pp. 16-17.

9. D. G. Gadzhanov, "Pŭtuvane na Evliia Chelebi prez sredata na XVII v.," PSBK 19, nos. 9-10, (1909):689-91.

10. I. Batakliev, "Geografskite usloviia na gr. Plovdiv," in *Iubileen sbornik na devicheskata gimnaziia* (Plovdiv, 1898), pp. 216-24; St. Shishkov, *Plovdiv v svoeto minalo i nastoiashte*, p. 223.

11. The wool that was sent to Dubrovnik was gathered first in Sofia and Salonika. At the end of the 16th century, with the decline of the textile industry of Dubrovnik, the import of wool from the Balkan Peninsula was forbidden. See P. Matković, "Putovanja po Balkanskom poluotoku iz XVI vijeka," *Rad Jugoslavenske Akademije znanosti i umjetnosti* 62 (1882):102-4 and 124 (1895):87; and D. Roller, *Dubrovački zanati u XV i XVI stoljeću*, pp. 22, 23, 34.

12. N. Mikhov, *Rapports consulaires français*, vol. 3 of *Contribution à l'histoire du commerce de la Turquie et de la Bulgarie*, pp. 27, 35, 64.

13. Ibid., pp. 25, 40.

14. There are different views on when and where the iron-toothed wheel first appeared in the Bulgarian lands, but without doubt it was in widespread use in the first decade of the 19th century and that the ironworkers of Gabrovo were the major producers of this machine for Kalofer, Karlovo, Sopot, Pirdop, and Samokov. See P. Tsonchev, *Iz stopanskoto minalo na Gabrovo*, pp. 283-84.

15. Mikhov, *Rapports consulaires français*, pp. 35-59; I. Sakŭzov, "Razvitieto na gradskiia zhivot i zanaiatite v Bŭlgariia prez XVIII i XIX v.," in *Bŭlgariia 1000 godini, 927-1927*, p. 691; *Istoriia na Bŭlgariia* 1:301-8, 332-36; *Istoriia Bolgarii* 1 (Moscow-Leningrad, 1954):215-36. Konstantin Jireček, *Kniazhestvo Bŭlgariia: Negovata povŭrkhina, priroda, naselenie, dukhovna kultura, samoupravlenie i noveisha istoriia* (Plovdiv, 1899), p. 236, also attached a great deal of importance to the ties with the wide markets of the Ottoman Empire for the development of the Bulgarian textile industry.

16. K. Moravenov, *Pamiatnik za Plovdivskoto khristiansko naselenie v grada i za obshtite zavedeniia po proiznosno predanie podaren na Bŭlgarskoto chitalishte v Tsarigrad 1869 g.*, p. 28. The work in question was a limited edition of a manuscript written in 1869 and preserved in NBKM, BIA, no. 377.

17. M. Apostolidis and A. Peev, "Kondika na Plovdivskiia abadzhiiski esnaf," *Godishnik na Narodna biblioteka i muzeia v Plovdiv za 1928-1929*, pp. 6, 14, 51-62, 68, 71, 72, 75, 78, 79, 81, 82, 86, 90, 103, 151, 164, 165; Moravenov, *Pamiatnik*, pp. 19, 28, 48-50, 144-45, 160, 170.

18. I. Snegarov, "Grŭtski kodeks na plovdivskata mitropoliia," *Sbornik na BAN: Klon istoriko-filologichen* 10, nos. 1-2 (1949):225.

19. Ibid., pp. 223-24.

20. Moravenov, *Pamiatnik*, p. 27.

21. Apostolidis and Peev, "Kondika" (1928-29), pp. 119, 129, 144, 150; ibid. (1930), pp. 3, 4, 6, 8, 9, 11, 14, 16, 20, 76; Moravenov, *Pamiatnik*, p. 166.

22. Apostolidis and Peev, "Kondika" (1930), pp. 20, 69. For more details on the testir in general, see V. Gordlevskii, "Derishi Akhi Evrana i tsekhi v Turtsii," *Izbrannye sochineniia* 1:289-306; and a 1900 manuscript of K. Tuleshkov entitled "Testiria," and contained in NBKM, BIA, f. K. Tuleshkov, ed., V, 1. 82-115. Tuleshkov himself took part in the final testir held in Tŭrnovo in 1851.

23. I. Batakliev, *Grad Tatar-Pazardzhik, Istoriko-geografski pregled*, p. 162; I. Chomov, *Pravoviiat red na esnafskite organizatsii v niakogashna Bŭlgariia*, p. 24.

24. P. Dorev, ed., *Dokumenti iz turskite dŭrzhavni arkhivi, 1564-1908*, 1:86, 166, 200, 247. In various years and in various regions one roll contained a varying number of meters in length of cloth (from seven to fifteen and more). But in Plovdiv at about that time one roll of cloth was about ten meters in length.

25. M. Madzharov, *Spomeni okolo epokhata 1854-1878* (Sofia, 1942), pp. 49-51, 56-77; L. Oleskov, "Koprivshtitsa," *Iubileen sbornik po minaloto na Koprivshtitsa* 1 (Sofia, 1926): 512 ff.

26. I. Govedarov, *Koprivshtitsa v svrŭzka s dukhovnoto i politichesko vŭzrazhdane*, pp. 67-68.

27. The kircalıs were bands of mostly Turk and Albanian brigands.

28. Oleskov, "Koprivshtitsa," pp. 487-89.

29. V. Aprilov, *Dennitsa novobŭlgarskogo obrazovaniia*, p. 108.

30. Mikhov, *Rapports consulaires français*, pp. 21, 24, 28, 39; Tsonchev, *Iz stopanskoto minalo na Gabrovo*, p. 489. See also the interesting descriptions of Engeholm (1839) and Poaie (1859) about Sliven and its population, its production, and its trade ties. The first wrote that in the 1820s cloth was exported not only to Asia Minor and Istanbul, but also to Hungary. Poiae reported that the taxes collected in the city for the state treasury reached 2,500,000 kuruş. See Mikhov,

Rapports consulaires français, pp. 80-81; and A. Ubicini, *Lettres sur la Turquie*, 1:273.

31. G. Kozarov, *Dobri Zheliazkov-Fabrikadzhiiata, rodo-nachalnik na bŭlgarskata tekstilna promishlenost*, p. 13.

32. Dorev, *Dokumenti iz turskite dŭrzhavni arkhivi* 1:117.

33. Ibid.

34. Ibid., p. 187.

35. See chap. 14.

36. Mikhov, *Rapports consulaires français*, p. 338.

37. Dorev, *Dokumenti iz turskite dŭrzhavni arkhivi* 1:220.

38. Aprilov, *Dennitsa*, p. 131.

39. N. Todorov, "Svedeniia za tekhnologiiata na sliven-skite tekstilni izdeliia ot 30-te godini na XIX v.," SNU, *nauka i knizhnina*, 50 (1963):406. The whole report is pub-lished, since it provides the earliest technical description of the production of textiles in the Balkans.

40. M. Arnaudov, "Iz minaloto na Kotel: Zaselvane, be-lezhiti lichnosti, stopanski zhivot, folklor," GSUIF 27 (1930-31):5, 26, 33.

41. M. Draganov, *Spomeni za izgoreliia grad Kotel ili istoricheski geografski, etnograficheski i dr. belezhik za gr. Kotel* (Varna, 1898), p. 39.

42. K. Rakovski, "Stranitsi iz bŭlgarskoto vŭzrazhdane," *Misŭl*, no. 1 (1910), pp. 152-57; Arnaudov, "Iz minaloto na Kotel," pp. 51-56.

43. D. Konstantinov, *Zheravna v minaloto i do dneshno vreme: Istorikobitov pregled* (Sofia, 1948), p. 77.

44. Ibid., pp. 64-66, 76.

45. Kh. Semerdzhiev, *Samokov i okolnostta mu*, pp. 207-16.

46. M. Vlaikov, *Belezhki vŭrkhu ikonomicheskoto polo-zhenie na grada Panagiurishte predi i sled vŭstanieto*, p. 19.

47. K. Jireček, *Kniazhestvo Bŭlgariia* 1:238.

48. Vlaikov, *Belezhki vŭrkhu ikonomicheskoto polozhenie na grada Panagiurishte*, pp. 17-20.

49. NBKM, BIA, f. K. Tuleshkov, ed. 1, l. 73 ("Test-iria").

50. Ibid., l. 86.

51. Ibid., ll. 61-71.

52. Shumen, Arkhiv na Shumenskoto chitalishte "Dobri Voinikov," inventory number 19/1949 (the memoirs of Iliia Dimitrov on the commerce and handicrafts of the city of Shu-men, as gathered by N. Mikhov in 1915).

53. M. J. Barbié du Bocage, "Description de la ville Chumla et ses environs," *Journal des voyages, découvertes et navigations modernes aux archives géographiques du XIXe siècle*, no. 119 (September, 1828), pp. 257-88.

54.   A. Papadopoulos-Vretos, *La Bulgarie ancienne et moderne*, pp. 10, 11.

55.   Kh. Gandev, "Tŭrgovskata obmiana na Evropa s bŭlgar-skite zemi prez XVIII i nachaloto na XIX v.," GSUIF 40 (1943-1944):1-36: V. Paskaleva, "Kŭm istoriiata na tŭrgovskite vrŭzki na Makedoniia sŭs Sredna Evropa prez XIX v.," IZII 11 (1962):51-80.

56.   Mikhov, *Rapports consulaires français*, pp. 52-104.

57.   Ibid., pp. 104-5.

58.   Ibid., p. 109.   Each bale weighed about 150 kilo-grams.   Cf. F. Beaujour, *Tableau du commerce de la Grèce, formé d'après une année moyenne depuis 1787 jusqu'en 1797* 1:155.   Macedonia exported about 27,000 kuruş worth of wool.

59.   Sarç, "Tanzimat ve sanayimiz," p. 424.

60.   D. Urquhart, *La Turquie: ses ressources, son organisation municipale, son commerce, suivis de considérations sur l'état du commerce anglais dans le levant*, 1:206-23.

61.   P. Masson, *Histoire du commerce français dans le Levant au XVIII s.*, p. 475.

62.   O. Köymen, "The Advent and Consequences of Free Trade in the Ottoman Empire (19th Century)," *Etudes balkaniques*, no. 2 (1971), pp. 47-55.

63.   Turkish tariffs, which had originated in a tithe impost on trade commodities established by the şeriat at the time of the early Arab caliphate, in the Ottoman period underwent a change in both their essence and form.   Their collective designation was *gümrük*.   Under various names they were collected on goods that were transported by land or by sea: the *amediye* was levied on goods transported from one place to another within the Ottoman Empire; the *reftiye* was an impost on merchandise in transit; the *masdariye* was a tariff on goods designated for sale in a given locality.   Later, the names of these customs duties were changed to the *ithalat* (import duty), *ihracat* (export duty), and *sarfiyat* (market duty).   The *müruriye* was the duty imposed on the goods of foreign merchants that simply passed through the Ottoman state without being sold (see Karamursal, *Osmanlı mâlî tarihi hakkında tetkikler*, p. 191).

64.   F. E. Bailey, *British Policy and the Turkish Reform Movement: A Study of Anglo-Turkish Relations, 1826-1855*, p. 74.

65.   Ibid., p. 40.

66.   The evidence of Urquhart (repeated by Ubicini), that the number of weaving looms in Tŭrnovo fell from 2,000 to 200 from 1812 to 1841, has frequently been cited in this respect. This information, however, concerned the weaving of cotton textiles, a craft that began to decline earlier than other handicrafts.   Also, the Tŭrnovo in question was not the city in northern Bulgaria but a village in Macedonia, located in an

area in which the artisan manufacture of cotton textiles had prospered to the end of the 18th century. See Urquhart, *La Turquie* 1:215; and Ubicini, *Lettres sur la Turquie* 1:387.

67. Madzharov, *Spomeni okolo epokhata 1854-1878*, p. 99.

68. It was only in the second half of the 19th century that these crafts began to disappear. The causes, however, were not only imported goods, but also the equally significant competition of local factories and manufactories, which became the dominant forms in certain areas of production. There is evidence of this in the spontaneous protests against machines on the part of artisans, weavers, and spinners who worked in cottage industry. In Sliven, the personal failures and then the illnesses of Dobri Zheliazkov, the founder of the large state textile factory there, were for a long time attributed to the curses of the small producers--weavers and others--who had been affected by the mill. Also characteristic in this regard was the 1851 rebellion of the Samokov women weavers and spinners. Armed with hoes, axes, shovels, and staffs, they attacked the Samokov workshop of Shtongar, who had installed mechanical combing machines. The women were pacified only after the police assured them that the machines would be re-moved. See Kozarov, *Dobri Zheliazkov Fabrikadzhiiata, rodo-nachalnik na bŭlgarskata tekstilia promishlenost*, pp. 39, 46; and *Tsarigradski vestnik*, 4, no. 2, October 13, 1851.

69. Apostolidis and Peev, "Kondika" (1928-29), pp. 56-60.

70. Ibid., pp. 62, 83, 104, 109, 151.

71. In the 1760s 1 kuruş was worth 5 francs, at the end of the century 2.5 francs, at the beginning of the 19th cen-tury 2 francs, and in the 1840s it took 4 kuruş and 10 to 15 para to equal 1 franc (a para was a small coin equal to one-fortieth of a kuruş). See M. Belin, *Essais sur l'histoire économique de la Turquie*, pp. 27, 35, 245, 251; and Mikhov, *Rapports consulaires français*, pp. 180-214.

72. Apostolidis and Peev, "Kondika" (1928-29), p. 14.

73. NBKM, Oo, Skr, S₄, ł. 1a-II, 1b-III, 3a-II, III.

74. "And if anyone enters into partnership with another who is not a master, let the one and the other be punished according to the customs of the masters--with the entertain-ment of all masters, small and large" (Apostolidis and Peev, "Kondika" (1928-29), p. 78).

75. Ibid., pp. 12-23.

76. Ibid., p. 78.

77. Ibid., p. 169.

78. Snegarov, "Grŭtski kodeks na plovdivskata mitropol-iia," p. 241.

79. For translations of the ferman see Tsonev, *Kŭm vŭ-prosa za razlozhenieto na esnafskite organizatsii*, pp. 31-38; and D. Ikhchiev, "Esnafski dokumenti i esnafski organizatsii v

tursko vreme," SBID 11, no. 7 (1907):445-61. Until recently
researchers have been misled by Ikhchiev's inexact translation. On the whole, Ikhchiev preserved the spirit of the
document, but on several occasions he arbitrarily expanded it
by adding his own explanations to the text. Here the translation is given according to the original text of the ferman
as contained in NBKM, Oo, Vkr, 571, ℓ. 40-I.

    80. Two Greek translations are known, with only insignif-
icant differences between them. See D. S. Guinis, *Perigramma
historias tou meta-Byzantinou dikhaeou*, pp. 205-6.

    81. Sufficient information was provided in part 1 of
this work to show clearly that one or two centuries before the
ferman of Mustafa III the application of the "law of olden
times" had also been required for almost analogous reasons
and aims.

    82. Plovdiv, Narodna biblioteka "Ivan Vazov," Rŭkopisi,
inventory number 434. This document has been printed without
the signatures of the masters by K. M. Apostolidis, "Dyo engrapha ek tes Philippoupoleos," *Thrakika* 2 (1920):329.

    83. In all probability this provision concerned only
Turks. The Plovdiv abacı guild was a general one for Bulgarians and Greeks, and it also included some Serbian, Armenian,
and Syrian masters (see Apostolidis and Peev, "Kondika" [1928-
29], pp. 62, 78, 119, 130 ff.).

    84. The books of the abacı guild recorded fines paid
into the treasury. As a rule, however, the violations for
which these fines were imposed were not shown. Generally
speaking, the size of the fines and the resultant treasury receipts were not large. Only in two cases in 1813 were significant fines recorded, as well as the reason--violation of the
rule concerning the purchase of aba: "From the fine of hacı
Ivan for the purchase of aba, wherein he violated the law--
50"; and "From the fine of Vŭlko Dimitriu for the purchase of
aba and paid to the guild--250" (ibid., p. 134). By way of
comparison in the same year in Sofia a horse cost 17 kuruş and
29 para; a pair of oxen with a cart cost 89 kuruş and 39 para;
a place for a shop cost from 212 to 301 kuruş; a house cost
800 kuruş; and 5 carts of straw cost 8 kuruş and 20 para (see
NBKM, Oo, Skr, S31, p. 32-I, p. 33-I).

    85. Cited after I. Chomov, *Pravoviiat red na esnafskite
organizatsii v niakogashna Bŭlgariia*, p. 24.

    86. NBKM, BIA, Kondiki IIA7738, IIA7740, IIA7741 and
IIA7742.

    87. Ibid., Kondiki IIA7738, ℓℓ. 27, 29, 34, 45; IIA7741,
ℓ. 9; see also Apostolidis and Peev, "Kondika" (1928-29),
pp. 65-66.

    88. In his *Handbook of the Plovdiv Diocese*, which he
published in Greek in Vienna in 1819, Bishop Constantine wrote
that in Karlovo "there are about 1,000 families, of which one-

fourth are Christian and the rest are Turks. Here, on every
sixth day of the week, i.e., on Friday, there is a market day.
There are various workshops located here. Karlovo and its
surroundings also have many rose farms; and the roses are used
to make rose water and attar of roses. Gunpowder is also produced here. The women in Karlovo weave woolen fabrics, the
so-called *griza* (the Greek term for aba)" (see *Izvestiia na
Bŭlgarskoto geografsko druzhestvo*, no. 3 [1935], p. 197).
Several decades later the Bulgarian activist Ivan Bogorov furnished a somewhat different picture of Karlovo: "Its population, about 15,000 in number, are Turks, Bulgarians and Jews.
. . . A few of the Bulgarians are engaged in trade in all
sorts of goods, for which they have stone-built warehouses in
the marketplace, and the remainder make their living by producing braid, as (do the Bulgarians) in Kalofer. . . . The
Stara River flows by Karlovo and it drives many of the wheels
(used) in the making of braid, and in several fulling mills
and several water mills: (see Ivan Bogorov, *Niakolko dena
razkhodka po bŭlgarskite mesta* [Bucharest, 1868], pp. 21-22).
    89. V. Aleksandrov, "Iz istoriiata na edin zapadnal
pominŭk: Gaitandzhiistvoto v Karlovsko," SBID 9, no. 1
(1905):82-85.
    90. In the 1830s the father of the Bulgarian activist
Ioakim Gruev went every week to the market in Karlovo to sell
wool. See I. Gruev, *Moite spomeni*, p. 1.
    91. The guild books preserved their previous names:
"Guild of the Abacıs" (1827-45); "Defter of the Abacıs for
Masters Who Have Begun to Work Independently" (1844-49);
"Guild of the Abacıs on Fines" (1844-61); "Guild of the
Abacıs: For Those Who Hire Boys and Entice Journeymen" (1835-
71). See NBKM, BIA, Kondiki IIA7741, IIA7740, IIA7738,
IIA7742.
    92. Ibid., Kondiki IIA7741, ℓℓ. 23a, 24 and 34b.
    93. Ibid.
    94. Ibid., ℓℓ. 1 and 45.
    95. Tsonchev, *Iz stopanskoto minalo na Gabrovo*, pp. 610-
12; Khristo Gandev, "Kŭm istoriiata na promishleniia kapitalizŭm u nas prez Vŭzrazhdaneto," IP 10, no. 4 (1954):94-104.
    96. B. A. Rybakov, *Remeslo drevnei Rusi*, p. 739.
    97. Shumen, Okruzhen naroden muzei, Kondika na terzii-
skiia esnaf, I, II, ℓ. 61; Apostolidis and Peev, "Kondika"
(1928-29), pp. 162, 169 ff.
    98. Ibid., pp. 130-50.
    99. Ibid., pp. 132, 158, 160, 162.
    100. Ibid.
    101. Moravenov, *Pamiatnik*, pp. 12-14.
    102. Ibid., p. 39.
    103. Snegarov, "Grŭtski kodeks na plovdivskata mitropol-
iia," pp. 230-32; cf. *Plovdivski obshtinski vestnik*, nos.

195-96 (1937), pp. 15-16.

104. *Tsarigradski vestnik*, 3, no. 31, January 7, 1850.
Toma Stefanu was elected as head of the board of the Bulgarian
church of "St. Stephen" in Istanbul. See chap. 13.

105. N. Todorov, "Za naemniia trud v bŭlgarskite zemi kŭm
sredata na XIX v.," IP 15, no. 2 (1959):13-16.

106. See the contract between Atanas Milusi (Milush) and
M. Gümüşgerdan of October 10, 1839 in TsDIA 1b 4; and Moravenov, *Pamiatnik*, p. 132.

107. Shumen, Okruzhen narodon muzei, I, 1. Tsŭrkovno
uchilishtna kondika, ℓℓ. 7, 8, 11; Kondika na terziiiskiia
esnaf, ℓℓ. 8, 14. See also a notebook with information on the
history of Shumen containing the notes made by S. Dzhumaliev
in an interview with Nadezhda Simeonova.

108. P. Kisimov, "Istoricheski raboti: Moite spomeni,"
Bŭlgarska sbirka (1897-1898), pp. 4, 14, 25, 126, 508, 515,
637 ff.

109. NBKM, BIA, f. K. Tuleshkov, manuscript entitled
"Tŭrnovo v tŭrgovsko-industrialno otnoshenie," notebook 1, ℓℓ.
5 ff., 61, 79, 81.

110. S. Samokovliev, "Rodoslovie na starite golemi rodove
v Plovdiv," *Plovdivski obshtinski vestnik*, nos. 168-69 (1934),
p. 10.

111. In Tŭrnovo the wooden stamps used to decorate the
woven cloth were made by the journeymen themselves on Sundays,
their supposed day off. See NBKM, BIA, f. K. Tuleshkov,
"Tŭrnovo v tŭrgovsko-industrialno otnoshenie," ℓℓ. 47-48.

112. *Tsarigradski vestnik*, no. 56, October 13, 1856.

113. Corbacıs and dzakis were rich non-Muslims who held
minor local offices.

Chapter 13

1. In 1869 K. Moravenov wrote that the Gümüşgerdans
came from the village of Boikovo in the Plovdiv region and
that their family name was Kalmukov (*Pamiatnik za Plovdivskoto
khristiiansko naselenie v grada i za obshtite zavedeniia po
proiznosno predanie, podaren na Bŭlgarskoto chitalishte v
Tsarigrad 1869 g.*, p. 129). S. Samokovliev, on the other
hand, wrote that the Gümüşgerdans sprang from certain Rhodope
villages ("Rodosloviia na starite golemi rodove v Plovdiv,"
Plovdivski obshtinski vestnik, nos. 172-73 [1934], p. 11).
K. Apostolidis, who was personally acquainted with the Gümüşgerdan family, noted that they were from the city of Veroia in
Macedonia. For a long time the father of Atanas sought to go
to Plovdiv, and to that city he sent his brother and then his
son (see K. M. Apostolidis, *He tes Philippoupoleos historia*,
p. 688).

2. M. Apostolidis and A. Peev, "Kondika na Plovdiv

abadzhiiski esnaf," *Godishnik na Narodna biblioteka i muzeia v Plovdiv za 1928-1929*, p. 57.

3. I. Snegarov, "Grŭtski kodeks na plovdivskata mitropoliia," *Sbornik na BAN: Klon istoriko-filologichen* 12, no. 21 (1949):218-20.

4. Apostolidis and Peev, "Kondika" (1928-1929), p. 83.

5. Ibid., p. 137.

6. Snegarov, "Grŭtski kodeks na plovdivskata mitropoliia," p. 257.

7. Ibid., p. 260.

8. Apostolidis and Peev, "Kondika" (1928-29), p. 80.

9. The words chiseled into his tombstone (and reported by Apostolidis), indicated that Atanas Gümüşgerdan was married to the daughter of the prominent abacı Mikhal Kiro. The tombstone stated that he died at the age of sixty, which would imply that he had been born in 1778. In all probability he was born several years prior to 1778, since he could hardly have become a master at the age of fifteen. As a rule, when someone died his or her age was rounded off and reduced.

10. TsDIA, f. 161, defter 1, pp. 2, 3, 4, 6, 9, 14, 15, 19, 20.

11. Ibid., pp. 2, 7, 9, 14, 19, 20.

12. In different regions of the country over different years a roll of aba contained a varying number of arshin of cloth. With regard to Gümüşgerdan, the figures cited above have been calculated by the author on the basis of dozens of examples from the same villages and cities for the period from 1837 to 1850 (ibid., defters 29 to 84).

13. Apostolidis and Peev, "Kondika" (1928-29), p. 110.

14. Moravenov, *Pamiatnik*, p. 128; the acquiring of the name by Atanas is an obvious error since Georgi, his uncle, was known by that name as early as 1769.

15. Ibid., pp. 129, 161.

16. TsDIA, f. 161, 1b/7, receipt of September 22, 1832. The Plovdiv fair was held near Marash and lasted from July 15 to August 1.

17. Ibid., defter 1, p. 27; defter 8, pp. 1, 2, 4, 17, 27.

18. Ibid., defter 8, ℓℓ. 4, 9.

19. TsDIA, f. 161, defter 6 from February 4, 1837 to June 20, 1840; defter 7 from May 1, 1837 to November 1, 1838; and defter 9 from December 7, 1838 to March 16, 1845.

20. TsDIA, f. 161, defter 7, p. 1.

21. Calculated on the basis of several dozen examples. See ibid., pp. 29, 30 ff.

22. Ibid., pp. 2, 3, 5, 9, 38, 39, 40, 41.

23. On the Sliven mill see chap. 14.

24. P. Dorev, ed., *Dokumenti iz turskite durzhavni arkhivi 1564-1908*, pp. 87-88.

25. TsDIA, f. 161, defter 9, ℓ. 61.
26. Ibid., 161.
27. Ibid., defter 11, ℓ. 59.
28. Ibid., ℓℓ. 60, 61.
29. Ibid., defter 9, ℓ. 176.
30. Ibid., f. 161, 164, receipt of February 15, 1846.
"Çelebi" was a title of respect.
31. TsDIA, f. 161, receipt of June 13, 1846. A rupe was
a Greek measure of length equal to approximately 8 cm.
32. Contemporary atlases also refer to this village as
"Goren Palas" and "Dolen Palas."
33. TsDIA, f. 161, 164, receipt of April 24, 1859;
"şayak" was a gray aba.
34. TsDIA, f. 161, defter 9, ℓ. 176.
35. In another case the worker received 2 kuruş and 30
para for each roll of aba, whereas the ledger had foreseen a
payment of 4 kuruş per roll (268 rolls for 1,074 kuruş). See
ibid., defter 4, ℓ. 161. Similar kinds of payments were also
recorded in defter 7, ℓℓ. 4, 9, 28, 38, 39, 40, 41.
36. Ibid., defter 23, ℓℓ. 184, 185; defter 42, ℓℓ. 5-6.
37. Ibid., defter 42, ℓℓ. 9-10, 19-20, 51-52, 55-60.
38. Ibid., ℓℓ. 15-16; defter 23, ℓ. 219; defter 51, ℓℓ.
13-14.
39. Ibid., defter 7, ℓ. 21; defter 9, ℓ. 176; defter 37,
ℓ. 5; 1b4, receipt of February 15, 1846.
40. Ibid., defter 27 and many others from 1844 to 1849.
41. K. Marx, *Capital*, ed. F. Engels, trans. Samuel Moore
and Edward Aveling, 1:371.
42. Dorev, *Dokumenti iz turskite dŭrzhavni arkhivi* 3:86-
166.
43. Marx, *Capital*, 1:577-78.
44. TsDIA, f. 161, defters 23, 42, 51. Information on
hired wage workers is spread throughout all of these defters.
45. Ibid., defter 6, ℓℓ. 32, 33, 95-96; defter 23, ℓℓ.
42-47, 54-57; defter 21 deals specifically with the storehouses in Akhŭchelebi (called the store) where finished goods
were assembled.
46. Ibid., defter 42, ℓℓ. 15-16, 25-26, 31-32, 45-46.
47. Ibid., defter 23, ℓℓ. 48-49; and 1b5--(separate receipts and contracts between Gümüşgerdan and the guilds of
Karlovo, Kalofer, and Tatar Pazardzhik). These contracts will
be examined subsequently in detail.
48. Marx, *Capital*, 1:343.
49. V. I. Lenin, "Razvitie kapitalizma v Rossii," *Polnoe
sobranie sochinenii*, 3:354.
50. TsDIA, f. 161, defter 29, ℓℓ. 22-194: the total
amount of wool delivered for processing into aba cloth in the
Rhodope villages. The accountant who was copying the information on the number of rolls of aba missed the first digit (1)

in one of the columns, and instead of "17,876" wrote "7,876."
Thus, an incorrect total of 43,052 was entered instead of the
correct total of 53,052.

51. Ibid., defter 6, ℓℓ. 2, 3, 25-26, 43-65; defter 23,
ℓℓ. 13-17. Published information on the receipt of goods in
the Istanbul customhouses during 1846 shows that aba arriving
from Plovdiv represented the basic part of the goods sent
to the capital.

52. In September 1838, for example, the Gümüşgerdans
purchased 4,849 okka of wool for 5 kuruş per okka. By December they had sold 4,709.5 okka to various people in Tatar Pazardzhik for almost 6 kuruş per okka, and they handed over
another okka to be made into aba cloth. For examples of other
such transactions, see ibid., ℓℓ. 23, 33-35, 95 ff.

53. In 1837 aba was being sold in Istanbul at 27.9 kuruş
per roll, and in 1838 at 29.10 kuruş per roll. At the same
time, the Gümüşgerdans were buying it at prices that averaged
from 23 to 24 kuruş per roll, thus implying that they were
making a profit of not less than 3 kuruş per roll (after
taking into account transport and other expenses).

54. All of the expenses connected with the process of
production--the payment of labor, the loss of material, etc.--
amounted to about 3 to 4 kuruş per roll of aba. By adding to
this figure the cost of the wool itself (2.5 okka cost on the
average about 4 kuruş) and transport costs, one arrives at a
figure of about 15 kuruş per roll.

55. Moravenov, *Pamiatnik*, pp. 131-35.

56. N. Nemski, "Novi danni za eksploatatsiiata na naselenieto v Plovdivskiia krai prez XIX v.," *Godishnik na muzeite
v Plovdiv* 4 (1965):141-211.

57. One cubit equaled 100 cm and one alebiia equaled 64
cm.

58. P. Marinov, "Oshte za Rodopskiia bunt prez 1865 g.,"
IP 12, no. 5 (1956):79.

59. TsDIA, f. 161, defter 6, ℓℓ. 2-3, 25, 65; defter 10,
ℓℓ. 1, 6 (balance sheet).

60. *Tsarigradski vestnik*, January 7, 1850. Ranked after
the five members of the board (the head of which was T. Stefanu) were their twelve assistants, men who were also artisans
and merchants. These assistants included Dimitraki, the brother of Mihalaki Gümüşgerdan.

61. TsDIA, f. 161, defter 6, ℓℓ. 104, 105.

62. TsDIA, f. 161. Folder with documents in Turkish.
Letter of 13 Receb 1264 (July 16, 1848). A "vali" was the
governor of a vilâyet, in this case that of Plovdiv.

63. It should be noted, however, that the author has
not discovered any indication whatsoever of the Turkish government providing material subsidies for the construction of
the mill and the organization of factory production.

534   Notes: Chap. 13

64. The first information on the purchase of real estate
concerns from 1839 to 1840 (from February to February) and a
sum of 12,323 kuruş. The purchased properties included a
Turkish çiftlik bought for 4,000 kuruş. For the construction
of shops, houses, and flour mills, the Gümüşgerdans spent
50,401.31 kuruş. In 1847 property worth 60,939.27 kuruş was
purchased. TsDIA, f. 161, defter 6, ll. 47, 48; defter 27, ll.
47, 48; defter 27, ll. 47, 59, 156.
65. TsDIA, f. 161, 1b4: numerous folders containing receipts. In 1855 for the village of Kuklen alone 6,155.18
kuruş were spent for the cultivation of vineyards. For work
in the rice fields in various years sums were spent ranging
from 1,000 to 2,500 kuruş.
66. It is necessary to stress that in the 19th century
there existed no single concept as to what was meant by a
çiftlik. Any attempt to reduce the varied economic and other
features of çiftlik farming to a single kind of landowning
inevitably leads either to a schematized understanding of the
complex land relations that existed in the second half of the
19th century or to a definition so general that the concept
loses its concrete meaning. True, some çiftliks can be characterized as feudal estates. These were the çiftliks of
those representatives of the Turkish feudal class (former sipahis, officers, and officials) who prior to the destruction
of the sipahi system in the 1830s succeeded in transforming
into their own property part of the land that had been included in their fiefs (or who managed to buy land from the
state land fund at extremely low prices). By the force of
tradition and with the aid of venal officials, feudal or semi-
feudal methods of exploitation were preserved for a certain
period of time in some of these çiftliks. Others, however,
were the property of representatives of the urban bourgeoisie,
and quite a few of these were owned by wealthy peasants able
to use hired labor. Thus, defining the çiftlik as a feudal
estate is hardly appropriate.
67. TsDIA, f. 161, 1b. Contracts with the dyers' guild
of Karlovo of July 27, 1854; of Kalofer of July 23, 1854; of
Tatar Pazardzhik of March 21, 1853; and various receipts of
1853, 1854, 1856, 1859, and 1862.
68. Bulgarian sources seem to contain no mention of the
term "bakamı." From other sources, however, it would appear
that it was a cheap dye used to replace true blue dye. Thus,
for example, in Bursa in the 15th and 17th centuries the guild
and state authorities forbade the use of bakamı as a dye. See
M. Göker, "Türklerde sanayı," *Belleten* 2 (1938):7-8.
69. M. Madzharov, "Na bozhi grob predi 60 godini,"
Dukhovna kultura, nos. 34-35 (1927), pp. 205-35; no. 36
(1928), pp. 46-64; no. 37 (1928), pp. 136-48; idem, *Spomeni
okolo enokhata 1854-1878*, pp. 49-77.

70. S. Maximos, *He auge tou Hellenikou kapitalismou*; G.
Kordatos, *Historia tes neoteres Helladas*, vol. 1; N. Svoronos,
Le Commerce de Salonique au XVIIIe siècle; C. Euelpides, *Oiko-
nomike kai koinonike historia tes Hellados* (Athens, 1950).

71. In addition to the works already indicated, see also
P. Michalopoulos, *Ta Yiannena kai he neo-Hellenike anagennesis
(1648-1820)*.

72. In addition to the works on Ambelakia cited above,
see also Elias P. Geōrgiou, *Neotera stoicheia peri tes historias kai tes syntrophias ton Ambelakion*, p. 88; idem, *Historia
kai synetairismos ton Ambelakion*, p. 108; G. Kordatos, *Ta
Ambelakia kai ho mythos yia ton synetairismo tous*, p. 147.

73. Beaujour remarked that Ambelakia had an external
appearance resembling a small Dutch town.

74. B. Kremmydas, "Opseis tes Tsakonikes koinonias
(1784-1821)," *Chronika ton Tsakonon*, vol. 3 (1969).

75. Ibid., p. 22.

Chapter 14

1. At the Paris Exhibition in 1856 seven Ottoman state
factories demonstrated their products: broadcloth (Izmir),
fezzes and cotton prints (Istanbul), cotton textiles (Zeytun-
burun), velvet and silk (Hereke), two for arms (the Tophane
in Istanbul and one in Beykoz), and porcelain and glass (Beykoz). In addition, there was a paper factory in Izmir and the
broadcloth mill in Sliven. In the words of Ö. C. Sarç, a
Turkish historian who has worked on the economic consequences
of the Tanzimat, most of these factories "had no success and
were forced to discontinue their activities, since they had
become a heavy burden for the state." There is one case known
of a person entrusted with the construction of a factory who
misappropriated all of the funds involved. For a full year he
purchased finished merchandise that he then presented as being
produced in the nonexistent mill (see Sarç, "Tanzimat ve sanayimiz," in *Tanzimat* 1:434-37).

2. As before, "manufacture" and "manufacturing" are
terms used here to describe a definite form of capitalist production based on an internal technical division of labor but
employing hand production (i.e., the artisan method).

3. See pp. 247 ff.

4. See, for example, Zh. Natan, *Stopanska istoriia na
Bŭlgariia*, p. 200, where the author directly asserts that convicts worked at the Gümüşgerdan mill. Natan has obviously un-
derrated the importance of this factory, placing it in the
second half of the 19th century (even though at another point
he states that it was founded at an earlier--albeit still in-
correct--date, 1840).

5. For a survey of the views expressed on this question, see N. Todorov, "Za naemniia trud v Bŭlgarskite zemi kŭm

sredata na 19 vek," IP 15, no. 2 (1959):3 ff. In 1969 Oya
Sencer published a monograph entitled (in English), *The Working Class in Turkey: Its Emergence and Development*. In it
the author examined the development of the working class in
Turkey up to the First World War, and with regard to the history of the working class in the 19th century, shared the positions and conclusions expressed in the above-mentioned study
of the author on hired labor in the Bulgarian lands (see
Sencer, *Türkiye'de işçi sınıfı*; and the review of this work by
D. Khakov in IP 25, no. 6 [1969]:119-22).
        6. V. I. Lenin, *Polnoe sobranie sochinenie* 3:581.
        7. In Bulgarian historiography the view is widespread
that 1834 marked the start of factory production in the Bulgarian lands. This is based on the notion that the state textile factory that began operations in 1836 was a natural continuation of the workshop that Dobri Zheliazkov opened in
Sliven in 1834. Essentially, however, these were two different enterprises, and it is incorrect to fuse them. True,
there was a link in the person of Zheliazkov himself, while he
was the founder and the owner of the workshop (a specialized
enterprise with a manufacturing division of labor), his role
and place in the establishment of the factory was, as shall be
shown momentarily, quite different (cf. N. Todorov, "Pervaia
gosudarstvennaia tekstil'naia fabrika na Balkanakh," in *Genezis kapitalizma v promyshlennosti* [Moscow, 1963], pp. 330-
52).
        8. K. G. Fotinov, *Obshtoe zemleopisanie vkrattse za
sichkata zemlia*, p. 87.
        9. A. Boué, *La Turquie d'Europe*, 3:100.
        10. N. Mikhov, *Rapports consulaires français*, vol. 3 of
*Contribution à l'histoire du commerce de la Turquie et de la
Bulgarie*, p. 338 ("Lettre du Docteur Poyet à la société de
géographie, contenant la description du district d'Islimnia").
        11. V. Aprilov, *Dennitsa novobŭlgarskoto obrazavaniia*
1:131.
        12. P. Dorev, ed., *Dokumenti iz turskite dŭrzhavni ar-
khivi 1564-1908*, p. 117.
        13. Ibid., pp. 187, 201.
        14. Mikhov, *Rapports consulaires français*, p. 338.
        15. S. Tabakov, *Opit za istoriiata na grad Sliven* 1:49-
50.
        16. Dorev, *Dokumenti iz turskite dŭrzhavni arkhivi*, pp.
17, 159, 173, 189, 202, 204.
        17. Ibid., p. 173.
        18. Ibid., pp. 187, 189.
        19. G. Kozarov, *Dobri Zheliazkov fabrikadzhiiata rodo-
nachalnik na bŭlgarskata tekstilna promishlenost*, pp. 22-24.
        20. Ibid., pp. 27-30; Dorev, *Dokumenti iz turskite dŭr-
zhavni arkhivi*, p. 203. The ferman delivered to Zheliazkov is

one of the most beautiful documents preserved in the Oriental
Department.

21. Kozarov, *Dobri Zheliazkov*, p. 31.

22. Natan, *Stopanska istoriia na Bŭlgariia*, p. 200.

23. Kozarov, *Dobri Zheliazkov*, p. 30.

24. A barutcubaşi was an official in a military arsenal.

25. NBKM, Oo, Sliven, 9/7; ibid., OAK, 37/42.

26. NBKM, Oo, OAK, 18/25; Dorev, *Dokumenti iz turskite
dŭrzhavni arkhivi*, pp. 217-40.

27. The porte's trust in Zheliazkov is indicated by the
repeated journeys that the latter made to Istanbul to work out
various details on the construction of the mill and to discuss
the implementation of the suggestions made by the inspector
sent to examine the factory. See Dorev, *Dokumenti iz turskite
dŭrzhavni arkhivi*, pp. 203, 217, 240.

28. NBKM, Oo, OAK, 18/25.

29. Ibid., 37/65; 36/89; 36/9; f. 138, ed. 236; f. 138,
ed. 51; f. 138, ed. 58, ℓ. 2; f. 112, ed. 338.

30. NBKM, Oo, f. 138, ed. 51; f. 112, ed. 338; OAK, 18/25.

31. Ibid., OAK, 18/25.

32. Ibid., Sliven, 6/6.

33. Cf. Todorov, "Za naemniia trud," pp. 15-16.

34. I,BA, Cevdet Tasnifi, Iktisat, no. 969, 4, Safer,
1256. The author would like to thank Mehmed Genç for making
this document available.

35. Boué, *La Turquie d'Europe*, 3:101.

36. NBKM, Oo, OAK, 18/25; f. 138, ed. 57; OAK, 36/8.

37. Ibid., OAK, 36/8.

38. Separate buildings housed the kitchen, the dyehouse,
the metalworking shop, and the foundry. Each of these structures was about 10 arshin in length. There was also a covered
terrace, supported by posts and reached by a staircase.

39. These dimensions fully conform with the preserved
building itself, which has lasted to this day with no change
in its external appearance. Early in the 20th century, when
the mill was turned into a prison, the individual sections and
rooms of the factory were partitioned off. At present the
building is used to house a museum on the history of textile
production in Bulgaria (and some of the old prisoners' cells
have also been preserved for inspection by visitors). The
first factory building, however, was destroyed during a fire
that took place after the 1878 liberation of Bulgaria. A
building subsequently rebuilt on its foundations has been the
location for several decades now of a professional school for
textiles.

40. Kozarov, *Dobri Zheliazkov*, p. 49.

41. NBKM, Oo, f. 138, ed. 53, ℓ. 4.

42. Ibid.

43. Ibid., OAK, 18/25.

44.   Ibid.
45.   Ibid.
46.   Ibid., OAK, 37/42.
47.   Dorev, *Dokumenti iz turskite dŭrzhavni arkhivi*,
p. 240.
48.   NBKM, Oo, f. 138, ed. 51.
49.   Ibid., OAK, 37/42.
50.   Dorev, *Dokumenti iz turskite dŭrzhavni arkhivi*,
p. 250.
51.   Ibid., p. 267.
52.   NBKM, Oo, f. 138, ed. 62.
53.   Ibid.
54.   Ibid., f. 138, ed. 58, ℓ. 2.
55.   Ibid., OAK, 36/9.
56.   In the 1860s Kanitz (*La Bulgarie danubienne et le
Balkan: études de voyage, 1860-1880*, pp. 353-54) wrote that
the mill used 120,000 okka of wool; a consular report, on the
other hand, mentioned 250,000 okka (Mikhov, *Rapports consulaires français*, p. 610). This discrepancy may have been because the authors in question calculated the amount of wool at
different stages. Thus, one may have cited the amount of wool
before it was cleaned and sorted and the other may have used
the amount that remained after this initial processing.
57.   Dorev, *Dokumenti iz turskite dŭrzhavni arkhivi*,
p. 299.
58.   NBKM, Oo, f. 138, ed. 58, ℓ. 2.
59.   Ibid., ed. 236.
60.   Boué, *La Turquie d'Europe*, 3:101.
61.   Some of the eyewitnesses who visited Sliven in the
1860s and 1870s wrote that the factory employed 400 workers
who processed 250,000 okka of wool a year; others wrote that
the factory had 330 women workers while the looms were operated chiefly by men. These reports said nothing about the
size of wages received by the workers. See Mikhov, *Rapports
consulaires français*, p. 610; and Kanitz, *La Bulgarie danubienne*, p. 354.
62.   NBKM, Oo, Sliven, 9/7.
63.   I,BA, Cevdet Tasnifi, Iktisat, no. 969.
64.   According to local residents, some of whom worked in
the factory until the 1878 liberation of Bulgaria, the first
workers received uniforms and on their caps wore specially
prepared metal badges. Later on this special dress was discarded, and the workers in the state mill were in no way distinguishable from the workers of other factories. See Kozarov, *Dobri Zheliazkov*, p. 34.
65.   See Mikhov, *Rapports consulaires français*, pp. 80,
236, 338, for the descriptions of Sliven by Eneholm, Pouqueville, and other foreigners.
66.   See pp. 191 ff.

67. Boué, *La Turquie d'Europe*, 3:101, 103.

68. NBKM, Oo, OAK, 36/39.

69. TsDIA, f. 161, defter 27, ł. 155.

70. Ibid., defter 51, pp. 97-98, 139-40.

71. Ibid., pp. 7-8, 150-60 passim (German-language documents and a "contract" dated November 30, 1848).

72. Ibid., f. 161, 1b4 (contract dated October 10, 1849).

73. Ibid., f. 161, 1b4, 1b5 (contract for the reconstruction of the factory in 1853 and invoices for the machines purchased).

74. Ibid., 1b1 (documents in French).

75. Ibid., f. 161, 1b4 (documents in Turkish).

76. Ibid. (contract for the repair of the mill dated April 10, 1853, and receipts for the sums of money received).

77. Ibid., defter 136, pp. 23, 24, 38 ff. After the reconstruction of the mill it seems that its volume doubled. In the course of only six months in 1862 it produced 2,025 rolls of aba.

78. Ibid., defter 327, pp. 3-4.

79. Ibid., defter 104, p. 70.

80. Khristo Gandev, "Kŭm razvitieto na promishleniia kapitalizŭm u nas prez Vŭzrazhdaneto," IP 10, no. 4 (1954): 105.

81. The receipts and ledgers from which this information has been drawn were kept for all of the firm's hired workers as a whole. It was only several years later that the office began to use separate accounts for the mill workers. See TsDIA, f. 161, defter 51, pp. 7-8, 11-12, 13-14, 19-20, 27-28, 59-60, 65-66, 145-46, 253-54 passim; see also the receipts that have been preserved.

82. Ibid., defter 85, pp. 35, 42, 61, 62, 75.

83. Ibid., defter 177, łł. 8a, 22b.

84. In the report noted above, which dealt with proposed improvements to the Sliven mill, the inspector, though admitting the clear advantages of steam power, noted that spinning wheels driven by children produced yarn that was, all things considered, not bad (see NBKM, Oo, Sliven 9/7).

85. Ibid., 6/6.

86. Ibid., Razgrad, 3/2.

87. This information has been drawn from dozens of cases wherein the sources cited the price of staples sold at the kinds of grocers' shops where workers usually made their purchases. See TsDIA, f. 161, defter 177, łł. 9, 11, 11a, 13, 13a, 22a; *Dokumenti za bŭlgarskata istoriia. Tom 1. Arkhiv na Naiden Gerov*, ed. M. T. Popruzhenko, p. 33.

88. TsDIA, f. 161, defter 177, łł. 11a, 13a, 22a; defter 122, p. 13; defter 51, pp. 35-36.

89. Ibid., defter 27, p. 59.

90.   Ibid., lb4 (contract dated October 5, 1848, signed by hacı Teodosi, Nestor Nidyuv, and Kinu Kachuv).

91.   Ibid., defter 177, ℓℓ. 40-41.

92.   It is difficult to say how there arose in the scholarship the view that the Gümüşgerdans employed forced or convict labor in the mill. Perhaps, as sometimes happens, a reference to a specific incident or episode was picked up and turned into a generalization.

93.   TsDIA, f. 161, defter 177, ℓℓ. 39a-40a.

94.   NBKM, Oo, OAK, 94/38.

95.   F. Engels, "Vneshnaia politika russkogo tsarizma," *K. Marx & F. Engels Sochinenia*, 22 (Moscow, 1962):33.

Chapter 15

1.   E. Z. Karal, *Osmanlı İmparatorluğunda ilk nüfus sayımı 1831, Başvakâlet İstatistik um. Müd.*

2.   Pejanović, *Stanovništvo Bosne i Hercegovine*, pp. 29-31.

3.   A. Viquesnel, *Journal d'un voyage dans la Turquie d'Europe*, (Paris, 1842), pp. 43-44; N. N. Obruchev, *Voenno-statisticheskii sbornik za 1868 g.*, vol. 2 (cited by N. Mikhov, *Naselenieto na Turtsiia i Bŭlgariia prez XVIII i XIX vv.: Bibliografski izdirvaniia sŭs statisticheski i ethnografski danni* 5:96-98).

4.   For example, the Plovdiv consul Zolotarev, who had at his disposal the official figures on the number of households and on the taxable population in the sancak of Plovdiv, supplemented this material with new information that he acquired through questioning and observation. He specified the number of Bulgarians, Greeks, and of Grecized Bulgarians and he indicated the total number of residents of the city and of the villages by using a coefficient of five for each household. All of this information had been lacking in the materials from the census itself. See Mikhov, *Naselenieto*, 5:98.

5.   NBKM, Oo, Lom 20/7. Cf. N. Todorov, "Bŭlgarskoto naselenie na grad Lom prez 40-te godini na XIX v.," *Izsledvaniia v chest na Marin S. Drinov* (Sofia, 1960), pp. 579-92.

6.   *Tsarigradski vestnik* 6, no. 300, October 27, 1856.

7.   NBKM, Oo, Lom 20/7, ℓ. 6b.

8.   Ibid., ℓ. 6a.

9.   Ibid., ℓ. 5b.

10.   Ibid., ℓ. 10a.

11.   Ibid., ℓ. 7b, 33b, 38a.

12.   A. Ivić, "Po Bŭlgarsko pre sto godina," *Sbornik na BAN: Klon istoriko-filologichen i filosofsko-obshtestven* 31, no. 17 (1937):6.

13.   T. Kovačević, *Opis Bosne i Hercegovine* (Belgrade, 1865); 2d ed. (Belgrade, 1879).

14.   Otto Blau, *Reisen in Bosnien und Hercegovina.*

15. F. Kanitz, *Donau-Bulgarien und der Balkan: Historisch-geographisch-ethnographische Reisestudien aus den Jahren 1860-1879*, idem, *La Bulgarie danubienne et le Balkan: Etudes de voyage, 1860-1880.*

16. *Materialy dlia izucheniia Bolgarii*, 2 vols.

17. A. N. Moshnin, "Pridunaiskaia Bolgariia (Dunaiskii vilaiet): Statistiko-ekonomicheskii ocherk," in *Slavianskii sbornik*, vol. 2; V. Teplov, *Materialy dlia statistiki Bolgarii, Frakii i Makedoniia*; A. Ubicini and P. de Kurteil, *Sovremennoe sostoianie Ottomanskoi imperii* (St. Petersburg, 1877).

18. On the Bosnian census of 1876, see for example, Pejanović, *Stanovništvo Bosne i Hercegovine*, p. 37; on the 1871 census in Epirus and Thessaly, see A. Troianskii, "Naselenie Fessalii i Epira," as cited in Mikhov, *Naselenieto*, 5:130-31.

19. Kanitz, *La Bulgarie danubienne et le Balkan*, p. 42.

20. Teplov, *Materialy*, pp. 6,7.

21. Ibid., pp. 22, 23.

22. Recently the Soviet historian S. A. Nikitin has been working with materials he found in Soviet archives on a census of the population of Bulgaria by the Russian civil administration during the spring of 1879. His publications contain interesting data on the demography of the Bulgarian city immediately after the liberation of Bulgaria. See S. A. Nikitin, "K voprosu ob ekonomicheskom oblike bolgarskogo goroda vremeni osvobozhdeniia ot turetskogo iga (na osnove russkoi perepisi 1879 g.)," in *Ocherki po istorii iuzhnykh slavian i russko-balkanskikh sviazei v 50-70-e gody XIX v.*, pp. 7-65.

23. See p. 312.

24. Istanbul, Belediye kütüphanesi, Salname-i Tuna, 32/7, pp. 124-27.

25. Ibid., Salname-i Yaniya, 35/1, pp. 98-99.

26. Ibid., Salname-i Edirne, 13/7, pp. 113-15.

27. Pejanović, *Stanovništvo Bosne i Hercegovine*, p. 33.

28. Ibid., table 3 in the appendix.

29. Ibid., pp. 33-37.

Chapter 16

1. N. J. Polyzos, "Essai sur l'émigration grecque," *Etudes démographiques, économiques et sociales* 5 (1947):40.

2. *Statistike tes Hellados, plethysmos 1879*, pp. 24-25.

3. H. Haufe, *Die Bevölkerung Europas, Stadt und Land im 19. u. 20. Jahrhundert*, pp. 15-16.

4. A. Veber, *Rost gorodov v 19-m stoletii*, pp. 17-19.

5. *Statistike tes Hellados, plethysmos 1879*, pp. 50-56.

Chapter 17

1. NBKM, Oo, Rs 98/8. The document is divided into two parts, which is why it bears two inventory numbers. It is a

large sheet divided into ten major sections, each of which is
in turn divided into from two to ten subsections and columns.
The Turkish title of the document is "Cetvel-i mizan-i vergi
ve nüfus" (which translates as *Table of the Taxes and of the
Population*).

2. See chap. 15.

3. See the text of the law on the vilâyets and particularly on the Danubian vilâyet in *Suvetnik*, vol. 2, nos. 32-
34, 36, 38, 41 (from November 7, 1864, to January 9, 1865).

4. In the document this city is called Dupnishka Dzhumaia, though it was also known as Grona Dzhumaia (to be distinguished from Serska Dzhumaia, Dolna Dzhumaia, and Barakli
Dzhumaia--all located near the city of Serres).

5. *Dunav*, no. 40, December 1, 1865.

6. Ibid., no. 53, March 2, 1866.

7. Ibid., no. 391, July 6, 1869.

8. Ibid., no. 914, October 6, 1874.

9. The village of Chertovets existed in the environs of
Liaskovets until the 1878 liberation of Bulgaria.

10. The other eight nahiyes were not included in the
Table of the Taxes and of the Population. A later salname
described several cities as being nahiyes: Novi Pazar (the
sancak of Ruse), Kotel (the sancak of Tŭrnovo), Teteven (the
sancak of Sofia), and Mahmudie, Isaccea, and Kiliya in the
Dobruja.

11. See *Ikonomicheska geografiia*, vol. 2 of *Geografiia
na Bŭlgariia*, ed. A. S. Beshkov and E. B. Valvev, p. 297; and
A. Beshov and N. Minchev, "Ikonomo-geografsko raionirane na
Severna Bŭlgariia," *Sbornik v chest na chl.-kor. Iordan Zakhariev*, p. 13.

12. The physical geography of northern Bulgaria is di-
vided into the Danubian hilly plain, the Predbalkan, and the
Balkan Mountains (see *Geografiia na Bŭlgariia*, 1:19; and I.
Ivanov, P. Penchev and D. Dimitrov, "Fiziko-geografskoto rai-
onirane na Bŭlgariia," *Problemi na geografiiata v NR Bŭlgariia*
[Sofia, 1964], p. 97).

13. *Dunav*, no. 914, October 6, 1874.

14. One of the reports of the French consul in Ruse that
discussed this question in detail noted that groups of Cossacks from Russia had settled in the Dobruja at various times,
though chiefly in the 19th century.

15. *Dunav*, no. 914, October 6, 1874.

16. M. Franco, *Essai sur l'histoire des Israélites de
l'Empire ottoman*, pp. 21-23; S. Emmanuel, *Histoire des Israélites de Salonique* 1:46-47, 57-61, 133, 266-67.

17. A. Margos, "Izchesnalata armenska koloniia v grad
Provadiia," IVAD 14 (1963):93-102.

Chapter 18

1. The holdings of the Oriental Department are rather skewed, for they lack materials on other parts of the Balkan Peninsula. To help counterbalance this problem the author has tried to dig out and analyze material not only from whole registers and from those that have been in large part preserved, but also from single pages and fragments.

2. In speaking about the possibility of exaggerating the number of migrants, it should once again be noted that most of the material used here has been drawn from fragmentary and not from full registers.

3. Hesitations concerning the absolute size of several of the figures in question in no way invalidate the effort here to establish the patterns by nationality of those individuals who came to northeastern Bulgaria and the Dobruja in search of work. The two major groups among these migrants were the Bulgarians and the Turks. The Bulgarians represent about 75% of all migrants studied and the Turks make up the majority of the Muslim migrants. Given the general Bulgarian predominance of the population in this area--a predominance mirrored in the percentage breakdown between Bulgarian and Turkish migrants--there is no need to undertake a special discussion of this question. Rather, the more appropriate focus of study should be that the Turkish population was, like the Bulgarian one, under the influence of the same socioeconomic factors that gave rise to migration in the first place. Like their Bulgarian counterparts, Turkish urban and rural artisans, small merchants, and unskilled workers were seeking a livelihood outside of their native regions by moving from place to place.

4. NBKM, Oo, Tŭrnovo, receb 1282 (from November 20, 1865).

5. The income distribution of the individuals in question was as follows: 164 had incomes of up to 500 kuruş; 56 had incomes of between 501 and 750 kuruş; 27 had incomes of between 751 and 1,000 kuruş; and 23 had incomes of from 1,001 to 1,500 kuruş or higher. For 22 individuals the income cannot be determined.

6. In the documents such bakers are designated as *hamurkar* and *firinci tezgah*.

7. *Dunav*, 1, no. 9, April 28, 1865; 2, no. 138, December 28, 1866; 3, no. 204, July 27, 1867; 3, no. 206, September 3, 1867; 4, no. 318, October 9, 1868; 8, no. 696, July 26, 1872; 9, no. 778, May 27, 1873; 10, no. 900, July 18, 1874; 11, no. 975, May 28, 1875; *Tsarigradski vestnik*, 8, no. 369, March 8, 1858; *Turtsiia*, 1, no. 15, October 31, 1864; 3, no. 27, January 23, 1867.

8. In speaking of the driving forces of the Bulgarian

April Uprising of 1876, the Bulgarian historian Khristo
Gandev used the term "pre-proletariat" to characterize the
layer of landless hired workers composed of destitute peasants,
bankrupt artisans, and poor laborers who either went abroad
in search of work or who stayed in their native places. Gandev estimated the migration from villages alone to number some
150,000 persons (Gandev, *Aprilskoto vŭstanie*, pp. 17, 26).
Though rejecting the concept of "pre-proletariat" and denying
any idea of the formation of a new class, the Bulgarian economic historian Zhak Natan nevertheless wrote that according to
his own estimates during the same period "there were in the
country more than 100,000 semi-proletarians, proletarians,
hired hands in farming and others" (Natan, *Stopanska istoriia
na Bŭlgariia*, pp. 22, 225). It is not possible to verify the
figures cited by both these authors or to establish the origins of the hired labor in question. This information has
been cited simply to indicate that Gandev and Natan have dwelt
on this question and have reached certain conclusions concerning it.

9.   NBKM, Oo, Constanţa, Register no. 6, ℓ. 27; Varna,
Register no. 6, ℓ. 17; Bazargic, Register no. 2, ℓ. 90; Varna,
Register no. 6, ℓ. 18.

10.   Ibid., Bazargic, Register no. 2, ℓ. 22; Constanţa,
Register no. 6, ℓ. 54.

11.   Ibid., Constanţa, Register no. 1, ℓ. 81.

12.   Ibid., Varna, Register no. 1, ℓ. 71.

13.   Ibid., Constanţa, Register no. 13, ℓ. 58.

14.   Ibid., Register no. 1, ℓ. 82; Varna, Register no. 1,
ℓ. 20; Babadag, Register no. 1, ℓ. 9.

15.   Ibid., Varna, Register no. 1, ℓℓ. 91, 48; Bazargic,
Register no. 16, ℓ. 59; f. 161, ed. 1235, ℓ. 8.

16.   Ibid., Constanţa, Register no. 1, ℓ. 90; Varna Register no. 1, ℓ. 42. Here are some additional typical examples
from this income group: Hacı Ibrahim of Hemsiye (located near
Macin?), a so-called fabricator (i.e., factory worker) in
Macin, earned an income of 1,250 kuruş; Petre (the son of
Stamo of Balchik), as a factory apprentice in Bazargic earned
1,500 kuruş; Pavli (the son of Rizolski of Bucharest), who was
an artist in Silistra, earned 1,000 kuruş; Djar (the son of
Georgi of Samokov) who worked as a painter in Varna, earned
2,000 kuruş; Ibn Hacı Mustafa (of Kayseri), another painter
who worked in Varna, had an income of 1,000 kuruş. Two musicians from Wallachia--Yoni and Yori--worked in Tulcea for incomes of 250 kuruş each. See NBKM, Oo, Macin, Register no.
124, ℓ. 58; Bazargic, Register no. 12, ℓ. 9; Silistra, Register no. 4, ℓ. 6; Varna, Register no. 1, ℓℓ. 24, 60; Tulcea,
Register no. 7, ℓℓ. 17, 18.

17.   NBKM, Oo, Constanţa, Register no. 13, ℓ. 54; Register no. 3, ℓ. 85; Register no. 4, ℓ. 77; Varna, Register no.
1, ℓ. 4.

18. Ibid., Constanţa, Register no. 1, ℓℓ. 85-87.
19. There are other cases that indicate that individuals earning such high incomes were not just isolated businessmen but formed a definite social category. Together with large exporters and importers, this group included even some representatives of foreign firms. Thus, two employees of foreign companies in Constanţa (called "company servants" by Turkish administrators who used the same term to describe servants in taverns and other commercial establishments) also received incomes of 1,000 kuruş or more a year: Koicho (the son of Stoian of Skopje), earned 1,000 kuruş, and the French subject Panbar (of Toulon), made 3,000 kuruş a year. See NBKM, Oo, Constanţa, Register no. 1, ℓℓ. 22, 83.
20. NBKM, Oo, Constanţa, Register no. 2, ℓℓ. 2, 18, 28, 29, 32; Register no. 10, ℓ. 75; Babadag, Register no. 9, ℓ. 51; Register no. 11, ℓℓ. 52, 67; Tulcea, Register no. 7, ℓ. 19; Macin, Register no. 124, ℓ. 83; Provadiia, Register no. 11, ℓ. 32 passim.
21. The registers include one document from Babadag that explicitly states that migrant artisans, though registered in the city itself, worked in the nearby or more distant villages of the surrounding district.

Chapter 19

1. These sources are discussed in more detail on p. 340.
2. Contemporary records and sources list a large and diverse number of handicrafts (more than one hundred). In view of this fact, and also because for certain crafts the number of cases included in the sample is very small, it would be both impossible and inappropriate to discuss them all here. Rather, handicrafts have been assembled into kindred groupings, with individual trades discussed in the context of territorial patterns of handicraft activity.
3. NBKM, Oo, f. 20, ed. 522, Register no. 38, ℓ. 6.
4. Ibid., f. 171, ed. 1273, ℓ. 48.
5. Ibid., Constanţa, Register no. 8, ℓ. 26.
6. Ibid., Silistra, Register no. 12, ℓ. 72; Register no. 19, ℓℓ. 64, 79; Register no. 38, ℓ. 19; Register no. 68, ℓ. 11; Register no. 17, ℓ. 88.
7. Ibid., Lom, no. 36.
8. Ibid., Bazargic, makh. Cevizli, ℓ. 5.
9. Basically the dry-goods dealers (*manifakturist* in Bulgarian) dealt in textiles, making them similar to other cloth dealers called *bezazes*.
10. Additional statistical processing of the data whereby the confidence interval was calculated for the relevant percentages shows that the inferences drawn here on the basis of the observed cases can be applied to the two major groups

of the urban population, Muslims and non-Muslims, taken in
their entirety.

Chapter 20

1.   For a discussion of how this sample or study group
was assembled, see pp. 387-88.
2.   Arabacıs.
3.   *Karutsari* (in Bulgarian), distinguished from the
arabacıs by the type of cart they used.
4.   See pp. 396-97.
5.   "Bezazes," see n. 9, chap. 19.   9.
6.   See p. 397.
7.   See p. 394.
8.   *Iz arkhivata na Naiden Gerov*, ed. T. Panchev, 1:129.
9.   Ibid., p. 44.
10.   Ibid., pp. 57, 327.
11.   Ibid., p. 35.
12.   A. Daux and F. Le Play, "Forgeron bulgare des usines
à fer de Samokowa (Turquie Centrale): D'après les documents
recueillis sur les lieux en 1848 et 1849 par MM. A. Daux et F.
Le Play," in *Les Ouvriers européens: Etudes sur les travaux,
la vie domestique et la condition morale des populations ouvrières de l'Europe, d'après les faits observés de 1829 à 1855*,
6 vols.; 2nd ed., (Paris, 1855-78), pp. 231-71. This material
has also been used by Khristo Vladov in his monograph, *Analiz
na domakinskite biudzheti s ogled na predvizhdaneto na potre-
bitelskoto tursene* (Sofia, 1966), pp. 113 ff. The author of
the present work has published in full the information provided by Daux and Le Play in *Sbornik v chest akad. D. Kosev*
(Sofia, 1974).
13.   *Journal de Constantinople*, no. 124, October 29,
1848, p. 12.
14.   Ibid., no. 824, September 28, 1857, p. 3.
15.   Ibid., no. 67, January 11, 1843, p. 1.
16.   The movement of prices in the Balkans from the 15th
through the 19th century followed roughly the direction of
price movement in Western and Central Europe, although at
given stages the Ottoman price fluctuations were unique. In
the last quarter of the 15th century there was a trend toward
rising prices (in silver equivalent), which, after certain
fluctuations in the first half of the 16th century, led
by the end of that century to prices twice as high as those
of the middle of the 15th century (this Ottoman "price revolution," however, was weaker and less enduring than the one
in Europe). After a period of declining prices in the middle
of the 17th century, there was a new wave of increases in the
early 18th, followed by another decline in the middle of that
century, and another rise in the early 19th century. By this

period the price level (in silver equivalent) had risen on an
average of four to five times higher than the price levels
existing in the middle of the 15th century. The general price
index in terms of the coinage then in circulation reflected a
much greater increase, since the state had put into circulation coins of less weight and a smaller precious metal
content. Throughout the remainder of the 19th century the
price movement fluctuated extensively in connection with wars,
reforms, and the growing dependence of the Ottoman Empire on
Western Europe. The movement of prices in the Ottoman Empire
has been the subject of recent historical studies. See, for
example, L. Berov, "Dvizhenieto na tsenite na Balkanite prez
XVI-XIX vek i evropeiskata revolutsiia na tsenite," IP, no. 1
(1975), a study that includes an extensive bibliography.

Chapter 21

   1. NBKM, Oo, Tolbukhin (Bazargic), Meclis-i idare-i
kaza, I resm-i tapu, May 23, 1870.
   2. For a general treatment of the extent and role of
Balkan fairs, see T. Stoianovich, "The Conquering Balkan Orthodox Merchant," *Journal of Economic History* 20 (June, 1960):
234-313.
   3. *Dokumenti za Bŭlgarskata istoriia. Tom 1. Arhkhiv
na Naiden Gerov:* pp. 32-34.
   4. The assessments were made by a commission of six
members, which put its signature at the end of the document,
and the whole register was certified by yet another commission
headed by the kaymakam of the city. In certain cases corrections were made in the original assessments, but these changes
have been taken into account here only where there is an ex-
plicit explanation offered for the correction made (such cases
are individually noted).
   5. In exceptional cases, it is true, a çarşı would include a shop dealing in unrelated merchandise.
   6. The grocers were basically grouped in two places,
but there were some of them spread among the other çarşıs.
   7. The "Braşov" çarşı was composed of individuals who
did business in goods produced in that city or supplied
through Braşov merchants. The most well-known of the commodities involved were products made of wood, particularly specially crafted and decorated trunks and carts.
   8. The dealers in dry goods were the most numerous of
the fair's merchants, and they were therefore spread over several çarsış and among the saddlers, the slippermakers, and
others.
   9. For a more detailed presentation of the fair see N.
Todorov, "Iarmarka v gorode Khadzhioglu Pazardzhik v 70-k
godakh XIX v.," in *Slavianskii arkhiv* (Moscow, 1963), pp.

116-39; and L. S. Beshkov, "Panairŭt v Khadzhioglu Pazardzhik predi Osbovozhdenieto," *Nashiiat grad v minaloto* (Tolbukhin, 1966), pp. 34-42.

10. The term "Bulgarians" is used with some hesitation, since these merchants might have included several Greeks.

11. *Turtsiia*, no. 21, July 11, 1872 (supplement).

12. Erroneously recorded in the text of Gerov's report as 20,000,000.

13. *Dokumenti za Bŭlgarskata Istoriia* 1: pp. 37-39.

Chapter 22

1. The average property values cited here, which are based on the author's calculations using tax receipts, deviate only insignificantly from the figures based on data contained in the *Table of the Taxes and of the Population* (see pp. 324 ff.). For urban property values in the range of several thousand kuruş, the deviations for Shumen, Bazargic, and Provadiia are within the scope of plus or minus 150 kuruş. For Silistra the deviation is within the range of plus or minus 356 kuruş. Only for Varna and Lom are the deviations greater, amounting to more than 1,000 kuruş. For Varna, as based on the *Table*, the value of urban property per taxable resident amounts to 7,800 kuruş; as based on tax receipts, the figure is 5,969 kuruş. For Lom the respective figures are 4,240 kuruş and 2,729 kuruş.

2. NBKM, Oo, Rkr, R_{29}, R_{30}, R_{31}, R_{32}.

3. NBKM, Oo, Rkr, R_{27}, ℓ. 75b-1.

4. Ibid., R_{33}, p. 160-II.

5. Ibid., R_{27}, ℓ. 16a-11.

6. Ibid., R_{30}, ℓ. 21a-II.

7. Ibid., R_{27}, ℓ. 23a-II.

8. NBKM, Oo, Registers of Silistra, no. 18, ℓ. 37.

9. Ibid., no. 16, ℓ. 69.

10. NBKM, Oo, f. 25, ed. 251, Register no. 2, ℓ. 12.

11. NBKM, Oo, Varna, Register no. 40, ℓ. 15.

12. Ibid., Register no. 39, ℓ. 56; Register no. 40, ℓ. 7.

13. Ibid., Constanţa, Register no. 7, ℓ. 29.

14. NBKM, Oo, Varna, Register no. 40, ℓ. 89; Register no. 1, ℓ. 40.

15. NBKM, Oo, Varna, Register no. 39, ℓℓ. 9, 68; Register no. 1, ℓ. 65; Register no. 40, ℓ. 8.

16. The average value of a dönüm of vineyard in Provadiia and Bazargic was 250 kuruş. The higher value in Varna indicates a great demand for vineyards.

17. Indirect evidence for such an assertion can be found in records used here that indicate that a person holding three dönüm of vineyard valued at 925 kuruş was registered as being

poor (NBKM, Oo, Varna, Register no. 39, ℓ. 45; Register no. 40, ℓ. 58).

    18. V. I. Lenin, "Kharakteristike ekonomicheskogo romantizma: Sismondi i nashi otechestvennye sismondistry," *Polnoe sobranie sochinenii* 2:223-24.

GLOSSARY

Unmarked entries are Turkish. Whenever possible the current Turkish
spelling of words is given following the *New Redhouse Turkish-English
Dictionary: Redhouse Yeni Türkçe-İngilizce Sözlük* (Istanbul: Redhouse
Press, 1968). Other entries are noted as follows: A=Arabic; B=Bul-
garian; G=German; Gk=Greek; H=Hebrew; Sl=Slavic; Sp=Spanish.

aba	coarse woolen cloth for cloaks and other clothing
abacı	maker or seller of aba
ağa	chief; officer; master
ahi	head of fütüvvet (q.v.); usually from the knightly estate of Seljuk society
ahur	livestock sheds
akçe	basic silver coin of account in the Ottoman Empire
akıncı	mounted irregular soldier used as a scout or raider

alebiia (B)	64 cm.
alemdar	standard-bearer
ambar	granary; barn
ambarcı	barnkeeper
âmediye	import duty
amele	workers
angariia (B)	forced labor
araba	peasant wagon
arabacı	carter
arabacılık	work or condition of carting
armatole (Gk)	locally recruited Christian armed guard
arshin	71.1 cm.
aşçılar	cooks
aş evi	fireplace
at	riding horse
ateş değirmen	fire mills; i.e., steam boilers
avarız	extraordinary (special, temporary) tax
azap	ordinary member of a fortress garrison
bad-i hava	extraordinary tax collected for the benefit of a feudal lord, who thereby gained judicial immunity
bağçe	orchard
bakamı	a blue dye substitute
barutçubaşı	official in a military arsenal
basmacı	a maker or seller of printed cotton cloth
başçılar	vendors of brains
başmakçı	footwear maker or seller
bazarbaşı	market official
bedel-i mukataa	payment by a muhtesib (q.v.) in return for a berat (q.v.) and right to collect the ihtisab (q.v.)
bedel-i nüzul	sum of the nüzul (q.v.)
bedel-i öşr	equivalent to the tithe; collected from land alienated from agricultural use
berat	charter for possession of land or assumption of salaried post
beygir	draft horse
beylerbeyi	highest ranking Ottoman governor
beylerbeylik	province; largest administrative unit up to sixteenth century

beyt (A)	house or dwelling
bezaz	dealer in textiles
bezistan	covered market
boza	a beer made from fermented millet
börekçiler	pie makers
buyrultu	written order
bülükbaşi	small-unit commander
büryancılar	soup makers
celebi	armed man serving under a sipahi (q.v.)
celepkeşan	livestock contractor
cetvel-i mizan-i vergi ve nüfus	table of taxes and the population
chapadzhii (B)	cultivator
cizye	poll tax paid by non-Muslims
cubit (Gk)	100 cm.
çalgıcı	musician; piper
çardak	terrace
çardak odası	room or door to the terrace
çarşı	street with rows of merchant shops of one type
çavuş	sergeant; guild official who implemented decisions of assembly; later a public armed guard.
çehli	soft, expensive slipper
çelebi	gentleman; i.e., sir--title of respect
çırak	apprentice
çift bozan	tax for leaving the land
çiftlik	farm or privately owned estate
çizme	high boot
çizmeci	maker or seller of boots
çorbacı	rich non-Muslim holding a minor office; Christian notable
çukaçı	maker or seller of broadcloth
dahiliyese ve hariciyesi	external and internal parts of a house
dar	house or dwelling
defter	register

defterdar	chief treasury official
defterhane	treasury department
derbentçi	guard of a bridge, pass, or other strategic location
derviş	member of a Muslim religious order
devşirme	levy of Christian youths to serve in the Janissary corps
dirhem	3.148 g.
divan	holding of court; public sitting of a judge
doğancı	falconer, member of a military unit
dönüm	919.3 m.
dzaki	Christian notable
elhac	article before a name; title of respect
emin	head of a department
esnaf	guild
esnaf tezkeresi	permit to exercise a trade
eşkinci	person freed from other obligations in return for ancillary service in the army
ev	house or dwelling
eyalet	province (after the sixteenth century); same as earlier beylerbeylik (q.v.)
ferman	imperial edict
firinci tezgah	designation for a migrant baker (v. Hamurkar)
fokani ve tahtani	number of stories
futuwwa (A)	same as fütüvvet (q.v.)
fütüvvet	organization of religious and social character
fütüvvetname	medieval guild statute
gaitan (B)	braid
gaitancı	maker or seller of braid
gaitan-dzhiistvo (B)	braid making
gayri müsmere	orchard other than a fruit orchard
gedik	document of sole ownership needed by a guild master to set up his own shop
gesetzmäss-igkeiten (G)	regularities
gradove dzhud-zheta (B)	pocket cities; category based on number of inhabitants

griza (Gk)	same as aba (q.v.)
gümrük	tariffs, collectively
hacı	title of respect for one who has made a pilgrimage (hac) to Mecca
haffaf	maker or seller of cheap shoes
hallaç	cleaner or beater of cotton-wool
halvaçı	sweetmaker or seller of sweets
hamamcı	public bathkeeper
hamurkar	migrant bakers: journeymen, apprentices, or masters who did not have their own shops.
hane	house or dwelling
haraç	land-use tax; sometimes used as a synonym for cizye (q.v.)
has	possession of the sultan allotted to an official
hasha-i padişah defteri	registers of has holdings
havlu	courtyard
hayat (A)	covered courtyard
haydut	bandit; brigand
hergele	herding horse
hirfa (A)	guild
hisar (A)	same as kale (q.v.)
hizmet	service
hizmetkâr	servants, porters, stevedores
hüccet	document confirming delivery of livestock
ırgat	farmhand; day laborer
icmal defteri	register of fief holdings
ihracat	export duty
ihtisab	certain municipal dues
imam	religious leader
imaret	charitable institution
irade	rescript
ispence	land tax paid in money
işçi	worker
ithalat	import duty
kadı	Muslim judge
kadıasker	chief military judge; highest rank in judiciary

kadılık	administrative unit presided over by a kadı (q.v.)
kâfir	infidel; non-Muslim
kâgir	stone foundation
kâhya	warden of a guild
kale	1. fortress, citadel; 2. fortified city
kalemci	warper in a textile mill
kalfa	journeyman or assistant master
kantar akçesi	a tax paid by nonlocal butchers for slaughtering rights
kanunname	collection of laws
kapıcıbaşı	military officer
kapudan paşa	admiral; high officer
karutsari (B)	drayman
kasaba	unfortified settlement
kashkaval (B)	yellow cheese
kâtib	clerk
kaymakam	deputy to the grand vizier
kaza	smallest administrative unit; same as kadılık (q.v.)
kebe	thick woolen cloth
keçeci	maker or seller of horsecloth
kehâya	head of a shepherds' association
kepenk	shutter
kethüda	head of guild, elected by elders
kile	measure of dry weight (variable)
kileci	grain weigher
kiler	pantry
kiler evi	same as kiler (q.v.)
kiraçı	village carter
kircalı	Turk or Albanian brigand
kiyak hane	auxiliary building
kondika (B)	guild register
kömür odası	coalbin
kunduracı	maker or seller of footwear
kurdzhii (B)	itinerant merchants
kuruş	monetary unit introduced in the 17th century
kurpacı	cobbler
lekha (B)	229.8 sq. m.

levandiye	monetary tax paid by peasants engaged in seasonal work
liva	subdivision of a province; sancak (q.v.)
lonca	guild meeting
mağaza	warehouse
mahalle	quarter of a city
mahlul	inheritance that went to the treasury--no legal heir
mahzen	cellar
manifakturist (B)	dry-goods dealer
marrano (Sp)	Christianized Jew
masdariye	market duty
masurci	bobbin winder
matbah	kitchen
mayi	foundation, of a house
meclis	council
medrese	higher school of Muslim law
menzil	house; postal station
mesken	house or dwelling
millet	non-Muslim community organized under its own religious head
mîr-i alem	sultan's standard-bearer
miriliva	governor of a liva (q.v.)
molla	senior member among doctors of Islamic law
mufasal defteri	detailed register
muhassıl	individual in service of a sipahi (q.v.)
muhtar	village elder
muhtesib	assistant to a kadı (q.v.)
mukataa	special state levy of considerable size
mut	400-500 kg.
mutafçı	maker or seller of goat-wool cloth
mutasarrıf	administrative head of a sancak (q.v.)
müdur	an administrator or director
müdur zaptiye	commander of the police
müfti	official expounder of Islamic Law
mülk	private property, mostly land
müruriye	duty paid on goods in transit
müsellem	regular salaried cavalryman

Müslim	Muslim, "one surrendered to God"
müsmere	fruit
müstahfız	mounted fortress guard
nahiye	subdivision of a kaza (q.v.)
nahr	price norms
naib	deputy to a kadı (q.v.)
nasihatname	instruction
nazır	supervisor
nefs	lit., the very place; center of a nahiye (q.v.)
niyabet	extraordinary defense tax levied on the reaya (q.v.)
nüfus defteri	summary register
nüzul	extraordinary tax on non-Muslims; foodstuffs for the army
obshtina (B)	non-Muslim religious-municipal community organization
oda	room
oda evi	lit., the place of the room
odzhak (B)	hearth; a yuruk settlement
okka	100-400 dirhem (q.v.)
orta kol	middle wing of the Rumelian beylerbeylik (q.v.)
padişah	sovereign, monarch, emperor
palanka	place fortified with embankments and stakes
papuç	simple slipper made without a counter
papuççu	cobbler
para	monetary unit introduced in the seventeenth century
paşa	alternate title for a beylerbeyi (q.v.)
paşalik	same as eyalet (q.v.)
paşa sancak	sancak that was the seat of the beylerbeyi (q.v.)
pazar	small town of the kasaba (q.v.) type
pınar	well
pomeshchik (B)	landlord
pomeshchichii (B)	landlordship
predbalkan	foothill area north of Balkan Mountains
râya	same as reaya (q.v.)
reaya	ordinary subject(s) of the empire

receb	seventh month of the Muslim lunar calendar
reftiye	export duty
resm-i çift	agricultural tax
resm-i huk	monetary tax levied on pig owners
rupe (Gk)	8 cm.
sağ kol	right wing of the Rumelian beylerbeylik (q.v.)
saka	water-carrier
salhane	slaughterhouse
salname	census, yearbook, almanac, yearly statistical register
saman hane	auxiliary building
sancak	administrative division of the empire
sancakbeyi	governor of a sancak (q.v.)
saray	court
sarfiyat	market duty
sayban	lean-to
sayeban	same as sayban (q.v.)
sayfi oda	summer room
sĕphārad (H)	region usually identified with Spain
serasker	military commander
serdengeçti	high-ranking officer
shop (B)	peasant of the Sofia district
sicil	register kept by a kadı (q.v.)
simid	sweet white bread
sinif	singular of esnaf (q.v.); lit., kind, part, class
sipahi	cavalryman
sobalı odası	room with a stove
soba odası	same as sobalı odası (q.v.)
sol kol	left wing of the Rumelian beylerbeylik (q.v.)
sofa	hall
sofa evi	same as sofa (q.v.)
sokolar (B)	falconer, member of a military unit
subaşı	1. head of a fifteenth-century vilâyet (q.v.); 2. police chief
şaban	eighth month of the Muslim lunar calendar
şahbender	official who supervised wholesale merchants in Istanbul; assistant to the kadı of the capital
şayak	type of cloth; a grey aba (q.v.)

şehir	fully developed city
şehirli	townsman; city dweller
şeriat	system of Muslim religious-civil law
şeyh	similar to ahi (q.v.); presided over guild religious ceremonies
şitevi oda	room for use in the winter
taifa (A)	guild
takye	linen skullcap worn under a fez
takyeci	member of capmakers' guild
tanzimat	period of political reforms beginning in 1839
tărg (Sl)	small town of the kasaba (q.v.) type
terzi (B)	tailor
terziistvo (B)	tailoring
testir (B)	general guild meeting at which journeymen became masters
tezkere	permit to exercise a trade
timar	land grant
timariot	holder of a timar (q.v.)
timar ve zeamet defteri	register of timar (q.v.) and zeamet (q.v.) holdings
topçu	artilleryman
toptançı	wholesale dealer
tüccar	merchant
tüfekci	gunsmith
uc	frontier area
usta	master craftsman
ustabaşı	elected head of a guild
vakıf	trust established with a grant of land or other income-producing property to support a pious foundation
vali	governor of a vilâyet (q.v.)
varoš	Christian quarter of an Ottoman city
vekili	representative of the population in local Ottoman administrative organs
vezir	title given to beylerbeyi (q.v.)
vilâyet	1. unit larger than a nahiye (q.v.) in fifteenth-century empire; 2. largest administrative unit in late nineteenth-century empire

voynugan (B)	horse groom; member of a military unit
voynuk	non-Muslim serving as a horse groom in Ottoman army
voyvoda	kind of mayor
Vŭzhrazh-dane (B)	Bulgarian National Revival
yabancı	migrant artisan or merchant
yamak	auxiliary janissary
yağmurluk	type of broadcloth; cloak made from it
yazlık	covered yard
yazlık hayatı	combination of yazlık (q.v.) and hayat (q.v.)
yiğitbaşı	second-ranking member of guild after the elders
zâbit	police officer
zaim	one given a land grant (zeamet q.v.) in return for service
zakonomernost (B)	regularities
zaviye	small cloister with a hostel
zeamet	medium-size land grant
zebun (B)	type of jacket
zemlik (Sl)	a room dug out of the earth
zilhicce	twelfth month of the Muslim lunar calendar

BIBLIOGRAPHY

ABBREVIATIONS

APP   *Arkhiv za poselishtni prouchvaniia* [Archive for the study of settlements]

GIBH   *Godišnjak istorijskog društva Bosne i Hercegovine* [Annual of the Historical Society of Bosnia and Hercegovina] (Sarajevo)

GINI   *Glasnik na Institutot za nacionalna istorija* [Herald of the Institute for National History] (Skoplje)

GSUIF   *Godishnik na Sofiiskiia universitet: Istori-ko-filologicheski fakultet* [Annual of Sofia University: History-philology faculty]

IBID   *Izvestiia na Bŭlgarsko istorichesko druzhestvo* [Journal of the Bulgarian Historical Society]

IC   *Istorijske časopis*

[Historical Journal]
(Belgrade)

IG *Istorijski glasnik* [His-
torical Herald] (Bel-
grade)

IP *Istoricheski pregled*
[Historical Review]

IVAD *Izvestiia na Varnenskoto
arkheologichesko dru-
zhestvo* [Journal of the
Varna Archaeological
Society]

IZII *Izvestiia na Instituta za
istoriia* [Journal of
the History Institute]

PSBK *Periodichesko spisanie
na Bŭlgarskoto kni-
zhovno druzhestvo* [Pe-
riodical publication
of the Bulgarian Liter-
ary Society

SBID *Spisanie na Bŭlgarskoto
ikonomichesko dru-
zhestvo* [Journal of
the Bulgarian Econom-
ics Society]

SNU *Sbornik za narodni umotvoreniia* [Anthology of
Folklore]

Works in Bulgarian, Russian, and Serbo-Croatian

Aianov, G. *Malko Tŭrnovo i negovata pokrainina: Antrop-geo-
grafski i istoricheski prouchvaniia* [Malko Tŭrnovo and its
environs: Anthropo-geographic and historical studies].
Burgas, 1939.

Aleksandrov, V. *Iz istoriiata na grad Karlovo: Stopanski,
kulturni, prosvetni i drugi pridobivki ot 1903 do 1934 g.*
[From the history of Karlovo: Economic, cultural, educational and other gains from 1903 to 1934]. With addenda:
1. History of woolbraiding; 2. Karlovo and the Karlovo
district. Sofia, 1938.

Andreev, M. and D. Angelov. *Istoriia na bŭlgarskata feodalna
dŭrzhava i pravo* [History of the Bulgarian feudal state
and law]. Sofia, 1968.

Andreev, S. "Danŭchen spisŭk na kotlenskite zanaiatchii ot
1865 g." [A tax list of kotel artisans from 1865]. IBID
26 (1968):321-29.

Apostolidis, M. and A. Peev. "Kondika na Plovdivskiia abadzhiiski esnaf" [Chronicle of the Plovdiv tailor's guild].
Pt. 1, "From 1685 to 1772"; Pt. 2, "From 1722 to 1818";
Pt. 3, "From 1811 to 1856." *Godishnik na Narodna biblioteka i muzeia v Plovdiv. Nauchna chast.* [Annual of the
National Library and Museum in Plovdiv. Scientific sec-
tion]. Plovdiv, 1931-32.

Aprilov, V. *Dennitsa novobŭlgarskogo obrazovaniia* [Dawn of the
new Bulgarian education]. Pt. 1. Odessa, 1841.

Argirov, St. "Dva stari esnafski ustava" [Two old guild regulations]. PSBK 61 (1900):382-88.

Arnaudov, M. "Iz minaloto na Kotel: Zaselvane, belezhiti lich-
     nosti, stopanski zhivot, folklor" [From Kotel's past:
     Settlement, notable people, economic life, folklore].
     GSUIF 27, no. 1 (1931):1-100.

Arsh, Gr. *Albaniia i Epir u kontse XVII-nachale XIX veka* [Al-
     bania and Epirus at the end of the 18th and beginning of
     the 19th centuries]. Moscow, 1963.

-----, I. Senkevich and N. D. Smirnova. *Kratkaia istoriia
     Albanii* [A short history of Albania]. Moscow, 1965.

Atanasov, V. "Iz minaloto na esnafite ni" [From the history of
     our guilds]. PSBK 63 (1903):747-52.

Barjaktarević, M. "Prijepolje (prilog proučavanju naših
     varošica)" [Prijepolje (contribution to the study of our
     towns)]. *Zbornik Filozofskog fakulteta u Beogradu* [Anthol-
     ogy of the philosophy faculty in Belgrade] 4, no. 1
     (1956):353-72.

Batakliev, I. "Grad Bansko" [The town of Bansko]. GSUIF 25
     (1929):1-56.

-----. *Grad Tatar Pazardzhik. Istoriko-geografski pregled* [The
     town of Tatar Pazardzhik. Historico-geographic survey].
     Tatar Pazardzhik, 1923.

Begović, M. "Tragovi našeg srednjevekovnog prava u turskim
     pravnim spomenicima" [Traces of our medieval law in Turk-
     ish legal documents]. IC 3 (1952):67-84.

Berbenliev, P. and V. Partŭchev. *Bratsigovskite maistori-
     stroiteli* [Bratsigovo master builders]. Sofia, 1963.

Beshkov, A. and N. Michev. "Ikonomo-geografsko raionirane na
     Severna Bŭlgariia" [Division of northern Bulgaria into
     economic-geographic regions]. *Sbornik v chest na chlen.
     korespondent Iordan Zakhariev* [Anthology to honor corre-
     sponding member Iordan Zakhariev], pp. 13-28. Sofia, 1964.

Bitoski, Kr. "Prilog kon prouchuvanjeto na bitolskite esnafi
     i nivnata opshestvena uloga vo XIX v. [Contribution to the
     study of the Bitolj guilds and their social role in the
     19th century]. GINI 10, no. 1 (1966):137-63.

Blŭskov, I. *Material po istoriiata na nasheto Vŭzrazhdane gr.*

Shumen [Material on the history of our National Revival.
The town of Shumen]. Shumen, 1907.

Bobchev, S. "Elena i Elensko prez vreme na Osmanskoto vladichestvo" [Elena and the district of Elena during Ottoman
rule]. *Elenski sbornik* [Elena anthology] 2:1-74.

Bogorov, I. *Osnova zaradi naprava na edna fabrika da prede i
tŭche pamŭk v gr. Plovdiv* [The basis for construction of a
factory to spin and weave cotton in the town of Plovdiv].
Istanbul, 1863.

-----. *Sŭdruzhestvo za pamuchina fabrika v Plovdiv* [Partner-
ship in the cotton factory in Plovdiv]. Plovdiv, 1865.

Bokhachek, A. *Grad Nikopol prez vekovete* [The town of Nikopol
through the centuries]. Sofia, 1937.

Bonchev, G. "Staroto rudarstvo v Bŭlgariia i Makedoniia" [An-
cient mining in Bulgaria and Macedonia]. *Spisanie na
Bŭlg. Akademiia na naukite* [Bulletin of the Bulgarian Academy of Sciences] 19 (1920):1-50.

Bozhkov, L. *Sŭobshtitelnite sredstva na Bŭlgariia* [Means of
communication in Bulgaria]. Sofia, 1929.

Božić, I. *Dubrovnik i Turska u XIV i XV veku* [Dubrovnik and
Turkey in the 14th and 15th centuries]. Belgrade, 1952.

Bücher, K., G. Mayer, and G. Simmel. *Bol'shie goroda, ikh
obshchestvenoe, politicheskoe i ekonomicheskoe znachenie.
Sbornik statei.* [Large cities--their social, political
and economic significance. Collection of articles]. St.
Petersburg, 1905.

Chankov, Zh. *Naselenieto na Bŭlgariia* [The inhabitants of Bul-
garia]. Sofia, 1935.

Chechulin, N. D. *Goroda Moskovskogo gosudarstva v XVI v.*
[Cities of the Moscovite State in the 16th century].
St. Petersburg, 1889.

Cholov, P. *Istoriia na grad Drianovo* [History of the town of
Drianovo]. Sofia, 1969.

Chomov, Iv. *Pravoviiat red na esnafskite organizatsii v niakogashna Bŭlgariia* [The legal order of guild organizations
in former Bulgaria]. Sofia, 1928.

Damianov, S. *Lomskiiat krai prez Vŭzrazhdaneto. Ikonomicheski zhivot i politicheski borbi* [The Lom area during the National Revival: Economic life and political struggles]. Sofia, 1967.

Danailova, L. "Materiali za pravna i stopanska istoriia na grad Svishtov" [Materials for the legal and economic history of the city of Svishtov]. *Godishnik na Vissheto tŭrgovsko uchilishte v Svishtov* [Annual of the Higher Trade School in Svishtov] 6 (1941-42):1-72. Svishtov, 1944.

Deliradev, P. *Rodopite kato selishtna oblast i planinska sistema. Istoriko-geografski ocherk* [The Rhodopes as an area of settlement and as a mountain system. Historical-geographical essay]. Sofia, 1937.

-----. *Prinos kŭm istoricheskata geografiia na Trakiia* [Contribution to the historical geography of Thrace]. 2 vols. Sofia, 1953.

Derzhavin, N. S. *Istoriia Bolgarii* [History of Bulgaria], vols. 3-4. Moscow, 1947-48.

Dimitrijević, S. *Dubrovački karavani u južnoj Srbiji u XVII veku* [Dubrovnik caravans in southern Serbia in the 17th century]. Belgrade, 1958.

Dimitrov, P. *Vŭzpomenatelen istoricheski sbornik na Sofiiskoto branshovo tŭrgovsko bakelsko sdruzhenie "Tri svetiteli," 1718-1937* [A memorial historical anthology of the Sofia grain trade grocers' association "Three Saints," 1718-1937]. Sofia, 1937.

-----. "Kŭm vŭprosa za otmeniavaneto na spakhiiskata sistema v nashite zemi" [On the question of the transformation of the Spahi system in our lands]. IP 12, no. 6 (1956):27-58.

-----. "Za kasovoto razsloenie sred selianite v Severoiztochna Bŭlgariia prez 70-te godini na XIX v." [On class differentiation among the peasants of northeast Bulgaria during the 1870s]. IZII 8 (1960):226-71.

Dimitrov, Str. "Demografski otnosheniia i pronikvane na isliama v Zapadnite Rodopi i dolinata na Mesta prez XV-XVII vv." [Demographic relations and the penetration of Islam into the western Rhodopes and the Mesta valley during the 15th-17th centuries]. *Rodopski sbornik* [Rhodope anthology], 1:63-114. Sofia, 1965.

-----. "Dokumenti za ikonomicheskoto polozhenie na naselenieto
v Smoliansko prez XVII-XIX v." [Documents on the economic
condition of the inhabitants of the Smolian district in
the 17th-19th centuries]. *Rodopski sbornik*, 1:325-33.
Sofia, 1965.

-----, and Kr. Manchev. *Istoriia na balkanskite narodi* [His-
tory of the Balkan peoples]. Sofia, 1971.

Dinekov, P. *Sofiiski knizhovnitsi prez XVI v.* [Sofia writers
during the 16th century]. Vol. 1. Sofia, 1938.

Djordjević, T. *Arhivska gradja za zanate i esnafe u Srbiji od
drugog estanka do esnafske uredbe 1847* [Archival materials
on artisans and guilds in Serbia from the second uprising
to the Guild Act of 1847]. Belgrade, 1925.

Djurdjev, Br. "Osnovni problemi srpske istorije u periodu
turske vlasti nad našim narodima" [Basic questions of
Serbian history during Turkish rule over our peoples].
IG, nos. 3-4 (1950), Belgrade.

-----. "O uticaju turske vladavine na razvitak naših naroda"
[On the influence of Turkish rule on the development of
our peoples]. GIBH (Sarajevo) 2 (1950):19-82.

*Dnevnikŭt na Khans Dernshvam za pŭtuvaneto mu do Tsarigrad
prez 1553-1555 g.* [The diary of Hans Dernschwam about his
journey to Istanbul, 1553-1555]. Ed. V. Mutafchieva;
trans. M. Kiselincheva. Sofia, 1970.

*Dokumenti za bŭlgarskata istoriia. Tom 1. Arkhiv na Naiden
Gerov* [Documents from Bulgarian history. Vol. 1. Archive
of Naiden Gerov]. Pt. 1. Ed. M. G. Popruzhenko. Sofia,
1931.

Draganova, T. "Gradskata obshtina na gr. Veliko Tŭrnovo prez
XIX v." [The town council of Veliko Trnovo during the
19th century]. *Izvestiia na okrŭzhniia muzei* [Journal of
the district museum] (Veliko Trnovo) 3 (1966):73-96.

-----. "Ikonomicheskoto razvitie na gr. V. Tŭrnovo prez epokhata na Vŭzrazhdaneto. Kratŭk istoricheski pregled"
[The economic development of Veliko Trnovo during the
period of the National Revival. A short historical sur-
vey]. Pt. 1. *Izvestiia na okrŭzhniia muzei* 4 (1968):67-
89.

Drinov, M. "Istoricheskoto osvetlenie vŭrkhu statistikata na

narodnostite v iztochnata chast na Bŭlgarskoto kniazhestvo" [The light of history on the statistics of nationalities in the eastern part of the Bulgarian kingdom]. PSBK
(1884):1-24; 8 (1885):68-75.

Druzhina, E. *Kiuchuk-Kainardzhiiskii mir 1774 goda* [The treaty
of Kuchuk Kainarji of 1774]. Moscow, 1955.

Elenski sbornik. (Kniga za Elena i Elenskiia krai) [Elena anthology (A book about Elena and the Elena District)].
Sofia, 1968.

Eshkenazi, E. "Za khronikata na semeistvo Arie ot Samokov" [On
the chronicle of the Arie family from Samokov]. IZII 12
(1963):193-210.

-----. "Evreite na Balkanskiia poluostrov prez XV i XVI vek,
techniiat bit, kultura, masovi razsloeniia, pominŭk i
organizatsiia na obshtinite im" [Jews on the Balkan peninsula during the 15th and 16th centuries--their customs,
culture, mass stratification, occupations and organization
of governing bodies]. *Godishnik na obshtestvenata kultur-
no-prosvetna organizatsiia na evreite v NR Bulgariia*
[Annual of the General Cultural-Educational Organization
of Jews in PR Bulgaria] 3, no. 1 (1968):127-50.

*Evreiski izvori za obshtestveno-ikonomicheskoto razvitie na
balkanskite zemi prez XVI i XVII vek* [Jewish sources on
the socioeconomic development of the Balkan lands during
the 16th and 17th centuries]. 2 vols. Sofia, 1958-60.

Fadeev, A. "Grecheskoe natsional'no-osvoboditel'noe dvizhenie
i russkoe obshchestvo pervykh desiatiletii XIX veka" [The
Greek national liberation movement and Russian society of
the first decades of the 19th century]. *Novaia i noveishaia istoriia* [Modern and contemporary history] (Moscow),
no. 3 (1964), pp. 41-52.

Filipović, N. "Iz istorije Novog brda e drugoj polovini XV. i
prvoj polovini XVI v." [From the history of Novo Brdo in
the second half of the 15th and the first half of the 16th
century]. GIBH 4 (1952):5-146.

Firsov, N. N. "Istoriia russkogo goroda do kontsa XVII v. [The
history of the Russian town to the end of the 17th cen-
tury]. *Istoricheskie kharakteristiki i eskizy* [Historical
characterizations and sketches] (Kazan), 1 (1922):153-71.

Fotinov, K. *Obshtee zemleopisanie vkrattse za sichkata zemlia*

[A general short geographical description of the entire country]. Smyrna, 1843.

Frasheri, K. *Istoriia Albanii* [History of Albania]. Tirana, 1964.

Ganchev, St. *Svishtov. Prinos za istoriiata mu* [Svishtov. Contributions to its history]. Svishtov, 1929.

Gandev, Khr. *Faktori na Bŭlgarskoto Vŭzrazhdane 1600-1830* [Factors in the Bulgarian National Revival 1600-1830]. Sofia, 1943.

------. "Tŭrgovskata obmiana na Evropa s bŭlgarskite zemi prez XVIII i nachaloto na XIX v." [Exchange of trade between Europe and the Bulgarian lands during the 18th and beginning of the 19th century]. GSUIF 40 (1943-44):1-36.

------. *Aprilskoto vŭstanie* [The April uprising]. Sofia, 1956.

------. "Pronikvaneto i ukrepvaneto na bŭlgarite vŭv Vidin kŭm kraiia na XVII i prez XVIII v." [Penetration and consolidation of Bulgarians in Vidin toward the end of the 17th and during the 18th century]. *Izvestiia na Etnografskiia institut i muzei* [Journal of the Ethnographic Institute and Museum] 4 (1961):5-25.

------. *Zarazhdane na kapitalicheskite otnosheniia v chiflishtkoto stopanstvo na Severozapadna Bŭlgariia prez XVIII v.* [The origin of capitalist relations in the farm economy of northwestern Bulgaria in the 18th century]. Sofia, 1962.

Ganev, N. "Istoricheskoto razvitie na tŭrgovskoto pravo" [The historical development of trade law]. *Godishnik na Sofiiskiia universitet: Iuridicheski fakultet* 12 (1915-16): 27-32. Sofia, 1921.

------. *Stranitsi ot istoriiata na grad Sevlievo* [Pages from the history of the town of Sevlievo]. Pt. 1. Trnovo, 1925.

------. *Provadiia v svoeto minalo i nastoiashte* [Provadiia in the past and present]. Sofia, 1929.

Genezis kapitalizma v promyshlennosti. Sbornik statei [Genesis of capitalism in industry. Collection of articles]. Moscow, 1963.

Geografiia na Bŭlgariia. Vol. 1, Ikonomicheska geografiia
[Geography of Bulgaria. Vol. 1. Economic geography].
Sofia, 1961.

Georgiev, I. "Grad Vrattsa. Sbornik za narodni umotvoreniia"
[The city of Vraca]. SNU 20 (1904):1-75.

------. "Grad Elena." [The city of Elena]. PSBK 65 (1904):74-
99.

------, and B. Achkov. "Uzundzhovskiiat panair v svetlinata na
novoizdireni dokumenti" [The market at Uzundzhovo in light
of newly discovered documents]. IZII 19 (1967):167-92.

Georgiev, M. *Ikonomicheskoto minalo na grad Sofiia i Sofiisko*
[The economic history of the city and district of Sofia].
Sofia, 1926.

------. "Osmanoturski izvori za istoriiata na Sofiia" [Ottoman
sources for the history of Sofia]. *Serdika* 6 (1942), nos.
1-2:87-96; nos. 3-4:87-97; nos. 5-6:104-17.

------. *Turski izvori za istoriiata na pravoto v bŭlgarskite
zemi* [Turkish sources for the history of law in the Bulgarian lands]. Vol. 1. Sofia, 1961.

------, and D. Buchinski. *Staroto zlatarstvo vŭv Vratsa* [An-
cient goldsmithing in Vraca]. Sofia, 1959.

Gordlevskii, V. A. "Dervishi akhi Evrana i tsekhi v Turtsii"
[The dervishes of Akhi Evran and guilds in Turkey]. *Iz-
brannye sochineniia* [Selected works]. Istoricheskie raboty
[Historical works], vol. 1, pp. 289-306. Moscow, 1960.

------. "Gosudarstvo Sel'dzhukidov Maloi Azii" [The Seljuk
state of Asia Minor]. *Izbrannye sochineniia*. Istoricheskie raboty, vol. 1, pp. 31-218. Moscow, 1960.

Gorianov, B. T. *Pozdnevizantiiskii feodalizm* [Late Byzantine
feudalism]. Moscow, 1967.

Govedarov, I. *Koprivshtitsa v svrŭzka s dukhovnoto i politichesko Vŭzrazhdane* [Koprivshtitsa in connection with the
spiritual and political National Revival]. Plovdiv, 1931.

*Grad Troian. Yubileen sbornik po sluchai 100 godini ot obia-
viaveneto mu za grad* [The city of Trojan. Jubilee anthology on the 100th anniversary of its declaration as city].
Sofia, 1968.

Gruev, I. *Moite spomeni* [My recollections]. Plovdiv, 1906.

Gŭlŭbov, G. *Miusiulmanskoto pravo s kratŭk obzor vŭrkhu isto-
    riiata i dogmite na isliama* [Muslim law, with a short sur-
    vey of the history and dogma of Islam]. Sofia, 1924.

------. "Za osnovnite nachala na pozemlenata sobstvenost v Os-
    vanskata imperiia i spetsialno v Bŭlgariia pol tursko vla-
    dichestvo (po osvanoturski zakoni i dokumenti ot XVI, XVII,
    XVIII, i XIX v.)" [On the basic principles of landed prop-
    erty in the Ottoman Empire and especially in Bulgaria un-
    der Turkish rule (according to Ottoman laws and documents
    from the 16th, 17th, 18th and 19th centuries)]. GSUIF 43
    (1946-47):1-92.

------. "Dva turski dokumenta ot XVII v. za stopanskata i obsh-
    testvena deinost na bŭlgarskite zanaiatchii" [Two Turkish
    documents from the 17th century on the economic and social
    activity of Bulgarian artisans]. IZII 18 (1967):289-97.

Gunchev, G. "Poselishtno-geografsi prouchvaniia v Bŭlgariia.
    Postizheniia i zadachi" [Settlement and geographic studies
    in Bulgaria. Achievements and tasks]. APP 1, no. 1
    (1938):3-37.

------. "Bŭlgarskite selishta" [Bulgarian villages]. APP 2,
    nos. 3-4 (1940):263-73.

------. "Zhelezodobivnata industriia v Samokov" [The iron-
    smelting industry in Samokov]. APP 2, nos. 3-4 (1940):
    274-86.

Iaranov, D. "Preselničeskoto dviženie na bŭlgari ot Makedoniia
    i Albaniia kŭm iztočnite bŭlgarski zemi prez XV do XIX v."
    [The emigration movement of Bulgarians from Macedonia and
    Albania to eastern Bulgaria from the 15th to the 19th cen-
    tury]. *Makedonski pregled* [Macedonian review] 7, nos. 2-3
    (1931):63-118.

Iavashov, An. *Razgrad. Negovoto arkheologichesko i istori-
    chesko minalo* [Razgrad. Its archaeological and historical
    past]. Pt. 1. Sofia, 1930.

Ikhchiev, D. "Esnafski dokumenti i esnafski organizatsii v
    tursko vreme" [Guild documents and guild organizations in
    the Turkish period]. SBID 11, no. 7 (1907):445-61.

------. "Panairite i pazarnite dni v Iuzhna Bŭlgariia predi
    Osvobozhdenieto" [Markets and market days in southern Bul-

garia before the liberation]. SBID 12, nos. 9-10 (1908):
604-9.

Ikonomikata na Bŭlgariia do Sotsialisticheskata revoliutsiia
[Economy of Bulgaria in six volumes. Vol. 1, Economy of
Bulgaria up to the Socialist revolution]. Sofia, 1969.

Iordanov, I. *Istoriia na bŭlgarskata tŭrgoviia do Osvobozhdenieto. Kratŭk ocherk* [History of Bulgarian trade before
the liberation. A short essay]. Sofia, 1938.

-----. "Nachenki na nashata industriia predi Osvobozhdenieto"
[The beginning of our industry before the liberation].
SBID 37, no. 5 (1938):281-98.

Iotsov, D. *Kulturno-politicheska istoriia na Vratsa. Ot rim-
skata epokha do Osvobozhdenieto* [Cultural and political
history of Vraca. Vol. 1, from Roman times to the libera-
tion]. Sofia, 1937.

Ishirkov, At. "Grad Varna" [The city of Varna]. PSBK 65
(1904):191-236.

-----. "Istoriko-politicheskiiat element v gustotata na naselenieto v Bŭlgariia" [The historico-political element in the
density of population in Bulgaria]. *Sbornik Vasil Zlatarski* [Anthology for Vasil Zlatarski], pp. 91-97. Sofia,
1925.

Istoriia na Bŭlgariia [History of Bulgaria]. Vol. 1. 2nd ed.
Sofia, 1961.

Istoriia na grad Tolbukhin [History of the city of Tolbukhin].
Ed. Evl. Buzhashki. Sofia, 1968.

Istoriia na grad Stara Zagora [History of the city of Stara
Zagora]. Sofia, 1966.

Iz arkhivata na Naiden Gerov [From the archives of Naiden
Gerov]. Vol. 1. Ed. T. Panchev. Sofia, 1911.

Jireček, K. *Istoriia Bolgar* [History of the Bulgarians].
Odessa, 1878.

-----. "Stari pŭteshestviia po Bŭlgariia ot XV-XVIII stoletie"
[Travels in Bulgaria from the 15th to 18th century]. PSBK
vol. 2, nos. 3-6 (1882-83); vol. 3, no. 7 (1884).

-----. *Kniazhestvo Bŭlgariia: Negovata pŏvurkhnina, priroda, naselenie, dukhovna kultura, samoupravlenie i noveisha istoriia* [The kingdom of Bulgaria: Its terrain, natural attributes, population, spiritual culture, self-government and modern history]. 2 pts. Plovdiv, 1899.

Kabrda, I. "Raia" [The rayah]. IZII 14-15 (1937):172-85.

Karanov, E. "Opisanie na Kratovskata kaza" [Description of the Kratovo District]. PSBK 11-12 (1876):124-29.

Karanovski, I. "Karnobatska kondika [The Karnobat chronicle]. *Izvestiia na Narodniia etnografski muzei* [Journal of the National Ethnographic Museum] 1, nos. 3-4 (1926):204-14.

Kazanlŭk v minaloto i dnes [Kazanlik in the past and present]. *Godishnik na Kazanlŭshkata druzhba "Rozova dolina" v Sofiia* [The annual of the Kazanlik Society "Rose Valley" in Sofia]. 2 vols. Sofia, 1912-23.

Kazhdan, A. P. "Vizantiiskie goroda v VII-XI vv.," [Byzantine towns in the 7th to 10th century]. *Sovetskaia arkheologiia* [Soviet archaeology] 21 (1954):164-88.

Khinkov, Khr. *Stopanski faktori na Bŭlgarskoto Vŭzrazhdane* [Economic factors in the Bulgarian National Revival]. Sofia, 1947.

Khristov, Khr. "Niakoi problemi na prekhoda ot feodalizma kŭm kapitalizma v istoriiata na Bŭlgariia" [Some problems in the transition from feudalism to capitalism in Bulgarian history]. IP 17, no. 3 (1961):83-107.

Kniga zakanov sultana Selim [The book of laws of Sultan Selim]. A. S. Tveritinova, ed., trans. Moscow, 1969.

Koicheva, V. "Narodnostniiat oblik na Starozagorskata kaza okolo sredata na XIX v." [The national character of the Stara Zagora district about the middle of the 19th century]. PSBK 27 (1970):281-95.

Kolarić, M. "Kniga krštenih u Beogradu, 1729-1739" [The Belgrade baptismal book, 1729-1739]. IG 1, no. 1 (1949):83-86.

Koledarov, P. "Kŭm vŭprosa za razvitieto na selishtnata mrezha i na neinite elementi v sredishnata i iztochnata chast na Balkanite ot VII do XVIII v." [On the question of the development of village networks and their elements in the central and eastern parts of the Balkans from the 7th to the 18th century]. IZII 18 (1967):89-146.

Kondov, N. "Broiat na naselenieto v Bŭlgariia kŭm kraia na XIV
v." [The number of inhabitants of Bulgaria at the end of
the 14th century]. IP 24, no. 5 (1968):29-47.

Koniarov, G. *Prinos kŭm istoriiata na rudarstvoto i metalur-
giiata v Bŭlgariia* [Contribution to the history of mining
and metallurgy in Bulgaria]. Sofia, 1953.

Konstantin, Steward. "Narŭchnik za Plovdivskata eparkhiia ili
neinoto opisanie, sŭchineno ot. . . ." [Guide to the Plovdiv eparchy or its description, compiled by. . . .] Trans.
M. Apostolidis. *Izvestiia na Bŭlgarsko geografsko druzhestvo* [Journal of the Bulgarian Geographical Society] 3:
187-206. Sofia, 1936.

Konstantinov, N. "Stopanski formi i tekhnika na industriiata v
Bŭlgariia predi Osvobozhdenieto" [Economic forms and tech-
nology of industry in Bulgaria before the Liberation].
SBID 6, no. 4 (1902):264-78; no. 7 (1902):446-66.

Kopanev, A. I. "Naselenie Russokogo gosudarstva v XVI veke"
[Settling the Russian State in the 16th century]. *Istoricheskie zapiski* [Historical notes] (Moscow) 64 (1959):
233-54.

Kosev, D. *Lektsii po nova bŭlgarska istoriia* [Lectures on
modern Bulgarian history]. Sofia, 1951.

-----. "Kŭm iziasniavane na niakoi problemi ot istoriiata na
Bŭlgariia prez XVIII i nachaloto na XIX v." [On explaining
certain problems in Bulgarian history during the 18th and
beginning of the 19th century]. IP 13, no. 3 (1956):13-46.

Kosev, K. *Za kapitalisticheskoto razvitie na bŭlgarskite zemi
prez 60-te i 70-te godini na XIX v.* [On capitalist development in the Bulgarian lands in the 1860s and 1870s].
Sofia, 1968.

Kovačevic, T. *Opis Bosne i Hercegovine* [Description of Bosnia
and Hercegovina]. Belgrade, 1865; 2nd ed., 1879.

Kozarov, G. "Trima maistori--trima velikani, tri mŭchenika na
bŭlgarskoto stroitelstvo i stopanstvo--Usta Koljo Ficheto,
Dobri Zheliazkov Fabrikadzhiiata i Usta Todor Karakhris-
toolu" [Three masters--three giants, three martyrs of Bulgarian construction and economy--Master Kolio Ficheto,
Factor Dobri Zheliazkov, and Master Todor Karakhristoolu].

Arkhiv na Bŭlgarski dŭrzhavni zheleznitsi [Archive of the
Bulgarian National Railway]. 5 (1933):245-95.

-----. *Dobri Zheliazkov Fabrikadzhiiata, rodonachalnik na bŭlgarskata tekstilna promishlenost* [The factor Dobri Zheliazkov, progenitor of the Bulgarian textile industry].
Sofia, 1934.

Kozhukharov, G. *Bŭlgarskata kŭshta prez pet stoletiia: kraia
na XIV v-kraia na XIX v.* [The Bulgarian house through five
centuries: End of the 14th to the end of the 19th cen-
tury]. Sofia, 1967.

Krusev, N. D. *Istoriia na V. Tŭrnovskiia esnaf--dnes manifak-
turistko--galanteristko sdruzhenie spored kondikate mu
(1863-1919)* [History of the Trnovo guild--presently the
Manufacturing and Haberdashery Association--according to
its chronicles (1863-1919)]. Trnovo, 1942.

Kuzev, Al. "Grŭtski nadpisi ot XVIII i nachaloto na XIX v. ot
Varna" [Greek inscriptions of the 18th and early 19th century in Varna]. IVAD 11 (1960):119-30.

-----. "Korennoto naselenie na gr. Varna ot XIV do nachaloto
na XIX v." [The core population of Varna from the 14th to
the early 19th century]. IVAD 14 (1963):80-90.

Lishev, Str. *Bŭlgarskiiat srednovekoven grad* [The Bulgarian
medieval town]. Sofia, 1970.

*Lovech i Lovchensko. Geografsko, istorichesko i kulturno opi-
sanie* [Lovech and the district of Lovech. A geographic,
historical and cultural description]. 7 vols. Sofia,
1929-38.

Madzharov, M. *Spomeni* [Memoirs]. Sofia, 1968.

Makushev, V. "Bolgariia pod turetskim vladichestvom preimush-
chestvenno v XV-XVI v." [Bulgaria under Turkish rule, especially in the 15th and 16th centuries]. *Zhurnal Minis-
terstva narodnogo prosveshcheniia* [Journal of the Ministry
of Education] 163 (1872):286-329.

Margos, A. "Izcheznalata armenska koloniia v grad Provadiia"
[The vanished Armenian colony in Provadiia]. IVAD 14
(1963):93-102.

Marinov, D. *Zhiva starina. Etnografski izsledvaniia. . .* [Liv-
ing antiquities. Ethnographic studies. . .]. 4 vols.

Ruse, 1891-1907.

------. "Iz istoriiata na grad Lom" [From the history of Lom].
SNU 11 (1894):251-58.

Materialy dlia izucheniia Bolgarii [Materials for the study of
Bulgaria]. 4 vols. Bucharest, 1877.

Medzhidiev, A. *Istoriiata na grad Stanke Dimitrov (Dupnitsa) i
pokraininata mu ot XIV do 1912-1963 g.* [The history of the
city of Stanke Dimitrov (Dupnitsa) and its environs from
the 14th century to 1912-1963]. Sofia, 1969.

Miiatev, P. "Kŭm istoriiata na administratsiiata na nashite
zemi prez tursko vreme" [On the history of land administration during the Turkish period]. IP 5, no. 1 (1949):
95-101.

Mikhov, N. *Naselenieto na Turtsiia i Bŭlgariia prez XVIII i
XIX vv.: Bibliografski izdirvaniia sŭs statisticheski i
etnografski danni* [The settlement of Turkey and Bulgaria
during the 18th and 19th centuries. Bibliographic investigations with statistical ethnographic data]. 5 vols.
Sofia, 1915-67.

Mikov, V. *Proizkhod i znachenie na imenata na nashite gradove,
sela, reki, planini i mesta* [Origin and meanings of the
names of our towns, villages, rivers, mountains and other
locales]. Sofia, 1943.

Milkova, F. *Pozemlenata sobstvenost v bŭlgarskite zemi prez
XIX v.* [Landed property in Bulgaria during the 19th cen-
tury]. Sofia, 1970.

Miller, A. F. *Mustafa pasha Bairaktar. Ottomanskaia imperiia
v nachale XIX v.* [Mustafa Pasha Bairaktar. The Ottoman Empire at the beginning of the 19th century]. Moscow, 1947.

Minev, D. *Grad Liaskovets. Minalo, segashno sŭstoianie i dei-
tsi. Istoricheski i stopanski prinosi* [The town of Liaskovets. Past, present, notables. Historical and economic
contributions]. Varna, 1944.

Moravenov, K. D. *Pamiatnik za Plovdivskoto khristiansko naselenie v grada i za obshtite zavedeniia po proiznosno predanie, podaren na Bŭlgarskoto chitalishte v Tsarigrad 1869
g.* [A record of the Plovdiv Christian population within
the city and general institutions, according to oral tradition, presented to the Bulgarian reading room in Istan-

bul in 1869].   Plovdiv, 1930.

Moshnin, A. N. "Pridunaiskaia Bolgariia (Dunaiskii vilaiet):
    Statistiko-ekonomicheskii ocherk" [Danubian Bulgaria (the
    Danube vilayet):   Statistical-economic essay].   *Slavianskii
    sbornik* [Slavic anthology] (St. Petersburg) 2 (1877):346-
    407.

Mŭrzev, St. "Pokazalets na sotsialno-ikonomicheskata ni liter-
    atura.   Broshuri, statii i antrefileta po vreme na Osvo-
    bozhdenieto, 1877 g." [Index to our socioeconomic litera-
    ture, brochures, articles and notes at the time of the
    liberation, 1877].   SNU 24 (1908):1-295.

Mutafchieva, V. "K voprosu o feodal'noi rente v Osmanskoi im-
    perii XVII-XVIII v. (Prinuditel'nye vykupy)" [On the ques-
    tion of feudal rent in the Ottoman Empire, 17th-18th c.
    (forced redemption)].   *Kratkie soobshcheniia Instituta
    slavianovedeniia* [Short communications of the Institute of
    Slavic studies] (Moscow) 24 (1958):90-99.

-----. "Otkupuvaneto na dŭrzhavnite prikhodi v Osmanskata im-
    periia prez XV-XVII v. i razvitieto na parichnite otno-
    sheniia" [Redemption of state income in the Ottoman Empire
    during the 15th-17th century and the development of money
    relations].   IP 16, no. 1 (1960):40-74.

-----. "Za roliata na vakŭfa v gradskata ikonomika na Balkan-
    ite pod turska vlast (XV-XVII v.)" [On the role of the
    vakif in the urban economics of the Balkans under Turkish
    rule (15th-17th c.)].   IZII 10 (1962):121-45.

-----. *Agrarnite otnosheniia v Osmanskata imperiia prez XV-XVI
    v.* [Agrarian relations in the Ottoman Empire during the
    15th and 16th centuries].   Sofia, 1962.

Nachov, N. *Kalofer v minaloto, 1707-1877* [Kalofer in the Past,
    1707-1877].   Sofia, 1927.

*Nashiiat grad (Tolbukhin) v minaloto. Sbornik ot statii na
    Bŭlgarsko istorichesko druzhestvo klon Tolbukhin* [Our city
    (Tolbukhin) in the past. Collection of articles in the
    Bulgarian Historical Society, Tolbukhin chapter].   Tolbu-
    khin, 1966.

Natan, Zh. "Kŭm vŭprosa za pŭrvonachalnoto natrupvane na kapi-
    tala v Bŭlgariia [On the question of the initial accumula-
    tion of capital in Bulgaria].   IZII 1-2 (1954):13-46.

-----. *Stopanska istoriia na Bŭlgariia* [Economic history of
    Bulgaria].   Sofia, 1957.

Nedkov, B. "Orientalistikata v Sofiiskata narodna biblioteka" [Orientalia in the Sofia National Library]. *Godishnik na Bŭlgarski bibliografski institut* [Annual of the Bulgarian Bibliographic Institute] 1 (1948):226-39.

-----. "Orientalskiiat otdel na Dŭrzhavna biblioteka 'V. Kolarov'" [The Oriental section of the State Library 'V. Kolarov']. IP 10, no. 2 (1954):115-20.

Nevolin, K. A. "Obshchii spisok russkikh gorodov" [General list of Russian cities]. *Polnoe sobranie sochinenii* [Collected works] 6 (1859):27-96.

Nikitin, S. A. "Opisanie ekonomicheskogo sostoianiia iugo-vostochnoi chasti Bolgarii do 30-kh godakh XIX v." [Description of the economic conditions in southeastern Bulgaria to the 1830s]. *Slavianskoe Vozrozhdenie* [Slavic National Revival], pp. 161-203. Moscow, 1966.

-----. "Bolgarskii gorod v 1879 g. po dannym russkoi perepisi" [The Bulgarian town in 1879 according to Russian correspondence]. *Actes du Premier congrès international des études balkaniques et sud-est européennes*, 4:77-94. Sofia, 1969.

-----. "Neopublikovannyi proekt gosudarstvennogo ustroistva Bolgarii" [An unpublished plan of state organization of Bulgaria]. *Slavianskii arkhiv. Sbornik statei i materialov* [Slavic archive. Collection of articles and materials], pp. 12-38. Moscow, 1969.

-----. "K voprosu ob ekonomicheskom oblike bolgarskogo goroda vremeni Osvobozhdeniia ot turetskogo iga na osnove russkoi perepisi 1879 g." [On the question of the economic aspect of the Bulgarian town at the time of the liberation from the Turkish yoke, on the basis of Russian correspondence of 1879]. *Ocherki po istorii iuzhnykh slavian i russko-balkanskikh sviazei v 50-70e gody XIX v.* [Essays on the history of the South Slavs and Russo-Balkan connections in the 1850s to 1870s], pp. 7-65. Moscow, 1970.

Panagiurishte i Panagiursko v minaloto. Sbornik [Panagyurishte and the Panagyur district in the past. Anthology]. Sofia, 1956.

Panova, S. "Tŭrgovskata i finansova deinost na evreite na Balkanite prez XVI-XVII v." [Trade and financial activities of the Jews in the Balkans during the 16th and 17th centuries]. IP 23, no. 3 (1967):30-60.

Paskaleva, V. "Kŭm istoriiata na tŭrgovskite vrŭzki na Makedoniia sŭs Sredna Evropa prez XIX v. [On the history of
trade relations between Macedonia and Central Europe in
the 19th century]. IZII 9 (1962):51-80.

Peev, Al. *Plovdiv kŭm sredata na XIX v.* [Plovdiv in the mid-
nineteenth century]. Plovdiv, 1930.

Pejanović, B. *Stanovništvo Bosne i Hercegovine* [The population
of Bosnia and Hercegovina]. Belgrade, 1955.

Perekhod ot feodalizma k kapitalizmu v Rossii [The transition
from feudalism to capitalism in Russia]. Materialy vse-
soiuznoi diskussii [Materials of an All-Union discussion].
Moscow, 1969.

Petrov, V. "Stariiat dikidzhilŭk v gr. Shumen" [The old sewing
craft in Shumen]. *Izvestiia na Narodniia muzei--Shumen*
[Journal of the National Museum in Shumen] 1 (1967):113-
24.

Pliakov, Z. "Dokumenti za reglamentatsiiata na tŭrgovskata
deinost v bŭlgarskite zemi prez XV-XVII v." [Documents on
the regulation of trade activity in Bulgaria during the
15th to 17th century]. IZII 19 (1967):263-70.

------. "Za demografskiia oblik na bŭlgarskiia grad prez XV-
sredata na XVII v." [On the demographic aspect of the Bulgarian town from the 15th to the mid-17th century]. IP
24, no. 5 (1968):29-47.

Popov, A. and N. Kŭnev. *Popovo. Gradŭt i okoliiata mu. Istoriko-geografski ocherk* [Popovo. The town and its environs.
Historical-geographical essay]. Popovo, 1929.

Popov, D. *Lom. Gradŭt i okoliiata mu. Ikonomichesko pazvitie
s kratki geografski i istoricheski belezhki* [Lom. The town
and its environs. Economic development with short geographic and historical notes]. Lom, 1927.

Pranchov, S. *Koprivshtitsa ot tochka zreniia istoricheska
sotsialna i ikonomicheska* [Koprivshtitsa from the historical, social and economic points of view]. Plovdiv, 1886.

Problemy genezisa kapitalizma. Sbornik statei [Problems in the
genesis of capitalism. Collection of articles]. Moscow,
1970.

Rashin, A. G. *Neselenie Rossii za 100 let* [The population of

Russia for 100 years]. Moscow, 1956.

Razboinikov, A. Sp. "Svilengrad. Proizkhod na selishteto i stroezha na zhilishtata mu" [Svilengrad. Origin of the town and construction of its residences]. *Trakiiski sbornik* [Thracian anthology] 3 (1932):115-63.

Rybakov, B. A. *Remeslo drevnei Rusi* [Handicraft of Old Russia]. Moscow, 1948.

Šabanović, H. "O organizaciju turske uprave u Srbiji u XV i XVI vijeku" [On the organization of Turkish rule in Serbia in the 15th and 16th centuries]. IG 3-4 (1955):59-78.

-----. *Turski izvori za istoriju Beograda. Katastarski popisi Beograda i okoline 1476-1566* [Turkish sources for the history of Belgrade. 1. Tax lists for Belgrade and its environs, 1476-1566]. Belgrade, 1964.

Sakharov, A. M. *Goroda severo-vostochnoi Rusi. XIV-XV vekov* [The cities of northeastern Rus', 14th and 15th centuries]. Moscow, 1959.

Sakŭzov, I. "Tŭrgoviiata na Bŭlgariia s Ankona prez XVI i XVII v. ponovi izvori" [Trade between Bulgaria and Ancona in the 16th and 17th centuries, according to new sources]. IBID 9 (1929):1-44.

-----. "Razvitieto na gradskiia zhivot i na zanaiatite v Bŭlgariia prez XVIII i XIX v." [The development of urban life and artisans in Bulgaria in the 18th and 19th centuries]. *Bulgariia 1000 godini, 927-1927* [Bulgaria 1000 years, 927-1927], pp. 685-703. Sofia, 1930.

-----. *Stopanskite vrŭzki mezhdu Dubrovnik i bŭlgarskite zemi prez XVI i XVII stoletiia* [Economic ties between Dubrovnik and Bulgarian lands in the 16th and 17th centuries]. Stranitsi iz stopanskata istoriia na Bŭlgariia [Pages from the economic history of Bulgaria]. Sofia, 1930.

Samardjić, R. *Beograd i Srbija v spisima francuzkih savremenika 16-17 veka* [Belgrade and Serbia in the writings of French contemporaries of the 16th and 17th centuries]. Belgrade, 1961.

Sarafov, M. K. "Naselenieto na gradove Ruse, Varna i Shumen" [The inhabitants of Ruse, Varna and Shumen]. PSBK 3 (1882):20-59; 4 (1882):33-66.

Sbornik na Kaloferskata druzhba [Anthology of the Kalofer So-
ciety]. 3 vols. Sofia, 1908-31.

*Sbornik Trŭnski krai. Prinos kŭm izuchavane na zapadnite bŭl-
garski kraishta* [Anthology of the Tŭrn district. Contribution to the study of western Bulgarian districts].
Sofia, 1950.

*Sevlievo i Sevlevskiiat krai. Izsledvaniia, materiali i doku-
menti* [Sevlievo and the Sevlievo district. Studies, materials, and documents]. Comp. and ed. Khr. M. Ionkov.
Vol. 1. Sofia, 1967.

Semerdzhiev, Khr. *Samokov i okolnostta mu. Prinos kŭm minaloto
im ot turskoto zavoevanie do Osvobozhdenieto* [Samokov and
its environs. Contribution to its past from the Turkish
conquest to the Liberation]. Sofia, 1913.

Serbina, K. N. *Ocherki iz sotsial'no-ekonomicheskoi istorii
russkogo goroda* [Essays on the socioeconomic history of
the Russian town]. Moscow-Leningrad, 1951.

Sharkov, V. *Grad Gorna Dzhumaia. Minalo idnes* [The city of
Gorna Dzhumaya. Past and present]. Sofia, 1930.

Shishkov, St. *Ustovo. Akhŭchelebiiski okrŭg.* [Ustovo. The district of Akhŭchelebiia]. Plovdiv, 1885.

-----. *Plovdiv v svoeto minalo i nastoiashte. Istoriko-geografski i politiko-ikonomicheski pregled* [Plovdiv in its
past and present. A historical-geographical and politico-
economic survey]. Plovdiv, 1962.

Siromakhova, Zh. and S. Parmakov. "Ikonomicheskoto razvitiena
Ruse prez epokhata na turskoto robstvo" [The economic development of Ruse during the period of Turkish rule]. *Izvestiia na narodniia muzei--Ruse* [Journal of the National
Museum in Ruse] 1:17-49. Varna, 1946.

Siuziumov, M. Ia. "Vizantiiskii gorod (seredina VII--seredina
IX v.)" [The Byzantine town (mid-7th to mid-9th centuries)]. *Vizantiiskii vremennik* [Byzantine chronicle] 27
(1967):38-70.

Skarić, V. *Staro rudarsko pravo i tehniku u Srbiji i Bosni*
[Old mining law and technology in Serbia and Bosnia].
Belgrade, 1939.

Slaveev, S. and M. Monev. "Stopansko-geografsko razvitie i

tŭrgovski vrŭzki na Svishtov ot kraia na XVIII do nachaloto na XX vek" [Economic and geographic development and
the trade ties of Svishtov from the late 18th to early
20th centuries]. *Godishnik na Visshiia finansovostopanski
institut* [Annual of the Higher Finance and Economic Institute in Svishtov] 33 (1968):59-104.

Smirnov, P. P. *Posadskie liudi i ikh klassovaia bor'ba do sere-
dinykh 17 v.* [Tradespeople and their class struggle to the
mid-17th century]. 2 vols. Moscow-Leningrad, 1947-48.

Snegarov, I. "Stariiat Tŭrnovski tsŭrkoven kodeks" [The old
Trnovo church codex] *Godishnik na Sofiiski universitet
Bogoslovski fakultet* [Annual of Sofia University, theolo-
gical faculty] 12 (1934-35):1-48.

-----. "Grŭtski kodeks na plovdivskata mitropoliia" [A Greek
codex of the Plovdiv Metropolitanate] *Sbornik na BAN* [An-
thology of the Bulgarian Academy of Sciences] (History-
philology section) 10, nos. 1-2 (1949):179-399.

-----. *Turskoto vladichestvo-prechka za kulturnoto razvitie na
bŭlgarskiia narod i drugite balkanski narodi* [Turkish
rule--an obstacle to the cultural development of the Bulgarian and other Balkan peoples]. Sofia, 1958.

Sokolov, L. "Stopanstvoto na Kumanovo vo vtorata polovina na
XIX vek so oddelen pogled vrz abadzhiskiot zanaet i esnaf"
[The economy of Kumanovo in the second half of the 19th
century, with special reference to the tailor's craft and
guild]. GINI 1, no. 1 (1957):113-54.

Sokoloski, M. "Zakon za gradot Nish (1497 g.) i zakon za gradot
Krushevats (1536 g.)" [The law for the city of Niš (1497)
and the law for the city of Kruševac (1536)]. GINI 1, no.
2 (1957):195-202.

-----. "Kostur i Kostursko v sredinata na XV vek" [Kostur and
the Kostur district in the mid-15th century]. *Istorija*
[History] (Skoplje) 1 (1958):297-314.

-----. "Turski izvorni podatotsi ot XV i XVI vek za gradot Bi-
tola [Turkish source information from the 15th and 16th
centuries for the city of Bitolj]. GINI 7, no. 1 (1963):
127-56.

-----. "Gradsko i selsko naselenie so spetsialni zadolzhenija
vo del od Ohridskiot sandžak vo vtorata polovina od XVI
vek" [Urban and rural population with special obligations

in part of the Ohrid sanjak in the second half of the 16th
century]. GINI 10, , nos. 2-3 (1966):181-92.

Sopova, D. *Makedonija vo XVI i XVII vek. Dokumenti od Cari-
gradskite arhivi (1557-1645)* [Macedonia in the 16th and
17th centuries. Documents from the Istanbul archives
(1557-1645)]. Skoplje, 1955.

-----. "Koga Skopje bilo centar na sandžak vo periodot od padanjeto pod turska vlast do krajot na XVI v." [When Skoplje
was the center of the sanjak, in the period from the Turkish conquest to the end of the 16th century]. GINI 1, no.
1 (1957):89-92.

Stoianov, K. Khr. "Bŭlgarskite esnafi prez turskoto robstvo
(Istoriia, organizatsiia i deinost)" [Bulgarian guilds un-
der Turkish rule (history, organization, and activity].
Godishnik na Vissheto tŭrgovsko uchilishte [Annual of the
Higher Trade School, Varna] 16 (1942-43):1-103.

Stoianov, M. *Grad Pirdop v minaloto i sega* [The town of Pirdop,
past and present]. Sofia, 1941.

-----. *Bŭlgarska Vŭzrozhdenska knizhnina. Analitichen reper-
toar na bŭlgarskite knigi i periodichni izdaniia, 1806-1878*
[Bulgarian literature of the National Revival. An analy-
tic repertoire of Bulgarian books and periodical literature, 1806-1878]. 2 vols. Sofia, 1957-59.

Stoikov, R. "Novi svedeniia za minaloto na bŭlgarskite selishta prez XV i XVI v." [New evidence on the history
of Bulgarian villages in the 15th and 16th centuries].
IP 15, no. 6 (1959):77-83.

-----. "Bŭlgarski selishta s naselenieto im v turski registri
za Dzhizie ot XVII v. [Bulgarian villages and their inhabitants in Turkish cizye registers from the 17th century].
Izvestiia na dŭrzhavnite arkhivi [Journal of the State ar-
chives] 8 (1964):147-64.

Stojančević, V. "Leskovac kao administrativno produčje za pos-
ledni sto godina turske vlasti" [Leskovac as an administrative area during the last 100 years of Turkish rule].
Leskovački sbornik [Leskovac anthology] 3 (1963):62-65.

*Stopanska i sotsialna knizhnina v Bŭlgariia. Bibliografiia za
bŭlgarski knigi i statii ot nachaloto do dnes: 1850-1945*
[Economic and social literature in Bulgaria. Bibliography
of Bulgarian books and articles from the beginning to the

present: 1850-1945]. Ed. T. Vladigerov. Svishtov, 1948.

Strumilin, S. G. *Ocherki ekonomicheskoi istorii Rossii* [Essays on the economic history of Russia]. Moscow, 1960.

Sŭbchev, N. P. *Istoriia i etnografiia na grad Chirpan* [History and ethnography of the town of Čirpan]. Čirpan, 1938.

Tabakov, S. *Opit za istoriiata na grad Sliven* [An attempt at a history of Sliven]. 3 vols. Sofia, 1911-29.

Tadić, J. *Jevreji u Dubrovniku do polovine XVII stoleća* [Jews in Dubrovnik to the middle of the 17th century]. Sarajevo, 1937.

-----. "Grčka i Dalmacija v XVI veku" [Greece and Dalmatia in the 16th century] IČ 14-15 (1965):19-27.

Teplov, V. *Materialy dlia statistiki Bolgarii, Frakii i Makedonii* [Materials for statistics of Bulgaria, Thrace and Macedonia]. St. Petersburg, 1877.

Teoreticheskie i istoriograficheskie problemy genezisa kapitalizma [Theoretical and historiographic problems in the genesis of capitalism]. Materials of the scholarly conference held in Moscow, 11-13 May 1966. Moscow, 1969.

Tishkov, P. *Istoriia na nasheto zanaiatchiistvo do Osvobozhdenieto ni* [History of the artisans up to the Liberation]. Sofia, 1922.

Todorov, N. "K razvitii v manufaktury v Bolgarii vo Vtoroi chetverti 19-go veka" [On the development of manufacturing in Bulgaria in the second quarter of the 19th century]. *Uchenye zapiski Instituta slavianovedeniia* [Scholarly notes of the Institute for Slavic Studies] 16 (1950):109-50.

-----. "Za niakoi promeni v kharaktera na tsekhovata organizatsiia v nas prez XVIII i pŭrvata polovina na XIX v." [On some changes in the character of our guild organizations in the 18th and first half of the 19th century]. IP 14, no. 4 (1958):44-76.

----. "Zarozhdenie kapitalisticheskikh otnoshenii v tekstil'nom proizvodstve Bolgarii v pervoi polovine XIX v." [The growth of capitalist relations in the textile industry of Bulgaria in the first half of the 19th century]. *Kratkie soobshcheniia Inst. slavianovedeniia* [Short communications of the Institute for Slavic Studies] (Moscow) 23 (1958):74-87.

-----. "Iz istoriiata na Karlovskoto abadzhiistvo i gaitandzhiistvo (30-70-te godini na 19 vek)" [From the history of
the Karlovo tailor and wool-braiding industries (1830s-
1870s)]. *Izvestiia na Institut Botev-Levski* [Journal of
the Botev-Levski Institute] 3 (1959):141-57.

-----. "Za naemniia trud v bŭlgarskite zemi kŭm sredata na 19
v." [On wage labor in Bulgaria in the middle of the 19th
century]. IP 15, no. 2 (1959):3-35.

-----. "Za demografskoto sŭstoianie na Balkanskiia poluostrov
prez XV-XVI v." [On the demography of the Balkan Peninsula
during the 15th and 16th centuries]. *Godishnik na Sofiiskiia universitet: Filosofsko-istoricheski fakultet* [An-
nual of Sofia University, Philosophy-History Faculty] 1-3,
no. 2 (1959-60):191-232.

-----. "Bŭlgarskoto naselenie na grad Lom prez 40-te godini na
XIX vek" [The Bulgarian population of Lom during the
1840s]. *Sbornik izsledvaniia v chest na Marin Drinov*
[Festschrift for Marin Drinov], pp. 578-90. Sofia, 1960.

-----. "Po niakoi vŭprosi na balkanskiia grad prez XV-XVII v.
[On some questions of the Balkan town in the 15th to 17th
centuries]. IP 18, no. 1 (1962):32-58.

-----. "Iarmarka v gorode Khadzhioglu Pazardzhik v 70-k godakh
XIX v." [The market in Tatar Pazardzhik in the 1870s].
Slavianskii arkhiv [Slavic archive], pp. 116-39. Moscow,
1963.

-----. "Sotsialno-ikonomicheskiiat oblik na Provadiia prez 60-
te i 70-te godini na XIX v." [The socioeconomic aspect of
Provadiia in the 1860s and 1870s]. IP 19, no. 2 (1963):
70-84.

-----. "Iz sotsialno-ikonomicheskiia zhivot na Sofiia prez
XVI-XVII v." [From the socioeconomic life of Sofia in the
16th and 17th centuries]. IZII 14-15 (1964):215-33.

-----. "Vŭrkhu demografskoto sŭstoianie na Varna v sredata na
XIX vek" [Concerning the demography of Varna in the mid-
19th century]. *Izvestiia na Naroden muzei vŭv Varna* [Jour-
nal of the National Museum in Varna] 2 (1966):83-108.

-----. "Iz demografiiata na gr. Ankhialo (Pomorie). (Utorata
polovina na 19 v.)" [Of the demography of the town of An-
chialo (Pomorie) (Second half of the 19th century)]. IBID
25 (1967):159-80.

-----. "Ruski dokumenti za demografskoto sŭstoianie na chast ot Iztochna Bŭlgariia prez 30-te godini na XIX v." [Russian documents on the demography of part of eastern Bulgaria during the 1830s]. *Izvestiia na Dŭrzhavnite arkhivi* [Journal of the State Archives] 13 (1967):186-220.

-----. "Sotsialno-ikonomicheskiiat oblik na Varna prez 60-te i 70-te g." [The socioeconomic aspect of Varna in the 1860s and 1870s]. IVAD 14 (1968):119-31.

Todorov-Khindalov, V. "Dobrudzha v minaloto spored turski ofitsialni iztochnitsi" [Dobruja in the past according to official Turkish sources]. *Godishnik na Sofiiska narodna biblioteka 1926-1928* [Annual of the Sofia National Library, 1926-1928], pp. 199-284 (1931).

Traichev, G. *Grad Prilep. Istoriko-geografski i stopanski pregled* [The city of Prilep. Historical, geographic and economic survey]. Sofia, 1925.

Trifonov, I. *Istoriia na grad Pleven do Osvoboditelnata voina* [History of Pleven to the War of Liberation]. Pleven, 1938.

Tsonchev, P. *Iz obshtestvenoto minalo na Gabrovo* [From the social history of Gabrovo]. Monograph Studies. Sofia, 1929.

Tsonev, St. "Kŭm vŭprosa za razlozhenieto na esnafskata organizatsiia u nas prez epokhata na Vŭzrazhdaneto" [On the question of the condition of our guild organization during the time of the National Revival]. *Trudove na VINS* [Works of the VINS] (Varna) 1 (1955-56):1-56.

Tsukhlev, D. *Istoriia na grada Vidin i negouata oblast* [History of the city of Vidin and its district]. Sofia, 1932.

Tsvetkova, D. "Prinos kŭm izuchavaneto na turskiia feodalizŭm v bŭlgarskite zemi, chast 2: Zavisimoto naselenie i negovata borba protiv turskiia feodalen gnet" [Contribution to the study of Turkish feudalism in Bulgaria, pt. 2; The dependent population and its struggle against Turkish feudal oppression]. IZII 5 (1954):115-74.

-----. "Materiali za selishtata i stroitelstvoto v bŭlgarskite zemi prez XV-XVI v." [Materials on settlements and construction in Bulgaria during the 15th and 16th centuries]. *Izvestiia na Institut za gradoustroistvo i arkhitektura* [Journal of the Institute of Urban Design and Architecture] 7-8 (1955):459-518.

-----. *Izvŭnrednite danŭtsi i dŭrzhavni povinnosti v bŭlgar-skite zemi pod turska vlast* [Extraordinary taxes and state obligations in Bulgaria under Turkish rule]. Sofia, 1958.

-----. "Novye dannye o khristianakh-spakhiakh na balkansom po-luostrove v period turetskogo gospodstva" [New data on Christian-Spahis on the Balkan Peninsula during Turkish rule]. *Vizantiiskii vremennik* [Byzantine chronicle] (Mos-cow) 13 (1958):184-97.

-----. "Kŭm vŭprosa za pazarnite i pristanishtnite mita i taksi v niakoi bŭlgarski gradove prez 16 vek" [On the ques-tion of market and port customs and taxes in some Bulgarian cities in the 16th century]. IZII 13 (1963):183-257.

-----. "Za etnicheskiia i demografskiia oblik na Vidin prez XVI v." [On the ethnic and demographic aspect of Vidin in the 16th century]. *Izvestiia na Etnografskiia institute i muzei* [Journal of the Ethnographic Institute and Museum] 7 (1964):11-24.

-----. "Kŭm ikonomicheskata istoriia na gradovete v bŭlgarskite zemi prez XV v." [Toward the economic history of cities in Bulgaria in the 15th century]. IZII 14-15 (1964):243-62.

Turski dokumenti za makedonskata istorija [Turkish documents for Macedonian history]. 4 vols. Skoplje, 1951-58.

Turski izvori za bŭlgarskata istoriia [Turkish sources for Bul-garian history]. Ed. Khr. Ganchev and G. Gŭlŭbov. 2 vols. Sofia, 1959-60.

Turski izvori za bŭlgarskata istoriia, seriia XV-XVI v. [Turk-ish sources for Bulgarian history, mid-15th and 16th cen-turies]. 2 vols. Vol. 1, comp. and ed. B. Tsetkova and V. Mutafchieva; vol. 2, comp. and ed. N. Todorov and B. Nedkov. Sofia, 1964-66.

Udal'tsova, Z. V. *Sovetskoe vizantinovedenie za 50 let* [Soviet Byzantine studies over the last fifty years]. Moscow, 1969.

Undzhiev, I. *Karlovo. Istoriia na grada do Osvobozhdenieto* [Karlovo. History of the town up to the Liberation]. Sofia, 1962.

Vakarelski, Khr. *Bit na trakiiskite i maloaziiskite bulgari* [Customs of the Bulgarians of Thrace and Asia Minor]. Sofia, 1935.

Vasić, M. "Leskovac v XVI vijeku" [Leskovac in the 16th century]. GIBH 17 (1969):41-60.

Veber, A. *Rost gorodov v 19-om stoletii* [Growth of cities in the 19th century]. St. Petersburg, 1903.

Veber, M. *Gorod* [The city]. Ed. N. I. Kareev. Petrograd, 1923.

Veliki, K. "Izselvanetu ot Karnobat vŭv Vlashko prez 1830g." [Emigration from Karnobat into Wallachia in 1830]. IZII 16-17 (1966):453-66.

Vinaver, V. "Kraj dubrovačke trgovine na Balkanu" [The end of Dubrovnik trade in the Balkans]. IG 1, no. 1 (1956):21-60.

-----. "Monetarna kriza v Turskoj (1570-1650)" [The monetary crisis in Turkey (1570-1650)]. IG 3-4, nos. 3-4 (1958): 113-53.

-----. *Dubrovnik i Turska v XVIII veku* [Dubrovnik and Turkey in the 18th century]. Belgrade, 1960.

-----. "Dubrovačka trgovina u Srbiji i Bulgarskoj krajem XVII veka (1660-1700)" [Dubrovnik trade in Serbia and Bulgaria at the end of the 17th century (1660-1700)]. IČ 12-13 (1963):189-237.

-----. *Pregled istorije novca jugoslovenskim zemljama XVI-XVIII v.* [Survey of the history of money in Yugoslav lands (16th to 18th century)]. Belgrade, 1970.

Vlaikov, M. *Belezhki vŭrkhu ikonomicheskoto polozhenie na grada Panagiurishte predi i sled vŭstanieto* [Notes on the economic condition of the city of Panagyurishte before and after the uprising]. Plovdiv, 1906.

Vlakhov, T. *Kukush i negovoto istorichesko minalo* [Kukush and its historical past]. Sofia, 1962. 2d. ed., 1969.

Vostochnye istochniki po istorii narodov IUgovostochnoi i tsentral'noi Evropy [Eastern sources for the history of the peoples of southeastern and central Europe]. Ed. A. S. Tveritinova. 2 vols. Moscow, 1964-69.

Vučo, N. *Raspadanje esnafa u Srbiji* [The decline of guilds in Serbia]. 2 vols. Belgrade, 1954-58.

Vulchanov, Kh. *Sevlievo (1842-1942)*. 2 vols. Sofia, 1942.

Zakhariev, I. *Tatarpazardzhishka kaza. Geografsko-istorichesko opisanie* [The Tatar-Pazardzhik district. A geographic and historical description]. Vienna, 1870.

------. *Chiprovtsi. Poselishtno-geografski prouchvaniia s istoricheski belezhki* [Chiprovtsi. Geographic settlement studies with historical notes]. Sofia, 1918.

------. "Kiustendil. Prinos kŭm poselishtno-geografskite prouchvaniia na nashite gradove" [Kiustendil. Contribution to settlement and geographic study of our cities]. APP 1, no. 1 (1938):48-106.

Zhechev, N. "Niakoi statisticheski danni za Samokov ot 1878 g." [Some statistical data on Samokov from 1878]. IZII 14-15 (1964):405-10.

Zirojević, O. "Rajnold Lubenau o Beogradu i Srbiji 1587 godine" [Reinhold Lubenau on Belgrade and Serbia, 1587]. *Godisnjak grada Beograda* [Annual of the city of Belgrade] 13 (1966):49-63.

------. Kruševački sandžak v svetlosti turskog popisa 1530-1531 godine" [The Kruškevac sanjak in light of the Turkish census of 1530-1531]. *Leskovački zbornik* [Leskovac anthology] 8 (1968):221-28.

------. *Carigradski drum ot Beograda do Sofije (1459-1683)* [The Istanbul road from Belgrade to Sofia (1459-1683)]. Zbornik istorijskog muzeja Srbije [Anthology of the Historical Museum of Serbia], vol. 7. Belgrade, 1970.

Zlatarski, V. *Nova politicheska i sotsialna istoriia na Bŭlgariia i Balkanskiia poluostrov* [A modern political and social history of Bulgaria and the Balkan Peninsula]. Sofia, 1921.

Zlatev, T. *Bŭlgarskiiat grad prez epokhata na Vŭzrazhdaneto* [The Bulgarian town during the period of the National Revival]. Sofia, 1955.

------. *Bŭlgarskite gradove po reka Dunav prez epokhata na Vŭzrazhdaneto* [Bulgarian towns along the Danube during the period of the National Revival]. Sofia, 1962.

Zografski, D. *Razvitokot na kapitalisticheskite elementi vo Makedonija za vreme na turskoto vladeenje* [The development of capitalist elements in Macedonia during the period of Turkish rule]. Skoplje, 1967.

Works in Greek

Apographe tou plethysmou kata ten 27 Oktobriou 1907 [Population census of October 27, 1907]. Compiled by G. Chomatianos. 2 vols. Athens, 1908.

Apostolides, K. M. "Kodikes Anatolikes Thrakes" [Codices of East Thrace]. *Thracica* 18 (1943):93-160.

-----. *He tes Philippoupoleos historia* [The history of Philip-popolis (Plovdıv)]. Athens, 1959.

Georgiou, Elias P. *Historia kai synetairismos ton Ambelakion* [History and guild of Ambeláki]. Athens, 1951.

-----. *Neotera stoicheia peri tes historias kai tes syntrophias ton Ambelakion* [More recent facts about the history and the guild of Ambeláki]. Athens, 1950.

Guinis, D. S. *Perigramma historias tou meta-Byzantinou dikaeou* [An outline of the history of post-Byzantine law]. Pragma-teiae tes Akademias Athenon [Treatises of the Academy of Athens], vol. 26. Athens, 1966.

Kalinderis, M. A. *Hae syntechniae tes Kozanes epi Tourkokratias* [The guilds of Kozáne during the Turkish domination]. Thessaloniki, 1958.

Katsouyiannis, T. M. *Peri ton Vlachon ton Hellenikon choron B' Ek tou biou kai tes historias ton Koutsovlachon epi Tour-kocratias* [About the Vlachs of the Hellenic regions, vol. 2. From the life and history of the Koutsovlachs during the Turkish domination]. Thessaloniki, 1966.

Konstantinidis, M. "He Mesembria tou Euxeinou" [Mesembria of Euxeinos]. *Historia*, vol. 1 (1945).

-----. *Karavia, kapetaneoi kai syntronautae 1800-1830* [Ships, captains and partners 1800-1830]. Athens, 1954.

Kordatos, G. *Ta Ambelakia kai ho mythos yia ton synetairismo tous* [Ambeláki and the myth about their guilds]. Athens, 1955.

-----. *Historia tes neoteres Helladas* [History of modern Greece]. Athens, 1957.

Kougeas, S. B. *Ho metropolites Monembasias kai Kalamatas Igna-tios ho Tzablakos (1776-1802) kai tina peri autou engrapha*

[Metropolitan bishop of Monemvasia and Kalamata Ignatius
Tzablakos and some documents about him]. Athens, 1957.
Reprint from *Peloponnesiaka*, vol. 2.

Koukkidis, K. *To pneuma tou synergatismou ton neoteron Hellenon kai ta Ambelakia: Ho protos synetairismos tou kosmou*
[The spirit of cooperation of the modern Greeks and Ambe-
láki: The first guild in the world]. Athens, 1948.

Kremmydas. B. "Opseis tes Tsakonikes koinonias (1784-1821)"
[Views of the Tsakonic Society (1784-1821)]. *Chronica ton
Tsakonon* [Chronicles of the Tsacons] 3 (1969):17-29.

Maximos, S. *He auge tou Hellenikou kapitalismou* [The dawn of
Greek capitalism]. Athens, 1945.

Mertzios, K. D. *Mnemeia Macedonikis historias* [Monuments of
Macedonian history]. Thessaloniki, 1947.

Michalopoulos, Ph. *Ta Yiannena kai he neo-Helleniki anagenesis
1648-1820* [Ionnina and the modern Greek renaissance 1648-
1820]. Athens, 1930.

Mnemeia tes Hellenikis historias [Monuments of Greek history],
vol. 8, no. 1. Athens, 1956.

Nikolaos, I. *He Odessos* [Odessus (Varna)]. Varna, 1894.

Pantazopoulos, N. *Ekklesia kai dikaion eis ten chersoneson tou
Haimou epi Tourkokratias* [Church and law in the Balkan
Peninsula during the Turkish domination]. Thessaloniki,
1963.

-----. *Neon Hellenon syssomatoseis kata ten ten Tourkokratian* [In-
corporations of modern Greeks under the Turkish domina-
tion]. Athens, 1958.

Sarantis, M. A. [M.A.S.]. "Thrakikoi kodikes" [Thracian codi-
ces]. *Thracica* 10 (1938):122-36.

-----. "Kodikes tes Episkopes Metron kai Athyra" [Codices of
Bishopric Metron and Athyra]. *Thracica* 15 (1934):163-78.

Statistiki tes Hellados, plethysmos 1879 [Statistics of Greece,
population of 1879]. Athens, 1881.

Thesprotis, K. and A. Psalidas. *Geographia Albanias kai Epei-
rou* [Geography of Albania and Epirus]. 1964.

Vakalopoulos, A. E. *Historia tou neou Hellenismou*, B' [History of modern Hellenism, vol. 2]. Thessaloniki, 1964.

Vasdravellis, I. K. *Historica archeia Macedonias*, A' [Historical archives of Macedonia, vol. 1]. Archeion Thessalonikis, 1695-1912 [Archives of Thessaloniki, 1695-1912]. Thessaloniki, 1952.

------. *Archeion Veroias-Naousis 1598-1886* [Archives of Veroia-Naousa (Niaousta) 1598-1886]. Makedoniki Bibliothiki, vols. 13, 19. Thessaloniki, 1954.

Vayiakakos, D. B. *Schediasma peri ton toponymikon kai anthroponymikon spoudon en Helladi 1833-1962* [A sketch on the toponymic and anthroponymic studies in Greece 1833-1962]. Athens, 1964. Reprint from *Athena* 66 (1962):300-424; 67 (1963-64):145-369.

Vourazeli-Marinakou, E. *Hai en Thrake syntechniae ton Hellenon kata ten Tourkokratian* [The guilds of the Greeks in Thrace during the Turkish domination]. Thessaloniki, 1959.

Zakythenos, D. *He Tourkokratia* [The Turkish domination]. Athens, 1957.

Works in Other Languages

Actes du premier congrès international des études balkaniques et sud-est européennes. 7 vols. Sofia: Editions de l'Académie Bulgare des Sciences, 1967-71.

Akbal, F. "1831 tarihinde Osmanlı Imparatorluğunda idarî taksimat venüfüs" [The administrative divisions and their population in the Ottoman Empire in 1831]. *Belleten* [Bulletin] 15, no. 60 (1951):617-28.

Akdağ, M. "Osmanlı Imparatorluğunun kuruluş ve inkişafı devrinde Türkiyenin iktisadi vaziyetî" [The economic situation of Turkey in relation to the Ottoman Empire's establishment and development]. *Belleten* 13 (1949):497-568; 14 (1950):319-411.

Antoniadis Bibicou, H. "Byzance et le mode de production asiatique." *La Pensée* (Paris), no. 129 (1966), pp. 47-72.

Aristarchi Bey. *Législation ottomane ou recueil des lois,*

*règlements, ordonnances, traités, capitulation et autres
documents officiels de l'Empire ottoman.* 4 vols. Constantinople, 1873-78.

Arseven C. E. *Türk sanatı tarihi. Menşeinden bugüne kadar
Mimari, heykel, resim, süsleme ve tezyini sanatları*
[History of the Turkish arts: Architecture, sculpture,
painting, the decorative arts from their origins to the
present]. Istanbul, 1954-56.

Asdrahas, Sp. "Aux Balkans du XVe s. producteurs directs et
marché." *Etudes balkaniques*, no. 3 (1970), pp. 36-69.

Ayverdi, E. H. *Fatih Devri sonlarında Istanbul Mahalleleri
şehrin iskânı ve nüfusu* [The inhabitants and settlers of
the boroughs of Istanbul at the end of the conqueror's
rule]. Ankara, 1958.

Babinger, Fr. *Beiträge zur Frühgeschichte der Türkenherrschaft
in Rumelien (14-15 Jrh.).* Südosteuropäische Arbeiten, vol.
34. Munich, Vienna, 1944.

-----. *Mahomet II le Conquérant et son temps, 1432-1481.*
Paris, 1954.

-----. *Sultanische Urkunden zur Geschichte der osmanischen
Wirtschafts- und Staatsverwaltung am Ausgang der Herrschaft
Mehmeds II, des Eroberers.* Part 1, Das Qânûn-nâme-i sul-
tânî ber müdscheb-i öri-i osmânî. . . . Südosteuropäische
Arbeiten, vol. 49. Munich, 1956.

Bailey, F. E. *British Policy and the Turkish Reform Movement:
A Study of Anglo-Turkish Relations, 1826-1855.* London,
1942.

Baker, J. *Turkey in Europe.* London, Paris, New York, 1887.

Bajraktarević, F. "Turski spomenici u Ohridu" [Turkish documents in Ohrid]. *Prilozi za orientalnu filologiju* [Con-
tributions to Oriental Philology, Sarajevo] 5 (1954-55):
111-34.

Barbié du Bocage, M. J. "Description de la ville Chumla et ses
environs, etc." *Journal des voyages, découvertes et navigations modernes aux archives géographiques du XIXe s.*
(Paris), no. 119 (1828).

Barkan, Ö. L. "XV Asrın sonunda bazı büyük şehirlerde eşya ve
yiyecek fiyatlarının tesbit be teftişi hususlarını tanzim

eden kanunlar"[Laws reorganizing the establishment and en-
forcement of prices of household goods and foods in a few
large cities at the end of the 15th century]. *Tarih vesi-
kalari* [Historical documents (Istanbul)] 1, no. 5 (1942):
326-40.

-----. *XV ve XVI ıncı asırlarda Osmanlı Imparatorluğunda ziraî
ekonominin hukukî ve mâlî esasları* [The laws and fiscal
principles of the agrarian economy in the Ottoman Empire
in the 15th-16th centuries]. Vol. 1. Istanbul: Kanunlar,
1943.

-----. "Osmanlı Imparatorluğunda bir iskân ve kolonizasyon metodu olarak sürgünler" [Places of banishment related to the
method of settlement and colonization in the Ottoman Em-
pire]. IFM, vol. 11 (1949-50); vol. 13 (1951-52); vol. 15
(1953-54).

-----. "Quelques observations sur l'organisation économique et
sociale des villes ottomanes des XVIe et XVIIe siècles."
In *La Ville*, vol. 7. Brussels, 1955.

-----. "Türk Yapı ve Yapı Malzemesi Tarihi için Kaynakları"
[Sources for the history of Turkish construction and construction materials]. IFM 17, nos. 1-4 (1955-56):3-26.

-----. "1079-1080 (1669-1670), Mâlî yılına âit bit Osmanlı
bütçesi ve ekleri" [The Ottoman budget and supplements for
the year 1079-1080 (1669-1670)]. IFM 17, nos. 1-4 (1956):
225-303.

-----. "Osmanlı Imparatorluğu bütçelerine dair notlar" [Notes
concerning the budgets of the Ottoman Empire]. IFM 17,
nos. 1-4 (1956):193-224.

-----. "1070-1071 (1660-1661) tarihli Osmanlı bütçesi ve bir
mukayese" [The 1070-1071 (1660-1661) Ottoman budget and a
comparison]. IFM 17, nos. 1-4 (1956):304-47.

-----. "Essai sur les données statistiques des registres de
recensement dans l'Empire ottoman aux XVe et XVIe siècles."
Journal of Economic and Social History of the Orient (Leiden) 1, no. 1 (1957):9-36.

-----. "XVI-XVIII asirlarda Türkiye'de Inşâat Işçilerinnin
Hukukî-Durumu" [The legal position of construction workers
in Turkey in the 16th-17th centuries]. In *Sosyal siyaset
Konferansları* [Conferences on social policy], vol. 14.
Istanbul, 1963.

-----. "Şehirlerin teşekkül ve inkişafı tarihi bakimindan:
    Imaret sitelerinin kuruluş ve işleyiş tarzina âit araştır-
    malar" [The formation and development of cities from a
    historical point of view: Research concerning the estab-
    lishment of working methods of Imaret communities]. IFM
    23, nos. 1-2 (1963):239-398.

-----. "894 (1488-1489) yılı Cizyesinin Tahsilâtına âit Muha-
    sebe Bilânçoları" [Accounting balances relating to the ci-
    zye dues collection of 894 (1488-1489)]. Belgeler [Docu-
    ments] 1, no. 1 (1964):2-118.

-----. "Edirne Askerî Kassamı'na Âit Tereke Defterleri (1545-
    1659)." [The inheritance records of the military judge of
    Edirne (1545-1659)]. Belgeler (Ankara) 3, nos. 5-6 (1968):
    1-479.

-----, and E. H. Ayverdi. Istanbul vakıfları tahrîr defteri
    953 (1546) tarihi [The 953 (1546) registers of the Istanbul
    vakıfs]. Istanbul, 1970.

Barkley, H. Between the Danube and Black Sea, or Five Years in
    Bulgaria. London, 1876.

Beaujour, F. Tableau du commerce de la Grèce formé d'après une
    année moyenne, depuis 1787 jusqu'en 1797. 2 vols. Paris,
    1800.

-----. Voyage militaire dans l'Empire ottoman. 2 vols.
    Paris, 1829.

Behrnauer, W. "Mémoire sur les institutions de police chez les
    Arabes, les Persans et les Turcs." Journal asiatique 15
    (1860):461-508; 16 (1860):114-90, 347-92; 17 (1861):5-76.

Beldiceanu, N. Les actes des premiers sultans, conservés dans
    les manuscrits turcs de la Bibliothèque Nationale à Paris.
    Actes de Mehmed II et de Bayezid II du ms. fonds turc,
    ancien 39, vol. 1. Paris, 1960.

Belin, M. Essais sur l'histoire économique de la Turquie.
    Paris, 1865.

Belon, P. Les observations de plusieurs singularités et choses
    mémorables, trouvées en Grèce, Asie, Judée, Egypte, Arabie
    et autres pays étrangers, rédigées en trois livres
    par. . . . Paris, 1555.

Berkes, N. 100 asırda Türkiye. Iktisat tarihi [The history of

100 centuries of the Turkish economy]. 2 vols. Istanbul, 1969-70.

Blanqui, J. A. *Voyage en Bulgarie pendant l'année 1841*. Paris, 1845.

Blau, Otto. *Reisen in Bosnien und Hercegovina*. Berlin, 1877.

Bogićević, V. "Grada za proučavanje ekonomskih odnosa u Bosni i Hercegovini pred ustanak 1875 godine" [Materials for the study of economic relations in Bosnia and Hercegovina before the 1875 uprising]. GIBH 1 (1949):215-32.

Borè, E. *Almanach de l'Empire ottoman, années 1849 et 1850*. Constantinople, 1850.

Boscovich, R. G. *Giornale de un viaggio da Constantinopoli in Polonia dell'abate . . . con una sua relazione etc.* Bassaro, 1784.

Boué, A. *La Turquie d'Europe ou observations sur la géographie, la géologie, l'histoire naturelle. . . .* 3 vols. Paris, 1840.

Boulanger, F. *Ambelakia ou les associations et les municipal-ités hélleniques avec documents confirmatifs recueillis et mis en ordre*. Paris, 1875.

Brocqière, B. de la. *Le voyage d'Outremer de . . . premier écuyer tranchant et conseiller de Philippe le Bon, duc de Bourgogne*. Published and annotated by M. Ch. Schefer. Paris, 1892.

Brunschvig, R. "Urbanisme médiéval et droit musulman." *Revue des études islamiques* (Paris), 1947, pp. 127-55.

-----. Métiers vils en Islam." *Studia Islamica* 16 (1962):41-60.

Burbury, J. A. *A Relation of a Journey of the Right Honourable My Lord Henry Howard, from London to Vienna, thence to Constantinople*. London, 1671.

Busbecq, A. G. *Itinera Constantinopolitanum et Amasianum ab Augerio Gislenio Busbequii, &c. D. ad Solimannum Turcarum Imperatorem C. M. oratore confecta. Eiusdem Busbequii De acie contra Turcam instruenda consilium*. Antwerp, 1581.

Busch, M. Dr. *Die Türkei. Reisehandbuch für Rumelien, die*

untere Donau, Anatolien, Syrien, Palästina, Rhodus und Cyprien. Trieste, Literarish-artistiche Abteilung des österreichischen Lloyd, 1860.

Cahen, C. "Mouvements et organisations populaires dans les villes de l'Asie musulmane au Moyen Âge: milices et associations de Foutouwwa." In *La Ville* 7:273-88. Brussels, 1955.

Caravokyro, M. *Le Droit successoral en Turquie ab intestat et par testament codifié d'après le Chéri et le droit byzantin.* Constantinople, 1898.

Chesneau, J. *Le voyage de Monsieur d'Aramon, ambassadeur pour le Roy en Levant, escrit par noble homme.* Published and annotated by M. Ch. Schefer. Paris, 1887.

Le Comte de Marsigli. *L'Etat militaire de l'Empire ottoman, ses progrès et sa décadence.* Amsterdam, 1732.

Cook, M. H., ed. *Studies in the Economic History of the Middle East from the Rise of Islam to the Present Day.* London, New York, Toronto, 1970.

Curipeschitz, B. *Itinerarium der Botschaftsreise des Josef von Lamberg und Niclas Jurischitz durch Bosnien, Serbien, Bulgarien nach Konstantinople, 1530.* Innsbruck, 1910.

Cvetkova, B. "Les Celeps et leur rôle dans la vie économique des Balkans à l'époque ottomane (XVe-XVIIIe ss.)." In *Studies in the Economic History of the Middle East from the Rise of Islam to the Present Day*, ed. M. H. Cook, pp. 172-93. London, New York, Toronto, 1970.

Dalsar, F. *Türk Sanayi ve Ticaret Tarihinde Bursa'da Ipekçilik* [The silk industry of Bursa in the history of Turkish industry and commerce]. Istanbul, 1960.

Deane, Ph. *The First Industrial Revolution.* Cambridge: At the University Press, 1965.

Divitçioğlu, S. "Essai de modèles économiques à partir du M. P. A.: Premières sociétés de classe et mode de production asiatique." *Recherches internationales à la lumière du marxisme* (Paris), nos. 57-58 (1967), pp. 277-93.

------. "Modèle économique de la société ottomane (les XIVe et XVe ss.)" *La Pensée* (Paris), no. 144 (1969), pp. 41-60.

Djurdjev, B. "Prilog pitanja razvitka i karaktera tursko-os-
    manskog feudalizma--timarsko-spahieskog uredenja" [Contri-
    bution to the question of the development and character of
    Ottoman feudalism--the Timar-Spahi System]. GIBH 1 (1949):
    101-67.

-----. *Kanuni i Kanun-name za Bosanski, Hercegovački, Zvor-
    nički, Kliski, Crnogorski i Skadarski sandžak* [Laws and
    law codes for the sanjaks of Bosnia, Hercegovina, Zvornik,
    Klis, Montenegro and Skadar]. Sarajevo, 1957.

-----. *Dva deftera Crne Gore iz vremena Skender-bega Crnoje-
    vića* [Two defters of Montenegro from the time of Sken-
    derbeg Crnojevic]. Vol. 1. Sarajevo, 1968.

Dorev, P., ed., *Dokumenti iz turskite dŭrzhavni arkhivi, 1564-
    1908* [Documents from the Turkish state archives]. Sofia,
    1948.

Duda, H. and G. Galabov. *Die Protokollbücher des Kadiamtes
    Sofia*. Munich and Oldenburg, 1960.

Elezović, G. *Iz carigradskih turskih arhiva Mühimme defteri*
    [Mühimme defters from the Istanbul Turkish archives].
    Belgrade, 1951.

Emmanuel, J. S. *Histoire de l'industrie des tissus des Israél-
    ites de Salonique*. Paris, 1935.

-----. *Histoire des Israélites de Salonique*. Vol. 1. Paris,
    1936.

Eus. Fermendzin. *Acta Bulgariae ecclesiastica ab a. 1565
    usque ad a. 1799*. Zagreb, 1887.

Evlija Čelebi. *Putopis. Odlomci o jugoslovenskim zemljama*.
    Uvod H. Šabanović [Travels. Excerpts about Yugoslav
    lands.] Introduction by H. Šabanović. Sarajevo, 1967.

Fekete, L. *Die Siyaqat-Schrift in der türkischen Finanzverwal-
    tung. Beitrag zur türkischen Paläographie mit 104 Tafeln*.
    2 vols. Budapest, 1955.

-----, and Gy. Kaldy-Nagy. *Rechnungsbücher türkischer Finanz-
    stellen in Buda (Ofen), 1550-1580*. Budapest, 1962.

Filipović, M. S. "Ćilimi i ćilimarstvo u našim zemljama do
    sredine XIX veka" [Rugs and rugmaking in our lands to the
    middle of the 19th century]. *Glasnik Zemaljskog muzeja u*

Sarajevu [Herald of the State Museum in Sarajevo] 13
(1957):179-94.

Franco, M. *Essai sur l'histoire des Israélites de l'Empire
ottoman*. Paris, 1897.

Galt, J. *Voyages and Travels in the Years 1809, 1810 and 1811.
Containing Statistical, Commercial and Miscellaneous Observations on Gibraltar, Sardinia . . . Turkey*. London,
1812.

Gerlach, S. *S. des Aelteren Tagebuch der von zween Glorwürdig-
sten röm. Kaysern, Maximiliano u Rudolpho, beyderseits den
andern dieses Nahmens an die ottom. Pforte zu Constantinople abgefertigten Gesandschaften*. Frankfurt a. M., 1674.

Gibb, H. A. R. and H. Bowen. *Islamic Society and the West: A
Study of the Impact of Western Civilization on Moslem Cul-
ture in the Near East*. Islamic Society in the Eighteenth
Century, vol. 1, pt. 1. New York, 1950.

Gibbons, H. A. *The Foundation of the Ottoman Empire*. Oxford,
1916.

Gökbilgin, T. *XV-XVI ıncı asırlarda Edirne ve Paşa livâsi,
vakıflar, mülkler, mukataalar* [The grants, land, and
levies in Edirne and the Pasa Liva in the 15th-16th cen-
turies]. Istanbul, 1952.

-----. "Kanunî Sultan Süleyman Devri başlarında Rumeli eyaleti
livaları, şehir ve kasabaları" [The livas, cities, and
towns of the Rumeli eyalet at the beginning of the rule of
Sultan Süleyman the Lawgiver]. *Belleten* 20 (1956):247-94.

-----. *Rumeli'de Yürükler, Tatarlar ve Evlâdi Fâtihan* [Yürüks,
Tatars, and conquering families in Rumeli]. Istanbul,
1957.

-----. "Kanun Sultan Suleyman'in timar ve zeamet tevcihi ile
ilgili Fermanlar" [Fermans of Sultan Suleyman the Lawgiver
concerning the assignment of timars and zeamets]. *Tarih
dergisi* [Historical review] 17, no. 22 (1968):35-48.

Göllner, C. *Turcica. Die europäischen Türkendrucke des XVI.
Jrh.* 1 vol. Bucharest and Berlin, 1961.

Gölpinarli, A. "Islâm ve Türk Illerinde Fütüvvet ve Teşkilâti
ve Kaynakları" [Futuwwas, organization and sources in Is-

lamic and Turkish countries]. IFM 11, nos. 1-4 (1949-50):
3-354.

Göyünc, N. *Yüzyılda Mardin sancağı* [The sancaks of Mardin in
the 16th century]. Istanbul, 1969.

Griesbach, A. *Reise durch Rumelien und nach Brussa im Jahre
1839*. 2 vols. Göttingen, 1841.

Grothusen, K. D. "Das mittelalterliche Stadtewesen Südosteuro-
pas im Einflussbereich des italienischen und mitteleu-
ropäisch-deutschen Rechtsstädte." *Südosteuropa-Jahrbuch* 8
(1968):43-71.

Grousset, R. *L'Empire de Levant*. Paris, 1949.

Grunebaum, G. E. von. "The Structure of the Muslim Town." In
*Islam: Essays on the Nature and Growth of a Cultural Tra-
dition*, pp. 141-58. London, 1961.

Grzegorzewski, J. *Z sidzyllatów rumelijskih epoki wyprawy
wiedenskiej* [From Rumelian "sidzyllats" of the period of
the Viennese expedition]. Constantinople, Lwów, 1912.

Guboglu, M. "L'importance des matériaux documentaires orien-
taux existant dans les archives, bibliothèques et collections roumaines." *Studia et acta orientalia* 2 (1959):107-
18.

-----. "Les documents turcs de la section orientale de la bib-
liothèque 'V. Kolarov' de Sofia et leur importance pour
l'histoire des pays roumains." *Studia et acta orientalia*
3 (1961):93-115.

Gücer, L. "XVIII yüzyıl ortalarında Istanbulun iasesi için
lüzumlu hububatın meselesi" [The question of the cereal
supply needed for Istanbul in the middle of the 18th cen-
tury]. IFM, vol. 11, nos. 1-4 (1949-1950).

Hadschi Chalfa, Mustafa. *Rumeli und Bosna geographisch be-
schrieben*. Vienna, 1812.

Hadžibegić, H. "Bosanska kanun-nama iz 1565." [Bosnian law
code of 1565]. *Glasnik Zemaljskog muzeja* 3 (1948):201-22.

-----. "Kanun-nama sultana Sulejmana Zakonodavca" [The law code
of Sultan Suleiman the Lawgiver]. *Glasnik Zemaljskog
muzeja* 4, 5 (1950):295-381.

-----. "Tri fermana iz prve polovine XVI vijeka" [Three firmans
    from the first half of the 16th century]. *Prilozi za ori-
    jentalnu filologiju* 2 (1951):83-94.

-----. "Džizja ili harač" [Cızye or Harač]. *Prilozi za ori-
    jentalnu filologiju* 3-4 (1953):55-135; 5 (1966):43-102.

Hadžijahić, M. *Neki problemi bosanske privredne historije
    predkapitalističkog perioda* [Some problems in Bosnian eco-
    nomic history of the precapitalist period]. Sarajevo,
    1965.

Hadzimichali, A. "Aspects de l'organisation économique des
    Grecs dans l'Empire ottoman." In *L'Hellénisme contempo-
    rain. Le cinq-centième anniversaire de la prise de Con-
    stantinople*, pp. 261-78. Athens, 1953.

Hahn, J. G. *Reise von Belgrad nach Salonik nebst vier Abhand-
    lungen zur alten Geschichte des Morawagebietes.* Vienna,
    1868.

Hammer, J. *Geschichte des osmanischen Reiches.* 10 vols. Bu-
    dapest, 1827-35.

Han, V. "Les courants des styles dans les métiers d'art des
    artisans chrétiens au XVIe et durant les premières dé-
    cennies du XVIIe siècle dans les régions centrales des
    Balkans." *Balkanica* (Belgrade) 1 (1970):239-71.

Handžić, A. "Grad Šabac i njegova nahija u prvoj polovine XVI
    vijeka" [The town of Šabac and its nahiye in the first half
    of the 16th century]. *Članci i gradja za kulturnu istoriju
    istočne Bosne* [Articles and materials for the cultural his-
    tory of Bosnia], pp. 95-151. Sarajevo, 1961.

-----. "O islamizaciju u severoistočnoj Bosni u XV i XVI
    vijeku" [On Islamization in northeastern Bosnia in the 15th
    and 16th century]. *Prilozi za orijentalnu filologiju* 16-17
    (1966-67):1-48.

-----. "Zvornik u drugoj polovini u XV i XVI vijeku" [Zvornik
    in the second half of the 15th and 16th century]. GIBH 18
    (1970):141-96.

Haufe, H. *Die Bevölkerung Europas, Stadt und Land im 19 u. 20
    Jahrhundert.* Berlin, 1936.

Heidborn, A. *Droit public et administratif de l'Empire ottoman.*
    2 vols. Vienna-Leipzig, 1908-12.

Hervé, Fr. *A Residence in Greece and Turkey. With Notes of the Journey through Bulgaria, Serbia, Hungary and the Balkans.* 2 vols. London, 1837.

Hunter, W. *Travels through France, Turkey and Hungary . . . in a Series of Letters to His Sister in England.* 2 vols. London, 1796.

Historia e Shqipërise [History of Albania]. Eds. Selim Islami, Kr. Frasheri. Tirana, 1959.

İnalcik, H. *Tanzimat ve Bulgar Meselesi* [The Tanzimat and the Bulgarian question]. Ankara, 1943.

-----. "15 asır Türkiye iktisadî ve içtimai tarihi Kaynaklarî" [Sources for the economic and social history of 15th-century Turkey]. IFM, vol. 13 (1949-50); vol. 15 (1951-52); vol. 16 (1953-54).

-----. "Osmanlı Imparatorluğunda kuruluş ve inkişafı devrinde Türkiyenin iktisadî vaziyeti üzerinde bir tetkik münasebetiyle" [An investigation relating to the economic situation of Turkey during the establishment and development of the Ottoman Empire]. *Belletin* 15, no. 6 (1951):629-84.

-----. "Od Stefana Dušana do Osmanskog carstva" [From Stefan Dušan to the Ottoman Empire]. *Prilozi za orijentalnu filologiju i istoriju jugoslvenskih naroda pod turskom vladavinon* [Contributions to Oriental philology and history of the Yugoslav people under Turkish rule], vols. 3-4 (1952-53).

-----. *Fatih devri üzerinde tetkikler ve vesikalar* [Documents and investigations relating to the period of the conqueror]. Vol. 1 of 7 vols. Ankara, 1954.

-----. *Hicrî 835 Tarihli Sûret-i Defter-i Sancak-i Arvanid* [A copy of the account book of the Sancak of Arvin for the year 835 A. H.]. Ankara, 1954.

-----. "Bursa I. XV asır sanayi ve ticaret tarihine dair vesikalar" [Documents relating to the 15th-century crafts and trade of Bursa]. *Belleten* 24, no. 93 (1960):45-102.

-----. "L'Empire ottoman." In *Actes du Premier congrès international des études balkaniques et sud-est européennes,* vol. 3, pp. 75-104. Sofia, 1969.

-----. *Ottoman Policy and Administration in Cyprus after the Conquest.* Ankara, 1969.

-----. "The Foundations of the Ottoman Economico-Social System
    in Cities." In VB, pp. 17-25.

İnan, A. *Aperçu général sur l'histoire économique de l'Empire
    turc-ottoman.* Istanbul, 1941.

Itzkovic, N. "Eighteenth Century Ottoman Realities." *Studia
    islamica* (Paris) 17 (1962):73-94.

Jelavich, Charles and Barbara, eds. *The Balkans in Transition:
    Essays on the Development of Balkan Life and Politics
    since the Eighteenth Century.* Berkeley and Los Angeles:
    University of California Press, 1963.

Jorga, N. *Geschichte des osmanischen Reiches nach den Quellen
    dargestellt.* 5 vols. Gotha, 1908-13.

-----. *Byzance après Byzance.* Bucharest, 1935.

Joung, G. *Corps de droit ottoman. Recueil des codes, lois,
    règlements, ordonnances et actes les plus importants du
    droit intérieur et d'études sur le droit coutumier de
    l'Empire ottoman.* 7 vols. Oxford, 1905-6.

Kabrda, J. "Des anciens registres turcs des Kadis de Sofia et
    de Vidin et leur importance pour l'histoire de la Bulga-
    rie." *Archiv orientalni* [Oriental archives] 19 (1951):
    329-92.

-----. "Les problèmes de l'étude de l'histoire de la Bulgarie
    à l'époque de la domination turque." *Byzantinoslavica* 15,
    no. 2 (1954):173-208.

"Les documents turcs relatifs aux droits fiscaux des métropo-
    lites orthodoxes en Bulgarie au XVIIIe s." *Archiv orien-
    talni* 26 (1958):59-80.

-----. "Les documents turcs relatifs aux impôts ecclésia-
    stiques prélevés sur la population bulgare au XVIIe s."
    Archiv orientalni 23 (1958):136-77.

Kaleshi, H. and J. Kornurumpf. "Das Wilajet Prizren. Beitrag
    zur Geschichte der türkischen Staatsreform auf dem Balkan
    im 19. Jrh." *Südost-Forschungen* 26 (1967):176-236.

-----. "Zur Geographie und Infrastruktur des Kaza Pirot (Sehir-
    köyü) vor 100 Jahren." *Südost-Forschungen* 28 (1969):283-
    86.

Kanitz, F. *Reise in Süd-Serbien und Nordbulgarien. Ausgeführt
  im Jahre 1864*. Vienna, 1868.

-----. *Donau-Bulgarien und der Balkan. Historisch-geographisch-ethnographische Reisestudien aus den Jahren 1860-1879.
  2. neubearb. Aufl.* 3 vols. Leipzig, 1882.

-----. *La Bulgarie danubienne et le Balkan: études de voyage,
  1860-1880*. Paris, 1882.

Karal, E. Z. *Osmanlı Imparatorluğunda ilk nüfus sayımı 1831,
  Başvekâlet Istatistik um. Müd* [The first population census
  of the Ottoman Empire (1831)]. Ankara, 1943.

Karamursal, Z. *Osmanlı mâlî tarihi hakkında tetkikler* [Inves-
  tigations relating to Ottoman fiscal history]. Ankara,
  1940.

Keppel, G. Th. *Narrative of a Journey across the Balkan by
  the Two Passes of Selimno and Provadi*. 2 vols. London,
  1831.

Kissling, H. J. "Die türkische Stadt auf dem Balkan." *Südosteuropa-Jahrbuch* 8 (1968):72-83.

Kolerkilic, E. *Osmanlı Imparatorluğunda para* [Money of the
  Ottoman Empire]. Paris, 1958.

Köprülü, F. *Les Origines de l'Empire ottoman*. Paris, 1935.

Koray, E. *Türkiye tarihi yayınları bibliografyası, 1729-1945*
  [Bibliography of Ottoman historical publications, 1729-
  1945]. Ankara, 1952.

Köymen, Oya. "The Imperialism of Free Trade: The Ottoman Empire." Paper read at Fifth International Congress of Economic History. Leningrad, 1970.

Kraelitz-Greifenhorst, Fr. "Kanunname Sultan Mehmeds des Eroberers, die ältesten osmanische Straf- und Finanzgesetze,
  nach der einzigen Handschrift." *Mitteilungen zur osmanischen Geschichte* (Vienna), vol. 1 (1921).

Kreševljaković, H. "Kapetanije i kapetani u Bosni i Hercegovini" [Kapetanijas and Kapetans in Bosnia and Hercego-
  vina]. GIBH 2 (1950):89-141.

-----. "Prilozi povijesti bosanskih gradova pod turskom upra-
  vom" [Contributions to the history of Bosnian towns under

Turkish rule]. *Prilozi za orijentalnu filologiju* 2 (1951): 115-84.

------. *Hanovi i karavansaraji u Bosni i Hercegovini* [Inns and caravansaries in Bosnia and Hercegovina]. Sarajevo, 1957.

------. *Esnafi i obrti u starom Sarajevu* [Guilds and crafts in old Sarajevo]. Sarajevo, 1958.

------. *Esnafi i obrti u Bosni i Hercegovini* [Guilds and crafts in Bosnia and Hercegovina]. Sarajevo, 1961.

Kyrris, K. "L'Importance sociale de la conversion (volontaire ou non) d'une section des classes dirigeantes de Chypre à l'Islam pendant les premiers siècles de l'occupation turque--fin du XVIIᵉ s." In *Actes du premier congrès international des études balkaniques et sud-est européennes*, 3:437-62. Sofia, 1969.

Lampard, E. E. "Historical Aspects of Urbanization." In *The Study of Urbanization*, eds. P. M. Hauser and L. E. Schnore, pp. 519-54. New York, 1967.

Lapidus, I. M. *Muslim Cities in the Later Middle Ages*. Cambridge, Mass., 1967.

Lascaris, M. *Salonique à la fin du XVIIIᵉ s*. Athens, 1939.

Levitsky, Y. A. "Problems of the Methodology of Medieval Town History (Analyzed on the basis of the History of a West European Town). In VB, pp. 7-16.

Levy, M. *Die Sephardim in Bosnien. Ein Beitrag zur Geschichte der Juden auf der Balkanhalbinsel*. Sarajevo, 1911.

Levy, R. *The Social Structure of Islam*. London, 1962.

Lewis, B. "The Islamic Guilds." *Economic History Review* 8, no. 1 (1937):20-37.

Lusignan, S. *A Genuine Voyage to Smyrna and Constantinople, and a Journey from Thence Overland to England*. 2 vols. London, 1801.

Mackenzie, G. M. and A. P. Irby. *The Turks, the Greeks, and the Slavons. Travels in the Slavonic Provinces of Turkey in Europe*. London, 1877.

Mantran, R. *Istanbul dans la seconde moitié du XVIIᵉ s*. Paris, 1962.

Marçais, G. "La Conception des villes dans l'Islam." *Revue d'Alger* 2 (1945):517-33.

-----. "Considérations sur les villes musulmanes et notamment sur le role du Mohtasib." In *La Ville*, 7:218-62. Brussels, 1955.

Marx, K. *Capital*. Ed. F. Engels; trans. Samuel Moore and Edward Aveling from 3rd German ed. New York, 1967.

Massignon, L. "Les Corps de métier et la cité islamique." *Revue internationale de sociologie* 28 (1920):437-89.

-----. "La Futuwwa ou pacte d'honneur artisanal entre les travailleurs musulmans au Moyen Âge." *La nouvelle Clio* 4 (1952):171-98.

Masson, P. *Histoire du commerce français dans le Levant au XVIII s.* Paris, 1911.

Matković, P. "Putovanja po Balkanskom poluotoku XVI vijeka" [Travels on the Balkan peninsula in the 16th century]. *Rad Jugosl. Akademije znanosti i umjetnosti* [Works of the Yugoslav Academy of Science and Art, Zagreb], vol. 56 (1881); vol. 57 (1882); vol. 84 (1887); vol. 122 (1892); vol. 124 (1895); vol. 129 (1896); vol. 130 (1897); vol. 136 (1898).

Mehmet, M. A. "De certains aspects de la société ottomane à la lumière de la législation (Kanunname) du sultan Mohamet II (1451-1481)" *Studia et acta orientalia* (Bucharest) 2 (1959):127-60.

Mikhov, N., *Rapports consulaires français*, Contribution à l'histoire du commerce de la Turquie et de la Bulgarie, vol. 3. Svishtov, 1950.

Mikoscha, J. *Reise eines Polen durch die Moldau nach der Türkey*. Leipzig, 1793.

Mols, R. *Introduction à la démographie historique des villes d'Europe du XIVe au XVIIIe ss.* 3 vols. Brussels, 1954-56.

Moltke, H. K. B. *Briefen neben Zuständen und Begebenheiten in der Türkei aus den Jahren 1835 bis 1839.* Berlin, 1841.

Montagu, M. W. *The Letters of Lady . . . during the Embassy to Constantinople, 1716-1718.* Paris, 1841.

Mujić, A. M. "Položaj cigana u jogoslovenskim, zemlima pod osmanskom vlašću" [The position of gypsies in Yugoslav lands under Ottoman rule]. *Prilozi za orijentalnu filologiju* 3-4 (1952-53):137-93.

Mutafčieva, V., and Str. Dimitrov. *Sur l'état du système des timars des XVIIe-XVIIIe ss.* Sofia, 1968.

Naçi, S. N. "Le pachalik de Shkoder considéré dans son déve-loppement économique et social au XVIIIe s." *Studia albanica* (Tirana) 3, no. 1 (1966):123-44.

-----. "Le Facteur albanais dans le commerce balkanique." *II congrès international des études du sud-est européen.* Athens, 1970.

Nurudinović, B. "Bosanske salname (1866-1878 i 1882-1893)" [Bosnian yearbooks, 1866-1878 and 1882-1893]. *Prilozi za orijentalnu filologiju* 10-11 (1960-61):253-65.

D'Osson, J. M. *Tableau général de l'Empire ottoman.* 6 vols. Paris, 1788-1824.

Pakalin, M. Z. *Osmanlı tarih deyimleri ve terimleri sözlüğü* [Dictionary of Ottoman historical expressions and techni-cal terms]. 3 vols. Istanbul, 1946-55.

Pantazopoulos, N. J. "Aspect général de l'évolution historique du droit grec." *Revue internationale des droits de l'an-tiquité* (Brussels) 5 (1950):245-79.

-----. *Community Laws and Customs of Western Macedonia under Ottoman Rule.* Thessalonike, 1961.

-----. *Church and Law in the Balkan Peninsula during the Otto-man Rule.* Thessalonike, 1967.

Papadopoulos, Th. *Social and Historical Data on Population (1570-1881).* Nikosia, 1965.

Papadopoulos-Vretos, A. *La Bulgarie ancienne et moderne.* St. Petersburg, 1856.

Paskaleva, V. "Les relations commerciales des contrées bulgares avec les pays occidentaux et la Russie au cours de la pre-mière moitié du XIXe s." *Etudes historiques* 1 (1960):253-83.

-----. "Contribution aux relations commerciales des provinces balkaniques de l'Empire ottoman avec les Etats européens

au cours du XVIIIe et la première moitié du XIXe s."
Etudes historiques 4 (1968):265-92.

-----. "Die bulgarische Stadt in XVIII. und XIX. Jahrhundert."
Süd-osteuropa Jahrbuch 8 (1969):128-45.

Pere, N. *Osmanlılarda Madeni paralar* [Metallic monies of the
Ottoman]. Istanbul, 1968.

Perenyi, J. "Villes hongroises sous la domination ottomane aux
XVIe-XVIIe ss. Les chefs-lieux de l'administration ottomane." In VB, pp. 25-33.

Play, F. le, A. Daux. "Forgeron bulgare. Des usines à fer de
Samokowa. (Turquie centrale). D'après les documents recueillis sur les lieux, en 1848 et en 1849 par. . . ." In
*Les ouvriers européens. Etudes sur les travaux, la vie do-
mestique et la condition morale des populations ouvrières
de l'Europe*, pp. 231-71. 2nd ed., 6 vols. Paris, 1855-78.

Poliak, A. N. "La Féodalité Islamique." *Revue des études islamiques* 10 (1936):247-65.

Pollo, S. "Traits distinctifs fondamentaux du mouvement national albanais." Paper read at II congrès international des
études balkaniques. Athens, 1970.

Polyzos, N. J. "Essai sur l'émigration grecque." *Etudes démographiques, économiques et sociales* (Paris), vol. 5 (1947).

Pouqueville, F. *Voyage dans la Grèce*. 2nd ed., 6 vols. Paris,
1826-27.

Refik, A. *Onuncu asr-ı Hicride Istanbul hayatı* [Life in Istanbul in the tenth century after the Hegira]. Istanbul,
1914-15.

-----. *Hicri on birinci asırda Istanbul hayatı (1000-1100)*
[Life in Istanbul in the eleventh century after the He-
gira]. Istanbul, 1931.

-----. *Türk idaresinde Bulgaristan (973-1255)* [Bulgaria under
Turkish rule]. Istanbul, 1933.

Ramberti, B. *Libri tre delle cose dei Turchi*. Venice, 1539.

Reinhard, M., A. Armengaud, and J. Dupaquier. *Histoire générale de la population mondiale*. Paris, 1968.

Renard, G. and G. Weulersse. *Life and Work in Modern Europe (Fifteenth to Eighteenth Century)*. New York, 1968.

Riccaut. *Histoire de l'état présent de l'Empire ottoman.* . . . Amsterdam, 1672.

Rizaj, S. "Counterfeit of Money on the Balkan Peninsula from the XV to the XVII Century." *Balkanica* (Belgrade) 1 (1970):71-79.

Roller, D. *Dubrovački zanati u XV. i XVI. stoljeću* [Dubrovnik crafts in the 15th and 16th centuries]. Zagreb, 1951.

Šabanović, H. "Bosansko krajište 1448-1463" [The Bosnian areas 1448-1463]. GIBH 9 (1958):177-220.

-----. *Bosanski pašaluk. Postanak i upravna podjela* [The Bosnian pashaluk. Origin and administrative organization]. Sarajevo, 1959.

Sahillioğlu, H. "Bir mültezim zimem defterine göre XV. yüzyıl sonunda Osmanlı darphane Mukataaları" [Farmed-out Ottoman mints at the end of the fifteenth century according to the account book of a tax farmer]. IFM 23, nos. 1-4 (1963): 1-74.

-----. "Ikinci Keykâvüs'ün bir Mülknamesi" [A property code of the first sultan]. *Vakıflar dergisi* [Vaki review], no. 8 (1969), pp. 57-65.

-----. "XVII Asrın Ilk Yarısında Istanbul'da Tedavüldeki Sikkelerin Râici" [The predetermined value of coins in circulation in Istanbul in the first half of the 17th century]. *Belgeler* 1, no. 2:227-33.

Sakŭsov, Iv. *Bulgarische Wirtschaftsgeschichte*. Berlin, Leipzig, 1929.

Samardžić, R. "Belgrade, centre économique de la Turquie du nord au XVIe s." In VB, pp. 33-44.

Šamić, M. "Ekonomski život Bosne i Sarsjevo početkom, XIX vijeka" [The economic life of Bosnia and Sarajevo at the beginning of the 19th century]. GIBH 11 (1961):111-34.

Sarç, Ö. C. "Tanzimat ve sanayimiz" [Tanzimat and our industries]. In *Tanzimat*. Istanbul, 1940.

Sauvaget, J. *Introduction à l'histoire de l'Orient musulman.* Paris, 1946.

Schneider, A. M. "XV yüzyılda Istanbul'un nüfusu" [The popula-
    tion of Istanbul in the 15th century]. *Belleten*, no. 61
    (1952), pp. 35-48.

Schwarzfuchs. S. "Dans la Méditerranée orientale au XVIe s.,
    les marchands juifs." *Annales, Economies, Sociétés, Ci-
    vilisations* 12 (1957):112-18.

Sencer, O. *Türkiyede işçi sınıfı* [The working class of Turkey].
    Istanbul, 1969.

Şerban, C. "Le Rôle économique des villes roumaines aux XVIIe
    et XVIII^ess. dans le contexte de leurs relations avec
    l'Europe du Sud-Est." In VB, pp. 139-54.

Sertoğlu, M. *Muhteva bakimindan Başvekâlet Arşivi* [The prime
    minister's archives, according to its contents]. Ankara,
    1955.

Sestini, D. *Viaggi e opuscoli diversi di. . . .* Berlin, 1806.

Shaw, S. J. "Archival Sources for Ottoman History: The Ar-
    chives of Turkey." *Journal of the American Oriental Soci-
    ety* 8 (1960):1-12.

-----. *The Financial and Administrative Organization and De-
    velopment of Ottoman Egypt, 1517-1798.* Princeton, N. J.,
    1962.

-----. *Between Old and New: The Ottoman Empire under Sultan
    Selim III, 1789-1807.* Cambridge, Mass., 1971.

Shködra, Z. "Nouvelles données sur la législation des esnafs
    (corporation) en Albanie pendant les siècles XVI-XIX." In
    *Conférence des études albanologiques de l'Université
    d'Etat de Tirana,* pp. 3-13. Tirana, 1962.

-----. "Qytetet schqiptare gjatë dy shekujevë të parë të sun-
    dimit turk" [The Albanian city during the first two cen-
    turies of Turkish rule]. *Ekonomia popullore* [National eco-
    nomics] (Tirana), no. 5 (1963), pp. 65-85.

-----. "Le Marché albanais au XVIIIe s." *Studia albanica* (Ti-
    rana) 3, no. 1 (1966):159-72.

Şimşir, B. *Contribution à l'histoire des populations turques
    en Bulgarie (1876-1880).* Ankara, 1966.

Sjoberg, G. *The Preindustrial City: Past and Present.* New
    York, 1965.

Skarić, V. "Iz prošlosti Bosne i Hercegovine XIX vijeka" [From
    the history of Bosnia and Hercegovina in the 19th century].
    GIBH 1 (1949):7-41.

Skendi, St. "Crypto-Christianity in the Balkan Area under the
    Ottomans." *Slavic Review* 26, no. 2 (1967):226-46. Also
    in *Actes du premier congrès international des études bal-
    kaniques et sud-est européennes*, 3:563-65. Sofia, 1969.

Slicher, van Bath, B. H. "Les problèmes fondamentaux de la
    société préindustrielle en Europe occicentale. Une orien-
    tation et un programme." *A. A. G. Bijdragen* (Wageningen).
    12 (1965):5-46.

Sokoloski, M. "Le développement de quelques villes dans le
    sud des Balkans aux XVᵉ et XVIᵉ siècles." *Balkanica* (Bel-
    grade) 1 (1970):81-106.

Spaho, F. "Turski rudarski zakoni" [Turkish mining laws].
    Glasnik Zemaljskog muzeja, 24 (1913):133-44.

Spencer, E. *Travels in European Turkey in 1850 through Bosnia,
    Serbia, Bulgaria, Macedonia, Thrace, Albania and Epirus.*
    . . . London, 1851.

Stanić, R. "Prilog proučavanju starih mostarskih zanata" [Con-
    tribution to the study of old Mostar crafts]. *Glasnik
    Zemaljskog muzeja* (1967):145-60.

Stoianovic, T. "The Conquering Balkan Orthodox Merchant."
    Journal of Economic History 20 (1960):234-313.

------. *A Study in Balkan Civilization.* New York, 1967.

------. "Model and Mirror of the Premodern Balkan City." In
    VB, pp. 83-110.

Svoronos, N. *Le Commerce de Salonique au XVIIIᵉ s.* Paris,
    1956.

Tadić, J. *Dubrovačka arhivska gradja o Beogradu* [Dubrovnik ar-
    chival materials on Belgrade]. Vol. 1 (1521-1571). Bel-
    grade, 1950.

------. "Ekonomsko jedinstvo Balkana i Sredozemlje u XV veku"
    [Economic unity of the Balkans and the Mediterranean in the
    the 15th century]. *Zgodovinsk časopis* [Historical journal,
    Ljubljana] 19-20 (1965-66):197-204.

Taschner, F. "Futuwwa, eine gemeinschaftbildende Idee im mittelalterlichen Orient und ihre verschiedene Erscheinungs-
formen." *Schweizerisches Archiv für Volkskunde* (Basel),
52 (1956):122-58.

Tischendorf, P. A. *Das Lehnswesen in den moslemischen Staaten
insbesondere im osmanischen Reiche*. Leipzig, 1872.

Todorov, N. "La Genèse du capitalisme dans les provinces bulgares de l'Empire ottoman au cours de la première moitié
du XIXe s." *Etudes historiques*, vol. 1 (1960).

-----. "Quelques aspects de la structure ethnique de la ville
médiévale balkanique." In *Actes du colloque international
des civilisations balkaniques*, pp. 39-45. Sinaia, 1962.

-----. "Sur certains aspects du passage du féodalisme au capitalisme dans les territoires balkaniques de l'Empire ottoman." *Revue des études du sud-est européen* (Bucharest) 1
(1963):101-34.

-----. "Sur certains aspects des villes balkaniques au cours
des XVe-XVIe ss." In *Actes du XII congrès international
des études byzantines*, 2:223-31. Belgrade, 1964.

-----. "Sur la structure d'âge d'un groupe de citadins dans
les terres bulgares au milieu du XIXe s." In *Turkologi-
cheskii sbornik*, pp. 266-72. Moscow, 1966.

-----. "The Balkan Town in the Second Half of the 19th Century." *Etudes balkaniques*, no. 2 (1969), pp. 31-50.

-----. "La Différenciation de la population urbaine au XVIIIe
s. d'après des registres de cadis de Vidin, Sofia et Ruse."
In VB, pp. 45-62.

-----. "The Genesis of Capitalism in the Balkan Provinces of
the Ottoman Empire in the Nineteenth Century." In *Explo-
rations in Economic History*, pp. 313-24. Wisconsin, 1970.

-----. "19-- cu Yüzyılın ilk Yarısında Bulgaristan Esnaf Teş-
kilâtında Bazı Karakter Değişmeleri" [A few changes in the
nature of the organization of Bulgarian guilds in the first
years of the 19th century]. IFM 27, nos. 1-2:1-36.

-----., ed., *La Ville balkanique, XVe-XIXe ss*. Sofia, 1970.

Tomiche, N. "La Situation des artisans et petits commerçants
en Egypte de la fin du XVIIIe s. jusqu'au milieu du XIXe s."
Studia islamica 12 (1960):79-98.

Ubicini, A. *Lettres sur la Turquie*. 2 vols. Paris, 1853-54.

Ülgener, S. "14 üncü Asırdanberi esnaf ahlâki ve şikâyeti mu-
cip bazi halleri" [Some conditions caused by the conduct
and complaint of guilds in the 14th century]. IFM, nos.
1-4 (1950), pp. 388-96.

Urquhart, D. *La Turquie: ses ressources, son organisation municipale, son commerce, suivis de considérations sur l'état
du commerce anglais dans le levant*. 2 vols. Paris, 1837.

------. *The Spirit of the East, Illustrated in a Journal of
Travels through Roumelia during an Eventual Period*. 2
vols. London, 1838.

Uzunçarşili, Is. *Osmanlı tarihi* [Ottoman history]. 4 vols.
Istanbul, 1947-59.

------. "Osmanlı devletinin Merkez ve Bahriye teşkilâtı" [The
central and maritime organization of the Ottoman State].
Türk tarih kurumu yayınlarından [Publications of the Turkish Historical Association], vol. 8. Ankara, 1948.

Vacalopoulos, A. E. *A History of Thessalonike*. 1963.

Vasić, M. "Etničke promjene u Bosanskoj krajini u XVI vijeku"
[Ethnic changes in Bosnian lands in the 16th century].
GIBH 13 (1962):233-50.

La Ville, vols. 6-8 of *Recueils de la Société Jean Bodin*.
Brussels, 1954-58.

Visvisis, J. "L'Administration communale des Grecs pendant la
domination turque." In *L'Hellénisme contemporain*, pp. 217-
38. Athens, 1953.

Vryonis, S. "The Conditions and Significance of the Ottoman
Conquest in the Balkans." Paper read at II Congrès international des études du sud-est européen. Athens, 1970.

Walsh, R. *Narrative of a Journey from Constantinople to England*. London, 1828.

Wenner, A. *Ein gantz new Reysebuch von Prag aus bis Constantinople etc. . . .* Nuremberg, 1622.

Wirth, E. "Die soziale Stellung und Gliederung der Stadt im
osmanischen Reich des 19. Jrhs. In *Untersuchungen zur
gesellschaftlichen Struktur der mittelalterlichen Städte
in Europa*. Konstanz, Stuttgart, 1966.

Wittek, P. *The Rise of the Ottoman Empire*. London, 1938.

-----. "Devshirme and sharif'a." *Bulletin of the School of Orient and African Studies*, 1955, pp. 217-78.

Zaplata, R. "Privredne prilike u Bosni i Hercegovini polovinom XIX veka. (Iz povjerljive arhive austrijskog generalnog konzula u Sarajevu)." [Economic conditions in Bosnia and Hercegovina in the middle of the 19th century. (From confidential papers of the Austrian Consul-General in Sarajevo).] *Glasnik Zemaljskog muzeja u Bosni i Hercegovini* [Herald of the State Museum in Bosnia and Hercegovina], no. 45 (1933), pp. 77-90.

Zinkeisen, J. M. *Geschichte des osmanischen Reiches in Europa*. 7 vols. Hamburg, 1859-63.

Žirojević, O. "Vučitrnski i Prizrenski sandžak u svetlosti turskog popisa 1530/31 godine" [The sancak of Vucitrn and Prizren in the light of the Turkish census of 1330-31]. *Gjurmime albanologjike* [Research in Albanology] 2 (1968): 103-16.

-----. "Palanka." In VB, pp. 173-80.

INDEX